Boris Karloff
A Gentleman's Life

Boris Karloff, gentleman, early 1950s.

BORIS KARLOFF

A GENTLEMAN'S LIFE

the authorized biography
by Scott Allen Nollen

with the participation of
Sara Jane Karloff

Midnight Marquee Press, Inc.
Baltimore, Maryland

Cover Design: A.S. Miller

ISBN 1-887664-23-8
Library of Congress Catalog Card Number 99-70129
Manufactured in the United States of America Feb. 1999
Printed by Kirby Lithographic Company, Arlington, VA
First Printing by Midnight Marquee Press, Inc., February 1999

Acknowledgments: John Antosiewicz Photo Archives, Ronald V. Borst/Holly-
wood Movie Posters, Linda J. Walter

For

my parents,

Harold N. and Shirley A. Nollen,

who made this book possible

Table of Contents

Foreword

When Scott Allen Nollen first approached me about doing another Karloff book, I must admit that my first reaction was "Why another? So many have been done." And I knew my father's reaction would have been "What's the big fuss? Local boy makes good. So what?"

Since his death in 1969, wonderful books about my father have been written. Some cover just his career, while others blend the man and his work. That, of course, is the case with my godmother Cynthia Lindsay's warm and loving family-authorized *Dear Boris*.

However, after reading Nollen's book *Boris Karloff: A Gentleman's Life*, I realized just how beautifully he has captured the essence of my father. Nollen's lifelong study of Boris Karloff, his extensive research, combined with his use of heretofore unseen photographs and untold family anecdotes, has made this book the ultimate Boris Karloff biography.

I was particularly delighted to see that my mother, Dorothy Stine Karloff, is given her place alongside my father during the very important years of 1930-46. And what glorious years those were.

Boris Karloff was revered by his fellow actors, who referred to him as *"the consummate professional," "the actor's actor."*

Nollen's book *Boris Karloff: A Gentleman's Life* reminds those of us who knew and loved Boris Karloff just how lucky we were to have had him touch our lives.

Thank you, Daddy.

Thank you, Scott Allen Nollen. "Full marks!"

Sara Jane Karloff
Rancho Mirage, California
February 1999

Preface

This book is the realization of a lifelong dream. The son of two Boris Karloff admirers, I practically was born in a theater. At the age of two, I already was going to the movies with my parents, crying my eyes out because a *three*-hour epic like *The Sound of Music* left me wanting more.

When I was five, my mother, who had been thrilled by Universal's *Frankenstein* since the late 1940s, thought it appropriate to introduce me to the film. Amid tacky 1960s late-night commercials and the terrible puns of Omaha's *Creature Feature* host, I got my first glimpse of Boris Karloff, just as many filmgoers did in December 1931, in James Whale's brilliant three-shot montage that is permanently emblazoned on my brain. By the time the film ended, I was lying face down on the floor, pulling a blanket over my head and feeling very sad about the demise of the poor, abused Monster. When I got up the next morning, I was a dyed-in-the-wool *Frankenstein* and Karloff fan.

Every Saturday night thereafter, I was enthralled by Universal's horror films and, without doubt, Karloff's resurrection in *The Mummy* scared me the most. For several nights, I tossed and turned, with the image of his 3,700-year-dead eyes flickering open, his wizened arm slowly escaping the bandages, and the insane laughter of poor Bramwell Fletcher echoing through my mind. I began reading all the related books I could find in the school and local libraries—Mary Shelley's novel was quite a challenge for an 11-year-old—collecting Frankenstein Monster figurines, and buying every issue of Forrest Ackerman's *Famous Monsters of Filmland*.

Once, while watching *Bride of Frankenstein*, I fell asleep during the middle and woke up just in time to see the Monster declare, "We belong dead!" and blow up the watchtower. I really was horrified! But I didn't see *Son of Frankenstein* until exactly 10:30 p.m. on Saturday, July 3, 1976—a date of extreme significance, for my career, my purpose in life, was born that night. Home video recorders were not readily available at the time, so I propped a portable cassette recorder by the television speaker to capture the sound. The following morning—on the bicentennial of the United States—I began seriously to make the study of Boris Karloff's life and work my utmost concern. Soon after, I told my mother that I was going to be an author, and my first book was to be on the great Boris. She did *not* take me seriously. But while my teenage friends were participating in all those senseless extracurricular pursuits befitting the peer group, I was at home with Boris. (Instead of my real name, the moniker "Boris" was even embroidered on my school band shirt by this time.)

Beginning in 1977, I produced dozens of amateur horror films, going so far as to make up my parents as the Monster and Bride of Frankenstein (after we'd made our little cinematic opus, this costume effort won first prize at a local Halloween shindig). And the next year, I published the premiere issue of *Classic Monster Movies*, my own fanzine—supported by Forry Ackerman—that lasted for about two years before the money ran out. It was the official publication of the Horror Movie Film Club, whose members attended the course I "taught" on Karloff during 1978 and then acted in my extremely low-budget, feature-length "remake" of *Son of Frankenstein* later that year.

Before the video revolution, I was forced obsessively to peruse each issue of *TV Guide*, scouring the late-night listings for any mention of one of the classic Universal horror films. Only rarely did one turn up; in an act of sheer desperation, KMTV in Omaha, Nebraska, ran *Son of Frankenstein* during prime time one night, when a tornado knocked out regular network programming! But for several years, I was forced to contact other collectors just to obtain nearly unwatchable copies of Karloff films they had taped off local shock theaters or scammed from friends.

In 1979 the Horror Movie Film Club threw a birthday bash for Boris at my parents' home in Harlan, Iowa. Film clips from the Universal classics were shown, as well as *Charlie Chan at the Opera*, the only full-length Karloff film I had on video at the time. Lively discussion about the King of the Horror Films accompanied the cutting of a cake graced by the head of the Frankenstein Monster.

When I had a serious brush with the Grim Reaper in 1980, Karloff's picture stood vigil on my bedside stand at the hospital. People I hardly knew piled into the room to see me; and one (very strange) girl, looking at the photograph, incomprehensively asked if the 80-year-old Boris was *me*! By this time, things were beginning to take a bizarre turn.

While vacationing in London during the summer of 1981, I began a 12-year correspondence with Karloff's widow, Evelyn, who provided a great deal of encouragement for my book project. In her second letter to me, Mrs. Karloff enclosed a necktie worn by Boris, the only such garment now known to exist. Needless to say, it remains the jewel in the crown of my collection. In a November 1982 issue of London's Sunday *Times*, Evie spoke of "a fan in Iowa who watches a Boris Karloff movie every day," and at about the same time, she put me in touch with a woman who had met Boris on board the *Empress of Britain* in 1936. This kind soul, who gave me the autograph she had received from him nearly 50 years earlier, looked at my stationery featuring a portrait I'd painted of him, and became the second person who thought that Karloff was me. I was happily getting used to this odd reaction by now.

During the 1980s, I lived in various residences that all had one thing in common: a room dedicated solely to Boris. Filled with memorabilia and all my research materials, these rooms came to be known as the "Karloff Museum." In fact, in 1986, an old friend I hadn't seen in several years asked, "Do you still have that *museum*?" (More recently, his father asked, "Are you still doing all that research on *Bela Lugosi*?")

In 1984, while majoring in film studies at the University of Iowa, I often sat next to a marginal friend in a class taught by the eminent professor of communications, Dr. Samuel L. Becker. Observing the shiny black dress shoes I was wearing, my companion, who had pretensions to hipness, admonished, "It's all right for you to idolize Boris Karloff, but you don't have to *dress* like him!"

The following year, I had the great good fortune to befriend Dr. Edward Lowry, a visiting professor from Texas Christian University who taught a magnificent course on the horror film, as well as a superb introduction to the history of American film in general. An irrepressible Karloff fan, he and I agreed to co-write a book about Boris, but unfortunately he passed away before much work could be done. Determined to write the ultimate volume on the King of the Horror Films, I forged on alone.

Dedicated in part to the late Dr. Lowry, my 1991 book *Boris Karloff: A Critical Account of His Screen, Stage, Radio, Television and Recording Work* was written in the final incarnation of the "museum" in Iowa City. One reviewer called it "an important book," while another dubbed it "the definitive book on Boris Karloff." Most importantly, Evie Karloff and Ray Bradbury, who provided the foreword, were both impressed. I was pleased, but I knew the book was not *definitive*.

Without doubt, Boris Karloff has been the biggest intellectual influence in my life—more so, even, than Robert Louis Stevenson and Sir Arthur Conan Doyle. Therefore I *had* to write another book about him, this time a volume about the *real* man. For years I had tried to contact his daughter, Sara Jane, but choosing to defer Boris matters to her stepmother, she remained out of the picture until Evie passed away in June 1993. Shortly after, she contacted me, interested in my book and my relationship with the late Mrs. Karloff.

Being able to know and work with Sara Jane on this project has been a highlight of my career. Hopefully this book is the most thorough, accurate and entertaining chronicle of her father's fascinating life. Perhaps a few Karloff mysteries have been solved.

Sara Jane Karloff and Scott Allen Nollen, Rancho Mirage, California, March 8, 1997. (photograph by Jeff Clothier)

My first personal note of gratitude goes to the late Boris Karloff. Contrary to popular belief, which asserts that he did not collect any materials on his career, Boris—aided by Evie—while not saving much from his films, did indeed preserve scores of clippings and other items related to his stage and television performances. For their attention to detail, and handwritten identifications of individual articles, I offer my undying gratitude. I also must thank the late Dorothy Stine (Karloff) Rowe, Boris' fourth wife and Sara Jane's mother, who wrote dozens of informative letters to her mother, Louise, during the 1930s and '40s. Thank goodness they were saved!

Many individuals who knew, worked with, met or were related to Boris were very gracious in sharing their memories, and it is to them that I offer my thanks: Eddie Albert, Bob Beckham, Ray Bradbury, the late Henry Brandon, Bernard Coleman, Elisabeth Crowley, Ralph Edwards, Julie Harris, Rosamund James, the late Zita Johann, the late Evelyn Karloff, Angela Lansbury, Anna Lee, Christopher Lee, the late David Manners, K. Mary Maydwell, the late Sir Laurence Olivier, the late Vincent Price, Tony Randall, Nancy Sinatra Lambert and the late Ian Wolfe.

I also would like to acknowledge those who provided information and illustrations, aided in the research, offered their encouragement, or literally took care of business: Bart Aikens, my erstwhile major domo who first drove me to Sara's door; Buddy Barnett, memorabilia dealer, publisher of *Cult* Magazine, and Karloff buff; Ronald V. Borst, horror-film historian, writer, professional collector extraordinaire and one of the nicest guys in Hollywood; Carol Burnett, actress; Bob Burns, film editor, actor, curator, perhaps *the* nicest guy in Hollywood; Kathy Burns, photographer extraordinaire and Bob's lovely wife; Ron Chaney, grandson of Lon, Jr.;

Linda Chaney, Ron's lovely wife; Jeff Clothier, fellow knight of the road, writer and musician, whose sax stylings pleased Sara no end; Thomas ("Big Fat Guy") Fortunato, friend; Sir John Gielgud, actor; John Giriat, Karloff aficionado; Roy Peter Green, Monarchist League; Russ Jones, artist, screenwriter and guy who (rightfully!) likes the same films as I do; Fred Jordan, friendly film-industry executive with a particularly special Karloff collection (He made one of my childhood dreams come true!); Ken Kaffke, president of the *Thriller* Fan Club; Harold N. Nollen, father; Sean Ian Nollen, son; Shirley A. Nollen, mother; Jerry Rudman, Archivist and Headmaster of Meadhurst, Uppingham; Gordon Shriver, Karloff aficionado; Berny Stringle, Sara Jane's cousin; W.D.E. Thomas, Headmaster of Enfield Grammar School; Ron Waite, Karloff aficionado and former associate editor of *Famous Monsters of Filmland*; and Katherine Wallace, Angela Lansbury's assistant.

A special note of gratitude is conferred upon the staff of the Screen Actors Guild, who run a magnificent facility, one that Boris certainly would be proud of. After a wonderful lunch at Marie Callender's in Hollywood, remarkable assistance was provided by Director of Communications Katherine Moore, President Richard Masur and Midge Farrell, SAG's original secretary in 1933 and an old friend of Boris', whose wonderful memories were a true delight. But my eternal gratitude goes to SAG Archivist Valerie Yaros, a consummate professional who sought out every possible scrap of Karloff material and then was kind enough to proofread the chapter dealing with Boris' Guild activities. In other words, thanks for finding my mistakes, Valerie! You are (literally) an archivist's archivist.

Another major thank you goes to John M. Eccles, Jr., an Atlantic City attorney and radio buff, and his cohorts, Matt Bohn, Martin Grams, Jr., Steve Kelez, Michael Ogden, Gordon Payton, Steve Pickett, Tom and Melinda Read, and Kerry Wright, who provided invaluable information about Karloff's career on the airwaves. John dedicated many hard-earned hours to this book, and I forever will be in his debt.

I also am indebted to Cory Ann Nollen, who became my wife just as I was finishing this 23-year journey. For her unique spirit, and attempts to understand my various moods as I worked feverishly on so many projects, I give her Boris' accolade of "full marks."

Finally, I warmly thank Sara Jane Karloff, without whom I could not have returned to my favorite subject, and her husband, William ("Sparky") Sparkman. I am grateful for the opportunity, their opening of the family archives, their hard work and their gracious hospitality at Rancho Mirage, Lake Tahoe, and Los Angeles.

To paraphrase Colin Clive's Henry Frankenstein, "Think of the pleasure—to *recreate a man!*"

Scott Allen Nollen
Iowa City, Iowa
February 1999

Introduction

"Well, I've showed them, and nobody's paid any attention!"

Nineteen twenty-six was a busy year for Boris Karloff. After more than 15 years of performing on the stage and in front of motion picture cameras, he was playing parts in major Hollywood films. During that year alone, he appeared in 11 productions for 10 different companies, yet remained almost totally unrecognizable. In Paramount's big-budget epic *Old Ironsides*, he appeared on screen for three seconds, and almost no one who saw the same studio's *Eagle of the Sea* could even spot him on the crowded deck of Ricardo Cortez's renegade ship.

At 38, Karloff was accustomed to alternating backbreaking odd jobs such as truck driving and construction work with small film parts. But landing an occasional supporting role that allowed him to demonstrate his acting prowess and unique visage kept him trodding the boards. While playing bit characters he forgot about as soon as his grease paint was removed, he was asked to portray an eerie sideshow mesmerist in a screen adaptation of Emile Erckman and Alexandre Chatrain's popular play *The Bells*.

Now Karloff was able to discuss the art of acting with one of his favorite performers, Lionel Barrymore, whom he called "a stimulating man—a marvelous, a great man." While brainstorming with director James Young, he sat beside Barrymore as the multi-talented artist sketched a look for the mesmerist, an inventive variation on the makeup worn by Werner Krauss in the groundbreaking expressionist thriller *The Cabinet of Dr. Caligari*, filmed in Germany seven years earlier. Looking a lot like his mesmeric predecessor, Karloff stood out quite conspicuously in an otherwise pedestrian film, giving audiences a hint of the frightening talent that would flash across the screen five years later.

Continuing to toil as a blue-collar thespian, Karloff made the acquaintance of another Hollywood giant whose mantle he would subsequently—and unwittingly—inherit. While walking home from Universal Studios one evening, he was stopped in his tracks by the loud honk of a horn behind him. Standing his ground, he walked even slower until a gruff voice emanated from the offending automobile. Asked if he failed to recognize an old friend, Karloff finally turned around to see the grinning visage of the Phantom of the Opera behind the wheel.

Character actor William Taylor recently had introduced him to Lon Chaney, someone he considered more than an amazing mime and makeup man. Karloff appreciated Chaney's sensitivity toward the physically challenged, a group of people this son of deaf mutes had represented so well: Although many of his characterizations were horrific, he projected a tortured soul from beneath those painful layers of wondrous makeup.

While driving Karloff home that day, Chaney offered advice about perseverance and the types of roles a struggling actor should pursue. Although they did not develop a close relationship, Karloff and Chaney crossed tracks occasionally, sometimes at the Friday night fights held at Los Angeles' Legion Stadium. Having no extra money to squander on athletic events, Karloff stood outside the entrance, hoping someone would invite him in. A true boxing enthusiast, Chaney would spot his old "friend" and stop for a brief conversation.

Later in life, Karloff always spoke admiringly of the Man of a Thousand Faces, and viewed his ride in 1926 as a nearly prophetic event. And indeed, Chaney's advice casts an appropriate light on Karloff the actor and the man:

The secret of success in Hollywood lies in being different from anyone else. Find something no one else can or will do—and they'll begin to take notice of you. Hollywood is full of competent actors. What the screen needs is individuality!

Chapter 1

The Prolific Pratts

"I was supposed to go into the consular service in China...
and after I left school, I went to King's College, University
of London, to really cram for these exams, but I didn't
do a stroke of work because: A, I was quite sure I couldn't
pass the exams; and B, I didn't want to. I was determined
to be an actor..."

To all appearances, Edward John Pratt wanted to be a family man. A respectable gentleman of English and East Indian ancestry, stern temperament and proper upper-class demeanor, he kept procreating but rarely was around to play the father, instead concentrating on his duties as Assistant Collector for the Salt Revenue Service in Bombay, a post he held until his retirement in 1878.

Edward had followed in the colonial footsteps of his father, Edward John Pratt, Sr., who had supported the Empire as a lieutenant in the Honorable East India Company's Marines, but now, situated in the quiet London sub-district of Camberwell, his days of adventure were over. By November 1887, at the age of 60, he had married three times and sired 12 children, the latest of whom was expected to make his debut quite soon.

Flashback: Bengal, India, 1815

Edward John Pratt, Sr., joined the Marines in Bengal on October 15, 1815. While serving as a first lieutenant on the *Tenate*, he married Miss Margaret Sheals on July 20, 1818. Less than nine months later, on April 6, 1819, she gave birth to a daughter, Margaret Caroline Pratt; and by November 8, 1824, aged a mere 24, she lay dead at Gargaum.

Young Edward John Pratt took his first breath, perhaps in England, on October 15, 1827, the son of Edward, Sr., and an unidentified Indian woman. By Christmas Day 1829, when the London ship *Charles Kerr* reached Bombay, the two-year-old boy and his half-sister were being cared for by a woman named Mrs. Charlotte Bellasis. On April 7, 1833, when young Edward was five, Charlotte and her husband, John, adopted the children in Bombay. Having kept a low profile for some time, Edward, Sr. drew his last pension payment from the Indian Office on New Year's Eve 1834.

On April 10, 1849, while working as an uncovenanted civil servant, young Edward married a 17-year-old lass named Julianna Campbell in Gargaum. Nine months later—on January 12, 1850—Julianna delivered their first child, Emma Caroline Pratt; and before the baby had settled into her crib, she was pregnant again. Eleven months after Emma entered the world, tiny Edward Pratt III was born, but tragically died the next day, December 14, 1850. Saddened by this cruel blow, Edward was shocked even further when Julianna, ill and considerably weakened by the delivery, also passed away.

After living as a widower for about three years, Edward married a second time, to a woman called Charlotte, who gave birth to a girl, Eliza Julia, on August 18, 1855. Perhaps cursed with physically frail wives, Edward had also lost her by 1860. During the two years following her death, he began a relationship with another woman, who gave birth to Charles Rary Pratt on August 3, 1863, although no record of their marriage exists.

BORIS KARLOFF'S FAMILY TREE

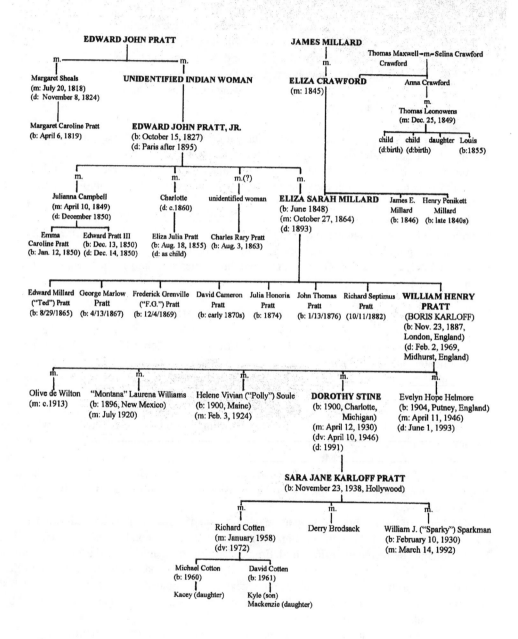

EDWARD JOHN PRATT

m. ——————————————— m.

Margaret Sheals
(m: July 20, 1818)
(d: November 8, 1824)

UNIDENTIFIED INDIAN WOMAN

Margaret Caroline Pratt
(b: April 6, 1819)

EDWARD JOHN PRATT, JR.
(b: October 15, 1827)
(d: Paris after 1895)

JAMES MILLARD

m.

Thomas Maxwell≈m≈Selina Crawford
Crawford

ELIZA CRAWFORD
(m: 1845)

Anna Crawford

m.

Thomas Leonowens
(m: Dec. 25, 1849)

child   child   daughter   Louis
(d:birth) (d:birth)   (b:1855)

m.   m.   m.(?)   m.

Julianna Campbell
(m: April 10, 1849)
(d: December 1850)

Charlotte
(d: c.1860)

unidentified woman

ELIZA SARAH MILLARD
(b: June 1848)
(m: October 27, 1864)
(d: 1893)

James E.   Henry Penikett
Millard   Millard
(b: 1846)   (b: late 1840s)

Emma   Edward Pratt III
Caroline Pratt (b: Dec. 13, 1850)
(b: Jan. 12, 1850) (d: Dec. 14, 1850)

Eliza Julia Pratt
(b: Aug. 18, 1855)
(d: as child)

Charles Rary Pratt
(b: Aug. 3, 1863)

Edward Millard   George Marlow   Frederick Grenville   David Cameron   Julia Honoria   John Thomas   Richard Septimus   WILLIAM HENRY
("Ted") Pratt   Pratt   ("F.G.") Pratt   Pratt   Pratt   Pratt   Pratt   PRATT
(b: 8/29/1865)   (b: 4/13/1867) (b: 12/4/1869)   (b: early 1870s) (b: 1874)   (b: 1/13/1876) (10/11/1882)   (BORIS KARLOFF)
                                                                                                                        (b: Nov. 23, 1887,
                                                                                                                        London, England)
                                                                                                                        (d: Feb. 2, 1969,
                                                                                                                        Midhurst, England)

m.   m.   m.   m.   m.

Olive de Wilton
(m: c.1913)

"Montana" Laurena Williams
(b: 1896, New Mexico)
(m: July 1920)

Helene Vivian ("Polly") Soule
(b: 1900, Maine)
(m: Feb. 3, 1924)

DOROTHY STINE
(b: 1900, Charlotte,
Michigan)
(m: April 12, 1930)
(dv: April 10, 1946)
(d: 1991)

Evelyn Hope Helmore
(b: 1904, Putney, England)
(m: April 11, 1946)
(d: June 1, 1993)

SARA JANE KARLOFF PRATT
(b: November 23, 1938, Hollywood)

m.   m.   m.

Richard Cotten
(m: January 1958)
(dv: 1972)

Derry Brodsack

William J. ("Sparky") Sparkman
(b: February 10, 1930)
(m: March 14, 1992)

Michael Cotton
(b: 1960)

David Cotten
(b: 1961)

Kacey (daughter)

Kyle (son)
Mackenzie (daughter)

Silver Street, one of Enfield's main thoroughfares.

On October 27, 1864, Edward began his third (perhaps fourth) marital union, with Eliza Sarah Millard, who was a mere two when he first became a father in 1850. Eliza, too, had strong connections to the East. Her mother, also named Eliza, was the daughter of Captain Thomas Maxwell Crawford, A.D.C. to the Commander of British Troops in Lahore, India, where he had been killed during a Sikh uprising in 1841. After Crawford's death, his wife, Selina, remained in India, where their second daughter, Anna, wed a young army officer named Thomas Leonowens on Christmas Day 1849.

Eliza, Anna and the King of Siam

After losing two children, Anna and her husband moved to London, where she gave birth to another daughter and son. In 1858, when Leonowens died of apoplexy brought on by sunstroke after a tiger hunt in Malaya, Anna opened a small school for the children of army officers, but abandoned it four years later. On March 15, 1862, she arrived in Siam with her seven-year-old son, Louis, to accept the position of governess and tutor in "English, science and literature" to the King's children. After leaving her position in July 1867, she wrote two heavily embellished "faithful accounts" of her experiences, claiming that her former employer, King Mongkut, was an eccentric and cruel barbarian—accusations that caused an uproar in Siam but soon were forgotten in England. [1]

Anna's prejudices also affected her family relationships, and she eventually disowned Eliza, who married Sergeant Major James Millard in 1845 and gave birth to a son, James E., the following year. Eliza Sarah was born in Poona, Bombay Province, in June 1848, two and one-half years before her father, now aged 44, was pensioned. One more son, Henry Pennikett, was born in Gargaum. Young Eliza's marriage to twice-widowed, half-Indian Edward Pratt at the age of 16 may have contributed to Anna's distaste for her sister.

Soon after their wedding, Eliza became pregnant and stayed that way for most of their married life. Their first child, Edward Millard, born in India on August 29, 1865,

Enfield Grammar School, where young Billy Pratt began his formal education.

William Henry Pratt, age 3 1/2.

was followed by two more sons, George Marlow on April 13, 1867, and Frederick Grenville on December 4, 1869. Three days before Frederick appeared, Edward was granted a medical certificate that would send him, on reduced salary, to Europe for 15 months.

A fourth son, David Cameron, joined the family prior to 1874, when Edward was appointed Assistant Collector of Salt Revenue and a lone daughter, Julia Honoria, was born. On January 13, 1876, Eliza gave birth to yet another boy, John Thomas, before Edward retired and moved the family back to England. The prolific Mrs. Pratt now benefited from a slight rest: Son number six, Richard Septimus, did not appear until October 11, 1882.

Billy Pratt

More than five years later, on November 23, 1887, at 15 Forest Hill Road in Camberwell, Eliza was awaiting the arrival of Edward's ninth child. Perhaps she wondered if the odds would change and a second girl would be added to the Pratt household.

It was another boy: William Henry, who, from his very first breath, had the cards stacked against him. His father was seldom at home, his workhorse mother was now in poor health and his brothers were upholding family tradition by preparing for the British consular service or other work abroad.

Young Edward, or "Ted," now 22, had attended Dulwich College and then joined the civil service in India, while Frederick, who had similar plans, enrolled at the same school. Charles eventually went to work for the French Cable Company in Brazil, but George, choosing to remain in England, became a medical student at London's Guys Hospital shortly before William, or "Billy," was born.

In 1893 the frail Eliza passed away. With Julia and John now approaching adulthood, and Richard an independent 12, five-year-old Billy began to feel even more isolated. His domestic life shattered, Edward perhaps thought that his family ties were no longer strong enough to hold him down—and something had occurred to make him feel uncomfortable in his homeland. On September 11, 1894, he wrote a letter to the India Office, in which he protested the "supercilious commiseration or compassion for the class of Coloured Englishmen to which I belong." Arguing that "Eurasia has yet to be discovered by the geographers," he claimed that he and his fellows deserved to be called "English or Indian." About a year later, he left 15 Forest Hill Road,

Ten-year-old Billy Pratt (front row, center) with his Enfield classmates, 1897.

never to return. Before sailing across the channel to France, he abducted Richard, but the family soon sent Ted to track him down at Calais and transport the lad back to England.

After this sudden abandonment, Billy knew nothing of his father, who eventually died in Paris. Now seven, Billy was taken in by his half-sister, Emma Caroline Pratt, a spinster only two years younger than his deceased mother, in Enfield, Middlesex, just north of London. First residing at 1909 Chaseview on Chase Green Avenue, they moved several times, to the Willows, Slade Hill and 38 Uplands Park Road, respectively.

Billy had inherited a dark, somewhat greenish, complexion from the Anglo-Indian Pratts, but his facial structure, prominent brow and brown eyes made him the very image of his mother. He was a quiet, lonely little boy, and struggled to overcome a stammer and lisp that affected his speech. Particularly adept at games and role playing, he enjoyed visiting other children in

Fircroft House, Uppingham. (1996 photograph by Sara Jane Karloff)

21

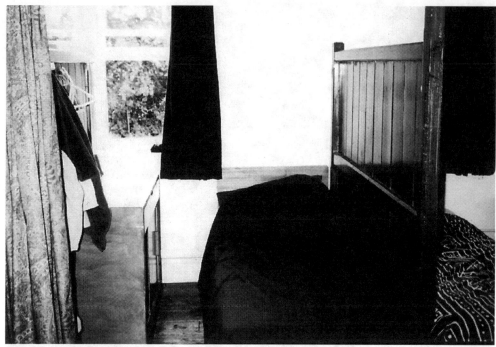
Billy Pratt's bunk in the Fircroft dormitory, Uppingham. (1996 photograph by Sara Jane Karloff)

the neighborhood to ride bicycles, play mumblety-peg or compete in a friendly round of field hockey. Running across the brickfields by Wormwood Scrubs Prison, he could be identified by his rhythmic, bowlegged gait.

Emma often was aided by Billy's coming and going brothers, whose contributions were not always welcomed. Still living at home, Richard received some hard knocks, usually remembering to pass them on to Billy. First and foremost, the elder Pratts saw to it that he received an education suitable for a career abroad. He initially attended the Enfield Grammar School, where academics were combined with athletics, the arts and religious studies to form boys of "rounded character." Founded in 1558 and located next to St. Andrews Catholic Church and the village market place, the school had a tradition of teaching self-discipline and moral values, but also the spirit of competition through games of cricket and rugby, two sports that Billy adored.

Although he was only one in a class of several dozen boys, his dark complexion and eyes made him stand out, and he appeared quite grim in school photographs, even when surrounded by a crowd of equally serious, properly uniformed schoolmates. Interested in the arts as well as athletics, he discovered that he had an aptitude for music and drama. Each Christmas, a parish play was performed at St. Mary Magdalene's Hall for two nights; and in 1896 he appeared in black tights and skullcap as the Demon King in *Cinderella*, an experience that whetted his appetite for the stage. After enthusiastically trying out for roles in two more parish productions, he raised the ire of his brothers who considered acting an unsuitable profession.

In 1899 Billy moved on to the revered Merchant Taylor's School, then located in London's Charterhouse Square. Richard had been educated there a few years earlier, and recalled having to memorize poetry and scenes from Shakespeare, a process that demonstrated the Pratt ability to retain and recite lengthy literary passages. As a respite from his studies, Billy enjoyed going to the theater, and he once saw his brother George, who used the name "George Marlowe," at the Strand, starring with Fanny Ward in the Napoleonic romance *The Royal Divorce*. The only brother who had forsaken foreign service, George worked as an actor, drama coach and partner in Elverstein and Company, a Swedish firm of paper pulp merchants, before earning his medical degree and a position at St. Bartholomew's Hospital.

22

Encouraged by his renegade brother, Billy was further determined to become a performer. But the other Pratt brothers knew how financially precarious the life of an actor can be, and George's middling success on the London stages added weight to their conservative arguments against such a career. Occasionally Billy would escape the oppressive brotherly atmosphere while visiting his sister, Julia, who had married a Suffolk vicar named Arthur Donkin. On the grounds of Semer Church, he enjoyed weekends with his niece, Dorothea, who was only eight years younger than he.

Graduating from Merchant Taylor's in 1903, Billy entered Uppingham, one of Britain's best boarding schools, located in Rutland. Founded by Archdeacon Robert Johnson in 1584, it originally was a small country school attended by children from the town of Uppingham and its environs; but in 1853 Headmaster Edward Thring, one of the greatest Victorian educationalists, transformed it into a major institution "providing a variety of musical, sporting and practical activities." To support its impressive academic schedule, the school also offered each student a safe, supportive environment and a sense of community involvement and responsibility.

Having experienced family strain and some rather uneven treatment at home, Billy could not have been placed into a more stable environment. The beautiful rolling landscape and quaint villages surrounding the school and small market town of Uppingham strengthened his lifelong love of the outdoors. At first he attended only during the day, but by January 1904 was boarding on a full-time basis. The houses on the campus were individual structures surrounded by well-tended grounds and gardens, and each boy was allowed his own private space, including a partitioned study and sleeping area, within the dormitory.

Living in Fircroft, Billy was advised by Housemaster Robert N. Douglas, Esq., who monitored both the academic and social progress of the two-dozen boarders in his care. Douglas was

Fircroft House hockey team, 1905. Billy Pratt stands far left, while his mate Geoffrey Taylor is seated, dead center.

Fircroft House photo, 1906. Billy and Geoffrey Taylor strike a pose of solidarity (back row, center).

assisted by his wife, Lina, and several "praeposters," or prefects, senior students who helped run the house and maintain order. During Billy's stay, the praeposters included Charles E. Raven, S.H. La Fontaine, G.S. Brock, and C.K. Archer.

Billy often found little to interest him in traditional academic subjects, but enthusiastically participated in the artistic and athletic offerings. Since Thring's arrival at Uppingham a half-century earlier, music had been a major part of the curriculum, and the school was proud to have established England's first director of music, Mr. Paul David. Billy particularly enjoyed voice and piano lessons, as well as speech and drama, and took part in a Fircroft show during the autumn of 1905. On July 6, 1906, the school's annual Speech Day, he won a prize for his performance in German.

Uppingham's athletic facilities were extensive, and the grounds included "The Middle," one of the largest unbroken stretches of playing fields in England. Located on the western side of Fircroft, this beautiful field expanded Billy's interest in cricket, and during the summer of 1905, he joined his housemates in matches against Meadhurst and F.A.E. Ashwell's XI. He also became a member of the Fircroft hockey team that year, joining 10 of his housemates, including J.G. ("Geoffrey") Taylor, a small, athletically able young man who became one of his closest friends.

Billy often walked to morning class with Geoff, who, being equally unconcerned about punctuality, joined him in running to the building, only to find the door shut and classes already under way. After a day's study, at which, according to Geoff, Billy did not distinguish himself, the pair would walk to a shop in Uppingham's High Street, where they would feast on fruit salads smothered in cream.

Geoff's athletic prowess far outdistanced Billy's, and he excelled in cricket, hockey, track and field and boxing. In the school's comprehensive sports competition for 1906, Fircroft was ranked fifth on the list of houses. Within the house, Geoff and Billy placed second and third, respectively, behind a chap named Selwyn, who, as an individual, placed fifth on the all-house list of 32 athletes. Participating in the routh cup and steeplechase, Geoff finished seventh in the all-house, while Billy, as a weightlifter, came in 17th. In their last Fircroft House photograph, taken in 1906, Geoff and Billy both stood proudly, their arms folded in manly fashion, side by side in the back row. As at Enfield, Billy's Indian features made him stand out conspicuously, but now he had someone with whom he experienced social solidarity.

Billy graduated from Uppingham after the spring term of 1906 and, that autumn, entered King's College at the University of London, ostensibly to study for the consular service examinations. With his mind set against such a career, and feeling that he was not capable of passing the exams, he ignored his assignments and headed for the West End whenever possible. In the gallery of His Majesty's Theatre, he was enthralled by the legendary Sir Herbert Beerbohm Tree in *Richard II*, *Antony and Cleopatra* and *The Tempest*, and enjoyed the performances of Lyn Harding, Constance Collier, Cyril Maude, George Alexander, Lewis Waller and other favorites of the day.

William Henry Pratt knew very little about acting, but it was the only profession he wanted to pursue. He had "the fire in his blood," which is all that mattered. After two years of hiding out in theaters to avoid the university, he celebrated his 21st birthday, realizing he could escape the oppressive shadow of his conservative brothers. At about this same time, Emma gave him a £150 inheritance left by his mother 15 years earlier. While collecting the money at the family solicitor's office, he debated over whether to emigrate to Canada or Australia and, after tossing a coin, chose the former. Having no idea what opportunities this unfamiliar country could provide for an aspiring actor whose only experiences were Enfield parish pageants and a show at Uppingham, he deliberately failed the consular service exam.

[1] Many decades later, in 1945, these accounts were revived by author Margaret Landon, making the late Mrs. Leonowens world famous as the heroine of *Anna and the King of Siam*, which later was re-worked as the musical *The King and I*.

Chapter 2

Canadian Pastures

"Well, I was determined to be an actor, and I knew so
little about the theater or anything connected with it,
that I went to Canada."

Poised to depart Liverpool aboard the *Empress of Britain* on May 7, 1909, William visited
the London offices of the Canada Company, claiming that he intended to become a farmer upon
his arrival in North America. Steaming to Montreal on this maiden voyage, he was smitten by
another type of maiden, although the romance must have been broken off while the *Empress* was
still at sea. A surviving marriage certificate bearing the name "William Henry Pratt" includes no
female name, nor any signatures.

After landing in Montreal on May 17, William set out for Toronto, where he was to report to
a Canadian official for an agricultural assignment. At "this damned place," he was sent to the
farm of Terence O'Reilly, eight miles outside Hamilton, Ontario. Excited about the prospect of
work, he hitched a ride on a buggy, but was greeted with a chilly reception. O'Reilly had never
heard of William Pratt and, to make matters worse, had no interest in a hired man. Knowing that
farm work would increase dramatically during the coming weeks, William convinced O'Reilly
to hire him at $10 per month, plus room and board, and he spent the late spring and early sum-
mer being roused out of bed by a pitchfork-wielding Irishman at 4:00 a.m. every morning. He
had no problem waking up after a few dashes of ice cold water from the pump, and after trying
to warm up in the itchy sweater O'Reilly gave him, he pulled on a pair of hobnailed boots and
headed into the fields. By 4:30 a.m., he was in the pasture and, knowing less about livestock
than he did about acting, attempting to round up the horses.

After three months at O'Reilly's, William had built up a stamina for hard physical labor, but
was pleased to leave horse breaking behind and head west. After enjoying "the rugged beauty
and impressive grandeur" of the Canadian Rockies, he stayed in Banff for a time. Accepting any
odd jobs he could find on farms and with construction firms, he eventually made his way to
Vancouver, where he earned 25 cents an hour digging a race track and a fairground. Nearly
broke, he skipped breakfast before reporting to work on the first day, and then blistered both
hands while operating a pick and shovel for 10 grueling hours. Prior to receiving his paycheck
on the following Saturday, he had managed to live on just four cents a day.

When his funds were nearly exhausted again, he serendipitously met up with Hayman Claudet,
a man who had attended Dulwich College with his brother John. Recognizing the Pratt visage as
he passed William on the street, Claudet wrote a note of reference to the Works Superintendent
of the British Columbia Railroad Company, where another pick and shovel were waiting. After
laying tracks for 10 hours a day, six days a week, he managed to save a whopping $16.80.

William then accepted Claudet's offer to help him land a job with a local real estate company.
Hoping to work his way up from "glorified office boy" to salesman, he began to make $10
payments on a lot of his own, but when this situation fell through, he laid streetcar tracks,
cleared land and shoveled coal for the British Columbia Electric Company, and then joined one
of their survey parties working near some lakes about 70 miles outside Vancouver.

While toiling in the British Columbian bush, William received a letter from Walter Kelly, a
theatrical agent he had approached during a previous trip to Seattle, stating that a small stock
company was looking for "somebody with just one head and a pair of legs" to fill a vacancy.

William had given up hope that Kelly would take him seriously, since his interview had consisted of nothing but lies about his performances in numerous London plays—those he merely had watched from the distant balcony.

Believing he was offered the position because no one else would accept it, he was told to join the Jean Russell Players in Kamloops, British Columbia, 250 miles away. On the train trip, he concluded that William Pratt was not the most advantageous name for an actor. Wasting little time mulling over pseudonyms, he chose "Karloff," which he thought was a maternal surname, and tacked on "Boris" because it fit.

Packing up in Kamloops, the company moved on to Nelson, where Karloff, the "experienced English actor," participated in his first rehearsals and made his stage debut in heavy makeup as Hoffman, the sexagenarian banker, in Ferenc Molnar's *The Devil*. Apparently his performance was so bad that Russell cut his $30 weekly salary in half before the final curtain fell the first night. But Boris made up for his inexperience by studying diligently, learning all his lines in the company's repertoire of 18 plays and doubling as assistant stage manager.

The Russell Players opened each new production on Monday, and after every evening's performance, they would retire to a back room or basement, remove their makeup and return to the stage to rehearse the following week's play. This regimen required the actors to report to the theater only once each day, and after completing all their work by around 3 a.m., they were free to catch some sleep before repeating the process again the following afternoon.

Boris stayed with the Russell Players for about 18 months, until the entire troupe was stranded by the manager. While traveling by train from Edmonton, Alberta, to Regina, Saskatchewan, on July 31, 1912, the company learned that a monumental cyclone had literally leveled their destination, killing 41 citizens, wounding 300 and leaving 3,000 homeless. Having no place to play, Russell vanished, leaving many of his actors, including Boris, penniless and with no prospect of future employment. Desperate for any sort of work, Boris helped to clear away the immense debris, somehow managing to find a place to sleep.

After working for six weeks to make Regina habitable, Boris labored as a baggage porter for the Dominion Express Company and in other toilsome jobs until, while thumbing through a theatrical trade paper, he noticed an advertisement calling for an experienced actor to join the Harry St. Clair Players in Prince Albert, Saskatchewan. He quickly wrote to St. Clair, who accepted him for a lengthy tour of Canada and the northern United States.

St. Clair's company was a bit ramshackle and often in dire straits financially, with no money to pay the actors. Boris described him as "truly honest...When he had the money, he paid us. When he didn't, he didn't have it." In fact, St. Clair, even when he wasn't able to pay his troupe, provided tuition-free dramatic lessons. Boris made the best of this work experience, and became very friendly with a married couple, Charlie and Connie Jackson, two fellow emigrant actors who hailed from Streatham, England, and had joined the company at the same time.

While on the road and in his room during the day, Boris further developed his formidable talent for memorizing entire plays and, as a result, began to land more prominent roles. At any time, he could take the stage and perform stock essentials such as *Charley's Aunt*, *East Lynne*, *Paid in Full* and *Way Down East*, and now was adding more titles to his growing repertoire.

Not having any spending money troubled him very little, since he had no time to squander, but he was forced to become particularly creative in the areas of attire and cuisine. Visiting local cleaners, he would buy abandoned suits and "press" them beneath his mattress during the few hours he slept each morning. Rather than eating in restaurants, he propped his traveling iron upside down and fried an egg or boiled the vegetables and broth from a can of mulligatawny soup, saving the meat for his next meal.

Boris was admitted to the United States on October 12, 1913, at Portal, North Dakota, by the U.S. Immigration and Naturalization Service. Prior to crossing the border, he apparently married a young English actress named Olive de Wilton, who was 11 years younger than he and probably about 14 at the time of their wedding. [1]

For over a year, the St. Clair Players, having no money to travel, were stranded in Minot, which then was a railroad town with a population of about 10,000. Performing in an opera house above a hardware store, Boris and his compatriots ran through their repertoire of 18 plays rather quickly and then began frantically rehearsing new ones in order to offer their audiences two full-length productions each week.

Boris' reputation as a quick study was solidified, and he frequently was given the thickest script after they had been spread out on a table in front of the actors, each of whom had three days to learn the dialogue and create the character. "I hate to think of what some of the performances were like, but at least you had to get on with the job," recalled Boris, who would use this rough and ready method—learning the dialogue and, rather than over-preparing his technique, allowing a certain amount of inspired improvisation—for the rest of his career. One of the plays he appeared in at the Minot Opera House had given him the acting bug back in Enfield—*Cinderella*—but this time, instead of the Demon King, he portrayed one of the hideous stepsisters.

The patrons who paid to see the St. Clair Players were very enthusiastic, and many farmers traveled by horse-drawn sled through 30 miles of snow just to catch the latest offering. But when only a dozen people managed to climb the stairs to the opera house, St. Clair would drop an entire act in order to close a little earlier. Having no transportation, Boris' own leisure activities were limited. After each evening's performance, he usually walked across the street to relax with a Coke at the drugstore fountain of George Magnussen, who kept the business open late to accommodate the troupe.

When World War I erupted in August 1914, Boris attempted to enlist in the British Army but was rejected when the doctor conducting his physical misdiagnosed a heart murmur. Thwarted in his patriotic effort, the 26-year-old actor returned to the safer environment of the stock company.

Believing he had learned enough to break out of the dead-end rut he had settled into, Boris, with a savings of $60, left the St. Clair Players in Kansas and headed for Chicago in 1916. On North Clark Street, he rented a small flat adjacent to one inhabited by his old friends, Charlie and Connie Jackson, who had left the troupe the previous year. For $4 a week, he even received a gas hot plate, but his fortune was meager, and he haunted the office of Milo Bennett, a theatrical agent, nearly every day.

After he had whittled his savings down to "about a quarter," Bennett placed him with another stock company for a 10-week tour of West Virginia. Completing that, he returned to Chicago with $50, which he lived on until only a dime remained. Something about the windy city terrified him, and he later confessed that "Chicago has always given me the willies, because the knife is really at your throat there." So he was more than happy to move on when a small troupe picked him up for a tour into Minnesota. Finding himself unemployed in St. Paul, he joined the Billie Bennett Company, who were touring across the Midwest performing Owen Wister's *The Virginian*. In the villainous role of Trampas, he performed in Iowa, Kansas, Colorado and Nevada before reaching California in December 1917.

Joining a stock company in San Pedro, he toured Southern California for about six weeks and then headed north to Vallejo for a jaunt in the San Joaquin Valley with the Maude Amber Players. In San Francisco, he worked with the Haggerty Repertory and other groups until a raging influenza epidemic closed down all the theaters in mid-1918. While waiting for the flu scare to end, he took a job loading trucks and freight cars at the Sperry Flour Mills.

Two months later, he bought a one-way passage on a lumber boat bound for San Jose, where his friend Alfred Aldrich was directing a vaudeville act. Unable to stomach the disgusting filth below deck, he spent his time attempting to find a place to sit or merely stand up for the duration of the voyage. Unfortunately, Aldrich's engagement was a brief one, and after the showman was unable to get a booking in Los Angeles, he loaned Boris enough money for food and lodging until another acting job could be found. Interestingly, even after arriving in the new movie capital, Boris "had no thought of getting into pictures. All my ideas were centered on a dramatic

Boris, age 26, in the Harry St. Clair Players production of *Paid in Full* (1914).

career, stage success"; but with a few of Aldrich's dollars safely in his pocket, he "made the rounds of the only possible outlet—the film studios."

---

[1] Although no official records of this union exist, Cynthia Lindsay, in her 1975 book *Dear Boris*, cites "oral reports" of the "dark and sallow" actress' "days of starvation as the wife of Boris Karloff." While Boris often recalled these stock company days, he never mentioned Miss de Wilton.

Chapter 3

Trial and Error

"If I'd stopped to light a cigarette, I wouldn't be sitting here. The whole point, I think, of an actor is, if you stay with it X number of years, you at least learn the ABCs of it. You learn something. You can't avoid it. Then it's 'Who's going to be lucky? Who's going to be on the right corner at the right moment?' And the opportunity comes along."

Between streetcar rides, Boris got a lot of exercise walking to and from the Hollywood casting offices, and his total earnings from film acting added up to a whopping $5, an extra's pay from appearing "in a crowd scene being directed by Frank Borzage at Universal."[1] Unable to find further work as an extra, he returned to San Francisco for a season with the Robert Lawrence Company at the Majestic Theatre, while Aldrich stayed behind, scouting for more possible film roles. James Edwards, who shared Boris' dressing room at the Majestic, later said:

> Boris was a very capable character actor... and he was tre-
> mendously popular with children. And it was a common
> sight to see Boris striding down Mission Street, smiling
> happily and always followed by an admiring group of six
> or eight small fry... I can still see Boris sitting in the dress-
> ing room, hour after hour, working with grease paint, nose
> putty, crepe hair and wigs, trying to perfect the art of chang-
> ing his appearance.

Three months later, Aldrich introduced Boris to Al MacQuarrie, an agent and actor who had played supporting roles in many of Douglas Fairbanks' lighthearted adventure films at Triangle. Fairbanks recently had formed United Artists with Charles Chaplin, D.W. Griffith, and his wife, Mary Pickford. *His Majesty the American* was the first film to be released by the new company. Co-written by Fairbanks and director Joseph Henabery, the film tells the tale of William Brooks, a young, thrill-seeking New Yorker who travels to Mexico in search of adventure. Threatened by revolutionaries after his arrival, he defeats them and wins the heart of a beautiful princess. An 8-reel extravaganza, this jingoistic film inspired by current events and politics (the Mexican Revolution and post-World War I propaganda) features trademark Fairbanks derring-do and acrobatics as his young Yank foils the evil Hispanic soldiers, one of whom is played by Boris.

When he managed to land the extra part in *His Majesty the American*, Boris was lodging in a rooming house on Bunker Hill, which overlooked downtown Los Angeles and was reached by riding up Angel's Flight, a steep funicular, or cable car system. His room and the other sur-rounding apartments and houses were actually re-developed mansions that had been prime real estate in the early days of the city. Paid $5 per day on the Fairbanks set, he worked for six days and was thrilled to earn more than he ever had in a single week on the stage. He had been a professional actor for a decade, and one job chasing an action star around a back lot had finan-cially outdone any role he had played in stock. He later recalled, "I thought I'd made my fortune."

The Deadlier Sex (1920). **Mahlon Hamilton protects chaste Blanche Sweet from the untoward advances of Boris' lecherous Jules Borney.**

But screen roles were nearly impossible to find, and even though he believed filmmakers were not interested in his particular "type," he kept making the rounds. Eventually a woman named Mabel Condon, who saw some promise in his looks and style, began spreading his name around the independent film companies.

Much to his delight, the "fortune" he had been paid for *His Majesty the American* soon increased 50 percent when he graduated to the $7.50-per-day extra ranks (perhaps in the 15-episode serials *The Masked Raider* and *The Lightning Raider*, both released in 1919). In late 1919 independent producer Jesse D. Hampton gave him a bit part in the William Desmond film *The Prince and Betty*, based on P.G. Wodehouse's novel and released by Pathé. A few weeks later, Hampton re-hired Boris, this time giving him a real character, the French-Canadian trapper Jules Borney, in *The Deadlier Sex* (1920), starring Blanche Sweet, Russell Simpson and Mahlon Hamilton. Filmed on location at Truckee, northwest of Lake Tahoe, this melodrama featured an authentic backwoods flavor and provided Boris with his first "heavy" character, a vicious, lustful brute who nearly murdered Hamilton before kidnapping Sweet, whom he imprisoned in a cave. In fine Victorian melodramatic style, Boris' Borney was about to commit rape just as Hamilton's hero ended Borney's rampage. Boris created a slight variation on this role for his next film, *The Courage of Marge O'Doone*, starring Pauline Starke and filmed at Vitagraph Studios during the spring of 1920.

Boris now was living at 327 South Hope Street in Los Angeles. In July, he married for the second time, to "Montana" Laurena Williams, a 24-year-old musician. Born in New Mexico, Laurena had moved to Phillipsburg, Montana, with her parents, William R. Williams and Annie Keeler, and then met Boris after finding employment in Los Angeles. Also present at the wedding were Charlotte Garbor and Holland F. Burr, who served as witnesses.

Later in 1920 Boris appeared in his first screen epic since *His Majesty the American*, and his role was nearly as insignificant. Heavily made up as a Huron Indian in director Maurice Tourneur's adaptation of *The Last of the Mohicans*, the first feature based on James Fenimore Cooper's sprawling novel, he was buried by the visual spectacle and Wallace Beery's typically bombastic star performance.

During 1921 Boris moved to 210 South Flower Street. At this time, casting directors began to take advantage of his dark complexion and somewhat exotic features, as he portrayed villainous Arabs in three of his four films that year. In Universal's *Cheated Hearts*, starring Herbert Rawlinson and Warner Baxter, he and his old friend Al MacQuarrie both played Middle Easterners. In 1922 he alternated his Arabs with a South Sea Islander and another French-Canadian trapper. In *The Infidel* and *Omar the Tentmaker*, he was directed by James Young. He also relocated again, to 1225 McCadden Place in Hollywood.

Truckee, California, in the 1920s. Here Boris played his first notable film character, Jules Borney, in *The Deadlier Sex*.

In 1923 Boris played nothing more exotic than a cowboy who is gunned down by Western star Hoot Gibson in Universal's *The Gentleman from America*. For his only other film that year, he returned to more mysterious type as "Prince Kapolski" in *The Prisoner*, shot at Universal by future MGM director Jack Conway from a script by prolific screenwriter Edward T. Lowe, Jr.

Although his roles were still fairly small, Boris now was making about $150 per week *when* he was working. Unfortunately a slump in production during 1923-24 forced him to look for a job outside the film industry. He believed he was better off waiting for more $150 roles to become available at the studios rather than slipping back into the extra ranks and risking the reputation he had established. Subsequently, he signed on with George Eastman, who operated three Los Angeles building material yards, one at Highland Avenue, one downtown and one at Westin and Slausen, where he became a warehouse man for 40 cents an hour. To keep up with the current boom in subdivision development, the yard was operating at full capacity, and Boris moved 100-pound sacks of concrete from boxcars to waiting delivery trucks until Charles Curtis, a fellow Englishman who drove a big Mack, asked him if he wanted to operate the small truck he was adding to the fleet. Boris later described what went through his mind at that moment:

> [H]e was going to put on a second truck, because the yards were so busy. And he bought an autocar, a little autocar truck. Those awful little things where the engine is under the seat, and they run on two cylinders, and always foul up and wind up on one cylinder, and you've got to crank, and there were no starters, and hard tires, you know. And he asked me if I'd like to drive his new truck, and I immediately said yes, in spite of the fact that I'd never driven anything in my life. Nothing. I had nothing to do with automobiles in those days. It was all streetcars.

To land the new position—and to avoid making a complete fool of himself—Boris went home (now 1404 North Catalina in Hollywood) that Saturday determined to learn how to drive. Luckily he persuaded a friend who owned a car to give him a lesson in a large vacant lot the following afternoon. Explaining the back wheel from the front and how to operate the gearshift, his instructor "practically gave up in despair" but taught him enough to get by. Bright and early on Monday morning, Boris was back in Eastman's yard, helping the warehouse man load the autocar with two tons of cement before "sailing up Slausen Avenue... the traffic scattering in all directions."

Boris drove the truck for the next 18 months, transporting cement from the yard to building sites all over the area. Still earning 40 cents an hour, he parked at each site and carried the 100-pound sacks to the cement mixer, which was often up to 50 yards away—a procedure that further honed his lean, muscular physique and tanned his complexion to an even darker tone. Another building material that he handled on a regular basis was the "delightful" plasterers' lime putty that was stored in 300-pound tin cans—the unloading of which was so savagely back-breaking that it paid *50* cents an hour!

Boris' struggle with the truck was lightened somewhat by his renewed friendship with his niece, Dorothea ("Dorrie") Donkin, who had moved to California to work as a governess. Earning more than he did, Dorrie would treat her long-lost uncle to an occasional meal.

Boris didn't abandon acting during this period, and appeared in villainous roles in seven films, including the ludicrous boxing comedy *Dynamite Dan* (1924), in which he had a conspicuous role as a man who robs his employer, *Parisian Nights* (1925), on which Robert Florey worked as an assistant director, and *Forbidden Cargo* (1925), a Prohibition adventure in which he played first mate on Evelyn Brent's rum-running ship. But he rarely went to see one of his films when it was released, and he apparently forgot about those he made during his stint at Eastman's, although he must have arranged leaves of absence to appear in them.

Another pursuit he hadn't given up was matrimony. Although no record of their divorce exists, Boris and Laurena's relationship lasted no more than three and one half years, as he was free to marry again on February 3, 1924. Helene Vivian Soule, a 23-year-old stage actress and dancer known as "Polly," became the third Mrs. William Henry Pratt, a.k.a. Boris Karloff, and moved in with him at 951 Venego Avenue after a civil ceremony was performed by Los Angeles Justice of the Peace J. Walter Hanby. Born in Maine, she had lived in Massachusetts with her parents, Greenwood E. Soule and Etta Rich, before seeking work in tinsel town. By 1925 Boris had found yet another residence, at 1549 Western Avenue.

Most of Boris' film roles held no special significance for him, but he remembered receiving a phone call from someone at Cosmopolitan about William Randolph Hearst's production of *Never the Twain Shall Meet* in mid-1925. Adapted by Eugene Mullin from Peter B. Kyne's novel, this major MGM release was directed by Maurice Tourneur, whom Boris had worked for briefly in *The Last of the Mohicans* five years earlier. Although he was assigned a small part as a villain, he asked for a week's leave from Eastman and joined the cast, including Anita Stewart, on location in San Francisco, where they were given $25 rooms at the beautiful Palace Hotel and another $5 per diem for meals. Since his scenes were shot out in the bay, Boris ate lunch on the boat and, ordering only a small dinner, still had most of his $5 when turning in each night.

He remained in San Francisco for three weeks, until Tourneur completed the shoot and the cast and crew returned to Los Angeles. Having saved the majority of his allowance, he was in good spirits; but upon returning to the Eastman yard, he learned that his two-week AWOL status had resulted in his substitute returning to the warehouse and a new man being hired to drive the truck.

During the summer of 1925 Boris again played opposite Evelyn Brent, in *Lady Robin Hood*, an interesting mixture of English outlaw legends and the American Southwest directed by Thomas Ince's brother, Ralph, for R.C. Pictures, the same company that had made *Forbidden Cargo* earlier in the year. Boris' character, Cabraza, paralleled the Sheriff of Nottingham, while William Humphrey's evil Governor represented Prince John. Brent's dual character of Catalina and

La Ortiga, who rescued the oppressed Californians from the two villains, was a clever female hybrid of Robin Hood and Zorro. Friar Tuck also was present in the form of D'Arcy Corrigan's Padre.

Over the next nine months, tolerable film roles became even harder to find, so Boris broke his seven-year hiatus from the theater by appearing in British actor-producer Reginald Pole's staging of *The Idiot*. In the spring of 1926 he played a small part in First National's *The Greater Glory*, starring Conway Terle and Ian Keith, and then did a third job for R.C. Pictures in *Her Honor, the Governor*, produced by Joseph Kennedy and starring Pauline Frederick. He was particularly effective in the latter film, portraying Snipe Collins, a treacherous dope addict, a characterization he would repeat over the next few years.

1835 Wilcox Avenue, Los Angeles. Boris moved into this building in 1928. (1996 photograph by Scott Allen Nollen)

It was after *Her Honor, the Governor* that he was chosen to appear in *The Bells* with Lionel Barrymore; and Boris' eerie sideshow mesmerist, a visual symbol of a murderer's guilty conscience, became one of the stagy film's few saving graces. After receiving fifth billing in *The Bells*, he lapsed back into bit parts in *Eagle of the Sea* and *Old Ironsides*, but still forged ahead, heartened by lucky coincidences such as his meeting outside the Universal gate with Lon Chaney.

Now living at 1012 Larrabee Street in Sherman, he applied for membership in the Masquers Club on March 7, 1926. Referring to himself as a "professional actor," he continued to make as many connections as possible, and was recommended by Guy Coburn and seconded by F. Esmelton for acceptance into the organization, which then met at a clubhouse at 6735 Yucca Street in Hollywood.

During that year he also played the first of his many "masher" roles, a lecher on a park bench who attempts to pick up the innocent Mabel Normand, in *The Nickel Hopper*, a Hal Roach three-reeler and his only silent slapstick comedy. While making the film, he rubbed shoulders with

Boris' half-brother Charles Rary Pratt, Guernsey, England, 1928.

Roach regulars Oliver Hardy and James Finlayson, who began appearing in the long-running series of Laurel and Hardy comedies the following year.

In 1927 Boris was on the move again, this time settling into an apartment at 6040 Eleanor Avenue in Hollywood. Like so many aspects of his career, he dismissed his films from this period, recalling only *The Bells* as being of any merit. During these "forgotten years," he played a native chief in *Tarzan and the Golden Lion* (1927), based on Edgar Rice Burroughs' novel, had a small role as a ship's purser in *Two Arabian Knights* (1927), the first film to win an Academy Award for Best Comedy Direction (Lewis Milestone), and appeared in four more Westerns. He also accepted the role of Artem Tiapkin in the play *Window Panes* at the Eden Theatre.

Boris' only sister, Julia Honoria Pratt Donkin (right), and her daughter, Dorothea, in the vicarage garden, Semer, England, 1930.

For many reasons, financial, matrimonial, and vocational, Boris could not establish any permanent roots. In 1928, he found a nice apartment at 1835 North Wilcox Avenue in Los Angeles, where he actually remained for some time. But on November 20 that year, William Henry Pratt, Defendant, was ordered by a Los Angeles judge to pay Helen V. Pratt, Plaintiff, a particular sum of money, apparently alimony (though no official record of their divorce exists). Failing to do so, he was ordered back into court on December 5 to answer a charge of contempt. And on July 10, 1929, he again was in court, having refused to pay attorney's fees and alimony to Helen V. Pratt, Plaintiff. This time the judge offered to drop the contempt charge in return for his payment to the plaintiff of $100 cash and an additional $240 in installments of $50 per month, plus $15 per week for a total of 54 weeks and the assumption of all bills held in common. After three marriages and divorces, Boris' track record with wives was rivaling his hit-and-miss career in the movies, but his luck in both of these areas was about to change.

Less than two weeks before the third court-ordered appearance, his first sound film, *Behind That Curtain*, was released by Fox Pictures. Based on a story by Earl Derr Biggers, it also marked the film debut of Charlie Chan (E.L. Park), who appeared in a secondary capacity alongside stars Warner Baxter and Claude King. Under the direction of Irving Cummings, Boris played a Sudanese servant, but now had to add a convincing accent to his familiar Arabic characterization. A few months later, he finished out his 1929 screen appearances as Abdoul, a "Hindu" servant, in MGM's *The Unholy Night*, a turgid drama directed by Lionel Barrymore in which a group of World War I buddies fake their own deaths to claim insurance money. Although based on a story by Ben Hecht, the film is heavy on dialogue and lacking in action; even Roland Young (in his talkie debut) cannot salvage it. And Boris, in a conspicuous role, overacts badly while affecting a very *un*convincing accent.

Two other events during this period were far more significant for Boris. One was a return to San Francisco to play the major role of Kregg in Chester DeVonde and Kilbourn Gordon's *Kongo* at the Capitol Theatre, and the other was attending a dinner party in Los Angeles where he was introduced to a young woman who helped him forget about his previous troubles with the opposite sex.

Dorothy Stine was a librarian for the Los Angeles City Library Central Supply System and lived in Hollywood with her mother. Slender, elegant and very intelligent, she possessed the qualities Boris liked, so much so that the two were married at the Hollywood Presbyterian Church on April 12, 1930. Like his previous marriages, he began this one after a very brief courtship, and did not tell his new wife about the former Mrs. Pratts. Dorothy, born in Charlotte, Michigan, to William F. and Louise M. Stine (whose maiden name, incidentally, was *Pratt*), also had been married previously, to a man named Kelly; and she, too, did not discuss earlier relationships. Unable to afford a honeymoon, the new couple drove Boris' broken-down Ford to a little home, which Dorothy called a "shack," above Laurel Canyon, where they lived for the next two years.

During 1930 Boris landed small roles in several films, including MGM's *The Sea Bat*, a realistic, earthy film shot on location off the California coast, in which he played an ill-fated Corsican sailor, and Tiffany's *The Utah Kid*, his first and only sound Western, but none of them brought him much attention. For several months, he was out of work, and one day while waiting for his agent to return, he walked over to the Actors' Equity office to inquire about his mail. After being told that nothing had arrived, he turned to leave, but the young woman behind the desk stopped him.

"By the way, are you working?" she asked.

"No," Boris replied, almost as a matter of course.

"There's a part in a play called *The Criminal Code*, a small part," she revealed, suggesting that he report downtown for a tryout.

Boris wasted no time getting to the audition, and because he had been "on the right corner at the right moment," won the colorful role of Galloway, the murderous prison trusty, in Martin Flavin's gritty play. *The Criminal Code*, with Arthur Byron in the lead role of Warden Brady, had been a big hit in New York before the entire company, with the exception of a few supporting actors, was transplanted to the West Coast for shows in San Francisco and Los Angeles. Although Galloway appeared in only four scenes, he motivated the most dramatic events in the play. When accepting the part, Boris told himself, "Well, by golly, here I go. I'm going to show these chaps."

After opening night at the Belasco Theatre in downtown Los Angeles, he left the door of his dressing room open as he sat inside, "expecting all the producers and agents in town to come pouring in." Disappointed that no one raved about his powerful performance, he was grateful for the good reviews he received in the next day's papers, as well as the $350 weekly salary he was beginning to earn.

About three months later, Howard Hawks was preparing to film Fred Niblo, Jr., and Seton I. Miller's adaptation of *The Criminal Code* at Columbia. Hawks had seen one of the performances at the Belasco, and since he was casting the film with talent from outside the studio, asked Boris to test for the same character. Impressed by his self-effacing, professional manner and his nonverbal acting capabilities, particularly the subtle menace he could evoke with facial expressions and bodily stance, Hawks, who had increased Galloway's role in the screenplay, gave him seventh billing and the opportunity to share scenes with Walter Huston, who chewed the Columbia scenery as Warden Brady, the role originally portrayed by Arthur Byron.

Boris and Hawks developed an excellent working relationship during the production, and the director allowed his supporting player to make suggestions about how his performance should be filmed. The high point of *The Criminal Code*, a scene in which Galloway stabs Runch (Clark Marshall), a fellow prison trusty, resulted from one of Boris' recommendations. Framed within a single dolly shot, Boris, with his back to the camera, slowly walks toward his victim, first trapping him with a single gesture (thrusting out his left arm, knife in hand) and then backing him into a closet, where the stabbing occurs off-screen. When Hawks requested that Boris recreate his facial expressions for a close-up, he persuaded the director to stick with the single long take, and portray it just as it had been done on the stage. Boris later explained:

Boris as Ned Galloway in *The Criminal Code* (1931).

The audience couldn't see my face. But they were imagining the most terrifying expressions on it, far more spine-chilling expressions than I could possibly have achieved. I simply provided the frame; they had filled in the picture... I knew that a single shot showing my face would have spoilt the effect. Imagination alone provided those thrills.

Here, Boris provided a specific example of his artistic vision, a philosophy influenced by the writings of his favorite author, Joseph Conrad, and one that served him well throughout his career: a "less is more" approach that stirs the viewer's imagination with dramatic subtlety rather than a graphic depiction of action, violence and mayhem.

Released on January 3, 1931, *The Criminal Code* was only one of 18 films in which Boris appeared that year. Haunting Columbia for several months after Hawks wrapped the prison extravaganza, he managed to land tiny parts in two Jack Holt vehicles, *The Last Parade*, directed by Erle C. Kenton, and *Dirigible*, the only film in which he was directed by Frank Capra. Although he helped make *The Criminal Code* a hit, Columbia did not offer him the contract he hoped for, and he returned to free-lancing, rather successfully, at RKO-Radio and Warner Bros.

At RKO, he appeared in three films, as a "revolutionary" menacing Bert Wheeler and Robert Woolsey in *Cracked Nuts*, directed by Buster Keaton's former collaborator Edward Cline; as "Cokey Joe," a dope pusher who tries to corrupt young Jackie Cooper but is foiled by Richard Dix, in *Young Donovan's Kid*; and as the "Professor," one of his first masterfully eccentric cinematic performances, in *The Public Defender*, another Richard Dix vehicle. But at Warner Bros., he landed roles in two major releases featuring the versatile and volatile Edward G. Robinson, who had shot to stardom in *Little Caesar* the previous year.

James Cagney, appearing as Robinson's pal in *Smart Money*, began a lengthy friendship with Boris, who played "Sport Williams," a down on his luck gambler, in one early sequence. Although so brief that a blinking viewer may miss him, Boris' performance is memorable and the first of his several gangster roles.

Boris' second Warners film with Robinson was achieved, in part, through the assistance of his friend George E. Stone, who was appearing in *Five Star Final* at the studio. Stone approached director Mervyn LeRoy and convinced him to cast Boris as reporter "Reverend" T. Vernon Isopod, an expelled divinity student.

Byron Morgan and Robert Lord adapted their screenplay from *Late Night Final*, a London-based play by Louis Weitzenkorn, former managing editor of the *New York Evening Graphic*, a scandal-mongering tabloid. In the film, Robinson plays Joseph Randall, editor of the *New York Gazette*, who is ordered to boost circulation by serializing the scandalous story of a society woman who murdered a man 20 years earlier.

Isopod is hired by Randall to interview the "murderess" (Frances Starr) and, disguised as a minister assigned to perform the marriage of her daughter (Marian Marsh) to a wealthy socialite (Anthony Bushell), he discerns her present situation. Reporting back to Randall, Isopod starts a chain reaction that culminates with the double suicide of the woman and her husband (H.B. Warner).

Within the film's milieu of immoral muckraking, Boris' character, whom he plays in an exaggerated, theatrical style, is the only one who exhibits no redeeming features. Even after the double suicide, Isopod, who previously was expelled from divinity school for drunkenness and womanizing, approaches his employers, intending to extract further information from the hysterical, orphaned daughter.

Produced for $290,000, *Five Star Final* became Warners' longest-running and most profitable release of 1931, was rated seventh in the annual *Film Daily* critics' poll and captured a nomination for the Best Picture Academy Award. Providing Boris with a colorful and substantial role that embodied the "lowlife" aspect of Warners' social problem genre, the film brought him more public and critical recognition than *The Criminal Code*.

Boris' third film with Warners involved an interview with the formidable Michael Curtiz, who was on the verge of becoming Hollywood's most prolific and tyrannical director. Casting *The Mad Genius*, a *Svengali* follow-up for John Barrymore (whose salary doomed this esoteric film to a quick box office death), the Hungarian filmmaker called in Boris, thinking he was Russian, and was instantly disappointed when he was answered with a slightly lisping but distinctive and very gentle English voice. Knowing that time was money to his Warner overlords, Curtiz awarded him a one-scene character: an abusive father thwarted by Tsarakov (Barrymore), a club-footed puppeteer who, having been unable to realize his dream of becoming a famous ballet dancer, creates a similar career for the abuser's son (Frankie Darro).

Boris' experiences at Warners were the beginning of the end of his career as a free-lance actor who occasionally landed a role that an audience might remember on the ride (or, during the Depression, walk) home. Here, he had worked with Alfred E. Green, Mervyn LeRoy and Michael Curtiz; he had also done minor stretches at Roach Studios, taking direction from James Parrott in the French foreign-language version of Laurel and Hardy's *Pardon Us*, and at Fox, speaking dialogue by Jules Furthman in *The Yellow Ticket*, a Raoul Walsh production featuring Laurence Olivier, a young stage actor who disliked films and did not share any scenes with his future friend and cricket comrade. (Olivier later wrote, "I remember Boris Karloff extremely well and I liked him very much, [but] I have no memory of his being in the picture.") Having established a great rapport with Howard Hawks, he also was cast as Gaffney, the enemy of Tony Camonte (Paul Muni), actually Chicago's Al Capone, in the director's urban crime masterpiece, *Scarface*, which was filmed in mid-1931 but, for censorship reasons, left unreleased until the following March.

Although his 21 years of acting on stage and screen had yet to catapult him to stardom, Boris' hard work had earned him a certain degree of respectability. No longer was he economically dividing cans of mulligatawny soup or heaving 100-pound sacks of concrete. He and Dorothy were hitting it off rather splendidly, having abandoned the shack of Laurel Canyon for a house on Las Palmas Avenue in Hollywood. But 92 steps were not welcomed by an actor working into the wee hours of the morning, and the new dwelling soon was left behind in a move to the San Fernando Valley.

Boris' face now was recognized at the respectable minor (Universal and Columbia) and some of the major (Warner Bros., RKO, and MGM) studios in Hollywood. He now stood out from the crowd a bit: a distinctive voice in the wilderness of would-be actors who aspired to that one role that would, in his words, "kick the goal." He knew that every professional worth his salt must pay his dues to deserve both popular and artistic success.

William Henry Pratt *had* paid his dues, more so than many. But there would be another major payment before he really could reap the benefits of toil. Bowlegged but well-built from all the years of physical labor, graying but still holding his hair, hard tanned but rarely able to enjoy the freedom of holidays in the sun, he rose one morning, started his Ford coupe and drove off to Universal City, ready to play Joe Terry, a waterfront henchman, in *Graft*.

---

[1]Late in life, Boris could not recall the name of the film, and it is doubtful that the scene in question was directed by Borzage, whose nine directorial efforts in 1918 were released by the Triangle Film Corporation. When Triangle folded late that year, the director moved on to William Randolph Hearst's Cosmopolitan Productions and then to First National. It is possible that one of these companies could have rented Universal's back lot to shoot a scene, but the fact is that the name of this first Karloff film probably will never be discovered. (Most of Borzage's silents no longer exist.) For years, biographers and film historians claimed Boris' cinematic debut occurred in the 1916 Anna Pavlova adventure *The Dumb Girl of Portici*, a non-Borzage film produced at Universal more than a year before the struggling actor reached California.

Frankenstein (1931). A Universal publicity shot of Boris as the Monster.

Chapter 4

The Right Corner

"I have to be very grateful to him, to the Monster, who's really my best friend. I'd been at it for 20 years when he came along, and he really changed the whole course of my life."

Portraying another criminal was an easy task for Boris. He was getting used to doing his thug routine by the summer of 1931, and Joe Terry in *Graft* was no exception. Perhaps collecting his $350 paycheck each week was the most exciting aspect of making the film, for its production was being heavily overshadowed by Carl Laemmle, Jr.'s intention to create a blockbuster follow-up to Tod Browning's *Dracula*, which had opened to packed houses over the Valentine's Day weekend.

Bela Lugosi, whose American reputation had been almost as obscure as Boris' before he appeared in the vampire opus, was now a hot property. But he had become difficult, scoffing at Robert Florey's screenplay for the new film and rejecting a character who would be covered with makeup and given no lines to speak. He was a classically trained *actor*, a very popular one at the moment, and not about to lower himself to the level of a "half-wit" performer. While appearing in an elaborate screen test shot on June 16-17, 1931, by Florey and cinematographer Paul Ivano, he considered obtaining a physician's certificate to exempt him from the distasteful role, but eventually just quit the project. After Laemmle, Jr., and Florey attempted to cast other actors, including John Peter Richmond (later known as John Carradine), who echoed Lugosi's reasons for turning it down, the film was shelved.

In the midst of all this controversy, Boris continued to work on *Graft*, quietly walking from the soundstage to the commissary each day for lunch. The buzz around the studio was that the former Lugosi follow-up had been resurrected by James Whale, an English director who recently had scored a big hit with Tiffany's anti-war drama *Journey's End* (1930), and now was putting the finishing touches on Universal's *Waterloo Bridge*. As Boris was eating one afternoon, an assistant to Whale inquired if he would like to join the director for coffee. Accepting the invitation, he received not only a free cup of java but also an offer to test for the Monster in *Frankenstein*. While Carl Laemmle, Sr., who was worried about the studio's poor financial status, was still campaigning for Lugosi, Whale decided to give Boris a chance.

"Of course I was delighted," Boris recalled, "because it meant another job, if I was able to land it. Actually that's all it meant to me. At the same time, I felt rather hurt, because I had on a very good straight makeup and my best suit, and I was being tested for the Monster, but that was that! I was very grateful for the opportunity."

Boris now was acting in *Graft* during the day, reporting to the Universal makeup department in the evening and attempting to re-read Mary Shelley's novel whenever he had a few spare minutes. Assigned to transform him into the Frankenstein Monster, former baseball player and resident makeup wizard Jack P. Pierce experimented extensively with various designs and materials, building upon sketches Whale had made of Boris' head. Prior to these nightly sessions, Pierce had spent many hours researching human anatomy, surgery, medicine, criminology, burial customs and electrodynamics. Learning that a surgeon could open the cranium six different ways, he chose the simplest, to "cut the top of the skull off straight across like a potlid, hinge it, pop the brain in, and then clamp it on tight." After creating a large scar for the right side

Frankenstein. Original lobby card for the film's theatrical re-issue, 1951.

of Boris' forehead, which he built up with layers of cheesecloth and cotton strips soaked in collodion, he added small metal clamps to hold the skull together and a metal stud for each side of the neck, the inlets for the electricity that would bring the Monster to life. (One of Pierce's early experiments also included clamps that looked like eye screws—one on each side of the forehead—surrounding large exposed veins.) When the facial makeup was nearly completed, Boris looked in the mirror and noticed that his eyes were "too normal and alive and natural," prompting Pierce to deaden them by adding a layer of mortician's wax to his eyelids. Pleased with the result, Boris then removed a dental bridge from the right side of his mouth to sink in his cheek and give the Monster an even more cadaverous appearance.

Pierce also made up Boris' arms, blackening his fingernails with shoe polish and adding sutures and metal slats to make it look as if his hands were sewn and clamped to his wrists. Any exposed parts of his body, including his face, arms and hands, were covered with a blue-green grease paint that photographed a lifeless gray. Considering that the Monster was pieced together from the corpses of executed felons, Pierce, who read that criminals bound and buried alive by the Egyptians had been discovered with greatly extended extremities, made his arms look longer by shortening the sleeves of his coat. As final touches, his torso was filled out and made more rigid with a double-quilted suit and a steel rod running along his spine, his legs were stiffened with steel struts and two pairs of pants, and his feet were burdened with asphalt spreader's boots weighing 13 pounds each. The entire outfit added nearly a foot to his height and an additional 48 pounds for him to carry.

Although he had begun a truly torturous professional relationship with Jack Pierce, Boris knew that his new friend could only benefit his career. Appropriately, the makeup man's experiments in bringing the Monster to life would rival those of Dr. Frankenstein in the film: By the time the final look for the creature was completed, they had stalled Boris' screen test for three weeks, allowing him ample time to prepare, both physically and mentally. Ironically, Boris' addition to the makeup proved effective only as a cosmetic touch, for his wonderfully expressive eyes cut right through the pall of mortician's wax. Observing him in all his moribund regalia, the Laemmles enthusiastically approved, admitting, "Karloff's eyes mirrored the suffering we needed."

Characteristically giving all the credit to Pierce, Boris later recalled, "If I'd have asked for [a delay], I would have been thrown out on my ear. But in his position, he was able to do it. And when he felt he was quite ready... he said, 'All right, we can shoot it,' and they did. And thank heavens, they liked his work and I got the part."

Pierce had been able to gain preparation time for Boris, but after three weeks, it is doubtful if the Laemmles would have waited any longer. The other roles had been cast by Whale and approved by the front office, Herman Rosse's expressionistic sets were ready, and Lugosi's name was still being bandied about, since he was not scheduled to begin his scenes for Robert Florey's "consolation film," *Murders in the Rue Morgue*, for another two months.

Florey's original *Frankenstein* screenplay had been revamped by Whale (who saw to it that the Frenchman received no credit for his work), and Carl Laemmle, Jr., approved Garrett Fort and Francis Edwards Faragoh's final script on August 12, 1931. Twelve days later, with a $262,000 budget and 30-day shooting schedule, Whale began production on a soundstage dressed as a lonely mountain cemetery in which Henry Frankenstein (Colin Clive) and his hunchback assistant, Fritz (Dwight Frye), steal a freshly buried corpse.

Filming began at 9:00 each morning, but due to Pierce's lengthy makeup applications, Boris had to report at 4:00 a.m. to Dressing Room No. 5, a one-room "shack with a shower bath" which became known as "The Bugaboudoir" due to its use as a monster preparation zone since 1922. Lon Chaney had used it during the filming of *The Hunchback of Notre* Dame (1923) and *The Phantom of the Opera* (1925), and Conrad Veidt had moved in to receive his hideous grin for *The Man Who Laughs* in 1928. And during the previous autumn, just before Boris settled in for Pierce's handiwork, Lugosi had applied his *Dracula* makeup within its four austere walls.

After four to five hours in Dressing Room No. 5's makeup chair, patient Boris forged ahead with a full day's work in the blistering summer heat. Because of his hideous appearance, he would sit in his dressing room during the lunch hour, a respite that allowed him to strip off the suit and sweat-soaked undergarments. Managing to wolf down a Spartan meal, he then put on dry underwear and another quilted suit before replacing the outer costume. Each day, he also was allowed a few tea and cigarette breaks, during which the flow of sweat would subside a bit. He recalled, "I felt, most of the time, as if I were wearing a clammy shroud. No doubt it added to the realism!"

While trying to cool off one morning, he walked onto the lot and frightened a studio secretary, who promptly passed out. When Carl Laemmle, Sr., heard of the incident, he expressed his concern for "nice little secretaries" who might be pregnant, requiring Boris to wear a light blue veil over his head whenever he ventured outside. Of course, posting two guards at the soundstage door eliminated any unsupervised strolls, and while appearing in outdoor scenes, he was led back and forth by Pierce, who stayed by his side, ready to touch up the makeup at a moment's notice. Often the mortician's wax would dry out and fall into his eyes, causing excruciating pain until Pierce could extract it and apply a fresh coat.

Even more appalling was the hour-long removal of the makeup that took place each night after everyone else was dismissed. Exhausted from the heavy costume, the heat and performing on his feet much of the day, Boris patiently sat in the chair as Pierce removed the appliances, cheesecloth, collodion and other foul substances with even fouler oils and acids. Boris claimed that he issued forth streams of profanity as his pal nearly skinned him alive each evening, but his coworkers testified that he accepted his agonizing lot with much humor and no complaints.

When conferring with Whale, who spoke in a very quiet, controlled manner, he patiently nodded his head before "doing the shot," sometimes receiving a playful push from the director. But one workday in particular made Boris wonder about Whale's motives, and ultimately led to a disagreement between them. On September 28, Whale, his crew, Boris, seven-year-old Marilyn Harris (who played Maria, the little girl), her mother, character actor Michael Mark and a trained kitten headed for Malibu Lake to shoot the scene in which the Monster and Maria take turns tossing flowers into the water.

Tiny Marilyn was not afraid of the huge, gruesome Monster as she rode to the lake with Boris, whose love of children instantly was apparent to her. Unfortunately she *was* terrified of her abusive mother, whose sadistic behavior added to the confusion during the location shoot. Boris liked the scene because it gave the Monster his one and only moment of pleasure, but he was very displeased with how it ended, transforming happiness into horror when the Monster drowns the child. When he and some members of the crew asked Whale if the scene could be altered, the director insisted that it be shot as written: Allowing the girl to live would destroy the shock the incident would give to the audience.

Actually, Whale's conception of the scene depicted the Monster, not as a killer, but as an infantile creature who, thinking the child will float like the flowers, makes a terrible mistake. He did not ask Boris to throw the child into the lake as a violent and deliberate act, but to toss her gently, like he had done with the flowers, as she cries, "No, you're hurting me." With Arthur Edeson's camera placed so that the drowning girl was blocked by Boris' body, the audience would not see, but only hear, her death. As shot by Edeson, the Monster, after tossing her in, attempts to find her, placing his hands in the water several times. When she does not re-appear, he turns and runs away from the lake and into the trees, his expression not one of malice, but of abject horror at what has occurred.

Reportedly the initial take of Boris tossing her in did not satisfy Marilyn's mother, who insisted that he do it again, this time with more force so that she would fly farther into the water. Whale consented, but Marilyn, whose back was hurting, refused. Promised anything if she would take another plunge, the child relented and, being on a strict diet, asked for a dozen hard-boiled eggs. When Boris got out of the situation, rightly claiming that his heavy costume restricted his movement, Whale ordered two crew members to do the honors. Marilyn went sailing in again, and this time failed to surface for several seconds.

Frankenstein. **Jack Pierce works his Monster magic on Boris.**

By the time Whale wrapped the scene, Boris had been in makeup since 3:30 a.m., having reported even earlier than usual for the drive to the lake. Dehydrated from the blazing sun and liable to catch a pneumonia-inducing chill, he arrived back at the studio around supper time. But, on this occasion, when he removed his costume and undergarments, it was not to have Pierce remove his makeup. Whale had fallen behind schedule and needed to shoot the climactic scene *that night*. Allowed a rest in his dressing room, Boris ate and then reported to the soundstage to run through the fake mountains with the bloodhounds nipping at his heels.

Worse than the re-shooting of Maria's drowning was Whale's insistence that Boris, who was not afforded the luxury of a double, carry Colin Clive up a hill to the old windmill over and over until "an acceptable take" was achieved. His bowed legs about to give out, Boris did not object, although this "savagely hard work" precipitated almost 40 years of back problems for him. At 5 a.m., he finally was allowed to collapse into Pierce's chair for removal of makeup he had been wearing for 25 hours.

The ridiculous events of September 28-29 did not recur, but the fact that he was forced continually to work 15 to 16 hours per day induced him to contact the Academy of Motion Picture Arts and Sciences, which required that no actor put in more than 12 hours unless given an expanded period of rest between studio calls. The Laemmles soon eased up a bit, moving the start of his workday to 5:30 a.m. and dismissing him a little earlier each night; but by that time, the filming was nearly over.

When Whale wrapped with shots of Frankenstein's watchtower laboratory on October 3, 1931, the production was five days over schedule and nearly $35,000 over budget. Having sweated off 25 pounds, Boris bid adieu to Jack Pierce, hoping that his performance, which he had viewed in some of the rushes, would lead to more work at the studio.

After Maurice Pivar finished editing the film, *Frankenstein* was previewed for the trade press by the Laemmles. Some reviewers were so shocked by certain scenes, particularly the drowning of Maria, that several cuts were ordered. Now the lake scene ended with the Monster reaching for the little girl, leading to a sequence showing her grief-stricken father, Hans (Michael Mark), carrying her lifeless body into town during the wedding celebration of Henry and Elizabeth (Mae Clarke)—a juxtaposition that allowed viewers to fill in the gap with their own interpretations, some surely more horrific than what Whale had shot. Incredibly, Boris, a relatively unknown actor who was not even invited to the premiere, later claimed that he instigated the removal of the "offending" footage:

> My conception of the scene was that he [the Monster] would look up at the little girl in bewilderment, and, in his mind, she would become a flower. Without moving, he would pick her up gently and put her in the water as he had done with the flower—and to his horror, she would sink. Well, Jimmy made me pick her up and do that [motioning violently] over my head, which became a brutal and deliberate act. By no stretch of the imagination could you make that innocent. The whole pathos of the scene, to my mind, should have been—and I'm sure that's the way it was written—completely innocent and unaware. But the moment you do that, it's a deliberate thing... and I insisted on that part being removed.

Ironically, Boris' own interpretation of the scene *is* the way Whale filmed it: In the original footage (finally restored to the film for MCA's 1987 video release), the Monster does pick up Maria and toss her into the lake like a flower. He does *not* hold the child above his head and then deliberately drown her. The simple fact is that an actor of Boris' status in late 1931 could not have had editorial power over any of the films in which he appeared.

Frankenstein. **Boris' Monster lies dying in the blazing windmill.**

The sanitized version of *Frankenstein*, shorn of Maria's drowning, close-ups of Fritz tormenting the Monster, an extreme close-up of Dr. Waldman (Edward Van Sloan) making an injection in the Monster's back, Henry's exclamation "Now I know what it feels like to be God" and an entire closing scene in which Henry was killed by the Monster (replaced by a happy ending showing Elizabeth tending to the recuperating Henry) opened at the Mayfair Theatre in New York's Times Square on Friday, December 4, 1931. Attracted by Universal's lavish publicity campaign, people lined up in the rain to buy tickets. During its first week at the Mayfair, the film raked in a record-breaking $53,000, selling out the theater's 1,734 seats a number of times, prompting the owners to schedule additional shows.

Rather than including Boris' name in the opening credits of the film, Universal, aping an early stage version of *Frankenstein*, indicated the player of the Monster with a mysterious question mark. However, in the official pressbook sent to all exhibitors of the film, Boris was called the successor to Lon Chaney, a "truly great character actor," and "a brilliant Englishman." Making bold embellishments on the facts, the publicity department described his nonexistent "long list of brilliant successes on the London and European stages" and his graduation from King's College! Considering that Boris did not bother to see most of his films, he probably never read any of the materials designed to promote them; had he read this pressbook, he certainly would have retched.

But Universal did not need to create such myths about him. Although he was billed fourth (at the *end* of the film), critics across the nation instantly realized that he was the true star. *Motion Picture Herald* likened him to Chaney, and *Variety* referred to his performance as "a fascinating acting bit of mesmerism."

Around Christmas, while visiting one of Dorothy's old schoolmates in San Francisco, Boris finally saw the completed film at a theater in Oakland. Enthralled by the effect his monstrous appearance had on the audience, he was brought back to reality when Dorothy's friend grabbed her by the shoulder and whispered, "Dot, how can you live with the *creature*?"

Boris first appears as the Monster in his "pre-birth" state, lying on Frankenstein's laboratory table prior to the magnificent, storm-lashed creation scene. Filmed in an era when many special effects had to be created during the actual filming, rather than printed in afterward, the electricity used to give the Monster life could have ended the actor's existence. Boris recalled:

> The scene where the Monster was created amid booming thunder and flashing lightning made me as uneasy as anyone. For while I lay half naked and strapped to Dr. Frankenstein's table, I could see directly above me the special effects men brandishing the white-hot scissors-like carbons that made the lightning. I hoped that no one up there had butterfingers!

As the newly born Monster, Boris made the most famous debut in the history of horror films. Photographed in a medium long shot, the creature *backs* through the laboratory door and slowly turns to face the camera. Here, in a classic example of James Whale's visual style, the scene cuts to a close-up and then closer still, so the viewer can get a good look at the Monster's haunting face. In 1931 this was a brilliant way to introduce filmgoers to the character, and no actor could have asked for a better entrance.

Very little of Mary Shelley's 1816 novel was adapted by Florey, Whale, Ford and Faragoh, but the author's essential theme of intellectual progress and its social ramifications is apparent throughout the film. One scene in particular, depicting Dr. Waldman's conservative resistance against Henry Frankenstein's desire "to look beyond the clouds and the stars, or to know what causes the trees to bud—and what changes the darkness into light," captures the thematic essence of her philosophical tale.

With 20 years of stage and screen experience behind him, Boris summoned up a wide array of emotions for

Original one-sheet poster for *Frankenstein*.

the characterization, ranging from a groping newborn, to a laughing childlike innocent, to a confused, terrified creature attempting to protect himself through violence, always ignorant of the consequences of his actions. And, as a seasoned dramatic artist, he knew that these emotions, like the Monster's physical parts, had to be linked by a common thread. Instinctively, he held them together with nonverbal techniques—quickly moving his head from side to side and allowing his arms to swing slowly to and fro—demonstrating the creature's total bewilderment when encountering unpleasantness and abuse. This aspect of his performance, resembling the behavior of a caged animal, conveys the confusion of a Monster who, in Boris' words, was "deserted by his god," placing him in the pantheon of great cinematic mimes including Charles Chaplin, Buster Keaton and Stan Laurel. In fact, his performance technique—an almost "invisible" style of pantomime that conveys deep emotion while hiding conscious intent—closely resembles that of Laurel, whose itinerant music hall training (primarily with the legendary Fred Karno) was similar to Boris' stock company experiences.

With only these nonverbal techniques and the "grunting" that so exasperated Bela Lugosi, Boris effectively communicates the same philosophical message that Mary Shelley's Monster relates through pages of sophisticated Oxfordian discourse. *Frankenstein* provided Boris with his first cinematic opportunity to impart profundity through artistic understatement, a chance to integrate the style of Joseph Conrad into a filmed performance.

One of Robert Florey's scripted ideas that survived in the finished film—the simplistic device of attributing the Monster's degeneracy to the dysfunctioning of a criminal brain—has been heavily criticized. However, Boris based his performance on the idea that the creature was a newborn human being, not a depraved criminal:

> Whale and I both saw the character as an innocent one.
> Within the heavy restrictions of my makeup, I tried to play
> it that way. This was a pathetic creature who, like us all,
> had neither wish nor say in his creation and certainly did
> not wish upon itself the hideous image which automati-
> cally terrified humans whom it tried to befriend.

The physiology of the Monster's gray matter has little to do with his actions. A brain pickled in alcohol, regardless of prior features, would not produce the best behavior in any situation. From the time the Monster is "born," he is subjected to constant abuse: Fritz's savage taunts, Dr. Waldman's attempted dissection, and a screaming, torch-wielding lynch mob.

The fan letters Boris received after *Frankenstein* reinforced his interpretation of the character whom he referred to as "the poor old thing." Youngsters, in particular, "could see right through the makeup and could see the tragedy of this poor figure, and express great compassion for him." With a role he initially had viewed as just another in a long string of acting jobs, he managed to achieve both artistic satisfaction and public notoriety.

From the time Jack Pierce removed the last of the Monster makeup until *Frankenstein* was released, Boris returned to supporting roles in films for several companies. Shot on the heels of his torturous terror performance, Columbia's *The Guilty Generation* (1931) offered him his second major mobster, Tony Ricca, who, attempting to gain control of a prominent bootlegging operation, declares war on his rival, Mike Palermo (Leo Carrillo). A gangster variation on Shakespeare's *Romeo and Juliet* and released just two days before the premiere of *Frankenstein*, the film is an exciting crime melodrama well directed by Rowland V. Lee.

In November, after playing the tiny role of a waiter in the Gloria Swanson–Melvyn Douglas romantic comedy *Tonight or Never* (1931), he returned to Columbia for the Jack Holt vehicle *Behind the Mask*, which offered him another colorful criminal role, Henderson, a member of an insidious gang of dope smugglers. When this film was released in February 1932, the advertisements referred to Boris as "the man who made America 'monster-minded'," and printed his name in type nearly as big as Holt's.

Much to his delight, Universal, still raking in the proceeds from *Frankenstein*, signed him to a star contract before the end of 1931. Soon after, plans to feature him in an adaptation of H.G. Wells' *The Invisible Man* were announced. To publicize the signing of his contract and play up his image as a master of the macabre, the studio assigned photographer Ray Jones to shoot publicity shots of him posing with Bela Lugosi at Universal City.

On the day of the publicity stunt, a light rain began to fall, but the ever punctual Boris arrived ahead of Bela, dressed to the nines in a black tuxedo covered by a dapper overcoat. After Lugosi joined him, the two "monster men" posed for several staged photos, both smiling or toasting each other with German beer steins. For one shot, Boris put his arm around Lugosi; for another, Bela placed Boris in his hypnotic "Dracula trance." For the benefit of journalist Ted LeBerthon, who published his account of the summit in the October 1932 issue of *Weird Tales*, they regaled one another with villainous badinage, going so far as to bet which one could scare the other to death.

But before he could begin any star appearances for Universal, Boris had to honor his commitments to other studios. In an effort to rush him into a film as soon as possible, Laemmle, Jr., gave him a cameo as himself in *The Cohens and Kellys in Hollywood*, in which he appears with Lew Ayres, Sidney Fox and Genevieve Tobin in a scene set at Hollywood's Coconut Grove. At Warner Bros., he made a brief appearance for Michael Curtiz in *Alias the Doctor* (which ended up on the cutting room floor), and he played small roles in Fox's Will Rogers comedy *Business and Pleasure* and Paramount's *The Miracle Man*, in which John Wray appears as "the Frog," a character created by Lon Chaney for the 1920 silent version.

When he reported back to Universal in March 1932, the Laemmles had not developed a suitable follow-up to *Frankenstein*. Rather than keep him waiting for another month, they gave him third billing in the omnibus melodrama *Night World*, a cinematic soap opera set in the

9936 Toluca Lake Avenue, North Hollywood. Boris and Dorothy lived here from 1932-34. (1996 photograph by Scott Allen Nollen)

Wearing his cricket attire, Boris poses with a favorite book in his Toluca Lake home, 1932. (Note the copy of *Frankenstein*, third shelf, center.)

nightclub of "Happy" MacDonald, a well-mannered gentleman who attempts to remain independent from the local bootlegging rackets. Although expected to play second fiddle to the romance of Lew Ayres and Mae Clarke (who had received a grapefruit in the face from James Cagney in Warner Bros.' *The Public Enemy* [1931] before appearing in *Frankenstein*), he was given a fair amount of screen time in a role intended to attract audience sympathy.

Carl Laemmle, Jr., was still trying to get *The Invisible Man* off the ground, but when he asked Robert Florey to write a treatment of the novel, his unwillingness to offer an ironclad contract frustrated the Frenchman, who did not want to repeat the *Frankenstein* experience. In the meantime, Universal arranged an interview for Boris with Mary Sharon, a young reporter for a movie fan magazine. Although she was not enthusiastic about interviewing an actor she assumed would be like the villainous characters he portrayed, Sharon set out for the job, only to miss the streetcar that ran to Universal City. Reaching a phone, she called the publicity department and was told to wait for a car to pick her up. Ten minutes later, a thin man in an old Ford pulled up to the curb, and she climbed into the passenger side, expecting to be driven to the studio but finding herself face to face with the terrible Monster himself. Maintaining the erroneous assumption that the actor and his characters were one and the same, Miss Sharon was perhaps the first in a long line of individuals to be pleasantly surprised when meeting him. In her report of their encounter, she wrote of his suave, distinguished personality and his interest in Joseph Conrad, claiming, "You can easily picture him in a romantic role. He is tall, well-built and very dark-skinned... the sort of fellow that would cause you to turn around, even on Hollywood Boulevard."

Carl Laemmle, Sr., had met James Whale's friend and colleague Benn W. Levy during a recent trip to England, inviting him to Universal City to write the screenplay for *The Invisible Man*. But Laemmle had not bothered to inform anyone at the studio of his decision, and Levy soon was loaned to Paramount to script *The Devil and the Deep*. After completing his work for Paramount, Levy returned to Universal and, trying to select a suitable vehicle for Boris, suggested J.B. Priestley's *Benighted*, a novel published as *The Old Dark House* in the United States. Whale was attracted to the bizarre British characters in the story, and Laemmle was pleased that one of them, a mute butler called Morgan, provided an excellent follow-up to Boris' Monster.

Assured top billing for the first time in his career, Boris reported to Jack Pierce's familiar makeup shop when shooting began in mid-April 1932. After discarding a more horrific, hirsute makeup that extended his brow in *Frankenstein* fashion, Pierce settled on a long scar running from the right side of his forehead to the bridge of his nose and a full, dark beard and eyebrows, giving Morgan a primitive look that visually symbolizes a line from Priestley's novel: Commenting on the butler's behavior, Horace Femm observes, "Being little better than a brute, he is very close to Nature... "

Although he was given star billing, Boris quickly realized that his non-speaking character would be overshadowed by Whale's quirky humor and the performances of two superb, eccentric actors who had worked with the director in England: Ernest Thesiger (as Horace Femm) and Charles Laughton (as Sir William Porterhouse). Focusing on five stranded travelers forced to spend the night in the Welsh country house of five people afflicted with various states of madness, Levy's darkly humorous version of Priestley's tale relegated Boris to a minor position, but Whale, again working with cinematographer Arthur Edeson, consistently emphasized Morgan's presence with dramatic and atmospheric close-ups.

The Old Dark House (1932). **An atmospheric publicity shot of Boris as Morgan, the mute butler.**

Whale shot Morgan's entrance, in which his face appears behind the partially opened front door of the Femm home as the travelers seek shelter, in a style aping the Monster's first appearance in *Frankenstein*; and for a later scene, he again filmed a series of three shots (all of them extreme close-ups of Boris' face) that recall that famous montage. Boris was able to steal a little thunder during the shooting of the film's climax when the intoxicated Morgan releases the eldest Femm sibling, Saul (Brember Wills), a dangerous pyromaniac, from a locked room on the top floor. After Saul sets the house ablaze and is killed in a struggle with Roger Penderel (Melvyn Douglas), Morgan cradles his body and then carries him up the staircase—the only moment in the film that allowed Boris effectively to inject some compassion into his "heavy" role.

Truth to tell, James Whale was beginning to develop a jealousy toward Boris, who had garnered the lion's share of critical praise for *Frankenstein*. But regardless of the director's attitude, and the fact that his character existed merely to add some shocks to a film wonderfully played by other fine actors, Boris maintained his usual degree of professionalism, turning in the best performance possible. Gloria Stuart, who played Margaret Waverton in the film, recalled:

> I understand that Boris and James were not great friends at that point. I didn't know that—I was not aware of it— and I don't think that anyone in the cast was aware of it... I think that James gave him his due. I think that James wanted him in every scene that he was written into—and larger than life, and giving a great performance. I never had the feeling that there was any difficulty at all between James and any of the cast... and I was on the set almost every day.

Daily, the English actors congregated, rather pretentiously, for their 11 a.m. and 4 p.m. tea times, while Stuart and Melvyn Douglas took an "American" break together. Stuart remembered that "there were no fun and games on that set, like there were on many, many sets. The scene was rehearsed, the cameras were set, the scene was shot. It was a very tight company."

Dorothy feeds the ducks at Toluca Lake, 1932.

Boris, relaxed and quite dashing, in a 1932 Henry Freulich portrait.

Whale was very satisfied with having the opportunity to create such a personal work highlighting his taste for the bizarre (so brilliantly evoked by Ernest Thesiger, who was unknown to American audiences at the time), but when the film was previewed in early June 1932, it was called "a somewhat inane picture" by the *Hollywood Filmograph*. Although Boris played a minor role, the Universal publicity department emphasized his star billing and included the following pre-title assurance to the audience:

> PRODUCERS NOTE:—Karloff, the mad butler in this production, is the same Karloff who created the part of the mechanical monster in "Frankenstein." We explain this to settle all disputes in advance, even though such disputes are a tribute to his great versatility.

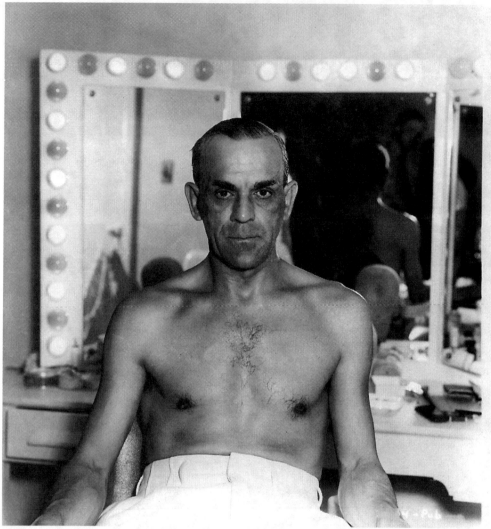

Waiting for makeup to be applied, Boris, at the age of 44, reveals the lean physique for which he was famous, 1932.

This statement simultaneously hypes Universal's new star and seems to apologize in advance for his not being on-screen long enough for viewers to determine if it is really the great Karloff under Pierce's makeup.

The Old Dark House did receive primarily favorable reviews after it was released on October 20, 1932, but box office receipts dropped dramatically after the public learned of Universal's deceitfulness in promising but not delivering a real star performance by Boris. Not even the combined acting prowess of Thesiger, Laughton, Douglas and Raymond Massey made up for this disappointment. And audiences were alienated further by the odd British humor so beloved by Whale and his compatriots. They wanted more horror, and Morgan's drunken rampage, followed by Saul's manic blaze, was not enough to satiate their expectations. [1]

After a well-deserved rest, Boris was loaned to MGM in August 1932 to star in *The Mask of Fu Manchu*, an outrageous mixture of comic-book characters, serial thrills and anti-Asian sentiments. When first handed the script, he realized that no one could possibly take the film seriously, so he approached the evil Chinese genius with tongue firmly in cheek, turning in one of his most deliberately overplayed performances.

But actually receiving a copy of the screenplay was the first obstacle in a production fraught with problems. About a week before Charles Vidor began shooting, Boris was still wondering if he would get to read his dialogue before delivering it. Literally hours before the cameras rolled on the morning of August 6, he was sitting in Cecil Holland's makeup chair, suffering through the application of "extremely bad" Oriental facial appliances, including a set of "thin shell teeth," when someone handed him four sheets of paper containing a lengthy speech, written in impeccable English, with which he was to open the film. Boris could learn dialogue very quickly, but no actor could memorize such a soliloquy in a matter of minutes. He refused to do it.

The Mask of Fu Manchu (1932). **Boris, graced by one of Myrna Loy's steamiest Asian temptresses, Fah Lo See, Fu's nymphomaniacal daughter.**

The Mask of Fu Manchu. **Boris, joined by his colleagues, proudly presides over a visiting group of Australian cricketers. The group includes director Charles Brabin (far left, back row), Lawrence Grant (between Brabin and Boris), Myrna Loy, David Torrence and C. Aubrey Smith (right, front row) and legendary bowler Don Bradman (behind Smith).**

A short time later, with his eyes altered to look like little swimming fishes and a ridiculous, drooping mustache framing his mouth, Boris was accosted on his way to the soundstage by another messenger, who handed him a replacement for the speech, this time written in pidgin English. "They had five writers on it, and this was happening all through the film," he recalled. "Some scenes were written in beautiful Oxford English. Others were written in—God knows what!"

No version of the script made sense. Characters appeared suddenly, only to deliver a few meaningless lines and then disappear. None of the major characters were developed beyond simple stereotypes, particularly Fu Manchu, relegating Boris to speaking insipid lines and registering a few sneering facial expressions.

Utilizing the talents of master cinematographer Tony Gaudio and art director Cedric Gibbons, MGM lavished its usual glossy production values on the film, particularly in the scenes set in the ancient tomb of Genghis Khan and in Fu Manchu's secret headquarters. And for a horror melodrama, Boris could not have asked to be surrounded with finer acting talent, including Myrna Loy, Lewis Stone, Jean Hersholt and Karen Morley. Loy, who specialized in exotic Asian temptresses early in her career, shared Boris' tongue-in-cheek approach to the absurd material, and played Fu's nymphomaniacal daughter, Fah Lo See, with obvious relish.

Irene Kuhn, Edgar Allan Woolf and John Willard, who were given credit for the final screenplay, made certain that the Asian characters (the majority of which were played by white actors, a standard casting practice at the time) espoused racist sentiments more often and with more severity than their Caucasian counterparts, with Fu continually referring to his desire for eliminating "the entire accursed white race!"

White audiences did not take *The Mask of Fu Manchu* seriously, but some Chinese Americans viewed it as a racial slur. Considering its cartoon plot and outlandish atmosphere and performances, Boris later commented that protest seemed "utterly ridiculous."[2]

Two weeks into production, the confusion mounted to the point where major script revisions were ordered, and Charles Vidor's director's chair was handed over to *Rasputin and the Empress* refugee Charles Brabin, who wrapped the picture on October 21. But not all the disorder was aggravating. Boris enjoyed posing for several publicity photos, projecting Fu's controlled megalomaniacal aura as the sexy Loy registered some of the steamiest facial expressions ever captured on film. And one day, while shooting Fu's sadistic experiment on Terence Granville (Charles Starrett), Brabin was forced to send Boris and Charlie home when they became incapacitated with laughter. While injecting "tarantula venom" into a baked potato behind Charlie's neck, Boris had caused the vegetable to explode, covering them with starchy shrapnel.

As the Great Depression raged on throughout 1932, Boris was earning $750 per week under his new contract with Universal. Enjoying the economic benefits of steady work and the notoriety of his first starring roles, he and Dorothy purchased their first real home at 9936 Toluca Lake Avenue in North Hollywood, where Bette Davis, W.C. Fields, Mary Astor, Bing Crosby and Bob Hope also were seeking solace from the hectic pace of stardom.

Another high point of the year was C. Aubrey Smith's formation of the Hollywood Cricket Club, which attracted several athletically inclined Englishmen who worked in the film industry. The passion for sports Boris had developed as a child never left him, and he spent much of his free time either watching rugby or playing cricket, field hockey and tennis, a game at which he was very proficient. He had been playing loosely organized cricket with the Overseas Club since 1919, and when he heard of Smith's efforts to start a serious organization, he became a charter member, playing every Sunday alongside Clive Brook, Ronald Colman, R.C. Sherriff, H.B. Warner, Basil Rathbone and his good friend Nigel Bruce. Six months after Smith began recruiting members, the club boasted five flourishing chapters and excellent playing grounds that were maintained for a five-month season. Some in Hollywood saw the club as evidence of a strong "British colony" in the film industry, but only a few English actors actually joined or even banded together in other activities off the field. Boris considered such a nationalistic congregation to be a myth:

> I don't know if there really was an English colony. I think
> that's an American phrase. There were a lot of English
> actors out there, but, I mean, I had friends, English, Americans. You know, you don't cling together quite as tightly
> as that. At least I hope not. It would be too provincial.

Cricket is, of course, an English game, but the club welcomed American members as well. Regardless of its social *raison d'être*, Boris was very proud of his membership, and he could be seen after a Sunday match, arriving home at Toluca Lake with "Hollywood Cricket Club" adorning the tire cover of his Ford.

The club negotiated a deal with UCLA, agreeing to coach students in return for the use of a well-maintained cricket ground. South African cricketer and UCLA student Eugene Walsh remembered Boris' avid participation:

> He spent much of his spare time teaching students at UCLA
> how to play cricket... He was not a great bat or bowler
> himself, but he was an excellent coach. He had a very
> wide knowledge of the game, and I remember many times
> we sat up to the early hours of the morning discussing
> cricket. In my opinion, Boris was one of the greatest ambassadors that England had in California.

The Mummy (1932). Boris, wearing his Ardath Bey makeup, poses in his personalized "director's chair."

While Boris was indulging his love of athletics, Carl Laemmle, Jr., was concentrating on casting him in the next Universal terror blockbuster. Intrigued by the "curse" of Tutankhamen that fatally befell members of Howard Carter's expedition to Egypt's Valley of the Kings 10 years earlier, Laemmle had assigned Richard Schayer and Nina Wilcox Putnam to write a story on the subject. The result, "Cagliostro," a nine-page treatment describing the murderous activities of a 3,000-year-old Egyptian magician who prolongs his life with nitrate injections, was then handed over to John L. Balderston, who had contributed to the screenplays for *Dracula* and

Frankenstein. While Schayer and Putnam had set their tale in San Francisco, Balderston immediately moved the action of the screenplay back to Egypt, basing the eternal life premise, not on pseudoscience, but on ancient Egyptian religion. Changing the title from "Cagliostro" to "The King of the Dead," he created a new lead character, a 3,700-year-dead mummy who rises from his sarcophagus to claim the reincarnated form of his ancient lover. When Balderston submitted the shooting script on September 12, 1932, the proposed film was titled "Im-Ho-Tep" and assigned to the great German cinematographer Karl Freund, whom the Laemmles had promoted to the director's chair on August 29.

In the early autumn, when Boris returned to Universal City to begin acting in *The Mummy* (the fourth and final title of the new film), he was handed his first true starring role, a beautifully written character that would earn him the rare honor of being billed on all advertising materials by his surname only, as "KARLOFF the Uncanny." But before he could give his preternatural performance, the soon-to-be uncanny one had to experience what he described as "the most trying ordeal I have ever endured."

Repeating the painful process he first suffered through for *Frankenstein*, he again placed himself at the mercy of Jack Pierce, who created an awe-inspiring makeup that made him literally look like a well-preserved mummified corpse. This time, Pierce's meticulous artistry took eight hours to apply, twice as long as his earlier Monster creation. Luckily for Boris, only one scene, showing Imhotep's terrifying resurrection from the dead, required him to appear in full mummy trappings.

On the day the scene was filmed, he reported to the makeup department at 11 a.m. First his ears were glued back; then his face was covered with cotton strips, collodion, and spirit gum. After Pierce set this mixture with a blow dryer, he then smeared his hair with beauty clay and, after allowing it to harden, covered it with rubber cement.

Using 150 yards of linen that had been rotted with acid and heated in an oven, Boris was wrapped horizontally, vertically and diagonally over his bare skin until he was completely covered and could hardly move or speak. Several hues of grease paint were applied to his face and hands so that they would match the color of the bandaging. As a final touch, his entire body was covered with a layer of Fuller's earth, a substance used in the manufacturing of paint.

At 7 p.m., a proud Pierce helped his new work of art to the soundstage and into a sarcophagus designed by Willy Pogany, whose impressive sets helped to create the film's eerie atmosphere. For the next seven hours, Boris performed his best impression of an ancient Egyptian who had been buried alive 3,700 years earlier, as Karl Freund, cinematographer Charles Stumar and crew, and actors Edward Van Sloan, Arthur Byron, and Bramwell Fletcher filmed all the setups for the scene. Photographed in the background of several shots, he also was given close-ups when examined by Van Sloan and while slowly stirring to life during the reading of the magical Scroll of Thoth by Fletcher. But Freund intended the scariest shots to show only the mummy's right hand as it reaches for the scroll and then a trail of bandages as it shuffles out the door—a visual strategy reflecting Boris' own subtle artistic style. Freund created unrivaled terror by juxtaposing these images with the shocking scream and insane laughter of Fletcher, whose archaeologist character, Norton, goes mad after seeing the unholy creature.

Except for a tea break with Dorothy, who visited the set to witness her husband's excruciatingly uncomfortable ordeal, Boris dutifully stayed in his coffin until Freund, having achieved remarkable results, wrapped at 2 a.m. To have the makeup removed, he then patiently sat for another two hours in Pierce's chair before returning to Toluca Lake around 5 a.m., pleased to be finished with a grueling 18-hour workday (but falling seven hours short of his longest day on *Frankenstein*). But perhaps the worst element of his ordeal, thanks to a Pierce oversight, was that he had been unable to relieve himself for 18 hours.

Freund and Balderston set the remainder of *The Mummy* in 1932, 10 years after the discovery and assumed theft of Imhotep (and the actual plundering of Tutankhamen's tomb). In most of his scenes, Boris appeared as Ardath Bey, Imhotep's contemporary alter ego, a mysterious Egyptologist who leads an archaeological team to the burial ground of Princess Anck-es-en-amon, the mummy's ancient lover. To become Bey, he was required to spend a mere hour in Pierce's chair each morning, receiving a somewhat less painful, toned down version of the "mummification."

One of Freund's most impressive scenes—perhaps the best in his entire Hollywood career—is the flashback to ancient Egypt that Anck-es-en-amon's reincarnated form, Helen Grosvenor (Zita Johann), experiences in Bey's magical pool, wherein she learns how, in ancient Thebes, he was stripped of his title and buried alive for attempting to raise her from the dead. Freund shot the entire sequence in the manner of a German expressionist silent, abandoning dialogue in favor of a narration that Boris recorded before the footage was edited. Ably executed by Stumar, the lighting of the shots was increased to produce a harsher contrast, while the rest of the film features the more subtle gray tones common to films of the period.

Wearing a straight makeup, an Egyptian gown and headdress of stark white, elaborate jewelry, and sandals, Boris appeared quite majestic as he performed the blasphemous act of stealing the sacred Scroll of Thoth to raise his beloved from the grave. And he summoned up one of the most agonizing and terrifying expressions of his film career as the unfortunate Imhotep was wrapped in linen bandages, a last strip being drawn across his eyes, to be buried alive.

Freund and Balderston intended the flashback to comprise a major portion of the film, including scenes of Anck-es-en-amon's various reincarnated forms throughout the ages. After her death in Thebes, she was to return as a 1st-century Christian being fed to the lions in Rome, an 8th-century Saxon princess who commits suicide to escape the marauding Vikings, a 13th-century noblewoman bidding adieu to a group of Crusaders and an 18th-century French aristocrat resembling Marie Antoinette. All the footage was shot, but after Freund wrapped the production in late October, Carl Laemmle, Jr. ordered that all the post-Egyptian reincarnation material be cut. Apparently these scenes slowed down an already brooding, poetically paced film; and, although the character of Anck-es-en-amon was important to the plot, the historical detail did not advance the narrative, but only distracted attention away from Boris, who would have disappeared for far too long.

Making his directorial debut, Freund was a bit tyrannical on the set, shooting for lengthy periods of time without breaks and, at one point, causing Zita Johann to collapse from exhaustion; but he brought the film in on schedule and under budget, making *The Mummy* a bargain at only $196,000. The publicity department began to ship out its striking full-color posters hyping KARLOFF the Uncanny in huge type, and on November 29, 1932, the Laemmles previewed the final cut of the film for the press.

Accompanied by Eugene Walsh, Boris, curious to see an audience's reaction, went to see the film at the Pantages Theatre. Walsh claimed:

> As we entered the foyer, a middle-aged lady came out of the theater... She seemed very apprehensive and nearly bumped into us. Then suddenly she sank to the floor and Boris helped the attendant to revive her. I don't think the lady had any idea who Boris was, but she was most grateful for the help he had given her.

In New York, a huge electrical image of Boris' mummified face beamed out eerily from the marquee of the Mayfair Theatre, catching the glance of anyone who crossed through Times Square. He was now as big a star as Hollywood could possibly produce, a fact demonstrated by *The New York Times*, whose critic suggested that the huge crowds turning out on opening day proved "that there is a place for a national bogey man in the scheme of things." In part because of his magnificent makeup, he again was called the new Lon Chaney by several papers, including *The Los Angeles Times*, which also reported that the film "is one of the most unusual talkies ever produced."

The Mummy. Boris' Ardath Bey prays over the "magic pool" designed by art director Willy Pogany.

Truly a unique cinematic experience, *The Mummy* is enhanced by an elegiac atmosphere created by Freund's austere pacing and the eerie, morose musical score (highlighting an oboe in low register) that primarily was culled from "canned" music in Universal's sound library. Boris' performance perfectly matches the overall pace, as his delivery is slowly, precisely presented in a graceful, dream-like manner. Portraying a long-dead being whose ability to move and speak is hampered considerably, he chose a voice and performance style that matched the character's physical condition. At certain moments, he punctuates this restrained approach with moments of understated viciousness, either recoiling his wizened, moldy arm away from a person's touch or attempting to use his hypnotic power upon Helen, Sir Joseph Whemple (Arthur Byron) or Frank Whemple (David Manners).

Like the Frankenstein Monster, Imhotep/Ardath Bey has no control over his resurrection, is tragically misunderstood by society and is eventually destroyed. But whereas the Monster has no premeditated plans for violence, the mummy, longing for his ancient lover, intends to remove all obstacles in his path. Distinct tones of necrophilia are present in the 3,700-year-dead creature's desire to attract the reincarnated form of his mate. And there are similarities between Balderston's screenplay and the plot of *Dracula*, but Boris' mummy, who uses hypnotism to kill from a distance, possesses a supernatural power that Lugosi's neck-biting vampire does not.

Despite, or perhaps because of, the severe conditions he experienced while making the film, Boris created his second unforgettable terror performance in *The Mummy*, fashioning a characterization of incredible subtlety and power. While the Frankenstein Monster is a re-animated patchwork of corpses struggling for identity and seeking compassion, the undead Imhotep is repulsive, yet elegant and regal, alternately sympathetic and iniquitous, and one of the most complex, beautifully acted roles of his career.

When *The Mummy* was released on December 22, 1932, Boris was reaching the end of his current contract with Universal, which had assured him $750 per week for an 18-week period. When that period elapsed, the studio was to begin considering six-month options to raise his salary $250 per week each time. In January 1933, knowing that the studio had lost $1.7 million during the previous year, he decided to waive his increase to $1,000, on the condition that his salary would be raised to $1,250 per week on the next option date.

During his contract discussions, several story properties were considered as KARLOFF the Uncanny starring vehicles, including "The Red Planet," Robert Louis Stevenson's *The Suicide Club*, Daniel Defoe's *Robinson Crusoe* and remakes of two classic silents, *The Wizard* and *The Hunchback of Notre Dame*. None of these proposals were taken seriously, however, and James Whale, in particular, considered them inferior to *The Invisible Man*, although there were numerous technical problems that needed to be solved before H.G. Wells' classic could be scripted. In September 1932 Whale had replaced E.A. Dupont as proposed director of the science-fiction opus, and once again wanting to emphasize quirkiness over straightforward terror, was not keen on using Boris in the title role.

As the front office debated over what to do with the uncanny one, he was loaned out again, this time to a company whose offer included an irresistible opportunity for him and Dorothy. The job and related travel should last until his next Universal option, he thought, as he prepared to set foot in a land he had not seen for nearly a quarter century.

---

[1] After the film was re-issued in 1939, it literally disappeared until 1968, when a gallant rescue effort by Whale's friend Curtis Harrington resulted in a restoration. Today it is considered a cinematic treasure and the best example of James Whale's idiosyncratic style.

[2] Many years later, character actor Henry Brandon, who played the same character in the 1940 Republic serial *Drums of Fu Manchu*, expressed a similar opinion, calling Sax Rohmer's novels "fairy tales" and noting that he had "played countless heavies of various nationalities," never feeling that he "was maligning any race by doing so."

Chapter 5

Milestones

"We'd had a great deal of trouble over the years in actors'
conditions, and I went to the first meeting of six people,
and out of that sort of grew the Screen Actors Guild, which
has done wonders for actors. I'm very proud of that."

At approximately 9 a.m. on Thursday, March 2, 1933, Dorothy Karloff answered the telephone. On the other end of the line was someone at Universal, claiming that, to board the S.S. *Paris* in New York only two days hence, she and her husband must catch a flight from Los Angeles at 4:30 *that* afternoon. As Dorothy recalled, "Neither of us had flown before, neither of us had passports, neither of us had any money." But, placing their domestic affairs in the capable hands of her mother, Mrs. Louise Stine, she began to pack.

Herbert Hoover was still president, and millions of Americans who blamed him for the worsening ravages of the Great Depression could not wait for Franklin D. Roosevelt to assume the throne on Saturday, when Boris and Dorothy were to sail on the *Paris*. Due to the devastating economic situation that had escorted previously well-off Americans onto the streets and into makeshift dwellings derisively referred to as "Hoovervilles," even a skyrocketing star like Karloff the Uncanny could not get his hands on ready cash. Neither could the Laemmles nor anyone else at Universal. Banks in 20 states already had declared "holidays" to prevent panic withdrawals, and now New York's Governor Lehman closed all banks and stock exchanges in the state.

But, on the other side of the Atlantic, Gaumont-British Pictures expected the arrival of a famous prodigal son to star in *The Ghoul*, England's first major sound horror picture. So, after cleaning out all the pay telephones at the studio, a Universal representative handed Boris a paper bag containing $12 in change, assured him that additional funds would be wired for and escorted him and his equally terrified wife to a small Ford tri-motor aircraft in which they would cross the country. In a letter to her mother, Dorothy wrote:

> The plane trip was no fun at all—more like a nightmare as
> we look back at it now—but a nightmare with no sleep
> attached. Never ever have I sat in harder seats, or been so
> rushed and pushed about. The plane came down only for
> from 5 to 15 minutes at a time to allow you to stretch and
> grab a bite of horrible food at some terrible lunch stand
> miles from anywhere.

Plagued by severe atmospheric conditions that rivaled the deteriorating economic situation, they spent five miserable hours in Cleveland before miraculously reaching New York at 9:30 a.m. on Saturday, but without having received a single dime for the transatlantic trip. The banks at all their refueling locations had closed ahead of them.

The "nightmare" only worsened in New York. Rushing from the immigration bureau to the headquarters of the S.S. company, and then to Universal's office, the disheveled couple finally were escorted to the harbor by some of the N.Y.P.D.'s finest. Scrambling into a small boat at

Boris on the deck of the S.S. *Paris*, steaming back to England for the first time in nearly 24 years, March 1933.

2:45 p.m., they were sped through a great swell to reach the *Paris*, which had taken on all its passengers nearly three hours earlier.

Just as the gangplank was re-lowered to accept them, an event of true serendipity bordering on Hollywood melodrama occurred. Glancing into the crowd, Dorothy recognized three faces, those of a show business family they had met in tinsel town: veteran actors James and Lucile Gleason, and their 25-year-old son, Russell. Striking up an instant friendship with their fellow travelers, they enjoyed many a laugh during the voyage as they shared pheasants and caviar at the dinner table and took long walks around the deck. None of them got seasick, but sleep often was hard to come by, as the rough sea rocked them from their berths during the night.

Entertainment was plentiful, including a daily "Punch and Judy" show at 3 p.m. and a feature film at 5:00 p.m. Boris particularly enjoyed seeing the Barrymore threesome, Lionel, John, and Ethel, in MGM's *Rasputin and the Empress*. During the evenings, the pitching of the ship contributed to their terpsichorean skills; and by the time the *Paris* landed at Plymouth on Friday, March 10, the two practically penniless couples had amassed "a spectacular bar bill."

As Boris descended the gangplank toward his native soil, Russell Gleason walked beside him, managing to snap a photograph of the feet of Frankenstein's Monster as they trod upon British soil for the first time in nearly 24 years. Escorted onto a boat train by four representatives from Gaumont, the party arrived in London at 10:30 in the evening, to be met by several photographers, a crowd of enthusiastic fans, and letters and wires from Boris' brothers. As they were being driven to the Dorchester Hotel, Boris may have asked himself why he had stayed away for so long. Dorothy wrote:

> We were... given a suite of rooms such as you've never seen. Champagne sent up and loads of people about. Boris was too excited to go to bed so we were taken to the Kit Kat Club—a very swell night club—then for a drive around the city until about 3 a.m.

Incredibly, Boris and "Jimmy" Gleason, character stars of the American screen, both had been hired by producer Michael Balcon at Gaumont, located in Shepherd's Bush. While the uncanny one was to join director T. Hayes Hunter to shoot *The Ghoul*, the thin, balding, rapid-fire Gleason (who, in delivering sheer syllables per second, could give James Cagney and Clark Gable a serious run for their money) was to check in with Walter Forde to film *Orders is Orders*, a cross-cultural comedy of errors about an American filmmaker's inept efforts to direct a British Army unit in a Foreign Legion picture.

During the weekend before filming was scheduled to begin, Boris and Dorothy took leisurely walks in Hyde Park, saw Charlotte Greenwood on the stage and joined the Gleasons for a posh party at Lady Ravensdale's. Having escaped from his overbearing siblings in long-ago

During their first day in London, Dorothy and Boris stroll through Hyde Park, March 1933.

Four brothers Pratt: Sir John, F.G. (Fred), Charles and Billy, Piccadilly Circus, March 1933.

1909, Boris decided to visit the remaining "respectable" Pratts, including David, who had worked for the Argentinean Railway but now lived outside London, and Fred, who had a house in town. Dorothy considered them "darlings—especially Fred," who had distinguished himself in the imperial service, first as District Magistrate and then Settlement Commissioner and Director of Land Records in Bombay, where he sat on the Legislative Council from 1915-25.

Prior to reporting to Gaumont at noon on Monday, March 13, Boris dropped in at the British Foreign Office and spoke with the amiable secretary before springing himself on John Pratt, knight of the realm and former Consul General at Tsinan, Nanking, and Shanghai, whom he now respectfully referred to as "My brother, the Sir." Transferred to the Foreign Office in 1925, Sir John had remained in London, where he was appointed Counsellor in Diplomatic Service four years later. Although Boris had not contacted his family for a quarter-century, he was impressed by his brothers' considerable accomplishments, and he agreed to meet with Sir John, Fred and Charles at a subsequent press party just off Piccadilly Circus.

On the afternoon of the reunion, Boris, expecting the event to be staid and stuffy, asked the cabby to drop him a few blocks away, so he could walk the distance with the real people of London before shifting back into proper upper-crust mode. He later admitted that the warm wishes of passers-by astonished him, making him feel more safely at home than he had prior to his emigration to Canada. At the party, he was alternately astonished and thrilled to witness all three brothers vying for the spot next to him when photographs were snapped. However, the old Pratt suspicion of the performing arts still remained: Drawing "Billy" aside, Sir John, in fine English fashion, informed him that such good fortune could not possibly last for a person engaged in "that sort of thing." (And the two brothers had another opportunity to discuss the subject when Boris and Dorothy spent a subsequent Sunday afternoon at "Jack's" home in Essex.)

66

Like Sir John, Charles also had achieved great success abroad, living in Buenos Aires, where he worked with David as an administrator for the Argentinean Railway. Absent from the reunion were George, who had passed away during the influenza epidemic at the end of World War I; Edward, who had served as a high court judge in Bombay; David; and Richard, who was still in China. John and Richard had experienced a political falling out while serving in China, the former having sympathized with the Communists while the latter organized the evacuation of women and children from the upper Yangtze in 1927. A staunchly conservative Victorian moralist, Richard became absolutely misanthropic, refusing to communicate with his family and turning down a knighthood. Boris' half-sister, Emma, had died on August 4, 1924; but his sister, Julia, still was living happily in Semer with her husband, the Reverend Donkin.

Growing tired of the Dorchester, which was "grand" but cost "about $20 a day," Boris—who never was overly fond of hotels—and Jimmy both rented service flats in a building on Duchess Street in the heart of Mayfair. Dorothy was particularly pleased with the size of the flat, which included a large living room, two bedrooms and a spacious dining room containing a pipe organ. The monthly rent also covered the services of a maid, butler, valet and cook. Boris had to pay Dorothy's expenses himself, but the studio provided a "very elegant" car and driver who allowed her "to go dashing around all day."

If *The Ghoul* was indicative of the direction Boris' cinematic future was to take, he may have been wise to listen to his brother, the Sir. Borrowing heavily from *The Mummy* in content and visual style, the production did not benefit from the slowly paced, uneven direction of T. Hayes Hunter, who was lucky to have landed Boris for the starring role. Performing his scenes with customary professionalism (and covered with German-silent veteran Herman Heitfeld's makeup combining elements of Paul Wegener's *Golem* [1920] with Pierce's *Mummy*), he soon realized that his character appeared only at the beginning and the very end of the film when "Professor Morlant" rises from his tomb to prevent the Eternal Light, an *Egyptian* jewel, from being stolen by various wily thieves. Even a superb cast including Ernest Thesiger, Ralph Richardson and Cedric Hardwicke (who also appeared with Gleason in *Orders is Orders*) could not save a turgid script, static camerawork and pedestrian direction—a dramatically deadly combination of elements given life only when Boris was allowed back into the mixture. Dorothy revealed:

> Boris as usual doesn't like the story—or his part—and
> they're having an awful time with the makeup. He says
> the makeup man doesn't know anything about Boris' type
> of work—is German besides and can't understand a word
> Boris says. So it's the same agony of starting a new pic-
> ture even if it's in England.

Dorothy did not hesitate to point out both the positive and negative aspects of their experience. She observed that Londoners were "so terribly nice... so polite and thoughtful about autographs," but that American staples had to be imported; more specifically, brought in by visiting Hollywood friends. In a letter to her mother, she suggested that Edith Havenstrite and her husband "bring in 200 Lucky Strikes for us... And if they want any decent coffee... bring a can with them—or 5 or 6 cans. The coffee is foul here."

But the lack of good coffee or the plot and overall quality of a mediocre film were the least of Boris' concerns. After a prolonged absence, he was back in his homeland, well regarded rather than reviled; acquainting his wife with the culture he still prized, even after his self-imposed exile. In the familiar streets of old London, he was building a wonderful camaraderie with Jimmy Gleason, a thorough Yank who shared similar professional goals and personal ideals. While Boris and Jimmy worked during the day, Dorothy, Lucile and Russell had ample time to tour all the sights—an activity that began to make the ladies feel guilty. Dorothy wrote:

Poor Boris—except for his two Sundays with his brothers, has seen nothing but the studio and the flat—but he gets a tremendous thrill about hearing about them every night... We never have dinner until 7:30 or 8—then we go for a walk every night—for its the only air Boris gets all day long—as the studios here are entirely enclosed—and he likes poking about the streets anyway.

The evenings also provided Boris with several visits to the West End, where he saw *Double Harness*, with Mary Ellis, and *Fresh Fields*, featuring Ivor Novello and *Ghoul* costar Anthony Bushell. However, one such outing was canceled due to a tragedy in Bushell's family. When Anthony's brother and roommate, Nicholas, failed to meet the Gleasons for a pre-theater dinner, Jimmy sent Russell to the Bushell flat, where the young man discovered "Nick's" dead body. According to Dorothy, no one knew why the apparently healthy Nick, a junior member in a London law firm, took his own life.

On Boris' "lazy" Sundays, they met Julia in Enfield, where Boris re-visited some of his old haunts, and took a second trip to "Jack's" home in Essex. On Monday, March 27, they spent the entire day in Enfield, at the cricket field, grammar school, family home—where they "poked around through the gardens"—and the cemetery, viewing the graves of George, Emma and Boris' mother. One Wednesday night was spent in pleasant dinner conversation with six members of David's family.

In fact, Boris spent almost all of his leisure time either attending plays or socializing. Whenever family members were unavailable, he and Dorothy went out or dined in with dramatic cohorts, including James Whale's colleagues R.C. Sherriff and Ernest Thesiger, whom Boris had befriended while working on *The Old Dark House* and *The Ghoul*.

Boris' brother Richard Septimus Pratt in his garden at Swatow, China, 1933.

In early April, Dorothy wrote to Louise:

Boris looks fine—he's so thrilled and happy all the time
that he looks heavier and more rested. But I don't think
he'll be contented to live in California ever again—not
really contented—he'll always want to come back to this,
I know...

There is still talk of a second picture here. Boris is
with the men now, talking about it. He'll be broken hearted
if we don't stay—Universal have given their permission,
but Gaumont couldn't start another picture until about the
first of May or later—so I don't know.

When Boris returned from his meeting at Gaumont, he borrowed his wife's pen, to add his
own perspective to the letter:

Hello, Mother dear... Don't you believe what Dorothy says
about my not being contented in California. She is the
one to distrust. She gets positively lyrical about everything, and everyone says, "What a charming wife you have
and how she has fallen into everything over here! We
never met anyone who enjoyed England so much." It is
lovely—the weather has been marvelous and the excitement of being here again is almost too much. But still I
have some pretty deep roots in California.

Plans for a second Gaumont film fell through, so in late April, with shooting on *The Ghoul*
completed, Boris and Dorothy had a week to plot their return trip to California. But these plans
also hit a snag when Dorothy was not allowed to re-enter the United States. She had written to
her mother numerous times, asking for a copy of her birth certificate, but no such document had
arrived. Ironically, Boris had no trouble obtaining his permit, even though he had never applied
for U.S. citizenship, while his wife, born in Charlotte, Michigan, was denied. Told that her
original birth certificate had been destroyed in a fire, Dorothy asked her mother to copy the
information written in the Stine family bible.

But by the first week of May, everything had been cleared up. Louise, discovering that her
daughter's birth certificate did indeed exist, had sent a copy to London; and not too soon, as
Dorothy was beginning to think she would be permanently exiled from her own country. Having asked relatives to swear that she actually had been born, she was relieved to write:

Needless to say I was glad to get it—for just that morning
I had been to the consul's, and he told me I'd have trouble
getting in—and might be held at Ellis Island until they
checked on those affidavits of yours and Cousin
Gertrude's. But now everything is fine.

Taking advantage of a 10-day salaried holiday provided by Gaumont, Boris and Dorothy
visited Canterbury, Dover, Warwick, Kenilworth, the Lake District, Windermere and the low-
lands of Scotland before re-crossing the Tweed to stay at York and then Rutland, including the
old schooling grounds of Uppingham. Luckily, they arrived during a holiday when all the boys
had gone home. Boris was relieved, admitting, "Oh, I'd be terrified to face the little wretches!"

Sailing for New York aboard the *Europa*, they were back in Hollywood by May 19, although Universal still had not developed the next Karloff project. R.C. Sherriff was busy writing a semi-faithful adaptation of *The Invisible Man*, but James Whale had no intention of using
Boris, even though the studio already had published advertisements billing him in the role.

So Boris concentrated on other things, including cricket. In May, he presided over the Cricket Club's annual dance to raise money for the upcoming five-month season. While "circumnavigating the floor" with a partner, he was approached in mid-dance by his friend, actor Kenneth Thomson, who was interested, not in the functions of the club, but in a different kind of organization. Many years later, Boris wrote:

> As he is not known for his prowess as a cricketer, I suspect that he had been lured there in the hope of knocking him over for a small financial contribution to the cause of cricket—to be rewarded, of course, with a fancy card proclaiming him to be a non-playing associate, non-voting, dues-paying member of the Hollywood Cricket Club.

Whispering into Boris' ear, Thomson asked him about the prospect of forming a new, stronger actors union, in part to combat the 50% pay cuts enacted by the studios just after he and Dorothy had left for England. Having endured some excruciating abuse during the past two years, Boris wasted no time in replying enthusiastically, but retained his "slow and stately manner" so as not to attract any unwanted attention. Desiring an alternative to the Actors Equity Association, which had been unable to fight the exploitation and contractual abuses being committed by the studios, Boris attended a meeting at Thomson's home at 8 p.m. the following Thursday evening. Jimmy and Lucile Gleason also were there, as well as Ralph Morgan, who presided over the gathering, Cricket Club members Noel Madison and Claude King, and Thomson's wife, actress Alden Gay.

Putting their careers on the line, these courageous few cautiously recruited others, primarily from the Cricket Club at first, for subsequent meetings held at a different home each week. To avoid drawing the attention of other actors who lived in the vicinity, they all parked on side streets some distance away. Only one or two new members signed on each week, but by the end of the first month, C. Aubrey Smith, Ivan Simpson, Murray Kinnell, Leon Ames, Bradley Page, Charles Starrett, Lyle Talbot and Alan Mowbray had joined the ranks. Boris later wrote:

> The general idea was to set the skeleton of an organization for film actors with a constitution and the machinery for making it work, get what recruits we could, but in the meantime sit back and hold the fort and wait for the producers to make the inevitable booboo that would enable us to interest the stars, without whose support we knew the Guild could not hope to function successfully.

On June 1, 1933, the screenplay for *The Invisible Man* was ready, and as James Whale thought of ways to persuade the Laemmles to cast his friend Claude Rains—a cinematic neophyte—in the title role, Boris, spurred on by his increasing activism, settled the entire affair. Having waived a $250 raise in January, he now expected Laemmle, Jr., to honor the agreement to increase his salary to $1,250, but when he was told that, due to further financial strife, his weekly $1,000 would now be *cut*, he would stand for no more of the studio's subterfuge. Karloff the Uncanny walked out.

Drafting a charter, Boris and his associates filed articles of incorporation for the Screen Actors Guild on June 30. Soon, he and Dorothy were hosting Guild meetings, attracting the interest of young friends like Eugene Walsh:

> I was present at one of the first meetings... at Boris' Toluca Lake home... Boris personally had everything to lose, but his determination to help other actors was the driving force

The first meeting of the original Board of Directors of the Screen Actors Guild, 1933. Seated (left to right): Alan Mowbray, Lucile Gleason, Boris, Ralph Morgan, Noel Madison. Standing (left to right): Kenneth Thomson, James Gleason, Ivan Simpson, Richard Tucker, Clay Clement, Claude King, Alden Gay Thomson, Bradley Page, Morgan Wallace, Arthur Vinton. (Courtesy of the Screen Actors Guild Archives.)

> behind his decision. After these meetings at Toluca Lake, I attended a meeting at a theater [the El Capitan] opposite Grauman's Chinese Theatre. By this time, however, everyone, including the big stars... wanted to join the Guild and support it.

As part of its by-laws, the Guild created a contract, specifying the rules for "Class A" membership, on July 8. Eleven days later, Boris applied, agreeing "to pay an entrance fee of $25.00, and... to abide and be bound by the Articles of Incorporation." On July 25, Kenneth Thomson wrote back, informing Boris of the Guild's "temporary headquarters," but more importantly, asking him to contribute two things, money and the willingness to recruit:

> As you know, we will soon have a rather large payment to make to the attorneys, and it will help us considerably if you can find it possible to send us your check for the full amount; or if that is not convenient, for the initiation fee and the first quarter's dues....
>
> In the meantime, if you know of anyone who might be interested in joining the Guild, please use all your persuasive powers, as we need members at once.

Only four days passed before Thomson had Boris' $25 check in his hands.

A Screen Actors Guild gathering, 1933. Boris shakes hands with his good friends James Gleason and James Cagney as Russell Gleason (back, left) and Robert Armstrong (back, right) look on.

On August 3, Arthur Vinton, chairman of the Guild's membership committee, contacted Boris to express his gratitude that they would be serving together in recruitment activities. "With a little diligent effort on your part," wrote Vinton, "we can get results." And the Guild meant *diligent.* By this point, the actors involved in SAG knew they were dealing with real union business. Like others on the committee, Boris was asked to phone, every second day, a list of members who supposedly were beating the Hollywood bushes. Vinton added, "Should any of your people contact actors or actresses who are important or semi-important, I will be very glad to arrange a get-together at Ralph Morgan's home."

Boris' career for the remainder of 1933 took a decidedly different turn. Walking out on Universal allowed him to free-lance for roles outside the horror genre with which he quickly was becoming synonymous. Having saved a few dollars, he was very particular about which scripts he accepted, a discriminating attitude that landed him strong supporting roles in two films that made all the major critics' 10-best lists during the following year.

On August 30, he boarded a train headed for Yuma, Arizona, joining his friend Reginald Denny and other fellow Britons Victor McLaglen, J.M. Kerrigan, Billy Bevan and Douglas Walton to shoot RKO-Radio's *The Lost Patrol*. At 6:30 the following morning, they assembled in nearby Buttercup Valley, a location dubbed "Abdullah Alley" by the crew. Boris had occasionally enjoyed a Scotch or two with John Ford, who preferred the company of Irish and English, but this grueling production in 120-degree desert heat was his first and only professional collaboration with the director he called "wonderful." When asked about the film, Boris merely replied, "That was directed by Jack Ford, who of course speaks for himself."

Ford was just beginning to make his mark as a major Hollywood director, but he already ran his location sets like a military general. A bugler awakened the company every morning at 4:30, breakfast was served promptly at 5:00 and then they all had time to visit the "six holer" latrine and six outdoor showers before reporting to Ford and cinematographer Harold Wenstrom at 6:30.

Given second billing behind McLaglen (who would win the best actor Academy Award for Ford's brilliant *The Informer* [1935]), Boris created one of his most unusual characterizations: Sanders, a British soldier and religious fanatic who goes mad in the Mesopotamian desert during World War I. For his final scene, in which he appears dressed in Christ-like garb and carrying a makeshift cross, he worked himself into a frenzy before wandering into the unguarded dunes to be gunned down by unseen Arabs.

Working from 6:30-11:00 a.m. and then breaking until 2:30 p.m. to avoid the worst heat of the day, Ford still managed to complete the entire location shoot in a mere two weeks, even though the oven-like atmosphere and constant sandstorms sometimes stressed the actors to the breaking point. When he was asked by RKO to speed up production by reducing the lunch break from three and one-half hours to 30 minutes, Ford refused. "I'm not going to have a lot of sick people on my hands—sunstroke and everything else," he explained. About an hour after defying the producer's directive, Ford discovered that his boss had been taken to the Yuma hospital to be treated for severe heat exhaustion.

The heat was sometimes stifling, but Boris played many of his scenes nearly naked, a vast improvement over the murderous Monster costume that had sweated off 25 pounds during the midsummer of 1931. Although the film was critically acclaimed, his performance was singled out as excessive by some reviewers. Although *The London Times* called him "outstanding," *The New York Times* commented that "with the exception of Boris Karloff, [it] was an exceptionally well-acted production"—a harsh criticism, considering that his character is fanatical at the beginning of the film and totally insane by the end!

Hollywood producers thought a large percentage of their stars were insane when, at about the same time *The Lost Patrol* was being lensed, a large group of high-profile performers deserted the Academy of Motion Picture Arts and Sciences (which, in 1927, had been established by producing executives to negate the influence of Actors Equity) and joined the Screen Actors Guild. The publication of President Franklin Roosevelt's National Recovery Act code in September prompted the move.

While the NRA hearings began in Washington, Guild members met frequently to develop a plan for battling the code's salary control regulation, which stated that "no actor, director or writer could make more than $100,000 a year" and that "the agents, who were supposed to be actors' agents, had to be licensed by the producers instead of the actors in order to function." At a special meeting held at the home of Ralph Morgan's brother, Frank, on Sunday, October 1, 14 leading actors, including Boris, declared their resignation from AMPAS. At 1:10 a.m., a mild earthquake briefly shook up the proceedings, which in turn rocked AMPAS later that day: The resignees had sent a telegram stating that only an actors' organization could deal effectively with the NRA code. Boris later called their actions "putting the cat among the pigeons and getting everybody into an uproar":

> The producers chose the moment when our evening quota
> of visiting nobility consisted of Groucho Marx and the
> late Charlie Butterworth. They, of course, knew what the
> row was about and we told them what we had been up to.
> Proudly we dangled our skeleton before them and trotted
> out the proud roster of our members... all 50 or 60 of them.
> That did it. They sent telegrams to every important star in
> the business and they all convened at Frank Morgan's
> house... and the Guild was off to the races at last.

At 8:30 p.m. on October 3, the Guild held another special meeting, at Kenneth Thomson's house, where the entire board of directors and officers resigned, allowing stars to fill the vacancies. The following evening at Frank Morgan's, the new regime was put in place. Eddie Cantor was elected president, while Adolphe Menjou, Fredric March and Ann Harding filled the three vice-presidential seats. Voted treasurer, the *very* active Groucho Marx was supported by the Karloffs' favorite, Lucile Gleason, as assistant treasurer. One of the high rollers to join at the meeting was Boris' friend "Jim" Cagney, who thereafter spent many an evening at the Karloff home. Decades later, Cagney wrote:

> The need for the Guild was dramatized for me by that
> very gentle gentleman, Boris Karloff (Boris playing mon-
> sters, by the way, was typecasting in reverse). Boris came
> to me one day saying, "Jim, I'm having a terrible time.
> Every morning I have to report three and a half hours be-
> fore work commences in order to put on these fanciful
> makeups. By day's end, I'm thoroughly exhausted, and
> then it's another hour getting the damned stuff off. Some-
> times they keep me working through to eleven or twelve
> o'clock at night. It's terribly, terribly trying." I said,
> "Boris, this is exactly what they're doing at Warner Bros.,
> too."

Following a mass meeting at the El Capitan on October 8, SAG's ranks swelled to a powerful 529. Armed with this growing support, Eddie Cantor traveled to Warm Springs, Georgia, to meet with his good friend President Roosevelt, who suspended the salary control and licensing regulations of the NRA code. Aided by FDR's order, the Guild continued to expand, and with the danger level decreased, members could now park in front of the homes of Boris, Jimmy Gleason, Jimmy Cagney and Robert Montgomery.

Not forgetting about paying work, Boris followed his role for John Ford with another project he considered a personal milestone, receiving second billing behind one of his acting heroes, George Arliss, in United Artists' *The House of Rothschild*, produced in December 1933 by Darryl F. Zanuck's Twentieth Century Company. Cast as the anti-Semitic Baron Ledrantz, the absolute opposite of his own personality and perhaps the most detestable non-horror role of his career, he persecuted Arliss' Nathan Rothschild, head of the famous European banking family—one of the consummate actor's many successful historical impersonations.

The House of Rothschild (1934). This original lobby card is the only movie poster pairing Boris with George Arliss, one of his acting heroes.

Partially filmed in three-strip Technicolor by Alfred Werker, *The House of Rothschild* was a commercial and critical success. A 10-best list favorite, it also was nominated for the best picture Academy Award. Of his admiring costar, Arliss later wrote:

> Most of the actors I knew well; I had either met them on the screen or played with them on the stage. The only one I had never met was the terrible Boris Karloff—the professional bogeyman. I was therefore considerably surprised to find him one of the most retiring and gentle gentlemen it has ever been my lot to meet.

The supporting cast of *Rothschild* was literally loaded with SAG founders: Boris, Noel Madison, Murray Kinnell, Ivan Simpson, Georges Renavent and Alan Mowbray. Paul Harvey, who later served as a Guild board member (1935-55), also made an appearance.

Boris' first major act of the New Year, on January 17, 1934, took place at Universal City, the studio he had forsaken six months earlier. But now professional admiration and common sense outweighed politics and fiscal shrewdness, for he could not miss attending Carl Laemmle, Sr.'s 67th birthday party, alternately a social and a public relations event. Even after walking out on Uncle Carl, he was welcomed back as a special guest by the Universal patriarch, who assigned him a seat next to the throne itself. Several publicity photos were taken, showing the diminutive Laemmle surrounded by his stars and dwarfed by an enormous chocolate cake sporting the Universal globe and airplane. Understandably uncomfortable, Boris was in uneasy company as B-Western star Ken Maynard attempted to make small talk, but he was saved by character actor Vince Barnett, whom he previously had met on the set of *Scarface*.

Boris attends the premiere of _The House of Rothschild_.

To promote _The Lost Patrol_, RKO had hired Boris, Victor McLaglen and Reginald Denny to re-enact scenes from the film on the October 7, 1933, broadcast of NBC radio's _Hollywood on Parade_. As a follow-up, Boris plugged the February 16, 1934, premiere by giving an additional "interview" to the show's host, Jimmy Fidler, on January 24, during which he read pre-written responses only the RKO publicity department could have devised.

Two weeks later, Carl Laemmle, Jr., enticed Boris back to Universal City with a flat rate of $7,500 to star in Peter Ruric's "adaptation" of Edgar Allan Poe's "The Black Cat." With his work time estimated at four weeks, he would be paid $1,875 per week, quite an increase over the $1,250 he was denied nine months earlier. At first reluctant to abandon his "straight" success to return to the monster route, he was convinced by the amount of money offered and Jack Pierce's promise to apply only a modicum of the painful makeup that had made him a star. His skin covered with white grease paint, his lips blackened by a particularly necrotic shade of lipstick, and sporting a triangular haircut that became the first in his long line of creative cinematic coiffures, Boris became Hjalmar Poelzig, a mixture of zombie and Satan himself.

As director for _The Black Cat_, Laemmle, Jr., had chosen his friend Edgar G. Ulmer, a unique stylist who previously had assisted many of Germany's expressionist dramatists and filmmakers, including Max Reinhardt and F.W. Murnau. Prior to firing up the cameras on the last day of February 1934, Ulmer co-wrote the final draft of the screenplay based on contemporary reports of a young couple who had encountered the bizarre cult of Satanist Aleister Crowley, and also designed the futuristic sets intended to compensate for Laemmle's tiny budget of $91,125.

It had taken Laemmle, Jr., a year to cast Boris in another thrill extravaganza, but he made up for lost time with additional firepower: Dracula himself, Bela Lugosi, whose rejection of _Frankenstein_ had paved the way for the success of Universal's uncanny but militant star. Lugosi had just finished a vaudeville tour of _Dracula_ and was about to begin rehearsals for another play, _Pagan Fury_, in New York when Laemmle offered him $1,000 per week for a guarantee of three weeks' work on _The Black Cat_. Bela abandoned his insufferably artistic dream of portraying a bohemian painter in the stage drama, and quickly caught the first train for California. Fortunately, Ulmer and Ruric provided him with a well-written role, Vitus Werdegast, one of his most convincing and realistic performances, including none of the artifice and flamboyance he would become associated with during his later career.

With both conservative Laemmles out of town, production supervisor E.M. Asher approved the shooting script on Tuesday, February 27, 1934. Pitting Karloff against Lugosi in a perverse tale of two former World War I comrades who become bitter enemies, it highlighted the unsavory elements of devil worship, sadism, murder and necrophilia! Incorporating a mandatory Hollywood romantic interest, it also featured David Manners and Jacqueline Wells as a couple who become wrapped up in the dire events during a Hungarian honeymoon.

76

On February 28, Ulmer and cinematographer John Mescall began filming *The Black Cat* with Lugosi, Manners and Wells. Two days later, they were joined by Harry Cording, Egon Brecher, Anna Duncan and Boris, who proceeded to craft the most evil character of his career. Adding his own measured technique to the restrained playing of his costar and the ballet-like pacing of Ulmer, he perfectly blended into the moribund atmosphere, rarely speaking but conveying his intentions with cunning glances and subtle bodily gestures—a remarkable performance, considering that he found it difficult to take the character seriously. Ulmer recalled:

> My biggest job was to keep him in the part, because he laughed at himself.... One of the nicest scenes I had with him, he lies in bed next to the daughter of Lugosi, and the young couple rings down at the door, and he gets up and you see him the first time in costume, in that modernistic set... he got into bed, we got ready to shoot, and he got up, he turned to the camera, after he put his shoes on, and said, "Boo!" Every time I had him come in by the door, he would open the door and say, "Here comes the heavy."

The Black Cat (1934). Boris' necrophilic Hjalmar Poelzig, perhaps his most thoroughly evil characterization.

David Manners remembered Boris being very pleasant during production: "He was a friendly, gentle person not at all like the monsters he portrayed. He and I had a kind of friendship—and he always spoke with a lisp."

Also joining the cast was the black cat that was to terrify Lugosi's Werdegast. To select the feline costar, the studio had held a "Black Cat's Parade," at which both Boris and Bela, fully costumed, helped to publicize the film while meeting the young contestants who had turned out with their pets.

Boris in the "Mexican-style" house at 2320 Bowmont Drive, Beverly Hills, 1935.

Each day, Boris was guaranteed his 4 p.m. tea break, during which he usually kept to himself as he enjoyed his English pick-me-up and a smoke. Sometimes he would talk with Ulmer about mutual interests such as music, but he did not socialize with Lugosi, although photographers took publicity shots of the two stars posing together. Fittingly, the final scene of the film had them grappling to the death, with Bela—in one of the classic horror genre's most savage sequences—skinning Boris alive on an embalming rack. Apparently Bela garbled his dialogue during the first two takes, therefore getting a chance to flay his rival at least three times before Ulmer was satisfied.

Ulmer wrapped *The Black Cat* on Saturday, March 17, but a week later was forced to reshoot some scenes deemed unacceptable by Laemmle, Sr. For three days, he filmed footage intended to tone down or lighten the mood of certain scenes, but he also achieved poetic justice by adding a sequence more disturbingly erotic than anything in the original cut. Boris, interestingly combining his own love for animals with his character's sickening voyeuristic necrophilia, gently caressed the black cat as he gazed longingly at the glass-entombed corpses of Poelzig's sacrificed lovers, one of them the former wife of Werdegast, in his subterranean mausoleum!

Although they owned no cats, plenty of other animals roamed Boris and Dorothy's new Beverly Hills estate at 2320 Bowmont Drive in Coldwater Canyon, which included a Mexican-style farmhouse previously owned by Katherine Hepburn. On March 31, 1934, William Henry and Dorothy S. Pratt, signing as joint tenants, purchased the home from Virginia Barnard, one of Dorothy's friends.

Although the Gleasons, who lived on Cherokee Lane in Beverly Hills, had been frequent visitors at the Toluca Lake house, they spent even more time at 2320, often admiring their son's

Playing the piano was one of Boris' favorite less-strenuous hobbies, 1935.

photographic masterpiece showing Boris' big feet returning to Old Blighty. The hardwood bar, a small alcove surrounded by glassware-lined shelves and fronted by two stools, was Boris' favorite perch during get-togethers; and whenever a guest was bold enough to prepare a pitcher of martinis, he would warn, "Please, don't *bruise* the mixture!"

Joining the Karloff-Gleason clique at this time was a young swimmer and burgeoning stunt woman named Cynthia Hobart, who had met Boris through Russell Gleason, her then-boyfriend and future husband. Describing her first experiences with Boris, Hobart (later known as Cynthia Lindsay) recalled:

> When I first met him, I think I was 19 or 20, and he just absolutely took me in. Not because the Gleasons were mutual friends of theirs, but he was just wonderful with me. And I adored his looks. He was a wonderfully handsome man—brilliantly handsome.

Another youthful friend of the Karloffs during this period was Bob Beckham, a Beverly Hills High School student whose mother, Mae Baldwin Beckham, had been one of Dorothy's bridge partners since the late 1920s. Beckham also was close with the Gleasons and became a

The 2320 bar, Boris' favorite perch during friendly get-togethers. (1996 photograph by Scott Allen Nollen)

member of the inner circle at Cherokee Lane, spending "many Sunday afternoons with Boris and the boys who had been playing cricket out at UCLA."

Boris diligently pursued his many hobbies on the estate's two and one-half acre "farm," particularly his insatiable love of gardening. Not only did he spend every available moment carefully tending to the lawn and extensive flower beds (often wearing swimming trunks and a top hat as he watered), but he also grew plums, oranges, grapefruits, limes, lemons, peaches, apricots and avocados in a small fruit orchard. Bob Beckham remembered one Sunday at the Gleason home when Boris, who had brought some of his produce, walked in holding two pieces of fruit: "He had two plums in his hand, and he said, 'The birds have left us these plums, and we are very grateful'."

At Toluca Lake, Boris and Dorothy had kept Scottish terriers as pets, but now their love of animals was taken to extremes. Whisky and Soda, a pair of Scotties, soon were joined by two Bedlington terriers, Agnus Dei and Silly Bitch, as well as a tortoise named Lightning Bill, a parrot, ducks (two of them named Donald), chickens, turkeys, a cow named Elsie and one other barnyard pet that became a favorite of guests, including Cynthia Hobart:

> Somebody gave him an enormous pig, whose name was Violet. And my mother, who knitted, made Violet a garment of rainbow colors, and she used to walk around the garden with this trailing garment, with reds and blues and purples going behind her. And Boris would walk along with his hand on her shoulder, walking around the garden, picking off things and patting Violet as he went. It was a good sight, especially when he was in makeup.

Violet, a Poland China sow, had been a joke gift from a banker friend of Boris and Dorothy's. Unable to use their pork present in standard fashion, they let her grow to over 400 pounds!

The dogs roamed the house freely, often wandering into the study to share the sofa and the warmth of a fire as Boris settled in to read for the evening. Jeffrey Williams, an old stock company friend who had met Boris during the truck driving days, was once in the study when Agnus Dei paid a visit. Boris had poured Jeff a stiff Scotch and just stepped out for a moment when the dog decided to relieve itself on one of the expensive overstuffed chairs. After glancing at Jeff, who silently shook his head, the animal paused, slowly lowered its leg and crept out of the room. When Boris returned, absolutely nothing seemed out of the ordinary.

The Laemmle-approved final cut of *The Black Cat* premiered at the Pantages Theatre on Thursday, May 3, 1934, where 3,000 patrons responded to Universal's colorful posters heralding "KARLOFF and BELA LUGOSI in EDGAR ALLAN POE'S 'The BLACK CAT'." Boris and Dorothy attended, as did the Lugosis and Jacqueline Wells. Two weeks later, it opened at the Roxy Theatre in New York. Critics on both coasts derided the film as tasteless and dull, but agreed that pairing the two horror stars was a wise box-office move.

Although the perversion of *The Black Cat* was slightly altered by Laemmle's personal censorship, its opening two months prior to the establishment of the Production Code Administration saved it from further emasculation. If it had been released after July 15, 1934, PCA director Joseph I. Breen, like Werdegast to Poelzig in the film, would have skinned it alive. The Satanic elements would have been downplayed and the erotic nature of Boris' character—a rare quality in his cinematic canon—might have been eliminated.

Soon after *The Black Cat* was finished, Boris and Bela spoofed their horror images in a segment of *Screen Snapshots #11*, a Columbia short spotlighting stars, including James Cagney and Eddie Cantor, who were involved in Hollywood charity efforts, primarily the "Film Stars Frolic," an elaborate show that raised money for the Screen Actors Guild. In the film, Boris, whose Sa-

Boris on the tiled staircase leading to the second floor at 2320, 1935.

tanic crew cut was just beginning to fill in, and Bela addressed each other as "Dracula" and "Frankenstein," recalling a scene from *The Black Cat* by pretending to play a game of chess.

Proving his indispensability to the Guild, Boris was re-elected to the board of directors, this time for a three-year term, and was mentioned in the May 15, 1934, issue of *The Screen Player*:

> Jimmy Cagney is handling the reins in connection with the arena activities. He's Jimmy-on-the-spot, and the circus and rodeo performers will whirl and tumble in merry style under his guidance.

Then there's Boris Karloff, who has been placed in charge of special events. Not only these events, but also on the radio and in innumerable ways, Karloff is busy spilling the news about the Frolic.

An article by Boris, "Cricket in California...," was published in the same issue. Incorporating a brief history of the game, he focused on the American version, principally how the Hollywood Cricket Club was established through a sheer "miracle": "For don't forget that this is a foreign game which in the main holds no interest for Americans." Opening his essay, Boris cuts to the chase: "In addition to having a most conservative nature, I am also a stickler for the plain, unvarnished truth, so I feel quite safe in prefacing my remarks by the simple statement that cricket is the finest game in the world."

Universal had planned to star Boris in "A Trip to Mars," an R.C. Sherriff screenplay that James Whale presented to Laemmle, Sr., after a two-month visit to England. Originally announced as "The Red Planet," the production was to begin as soon as *The Black Cat* wrapped, but even after the reliable John Balderston revised the script, the disgruntled Laemmle canceled it, shifting Whale to "The Return of Frankenstein." Earlier assigned to German director Kurt Neumann in mid-1933, the *Frankenstein* sequel had been postponed when the studio's books indicated a $1 million loss at the end of the fiscal year—a setback that pleased Whale, who had insisted that the project be saved for him.

The box-office success of *The Black Cat* also induced the Universal publicity machine to announce upcoming Karloff-Lugosi projects such as Stevenson's *The Suicide Club*, "Dracula's Daughter" and "The Return of Frankenstein," but the only other 1934 film that joined the two horror maestros was *Gift of Gab*, an insignificant musical romance featuring cameos by several Universal contract players. Directed by Karl Freund, it starred Edmund Lowe and Gloria Stuart, included high-priced radio talent such as Phil Baker and Ruth Etting and only briefly worked in

Boris in the master bedroom at 2320, 1935.

Boris and Bela, who were paid $500 and $250, respectively.

Boris dedicated the second half of 1934 to his home, hobbies and the Screen Actors Guild, while Whale and Balderston hammered out a story adaptation for "The Return of Frankenstein." Whale, who had no intention of repeating himself, wanted to blend the horror elements of his first monster opus with the eccentric, perverse humor he had developed in *The Old Dark House*; and, although he did none of the actual writing, he had an enormous influence on William Hurlbut's complex, bizarre screenplay. At the end of the year, when the production, which was budgeted at $293,750, was set to begin, its monstrous star joined a group of fellow Universal players at Los Angeles' Shrine Auditorium for the annual Christmas benefit sponsored by the *Examiner* newspaper.

Although the estimate for "The Return of Frankenstein" was only a few thousand dollars more than the price tag of its 1931 predecessor, Boris now was guaranteed $12,500 for five weeks' work. Accompanied by a

Boris enjoys the company of one of his Bedlingtons on the patio at 2320, 1935.

Boris, posed but relaxed, in the yard at 2320, 1935.

Boris dapperly dressed for a match at the Hollywood Cricket Club, Griffith Park, 1935.

huge publicity campaign, the casting of the actress who would play his "bride" became a major media event. Universal mentioned several names, including Phyllis Brooks, Arletta Duncan and Brigitte Helm, but Whale, as usual, had only one choice: Elsa Lanchester, prominent English stage and screen performer, fellow eccentric, and wife of actor Charles Laughton.

Once again, Boris was back in Pierce's torture chamber. And though he now was ensured a 12-hour workday by the Screen Actors Guild, which became part of the American Federation of Labor on January 16, 1935—two weeks after production of "The Return" began—he still suffered through an agonizing schedule.

At 4:30 every morning, as Dorothy still slept, he staggered from the bed to the bathroom, where he took a very cold shower—the first step in bringing the Monster back to life. Just after 5 a.m., he had a Spartan breakfast of toast and black coffee before driving to the studio, where Pierce was ready to work his magic at around 6:00.

For the next six hours, the familiar makeup was applied, this time with alterations accounting for the terrible fire at the end of *Frankenstein*: singed hair, blood wounds on the scalp and burned facial and arm skin. At 12:30 p.m., Boris put on the steel braces, padding and suit, and the heavy asphalt spreader's boots. An hour later, he finally ate lunch, but only a sandwich and cup of tea. Shooting ran from 2 p.m. to about 6:30 or 7:00, when Pierce and two assistants, using oils and acetic acid, removed the makeup, which already had begun to close off the pores of his skin.

Still at the studio, he took another cold shower and ate a light dinner before driving home. Due to a hip dislocation that occurred while falling into the underground windmill set during the first week of production, he underwent a massage and infrared ray treatment before turning in at about 9:30 to study his scenes for the following day. He recalled:

> The watery opening scene... was filmed with me wearing a rubber suit under my costume to ward off chill. But air got into the suit. When I was launched into the pond, my legs flew up in the air, and I floated there like some obscene water lily while I, and everyone else, hooted with laughter. They finally fished me out with a boat hook and deflated me.

84

Working over the Guild's 12-hour requirement by about an hour—but never having to endure another 25-hour session as he did on *Frankenstein*—the 47-year-old Boris, at times resting in a special "Monster chair" that was built for him, enjoyed the month-long experience, particularly when he took breaks with fellow-Britons Colin Clive, who reprised his Henry Frankenstein characterization, Valerie Hobson, who took over as Elizabeth, and Lanchester, who later wrote:

> I was bound in yards and yards of bandages most carefully wound by the studio nurse. I did not particularly want to be seen by anyone. Nor did Boris Karloff. We weren't trying to be secretive. We just didn't want to be stared at. Poor Boris Karloff! When he ate in the studio commissary, he would cover up his head and shoulders with a piece of butter muslin, lifting it quickly like a curtain to pop some food into his mouth.

On at least one occasion, the challenging assignment affected his participation in SAG activities. After he wired the Guild that he would be forced to miss an important meeting, Kenneth Thomson wrote back on January 19, assuring him that his colleagues "realize the difficulties under which you are working." But, as always, Boris had a chance to "do his part," as Thomson elaborated:

> I don't suppose with that make-up you get much chance for conversation while you are working, but according to the [Hollywood] Reporter the following members of your cast are not Guild members:
>> Colin Clive
>> Valerie Hobson
>> Elsa Lanchester
>> O.P. Heggie
>> E.E. Clive
>> Ernest Thesiger
>
> We are making a determined effort to increase our membership, and if you can do anything we would appreciate it. I am enclosing a few membership blanks just on the chance.

Required to give the Monster a voice—a development he did not agree with—Boris delivered another powerful yet sensitive performance as his character became the tool of Dr. Pretorius (Whale's favorite, Ernest Thesiger), who coerces Frankenstein into creating "a woman—that should be *really* interesting." While his workdays were shorter, he actually was put through more taxing physical action as the Monster was pursued by a lynch mob, taunted, screamed at, shot, beaten with clubs, trussed to a pole, chained and, finally, blown up.

And, as part of Whale's radical thematics, which include a bizarre mockery of Christianity, he became a sort of twisted pseudo-Christ on four occasions: in a scene where the Monster is figuratively "crucified" by the villagers; when he is taken in by a blind hermit (O.P. Heggie); a shot where he stands next to a similarly posed statue of Jesus; and when, in a cemetery, he is paralleled with a huge crucifix as he angrily topples the statue of a bishop. Whale had intended to depict the Monster attempting to rescue Jesus from the cross, but, for unknown reasons, the scene eventually was toned down. Although Boris, who was not a religious man, never commented on this content, it is improbable that he did not notice it, considering that Whale is blatant in his depiction of Frankenstein *as* God, creating the Monster from the "dust of the

Bride of Frankenstein (1935). **Boris enjoys a smoke while relaxing in his "Monster chair."**

dead" and then giving him an Eve, with help from Dr. Pretorius, who, at one point, compares himself to "the very Devil."

However, the "evolution" of the Monster seemed unnecessary to Boris, who said, "The speech... stupid! My argument was that if the Monster had any impact or charm, it was because he was inarticulate... this great lumbering creature." By contrast, Whale saw the addition of dialogue as a further connection to Mary Shelley's novel, in which the Monster attains quite eloquent and philosophical speech patterns and highly advanced views on the horrors committed by human society. But, whereas Shelley's Monster requires pages of text to communicate his opinions, Boris achieved the same results with a few rudimentary words and phrases, again relying on nonverbal gestures and expressions.

Whale believed that the Monster's speech, which resembles that of a young child—a progression from the infantile creature of the first film—added another layer of depth to the character. And, regardless of Boris' purist protest, his performance impressed everyone who worked on the film *and* the critics who reviewed it.. Valerie Hobson said:

> It was Boris' kind eyes—he had the kindest eyes! Most monsters have frightening eyes, but Boris, even in makeup, had very loving, sad eyes. The thing I remember best about him was his great gentleness... he was awfully quiet, softly spoken, and always interested in one's problems, but still had his reserve. He was a dear man... Karloff is so moving—like one of the great clowns who make you cry, he did make you cry. The makeup is wonderful, but it was almost clown-like in its extremeness. You really felt that here was one whose heart was absolutely bleeding to get out of his monstrous self and find someone to love and who would love him. Very moving.

Whale, his healthy ego bristling to peak proportions during this production, still regarded Boris as a lowly laborer and truck driver who aspired to the thespian art. And when the film opened as *Bride of Frankenstein* at the Pantages Theatre on April 20, 1935, Universal's billing of him as KARLOFF on posters and huge billboard displays only irked him further. *Variety* noted that Boris displayed "some subtleties of emotion that are surprisingly real and touching," while *The New York Times* regarded him as "so splendid," but Whale also captured his deserved degree of praise in an age that often overlooked the director: *Variety* added, "James Whale... has done another excellent job; the settings, photography, and the makeup... contribute their important elements to a first-rate horror film."

Although Boris preferred his first performance as the Monster, film critics and historians have singled out his *Bride* turn as his finest heavy makeup characterization, a thoroughly convincing and deeply moving creation. The realistic to and fro movement of the head, arms and torso he created in the first film is again in evidence, this time intensified during the scene when the Monster is waiting for his mate to be "born": Boris emphasizes the creature's nervous state by gradually increasing this nonverbal technique.

Universal again publicized the unique quality of Pierce's makeup, repeating the stories of Boris being confined to his dressing room and led to the set with a veil of cheesecloth draped over his head. In fact, the pressbook, which described him as "the screen's most distinctive character actor," claimed that, due to the fire at the end of *Frankenstein*, Pierce had so altered his makeup that another campaign of secret security precautions was warranted.

During production, artist Rolf Armstrong, who had built a home and studio in Coldwater Canyon, painted a stunning neo-realistic portrait of Boris as the Monster. The uncle of actor Robert Armstrong, with whom Boris collaborated on the Screen Actors Guild, Rolf enjoyed visiting his Beverly Hills neighbors, playing tennis with the Karloffs and painting a handsome portrait of the ubiquitous Jimmy Gleason.

The publicity department, which previously had emphasized Boris' remarkably ghostly screen presence, also began to advertise his actual qualities, contrasting his intelligent and gentle per-

Bride of Frankenstein. **Boris enjoys an English tea and cigarette break with countryman Colin Clive.**

Bride of Frankenstein. **Colin Clive, Elsa Lanchester, Boris and Ernest Thesiger in the famous climactic scene.**

sonality with the terrifying creatures he portrayed. In a feature titled "The Monster Has a Heart," the pressbook emphasized, "And it is not the one with which the hideous creature was supplied when he was constructed by a scientist from parts of dead bodies and fused with life at the height of an electrical storm. Actually he is a man filled with sentiment and tender emotion."

Having endured a lengthy second round of Pierce's prosthetics, Boris fled the Universal lot as fast as his increasingly arthritic bowlegs could take him. For most of March 1935, he concentrated on his flowers, lovingly tending to his garden, which Jimmy Gleason could only refer to as "remarkable" as he arrived for a Saturday evening visit. Sometimes Nigel Bruce and his wife also were there, expressing their admiration when Boris would nudge out the hired cook to take up the skillet.

While Boris was providing sustenance for his guests, he also was thinking ahead to future projects, momentarily to *Werewolf of London*, a project announced for him and Lugosi, but quickly reduced to low-budget status with a Karloff-level contract for New York actor Henry Hull and a supporting role for current Charlie Chan Warner Oland. As a replacement project, he was offered *The Raven*, a convoluted, serial-like Edgar Allan Poe "adaptation" by David Boehm, who incorporated a modicum of the classic poem with the generic misunderstanding of its alcoholic, psychotic, misanthropic and suicidal author. Boris said, "Here was an attempt to pile on the thrills without much logic," adding that the Raven "was nothing but a bloody stuffed bird on Bela Lugosi's desk!"

The illogical quality of Boehm's script was created by seven different writers who had made contributions over the course of eight months before Laemmle, Jr., accepted it. While Bela was guaranteed $5,000 for the film, Boris was given $10,000. Director Louis Friedlander (later known as Lew Landers) began shooting on March 20, but hardly anyone was enthusiastic about the project.

Boris was distracted by the acting requirements of a film that luckily awarded a healthy paycheck. Realizing the "penny dreadful" tone of a story that transformed a fleeing criminal (via Lugosi's crazed plastic surgeon) into a hideous beast, he combined elements of his earlier gangster characters with the more blatant traits of the Frankenstein Monster.

From the outset, Boris did not relish making the film, which he viewed as a definite come-down from Whale's previous prestige production. Joining him on the set was Ian Wolfe, a severely balding 38-year-old character actor, whose considerable stage experience had led him to Hollywood. Later, Wolfe, a long-time member of the Screen Actors Guild, remembered Boris as "one of the most gentle, most kindly men imaginable, and thoughtful regarding other actors." But their initial meeting occurred on a somewhat less pleasant footing.

Arriving at Universal City early on his first day of work, Wolfe was wandering about, unsure where *The Raven* soundstage was located. In a state of confusion as the sun began barely to light the back lot, he strolled about the desolate corridors as he met a solitary man who was waiting for a makeup technician to arrive. Recognizing the man as none other than the star of *The Raven*, he asked, "Mr. Karloff, could you tell me where I may find the toilet?"

Pacing in an impatient manner, Boris, again troubled by a Laemmle contractual subversion, replied that the entire studio was a toilet before walking back into the makeup department, where he waited for Jack Pierce's unprompt assistant to arrive. During Fried-lander's shooting of the film, Wolfe, a supporting player reporting on a different schedule, "had little contact with" Boris, but saw "enough to know that, indeed, he was thoroughly disgruntled," and "had no contact whatsoever with Bela Lugosi."

Although Bela only received half as much pay as Boris, he was given more screen time, and he saw to it that audiences would never forget his performance as the megalomaniacal Dr. Vollin, whose obsession with Poe leads to sadism, torture and murder. Echoing the scripted material that stresses the

The Raven **(1935). Boris as the tragic Edmond Bateman.**

doctor's ever-increasing insanity, he dominates the film with an outrageously overplayed performance that must have rattled the very foundations of Albert D'Agostino's low-budget sets. By contrast, Boris' Edmond Bateman is the type of character for which he soon became famous: an essentially innocent man turned into a criminal by uncontrollable circumstances. He is the Frankenstein Monster set in a different location and time, a character who is unattractive in a normal sense, frightens those whom he meets and ultimately is controlled by someone who induces his antisocial and dangerous behavior.

Two weeks before the film was released, a ridiculous newspaper story was published, claiming that a real bullet was fired at Boris during the final scene in which Bateman rescues the kidnapped young couple (Lester Matthews and Irene Ware) from Vollin's clutches. The article reported that, while Bela shot blanks, a marksman (appropriately named Hugh Ames) fired an Enfield rifle at Boris, who was outfitted with a 50-pound bullet-proof vest. Instead of missing him, the bullet whizzed off mark a wee bit, grazing his left side. The idea that the Laemmles would be dangerously reckless with their top adult star is incredible; and, asked to recall the incident nearly 30 years later, Boris denied it ever happened.

Friedlander wrapped production on Friday, April 5, 1935, and the film premiered on Independence Day at New York's Roxy, where Lugosi made a personal appearance before sailing to England to star in *The Mystery of the Mary Celeste*, the seminal Hammer film. In the opening credits, Boris and Bela were both billed by surname only, but in the list of players at the beginning and the end, the former remained "KARLOFF," while the latter was again "Bela Lugosi," a reflection of the disparity in their Universal contracts and levels of stardom. While filmgoers turned out in great numbers to see *The Raven*, critics referred to it with such superlatives as "absurd," "dreadful" and "the worst," primarily objecting to the extremity of Vollin's torturing of his victims, an element that also troubled censors across the nation.

Boris didn't care. He had worked hard on *The Raven*, just another film in a continuing series of cinematic works he could not refuse, for the simple reason that it was *work*. A working actor did his job—as long as he was properly paid for it—and doing that job involved another loan out by Universal during May 1935 to appear in Columbia's "The Black Room Mystery," an atmospheric period piece filmed over the ensuing month but actually released before *The Raven*, which had been delayed by various post-production problems.

After doing all he could with a criminal-monster in a melodramatic penny dreadful, Boris was pleased to sink his teeth into a real acting challenge: twin brothers with opposing personalities—a psychological dichotomy borrowing elements from Alexandre Dumas' *The Man in the Iron Mask* and Robert Louis Stevenson's *The Strange Case of Dr. Jekyll and Mr. Hyde*—in a film inspired by a Hungarian legend about a noble family in which one son murders the other. Required to create two separate characters with disparate personalities, he attempted to imbue each of them with subtlety and restraint, ensuring that one was not too evil and the other too kind. And after appearing in a scene in which the bad brother murders the good one and then assumes his identity, he carefully merged the two personae, rather than simply repeating his performance as the latter—in effect, portraying three characters in the same film.

This multi-character situation also posed technical challenges, especially acting in scenes that ultimately would show both of his characters interacting with one another: Not only did he have to interpret two characters, he also needed to follow director Roy William Neill's complicated blocking instructions when either conversing with a carefully positioned double or simply thin air (in shots marked for later double-exposure optical prints). In the finished print, cinematographer Al Siegler's work depicting two Karloffs as the De Berghman brothers is flawless, as are the actor's characterizations, one forcefully malignant, the other an interesting variation on his own gentle personality. Not only does the lustrous visual style create an evocative atmosphere, but Boris' physical appearance also adds to the ambiance of the film. While Anton, the kind brother, is well-groomed and formally dressed, his evil doppelganger, Gregor, wears long, unkempt hair and casual clothing that accentuates his lean physique—qualities that emphasize his less refined, more sensual characteristics.

The Black Room (1935). **Boris as the evil Gregor De Berghmann, disguised as his kind brother, Anton, about to murder Colonel Hassel (Thurston Hall).**

An impressive early 19th-century period piece, *The Black Room* also benefits from a superb supporting cast, including Thurston Hall, Edward Van Sloan and Marian Marsh, who portrayed Thea, the object of evil Gregor's desire. Marsh and her husband occasionally joined Boris and Dorothy for dinner at 2320, where she enjoyed seeing her costar romp about with the 400-pound pig in its "playpen." Another supporting actor, Torben Meyer, who played Peter, the servant, enjoyed working with Boris during the six-week shoot:

> We became good friends from the very beginning... later on, we met, had a chat or a lunch together... I remember once we talked about misuse and overwork of actors... by the studios... He said in a very subdued way: "Yes, I hate them."... He certainly paid for the glory of being a star. But he was strong... physically... I do not think anyone else could have done it... He was thankful for the chance he got at Universal. He said to me, "Torben, I never thought I'd be a star."

In July 1935 Boris' responsibilities for the Screen Actors Guild were increased when he was elected to a one-year term as assistant secretary. And his impressive acting in *The Black Room* did not go unnoticed by the union, whose members awarded him honorable mention in the "best performance of August" contest. Only the recently deceased Will Rogers (as Dr. John Pearly in John Ford's *Steamboat Round the Bend*) and Henry Fonda (as Don Harrow in Victor Fleming's *The Farmer Takes a Wife*) received more votes in an election involving 20 actors.

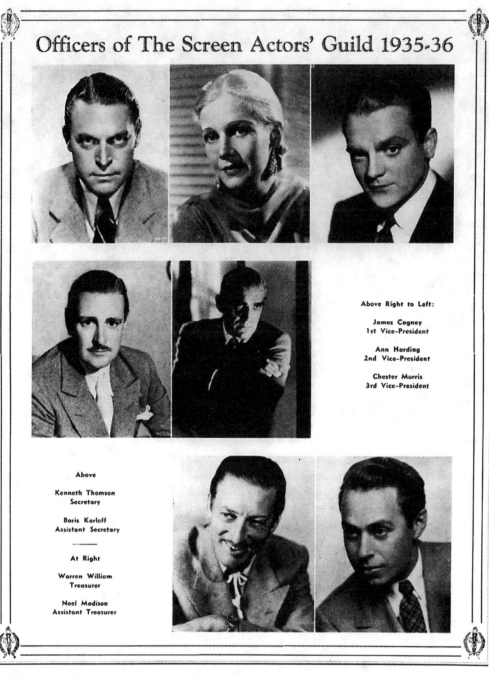

Officers of The Screen Actors' Guild 1935-36

Above Right to Left:

James Cagney
1st Vice-President

Ann Harding
2nd Vice-President

Chester Morris
3rd Vice-President

Above

Kenneth Thomson
Secretary

Boris Karloff
Assistant Secretary

At Right

Warren William
Treasurer

Noel Madison
Assistant Treasurer

Officers of the Screen Actors Guild, 1935-36. Originally published in the August 1935 issue of *The Screen Guild's Magazine.* **(Courtesy of The Screen Actors Guild Archives.)**

Boris also became a member of the Motion Picture Hall of Fame in July, appearing with a host of other veteran actors at the California Pacific International Exposition in San Diego, where they happily spoke with fans and signed innumerable autographs. Lucile Gleason acted as chairman of the Exposition Committee, on which Boris served with 33 colleagues, including Joan Crawford, Bette Davis, Joe E. Brown, James Cagney, Clark Gable, Jimmy Gleason, Fredric March and Robert Montgomery. Later that month, Hal Hall, in *The Screen Guild's Magazine*, wrote:

Richard Tucker, Dorothy and Boris at The Screen Writers' Dinner and Dance in the Fiesta Room of the Ambassador Hotel, Hollywood, August 1, 1935. (Courtesy of The Screen Actors Guild Archives.)

> The manner in which the visiting stars cooperate in making the building a success really amazes many people. An entirely new side of the picture folk is shown and it is a human side that is doing much for the industry for it reveals the players as regular men and women who gladly rub elbows with the public which patronizes their films and their exhibit at the fair.

Boris made what is considered his dramatic radio debut on the August 1, 1935, broadcast of *Shell Chateau* starring Al Jolson, whose declining career was reflected in this variety-show hodgepodge. Supported by Martha Creighton and Crawford Kent, Boris, in Fu Manchu mode, played a villainous, Anglophobic rajah in a skit adapted from *The Green Goddess*, William Archer's stridently anti-Asian 1923 play. Later that evening, he and Dorothy attended a dinner and dance held by the Screen Writers' Guild in the Fiesta Room of the Ambassador Hotel. Although most of the attendees were screenwriters, including SWG president Ernest Pascal, vice-president Nunnally Johnson and secretary Robert N. Lee, a few actors also showed their support.

Later that month, Universal, having scrapped plans to star Boris in David Diamond's production about the infamous strangler Bluebeard, announced that his next film, *The Invisible Ray*, would be produced by Edmund Grainger. Hoping to repeat the box office successes of the two previous Karloff-Lugosi vehicles, the studio cabled Bela in London before he and his wife had a chance to leave for a long-planned trip to Hungary, and offered him a flat rate of $4,000 to costar in the new film. (Boris already had been guaranteed $15,625 for a five-week shoot.) Based on "The Death Ray," a story by Howard Higgin and Douglas Hodges, this science-fiction thriller, budgeted at $166,875, was designed as a high-grade B picture and placed in the hands of Stuart Walker, who ran into problems after his request for a minor rewrite was refused by the

Laemmles. Having competently directed *The Mystery of Edwin Drood* and *Werewolf of London* for the studio, Walker would not agree to film what he believed was flawed material, and not only quit the project, but walked out on the studio.

Having little time to choose a replacement for Walker, Carl Laemmle, Jr., turned over the reins of *The Invisible Ray* to the efficient Lambert Hillyer, a Western and action specialist, who began shooting on Tuesday, September 17. Boris' portrayal of Dr. Janos Rukh, a Hungarian research scientist who discovers a powerful new element, initiated a Karloff archetype: a sincere man who intends to aid humanity, but after being exposed to the dangerous side effects of his work, mentally deteriorates and unwittingly causes destruction and death. Poisoned by "Radium X," the element he hopes to use as a cure for various diseases, Rukh becomes enraged when his former colleague, Dr. Benet (Lugosi), receives the credit due him. Required to depict a wide range of emotions, Boris again invested his characterization with the subtle gestures and expressions he had used to excellent effect in *The Black Cat*, *Bride of Frankenstein* and *The Black Room*; but, in depicting the obsessive and increasingly maniacal behavior of Rukh, he added touches of overplayed melodrama to certain scenes. Bela also was given an opportunity to create a convincing, sympathetic character, similar to Werdegast in *The Black Cat*, rather than the scenery chewing Vollin in *The Raven*.

The most interesting set in the film, a Paris church where Rukh destroys six religious icons with his radioactive power, was originally the cathedral built for Lon Chaney's *The Hunchback of Notre Dame* (1923). Other visual highlights were contributed by special effects artist John P. Fulton, who created Rukh's exploration of the Andromeda galaxy and a glow in the dark look for Boris, whose physical appearance—including curly black hair and a mustache courtesy of Jack Pierce—is very striking.

Although the majority of shooting took place on soundstages and the back lot, scenes set in Africa, where Rukh mines and develops Radium X, were filmed at outside locations. One particular scene, depicting Rukh gathering a specimen of the element, required Boris to wear a suffocatingly hot radiation suit while being lowered into a smoking pit. Since the shot in which he is suspended on the scaffold was filmed just before noon, the crew decided to play a practical joke on him. Frances Drake, who portrayed Rukh's beautiful wife in the film, recalled that, although he was left hanging by the technicians who broke for lunch, he was "a good sport" about it all.

But the good sport could also be quite aggressive when it came to performing with actors who had not joined the Guild. Taking his assistant secretary position very seriously, he increasingly viewed each new filmmaking situation as a recruitment opportunity. On September 22, only five days into the *Invisible Ray* shoot, he sent a letter to Kenneth Thomson, enclosing a completed SAG application and check from Frank Lawton, who played Mrs. Rukh's lover, Ronald Drake, in the film. "His wife, Evelyn Laye, undoubtedly will follow," Boris wrote, asking:

> Can you give me a report on the following:
> Frances Drake
> Beulah Bondi
> Violet Kemble Cooper

One month later, he again contacted Thomson, outlining his own plan of action:

> Enclosed is the signed application of Frances Drake. I am
> happy to report that with the addition two weeks ago of
> Frank Lawton this makes "The Invisible Ray" company
> 100%.
> I have found no resistance at all from the people I
> have worked with and I believe that by studying the casts

The Invisible Ray (1936). Boris' tragic Dr. Janos Rukh confronts Dr. Felix Benet (Bela Lugosi), the man he accuses of "stealing" his great discovery, Radium X.

as published in the Reporter, selecting some real member of the cast who is also in the Guild, firing them up and arming them with applications for immediate action, we can make each working unit 100% by working from within.

Much to the Laemmles' chagrin, the usually swift Hillyer took 36 days to shoot *The Invisible Ray*, wrapping a full 12 days over schedule on October 25, 1935. And by the time Fulton finished his elaborate special effects on November 20, the production had gone $68,000 over budget. Fulton's innovative work and the unusual science-fiction premise were emphasized in the pressbook and other promotional materials, including a *Universal Weekly* column in which Laemmle, Sr., advised patrons to "watch out for the technical effects."

When *The Invisible Ray* premiered at New York's Roxy on January 10, 1936, Universal's typically colorful posters billed Boris as "The Great KARLOFF," while his costar again was "Bela Lugosi," listed in much smaller type. The film proved popular at the box office and, although most critics faulted the fantastical premise, Britain's *The Cinema* noted that Boris "makes a curiously sympathetic figure of the stricken Rukh, and gives us no small insight into the tortured brain responsible for his later atrocities."

Having mentioned his recruitment plan to Thomson, Boris immediately put it into practice, asking Murray Kinnell, who was playing a doctor in MGM's *Kind Lady*, to sign the non-Guild members of the cast. On November 5, 1935, SAG mailed Kinnell a list of 12 names, which included Boris' future cricket colleague, co-star and union collaborator Basil Rathbone.

Later that month, Boris was loaned to Warner Bros., where he became re-acquainted with the versatile and dictatorial Michael Curtiz, who, after directing two of the best horror films of the early 1930s—*Doctor X* (1932) and *The Mystery of the Wax Museum* (1933)—had just completed *Captain Blood* (1935), the film that soon would make Errol Flynn a household name. Budgeted at $200,000 (with Boris guaranteed $3,750 per week), *The Walking Dead* was scripted as a gangster film (a Warners specialty) including elements of mythology and understated horror. Inspired by Boris' *Frankenstein* portrayals, screenwriters Ewart Adamson, Robert Andrews, Lilli Hayward and Peter Milne (whom Curtiz had added to the project) fashioned a sensitive story about John Elman, a meek musician who, after being framed, executed in the electric chair, and then revived, provokes the accidental deaths of each member of the gang who railroaded him. But, unlike Universal's fairy-tale horror movies, *The Walking Dead*, set in the real world of Depression America, was another installment in Warners' series of social problem films depicting a gritty world of unemployment and criminal racketeering.

Benefiting from Hal Mohr's expressionistic camerawork and lighting, Curtiz used the gangster plot to create a rapid pace, including a pseudo-*Frankenstein* resurrection scene (featuring Edmund Gwenn as the scientist) as additional excitement. He generated the "horror" of the film, not by depicting a rampaging monster, but by maintaining a consistent mood: a strange eeriness resulting from the combination of Boris' virtuoso performance, Mohr's cinematography and his own tendency toward urban realism. The believable character of John Elman is, like the Frankenstein Monster and Edmond Bateman, not really a monster, but a victim of social forces he cannot control. In this instance, crime and a corrupt justice system cause him to be condemned and put to death, only to be revived and turned into a zombie.

Curtiz inspired one of Boris' most memorable and powerful cinematic moments while directing the scene depicting Elman's walk to the electric chair—content he earlier explored with Spencer Tracy in *20,000 Years in Sing Sing* (1933). Using an overhead long shot with a slowly revolving ceiling fan in the foreground and a cello player at screen left, he created a strong sense of visual entrapment by having Mohr light the cell bars to throw long, web-like shadows across the floor. Closing the scene, he had Boris walk into the execution chamber, glance upward and say, "He'll believe me." As it turns out, *He* does believe Elman, as the Christian deity actually becomes part of the "monster" to punish the criminal gang who led him to his death.

After the resurrection scene (which incorporates the Lindbergh Heart, an actual device invented by the famous aviator and several researchers, including Dr. Alexis Carrel), Boris speaks very little dialogue, again relying on the nonverbal versatility of his eyes and mouth to depict Elman's emotions, particularly in an unforgettable, haunting scene in which he sits at the piano, playing Arthur Rubinstein's "Kammenoi Ostrow" as he stares into the faces of the terrified gangsters.

During production, Boris and fellow cast members Ricardo Cortez, Marguerite Churchill, Henry O'Neill, Barton MacLane and Warren Hull visited the neighboring set of *The Petrified Forest*, where Archie Mayo was directing Leslie Howard, Bette Davis and a rather obscure stage performer called Humphrey Bogart in Charles Kenyon and Delmer Daves' adaptation of Robert E. Sherwood's hit play. While directing the eerie cemetery scene that closes *The Walking Dead*, Curtiz's perfectionism resulted in extra days of shooting and an additional $47,000—a development that greatly irked head of production Hal B. Wallis—but he finally wrapped Boris' scenes at 2:30 a.m. on December 21.

In its promotional campaign, the Warners publicity department claimed that the new film would revive the public debate over capital punishment. Claiming that the cast had discussed the controversial issue, a pressbook article listed Boris and Barton MacLane as the only actors who were against the death penalty. But the studio did not have to resort to such tactics to sell the film: The public, impressed by the thoughtful thematics and Boris' masterful portrayal, plunked down $300,000 to see it.

Again, another "controversial issue" was Boris' performing with non-union actors. Just after production on *The Walking Dead* began, he received a letter from SAG, perhaps dictated by Kenneth Thomson, informing him that Warren Hull, Eddie Acuff, Addison Richards, Joseph King and Ruth Robinson had not joined. But even more unsavory than these non-members were

The Walking Dead (1936). Ricardo Cortez, Marguerite Churchill, Boris, Henry O'Neill, Barton MacLane and Warren Hull visit the set of *The Petrified Forest* at Warner Bros.

the attitudes of two other players; the letter concluded: "Mike Morita... has never paid a penny. Ricardo Cortez, as you know, has resigned."

On the evening of December 30, 1935, a radio program demonstrated the enormity of the stardom Boris had achieved during the four years since *Frankenstein* was released. Featuring his friends Murray Kinnell (as "his brother, the Sir," John Pratt) and Russell Gleason (in several parts), the show broadcast his "life history," starring Boris as himself!

Prior to the release of *The Walking Dead*, Boris received a second offer from Gaumont-British. Excited by the prospect of again returning to England, he agreed to star in another horror film, for $30,000 plus the bonus of a few days' paid leisure in New York. But by the second week of January 1936, the deal was in jeopardy: Pressured by restrictions on horror films enacted by the Middlesex County Council, Gaumont shelved the project and tried to buy off Boris with a cash settlement. Fortunately Boris could count on his agent, Myron Selznick, who negotiated for "another type story" for him to star in.

Allowed more travel time than they had been given three years earlier, Boris and Dorothy booked a berth on an eastbound train. But prior to boarding, they were feted at a Beverly Hills cocktail party organized by Jimmy and Lucile Gleason. At 7 p.m. on January 28, after all the drinks were downed, a Tanner bus pulled up to the Gleason home, and accompanying the Karloffs on their ride to the depot were dozens of their friends, including Mr. and Mrs. James Cagney, Basil and Ouida Rathbone, Nigel and Bunny Bruce, Mr. and Mrs. Frank McHugh, Pat and Eloise O'Brien, Mr. and Mrs. Kenneth Thomson, Mr. and Mrs. Murray Kinnell, Mr. and Mrs. Rolf Armstrong, Russell Gleason, Cynthia Hobart and 30 members of the Globe Theater Shakespearean Company.

Although avoiding the pitfalls of flying this time around, they did not arrive in New York without their share of unplanned adventures. From their room at the Algonquin Hotel on West 44th Street, Dorothy wrote to her mother:

> Well here we are and loving it—but what a time we had getting here. That N.Y. car on the Grand Trunk was certainly shoved about. They soon got bored with us and left us on a sideing until another train came along and took a fancy to us—and so it went on all night. However, we were lucky, for the train that dropped us at Hamilton, Ontario, had a wreck a few miles out of Hamilton and it was no night to be in a wreck—the thermometer what it was and my ears what they are. We got into N.Y. five hours late—and no train that got attached to us from 6 p.m. Monday night until we landed here at 2:30 p.m. Tuesday had any diner. We stopped somewhere in Pennsylvania for a cup of coffee and that's all. But we're here and everything's grand. A telegram waiting for Boris from the Selznick office for a 3 yr. contract at Warner Bros.— recognizing the Universal contract and to run together with it—a nice jump in salary too. Wasn't that a pretty grand greeting to N.Y.?

Before sailing from New York during the second week of February, they attended eight plays, visited with actor Melville Cooper and his wife, Rita, dined in a 5th Avenue penthouse and stayed out until the wee hours almost daily. In fact, their partying became so severe that Dorothy was forced to write, "have had no sleep—5 and 6 o'clock every morning—have cirrhosis of the liver, delirium tremens and nervous exhaustion."

On Wednesday, February 5, *New York Evening Journal* reporter Arthur Le Duc published an article about Boris, noting, "There was little of the 'monster' about him as he discussed domestic problems and let drop the astonishing news that instead of devouring babies in his spare time, he devoted it to raising pigs and chickens!" That same day, Boris rehearsed at NBC for an appearance on *The Fleischmann Hour*, which was broadcast the following evening at 8 p.m. A 60-minute program hosted by Graham McNamee, it featured him in a dramatic skit titled "The Bells." He also gave an interview to B.R. Crisler of *The New York Times*, who described him as an actor who, instead of being a monster, "would rather be like Bing Crosby, if [he] had any say so in the matter."

The wintry transatlantic voyage aboard the S.S. *Washington* often was a rough one, particularly while crossing the Irish Sea. Scheduled to reach Plymouth at 2 p.m. on Tuesday, February 18, the ship finally docked at 3 a.m. the following morning. Although he was very tired, Boris was thrilled when two Torquay girls who had stayed up all night came forward to request his autograph.

The press had also come out to meet him before he and Dorothy boarded a train bound for Paddington Station. Later that day, London's *Star* interestingly referred to him as a "rather serious-looking sunburnt Englishman," while the following day's *Daily Mirror* reported, "Karloff is still a British subject and does not intend becoming a naturalized American." And the February 20 *Morning Advertiser* combined two of his nicknames, calling him "King of the Uncanny."

Settling into their room at the Berkeley Hotel, Boris readied himself for the intelligent and witty *The Man Who Changed His Mind*, but was equally anxious to see his beloved England once again. Gaumont began paying his salary immediately, but after the studio decided to rewrite the script, his pay was suspended for a few days. Uncomfortable at the Berkeley, he and Dorothy briefly relocated to the Dorchester, but ultimately decided to re-visit the service flat at

Joined by other visiting members of the Hollywood Cricket Club, Boris and his colleagues challenged the Oxford University team during the 1936 trip to England.

#1 Duchess Street, where they had found such happiness three years earlier. "It seems like getting home," Dorothy wrote to Louise, adding that she and Boris had brightened up the gloomy weather by making the place look like a flower garden: "Have great branches of white lilac all over the room—and two bowls of tulips—and have snowdrops, violets or lily of the valley to wear every day. They're so beautiful and so cheap."

On Monday, February 24, Boris reported to the office of Harry Ham, the London representative of the Joyce-Selznick agency, to discuss the script situation before lunching with Godfrey Tearle at the Carlton Club and attending a pantomime of *40 Thieves* at the Lyric Theatre. He and Dorothy then enjoyed a fine dinner at the home of Robert Stevenson, the director of *The Man Who Changed His Mind*, and his wife, Anna Lee, who was cast as Boris' leading lady, before returning to the hotel at 2 a.m. Prior to meeting their supper companions, Dorothy had "read all of Boris' script, which is rotten," informing Louise that everyone involved with the project believed it would never be produced.

The following day, Boris again met with Ham before joining Dorothy for dinner and on to the movies to see Robert Montgomery in MGM's macabre *Night Must Fall*. Press photographers descended upon them Wednesday morning, before Boris reported to Gaumont for a one-hour meeting. Since the film still was not ready to go, they then filled the day with a matinee of *Out of the Dark*, dinner at the Bolivar and another trip to the theater to see *Antony and Anna*.

Thursday was even more of a party. Having eaten dinner with Paul England and his girlfriend, they went to the play *Call It a Day* and then ate again at the Dorchester, where the floor show kept them out until 3 a.m. The next morning, press photographers recorded Boris' purchase of cricket bats at Lillywhite's, and after lunch at the Bolivar, Dorothy drove him to the studio. The film was still on hold, so they again spent the day eating two dinners and attending a play, *Tovarich* this time, after which they visited backstage with Sir Cedric Hardwicke. Continuing to enjoy his free time in London, Boris, dapper in tie and tails, once more kept Dorothy out until 3 a.m.

On Saturday, February 29, they went to Twickenham to see the Army and Navy rugby game before dressing for dinner at the Carlton and *Round About Regent Street* at the Palladium. Turning in at 2:30 a.m., they were up again at 8:00 on Sunday morning for an 80-mile drive to Hastings, to view the battlefield where William the Conqueror defeated King Harold in 1066. Back in London at 6:30, they ate dinner in the company of Theodore Roosevelt, Jr., Alexander Woolcott and Alfred Werker, who had directed Boris in *The House of Rothschild*. Remarkably, they were in bed by 10 p.m.

It had been a very hectic but wonderfully satisfying week, although Boris had not worked or been paid a penny by Gaumont. On the morning of Monday, March 2, Dorothy wrote to Louise in Charlotte, Michigan:

> What a mess it's all been... he goes back on salary tomorrow... I'm trying to take care of his fan mail—about a hundred letters a day—and just opening, reading and sorting them is a job. I'm not answering them but just getting them ready to turn over to a secretary for answering. And up late every night as usual... Boris is at the studio now... but as soon as he comes we're going to lunch at Quaglino's—then to his tailor's—then to the Tower of London—then to dinner—then to see H.G. Wells' *The Shape of Things to Come*.
>
> However it will all quiet down as soon as he starts work which will be in about another week.

On the very day he went "back on salary," Boris wired the Guild about negotiations he had been carrying out with representatives of British Equity to link the two unions and create enforcement of standard actors' working conditions for both countries. Asking for information about "proposed... conditions for contract, freelance, and day players," he expressed his desire for a tentative agreement. The following day, Kenneth Thomson wrote to Harry Ham's office, advising Boris that he should be able to conclude with such an accord, "subject, of course, to the approval of the Board, which we are sure will be granted."

When shooting finally began on *The Man Who Changed His Mind*, Gaumont relegated the film to its factory in Islington, which Dorothy, in a letter to Nancy Smith, referred to as "a foul filthy hole if ever I saw one":

> The air inside the place is awful. The stage is way inside of a factory building and not one breath of fresh air all day. And Boris has been working with two chimpanzees, and although they are darlings—they don't help the air any. And the canteen there is no good so I've been taking his lunch down every day...

Dorothy occasionally watched Boris working on the film, and saw to it that he still had enjoyable nights on the town, including dinner with Gaumont producer John Holmes on Friday, March 13, and with Sir Cedric and Lady Hardwicke at the Savoy Grill, a meeting place for the city's theatrical elite, the next day. On Saturday, March 14, she also took some fruit to Boris' brother Fred who was ill with the flu.

Sunday again was a time to visit relatives, but rather than leading them to the south of England, this occasion involved a 100-mile drive up the east coast to Southwold on the North Sea, where a niece was attending school. They treated her to lunch at Lowestoft, an old fishing town about 13 miles north of Southwold, and then took a ferry down the Blyth River and out to sea, landing on Walberswick, a little island fishing village featuring remnants of ancient Danish culture. "Walked around there," wrote Dorothy, "loving every minute of it." At 8 p.m., they were back at Brentwood on the northeast edge of London, enjoying dinner with Sir John and Lady Edith Pratt.

On Monday morning, Boris was thoroughly immersed in *The Man Who Changed His Mind*, which now occasionally kept him at Islington until 8 p.m. Drawing inspiration from the work of 17th-century French philosopher Rene Decartes, the film cast him as Dr. Laurience, a surgeon who claims that the human soul exists independently of the brain. By the time he tackled this role, he had become an exponent of the "science versus society" theme in his two *Frankenstein* films, *The Invisible Ray* and *The Walking Dead*, but Laurience provided him with a more blatant philosophical voice. Intending to prove his theory that one person's mind may be transferred into the body of another, he is reprimanded by his young assistant, Claire Wyatt (Anna Lee), branded a charlatan by his colleagues and, after using his transference device for his own ends, commits murder. Just before he dies, Laurience, admitting that the soul is sacred, orders Claire to destroy his research.

Not wanting to merely repeat his characterization from *The Invisible Ray*, Boris created an acting style bordering on the surreal. In one scene set in Laurience's laboratory, he purposely emphasized his bowed legs and spinal curvature while subtly mimicking the physical appearance of the two chimpanzees. Anna Lee, who greatly enjoyed her collaboration with Boris, echoed Dorothy by claiming, "He wasn't too happy about the monkeys—the chimpanzees—that we had. They were not at all well trained. I know they inhabited the dressing room next to mine and they used to make an awful smell."

Malt House, the 17th-century Berkshire home Boris and Dorothy lived in from April-July 1936.

The Malt House dining room, spring 1936.

Boris often spent his lunch and tea breaks with Lee, who recalled:

> I remember him as a very kind and gentle man. We shared
> a great love of poetry. We used to have "jam sessions"
> together—he would start a poem, "Between the dark and
> the daylight... " and I would continue, "When the night is
> beginning to lower... " and go on until one of us got stuck!
> I forgot who usually won!

While making *The Man Who Changed His Mind*, Boris signed a one-picture deal with London's Twickenham Films, ostensibly to remain in his homeland for another three months. But he and Dorothy were growing tired of the city, so in early April, they spent a rainy weekend in the country, with Gordon Walker and George Simpson, at Moyleen Farm. And over the four-day Easter weekend, accompanied by their friend Eb Morgan, they stayed in the village of Hurley, Berkshire, on the Thames halfway between London and Oxford. Although their getaway was chilled by spring snow, their love for the area led them to rent a local 17th-century home, Malt House, which they moved into the Friday after Easter, just in time to see "the daffodils... making a wonderful show [and] the fruit trees... just beginning to burst." On Monday, April 25, Dorothy wrote to her mother, who recently had relocated from Michigan to the Beverly Hills estate:

> The house is too large for us but very comfortable, and
> the gardens are lovely—about eight acres—three garden-

ers and three indoor servants... There's a billiard room for
Boris, and since Eb is staying with us, I haven't yet had to
take up the game seriously.

We have a movie camera and are trying to use colour
film—so we can show you all this when we get back.

Dorothy informed Louise of $3,000 that had been sent to cover various expenses, as well as
several boxes (which were to remain sealed until their return) containing items they had acquired during their stay, particularly "priceless bits of English ashtrays accumulated at great
trouble... and each one will remind us of a great theft cautiously executed." In her letter, she also
mentioned Twickenham's utterly confusing film project:

He's happy to stay—and I hope by the time you get this
he will be happy about the picture. At the moment the
story is a mess and he's having the usual arguments with
them—but I'm certain it's bound to be straightened out.
It was nice for us, wasn't it, that he wasn't needed in Hollywood immediately after the last one?

The new picture is called *Juggernaut*—but is not the
story Bertie Anson wrote—isn't that a shame?

Beginning work on *Juggernaut* on April 25, Boris expected to be finished by June 6. Repeating the wifely duties she had carried out at Islington, Dorothy arrived at Twickenham to
have lunch with Boris, and when the work day ended, they often joined Sir John and Edith for an
interesting evening in London or returned to Berkshire for a drink and a round of darts at the
Chequers pub. Dorothy recalled:

We were entertained after hours by the proprietors. I can't
describe what fun it was or how different from anything
in America. All eight of us and an ancient dog sitting
around the parlor of an old pub with special police permission for late hours, eating cheese and watercress and
drinking ale. We didn't get home until the wee hours, and
I claim it to be a perfect night's entertainment.

On Wednesday, May 6, Boris and Dorothy drove to Oxfordshire for lunch and to watch a
cricket match between Oxford and the All-Indian team. The weather was beautiful, and Boris
was overjoyed to see such a first-class contest. Three days later, Mr. and Mrs. Murray Kinnell
arrived in Liverpool, wiring that they would reach London on Monday, May 11. Dorothy hoped
that they would be able to stay at Malt House the following weekend, as Boris' frequent time off
from the haphazard *Juggernaut* would allow them to visit with their old friends. Dorothy met
the Kinnells in London on the 11th, and Boris joined them and Eb Morgan for dinner after the
film wrapped for the day. Dorothy planned another solid week of socializing, capping it off with
the Kinnells' visit, during which they attended a cricket match, played tennis, went pub crawling
and sailed up the Thames with Harry Maynard, a friend from Yorkshire.

But such conviviality did not prevent Boris from maintaining a bit of union activity. On the
morning of May 15, the London *Daily Herald* reported, "Film Actors Linked Across the Atlantic—Boris Karloff as Negotiator," announcing that an agreement between SAG and Equity had
been signed:

Boris Karloff, the film star, played a leading part in the
negotiations, representing the Guild in the London dis-

cussions. George Arliss also took part.... Mr. A.M. Wall, general secretary of Equity, told the "Daily Herald" last night, "The agreement is highly satisfactory, in view of the fact that the motion picture industry, so far as English-speaking films are concerned, is becoming more and more dependent on the joint efforts of American and British artists."

Under the agreement, all Equity actors working in the United States automatically were granted membership in the Guild, while their American counterparts received Equity protection in Britain. And of course, Boris was, to paraphrase the *Daily Herald*, both an American and British artist.

On the day the article appeared, Boris clipped it from the paper and mailed it to Kenneth Thomson, along with a letter he typed during a break in the *Juggernaut* filming. Characteristically, he downplayed all the time and effort he had volunteered:

It is grand news, and I know it is a foregone conclusion that it will be accepted by the General Meeting on the 24th. I assure you that absolutely no credit is due to me because Equity on this side was so receptive that the agreement was to be had for the asking.

Juggernaut (1936). Boris as Dr. Sartorius, with Joan Wyndham, in Twickenham's absurd "thriller."

Then he offered to provide further assistance by joining "a Committee of Equity here to draw up a skeleton of working conditions for the studios."

The erratic production schedule at Twickenham also allowed Boris and Dorothy to attend a session of the House of Commons on Monday, May 18, where they were thrilled to hear speeches made by Anthony Eden, Winston Churchill, Stanley Baldwin, Neville Chamberlain and Ramsay MacDonald. Dorothy wrote another letter to Louise the next day, explaining that they might remain in England until August 1, ostensibly to establish a six-month residency and avoid paying U.S. state and federal income taxes on the money he had earned in London, which already had been taxed by the British government. Closing her missive, she admitted, "You're right about Boris. He does make life very beautiful for both of us, doesn't he? He's loving it here, too..."

Boris typed a lengthy letter to his mother-in-law on Tuesday, May 26. Apologizing for not writing sooner, he remarkably referred to himself as "a frightful man." He had been having problems with his back and one of his legs, but now claimed he was "feeling awfully fit" and "well rested." He and Dorothy now had decided to stay in England until the third week of August, having just received word from Universal that his loan-out to Twickenham had been extended. But he was more concerned, not with the relatively insignificant *Juggernaut*, but with his garden back at 2320—and even more so with one of his most beloved pets:

> About poor old Violet: I am sure I don't know what to do.
> I have planned to fence in part of the hill so that she and
> the chickens can have that to run in, but I don't like to
> start that until I actually get home, because we have to
> decide very carefully just what part of the hill to fence in.
> If the old girl can keep her figure and not die of fatty de-
> generation of the heart before I return, all will be well. I
> think I would consult Earle about that, and maybe we could
> board her out on a ranch somewhere where she would get
> a bit of exercise.

Although Louise had been staying at 2320, she had not been handling their financial affairs properly. Dorothy had penned several letters, featuring Boris' own handwritten suggestions, advising her who to contact and what funds to use, but she had been reluctant to spend the money. Boris again explained the process in great detail, coloring the situation with a bit of humor:

> I don't want to hear any more nonsense such as you wrote
> to Dorothy about having $500 left and leaving it in the
> bank to draw interest; you know perfectly well that the
> pennies we send you are to be spent—but please don't
> use it all for whiskey!

Juggernaut was finally in the can, but Boris was informed that he needed to report back to Gaumont for a few retakes to complete *The Man Who Changed His Mind*. Although he did not mind a little additional work on this interesting film, the best thing that can be said about *Juggernaut* is that he never had to see it. He had not been in such a bad film since the early silent days, and it is doubtful that he would have accepted such an atrocious script had he been back in Hollywood. Regardless of his intentions or approach to the character of Dr. Sartorius, a one-dimensional research scientist, he gave one of his worst cinematic performances, affecting a few melodramatic scowls as he uttered painfully banal dialogue.

With two months left in their self-imposed "tax exile," they planned to spend the majority of July touring through France. By the time they had their plans solidified, two weeks of that

84 LA BAULE. — Vue générale de la Plage prise de l'Hôtel Adriana, vers le Pouliguen

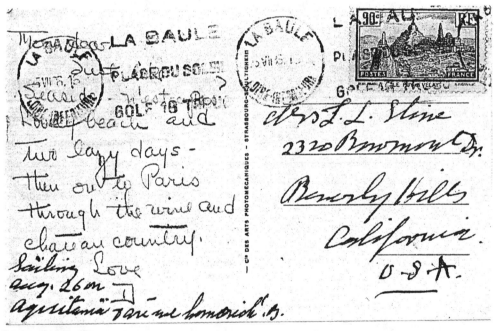

During their holiday in France, Boris and Dorothy sent this postcard to Louise Stine. Postmarked July 25, 1936, it includes Boris' admission to his mother-in-law that they are quite homesick.

month had passed, and on the 14th, they ferried from Dover to Calais, where, according to Dorothy, they would "just turn the nose of the car loose for four weeks." They spent the first night at Amiens, the next two days at Rouen and then drove through Liseaux, Villedieu, and Auvrauches to the Hotel de l'Univers in St. Malo on Friday, July 17. On the following Wednesday, they traveled 17 miles to Mont St. Michael, and then to Quimper in the heart of Brittany. By Thursday, July 23, they were in the seaside resort of La Baule, planning to drive through "wine and chateau country" to Paris, where they would spend the last 10 days of their holiday.

But before reaching Paris, they spent the night of Saturday, July 25, at the Hotel de l'Univers in Tours. The next morning, Dorothy wrote to her mother:

> One of the funniest things of the whole trip happened last night. After you've been two weeks in rural France—with not even a newspaper to know what's going on—except trying to decipher the French headlines—you feel thousands of miles from anything American.
>
> Last night we came out of the restaurant after dinner—and in the lobby of the hotel stood two American sailors waiting for Boris' autograph. When you realize Tours is miles inland—and isn't exactly the place you'd expect to find anything in a sailor suit—then to have these two off the U.S.S. *Wyoming* waiting there was a shock—and a very funny feeling it was.

At the end of this letter, Boris appended, "Corrected, passed and approved by the family linguist... Boris."

On July 27, Boris drove to Paris, where they spent the next nine days in a top-floor suite at the Hotel George V. They absolutely loved touring the city, but both were homesick and anxious to start back via Rheims. Due to inclement weather, their plans to drive to London via Cornwall and Devonshire were scrapped, and as soon as they reached Dover on August 9, they went straight to the Hotel Washington in Mayfair. The next day, Boris took Sir John's daughter, Diana, to see a cricket match at the Oval pavilion in London.

On August 22, they boarded the *Empress of Britain* for the return voyage to North America. Originally planning to sail aboard the *Aquitania* on August 26, Boris instead chose the earlier departure, because the *Empress* was scheduled to land in Quebec, near enough to Toronto, where he would take part in another *Fleischmann Hour* radio broadcast on September 3.

The word that Boris was on board the *Empress* spread among the passengers like wildfire, and he handled the excitement with his usual good cheer. One 11-year-old girl, who was seeing her grandparents off on the first leg of their journey to the Congress of the British Empire Chambers of Commerce in New Zealand, heard of the uncanny one's presence and immediately desired a memento. Many years later, K. Mary Maydwell wrote, "my grandfather, a very lively, friendly man, succeeded in finding him, no doubt aided by ship's officers, and had him very kindly sign [his] autograph, to the enormous delight of the little girl I was."

Apparently, "enormous delight" also was had on the other side of the Atlantic, by Screen Actors Guild colleagues who had not seen one of their founding members for several months. During his lengthy absence, Boris had been retained as assistant secretary of SAG for another year.

Chapter 6

Son and Daughter

"I was in *Frankenstein*, *The Bride of Frankenstein*, and
The Son of Frankenstein. It was all proper order. It was
all quite respectable. The bride came first."

When Boris returned to Los Angeles in September 1936, he discovered that the horror
genre had died an amazingly quick death. Due to changing public interest and constant pressure
from the Production Code Administration, uncomplicated, upbeat stories had replaced the austere and "pessimistic" themes featured in the films that had made him famous.

Due to his well-known versatility, Boris was offered a non-horror, but still very heavy, role
as a crazed classical singer in Twentieth Century-Fox's *Charlie Chan at the Opera*, filmed during October 1936. As Gravelle, he was only a red herring, but provided a welcome challenge to
Warner Oland's mock-Chinese detective. Driven by madness, revenge (against those who locked
him in a burning dressing room 12 years earlier) and a passionate love of opera, Gravelle appears as Mephistopheles in Oscar Levant's *Carnival*, and is seriously wounded by a trigger-
happy policeman before the ever intrepid Chan unmasks the real killer. At one point in this
solidly campy melodrama, the director of the production proclaims, "This opera is going on
tonight, even if *Frankenstein* walks in!" Mouthing the libretto of the opera as well as playing
tender scenes with Gravelle's long-lost daughter (Charlotte Henry), Boris, unable to take the
story seriously, chewed the scenery as if he was still trapped at Twickenham.

After drawing upon his old Uppingham musical training for the Charlie Chan episode,
Boris spent the next three months primarily at 2320, often catching up on his reading. The
shelves in his library rapidly had been filling up with volumes of excellent English literature, but
he rarely had been home to crack their covers. Settling into his cozy study, with one of the
Bedlingtons snuggled at the foot of the chair, he perused Conrad's *Heart of Darkness* and "The
Secret Sharer," re-acquainting himself with the profound but subtle allusions of the Polish writer
who had mastered English as few Britons or Americans ever could.

Planning to accompany Dorothy to the Hollywood Cricket Club's annual dance, held at the
Miramar Hotel in Santa Monica, Boris was approached by Eugene Walsh, who still was alternating cricket with courses at USC. Walsh's finances were meager, and after mentioning that he
would have to clean up his "old Model A Ford" before picking up his date, Boris offered to loan
his car, a beautiful Auburn. Walsh recounted:

> Tragedy struck as I was driving down Wilshire Boule-
> vard, and a car collided with me, denting in the doors of
> Boris' car. I was able to drive the car to the dance, but it
> took me two hours before I had plucked up enough cour-
> age to tell Boris about the accident. His immediate reac-
> tion was his deep concern that neither of us was hurt, add-
> ing "Don't worry about the car. I'll get it fixed." His
> kindness and generosity of spirit on this occasion is some-
> thing I shall never forget.

Night Key (1937). **Boris reads his fan mail during a break at Universal.**

In February 1937 Boris finally was summoned back to the studio that had made him a star. His contract with Uncle Carl tossed to the four winds, he now faced the owner of the *New Universal*, J. Cheever Cowdin of Wall Street's Standard Capitol Corporation, a specialist in pouncing upon destitute companies, who had taken control of the studio after the Laemmles had spent it into receivership.

Carl Laemmle, Sr., had seen the last of his filmmaking days. And his son, made a ceremonial chairman of the board, was not long for the professional world. Cowdin, who had hired Robert H. Cochrane as president of the New Universal, immediately sacked 70 employees and revamped most of the films the studio had on its docket.

Boris was no longer KARLOFF or Karloff the Uncanny, a reduction in billing that he ignored absolutely. Freed from the contractual difficulties of the Laemmle regime, he still was considered one of the studio's major personalities. In an attempt to re-work Boris' image but still capitalize on his villainous reputation, Cowdin and Cochrane, offering above-the-title billing, rushed him into *Night Key*, the tale of a misunderstood burglar-alarm inventor who runs afoul of local racketeers. In another film mixing tenets of the gangster and horror genres, Boris emerged as the hero, even though the production suffered from Cochrane's $175,000 budget and Lloyd Corrigan's pedestrian direction.

During the filming of *Night Key*, Boris objected to Universal's attempt to work him more than eight hours per day, reflecting the increased activism of the Screen Actors Guild. One particular incident, resulting from the studio's order that he report for night shooting, culminated with his refusal to appear the next day, a "militant" act that enraged the front office.

On March 8, 1937, Boris returned to Warner Bros. to play Wu Yen Fang, another counterfeit Asian, in *West of Shanghai*, the story of a Chinese warlord who prevents two American finan-

Boris is joined on the tennis court by (left to right) Rolf Armstrong and his wife, Dorothy and her mother, Louise Stine, and Rolf Armstrong's brother, c. 1938.

ciers from foreclosing on a local oil field. An Eastern version of Porter Emerson Browne's play *The Bad Man*, the film allowed him to indulge his comic abilities in an absurd but well-developed characterization that was lauded by several major publications, including *The New York Times*, whose critic praised his economical and subtle style, calling Fang "lovable, charming and ridiculous."

Finally, in April—two months after *Night Key* wrapped—threats of mass support for a film-industry strike began to be voiced. On May 1, 3,000 technicians and workers picketed the major studios, inducing the Guild to throw its weight behind the effort. Ninety-six percent of the major stars and contract players were ready to strike. Among those who ignored the militancy and crossed the picket lines were several heavyweights: Clark Gable, William Powell, Jean Harlow, Jeanette MacDonald and Greta Garbo, all complaining because they had received no breakfast from chefs who had walked out. Managing to eat their early morning meal elsewhere, Jack Benny, Bing Crosby, Martha Raye, Irene Dunne, Jean Arthur and Randolph Scott also disregarded the stand of their fellow performers.

Proposing a contract for actors working in feature films—including a closed shop, minimum wage rates, a 10-percent pay increase for extras and a 12-hour rest period between calls—the Guild successfully negotiated with RKO, Paramount, MGM, Twentieth Century-Fox, Universal and Columbia without resorting to an actual strike. On May 15, the new agreement, signed by 13 producers, went into effect. Two weeks later, when the Guild re-elected Boris to another one-year term as assistant secretary and to the board of directors for another three, he was more than enthusiastic in his support of president Robert Montgomery and vice presidents

110

Members of the Hollywood Cricket Club, late 1930s. Founder C. Aubrey Smith is seated (center). Among those standing are Herbert Marshall (third from left), Nigel Bruce (center) and Boris.

Joan Crawford, Chester Morris and James Cagney, whom *The New York Times* had described as "the most ardent proponent of unionism among the stars." Among the most vociferous supporters of the effort were some of Boris' colleagues and friends: Edward G. Robinson, Humphrey Bogart, Victor McLaglen, Paul Muni, Peter Lorre and Bela Lugosi.

Having developed a friendship with director John Farrow during the making of *West of Shanghai*, Boris returned to Warners in October 1937 to appear as the alcoholic Jevries, another red herring, in *The Invisible Menace*, a film about military police brutality. Marred by a leaden pace and inappropriate comedy relief, the contrived screenplay offered Boris a sympathetic character, but little else. He did his best to make the role interesting, giving a very subtle performance, but the studio misled the public by promoting the film as a horror thriller. When it was released two months later, *The New York Journal-American*'s Rose Pelswick noted, "Customers who settle down expecting to be scared will find themselves feeling sorry for him."

On November 23, 1937, Boris turned 50. To commemorate the event, 20 close friends, including Jimmy Gleason, Murray Kinnell and John and Betty Reinhardt, converged upon Coldwater Canyon, filling 2320 with warm birthday wishes and superannuated humor.

The following January, Boris returned to radio, scaring those who tuned in to hear Edgar Bergen and Charlie McCarthy on *The Chase and Sanborn Hour*. Reading "The Evil Eye," an adaptation of Poe's "The Tell-Tale Heart," he used his eerie voice to such good effect that it was discussed during a session of the United States Senate the following week. Commenting on the gruesome nature of the broadcast, Iowa Senator Clyde LaVerne Herring, who served one term from 1937 to 1943, called for FCC censorship of such material, but his proposed bill received little support.

About six weeks later, Dorothy returned from a doctor's appointment to inform the 50-year-old actor that he soon would add *father* to his long list of roles, a development that kindled joyful anticipation in a man who had loved children all his life. But on March 13, 1938, he reverted to type as Hollywood's preeminent bogeyman, teaming with Bela Lugosi for the radio show *The Baker's Broadcast*.

Featuring Ozzie and Harriet Nelson, and hosted by Feg Murray, *Baker's Broadcast* gave its listeners brief insights into the personal lives of the "Titans of Terror." While Boris read Rudyard

Boris, the "gentleman farmer" as Dorothy called him, feeds his flock of turkeys at 2320, 1938.

Kipling's poem "The Supplication of the Black Aberdeen" as a tribute to one of his Scottish terriers, Bela (who called Murray "Fag" at one point) made the tongue-in-cheek claim that watching *Dracula* sent him to bed for a week! Ending their collaboration on a truly absurd note, they poked fun at their horror personae, in a duet called "We're Horrible, Horrible Men":

> *Boris and Bela:*
> We're horrible, horrible men.
> We're horrible, horrible men.
> We're villainous, killinous, lecherous, treacherous,
>   toughiest, roughiest men.
>
> *Bela:*
> To the grave we come in,
> 't would make strong men afraid.
> You can't blame us for it,
> for the rent must be paid.
>
> *Boris and Bela:*
> We're horrible, horrible, horrible, horrible, horrible, hor-
>   rible men.
> We're horrible, horrible, horrible, horrible, horrible, hor-
>   rible men.
> We're villainous, killinous, treacherous, lecherous,
>   roughiest, toughiest men.
>
> *Boris:*
> Though the movies would make me
> a terrible brute
> When my makeup is off,
> I am really quite cute.
>
> *Boris and Bela:*
> We're horrible, horrible, horrible, horrible, horrible, hor-
>   rible men.

Boris cooling off in the 2320 pool, 1938.

Ten days later, Boris flew to Chicago to begin a series of five weekly guest appearances on Arch Oboler's *Lights Out*, the nation's most popular radio horror show. In the first episode, "Darrell Hall's Thoughts," broadcast on March 23, he played a college professor who had never dreamed. But after revealing his secret to his doubting colleagues, he experienced a recurring nightmare in which spirits moaned and a female apparition with "a face from hell" chanted, "Kill," eventually driving him to murder his fiancée. Realizing that the moaning spirits had tried to warn him not to be coerced by the apparition, he learned that he must die on the gallows or be doomed to serve her for all eternity. After being sentenced to death, however, he succumbed to a heart attack, appearing as if "he were looking at the devil himself."

For the April 6 episode, the truly frightening "Cat Wife,"

Boris spent as much time as possible in 2320's greenhouse, 1938.

113

Boris' workaholic lifestyle and love of sports kept him trim at the age of 50, 1938.

Boris gave one of his most memorable radio performances, as John Taylor, an unhappy man who caused his spouse to transform after calling her a "cat." Married to a human-sized feline whose communication skills were limited to meowing and scratching, Taylor eventually shot the beast after she clawed out his eyes. In a shock ending, the poor man heard her call out his name just before she died. Echoing many of his horror-film roles, these *Lights Out* characters were men doomed by forces they could not control.

Later that month, he was on the road, narrating a 55-minute stage production incorporating "The Tell-Tale Heart." His first stint with a touring company in nearly two decades, this play, combined with his increasing radio work, offered a welcome respite from the grind of filmmaking.

In June 1938 he reported back to Warner Bros. to star in *Devil's Island*, a social problem film inspired by the French government's closing of the notorious penal colony the previous year. Originally selecting George Raft to play Dr. Charles Gaudet, a physician who is incarcerated and abused after treating a political revolutionary, producer Bryan Foy instead turned to Boris when the decline of the horror genre killed off the proposed thriller *Witches' Sabbath*. Shot quickly by director William Clemens, the film was ready for release in September, but was delayed by a French propaganda campaign.

While Boris was working on the Warners lot, the success of Oriental detective films, inspired by popular magazine stories, was attracting the attention of producers at the minor studios. The "poverty row" studios, too, caught wind of this trend, and in September, Monogram, having acquired the screen rights to Hugh Wiley's "Mr. Wong" stories, approached Boris, hoping that his search for non-horror roles might include a series detective. Indeed it did, and he signed to appear in four adaptations of Wiley's *Collier's* magazine tales. Merging Warner Oland's character from *Charlie Chan at the Opera* with fond memories of Conan Doyle's Sherlock Holmes stories, he fashioned a very subdued, highly educated detective who solved crimes with brains rather than brawn.

After finishing *Mr. Wong, Detective*, which was released on October 5, he received a call from Universal, where yet another management team had taken over. When Robert Cochrane had turned over the presidential reigns to Nate Blumberg in February, the horror genre was still considered box-office poison. But after the owner of the Regina, a failing Los Angeles theater, exhibited a triple bill of *Dracula, Frankenstein* and RKO-Radio's *Son of Kong* (1933) on August 5, things began to change. Booking all three films for only $99 per week and running several large advertisements in local newspapers, the exhibitor was delighted to see huge lines form around his theater every time he showed them between 10 a.m. and 3 a.m. Taking advantage of the situation, Blumberg and vice-president Cliff Work re-issued 500 official Universal prints of *Dracula* and *Frankenstein,* in a

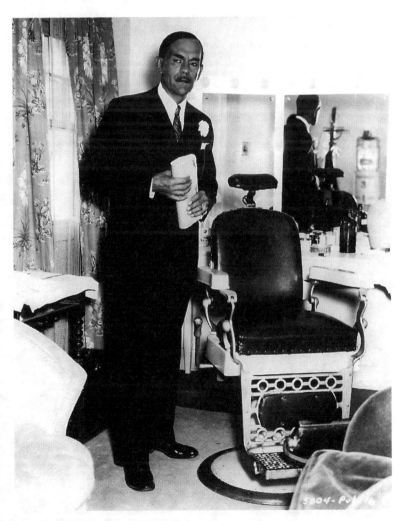

Boris, script in hand, poses in Monogram's makeup shop during the filming of the "Mr. Wong" series (1938-40).

double-feature package. Regardless of the PCA and Great Britain's dreaded "H" certificate, which barred persons under 16 from seeing scary films, horror was back.

Anxious to capitalize on the tremendous public response, Blumberg and Work made preparations for another Frankenstein sequel. Hoping to rush the new film into theaters as quickly as possible, they allocated only $250,000 to the production and chose costume-drama specialist Rowland V. Lee to double as producer and director. Now that James Whale, whose eccentric lifestyle had not impressed the *New* Universal, was gone, Lee was the studio's number one filmmaker—a fact the director did not hesitate to mention as he demanded that the budget for *Son of Frankenstein* be enlarged considerably.

On October 13, 1938, *Variety* reported that the new terror project, being written by *Lights Out* veteran Willis Cooper, would star Karloff, Lugosi and Peter Lorre, who was being loaned by Twentieth Century-Fox. Having squeezed more money out of the new conservative regime, Lee then insisted that Henry Frankenstein's son be played, not by the diminutive, bizarre Lorre, but by villain extraordinaire Basil Rathbone, who, at $5,000 per week, was Hollywood's most expensive free-lance actor. Interestingly, Boris, who was no longer the KARLOFF of the previous Frankenstein picture, not only accepted second billing, but also received $1,250 per week less than Rathbone.

Having no problem deferring to his Shakespearean countryman, Boris, however, did object to the way Cooper had depicted the Monster. Added to the creature's speech—which he had performed under protest in *Bride*—were his violent encounter with a modern army and ludicrous attempt to perform *brain surgery*! Aware of his star's distaste for the screenplay, Lee rejected it after plans to shoot the film in Technicolor were scrapped: Jack Pierce's gray-green

Son of Frankenstein (1939). Basil Rathbone and Boris enjoy a laugh during Boris' 51st birthday celebration, November 23, 1938.

grease paint, which made Boris appear so realistically cadaverous in black and white, looked like a coating of bad makeup in color.

Regardless of these major setbacks, Lee, pleased that the front office's original conception had been abandoned, began shooting *Son of Frankenstein* without a script on November 9. Having hired former mad doctor Lionel Atwill to play the Teutonic Inspector Krogh, Lee then concentrated on Lugosi, who had been signed for a nonexistent role. Working closely with Cooper, the director fashioned the character of Ygor, a broken-necked blacksmith who uses the Monster to exact revenge on his enemies. Menacing, yet sympathetic and humorous, Ygor gave Lugosi a rare chance to demonstrate his considerable talent, plus a $500 salary that Lee insured he would receive for several weeks, rather than the one Universal had slated. Only 11 months old when he visited his father on the set, Bela Lugosi, Jr. later wrote, "Ygor... was one of my father's most enjoyable and physically demanding roles."

Universal production manager Martin F. Murphy, who projected a $300,000 budget and 27-day shoot with a wrap on December 10, was destined for disappointment. However, the cast, which also included Josephine Hutchinson as Mrs. Elsa Frankenstein and Donnie Dunagan as little Peter Frankenstein, had a pleasant time indeed, with Boris and Basil often taking tea together and discussing their mutual love of cricket and practical jokes.

Boris again arrived at the makeup lab at 5 a.m. to undergo a four-hour transformation; although, since the production of *Bride of Frankenstein*, Pierce had developed pre-made appliances such as a head piece to cover his scalp. In official publicity, Universal reported that the entire costume, including the asphalt-spreader's boots, added eight inches to his height and 64 additional pounds for him to carry.

Two weeks into production, on Wednesday, November 23, 1938, Boris celebrated his 51st birthday. Much to his delight, the cast and crew threw a surprise party that began *during* the shooting of a powerful scene in which Frankenstein is startled by the Monster, who grabs him from behind. When Boris placed his hand on Basil's shoulder, Rathbone moved aside to reveal a huge cake on the laboratory table. During the festivities, Boris made certain to smear a quantity of white frosting across the dreaded sheepskin vest he had reluctantly worn in all his scenes. (He later referred to it as "furs and muck.")

But there was more than one Karloff nativity to celebrate. At Hollywood Presbyterian Hospital at 10:50 that morning, Dorothy had given birth, via a Cesarean section performed by Drs. Thompson and Branch, to a 6 lb. 2 oz. girl, Sara Jane Karloff Pratt—an event commemorated by Rowland, Basil and Bela's presentation to Boris of a tiny pair of Frankenstein Monster boots! Dorothy, in the meantime, was literally deluged with telegrams from friends, well-wishers and Boris' colleagues, including actors Alan Mowbray and Henry Stephenson, the *Son of Frankenstein* camera crew, Scott R. Dunlap of Monogram, and, of course, Mr. and Mrs. Jimmy Gleason and Mr. and Mrs. C. Aubrey Smith.

Among the first regards was a wire from Mae, Rob and Bob Beckham in San Francisco: "Congratulations on the wonderful news—came just as we were drinking to Boris' birthday—we are thrilled to pieces—can hardly wait to see the young lady—godmother telephoning her godchild in a few days—a heart full of love and best wishes." Another San Franciscan message, signed "Marion and Lou," made a clever play on Boris' real name: "What a swell wife you are to hand the old gent that kind of a birthday gift—love to you and Boris—give the Dot a loving pat on the prat... " And from Los Angeles, a wire from Ed Thomas read, "Congratulations to mama and papa and the daughter of Frankenstein."

A few days later, Lugosi brought his wife, Lillian, and Bela, Jr., to the soundstage, where they presented their own baby gift to Boris. But even his cheerful response could not prevent little Bela from crying in terror at the sight of the Monster makeup.

Boris and the baby were doing well, but Dorothy had been weakened considerably by the birth. According to Sara Jane, she "had to stay in the hospital, something like 10 days or two weeks, because she had to have transfusions when I was born. She was very sick and nearly died... I am assuming I stayed in the hospital most of that time and went home with a nurse."

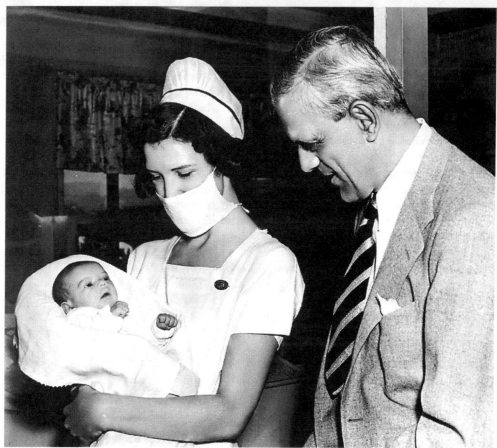

Boris visits newborn Sara Jane for the first time, Hollywood Presbyterian Hospital, November 1938.

On November 26, Martin Murphy reported to the front office that Rowland Lee's slow, meticulous methods were creating "the most difficult conditions... that is, without script which prevents us from laying out schedule or figuring a budget." Now considering a total shooting period of 39 days, to end by Christmas Eve, Murphy knew that his $300,000 estimate was out the window. The production manager also mentioned that Boris had gone AWOL to visit his wife and newborn daughter on the 23rd, an action that required him to play his last day as the Monster for free. Like the Screen Actors Guild, the studios, too, expected fair treatment.

On December 10, Murphy expressed concern that Lee would not complete the shoot within the following two weeks: "Of course, we still have no script upon which to base this contention, and unquestionably Lee should be in a better position than we are to know just how much he has left to do because the story appears to be altogether in his mind." In his production report, Murphy now estimated the budget of *Son* to be $347,100, contingent upon a Christmas Eve wrap.

As filming continued, Boris grew more concerned that his characterization of the Monster was being overshadowed by Lee's emphasis on the activities of the other characters, particularly the scenery-chewing clash of wills between Wolf Frankenstein and Inspector Krogh. He later recalled:

> I thought I could (and I was right as it turned out) see the
> handwriting on the wall as to which way the stories were
> going... that they would go downhill. There was not much
> left in the character of the Monster to be developed; we

had reached his limits. I saw that from here on, he would
become rather an oafish prop, so to speak, in the last act
or something like that, without any great stature.

However, having convinced Lee to drop the Monster's dialogue, he was able to return to the subtle, pantomimic performance style he had used to great effect in the first Frankenstein film.

Physically the Monster is considerably larger in *Son*, due primarily to a padded undergarment that broadened Boris' shoulders and extended his chest, and the heavy leather coat and sheepskin vest that replaced his original suit jacket. Although the official pressbook describes Boris as six feet tall and weighing 170 pounds, he looks more robust, even when accounting for the makeup and 27 pounds of clothing.

For James Whale, Boris had fashioned a formidable but gentle character with human vulnerability; for Rowland Lee, he became a superhuman, indestructible force that could be revitalized with another jolt of lightning. When Wolf first encounters the comatose Monster, Ygor reveals that he "cannot be destroyed—cannot die," adding, "Your father made him live for always." Later, during the creature's lengthy "physical," Wolf claims, "No human heart could possibly function like that. It's beating at over 250 per minute"—a strange diagnosis, considering that his father had used only human parts that he took "from graves, from the gallows, anywhere" in his original construction of the Monster.

To recognize the Christmas holiday, Universal usually shut down all production by noon on December 24. However, Lee kept George Robinson's camera rolling until 6:15 that evening, an effort that still fell far short of wrapping what was becoming a truly monstrous nightmare for poor M.F. Murphy.

Four days later, actor Perry Ivins, who was cast as the servant Fritz in the film, presented one-month-old Sara Jane with a slightly belated Christmas present, a poem satirizing her famous father's persona:

> "Mother Goose-Flesh Rhymes for
> Miss Sara Ann [sic] Karloff"

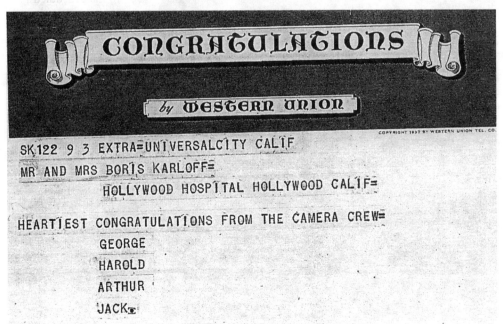

Boris and Dorothy received this telegram, congratulating them on the birth of Sara Jane, from the *Son of Frankenstein* **camera crew, November 1938.**

Rockabye baby, don't stare at your pop,
For if you do, your blood pressure'll drop!
When he grimaces, gurgle with glee,
His faces finance your family tree.

Ride a nightmare to opening night,
To see the old ladies get pallid with fright.
With belles all a-swooning, as well as their beaux,
Your dad'll make money wherever he goes.

On December 14, Jimmy Gleason had contacted Sara Jane via Western Union. His jocular telegram read, "Have you an agent—if not see me before you do any business with anyone else—I can place you usual ten percent—my kindest regards to your father—my love to your mother—J. Feldman Blum Gleason." Two weeks later, writing under the guise of his infant son, he was at it again, even more nonsensically: "Madame: providing proper dowry of forty seven cents can be suitably arranged—I have the honor to ask for your hand—respectfully, Michael Morgan Gleason."

On New Year's Eve, the ever-frazzled M.F. Murphy reported that, after guaranteeing a December 28 wrap of *Son*, Lee had not come through, further increasing the budget to pay the high-salaried actors. On December 29, only Boris, Bela and young Dunagan still had scenes to perform, but even these drove the shoot toward a completion date of January 4, 1939, only three days before the scheduled preview.

True to form, Lee stretched production a few hours past the new proposed deadline, finally wrapping at 1:15 a.m. on January 5. In a truly Herculean effort, Maurice Pivar's editorial department and Charles Previn's music department, including composer Frank Skinner and Austrian composer and orchestrator Hans J. Salter, worked nonstop until the picture was completed, *on* the preview date of January 7, 1939. Taking his expressionistic opus 19 days over schedule, Lee had increased the budget by $120,000.

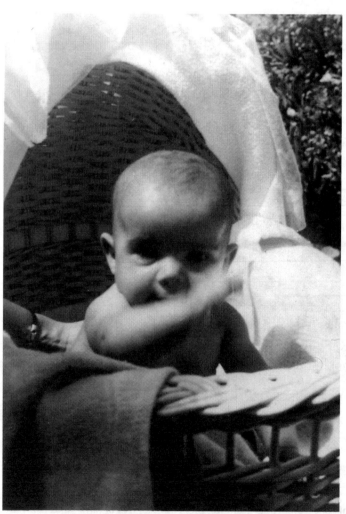

Sara Jane in her basket at 2320, spring 1939.

However, much to Universal's relief, shortly after its premiere at the Pantages Theatre on January 13, 1939, and New York release on January 28, *Son of Frankenstein* became a box-office smash, inaugurating a second "cycle" of Hollywood horror films.

With his final Frankenstein performance in the can, Boris returned to the steady, relatively unchallenging Mr. Wong series at Monogram, which perhaps was a blessing, considering that now he was getting less sleep than usual. At the age of 51, he was being roused out of bed at 4 a.m., not by a wake-up call to put on a horrendously painful makeup, but by a hungry infant. And, on Easter Sunday—April 9, 1939—he and Dorothy invited 30 of their closest friends to attend Sara Jane's christening.

Only a few film industry personalities attended. Betty Rhineheart, who would go on to co-write *Laura* in 1944, was there, as well as the newly wed Cynthia Hobart and Russell Gleason, who acted as godparents to the child, along with Mae Beckham, Edward Hayman and Adam Hulton. Other guests included Dorothy's mother, who recently had lost her sight after being hit by a car; Boris' friend and intellectual compatriot, Professor Raubenheimer of USC, and his wife, Mary; the Kinnells, the Gleasons and the Aubrey Smiths. Dressed in a white christening gown, baby Sara Jane, peering up at the guests with dark eyes unmistakably inherited from her proud father, wore a tiny orchid corsage to match the one displayed by her equally spirited mother.

Sara Jane's christening, Easter Sunday 1939. Dorothy, Boris and Sara Jane are joined by friends and family, including C. Aubrey Smith (center of group), Cynthia Gleason (later Lindsay, in dark hat, behind smiling boy), James Gleason (back row, far right), Russell Gleason (in front of James), Lucile Gleason (beside Boris), Louise Stine (wearing dark glasses) and William Stine (beside Louise.)

Although the christening was overseen by Dr. J.H. Lash, a Presbyterian clergyman, it was primarily a secular affair, as Boris, whose philosophical anarchism also encompassed religion, was an agnostic all his life. "He allowed everyone to hold whatever views they might," Sara Jane remembers. "I don't think he knew exactly what his own beliefs were."

Karloff family portrait, 1939.

Sara Jane made her first foray into the outside world—beyond Boris' garden, that is—in early May 1939. Safely cradled in Boris' Buick, she rode with her parents to the C. Aubrey Smith residence. Although the old boy himself was out, Mrs. Smith presented her with a locket that had belonged to C. Aubrey's mother. Loot in hand, they then drove to the Gleasons' on Cherokee Lane, where Jimmy, Lucile, Russell and Cynthia all took turns making baby talk.

At this stage of her young life, the only major obstacle Sara Jane posed to her rather strict mother was a penchant for thumb sucking. To "correct" the problem, Dorothy tied coverings of canvas and plastic to her daughter's tiny hands, making the thumbs inaccessible.

After acting in *The Mystery of Mr. Wong* and *Mr. Wong in Chinatown*, Boris reported to Columbia for *The Man They Could Not Hang*, the story of a humanitarian research scientist who, because of societal misunderstanding, is turned from a career of helping others to one of vengeance and murder. The first of a four-film series that explores one basic theme, this B picture built upon his previous work in the "misunderstood scientist" sub-genre, solidifying the screen image he would be identified with for the rest of his life. Upon completion of this programmer, he returned to Universal to honor a two-picture extension of his contract. For his first project, Rowland V. Lee planned to create a follow-up to *Son of Frankenstein*: the Rathbone-Karloff blockbuster *Tower of London*, a mixture of historical fact, Shakespearean tragedy and 1930s horror.

On August 11, 1939, Lee, armed with a $500,000 budget, 36-day shooting schedule and his brother Robert N. Lee's meticulously researched screenplay, began production. To support Rathbone's humpbacked Richard III, Boris was cast as Mord, a bald-pated, club-footed executioner resembling John Holland, who was Constable of the Tower of London during the 1440s. Once again placing himself at the mercy of Jack Pierce, he underwent a true indignity this time, having his hair completely shaved off. Then his eyebrows—the only growth left on his head— were waxed and curled to add to Pierce's other distortions: a large, hooked nose; built-up, taped-back ears; and the club foot created with leg padding and a huge shoe. The shaving, which also rendered his hands and wrists hairless, was repeated every other day.

After lunch at Universal on August 19, Boris received a telegram from Dorothy, who had wired using the baby's name: "Excitement of your starting picture produced first tooth— love—Sara Jane." Turning the Western Union form over, he wrote in pencil on the back—"Sara Jane Karloff, 2320 Bowmont Dr., Beverly Hills. Upper or lower. Suspense holding up production. Congratulations and love, Daddy."—and wired the message from the studio at 3:02 p.m.

Truly excited about the film and his little girl, Boris, devising a bizarre father-and-daughter project,

Tower of London (1939). Boris' formidable Mord the Executioner receives from Richard, Duke of Gloucester (Basil Rathbone), the dagger with which he will assassinate mad King Henry VI.

was inspired to make her look just like him. However, according to Cynthia Lindsay, the experiment was not a hit, and after Dorothy observed Boris with a totally bald Sara Jane, "she absolutely flew off the handle":

> She was furious. She said, 'Boris, how dare you? It's going to take years to grow out.' Well, it didn't, and she looked kind of cute, but it wasn't really the thing to do—but it amused him to do so. Whether he'd done it to annoy Dorothy, or to make her laugh—she did not laugh—I don't know.

Boris attends a Screen Actors Guild meeting during production of *Tower of London*. Among the group are Hugh Herbert (front, second from left), Pat O'Brien (front center), Frank McHugh (to Boris' right) and Ronald Reagan (top corner). First published in the September 1940 issue of *Screen Actor*. (Courtesy of The Screen Actors Guild Archives.)

Perhaps some of Boris' colleagues got a chuckle or two at *his* expense during the *Tower of London* shoot, particularly when he sat with Frank McHugh, Pat O'Brien, Hugh Herbert, and Ronald Reagan at an important Guild meeting, quite a sight without a single hair on his head!

Shooting location scenes for *Tower of London* was a similar disaster. Attempting to film authentic re-enactments of the Wars of the Roses battles of Tewkesbury (1471) and Bosworth (1485) at a ranch in Tarzana, Lee's 300 extras were plagued by wind, blazing summer heat and cardboard armor that was destroyed by sporadically functioning rain machines. Behind schedule, over budget and forced to cut corners, Lee attempted to complete the high-salaried actors' scenes first, but still had to be bailed out by second-unit director Ford Beebe, who wrapped the film on September 4 at a final cost of $558,000.

An enjoyable scene for both Boris and Basil was one in which Richard and Mord drown George, the Duke of Clarence, in a butt of malmsey wine. One of several scenes based on material in Shakespeare's *The Tragedy of Richard III* (first staged in 1597), it gave the two veteran actors a chance to really terrify relative neophyte Vincent Price, who was appearing in his third Hollywood film. Tossed into the wine butt (which was filled with soda) by Boris and Basil, Vincent was told to grasp an iron bar at the base and count to 10 before resurfacing. However, when the enthusiastic Boris jumped up and sat on top of the barrel, the lid became stuck and studio technicians were unable to pry it loose. According to the original pressbook, crew members, wielding axes, managed to free the nearly drowned actor. The drinking scene leading up to the drowning, in which Rathbone provides a subtle, nonverbal contrast to Price's rampant overacting, is a highlight of the film.

No doubt some overacting also occurred on November 23, when a double birthday party was held at 2320. Boris was 52, hardly a milestone age, but little Sara Jane had turned one, an event considered momentous by the usual gathering of Gleasons.

Tower of London premiered at San Francisco's Warfield Theatre on December 15, 1939. Introduced by actor Mischa Auer, Boris and costars John Sutton and Nan Grey were joined on stage by Lugosi, whom Universal had hired as an additional drawing card. Although some reviewers criticized the film for bastardizing history, most of its content was based on solid historical evidence, its distortion of certain events and personalities borrowed from Shakespeare, who based his play on propagandistic accounts written by Tudor historians. A personification of Richard III's evil side, Boris' Mord is similar to his Monster in *Son of Frankenstein*, a villain who carries out criminal activities planned by his master, exhibiting moments of humanity along the way.

Later in life, Vincent Price recalled that his collaboration with Boris was an educational one:

Boris, the proud father, with little Sara Jane at 2320, 1939.

I identified with him immediately, as somehow I knew the villain was to be my role in movies, too, as already the mumble school of acting was being imported and the people who used English well were on their way out. Boris was a formidable star at that time... but he went out of his way to make me feel welcome to a business I knew I was going to like.

125

```
SG119 9=TDS BEVERLYHILLS CALIF AUG 19 1939 1253P

BORIS KARLOFF,
          ,TOWER OF LONDON SET UNIVERSAL STUDIO=

:EXCITEMENT OF YOUR START·ING PICTURE PRODUCED FIRST TOOTH
LOVE=
          SARA JANE·100PM··
```

Christmas 1939 delivered another milestone for Sara Jane: her first steps, witnessed by Dorothy's parents and her godfather Tom Forgan. Dorothy, who had put up a separate tree in Sara's nursery, wrote that she "got many lovely presents—a very happy and exciting day."

Following a stint at Monogram to film *The Fatal Hour*, another Mr. Wong programmer, Boris completed his Warner Bros. contract, playing a World War I German spy in the convoluted, jingoistic, but occasionally interesting *British Intelligence*. Originally titled *Enemy Agent*, the film replaced two other vehicles planned for Boris: a horror opus called *Dark Tower*, which was not produced, and *The Return of Dr. X*, which was made with a *very* miscast Humphrey Bogart in the title role. During the *British Intelligence* shoot, Boris was interviewed on the set by 18-year-old Sue Clark, who later wrote that she "was so impressionable and he was so kind. He was... so excited about Sara and kept telling me the wonder of it all."

Back at Universal on December 28, 1939, Boris prepared for his second *Son* follow-up, a gangster-horror film called *Friday the Thirteenth*. Scripted by Curt Siodmak, the new thriller

```
SQ244 10=WUX IF UNIVERSALCITY. CALIF 19  30 2P '939 AUG 19  PM 3  39

SARA  JANE KARLOFF=
     2320 BOWMONT DR DR BEVERLYHILLS CALIF=

UPPER OR LOWER? SUSPENSE HOLDING UP PRODUCTION.
CONGRATULATIONS AND LOVE=
          DADDY.
```

While filming *Tower of London* on August 19, 1939, Boris received a charming telegram (top) sent by Dorothy for little Sara Jane. During a break that afternoon, he replied, also via Western Union (bottom).

was to recreate the popular Karloff-Lugosi combination of the mid-1930s by depicting the story of a research surgeon who transplants the brain of a notorious gangster into the head of a mild-mannered English professor! Bela originally was slated to portray Ernst Sovac, the surgeon, with Boris in the Jekyll-and-Hyde part of Professor Kingsley (roles similar to those the duo had played in *The Raven*). However, after production began, director Arthur Lubin became dissatisfied with Boris' interpretation of professor-cum-gangster Red Cannon and decided to recast the characters. Assigning the Kingsley-Cannon role to the versatile Stanley Ridges, Lubin gave Boris the Sovac role, and Bela was reduced to playing Eric Marnay, a gangster who orders a hit on Cannon.

Incredibly, Boris and Bela did not act in any scenes together, and Lubin handled the action sequences in a totally uninspiring manner. (Perhaps the tiny $130,750 budget had something to do with the claustrophobic sets and pedestrian direction.) Saddled with inadequate production standards, Lubin tried to complete the picture as quickly as possible, and once again Boris objected to the studio's attempt to keep him on the soundstage for more than eight hours per day.

After the film wrapped on January 18, 1940, Universal issued advertisements, including a coming attractions trailer, claiming that Lugosi had been placed in a hypnotic trance by Dr. Manley P. Hall prior to a scene in which his character suffocates in a closet. Even *The New York Times* reported that "Universal is convinced that entirely new and unexpected vistas have been opened to the cinema," although its report facetiously described the absurdity of the affair:

> To reassure doubters, Boris Karloff... stated he was positive Lugosi was hypnotized because he had never seen his fellow actor keep his back to the camera for so long...
>
> Hall went over the script once with the hypnotized man, the cameras turned, Hall whispered, "Now you're suffocating," and Lugosi began to nose the cracks in the door, demanding. "Let me out!"...His voice became shrill and he screamed his lines. With his shoulder against the door, the set began to give, and then he slumped to the floor. A doctor who was in attendance stepped in, took his pulse, which had increased from normal to 160, which... would be actual in a suffocating person. They carried Lugosi to a chair, where Hall awakened him... Arthur Lubin... said that the scene was 100 percent better than it had been in the afternoon without hypnosis.
>
> The one flaw in the experiment was revealed when the cameraman said that he had run out of film when the thing was half over.

Lubin's remark to a journalist that he "never saw a man die so horribly on the screen— I nearly died watching him," and photographs showing Boris, Stanley Ridges and others observing the hypnotism were proved bogus many years later, when the director unveiled the entire affair as a publicity hoax.

Released as *Black Friday*, the film marked the third time one of Boris' characters was capitally executed (along with John Elman in *The Walking Dead* and Dr. Henryk Savaard in *The Man They Could Not Hang*) and the fifth time he was sentenced to or recommended for the punishment. Although he may have proved effective in the Kingsley-Cannon role, Stanley Ridges stole the show, giving two very different performances: one scholarly and gentle, the other powerfully violent.

Soon after frying in Universal's electric chair, Boris was back at Columbia to play Dr. Leon Kravaal, another research scientist with questionable ethics, in *The Man with Nine Lives*. Unlike *The Man They Could Not Hang*, this screenplay by Karl Brown did not rely on his delivery

In costume and hot makeup for the Celebrity All-Star Baseball Game at Los Angeles' Gilmore Stadium, Boris is visited by Evelyn Helmore, summer 1940.

of lengthy speeches, but revealed his character's many facets gradually, through actions rather than rhetoric. Although much of the story, which involves a form of cryogenics used in the treatment of cancer, includes recycled material from the earlier film, Boris' less intense characterization is thoroughly believable.

Following his turn as Dr. Kravaal, Boris took a much needed rest, spending the spring and early summer of 1940 with little Sara, who now was at the playful age of 18-20 months. Although *Black Friday* and *The Man with Nine Lives* both premiered in April, he characteristically ignored them, as he did *Devil's Island*, when Warners finally released the final cut, including a prologue describing how France was reforming its penal system, on July 11.

Having sworn off the Frankenstein Monster makeup, he graciously allowed Jack Pierce to torture him one final time for a bizarre public appearance at Los Angeles' Gilmore Stadium that summer. To raise money for charity, Boris joined the team of "leading men" who had challenged the "comedians" team to an "all-star" baseball game. Barely bunting the ball, he managed to score a home run when the ineptitude of the infield (the Three Stooges) and the catcher (Buster Keaton) allowed him to round the bases in his heavy (and very hot) costume! At some point that day, Boris, in full makeup, was photographed with family friend Evelyn Helmore, the wife of English actor Tom Helmore, who worked as an assistant to producers David O. Selznick and Maurice Evans.

In midsummer, he made his final appearance as Mr. Wong in Monogram's *Doomed to Die*. Also in the cast was his friend Henry Brandon, whose "chief memory of the shooting of a mediocre little film at a very shabby little studio was that I had played the villain in a picture in which the arch-villain, Karloff, had played the hero."

In September, Boris was re-elected to yet another three-year term as a director of the Screen Actors Guild. Over the next six months, he completed his Monogram contract with *The Ape*, and the "mad doctor" series for Columbia with *Before I Hang* and the very eerie *The Devil Commands*. His silliest film since *Juggernaut*, *The Ape* cast him as a scientist who develops a polio serum made with human spinal fluid that he obtains by dressing in a gorilla's skin and committing murder!

Missing a chance to costar with Peter Lorre two years earlier, Boris was able to play some deadpan scenes with the diminutive Hungarian while filming *You'll Find Out* at RKO in August and September 1940. Originally signing for a three-week shoot at $12,500, he ultimately earned much more, receiving special billing in a cast including Kay Kyser and his band, Ginny Simms and Bela Lugosi. Directed by David Butler, this $400,000 musical-mystery-thriller is unique in offering Karloff,

Sara Jane exploring the backyard at 2320, 1940.

Lugosi and Lorre as cohorts in crime, but also drags interminably as Kyser and his Kollege of Musical Knowledge drone on with their insipid songs and *shtick*. Having met Lorre (who was born Ladislav Loewenstein) a few times prior to their teaming, Boris developed an almost immediate friendship with him. While production was destined to run over schedule, the three horror maestros gave the film an early plug on Kyser's NBC radio show on Wednesday, September 25.

On November 23, 1940, Sara Jane turned two. Although he had been characteristically busy, Boris attempted to spend as much time as possible with his daughter. Of this period, she recalls:

> I have a lot of memories of him at... 2320... I know he used to keep his wire-rimmed glasses by the bed at night. He was wonderful with animals. I can remember being in the pool with him...
>
> I can remember picking out a rabbit with him, from some family friends. They had a lop-eared rabbit that I didn't pick, and I was allowed to make my own selection. But he said to me, afterwards, that he would have picked that one because it looked like it needed a home.
>
> He was an avid reader and a devoted father. I have loads of children's books from him, so I certainly think that he read me bedtime stories—but nothing grisly.

Regardless of the dramatic quality of his recent films, Boris appreciated the sheer volume of work that was being sent his way. But as 1941 dawned, he had no idea that he soon would be able to shed the silliness of overblown "prestige" pictures such as *You'll Find Out* for one of the greatest acting challenges of his career, in an environment alien to him, and as far away from Hollywood as he could go without again crossing the Atlantic.

Chapter 7

Doing His Part

"I was rotten and I knew it. I wanted to say, 'I can't go through with it—let me go back to Hollywood.'"

Boris first met theatrical producer Russel Crouse at a party in 1940. Later that year, Crouse telephoned 2320, inviting him and his agent to lunch at Lucey's Restaurant in Hollywood. Even before the food reached their table, Crouse and his partner, Howard Lindsay, revealed the true nature of the meeting.

"How would you like to do a play in New York?" Crouse asked.

Unhesitatingly, Boris answered, "No."

"Then what on earth are we having lunch for?" Crouse countered.

Years later, Boris recalled how he handled the situation:

> I said, "Wait a minute—let me explain. If you mean exactly what you said: *do* a play in New York, I wouldn't think of it, because I haven't been in a play in heaven knows when—and I haven't been in New York." And that sounds, you know, rather pompous. "But if you've got a play where there's a good part for me, and there are at least two other parts in the play that have to carry the ball a little more than I do, I'd be delighted to have a shot at it, because this is my first time in New York."

Boris believed that his reputation as a Hollywood film actor would not carry any weight on Broadway, particularly if the success of a play rested squarely on his shoulders. Crouse was delighted to inform him that his part would be conspicuous, but, as far as stage time was concerned, two other roles—insane old women to be played by Josephine Hull and Jean Adair—would far outdistance his.

The play was *Arsenic and Old Lace*, Joseph Kesselring's dark comedy about a bizarre family headed by two aunts who poison destitute men out of empathy. Though Hull and Adair would be on stage most of the time, Boris would steal the show as desperate criminal Jonathan Brewster, the family black sheep, who returns to the Brooklyn homestead with his strange friend, a plastic surgeon named Dr. Einstein.

Boris continued:

> And he [Crouse] went a step further, and he explained to me that before I'd been on the stage five minutes, the other character, Dr. Einstein, with whom I played intimately, said—about a man we'd sort of given a ride to in the car— "You shouldn't have killed him, Johnny. Why did you do it?"
>
> And my reply was, "He said I looked like *Boris Karloff!*" So, as soon as he told me that line, I said, "You're

on. I'll do it." And I knew that would dissolve an audience immediately—if you go and cod yourself.

Lindsay and Crouse planned to open *Arsenic and Old Lace* at New York's Fulton Theatre on January 10, 1941, with rehearsals to begin about a month earlier. During the first week of December, Boris was still working on *The Devil Commands* at Columbia, but he persuaded neophyte director Edward Dmytryk to rush the final takes on the last day of shooting, acting until well after midnight before speeding to the airport to catch his flight.

On the morning of December 10, he stepped off the plane, "terrified... of being in a play in New York." Crouse greeted him, picked up his bags and whisked him off to the Algonquin Hotel on West 44th Street, where they met Howard Lindsay. Pouring coffee into the exhausted actor, the producers discussed the first rehearsal scheduled for that afternoon.

"Oh, no, not for a week," Boris pleaded. "Give me time!"

After buying lunch at the Oak Room, Lindsay and Crouse accompanied him to the nearest subway station. Boris later said that Lindsay insisted on taking the train "because he wanted to see people recognize me. And thank God somebody did, or I'd have got the sack. On the spot!"

Already fatigued and nervous, Boris nearly fell apart when they reached the Fulton:

> Well, we got to the theater, and there was Bretaigne Windust, who directed it—a wonderful man. And this wonderful company, but they all looked like ogres to me,

Arsenic and Old Lace (1941). **The cast on stage at the Fulton Theatre, New York City.**

because they were New York actors. And I was introduced, and I was shaking, and tired from the ride and everything else, and my nerves were gone.

And then we did a thing... that I had never done before. The company sat down in a semicircle: Howard and
Russel sat there with Windy, with the play. They read the
stage business and you read the play. Well, I'd never done
anything like that. You just were on your feet, in blind-
folds. Well, I was so nervous and I was so frightened, I
couldn't get a word out. I literally couldn't speak. I was
stammering. I was stuttering. I was trying to read ahead,
and I'd see a word... and I'd say, "That word's going to—
I know that word'll throw me," and in my mind I'd substitute another one... and I'd see these three heads come
up and I'd read a word that wasn't in the script, you see!

Ending the initial run-through, Windust asked Boris to return at 8 p.m. for an actual rehearsal. Back at the Algonquin, he paced his room, asking himself, "Oh, my God, what am I
going to do?" and then answering, "Well, it'll be all right when I get on my feet." Unable to rest,
he soon was back at the Fulton, more agitated than ever:

So we rehearsed that night at 8 o'clock, and I was just as
bad. I *really* had a case of nerves. I just couldn't get a
word out. I was stammering and stuttering. I'd stick and
I'd have to change words, and do this, and all sorts. Well,
this went on for two and a half days, and I was getting no
better, and they were marvelous. They paid absolutely no
attention to me...

After a session on the third day of rehearsals, he returned to the hotel for dinner, but was
unable to sleep later that evening. Heading out into the streets of Manhattan, he walked long
into the wee hours, up Fifth Avenue to Greenwich Village, wrestling with his dilemma:

I thought, "There are only two things I can do. I know
that I've always had this little thing, if I... go way below
par. It has never troubled me, but now, in the tight spot, it
has caught up. And only one or two things that I can do.
One is to go to them in the morning and say, 'Well, I'm
terribly sorry, but we've all made a mistake. You've seen
what's been going on. You've been very kind and haven't
said anything, but it's just no good. I can't make it. How
much do I owe you?'"

And then I thought, "Well, if that happens and I go
back to Hollywood, I'm just about done there—because
there's been a flourish of trumpets and all that, and a week
later, I come back with my tail between my legs and that's
it." So I thought, "Well, I've just got to make myself do
it. I've just got to force myself to do it."

Around dawn, he found himself back at the Algonquin, exhausted enough to get a few
hours' sleep before reporting to the theater for the 2 p.m. rehearsal. Determined to overcome his
stage fright, he concentrated on words that had thrown him during the previous rehearsals, fall-

Arsenic and Old Lace. **Dr. Einstein (Edgar Stehli) and Jonathan Brewster (Boris) during a live performance.**

ing back on his method of learning dialogue and then letting his actions develop naturally during the performance. By the time he returned for the 8 p.m. session, his acting was "all right."

Following extensive rehearsals, the entire company moved down to Baltimore for a two-week trial run at the Maryland Theatre before the January 10 Fulton premiere. Prior to opening the road version on December 26, Boris received a telegram from Eddie Cantor, Kenneth Thomson and the SAG Board of Directors, who wished they "could all be there to cheer you on tonight. You know our thoughts are with you and our best wishes for a smash hit." Although the local critics called the play "odd," noting that it "may not appeal to some mundane souls," they also praised its unique style, hilarious dialogue and "ideal" casting.

Dorothy, having left Sara Jane with her nanny, reached New York, where Boris had rented an apartment at the Lombardy on East 56th Street. On the morning after *Arsenic* opened at the Fulton, she wrote to her mother:

> The audience was all very exciting—all the critics in the first few rows, Charlie Chaplin was there, and all sorts of people. But from the moment the curtain went up you knew it was going over. The audience started to laugh— and just never stopped. They were the most wonderful audience I've ever seen—they applauded and cheered and yelled, "Bravo" and "Speech"—and after about the 15th curtain call, Boris and the two old ladies had tears streaming down their face—and I was weeping—and it was just colossal—the whole thing.

Following the performance, Boris and Dorothy joined Lindsay and Crouse at a party held in the Park Avenue apartment of one of the show's backers. Although they did not return home until 3 a.m., they were up bright and early to read the reviews in the New York papers, all of which concurred that *Arsenic and Old Lace* was a bona fide hit. While the *Herald Tribune* considered the formerly terrified Hollywood horror star "a really expert performer," the *World-Telegram*'s Sidney B. Whipple judged him "excellent in every respect," and John Anderson claimed that "he is overpoweringly sinister in a performance that would, I should think, scare the other actors out of their makeup." Every critic found the play a laugh riot, including Robert Coleman, who wrote, "A lot of first nighters are going to have wrinkles in their faces today from laughing so hard last night." But it was Louis Kronenburger of *PM Reviews* who pointed out the true significance of Kesselring's work:

> The theater, which is several thousand years old, has never produced anything quite like *Arsenic and Old Lace*. And in case you're not impressed by the fact that it's different and unusual, you might like to know it's also screamingly funny.
>
> There have been farce melodramas in the past, and burlesque thrillers, and tongue-in-cheek murder mysteries, but after Friday night they don't count. For on Friday night certain truths came to light at the Fulton Theater which nobody could possibly have guessed before, and which psychologists may wish to ponder. It can now be positively stated, for example, that horror is the mother of hilarity; that corpses are as comical as Ed Wynn; and that maniacs are the salt of the earth.

Even Frank Sullivan, one of the show's backers, published his "review," commenting on Boris' contributions:

> I really believe that the feeling of security an angel like me gets from owning a part of an actor like Boris Karloff is a tonic worth a dozen bottles of beer, iron and wine; or six hours with a psychoanalyst... On Halloween I suggested that it would be fun if I could take out Mr. Karloff, who was not rehearsing that night, and scare people with him. My request was denied on the ground that Boris Karloff is frightened of jack-o'-lanterns.

And word of mouth was just as effective as the critics' notices. The line in front of the Fulton box office began to form at 9 a.m., and by 10:30, it had stretched halfway down the block. All the seats sold out so fast that the manager agreed to add standing-room-only tickets at $2.65 each. After the evening performance, photographers from *Life* arrived to take pictures for a feature on Boris. At 12:30 a.m., a large group of cast and crew members went to Sardi's to celebrate.

Each evening, audiences laughed uproariously at Mortimer Brewster's (Allyn Joslyn) comment that his brother "liked to cut worms in two—with his teeth." Upon his return to Brooklyn, Jonathan was not recognized by his two aunts, who later inquired about his altered face. Explaining that he was responsible, Dr. Einstein (Edgar Stehli) informed them that he had seen a film just before performing the plastic surgery. "I was intoxicated at the time," he adds. This explanation of how Jonathan was made to look like Boris Karloff never failed to raise the largest and longest laughs.

On the morning of Sunday, January 12, Boris and Dorothy visited Maurice Evans' country home, where they "had a beautiful lazy day." It was the first time Boris had relaxed in over a month, since Bretaigne Windust had been rehearsing *Arsenic* seven days a week. The next day, Dorothy wrote to Louise:

> And apparently the play is here to stay. We're both afraid someone will pinch us and we'll wake up—'cause Boris has a straight salary—plus 10% of the box office—plus a 10% interest in the whole thing which includes the movie rights—for which they're offering colossal figures already.

Tickets for *Arsenic*, ranging from 55 cents to $3.30, now were selling eight weeks in advance. Nearly every theater lover who lived in or visited New York saw the play. Future actress Julie Harris attended, as did Boris' faithful follower Henry Brandon, who later wrote:

> Whoever had the inspired idea of getting Karloff to play Jonathan Brewster in *Arsenic and Old Lace* should be awarded some kind of medal. I was lucky enough to be in New York during its run. He was magnificent in it!... Of course, the audiences were charmed and delighted that he had no compunction about ridiculing his own appearance.

Boris' role as Jonathan did not ridicule his appearance as much as it commented on his screen persona. After a decade of horror roles and memorably immortal and grotesque characters, his image already was known to the public; but the success of the play soon increased his status as a household name. About a month after the premiere, he noticed that his famously gaunt physique was becoming even leaner: "I got on the scales and I had lost twenty-six pounds—in sheer fright."

Between performances, Boris starred in several radio programs, including Ernest Kinoy's hour-long abridgment of *Arsenic*, which ran on NBC's show *Best Plays*. Joining him in the broadcast were fellow stage colleagues Jean Adair and Edgar Stehli. He also appeared on *Stars on Parade* and the quiz show *Information Please*, which featured a panel of four men answering the questions of audience members who tried

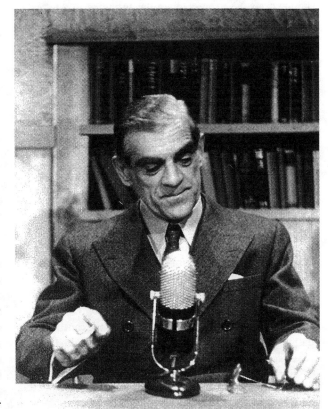

Information Please (1941). Boris ponders an answer on the popular radio quiz show.

to stump them. Each week, a guest would join the three regular panelists: *New York Post* columnist Franklin P. Adams, *New York Times* sportswriter John Kieran and musician and celebrated wit Oscar Levant. During Boris' appearance on January 24, 1941, he astonished both the panel and the studio audience by correctly identifying dialogue from the 19th-century melodramas *Bought and Paid For*, *Ten Nights in a Barroom* and *The Death of Lady Isobel in East Lynne*, all of which he had memorized during his early stock company days.

Just in time for February 14, Boris received a valentine from his mother-in-law. He always had been very fond of Louise—developing a relationship rare among husbands and mothers-in-law—and when writing, apologized profusely for being so negligent in answering her frequent missives. On February 22, he wrote, conveying simultaneously his gratefulness, astonishment and humor (particularly his tendency to mention alcohol when writing to her):

> I'm afraid sending a wire is a rather lazy way of reminding you that I love you and am thinking of you. But by this time Dorothy has probably told you that life has been a little hectic, to say the least! The hardest thing is to get used to a completely new set of hours, then comes having to be dressed with your neck washed before you can put your nose out of doors, and then comes only one martini before dinner, and some time before dinner at that! There are no retakes from 8:40 to 11:15! But it's all very exciting and really too good to be true. I still can't believe half that has happened, or that I am so absurdly lucky.

The next day, he expressed similar thoughts in a letter to Guild-mates Pat Somerset and Jack Dales:

> The play is really a peach and I am damned lucky to be in it. It looks as though I'll be away for a quite a while and believe me I'm going to miss all of you. Very slowly I'm getting over the worst of the terrors and can take time out to look around and get off a few notes really overdue.

In April, Dorothy and a friend drove 1,900 miles down the East Coast, touring through Virginia and the Carolinas, including visits to Washington, D.C., Virginia City, Charleston, and many Revolutionary and Civil War battlefields. Back in the North, she and Sara Jane settled into "Blue Spruce," the house they now were renting in Darien, Connecticut, just north of Long Island Sound, while Boris continued to experience the terror and triumph of his first months on Broadway. The evening show ended at 11 p.m., which gave Boris an hour to catch the midnight train to Darien, arriving home around 1:30 a.m.

The popular radio horror show *Inner Sanctum Mysteries* featured Boris in yet another adaptation of Poe's "The Tell-Tale Heart" on August 3, 1941. As Simon, a man recently cured of deafness, Boris gave a restrained performance, quietly depicting his descent into murder and madness. As in the short story, the victim, killed because of his unmitigated hatred for others, was concealed under a floor, only to cause the murderer to confess after he "heard" the incessant beating of the corpse's heart. However, in a twist ending extraneous to Poe, the murder was proved to be a figment of the still-deaf Simon's imagination.

Early one evening during the *Arsenic* run, Boris phoned Bob Beckham, who had been assigned to New York by his employer, the Etna Casualty Insurety Company, asking him to attend a dinner party after the performance. When the very eligible bachelor was told that an escort would be provided, he jumped at the chance. Arriving at the party later that night, he was thrilled when Boris introduced him to his date, Hollywood starlet Heather Angel. Remembering her as a "super young girl," Beckham added, "It was also the first time... that I met Maurice Evans, along with Lindsay and Crouse. So those were heady days for a 22-year-old boy who was really from California, in New York with celebrities and on the Great White Way, and everything was exciting."

Just before the evening performance of *Arsenic* on November 11, Boris received a telegram at the Fulton from Lloyd Almirall, who wired: "First part Henry Sixth—act five—scene two—line eight and nine." If Boris had a folio of Shakespeare handy, he perhaps read the following: "Success unto our valiant general, And happiness to his accomplices!"

On Sara Jane's third birthday—Sunday, November 23, 1941— Boris and Dorothy threw a party at Blue Spruce. Sara Jane received a "sleepy head doll" and a Dumbo stuffed animal resembling the animated creature in the current Disney extravaganza, but the date marked Boris' nativity, too. The phone rang just after little Sara Jane went to bed, but, having been awakened, she was al-

Arsenic and Old Lace. **A publicity photo of Boris as Jonathan Brewster.**

lowed to cut Boris' cake, which had been designed to feed the multitude who had crowded into the room. But Dorothy had planned everything to the letter, ordering salad and rolls, beefsteak and kidney pie, Virginia ham (with aspic and ham mousse inside) and seafood Newberg, which was so elegant that anyone in attendance hated to disturb its magnificence. Boris' present to his daughter was a five-foot house facade, consisting of a front and two sides, with a Dutch door and a window with curtains, that sat in front of her closet, transforming it into a roomy playhouse. As so many parents do for their pre-literate children, Dorothy conveyed Sara Jane's sentiments when she wrote to Louise, "I am a great big girl—I can give myself a bath."

On Wednesday, November 26, Boris and Dorothy attended a breakfast held at the Waldorf-Astoria by the Limited Editions Club, an organization that presented a gold medal to "the author of the book most likely to become an American classic." Among the attending writers and publishers were Charles Scribner and Sinclair Lewis, who explained why Hemingway's *For Whom the Bell Tolls* had been chosen. Dorothy wrote that it was "the most fascinating speech I've ever listened to. It just poured out of him, and was most exciting."

The day after the Waldorf gathering, Boris purchased two tickets for the annual Army-Navy football game in Philadelphia. Knowing that he could not attend because of his *Arsenic* commitment, he suggested that Dorothy go with Bob Beckham. Having less than two days to plan the trip, she made arrangements, scheduling their departure for Friday night, to avoid the mob that would form during the parade on Saturday morning. Adding an interesting twist to the incident, Bob later suggested that Dorothy took advantage of the Philadelphia trip to visit a prominent attorney from San Francisco to whom she had been introduced by his parents, Mae and Rob:

> Dorothy said, "I have two tickets. Would you like to go with me?" So I accompanied [her], and we went to Philadelphia on the train to see the Army-Navy football game the big weekend in November. And, lo and behold, as we got into the lobby of the hotel where we were staying, Dorothy said, "Well, what a surprise! There's Edgar Rowe, of all people!" So they had a very nice rendezvous in Philadelphia. Obviously, it was all arranged. I was the escort for Dorothy, and probably the excuse so she could get out of town and meet Edgar for a little rendezvous in Philadelphia.

Mae Beckham stayed at Blue Spruce for a time, particularly enjoying a chance to take care of Sara Jane, whom she called "*our* baby" and "without a doubt the cheeriest little soul... *so* smart and sweet." Mae and Dorothy loved to talk in front of the roaring log fire as they waited for Boris to return from New York. Ravenous after an evening's work, Boris would usually cook up a 2 a.m. meal, sometimes a wonderful oyster stew that Mae was fond of.

Boris Claus

By the end of the year, *Arsenic and Old Lace* had become one of the most successful productions in Broadway history, ranking behind only six other shows that had run longer. Just in time to avoid the onset of heavy winter weather, Boris, Dorothy and Sara Jane moved into a house at 124 East 62nd Street in New York, which they had leased for the remainder of the play's run.

At Christmas, Boris briefly exchanged his Jonathan Brewster persona for that of old Saint Nick to bring good tidings to a group of grateful youngsters recuperating at the Beekman Downtown Hospital. In their excitement to meet "Boris Claus," some of the more active patients toppled the huge Christmas tree that had been set up in the children's wing.

On the evening of January 10, 1942, Howard Lindsay and Russel Crouse hosted a party, honoring the one-year anniversary of *Arsenic*, at the Cottage Club near the Fulton. An entire program was acted out, including Lindsay and

Crouse singing a song about the show and its backers, and a scene from the play in which Boris and Edgar Stehli played the two old aunts, and Josephine Hull and Jean Adair portrayed Jonathan and Dr. Einstein, respectively! "The party was lots of fun," recalled Dorothy.

Since the Japanese attack on Pearl Harbor a month earlier, the Karloffs' hectic schedule, like those of most American families, had become even more complicated. While Boris forged ahead with the show, Dorothy became involved in the war effort, selling defense bonds, participating in Red Cross drives and taking an Army course on aircraft spotting. In between "doing her part," she took Sara Jane sledding "until her cheeks and nose were as red as strawberries" and went ice skating in the outdoor rink at Rockefeller Center, "down at the bottom of those towering skyscrapers—and when we'd look up and see the moon shining away and those buildings right up to the moon, you felt like you were in another world entirely." And during the afternoon of January 30, 1942, they joined Maurice Evans and his assistant, Evelyn Helmore, to see 12-year-old Pat Hitchcock, daughter of Alfred and his wife, Alma Reville, starring in a new play "for which she got rave notices."

Boris and Dorothy hung small flashlights around the 62nd Street house and mailed some additional units to Louise at her Hollywood apartment. On February 3, Boris wrote to his mother-in-law, mentioning blackouts and two causes of them—wartime measures and John Barleycorn:

> Your account of your air raid drill is really one of the funniest things I have ever read. We simply howled over it. All you need to make it complete is to be balancing a bowl of goldfish on your head as you go up the ladder. I am having a copy typed as it is much too good to keep to myself. The trays work overtime. Our Robert always provides us a little fancy bite to go with the cocktail, and one of the wooden trays takes care of that, and I use the metal one for the glass and shaker. So you see you are directly responsible for the continuance of my alcoholism.

In the letter, Boris also revealed his fatherly concerns:

> Sara Jane was completely gone over yesterday by her doctor who pronounced her A number one. Three foot two inches and thirty and a half pounds. Three pounds under normal weight, but as he says, she is tall and her mind dominates her body! At the moment she is having her bath after helping me to count and sort the contents of her silver pig. A monthly proceeding which incidentally nets her an average of three twenty-five dollar defense bonds a month. Not bad for all my loose change at night!

The continuing success of *Arsenic and Old Lace* sometimes helped Boris to forget about the war, a fact he mentioned in his remarks to Louise: "The play is still wonderful and our business is steadily growing back to normal each week after the first shock of the war. We are lucky in that our show is one where people can really laugh and relax for a few hours, and that is always good medicine."

On February 20, 1942, Boris and Dorothy spent the afternoon at a New York police station, where they were fingerprinted and photographed for Civilian Defense work. That evening, he made another appearance on *Information Please*, this time augmenting his erudition with some keen humor. When asked, "Name something which you can approach but never reach," he quietly responded, "Garbo."

Arsenic and Old Lace. **Dr. Einstein helps hide the body of a man who told Jonathan he looked "like Boris Karloff."**

This particular broadcast of the program added an extra participant to the panel: fellow screen villain John Carradine. When the panel was asked to "identify a victim of treachery who was shot in the back of the head," Boris answered, "Jesse James."

Clifton Fadiman then queried, "Who shot him?"

"I did," Carradine replied, raising an enormous laugh from the audience, who recalled when, as Bob Ford, he killed the outlaw (Tyrone Power) in Twentieth Century-Fox's *Jesse James* (1939).

Boris was not entirely at ease on the show, and after he agreed to make a second appearance, wrote, "What an ass I am. I was so lucky the last time that I swore I'd never do it again, but Russel Crouse talked me into it, the scoundrel." Dorothy wrote to Louise, "Boris was again excellent... He seemed and looked very easy and comfortable but said he was even more scared than the first time. It's a grand program to watch."

They continued socializing with Maurice Evans and Evie Helmore, and, during the weekend of February 21-23, were guests at Evans' country home, where Dorothy looked forward to riding and more ice skating. They all stayed up late, talking each night, and on Monday morning, attended an auction where Boris paid $15 for a beautiful pine, four-poster bed. "Don't ask me what we'll do with it," Dorothy admitted to Louise.

Dorothy's first position with Civilian Defense was as a secretary at Air Warden Sector Headquarters, where she answered the phone and gave out pre-approved information. In the evenings, while Boris was at the Fulton, she would drop in at the Seaman's Institute to dance with the sailors. On one occasion, after Boris was finished with the *Arsenic* performance, he joined her for another play and dancing before capping off the day with a 3 a.m. visit to Hamburger Heaven, "eating hamburgers and drinking milk!"

On the evening of March 10, 1942, Boris took part in a Navy Relief Show at Madison Square Garden. Among the all-star acts who performed, the "Floradora Sextette" featured Boris, Vincent Price, Danny Kaye, Clifton Webb, Ed Wynn and Eddie Cantor as drag queens—in front of 21,000 cheering fans! Opposite them strutted Sophie Tucker, Lenore Aubert, Luise Rainer, Tallulah Bankhead and Eve Arden dressed as men. Dorothy wrote to Louise:

> Boris had a yellow dress made entirely of sequins—with just straps over the shoulders—and a large yellow hat. Vincent Price looked the funniest of the lot—because he's so tall anyway—about 6 ft. 3—and he had a beard which he has to have for *Angel Street*.

While performing in *Angel Street*, Vincent often met with Boris and other English actors, including Cedric Hardwicke and Philip Merivale, to play cards. Much to his delight, he was being accepted into the "British Colony."

Three days after the Relief Show, appropriately on Friday the 13th, Boris threw a "party," staged for the press by the *Arsenic* company, in a brownstone near Gramercy Park in Manhattan. Such horrific concoctions as "strychnine stingers" and "formaldehyde sidecars" were served to members of the cast and crew, as well as other actors, including Ed Wynn, Nedda Harrigan, Sophie Stewart and Leonora Corbett, who was starring as the ghost in *Blithe Spirit*.

That following Sunday, Boris and Dorothy joined Lindsay and Crouse, their wives, and other friends at a cocktail party held aboard a ship at the Brooklyn Navy Yard, which she described as "a wonderful sight": "to see all the destroyers, cruisers, airplane carriers being built. The big cruisers are the most impressive sight you'd ever want to see—and pretty deadly looking."

At 1 a.m. on March 20, Boris wrote to Louise, giving her "ten guesses as to where I am writing from." He had begun his career as an air-raid warden holed up at sector headquarters in the basement of the Hotel Beekman, just around the corner from their house on East 62nd. Scheduled to be on duty every third Thursday from midnight until 8 a.m., he promptly arrived with a pillow and blanket tucked under his arm. While many men might consider such accommodations quite uncomfortable, Boris made the best of it, viewing his tour of duty as an opportunity to read, write letters and relax with "a lunch... that would feed an army." Constantly involved with *Arsenic* performances, nights on the town with Dorothy and playing with Sara Jane, he found little time for literature, but now was immersed in former Ambassador Joseph E. Davies' pro-Soviet book *Mission to Moscow*, after which he had "a date with Steinbeck's *The Moon is Down*." But his apparent contentment in New York was underlaid by a desire to return to California:

> Really good news about the family at last. They are all leaving for home the last of April to open up the house, etc., and I'll be home the end of June to do the Columbia Picture and then take a three weeks' vacation, and could I use it! After that, back to the play most likely on the road and perhaps opening in San Francisco, so you'll have a chance to see it at last in Los Angeles! Honestly I'm so homesick I could burst, and the closer it gets to seeing all of you again the harder it is to wait. Dorothy and Sara Jane are fine. The last one knows so much and talks so much—she springs a new surprise every day!

One of Boris' fellow air-raid wardens was a young woman named Nancy Farrell, a New Yorker who, as a teenager, had been frightened by *Frankenstein*, and now was impressed by the former Monster's punctuality and dedication:

> He was always ahead of his time when he reported for his watch, which began at midnight. Our post was in the Beekman Hotel at 63d Street and Park Avenue—a basement room with cement floor and walls and pipes overhead. As Karloff entered, he said, "Good evening. I've brought my *suppah*." His voice, with its variety of pitch and its resonance, was friendly and reassuring...
> In the air raid post, Karloff kept on his conservative coat of good British tweed. He wore rimless glasses. He

looked thin and not especially tall. He urged us two wardens to hurry home and assured us he was glad to go on duty early... I thought only of the calmness and dependability of this courteous man who was responsible for the lives of thousands of his neighbors. I felt that he would rather be an air-raid warden in London and that he was imposing on himself the same discipline that he would have observed in the blitz.

During the second week of April 1942, Dorothy met with Ilka Chase, Mrs. Lawrence Tibbetts, Nedda Harrigan and Katherine Cornell to raise money for a canteen operated by the American Theater Wing. Organizing a committee, they planned to meet frequently until a coherent fund-raising plan was adopted. On the 12th, she and Boris appropriately celebrated their 12th wedding anniversary, for which he presented her with "a dozen beautiful monogrammed handkerchiefs, a dozen guest towels and a dozen sheets and pillow cases—all the most beautiful linen and monogrammed." On Easter, she took Sara Jane to see the defense workers' parade and then joined Boris for the annual show at Radio City Music Hall.

Again writing to her mother from sector headquarters, Dorothy humorously mentioned one of the pitfalls of defense work:

> There's an old fool sitting here shouting and chewing on a cigar. He's an air warden—an elderly man—who is retired—and has nothing to do—and comes in here just to sit and gabble—and he drives us crazy. He stayed for two hours last Monday. Today I've tried to keep on writing—but every other line or two he shouts, "Isn't that so, Mrs. Karloff?" At the moment he's giving a dissertation on the morals of the Army and of Red Cross nurses, etc.—and he's such a bore. But he's shouting, so I can't keep my mind on my letter any longer...
>
> I may slay this man at any moment!!

On April 16, Boris was back at his duty post in the Beekman basement, faithfully writing to Louise. But now he had more concrete details to relate about his upcoming Columbia film, *The Boogie Man Will Get You*, in which he would costar with his old friend Peter Lorre:

> They will all be home by June first and I am following a month later. The picture is definitely set for July 6 with a possible leeway in starting till July 27. If it starts July 27 I'll get my vacation beforehand, but if it starts July 6 then I'll get my three weeks afterwards before re-opening in the play.... I've signed for five more Sunday nights on *Inner Sanctum* beginning this coming Sunday which doesn't leave a lot of time for all the things that still have to be done.

On May 3, Boris began his new stretch on *Inner Sanctum* with the episode "Study for Murder," the far-fetched story of Dr. Herbert Lodge, a psychiatrist who tried to discover what drives ordinary people to kill. After forming a criminal gang to provide him with firsthand test cases, Lodge was instructed by a victim's ghost to commit murder himself. But after realizing that his studies would never be complete, the enraged doctor accidentally killed his wife and was sentenced to die in the electric chair.

Arsenic and Old Lace (1942). **Boris arrives at the West Point Military Academy for a historic stage performance.**

The following week, Boris and Dorothy were joined by Mr. and Mrs. Howard Lindsay at a performance of *Arsenic* staged by the dramatic club of Washington, D.C.'s Gallaudet College, the nation's only school of higher learning for the deaf. The majority of the 800 audience members at the Fulton also were hearing impaired, the first such public gathering ever assembled for a stage show. As Dorothy wrote to Louise, all of them found it thoroughly fascinating:

> It was really terrific to watch. And we sat through the
> whole show which lasted about 1/2 hour longer than the
> regular performance. I wouldn't have missed it for any-
> thing. They all have great talent—and of course are mag-
> nificent pantomimists.

At the close of the last act, Boris approached Eric Malzkuhn, who played Jonathan, and after using pantomime to communicate with him, joined the 14 deaf actors for a curtain call.

Arsenic indeed was making history, as Boris and his colleagues also traveled 50 miles north of New York City to perform at the West Point Military Academy. Greeted at the bus by enthusiastic cadets, Boris was proud to join them in the mess hall before performing in the first Broadway play staged at the academy in 139 years.

On Saturday, May 16, Boris sat down at his typewriter to compose the foreword for *Drawn and Quartered*, a book of drawings by artist Charles Addams. One evening not long before, he had expressed his "whole-souled admiration" for Addams to his neighbor, Random House's Bennett Cerf, who soon persuaded him to write the introductory essay. In a publisher's note to the foreword, Cerf explained:

> What more natural than that I should vault the fence that
> separates his New York dwelling from mine, and pin him

Arsenic and Old Lace. **Although his aunt and Dr. Einstein also commit illegal acts, the malevolent Jonathan makes them recoil with fright.**

down to the task?... I found the fearsome Mr. Karloff engaged in singing nursery rhymes to his little three-year-old daughter. I hope it will not disillusion you to know that he is the second most gentle character I have ever met. The gentlest, and the kindliest old schizophrene, by a wide margin, is the creator of these drawings—Mr. Charles Addams.

In the original draft of his foreword, Boris, while analyzing the style of Addams' work, characteristically shed some light on his own artistic philosophy. The qualities that attracted him to Addams' work were similar to those he admired in the literature of Joseph Conrad and projected in his own portrayals of the Frankenstein Monster, Ardath Bey, Hjalmar Poelzig and other subtly wrought characters:

Why a collection of the drawings of Charles Addams should need any written introduction at all is as far beyond me as the writing of one! Addams seems to me to be the one comedic artist today whose drawings need no letterpress at all. Supremely he has achieved the primary and essential purpose of any drawing serious or comic, which is to tell a story graphically in one blinding flash without a single written word of explanation. While it is true that the general development has been consistently away from the style of the comic artists of *Punch* in the last century and even in the early part of this one, when every drawing was followed by five to ten lines of print containing an elaborate joke which often bore no relation to the drawing at all, few men have realized and practiced the earliest and most eloquent of all forms of storytelling as has Addams.

Continuing his analysis, Boris makes a remark that echoes his criticism of the Monster's speech in *Bride of Frankenstein*: "And even when the written comment does add a little spice, the drawing really does not need it."

On the evening of Sunday, May 17, Boris and Dorothy threw a farewell party for, as he wrote to Louise, "All the people who have been so nice to us here. I may say that your daughter has made a great stir both here and in Connecticut!" Dorothy rented a Victorian suite at the Carlyle Hotel and hired a guitarist and an accordion player to entertain the 30 guests.

Dorothy and Sara Jane departed for Los Angeles aboard *The Chief* on Sunday, May 31. Much to their pleasure, they were able to share a car with their old Darien friends Bob and Barbara Wilkin and their three children. Before leaving, Dorothy wrote to Louise:

> I don't want anyone to meet us—what with the rubber situation and train schedules. People have been anywhere from 6-20 hours late in these transcontinental trips, having cars and whole trains sidetracked for the Army—which is quite right. The travel agency won't even guarantee or tell you any time of arrival...

After playing Jonathan Brewster for 18 months, Boris set out for California on June 27. Intended to capitalize on his success in *Arsenic*, *The Boogie Man Will Get You*, in which Peter Lorre aids him in creating "supermen" for the United States war effort, uneasily mixes horror and comedy with the anti-Nazi propaganda that, courtesy of the Office of War Information, seeped into nearly all films released during 1942.

Back in Hollywood, Boris was pleased to see old friends, particularly many of his English colleagues. On one afternoon, he and Dorothy attended a tea party at the home of Sara Allgood, the Irish actress of Abbey Theatre fame who recently had appeared as Mrs. Morgan in John Ford's masterful *How Green Was My Valley* (1941). Also among the guests that day was English stage and screen actress Moyna MacGill, who had moved to Hollywood from New York, where she and her children had lived after the Nazi blitz drove them from London in 1940. Accompanying her mother, a strikingly beautiful, 16-year-old, aspiring actress named Angela Lansbury was quite taken with Boris: "I was blown away to meet a full-blown movie star. He was King of the Horror Movies—the great Frankenstein. But what impressed me at the time was that he was the dearest, sweetest, most soft-spoken gentleperson that I'd ever met. He was enormously encouraging to me."

Miss Lansbury encountered Boris at several Hollywood social functions during the summer of '42:

> I saw him on a number of occasions. Nigel Bruce and his wife used to throw their house open to the servicemen on weekends. And they had a nice, big back yard. They lived on the flats in Beverly Hills... And Boris and Dorothy would be at those teas, greeting the boys and being generally available... for autographs and that kind of thing. I used to go along and help to serve. I didn't have any position, other than just being a guest.

During Boris' absence, Lindsay and Crouse kept *Arsenic and Old Lace* running, hiring Erich von Stroheim, who had been playing Jonathan with a Chicago company, to fill in for him. And when director Lew Landers wrapped *Boogie Man* at Columbia, the producers sent the New York company to Los Angeles, where Boris re-joined them for a 66-week national tour to begin at the Biltmore on August 15 and then move to San Francisco, Sacramento, Portland, Denver, Salt Lake City and many other cities across the country before returning to New York in mid-1943.

In October, the company reached San Francisco, where Boris and Dorothy stayed for two weeks in a beautiful room on the 19th floor of the Hotel Sir Francis Drake. One evening, they attended a cocktail party at the lovely Nob Hill apartment of Mae and Rob Beckham, enjoying warm conversation with a dozen other guests, including the attorney Edgar Rowe and his wife, Sara. Before leaving the city, Dorothy and a friend joined Rowe for an afternoon round of bridge at the San Francisco Bar Association—a gaming get-together she repeated, accompanied by her friend Ruth Swaney, at Rowe's home that evening, and again at the Bar Association the

The flagstone patio that Boris installed in front of 2320 greatly exacerbated his back problems. (1996 photograph by Scott Allen Nollen)

next day. One day prior to moving on to Sacramento, Dorothy, referring to her husband's exhausted condition, wrote:

> "It's 12:45—a matinee day—and I've called Boris since
> 11:30 trying to get him up. Guess I'll have to resort to the
> cold water method—cause he still has packing to do. But
> he just says he has plenty of time."

For several weeks during late 1942, a different supporting cast joined Boris on the road. Another movie studio—Warner Bros. this time—negotiated with Lindsay and Crouse, but rather than getting the big-name star, took some of the supporting players and left Boris, much to the producers' delight, to keep packing theaters across the land. Frank Capra was chosen to direct the film adaptation of *Arsenic*, and Boris' *Old Dark House* costar Raymond Massey was given his Jonathan role. (Peter Lorre and a scenery-chewing Cary Grant also dominate the Capra version.) After Lindsay and Crouse practically had pleaded with Boris to take the Broadway assignment, they refused to allow him to immortalize the performance on film. Regardless of the $2,000 he was earning every week, he was disheartened by the actions of his supposed friends; but his professionalism did not allow him to jeopardize the success of the tour.

Of course Boris took time to celebrate Christmas with his family. On December 8, Dorothy had written a Santa Claus letter for Sara Jane, who asked for a whole array of things and received "a pinafore... a doll with curls in front and braids in back... and PJ's for my Linda doll."

When *Arsenic* reached Minneapolis, Boris again ran into his old Harry St. Clair colleague Charlie Jackson, who now worked as a regional representative for Warner Bros. Happy to reminisce about the lean years in Prince Albert, Minot and Chicago, he joined the Jacksons for dinner "two or three times."

While on the road, Boris added the title of literary scholar to his lengthy resume, reading dozens of short fantasy stories and selecting 14 for World Publishing Company's anthology *Tales of Terror*. To introduce the works by Bram Stoker, Ambrose Bierce, O. Henry, William Faulkner, Edgar Allan Poe and others, he wrote a lucid six-page essay describing the genre and the specific examples he had chosen. Of course, he included Joseph Conrad; and when referring to his favorite author's style, again described his own artistic philosophy:

> All my reading life I have been devoted to this great mas-
> ter of English prose. He too had the power of creating
> suspense and terror through suggestion. But he added one
> ingredient which drives his stories home. Compassion.
> He knew that compassion is the touchstone of our com-
> mon humanity, and he never fails to make us share and
> understand the sufferings of his characters persevering
> hopelessly but gallantly in an unequal struggle.

In November 1943 Boris was re-elected to a fourth consecutive three-year stint as a director of the Screen Actors Guild, even though he had been absent for most of the previous term. And when he arrived back in Hollywood in early 1944, he had appeared in only one film in nearly four years. During his absence, the nation had become involved in a global war, forcing the major studios to adjust their production schemes to fit a wartime economy and the propaganda dictates set down by the Roosevelt administration. Concentrating on releasing prestigious A productions, most studios tightened their budgets by reducing the number of B films they would churn out each year.

Filling the low-budget void, Universal, who had made two more Frankenstein sequels (as well as a score of other horror programmers) during Boris' *Arsenic* run, immediately signed him to a two-picture deal, guaranteeing $5,000 weekly for a period of 13 weeks. The first film, however, was not a B programmer, but a prestige production. On February 1, 1944, Boris began an eight-week stint in *The Climax*, his first Technicolor film and a $750,000 follow-up to the studio's Academy Award-winning Claude Rains opus of the previous year, *The Phantom of the Opera*. A ponderous but visually impressive effort starring Boris as a Svengali-like doctor who tries to dominate a young opera singer (Susanna Foster), it was followed by "The Devil's Brood," an all-star, medium-budget ($354,000) production featuring a mad doctor (Boris), Dracula (John Carradine), the Wolf Man (Lon Chaney, Jr.), a hunchback (J. Carroll Naish) and the Frankenstein Monster (Glenn Strange). Early on, producer George Waggner and screenwriter Edward T. Lowe wanted to call the film "Chamber of Horrors" and carry their potluck approach further by working the Mummy, the Invisible Man and the Mad Ghoul into the script!

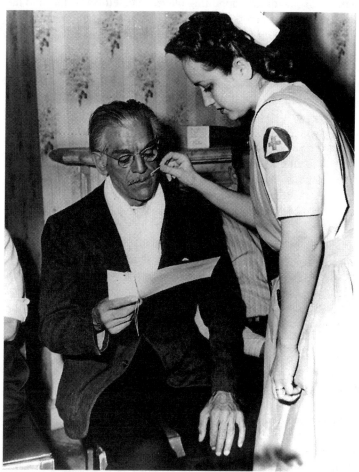

The Climax (1944). **An ailing Boris is monitored by a Universal studio nurse.**

Boris began experiencing severe back pain during the making of *The Climax* and "The Devil's Brood" (which eventually was released as *House of Frankenstein*), and his gaunt, tired condition became noticeable throughout both films. Unable to perform in some of the latter film's more strenuous sequences, he ate soda crackers and drank quarts of milk on the set, attempting to compensate for his own lack of energy by coaching Glenn Strange on how to do the Monster's famous walk.

One of his most uncomfortable moments on the *House of Frankenstein* set occurred during the shooting of the climactic scene at 3 a.m., Tuesday, April 25, 1944, when Strange's Monster pulled him under a bog of studio quicksand. By the time he was lifted out of the mire, he had put in a 14-hour day—a curious effort, considering that a few years earlier, when in much better health, he had become known for his objections to night scenes and refusals to work more than eight hours per day. But he was back the following afternoon to shoot a scene in the glacial ice cavern where the Monster is discovered. More amazing yet, that evening he was still on his feet, reporting to NBC studios to host his regular radio series *Creeps By Night*. At 4:30 p.m. on Saturday, April 29, while filming a scene in which Dr. Niemann demonstrates "the world's most astounding horrors," he completed his Universal commitment.

The *House of Frankenstein* pressbook, briefly revealing that Boris was "trying to gain weight," included an atypical amount of information about his personal life. Playing up the

House of Frankenstein (1944). **In this "all-star monster rally," Boris is most effective in the early scenes, playing the incarcerated, hirsute Dr. Gustav Niemann with the quiet intensity that made him famous.**

angle that he was a "devoted husband and father," one article claimed the following about little Sara Jane, who was five when the film was made:

> The child is totally unaware that her father has earned a tidy fortune by his genius for scaring people. The only movies she has been taken to see to date have been the cartoon fantasies *Dumbo* and *Bambi*.
>
> Sara Jane doesn't even know her father is an actor, but having been informed that he works in a place called a

Boris "does his part" serving soup to servicemen at the USO's Hollywood Canteen, 1944.

"studio," she frequently asks him: "When is that man going to give you a day off?"

While appearing in *House of Frankenstein*, Boris attended a meeting at RKO, where he discussed a potential contract with executive producer Jack J. Gross, director Mark Robson and producer-writer Val Lewton, who, over the past two years, had almost single-handedly rescued the horror genre from a state of total absurdity. While Universal had been grinding out imitations of its earlier successes, Lewton and his production team created a new strategy emphasizing the terror existing in the natural world, rather than monsters from a supernatural realm. Made on budgets of $150,000, films like *Cat People* (1942), *I Walked with a Zombie* (1943) and *The Leopard Man* (1943) had been big hits; and as the profits rolled in, Gross thought it might be even more lucrative to add the world's greatest horror star to the mixture.

Lewton, who wanted to keep his films fresh and devoid of any Universal trappings, initially rejected the idea, but after his first meeting with Boris, quickly changed his mind, setting to work on developing ideas for two films. Deciding to base one of them on *Isle of the Dead*, an Arnold Bocklin painting that had fascinated him all his life, he chose Robert Louis Stevenson's 1881 short story "The Body-Snatcher" as resource material for the other.

Boris signed his two-picture, $6,000-per-week RKO contract on May 18, 1944, expecting to report two months later to begin work on *Isle of the Dead*. While he concentrated on working in the garden at 2320, Dorothy and Sara Jane headed north to San Francisco and then to Lake Tahoe, where they planned to spend part of the summer at Brockway Hot Springs. Sara Jane enjoyed fishing in the lake, using a bent pin and bread for bait, and did not appear too disappointed when the fish only nibbled and then swam away. She also began to develop a considerable prowess for swimming and riding horses.

On Thursday, June 18, Dorothy wrote to Boris that she "was ready to come home any-time—but that I knew it was grand for Sara Jane. It really is because she has a freedom she could never get anywhere else." But the next day, she sent a long letter to Louise, informing her about the busy leisure and social schedule she enjoyed each day:

> In the mornings right after breakfast we usually do our washing and rowing—then about 10:30, down by the pool for a sun bath and to get the morning paper which arrives at 10:30—maybe a game of badminton—then it's time to clean up for lunch. Then in the afternoon we ride—or swim—or play more badminton—and then it's time to dress for dinner. Everyone meets in the bar for a cocktail first. Then after dinner there's always a bingo game—or someone wants to play gin rummy—and by 10 or 10:30 it's bedtime.

Closing her letter with eloquence, Dorothy was clearly inspired by the awesome beauty of the Tahoe area: "The nights up here now are simply gorgeous—with the moon over the lake—and the stars so close you can almost touch them."

On June 24, Sara Jane was bedridden with a cold, dictating a letter to her nanny, Mary Jane. Informing her grandmother that Dorothy's cold was getting much better, she said that Mary Jane had fibbed to her friends that she had been stricken with "ammonia." During the first week of July, as they were preparing to return to Los Angeles, she told Dorothy that she wanted to live at Tahoe, "didn't ever want to go home."

Dorothy spent the evening of the Fourth of July holiday at the Cal-Neva casino, where she only broke even financially, but again was inspired to wax poetic: "Cal-Neva is the most beautiful place—built on a hill right over the lake, and last night there was a full moon—and the most beautiful view—the lake absolutely silver—and the snow on the mountains shining so wonderfully in the moonlight."

Although she had written to Boris claiming she could return home at any time, Dorothy was in no great hurry to do so, stopping again in San Francisco on the way back. Although Dorothy's frequent letters to her mother do not suggest that she and Boris were experiencing marital problems, his traveling with *Arsenic*—as is the case with many "road" performers—could not have strengthened their relationship. In fact, the three-year *Arsenic* experience, involving 1,444 performances, was a complicated, mixed blessing for him. On one hand, he had greatly enhanced his career, earning an excellent salary (plus returns on $2,500 that Lindsay and Crouse had invested for him), tremendous reviews and the satisfaction of taking Broadway by storm in one of the most successful shows in theater history. On the other, he probably had damaged his personal life by working so incessantly.

And now Boris was being separated from his wife and child for another considerable period of time. Apparently having met with Edgar Rowe at Philadelphia in November 1941, Dorothy had seen him again in San Francisco a year later; and although she cannot recall exact dates, Sara Jane does remember seeing him at some point during her Tahoe experience. And then there was the presence of Evie Helmore in Boris' life, as early as the charity baseball game during the summer of 1940, perhaps another sign that their marriage was in jeopardy.

When the July 14 shooting date for *Isle of the Dead* arrived, Boris' back pain returned with a vengeance. Spending two months in the garden had only added to his physical problems, and even a wheelchair and Mark Robson's understanding direction failed to keep him on his feet. On July 21, Val Lewton shut down production and Boris entered the Good Samaritan Hospital to undergo a risky and debilitating spinal fusion: All of his ceaseless work literally had ground down some of his vertebrae. Originally expected to be dismissed after a two-week stay, he still was recuperating a month later, with plans to rest another two weeks at home before returning to work.

With his star bedridden, Lewton, fearing that *Isle of the Dead* would have to be postponed, worked on the script for *The Body Snatcher*, expanding Stevenson's frightening fictionalization of the murders committed by Burke and Hare in 1828 Edinburgh, to be ready for RKO's October 13 start date. Using the pseudonym Carlos Keith (which he had used earlier in his writing career), he co-wrote the screenplay with Philip MacDonald, author of *Patrol*, the novel on which *The Lost Patrol* was based, and selected Robert Wise to direct it.

With the family back at 2320, attention was turned to domestic affairs, including Sara Jane's education. She had begun at Miss Buckingham's Nursery School before attending kindergarten at the Wilshire Methodist School; and during the fall of 1944, entered Hawthorne Primary School in Beverly Hills, which was located near the C. Aubrey Smith residence: "Often I would go over to their house in the afternoon after school, waiting to be picked up to go home." Of her relationships with other students, she remembers, "I went to school with the children of other people who were in the entertainment industry... I knew the Cagney children, and I knew Anthony Perkins."

Of course, Sara Jane also received certain instruction from her parents. One day, after committing a series of crimes against family discipline, she sat down to compose a list of things she either would or would not do in the future:

> 1. I won't tell feds [sic].
> 2. I won't ask the girls to come up.
> 3. I will do things when I'm ask [sic] to do them.
> 4. I will be helpful.
> 5. I will wash my face every morning.
> 6. I will brush my teeth every morning.
> 7. I will brush and comb my honey every day.
> 8. I won't pull the cat's tail.

Although it is not on the list, Sara Jane also liked to climb up on the window seat in her room and out the second-storey window that led down to the swimming pool. Her playmates at this time were John Lipscomb, Andrew Cronin, Beverly Clothier and Jimmy and Lucile Gleason's son, Michael Morgan. She also loved to spend time with Smokey, the Bedlington terrier, Rocky, the white Persian cat and Tony, the parrot.

In *The Body Snatcher*, John Gray, a cab driver who resorts to grave robbing to put food on the table, offered Boris a cinematic opportunity he had not found since *Frankenstein*. Being typecast in the horror genre for nearly 15 years, he seldom had the chance to interpret such a magnificently complicated and literate character. Like his finely textured performance as the Monster, his characterization of Gray, who was based on a witness in William Burke's 1829 trial, constantly involves the viewer: He is genuinely frightening but actually draws the audience to him each time he appears.

Boris appreciated the opportunity to play a character of great depth, one whose evil behavior was begotten by the rigid class-based environment in which he was raised. Near the end of the film, when Dr. "Toddy" MacFarlane (Henry Daniell) attempts to bribe Gray to stop tormenting him and live a "respectable" life, the body snatcher replies:

> I am a small man, a humble man and being poor, I have
> had to do much that I did not want to do. But so long as
> the great Dr. MacFarlane jumps at my whistle, that long
> am I a man—and if I have not that, I have nothing. Then
> I am only a cabman and a grave robber.

The Body Snatcher (1945). Original lobby card featuring the scene in which Gray delivers the body of the street singer to Donald Fettes (Russell Wade).

In several scenes, Boris was able literally to integrate his own personality into the multifaceted Gray, exhibiting sincere gestures of kindness, even gentleness, toward Georgina Marsh (Sharyn Moffet), a disabled little girl whose only hope is Dr. MacFarlane, who is reluctant to perform a corrective operation on her spine.

But much like his other effective horror portrayals, Boris invested Gray with a genuinely frightening quality, actually helping to create the mood of the film. For the scenes that pose Gray and MacFarlane against each other, he and Henry Daniell gave impeccable performances, beautifully interpreting Lewton and MacDonald's Stevensonian dialogue. Recalling this aspect of the production, Robert Wise said:

> What intrigued me about it, and it intrigued Boris Karloff particularly, was the relationship between the cab driver and the doctor, because there's some marvelous antagonism from [them]... the duel that went on—marvelous scenes between the two. And Karloff realized, or felt, that this was a chance for him to show that he... was an actor, and not just some kind of monster to be in films— that he could really hold his own with top actors in town. And he had to prove that with a man named Henry Daniell, who was one of the top English character actors in Hollywood at the time... And so Karloff saw this as a chance; in those scenes, the kind of duels between the two—duels of personality and viewpoint and dialogue—that he could hold his own with Daniell, and he did. Some of the best

parts of the film, for me, are those two or three sequences where they're kind of... dueling with each other, in terms of their philosophies. So that's one of the things that intrigued me very much about the thing.

In his second directorial assignment, Wise appreciated the fact that Boris, regardless of the circumstances, never held up production:

Karloff was not particularly well at the time. He was having a lot of back problems, but he didn't let that stop him at all. He was in there working as hard and as steady and as strong as he could... seriously, he never complained... he just gritted his teeth and did it. And one of my best experiences—he was quite a different man than he appeared on the screen. He was very well educated, a very sensitive man, a very tasteful man... He was a very, very, very lovely person—very warm and very kind. We got to be quite friendly for a period of time...

Appearing opposite Boris for the eighth and final time was Bela Lugosi, whom Lewton reluctantly worked into the script after the RKO front office decided to reunite them for added box-office appeal. With typical Lewton inventiveness, he wrote the character of Joseph, an assistant in Dr. MacFarlane's medical school, and provided Bela with his first quality role in many years. Wise remembered:

Lugosi... was not well... It was a small part. It didn't require too much out of him, but I had to kind of nurse him through the whole role, such as it was. And I always appreciated Karloff's sensitivity when it came to the scene where they played together... where the Lugosi character came to see the Karloff character. Boris was very, very gentle with him. And I always respected Karloff for that, for the sensitivity in that situation. I have heard that he [Lugosi] was on drugs at the time. I think it might have been drugs, because he was in pain, but he got through it—it was all right. But Karloff was very, very helpful in getting him through the sequence that I had to do with them.

Although he was signed for only one week, Lugosi was paid $3,000, much more than he received for his work in many grade-Z penny dreadfuls during that period. In his brief role as the doomed Joseph, who is suffocated by Gray in one of the film's most powerful scenes, he gave a totally convincing and moving performance, his best since Ygor in *Son of Frankenstein*. "He was a little vague," Wise added. "He was not quite on it—which was all right for the role, because he played a not very bright guy... I think his whole mental and emotional condition maybe helped to contribute to that."

Boris' final scene with Bela inspired some of his finest acting, including one of the most profound gestures in his entire cinematic career. As Joseph lies expired upon the floor, Gray removes his hands from the victim's mouth and gently reaches over to pet "Brother," his cat, allowing the animal's tail to slide slowly through his palm—a subtle recurrence of an earlier thematic juxtaposition: Gray's killing of a little Scottish terrier that guards its master's grave is followed by his gentle petting of Brother as he speaks with MacFarlane's assistant, Fettes (Russell Wade).

As directed by Wise, Stevenson's harrowing climax is one of the most frightening four-minute scenes ever filmed, and the first sequence in a horror film to feature Boris, not as a resurrected corpse, but as a bona fide dead body. Having killed and dissected Gray, MacFarlane believes that he has seen the last of his tormentor; but later, as he and Fettes drive back to Edinburgh with the corpse of an old woman they have stolen, the doctor hears voices. Upon examining the face of the corpse, he sees the visage of Gray: an image that sends the horses bolting and MacFarlane to his death at the bottom of a gorge. When Fettes lifts the shroud from the corpse, he sees only the old woman's lifeless face. Shirtless and constantly drenched with studio rain machines as he bounced around inside the coach, grabbing at Henry Daniell, Boris was as uncomfortable as his appearance was hideously death-like.

Although he was in constant pain during the making of *The Body Snatcher*, Boris never let it show, thoroughly enjoying his excellent role and the company of a talented and friendly cast and crew. After Wise completed the shooting on Friday, November 17, 1944, Boris attended the wrap party at the studio. Provided with a stack of photographs by the RKO publicity department, he graciously inscribed them as mementos for his coworkers.

Having thought of Boris as a "type" prior to directing *The Body Snatcher*, Wise, who dined at 2320 on one occasion, had quite a different impression when the shoot ended:

> I realized how much more there was to him than those
> monster creatures with which he had been identified so
> strongly. I think [he] was absolutely first-rate... an excel-
> lent actor... And then to go to his home, to see his lovely

Isle of the Dead (1945). **This original lobby card depicts Boris' General Pherides being restrained by Marc Cramer and Jason Robards, Sr.**

155

home... books all over the place. And to talk to him, such a fine, fine, knowledge, fine background. Well read, well educated. It was such a contrast—his whole being and his own personal life to what you were accustomed to seeing on the screen.

Having shot only the early scenes of *Isle of the Dead* prior to Boris' back surgery, Mark Robson resumed production on the film, set in Greece during the Balkan War of 1912, on December 1, 1944. Situated within a context of war and Greek mythology, it is another of Lewton's explorations of how myth and death affect the human psyche, particularly how superstition and disease erode the rationalist beliefs of General Nikolas Pherides, a Greek general who believes he can fight an outbreak of septicemic plague by controlling those around him. Because of his illness, Boris was weary during the filming, but he again summoned up a complex and realistic characterization, a powerful, rigidly conservative military leader who, in time of turmoil, stresses a need for absolute control, yet loses his rational capabilities when faced by the overwhelming superstition and irrationality of his companions.

While filming a scene in which Pherides turns in for the night, Boris demonstrated the General's rigid adherence to military code: Stating that he has "learned to live without comfort," Pherides tosses the pillows and mattress from his bed before lying down upon the wire webbing beneath—an action consistent with the characterization, but certainly not a wise move for an actor recuperating from major back surgery.

Even during production, the cast and crew realized that *Isle of the Dead* would prove a dramatically uneven experience, but their stalwart work created several highlights that critic James Agee called "brutally frightening and gratifying." One scene, in which Mrs. St. Aubyn (Katherine Emery), one of the supposed plague victims—actually a woman suffering from catalepsy—awakens within her coffin, is the visual and narrative high point of the film, a well-mounted shock that Agee described as inspiring "the rest of the show into a free-for-all masterpiece of increasing terror... one of the best horror movies ever made."

Like his approach to so many of his other sympathetic villains, Boris created a subtle but concentrated menace for General Pherides, simultaneously evoking distaste for his rigid militarism and empathy for his intentions to save those around him. In a parallel to Gray's unpleasant end in *The Body Snatcher*, Pherides meets a violent death: Making the most of his character's gruesome demise, Boris slithered along the floor, coughing up blood as his head and gory torso filled the frame.

156

Chapter 8

Crossroads

"To live in Hollywood—it's a very much abused name, you know—it's exactly like any other place in the world. You can live in Hollywood, you can work in Hollywood, like I did, and you can live entirely your own life. And I lived in Hollywood in all sorts of ways... as an extra... as a lorry driver, as a small part player, and... as a so-called star. And I lived entirely my own life. I did exactly the things that interest me. I didn't go to nightclubs, because they didn't interest me...

All told... in Hollywood, there are probably twelve- or fourteen-thousand people who earn their living in front of the camera... Now, out of that... there are possibly five hundred who, shall we say, are newsworthy. There are also seven- or eight-hundred people connected with newspapers and magazines and syndicates... whose business— whose bread and butter—depends on writing something about the five hundred. So you can see what that leads to. If there's nothing to write, they want to eat, so they make something up, and that accounts for the extraordinary reputation that Hollywood has."

When the Japanese bombed Pearl Harbor on December 7, 1941, Boris was 54 years old. Rejected because of a nonexistent heart murmur during World War I, he was too old to enlist in World War II. Although he truly admired the United States, he never became a citizen; his ties to Great Britain were too strong. But his fondness for the former colonies was considerable, and bolstered by his hatred for totalitarian regimes he considered worse than the flaming torch-bearers in *Frankenstein*, he had "done his part" as an air-raid warden in New York and with the USO, serving food at the Hollywood Canteen.

Early in 1945 Boris and Dorothy were visited by Evie Helmore. Maurice Evans, now an Army major in charge of the entertainment section in the Central Pacific, asked Evie to send a photograph of Boris as Jonathan Brewster, so the actor in the military troupe's version of *Arsenic and Old Lace* could pattern his appearance after the original.

Boris, with characteristic self-deprecation, wrote to Evans, offering, "If you can stand it, I can arrange to come out and do it myself," and then instructed his agent to turn down any film or radio work for the next several months. He again had a chance to perform in *Arsenic*, this time for the ultimate director, Uncle Sam.

Prior to flying into the Pacific theater, however, he formalized a new contract with RKO, agreeing to appear in three more films for $100,000. Arriving in Hawaii under the auspices of the USO Camp Shows, Inc., he was the only professional actor in the outfit, aside from three local women who had been recruited to play the female roles. Appearing as Dr. Einstein was a young private named Werner Klemperer, the son of orchestral conductor and German émigré Otto Klemperer, whose experience in the play would give him (as Boris would say) "the fire in the belly" for acting.

Boris arrives in Honolulu to begin his USO-sponsored tour of *Arsenic and Old Lace*, spring 1945.

After the group adjusted to the shock of having a true Hollywood star in their midst, they buckled down for serious rehearsals with director Sergeant George Schaefer (who also played "Teddy" Brewster), as they were scheduled to trod the boards within days of Boris' arrival in Honolulu. Performers who entered a war zone also had to undergo a simplified version of "basic training," and Boris, donning military fatigues, became an honorary Marine as he learned infantry techniques, including amphibious maneuvers and the proper use of weapons.

On February 21, 1945, Boris wrote to RKO, asking for two 16mm prints of *The Body Snatcher*, which had been previewed for the press a week earlier. Having contributed a live performance to entertain the troops, he also wanted to show them one of his cinematic efforts.

For the next three months, Karloff and company performed *Arsenic* at every military facility on Oahu, including Scofield Barracks for a three-week run, before heading out to Midway, the Marshall Islands, Canton and Christmas Island, where grateful troops cheered the first production they had seen in two years. All told, Schaefer's troupe played 96 camps, airstrips and naval stations.

While heading to the Marshalls, they docked at Johnson Island, described by Boris as "a landing strip about 300 yards long and maybe 100 yards wide," where they played for two nights in a tiny theater built next to an aircraft loading area. He fondly remembered that "they used to rev the planes up before they went out on the runways; so always on your best line, there would be a blast of engines... right next door! It was a wonderful experience... I wouldn't take anything for it."

During his second day on Johnson, Boris set out across the island on foot. Attracting little attention, he eventually bumped into a Marine who recognized him:

> This kid... he said, "What are you doing here?" and I said, "I'm here in a show," and told him what it was. And he said, "Are you playing here tonight?" and I said, "Yes." He said, "My gosh, I think I'll take it in. Do you know, I haven't been downtown in two weeks." You know, just marvelous—perfectly serious.

Even after experiencing the enormous Broadway and touring successes of *Arsenic and Old Lace*, he was thrilled to be able to interest a lone serviceman in one of his performances. By the end of the tour, 196,000 military personnel had seen it.

Another kind of thrill—one appealing to Boris' love of animals—occurred on the Marshall atoll of Kwajalein:

Boris is welcomed by grateful servicemen, Honolulu, spring 1945.

Boris confers with a Marine officer during his "basic training," Hawaii, spring 1945.

Boris learns some basic combat principles, Hawaii, spring 1945. (Standing behind Boris is Pvt. Werner Klemperer, who played Dr. Einstein in the *Arsenic* production.)

Boris enjoys the amphibious portion of his training, Hawaii, spring 1945.

The Seabees had asked us to play their end of the island and said they'd build us a stage. They were marvels. They built the stage in a couple of hours and erected the set—a Victorian living room. And then the most astounding thing happened—on that dreary, wasted island. A cat emerged from the kitchen door of the set. He looked around the living room—and, bless me, walked calmly out the living room door as if he'd lived there all his life.

Back on Oahu, Boris visited several hospitals, cheering up soldiers who had been wounded or stricken in action. Also having joined the Marines by this time, Bob Beckham contacted him after the tour returned for another run in Honolulu: "I, of course, got in touch with Boris. He invited me over to see the show, and then came backstage and had my picture taken with the whole cast—a young first lieutenant in the Pacific, kneeling in front of Boris... a very memorable picture... "

One of Boris' fondest memories of the tour was traveling with George Schaefer, who, as well as directing and playing Teddy, also "drove the bloody truck." Boris recalled that his friend's triple duty "put us in the horns of a dilemma. Schaefer loved Gilbert and Sullivan and the only way we could keep him awake while he drove was to bellow out Gilbert and Sullivan at the top of our lungs."

By the time Boris returned from the Pacific, his crumbling marriage to Dorothy had reached an irreconcilable stage: The past five years of constant performing and traveling had only worsened the rift between them. On May 1, 1945, Boris sold 2320 to director Robert Siodmak, and Dorothy and Sara Jane settled into a home at 714 Foothill in Beverly Hills. Soon after, when Howard Lindsay and Russel Crouse were looking for a residence, Dorothy rented 714 to them before relocating to another house just down the street at 503 Foothill.

Having blazed new trails as an actor on Broadway, across America and hopping islands in the Pacific, Boris was not anxious to return to the cinematic stable where he had been confined a decade before. During his absence, his agents had negotiated a new three-film contract with Universal, which, combined with the three upcoming projects for RKO, would keep him working steadily for the next two years. However, upon his return to Universal City, things got off to a rocky start:

> I came home, and we went out to the studio, and to my horror, I found that the first film was a Frankenstein. And I said, "No." They were adamant, so we just kissed and parted, and I let the contract go because I was determined not to do that again—because it was no good...

At Hollywood's Hawaii Theatre on May 10, RKO premiered *The Body Snatcher* to the delight of both patrons and critics. Two weeks later, this success was repeated at New York's Rialto, inspiring James Agee to select the film as one of the best of the year.

Choosing to follow the Stevenson adaptation with another historical period piece, Lewton and Wise had discussed featuring Boris in a version of J. Sheridan Le Fanu's *Carmilla* set during the American Colonial period, but soon abandoned the vampire tale for a more realistic 18th-century subject: the savage mistreatment of the mentally ill.

Again using the nom de plume Carlos Keith, Lewton, inspired by a William Hogarth painting, co-wrote "Chamber of Horrors: A Tale of Bedlam" with Mark Robson, who also was slated to direct. More than doubling his usual budget, RKO promised Lewton $350,000, allowing him to focus even more attention on period detail; and on July 18, 1945, production on the re-titled *Bedlam* began.

Set at London's St. Mary's of Bethlehem Hospital in 1761, the film vividly chronicles the efforts of Nell Bowen (Anna Lee), the former companion of a Tory politician, to end the sadistic reign of Apothecary General George Sims, who charges visitors tuppence to view the "loonies" in their cages. Playing Sims made Boris somewhat uncomfortable, as he had to create a wantonly sadistic character who was capable of gaining audience sympathy. To justify Sims' iniquitous behavior, Lewton presented him as a living symbol of the deterministic

Seven-year-old Sara Jane poses for the 1945 Karloff Christmas card. Boris carried this photograph with him, in a small vinyl photo album that fit into his pocket.

Bedlam (1946). **Belying their pose in this publicity photo, Anna Lee and Boris were actually great friends.**

views that held precedence during the Enlightenment, or "Age of Reason": particularly the belief that a natural hierarchy placed each class of people in its "proper" place—that every individual deserved the life he or she led.

Regardless of the personal distaste he felt for the character, Boris gave a sterling performance, especially in his scenes with the equally talented Anna Lee. In a scene performed beautifully by both actors, Sims describes his faith in the hierarchy to Nell Bowen:

> They have their world and we have ours. Ours is a human
> world. Theirs is a bestial world, without reason, without

soul. They're animals. Some are dogs—these I beat. Some are pigs—these I let wallow in their filth. Some are tigers—these I cage.

Boris had to be entombed alive, à la Poe's "The Black Cat" and "The Cask of Amontillado," for the film's climactic scene, during which some of the inmates (including Ian Wolfe and Jason Robards, Sr.) seize control of the asylum, try Sims in a kangaroo court and stab him before bricking his body into a partially completed wall. For a shot depicting Sims' expression of mortal terror as the last brick is mortared in, Boris again used his eyes to create an unforgettable cinematic moment.

Although RKO feared that Lewton was diluting the horror content by concentrating on politics and social philosophy (an opinion supported by some critics), Boris appreciated his attempt to make another serious film devoid of the usual genre trappings. Anna Lee recalled:

> *Bedlam* was definitely one of the best parts that I have ever played. I loved it.
> Boris loved it too but he used to get quite annoyed if anyone referred to it as a "horror" film. Val Lewton felt the same way—he had taken great pains to establish it as an "historical" picture, which indeed it was, having been drawn from the Hogarth drawings of that period, and it turned out to be *so* historically accurate that it was banned in England for some years, as St. Mary's of Bethlehem was still used as an asylum and it was felt that Val's descriptions were too close to the truth! Val supervised every detail and was nearly always on the set with suggestions to Mark Robson...
> I thought that Boris gave one of his very finest performances in *Bedlam*. He was so sadistic and so unpleasant, but at the very end he became so pathetic and pitiful when he was pleading for his life and trying to explain what had caused him to be so cruel that one was almost sad to see him walled up!

After *Bedlam* wrapped on August 17, 1945, Lewton intended to produce "Blackbeard," another historical picture, starring Boris as "Captain Aguilar," an aging American pirate attempting to make a living in the Charleston area. As co-written by Ardel Wray and Mark Robson, the screenplay offered him a unique character, but the film was never made. Due to two deaths during 1945—those of RKO's head of production, Charles Koerner, in February, and the horror genre following World War II—*Bedlam* proved to be Lewton's final film for RKO and the end of his collaboration with Boris.

With his commitment to RKO temporarily on hold, Boris concentrated on radio work, including two more appearances on *Inner Sanctum Mysteries*. Broadcast October 23, 1945, "Corridor of Doom" cast him as a troubled man who nearly was murdered by his son-in-law (a very young Richard Widmark) for insurance money; while the Poe-influenced "The Wailing Wall," aired on November 6, featured him as Gabriel Hornell, yet another wife murderer. Relentlessly moribund, the latter episode, borrowing from "The Black Cat," "The Tell-Tale Heart" and "The Cask of Amontillado," had Hornell kill his spouse and place her body behind a basement wall, only to be haunted by a wail he believed was her spirit. Later, when his girlfriend asked what the eerie sound was, he also killed her and then shut himself up in the house for 40 years. Finally driven mad, he tore down the wall and discovered that the wail was actually the wind blowing through an external fissure. The broadcast ended with the institutionalized Hornell jumping 18 stories to his death!

Between the two *Inner Sanctums*, Boris was featured on the Halloween episode of *The Charlie McCarthy Show*, in which he escorted the dummy and his friends to a haunted house. And on December 8, 1945, he starred in "Angel Street" on CBS's *Textron Theatre*, playing the role made famous by Charles Boyer in the MGM film version, *Gaslight*, made the previous year.

While Dorothy was interested in Edgar Rowe, Boris had become attached to Evie Helmore, whom he had the opportunity to visit while appearing on radio in New York. Recently divorced from her husband, Evie was continuing to serve as production assistant to Maurice Evans, who was staging a modern version of *Hamlet* on Broadway. Combined with a great knowledge of the theater, her sophistication and English heritage proved irresistibly attractive to Boris.

Born Evelyn Hope in Putney in 1904, she was the oldest of three sisters. From an early age, she was interested in the stage, but only managed to land a few minor roles as an actress. After attending school, she accepted a job at a French dry cleaning establishment set up in London by Maurice Evans and Tom Helmore, who both had been unable to make a living as actors. Displaying a strong aptitude in mathematics and a keen business sense, Evie managed the Helmore-Evans operation for about a year before she and Tom were wed. Her marriage, association with Evans and familiarity with the London stage scene sparked many friendships with notable performers in England and the United States, where she found work on both coasts after Tom began to receive offers from Broadway and Hollywood. For several years, she was a successful script reader for David O. Selznick. By the time Evie moved to the United States, her mother, Lina, had married a kind man named Adamson, and the couple raised two additional daughters, Barbara and Kate, a talented artist who died quite young.

Evelyn Karloff, from an original photo that Boris carried in his pocket-sized album, mid-1940s.

In early 1946 Tom Helmore wrote a letter to Evie's mother, mentioning "Evelyn's forthcoming marriage to Boris... about 'the nicest person I have ever met'." On April 10, 1946, Boris and Dorothy's divorce was finalized; and the very next day, Evie and Boris, declaring his residence as Boulder City, Nevada, were married in Las Vegas by Justice of the Peace W.L. Hayward. Witnessing the union of William Henry Pratt and Evelyn Helmore were Perlie Morris and Hayward's wife, La. V. La. The marriage was officially recorded in the records of Clark County, Nevada, at 1:30 p.m. on April 22, 1946. Boris was charged $1.

At their rented Foothill home on April 11, Dorothy sat down with Sara Jane, who had stayed home sick from school, and told her, "Your father and I are divorced. Your father married Evie this afternoon." With that said, she got up and left the room. Only seven years old at the time, Sara Jane remembers very little about the divorce or the events leading up to it:

> I don't know why my mother didn't go with my father on
> tour. It could be that I was in school and it would have
> been inappropriate. It could be that, because he was on

tour, how could I go to school? I could be left with a governess. Or in anticipation of a divorce, or as a trial separation. I have no idea.

I know that my stepfather was in the picture before my father and mother were divorced, because I have memories of my stepfather and his daughters and their husbands around the pool at 2320. I don't know if his wife was with him or not... And of course Evie was a "friend of the family" for years and years before the divorce.

So I don't know if we didn't go on the road because they knew they were getting divorced or... because I was in school.

Cynthia Lindsay hadn't seen Boris for over a year when she received a telephone call from him on the day of the wedding. He was in Vegas and in desperate need of a favor. Lindsay clearly remembered:

He said, "Darling, will you do me a favor?"

I said, "Naturally."

And he said, "I have a hotel room in the Miramar in Santa Monica, and I'm bringing my bride in."

I said, "What are you talking about?" I didn't even know they were divorced.

He said, "Darling, I guess I didn't tell you. Dorothy and I were divorced... Evie and I are married, and I'm bringing my bride home. Would you put some flowers in the room? And I'll tell them to let you into the room."

I said, "Yes, of course"... this was Dorothy's best friend, who was around the house all the time, and it stunned me. So I went to the Miramar Hotel, and I put some champagne in it, and some caviar, and a Gideon Bible in the icebox, and put the flowers in the room, and left. And then he called me and thanked me for the Bible and the champagne and the caviar and the flowers. Couldn't have been more surprised. Came as absolutely, totally left field. Then I got used to it.

One day during their honeymoon at the Miramar, Evie answered the telephone to discover her ex-husband on the line. Having signed a contract with MGM, Tom Helmore and his wife, Mary, had just relocated from New York; and while they were searching for a house, the studio had booked them into the same hotel, in the room right next door! At Boris' suggestion, the Helmores joined them for dinner, an event that sparked an enduring friendship.

On a more stable note, Boris' second work as a literary scholar was published that same month. Three years earlier, *Tales of Terror* had sold out four printings, inducing World Publishing Company to contract him to edit a second volume of classic fantasy stories. For the new compilation, *And the Darkness Falls*, he gathered 68 works by 57 authors and, this time, wrote a separate introduction for each tale. An extremely diverse and remarkable collection of fantastic literature by Ivan Turgenev, Guy de Maupassant, Ambrose Bierce, Arthur Conan Doyle, Edgar Allan Poe, Jonathan Swift, William Butler Yeats, Nikolai Gogol and, of course, Joseph Conrad, it demonstrates Boris' vast knowledge of literary history and criticism.

In his introductions, he provides a short biography of each author, once again adding his own thoughts on how terror should be presented in a story. Commenting on *Night Fears*, a collection of short stories by L.P. Hartley, he writes, "In these he reveals a skill in word-economy, the ability to pack in a narrow space strikingly interesting studies of human nature, some cruel, some impish, a few rather humorous, but all of them touched with tenderness, sympathy and beauty." True to form, his comments about these literary works also describe his own portrayals in *Frankenstein*, *The Mummy*, *The Walking Dead*, *The Body Snatcher* and other horror films.

Mulholland Drive, Beverly Hills. Boris and Evie lived in this home following their marriage in April 1946.

After their romantic sojourn in Santa Monica, Boris and his new bride settled into Gregory Peck's former home on Mulholland Drive, high above Beverly Hills. Leaving her New York job, Evie effectively retired from the entertainment business to devote her full attention to one of its busiest icons.

In the fall of 1946 Sara Jane began second grade at Hawthorne Primary in Beverly Hills. She would remain there through the following year, until Dorothy married the now-divorced Edgar Rowe and relocated to San Francisco, where he was an attorney with the Bronson, Bronson and McKinnon law firm. Although Boris liked and respected Edgar, he and Dorothy were not particularly friendly, and she was not pleased when his workaholic lifestyle prevented him from seeing his daughter—a state of affairs encouraged by Evie, who, from the outset, was very possessive of her new husband.

Boris happily moves some odds and ends to the home on Mulholland Drive, 1946.

167

Boris confers with actress Louise Beavers at a Screen Actors Guild general membership meeting, Hollywood, September 13, 1946. (Courtesy of The Screen Actors Guild Archives)

Having been retained by the Screen Actors Guild as a board member for another three-year stretch, Boris attended a September 13 general membership meeting at the Hollywood Professional Building, where he was photographed conferring with African American actress Louise Beavers. Two weeks later, actors began to form picket lines at the major studios, and threats of a strike were voiced. On October 2, he joined 3,000 fellow performers, including Joseph Cotten, Gene Kelly, Walter Pidgeon, Jane Wyman, Glenn Ford and Frank Sinatra, at Hollywood's American Legion Stadium to discuss a potential walk-out with Ronald Reagan, vice-president Franchot Tone and legal counsel Laurence Beilenson, who "stressed that if the Guild as an organization voted to respect picket lines... it would be voting to strike." The walk-out eventually was averted.

Boris returned to the stage in November, as Julian ("Gramps") Northrup in Paul Osborn's *On Borrowed Time*, which had been filmed by MGM in 1939. Given the chance to play a cantankerous and lovable old man, he enjoyed projecting aspects of his own personality during performances in San Francisco and Hollywood, where Henry Brandon again caught him in the act:

Jane Wyman, Boris and Gene Kelly attend a Screen Actors Guild strike meeting at American Legion Stadium, Hollywood, October 2, 1946. (Courtesy of The Screen Actors Guild Archives)

He played the grandfather in *On Borrowed Time*, a beautiful play about the relationship between a wonderful old man and his grandson. One could see that he really relished playing that sweet old man who kept Death (Mr. Brink) in a tree so he couldn't take the little boy... Of course, Karloff's fantastically villainous features helped to provide him with great roles and enormous wealth. However, his own innate sweetness and gentility were much more akin to the grandfather role in *On Borrowed Time*.

Supported by Beulah Bondi, Ralph Morgan, Joseph Crehan, Margaret Hamilton and Tommy Ivo, Boris was delighted with every aspect of the play, and thereafter considered Gramps one of his favorite stage roles. But while the character was a total change of pace for him, he admitted feeling that "the audience was waiting for me to unmask and exterminate the rest of the cast."

169

On November 8, 1946, while playing the El Patio Theatre in Hollywood (where Jack Pierce did his makeup), Boris promoted *On Borrowed Time* on *That's Life*, a radio show hosted by Jay C. Flippen. For this particular broadcast, audience members had been invited to read limericks, and Boris, assuring them that he was portraying a sympathetic, non-horror character in the play, read his own composition:

> As a beauty I am not a star
> There are others more handsome by far
> But my face I don't mind it
> I'm safely behind it
> It's the people out front that I jar.

On Borrowed Time (1946). Boris as Julian ("Gramps") Northrup.

Having completed his scenes for *Bedlam* more than a year earlier, he ended his hiatus from the silver screen by accepting a prestigious non-horror role in Cecil B. De Mille's $4 million colonial epic *Unconquered*, which had been in the planning stages since 1945. Typically stressing historical detail and spectacle, De Mille persuaded Boris to study the Seneca language before reporting to Paramount to play Chief Guyasuta. Possessing a complexion appropriate for the role, he wore little makeup but was dressed in layers of fur costuming to cover a large brace that supported his spine and legs. Again suffering from intense pain, he was able to move only with great difficulty, so De Mille set up shots allowing him to lean against props or sturdy portions of the set. He also was assigned a wardrobe assistant who doubled as an historian of Native American culture. After helping Boris into his costume on one particular day, this remarkable deaf-mute man wrote a note to a coworker that read, "This man is as patient as a horse."

Less than a year into their marriage, Evie was beginning to act as Boris' private nurse, closely monitoring his work schedule and activities, and often accompanying him to the sets of films. During the spring of 1947, he accepted the physically undemanding role of "Dr. Hugo Hollingshead," a criminal henchman who poses as a psychiatrist, in the Danny Kaye opus *The*

Secret Life of Walter Mitty. Produced by Samuel Goldwyn, this big-budget comic fantasy was based on the James Thurber story and was released by RKO-Radio, who counted it as one of the two films Boris owed them from the Lewton contract. Shot in eye-popping Technicolor by Lee Garmes and giving free rein to the multi-talented Kaye, the film was an enjoyable one for Boris, who, in a typical understatement, recalled, "I was doing my old stuff, of course, in that... frightening Danny." (In fact, in one scene, while describing how to commit the perfect murder, he pushes Kaye out of a high-rise window.)   Briefly join-

Boris captured by a fan's camera as he attends a Broadway show, late 1940s.

ing him in two scenes, Virginia Mayo, who at one point appears bound and gagged in the psychiatrist's office, remembered her cinematic tormentor only as "a true gentleman."

Having returned to Los Angeles after the war, Bob Beckham was allowed on the set frequently, and Boris usually treated him to lunch at the Formosa Cafe on Santa Monica Boulevard. Beckham later said, "Danny Kaye was wonderful in those days, but... when I was involved in the Pasadena Tournament of Roses, he was the grand marshall, and I must say he was a pain in the ass."

Back in the insurance business, Beckham often visited his friend on Mulholland. Interested in helping out his young friend, Boris bought a special household policy covering Evie's jewelry and some of their expensive furniture, but Beckham nonetheless felt somewhat ill at ease:

> I remember Evie as being a little bit cold to me. She was not overly friendly, because of course I was involved with Dorothy in the old days, and my mother was a good friend of Dorothy's. So I was not particularly a favorite of Evie's. She was cordial and pleasant, but not overly friendly. And Boris seemed happy. She took very good care of him. She was very possessive, and also very supportive of him. And I thought they were a great pair.

Beckham was only one of Boris' old friends who experienced Evie's "pleasant but somewhat cold" attitude. She simply wanted to create an entirely new life for her husband and not be caught in the shadows of his past. Sara Jane concurs:

> She was pleasant and *seemingly* warm to everyone. She was very intelligent, very funny. My father had a won-

derful sense of humor. She would've had to have a sense of humor.

I never had any problem with her. I never *allowed* myself to have any problem with her...

She was awfully good to him, and he to her... but in analyzing it, from a different point of view, she really engineered his life so that I was as little a part of it as possible... She never, ever put anybody in touch with me. I was just something left over from another era. I couldn't be *totally* ignored, but she engineered it so that I spent a minimum amount of time with my father.

Evie was a very gracious host to new friends at Mulholland Drive, often entertaining neighbors Collier and Meg Young, and fellow Britons like Mary and Francis Hope, who was very fond of Boris:

I was always very deeply impressed by his enormous kindness and gentleness, always seeming to have all the time and attention in the world for anybody. I particularly remember an evening... when... Boris and I talked about county cricket, and he told us about some filming he'd recently done, which involved taking a lion for a walk. Afterwards Mary said to me that he had obviously taken more trouble and put up with more inconvenience in filming that one scene than most young actors would do for a whole film. "He must be a director's dream," she said: to have such a huge reputation and still be ready to take on anything and do whatever they ask, perfectly. I can't think of a more striking combination of talent and goodness.

Boris' "goodness" even continued to be demonstrated toward Louise Stine, who now had been his *ex*-mother-in-law for over two years. Having suffered from blindness for nearly a decade, she still lived in number 302 at the Garden Court Apartments on Hollywood Boulevard, but was experiencing some problems with her finances. Still unusually devoted to her, Boris paid the monthly bill for her rent, phone and newspapers. He also visited with his new mother-in-law, Mrs. Lina Adamson, during this time, particularly when she and Sara Jane joined him and Evie for a stay with Mr. and Mrs. C. Aubrey Smith, who had rented a home on Rexford Drive in Beverly Hills.

On the heels of *Walter Mitty*, Boris appeared as a red herring in *Lured*, directed by Douglas Sirk and costarring George Sanders, Lucille Ball and Charles Coburn. Continuing his sabbatical from monster movies, he did, however, share the screen with fellow Universal horror veterans Cedric Hardwicke, George Zucco and Alan Mowbray. After playing a mysterious London dress designer in this fog-shrouded United Artists release, he fulfilled his RKO contract with *Dick Tracy Meets Gruesome*. In this comic-strip potboiler, a policeman (Lyle Latell), puzzled over the disappearance of the supposedly deceased "Gruesome," takes a cue from *Arsenic and Old Lace* when he declares to Tracy (Ralph Byrd), "Smart? He's weird! I tell ya, if I didn't know better, I'd swear we were doing business with Boris Karloff!"

During the summer of 1947 Boris returned to truly gruesome form while hosting a four-week revival of *Lights Out* on ABC radio. And in September, he joined Gary Cooper and Howard Da Silva to promote the release of *Unconquered* on a 15-minute "Paramount Star Interviews" radio show that was syndicated throughout the United States. On October 29, he guest starred on Bing Crosby's *Philco Radio Time*, suggesting ways for the crooner to celebrate Halloween;

The Linden Tree (1948). **Atmospheric publicity shot of Boris as Professor Robert Linden, Music Box Theatre, New York City.**

and on the December 10 broadcast of *The Jimmy Durante Show*, he welcomed the frightened comic into "his spooky home."

During the waning days of the year, he received a script from Maurice Evans, who wanted him to return to the Broadway stage. After reading *The Linden Tree*, he fell in love with the play and the part of Professor Robert Linden, a traditional academic who is forced to retire, but doubted that such intellectual subject matter would play well in New York. Nonetheless, thinking "that if it ran for 10 weeks even, it would be worth doing," he accepted Evans' offer.

After all the arrangements were made, Evans had one last detail to attend to: receive author J.B. Priestley's approval of Boris in the lead role. "Good Lord, no!" Priestley responded. "Put his name on the marquee and people will think my play is about an axe murderer!"

Evans argued with Priestley, describing Boris' great versatility as an actor, his innate gentleness and scholarly interests, but the author still refused to accept such a genre icon as his sweet old history professor. Having persuaded Boris to do the play, Evans hated to relay the bad news.

"Well, that's all right. It's all off," Boris replied dejectedly; but after hanging up the phone, he thought of a charming way to melt Priestley's icy resolve. Cabling the playwright in London, he wrote, "Dear Mr. Priestley, I'm awfully disappointed that I'm not going to be in your play, and I give you my word of honor I would not have eaten the baby in the last act."

Soon after, Evans received a cable from Priestley, reading, "Let him play."

Boris and Evie flew to New York, where rehearsals began at the Music Box Theatre. Costarring with his old *Bride of Frankenstein* crony Una O'Connor, Boris again enjoyed working with director George Schaefer. Opening on March 2, 1948, the play was a mild critical success, but failed to attract much public support. Faulting Schaefer and some of the supporting players, reviewers reserved their praise for Boris. While George Freedly, of the *Telegraph*, called him "a superb actor" and *The New York Herald-Tribune*'s Howard Barnes described him as hard-working, sincere and giving "a fine account of himself," Brooks Atkinson, in *The New York Times*, wrote:

> Give it credit for one achievement. It proves that Boris Karloff, made up to look like a human being, is an extraordinarily winning actor. He plays the venerable academician with attractive humorsome conviction. Shaggy, tweedy, gray-haired, he has warmth and magnetism; and those beetling brows, which can scare you in his shiver plays, can soothe you with wisdom when he is in a benevolent mood.

Boris and Evie pose in the New Mexico desert during his brief run at the El Teatro de Santa Fe, summer 1948.

Boris had hoped *The Linden Tree* would run for 10 weeks. It closed after seven performances. Viola Keats, who portrayed his daughter, Jean, in the play, remembered, "Such a dear, kind man... his concentration and *warmth* are something I have never forgotten."

Back in Beverly Hills, he agreed to return to his old stomping grounds, now known as Universal-International, to play another Native American role, Tishomingo, an educated Choctaw, in *Tap Roots*, an adaptation of James Street's popular novel. Set in a Mississippi county that remained neutral during the Civil War, this Technicolor film, costarring Van Heflin, Susan Hayward, Julie London and Ward Bond, provided him with "the first character I've ever played on the screen who didn't come to a bad end."

Another atypical project was instigated by Ralph Edwards, who had been introduced to Boris and Evie by his producer, Al Paschall. Paschall was in the process of opening a new summer theater, El Teatro de Santa Fe, in New Mexico. Edwards recalled:

> We petitioned all of our acting friends to be a part of it. I opened the season with a week of *Goodbye Again*. Boris came the next week, and my mind fails for his vehicle. I have a picture of Boris with the cast. Boris and Evie stayed on for another week and then returned for the end of the season party at our house.

Hitting closer to home with Boris, Universal had just completed a film featuring a very dim reflection of the studio's most famous character: the Frankenstein Monster, who, along with Dracula and the Wolf Man, was set against the shenanigans of America's most popular comedy team. Although he did not join Bela Lugosi and Lon Chaney, Jr., in *Abbott and Costello Meet Frankenstein* (Glenn Strange played the Monster, as he had in *House of Frankenstein* and *House of Dracula* [1945]), Boris agreed to "promote" the film when it opened in New York.

But first he signed on for a week-long *Tap Roots* tour, beginning with the premiere in Philadelphia—an event that competed for attention (and hotel space) with the 1948 Democratic Convention. Joined by Evie, Boris became fast friends with Universal representative Philip Gerard, who remembered the experience as "a long, hot, noisy week":

> When tempers flared and patience wore, it was always Boris' good humor which brought our little troupe around...

Tap Roots (1948). **Sans makeup and wearing a sportcoat over his Choctaw shirt, Boris relaxes on the set with Evie.**

Van Heflin constantly worrying about photographers and his hairpiece—sulky Julie London—and affable Richard Long... I remember each town on that tour.

Frantic schedules, the trains, the planes and the rain. There was lots of rain.

Boris... represented and symbolized all the qualities and human values that are talked about but seldom fulfilled. He inspired all of us and gave us each something special that we shall always treasure.

The *Tap Roots* tour was only the beginning of Boris and Evie's friendship with the Gerards. Years later, Philip's daughter, Jennifer, would write:

As a child, I considered Boris an Olympian God. When I grew older, I realized, although not a god, he was nonetheless an exceptional human being. I have seldom experienced admiration of this sort. Boris radiated a special inspiring quality from within... his friendship has enriched me.

After the final *Tap Roots* appearance, Boris and Evie flew to the Big Apple, where Universal paid their expenses for a week. And while waiting for the July 28 premiere of the Abbott and Costello film, Boris gave an interview to Thomas F. Brady of *The New York Times*, emphasizing his latest role, as the "Choctaw sage... well disposed toward his white friends and learned in the healing arts." On July 25, his discussion with Brady was published under the headline, "Boris Karloff Views His Ghoulish Past And Finds He's Happier as an Indian."

Three days later, startled passers-by stopped and stared as he posed in front of Loew's Criterion Theatre, pointing at lavish posters and standing in the ticket line for *Abbott and Costello Meet Frankenstein*. In his interview with Brady, he claimed that, before leaving for New York, he said he would avoid seeing the film: "I'm too fond of the Monster. I'm grateful to him for all he did for me, and I wouldn't want to watch anybody make sport of him."

On October 17, 1948, Boris was back on the radio, starring in *The NBC University Theatre*'s adaptation of "The History of Mr. Polly," H.G. Wells' brilliant satire of 19th-century English society. As the timid window-dresser Alfred Polly, he aged several decades in 60 minutes, ranging from a Cockney-accented teenager to a middle-aged business failure who, through a series of tragicomic adventures, discovers his "duty" in life. The befuddled Polly provided Boris with one of his most challenging roles, and his multifaceted performance, reminiscent of Robert Donat's in the 1939 film *Goodbye, Mr. Chips*, proved that he was an actor of considerable range and subtlety.

In a radio segue from the sublime to the ridiculous, Boris was persuaded by Ralph Edwards to guest star in a special Halloween episode of the popular game show *Truth or Consequences*. Although Edwards was in Milwaukee, broadcasting a "road" version of the program for a week, Boris still agreed to help his friend pull a fast one on two unsuspecting locals, Mr. and Mrs. Earl Peterson.

Boris took *The Super Chief* train from Los Angeles to Chicago, where he was met by Edwards' assistant, Sue Clark Chadwick, whom he had met on the set of *British Intelligence* nine years earlier. Recalling the subsequent flight to Milwaukee, Edwards claimed that Boris was "still a bit leery of flying... Well, Sue said the plane was a six place job that flew low, so she held Boris' hand all the way. But being the good sport that he was, he was willing to return to Chicago the same way."

The broadcast of *Truth or Consequences* was almost as terrifying as the flight. Informing Mrs. Peterson that her husband would appear on stage disguised as a gypsy fortune teller, Edwards told her to kiss him passionately each time he correctly answered a question. After she was led off-stage, Edwards brought out Boris, introduced him to the audience and then disguised him as "Swami Hoozbando," replete with long robe and heavy beard. Masking his legendary voice with a high-pitched falsetto, Boris correctly answered three questions about the Peterson family, each time receiving a knock-out kiss, the audience roaring as he became the unwitting recipient of Mrs. Peterson's affection.

After the third embrace, Mrs. Peterson informed the audience that the swami was really her husband. "I knew those lips," she added, as the laughter increased.

Then Edwards asked the swami to remove his costume.

Boris turned his back, took off the robe and beard and faced her, unleashing his best Halloween groan.

Mrs. Peterson promptly screamed and ran off the stage, only to be brought back for a formal introduction to Boris. After Mr. Peterson was asked to re-join them, she received a Bulova wristwatch, $50 and a box of DUZ from the program's sponsor.

As the coup de grace, Boris, demonstrating that there were no hard feelings, playfully smooched her again, admitting, "Brother, have I been kissed!"

In November, Boris and Evie were in New York for another stab at the Great White Way. During the next two months, Boris reported to the Booth Theatre to rehearse with director Margaret Perry for Edward Percy's *The Shop at Sly Corner*. As former Devil's Island convict Decius Heiss, he again appeared oppo-

The Shop at Sly Corner **(1949). Boris as Decius Heiss, with Mary MacLeod as his wife, Margaret, in the Broadway production at the Booth Theatre.**

site Una O'Connor. Opening on January 18, 1949, the play fared even worse than *The Linden Tree*, closing after the fifth performance. "I fell into the usual actor's trap," Boris admitted. "A jolly good part for me in a very bad play."

Critics agreed that his role was the only bright spot in the play. All of the New York reviewers called him "excellent" or "skilled," with Howard Barnes of *The Herald-Tribune* again giving him high marks: "His portrayal... is persuasive and occasionally terrifying. It is altogether the best characterization he has achieved since he renounced horror films." (But Barnes' comment about "renouncing" horror is inaccurate, since Boris could not abandon a genre that no longer existed.)

Prior to flying back to Los Angeles, Boris made his television debut on the dramatic anthology *The Chevrolet Tele-Theatre*. Broadcast live from NBC studios on February 7, 1949, the 30-minute episode, "Expert Opinion," also featured

Dennis King and Vicki Cummings. One week later, he returned to radio in the clever "Birdsong for a Murderer" on *Inner Sanctum Mysteries*, playing a man who was killed by his wife, a homicidal maniac and asylum escapee, after he had devotedly hidden her from the authorities.

Later that month, he returned to the Universal lot, ironically to appear in *Abbott and Costello Meet the Killer, Boris Karloff*, a follow-up to the earlier monster comedy he had refused to see. When asked why he decided to appear with the comedy team, he replied, "Bud and Lou are wonderful chaps to work with, but we've all got to work, don't we? So the less said about this film, the better."

Whereas *Abbott and Costello Meet Frankenstein* poked fun at his most beloved character, the new film, like *Arsenic and Old Lace*, allowed Boris to make sport of *himself*, an entirely different matter. After being billed by surname only during the 1930s and having his name prominently featured in the dialogue of a smash Broadway play, he now was honored further by becoming part of a film's title.

By the time the Abbott and Costello picture was completed, Boris realized that more consistently interesting and challenging work was being offered by radio and, now, television producers. A year earlier, the Supreme Court, ruling on *United States vs. Paramount Pictures*, had ordered the film studios to reform their marketing practices. Combined with the increasing prominence of independent producers and the popularity of television, this decree literally killed the studio system. And the security of a multiple picture contract died along with it.

Boris and Evie both wanted to relocate to New York but knew that his status as a free-lance actor made such a move financially precarious. "Looking for an excuse to move," he was handed a golden one when ABC offered him his own television series, *Starring Boris Karloff*, to begin during the company's seminal autumn season. The package, designed as a weekly suspense anthology, was engineered by MCA and Boris' agent, David Susskind, who landed his client a producer's credit as part of the deal. When Boris was informed of this aspect of the contract, he refused to accept it, claiming that director-producer Alex Segal deserved the credit. Although MCA insisted on maintaining his producer status, Boris had them deduct $50 from his salary and add it to Segal's check every week. Wanting the series to be a success, he often worked overtime, helping Segal and George Axelrod rewrite the scripts and learning new dialogue at a moment's notice. He also collaborated with a different director, Charles Warburton, to produce a second version of each story for ABC Radio.

Starring Boris Karloff premiered on September 22, 1949, with "Five Golden Guineas" costarring Mildred Natwick. Although *Newsweek* hailed the "double duty" effort as "a good radio scare-show and an exceptional television program," it lasted only a half season, making its final broadcast on December 15. "Unhappily we were just too early for that sort of thing," recalled Boris, referring to the anthology style. "And we ran 13 weeks, but there were just no takers. But it gave me the peg to hang a move East on."

The following month, Boris starred in a revival of *On Borrowed Time*, directed by Gerald Savory at Atlanta's Penthouse Theatre, an in-the-round stage located at the top of a hotel. He loved playing Gramps again, and had the additional delights of costarring with 10-year-old Richard Wilson, a talented young actor from Atlanta's Peeples Street School, and the praise of critics and commoners alike. While George Goodwin called him "one of America's great actors," Paul Jones enthusiastically wrote:

> Many of us have lost sight of the fact that Mr. Karloff was one of the great actors of the theater when most of us were children... in *On Borrowed Time*, he has a real chance to display... fine dramatic qualities. He has a chance to show that he is one of the stage's true "greats."
>
> Many actors have performed before my eyes and before the eyes of thousands of theater regulars in the show world here in Atlanta during the past decade. But the tre-

mendous ovation accorded Karloff last night will ring in
his ears for many years as a stirring tribute from a discriminating audience to a great trouper.

Boris was impressed with Atlanta, as was Evie, who later wrote, "I have *very* fond memories of the time [we] were there. Gerald Savory was so nice, and we met some lovely people."
The lovely people presumably included the members of the Georgia House of Representatives,
to whom Boris was introduced. When a reporter asked him about his visit, specifically what he
thought of Georgia politics, he responded, "I think they've got very comfortable seats here."
Recalling his experiences, Savory wrote to Evie, "You were such a perfect combination and,
everywhere you were, radiated affection and a lovely feeling of civilization."

The "move East" finally occurred after Boris realized his greatest Broadway success since
Arsenic and Old Lace. In early 1950 Peter Lawrence and R.L. Stevens asked him to appear
opposite Jean Arthur in their lavish staging of Sir James M. Barrie's *Peter Pan*, not in a single
show-stopping role such as Jonathan Brewster, but in *two* major parts: the gentle, fatherly Mr.
Darling and the thunderous, bloodcurdling Captain Hook. Without a moment's hesitation, he
accepted, throwing himself into the rehearsals at the Imperial Theatre, where he experienced
none of the self-doubt that had wracked him a decade earlier.

Peter Pan opened on April 24, 1950, to rave reviews. The New York critics again lavished
high praise on Boris, who impressed them with his two *very* different characterizations and
seldom-utilized baritone voice on Leonard Bernstein's "Drink Blood" and "The Plank." One
columnist referred to his vocal technique as "unfaltering," quoting Boris' appreciation of musical conductor Ben Steinberg: "Thank heaven for Ben. When I get out on that stage and begin to

Peter Pan (1950). Boris, as Captain Hook, menaces a young friend in his dressing room.

sing, I keep an eye on that little man in the pit. His face and baton are my rod and staff, they comfort me."

Praising the broad style of the play, Brooks Atkinson of *The New York Times* wrote:

> Mr. Karloff is an actor of tenderness and humor, with an instinct for the exact inflection. His Captain Hook is a horrible cutthroat of the sea; and Mr. Karloff does not shirk the villainies. But they are founded on an excellent actor's enjoyment of an excellent part, and a relish of Barrie's inscrutable humors. There is something of the grand manner in the latitude of his style and the roll of his declamation; and there is withal an abundance of warmth and gentleness in his attitude toward the audience... Miss Arthur, Mr. Karloff and their associates have brought a purity of style and genuine affection to Barrie's winged fairy story. They have recaptured something that is priceless in the workaday theatre.

Jay J. Riley, who portrayed one of the pirates, remembered the experience as "a delightful time," but admitted that "even as a *pirate*, I was always *overacting!*"

Even while playing two characters every day, Boris still accepted additional assignments. At 7 p.m. on Sunday, September 17, he debuted his children's radio show *Boris Karloff's Treasure Chest* on WNEW. Mort Levin provided the continuity, and Boris greatly enjoyed telling stories and riddles, reading poetry and playing records for the youngsters of New York.

On Wednesday, November 15, he attended *The New York Times'* fourth annual Boys and Girls Book Fair at the American Museum of Natural History, where he read excerpts from *Peter Pan* to fifth grade students from Westchester's Thornwood School. Rather than relaxing on his birthday, which also happened to be Thanksgiving, he put on the Hook regalia and spent a portion of November 23 aboard Macy's "Pirate Ship" float in their 24th annual parade. And on Christmas Eve, he jumped at the chance to interpret Charles Dickens on NBC's *The Theatre Guild On the Air*. Costarring Richard Burton and Flora Robson, this one-hour radio version of *David Copperfield* (in which he played Uriah Heep) was his first recorded Dickensian performance.

After 321 performances of *Peter Pan*, during which the company recorded a Columbia LP featuring an abridged version of the play, they packed up and hit the road in late January 1951, touring the East and Midwest for the next three months. Like Boris' performance in *Frankenstein*, his *Peter Pan* effort was thoroughly appreciated by thousands of children who were attracted, not to the gentle Darling, but to the murderous Hook. Backstage, he often let youngsters try on his pirate hook; and later, when queried about the challenge of working with children on stage, he said:

> [G]ood gracious me, we had nine or ten little boys in that, and it was wonderful. I had great fun with them. Particularly doing *Peter Pan* in New York, because you were playing, then, to children who, by and large, were seeing their first play, which was a great excitement. And this, of course, was the one play that was going to capture their imagination. It was most exciting for us.

Among the happy children who came backstage were the daughters of producer Martin Manulis and his wife, Katie. Boris took time to describe the essential goodness of Captain Hook to the little girls and then gave the whole family an exclusive tour of the stage sets. Katie later wrote:

> I am so grateful... that our girls knew Boris a bit, and have
> him as part of their life experience... that Martin and I
> knew him, and that he was our friend, and we came under
> his good, loving spell. A man so wise and true, so dear...
> What a privilege to have shared moments now and then
> with him and his dearest Evie.

On February 5, 1951, the *Peter Pan* company (with Jennifer Bunker replacing Marcia Henderson as Wendy) opened at The Opera House in Boston. Two weeks later, they moved on to Philadelphia's Shubert Theatre; and by April 15, they were in Chicago. During the Broadway run, 12-year-old Sara Jane was scheduled to visit her father and stepmother in New York, but after a broken ankle prevented her from traveling, she caught up with Boris at Chicago's Opera House. In an effort to plug the play and boost its own business, Isbell's Restaurant on Rush Street graced the cover of its April menu with a photo of Boris and Evie dining with "beauteous Caren Doll."

Although Boris had arranged for Sara Jane to view the play from several vantage points, including the wings, she did not appear overly enthralled with his or the other actors' performances:

> When it was time for me to leave, he said, "I can tell you
> have no interest in becoming an actress, because you paid
> more attention to Nana, the dog, than you did to me." So...
> I think he was both disappointed and probably gratified
> that I didn't want to have [a] career on the stage.

Although the St. Bernard interested Sara Jane, its appeal was surpassed when Boris allowed her to "fly" across the stage on the rigging used by Joan McCracken (who had replaced Jean Arthur in the Peter role). And she also discovered one more appealing element: "I remember being enamored almost equally with Nana and the seven boys that were in the cast."

Sara Jane's *Peter Pan* experience was indicative of her relationship with Boris since the divorce and her move to San Francisco. Describing their twice-a-year meetings as "difficult," she remembers them as awkward situations in which her father and stepmother "didn't know what to do with an 11-year-old child roaming around the house." Prior to Boris and Evie's move to New York, she would visit them at Mulholland Drive when Edgar drove down to Los Angeles on business.

Evie was not keen on frequent reunions, but Boris' constant working and traveling was also a contributing factor:

> I was sorry that I didn't know him better—that time did
> not allow me to know him better. He and Evie had a very
> close relationship, and their lives were not accustomed to
> having a youngster in them. That's not a criticism, that's
> just an observation. And when I was with my father, I
> was acutely aware of trying to make it a normal relation-
> ship. And as an adult, I look back and I realize that's not
> the job of a child. But that's not to say that my father was
> not working equally hard at having a normal relationship.
> It just isn't possible in a divorce situation, made more dif-
> ficult by his fame.
>
> I don't feel that I made the best of it. I *had* the best of
> it. My stepfather was a wonderful man. I thought the sun
> rose and set on him, and my father was very comfortable

with the role my stepfather played in my life. And I think that, rather than have a child torn between two fathers, I think he left well enough alone. I think it was a decision my father consciously made, that he could not be a hands-on father, given his career and traveling, and that my stepfather would be the best stand-in possible. And he was. I was very fortunate.

After attending fourth grade at Madison School in San Francisco in 1949, Sara Jane had moved on to the Sarah Dix Hamlin School, a strict, all-female, college preparatory school. Attired in a uniform, studying French and Latin and leading a most non-Hollywood life, she sang in the choir, was elected president of the student body and lettered in several sports, including basketball and volleyball. Each year, her dedication to serious study landed her at the top of the class, and she had no time for the pop culture that enamored so many youths of the era.

By the late 1940s, when Boris was busy with stage, radio and television performances, "Karloff films" no longer haunted the theaters, and she and her friends, even if they had wanted to, did not have the opportunity to see him on the big screen. And when she did go out for an evening's entertainment with Dorothy and Edgar, she usually was treated to a stage play or the symphony, not to the current Hollywood fare:

> My main interest was in school. And I didn't go to a lot of films... I visited my friends at their homes, and they at my home. I did a lot of horseback riding. One of my friends, her family was well known in the polo circles—their name was Tevis—and they had a ranch outside of San Francisco. I spent a lot of weekends on the ranch, riding. And there was a riding academy not far from where we lived, and so I tried to ride three or four times a week. I had learned to ride English, and then later I switched to Western, did some gymkhana stuff and did a lot of shows—on a small scale. Never had my own horse. I taught riding, later. Sports, other than school, was one of the things I was interested in.

She did, however, retain the Karloff surname, which occasionally piqued the curiosity of schoolmates:

> When I moved to San Francisco... the name stood out more. It was more unique. And I suppose at that point, I realized the degree of his fame. Before moving, I really didn't have any concept of his fame, let alone the degree of fame that he had. People would just tease me about being the Monster's daughter and things. I was always glad that they made *Son of Frankenstein* and not *Daughter of Frankenstein*!

While visiting at Mulholland, Sara Jane was taught to play gin rummy, so Boris "would have someone to 'beat' unmercifully," but devising other activities was a constant challenge:

> He took me to a football game one time, and no one in the stands... at least in the stands around where we were sitting, could have told you one thing about the game, be-

cause they were all watching him. So it was difficult for him to have a relationship in public with a child. I mean, weekend fathers take their children to the movies, or they take them to a football game or they take them on an outing. But because of his recognizability, public outings were difficult, and so we'd be at his house, *their* house.

He was 51 when I was born. Therefore none of his friends had children my age. So they were kind of stuck with a kid sitting around and playing gin rummy, badly. They didn't know what to do with me. And I didn't know what to do with them.

After the *Peter Pan* tour closed in Minneapolis during the early spring of 1951, Boris and Evie drove back to New York. Jean Arthur had left the company to do a film in Hollywood, where Boris' realtor finally had sold the Mulholland Drive house. "So then we moved East completely," Boris said. "And I was up to my ears in television... on all the networks."

During the Broadway run of *Peter Pan*, he had made television appearances on *Masterpiece Playhouse*, *Lights Out* and *Paul Whiteman's Goodyear Revue*, and before flying back to Los Angeles for a film assignment, he appeared on the April 11, 1951, broadcast of *The Don McNeil TV Club*. Universal-International again had devised a multiple-picture deal, but this time offered to cast him in supporting roles requiring only brief time commitments.

For the first Universal vehicle, *The Strange Door*, writer Jerry Sackheim mixed a few references from Robert Louis Stevenson's short story "The Sire de Maletroit's Door" with every timeworn horror cliché he could recall. Thinking little of the hackneyed mess the studio called a script, Boris, who played his shuffling henchman in a measured tongue-in-cheek style, did appreciate being reunited with *Old Dark House* costar Charles Laughton, who expressed his opinion of the material by overacting outrageously in nearly every scene. While working on the film, Boris also starred in "The Big Man" on *Stars on Parade*, a syndicated radio show produced by the U.S. Army and Air Force.

More outrageous than any Hollywood B film was a second round of Communist witch hunts waged in tinsel town by the House Committee on Un-American Activities (HUAC) during 1951. Having begun its assault on the "Communist infiltration" of the film industry four years earlier, the committee, headed by J. Parnell Thomas, was certain that card-carrying pinkos had taken over the Screen Writers Guild to disseminate subversive propaganda through the film medium. Now, the second assault had resulted in a list of 90 Hollywood figures who were called to testify before HUAC.

Was Boris, the liberal thinker and union organizer, ever sought out by the committee? Cynthia Lindsay claimed, "He was slightly left wing, if you call being democratic left wing. And everybody then who wasn't a straight Republican in the industry was a 'pinko,' and he was definitely known as a pinko. He was not a pinko, but he was on the liberal side."

Evie revealed:

We were living in New York at that time, and we were very, very conscious of it [the HUAC witch hunts]. And... Lillian Hellman, the author... was a great target. But we never became involved in it in any way, although Margaret Webster, the director, was a very close friend. She was under surveillance all the time, and I remember her telephoning one night and saying to me, "I now know what the chill of fear in your bones means." But I never really had any closer contact with people in that, but of course it was shocking.

> Earlier than that, I took a course in motion picture
> directing in California, and I can't remember the names,
> but most of the people I had known on that course were
> under suspicion after that.

The move to New York ended Boris' participation on the board of the Screen Actors Guild. Since 1947 he had been serving under Guild president Ronald Reagan, who then was an FDR liberal. Years after embracing conservatism in 1962, he wrote a letter to Cynthia Lindsay describing Boris as "one of the warmest, kindest, most gentle human beings I have ever met, and at all times a perfect gentleman... He had great, good common sense plus a sense of fairness typical of his great integrity." Ironically, in an interview with London's *Sunday Times*, Evie later said of Reagan, "We thought he was very nice, but not very bright, even then."

Geographically distant from the focus of HUAC's attention, Boris and Evie purchased an apartment on the top floor of the legendary Dakota, located near Central Park on West 72nd Street. Here, Boris enjoyed returning from the television studios to find enthusiastic youngsters waiting for him, knowing that none of them knew anything about the Frankenstein Monster or horror films. Evie said:

> When we lived in the Dakota... there were a lot of chil-
> dren in the building at the time, and they didn't know who
> Boris was at all, but they all loved him... It was a wonder-
> ful building, because you could run all around... there were
> four elevators... They used to come knocking on the door
> all the time... They used to bang on the front door and say,
> "Mister, Mister, can I come in?"

A featured guest at a November awards ceremony held by the New York council of the Screen Actors Guild, Boris was presented with a gold card granting an honorary life membership for his "long and faithful" 28 years of service. After tearing up in the presence of his colleagues, he sat down and wrote to the Hollywood Board of Directors on November 20:

> Ladies and Gentlemen:
>
> You have just done me the greatest honour that any
> actor could receive from his fellows, and I am humbled
> and deeply grateful. I was only luckier than most in that I
> happened to be around when things got started. My best
> love to those who are serving now, but most of all to those
> who have gone ahead and those who will follow on... for
> actors. God bless you all.

During the autumn of 1951 Boris became a regular presence on television, doing comedy bits with Milton Berle on *The Texaco Star Theatre*, musical skits (including one in drag) on *The Fred Waring Show*, straight dramatic roles on *Robert Montgomery Presents*, *Studio One* and *Lux Video Theatre*, and demonstrating his knowledge alongside perennial panelist Kitty Carlisle on the quiz show *Celebrity Time*. He even spent Christmas Day performing in "The Lonely Place" on CBS's *Suspense*. And the New Year brought the same busy schedule, further allowing him to demonstrate his versatility as an actor, stage performer and comedian. On January 30, 1952, he gave his first television interview, to Sherman Billingsley, on CBS's talk show *Stork Club*.

In March, he and Evie made another trip to Los Angeles, to make *The Black Castle*, a second Gothic adventure film for Universal-International. Working with costars Richard Greene and Paula Corday (whom he had met on the set of *The Body Snatcher* seven years earlier) was a pleasant experience, and the effective atmosphere and serious tone established by director Nathan Juran was an improvement over Joseph Pevney's pedestrian handling of *The Strange Door*.

Finishing his sinister routine once again, Boris happily prepared for his first visit to England since 1936 and his first ever with Evie, who had moved to the United States in 1939. Producer Hanna Weinstein offered him a stab at another television series, asking him to fly to London to shoot three pilot films for *Colonel March of Scotland Yard*, in which he would star as John Dickson Carr's popular detective. Still owing one more film to Universal, Boris was loaned out for the summer, and the studio began to arrange for the comfort of its former superstar. But before departing, he appeared on two more *Inner Sanctum Mysteries*, a second performance of "Birdsong for a Murderer" on June 22, and "Death for Sale," another murder-for-the-insurance-money story, on July 13.

Advance notice was sent to Universal's London office suggesting that Boris' one major desire be fulfilled: Now unable to play the game himself, he wanted to see an authentic English cricket match. Luckily, a journalist in the office knew one of the nation's most knowledgeable cricket enthusiasts and frantically telephoned him, asking if he could possibly acquaint Boris Karloff with the current cricket scene.

Bernard Coleman, a successful 28-year-old pub manager, was a member of the Surrey County Cricket Club, one of the major clubs in England, and often attended matches at the Oval, a major test ground at Kennington in London. Arrangements were made for Coleman to meet Boris at a flat in Brompton Square, where he and Evie would be living during their stay; and after brief introductions, the pair set out for the Oval. High up in the huge Victorian pavilion that overlooks the cricket ground, they sat, enjoying a warm, sunny day and watching Alec Bedser, one of the nation's senior bowlers, put on an impressive display. Coleman recounted:

> We had exchanged a few pleasantries, but he'd said very little. And after possibly an hour, he suddenly turned to me and, in this beautiful voice of his, said, "This is like dying and going to heaven"—which I have always considered one of the great quotes of all time. He didn't talk very much, but we spent most of the day there.
>
> And I said to him, "Would you like to meet Alec Bedser?"
>
> And he said, "Yes, I would."
>
> Well, I knew Alec from the previous year... So I went down... and knocked on the dressing room door. Alec was one of the old-fashioned people who didn't know too much about anything that happened other than cricket. And I asked for him and said, "I've got a very famous film actor with me... who would like to meet you."
>
> So Alec said, "Well, I don't know anything about films."
>
> I said, "Well, it's *Boris Karloff.*"
>
> And Alec said, "Well, even *I've* heard of him!"
>
> So I duly took Boris down to the dressing room and introduced him, and he then, over a period, got to know all the Surrey players. And he used to sit on their balcony, and became very friendly with them, and used to umpire some of their charity matches. And he did become a great stalwart of the club.

With the three *Colonel March* pilots in the can, the Karloffs flew back to New York toward the end of 1952, and on December 16, Boris appeared with Don Ameche and Miriam Hopkins

Boris at sea, apparently fatigued from his fishing excursion off the coast of Acapulco, March 1953.

on another broadcast of Milton Berle's *Texaco Star Theatre*. But soon they were traveling again, this time to the warmer climes of southern Mexico during early March 1953. Evie loved combing the beaches of Acapulco, as well as joining Boris on a deep-sea fishing excursion during which they both landed enormous sailfish. Boris also caught a small shark, which was a challenge to remove from the hook, leaving him covered with more blood than he had encountered in any of his horror films.

During the spring and early summer of 1953, Boris continued to accept television roles, all of a dramatic nature, including return engagements on *Robert Montgomery Presents* and *Suspense*, which cast him as Grigori Rasputin in "The Black Prophet" on March 17. Now 14, Sara Jane began to view her father's work with an exacting eye:

I was critical when I'd watch him on television, because I could tell he was acting. And I thought, "Gee, a good actor—you shouldn't be able to tell that they're acting." But that's a dumb thing... He wasn't my father as I knew my father; he was acting. So I was consciously aware of his acting when he was on, in some of the roles he did on television. And that sort of discomforted me. I didn't think he was a bad actor. I just knew he wasn't my father up there...

The guest appearances were totally away from the characters that he played. When he had his series, he would play the heavy or the boogieman; but when he was doing guest appearances... there were a lot of comedic things that he did.

There's a lot of television that he did that I didn't see, not out of avoidance, and not out of a family policy, but really that it just wasn't part of my life. As a one televi-

186

sion household, we wouldn't sit around in the evening and watch my father.

Although the popularity of radio was being affected by the American public's increased interest in television, major stars still were attracted to the sonic medium. On April 5, 1953, Boris tackled another Dickensian role, Magwich, in the *U.S. Steel Hour*'s adaptation of *Great Expectations* for NBC radio. Joining him for this hour-long abridgment were Melville Cooper, Estelle Winwood, Anthony Kemble Cooper and Tom Helmore (in his only professional association with Boris).

When Queen Elizabeth II was crowned on June 2, Boris and Evie attended a coronation party at the lovely 57th Street home of Helen Bryson. While Boris was mingling with the other guests, Evie found her designated place at the table. Seated next to her, actor Alan Craig leaned over, read her place card and said, "If you're Mrs. Boris Karloff, then I'm Mr. Boris Karloff!" Evie and Helen laughed cheerfully as they pointed out the formidable Boris in the crowd.

Later that month, Boris fulfilled his Universal contract by again squaring off against the inimitable duo Bud and Lou in *Abbott and Costello Meet Dr. Jekyll and Mr. Hyde*. An improvement on the previous Abbott and Costello script, it of-

Evie and Boris with their catch from the *Pescadora*, Acapulco, March 1953.

fered him more screen time and an opportunity to build a semblance of characterization. By 1953 he had played nearly every horror part imaginable and now was able to add Dr. Jekyll and Mr. Hyde to his rogue's gallery. Director Charles Lamont followed the lead of his predecessor, Charles T. Barton, in *Abbott and Costello Meet Frankenstein*, smoothly incorporating the Jekyll-and-Hyde scenes with the team's shenanigans.

Surrounded by respectable period detail, Boris played his scenes with total conviction, presenting Jekyll as a man who already possesses some of Hyde's iniquitous traits. Now 65 years old and ever mindful of his sensitive back, he gladly stepped aside whenever the action became too physical. Although he underwent Bud Westmore's Jack Pierce-like makeup process for the transformation sequences, he also wore a heavy rubber mask, which stuntman Edwin Parker donned for the chase and fight scenes.

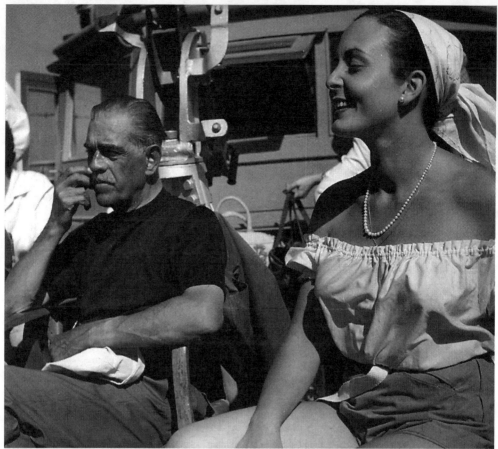

Il Monstro del Isola (U.S.: *Monster of the Island*, 1954). Sailing off the Italian island of Ischia, Boris conveys the futility and utter chaos he experienced during the production of this disastrous film, summer 1953.

After toppling to his death on a back lot sidewalk, he appeared in a few scenes for independent producer Frank Ferrin, whose film *The Hindu*, produced in India with popular juvenile actor Nino Marcel, needed a big-name star to attract a U.S. distributor. After joining his old mate Reginald Denny and character actor Victor Jory in shooting the additional sequences, he returned to New York, where he and Evie soon prepared for another flight to London. Hanna Weinstein had sold the *Colonel March* series to ITV and was preparing to film an entire season of episodes. While Weinstein tended to the extensive preproduction schedule, Boris signed a one-picture contract with Romana Films of Italy, and he and Evie flew to Rome.

Il Monstro del Isola (*Monster of the Island*) was produced at Rome's Paolis Studios, with some location scenes filmed on Ischia, an island off the coast of Napoli. The entire experience was a disaster for Boris. Being the only English-speaking actor on the set, he had scant knowledge of what was happening either in front of or behind the camera, and the plot involving a gang of international dope smugglers made even less sense. After director Roberto Montero wrapped the project, he and editor Iolanda Benvenuti could do little to improve the footage, and finally decided to overdub Boris' voice with that of another actor, resulting in "Don Gaetano Bronte" speaking in an accent that sounds like a mixture of British and gibberish.

And the Karloffs' generally pleasant adventures in the Italian capitol unfortunately were marred by the manager of the Hassler Hotel, whose attitude the usually tolerant Boris described as "venal." Having dropped in to see them at the Hassler, located at the top of Rome's Spanish Steps, their old friend Henry Brandon remembered:

Boris and Evie arrive in London, autumn 1953.

> The pompous old fool of a manager behind the desk had
> sent me to the wrong suite. I surmised it was his way of
> demonstrating that he was unimpressed by his illustrious
> guest... I had lived there a year and a half... The people
> whom the stranger meets in resort towns traditionally bite
> the hand that feeds them—the hotel clerks, tradesmen,
> landlords, bill collectors, taxi drivers, etc., etc.—and Rome
> is the greatest tourist trap in the world.

In October 1953 they returned to London, and Boris began to study the scripts for *Colonel March*, which was filmed from November until early 1954. Interest in the series was bolstered by *Colonel March Investigates*, a feature constructed from the three pilot episodes and released by Criterion Films. Twenty-six total episodes were produced, including one, "All Cats Are Grey at Night," in which Boris appeared with a 31-year-old English actor named Christopher Lee. Weinstein's company, Panda Productions, Ltd., had assembled a first-rate crew, including director Martin Ritt, who contributed moody visuals and a fluid pace to many of the 30-minute installments.

While working on *Colonel March*, Boris made a rare appearance on British radio, in "The Hanging Judge," actor Raymond Massey's adaptation of a novel by Bruce Hamilton. Broadcast on *The Play of His Choice* in December 1953, this drama, which bears similarities to *Weir of Hermiston* and other works by Robert Louis Stevenson, cast Boris as Sir Francis Brittain, a judge who must levy a sentence of capital punishment against a man who may be innocent. Although Brittain wrestles with a moral dilemma, he still upholds the law, believing the British judicial system to be infallible. In the closing moments, however, Brittain is revealed as a corrupt official leading a double life.

Returning to the comfort of the Dakota, the Karloffs spent the next 18 months in New York, where Boris appeared in a dozen live television shows, including a one-hour abridgment of *Arsenic and Old Lace* on the January 5, 1955, broadcast of CBS's *The Best of Broadway*. Playing Jonathan Brewster for the first time in a decade, he was surrounded by an excellent supporting cast including Helen Hayes, Billie Burke, Orson Bean, Edward Everett Horton and his good friend Peter Lorre.

On the February 19, 1955 *Donald O'Connor Show*, Boris again unleashed his warm baritone, on "The Human Thing to Do" and "'Arry and 'Erbert." Two days later, *Variety* thrashed O'Connor for "his weakest effort" of the season, claiming that he lacked the versatility to appear in skits with an actor of Boris' ilk:

Colonel March of Scotland Yard (1954). **Boris and Christopher Lee in the episode "All Cats are Grey at Night."**

If his writers sold him the idea of playing spooks with Boris Karloff, he's to blame for accepting it. Not even on paper could it have looked good... Three times Karloff was called on to sing and in the closing English music hall number poured into glittering habiliments to clog with O'Connor and five pairs of shapely stems... Maybe the banty comic-dancer is trying to do too much and should be content to do the performing and let others worry about the rest. Not even Gleason nor Gobel spread themselves so thin.

Having played detectives on the big screen and in television series such as *Colonel March*, which currently was being syndicated throughout the United States, Boris appeared as "Mr. Mycroft," a character based on Sherlock Holmes, in "The Sting of Death," an *Elgin TV Hour* adaptation of H.F. Heard's short story. This February 22 appearance as the retired investigator with an interest in bee culture was his only dramatic connection with the work of Sir Arthur Conan Doyle.

On March 12, 1955, Boris starred in another bona fide musical, Rodgers and Hart's adaptation of Mark Twain's *A Connecticut Yankee in King Arthur's Court*, on NBC's *Max Liebman Presents*. As a vocalizing King Arthur, he performed "Knight's Refrain" and "You Always Love the Same Girl," sharing the studio with Janet Blair and Eddie Albert, who remembered him as "a splendid actor." Nine days later, he signed with Kermit Bloomgarden to appear in *The Lark*, a Broadway production that Lillian Hellman was adapting from *L'Alouette*, a French play by Jean Anouilh. Several New York papers published articles about the signing, noting that Julie Harris would play Joan of Arc opposite Boris' "Inquisitor."

To top off a momentous month, Boris also accepted an invitation from Bernie Coleman, who wanted him to serve as the new president of the Castle Cricket Club, which represented a pub that Coleman owned in South London's Tooting district. Planning to take a brief holiday in England during May, Boris asked Bernie to book seats for the upcoming test match at Lord's. But before he and Evie could leave the country, he joined Susan Strasberg, Eli Wallach, Anthony Perkins and the man he had scared to death 22 years earlier in *The Mummy*, Bramwell Fletcher, for "Mr. Blue Ocean" on the May 1 broadcast of CBS's *General Electric Theatre*, which indirectly reunited him with Ronald Reagan, who hosted the program.

In early September, Boris and Evie made another transatlantic flight, a trip that was becoming habitual. But this time they went to London primarily for a holiday, to let Boris relax from the non-stop schedule he was determined to maintain in New York. Although he sometimes mentioned that a role in a West End play would make him feel like a truly successful actor, he made his only London stage appearance during this visit. In *Night of 100 Stars*, a benefit for the Actors' Orphanage, he trod the boards of the Palladium with Richard Attenborough, Marlene Dietrich, Alec Guinness, Jack Hawkins, Laurence Olivier, Michael Redgrave, his old costar Danny Kaye and Evie, who appeared as an extra.

Boris and Evie spent several evenings with Ralph and Barbara Edwards, who had flown to London to launch the television show *This Is Your Life*. Edwards remembered, "Well, of course the first guests at our quarters at St. James' Court were Boris and Evie, and we saw a lot of them during our six-week stay. They attended the show and were a part of the audience as I went down the aisle, looking for a 'victim'."

Just prior to leaving for England, Boris had solidified his commitment to *The Lark*. Perhaps a vacation in his homeland was the best move he possibly could have made at that point, for after returning the following month, he crafted the performance of a lifetime, which he thereafter referred to as "one of the most rewarding experiences of my life."

Chapter 9

Renaissance Man

"The only sort of point of view of that (*Boris Karloff's Treasure Chest*) program was that children are really the same the world over. And it was to try to... breed tolerance, you know, with prejudice—which has to be done in America, unhappily. There's a great deal of it."

In 1429 France, Joan of Arc was on the march, relieving Orleans from English occupation and attempting to recapture Paris. A year later she was captured and tortured by the English and their French collaborators, who, in 1431, burned her to death at Rouen for being a "witch" and a "relapsed heretic."

During the Nazi occupation of France, playwright Jean Anouilh wrote *L'Alouette*, paralleling his nation's World War II plight with Joan's ordeal during the Hundred Years War (1337-1453), as a message of hope for his countrymen. After the play was produced in Paris in 1953, the English dramatist Christopher Fry translated it for the London stage; and in 1955, the great American playwright Lillian Hellman, who also was persecuted for holding her own political beliefs, adapted it for Broadway.

When asked about his depiction of the historical Joan, Anouilh wrote:

> The play... makes no attempt to explain the mystery of Joan. The persistent effort of so-called modern minds to explain mysteries is, in any case, one of the most naive and foolish activities indulged in by the puny human brain since it became overstocked with shallow political and scientific notions, and can yield nothing in the long run, but the nostalgic satisfaction of the small boy who discovers at last that his mechanical duck was made up of two wheels, three springs and a screw. The little boy holds in his hands three springs, two wheels and a screw, objects which are doubtless reassuring, but he has lost his mechanical duck, and he has usually not found an explanation.
>
> For my own part I always refuse to tell children how things work, even when I know; and in the case of Joan I must confess that I did not know...
>
> You cannot explain Joan, any more than you can explain the tiniest flower growing by the wayside. There's just a little living flower that has always known, ever since it was a microscopic seed, how many petals it would have and how big they would grow, exactly how blue its blue would be and how its delicate scent would be compounded. There's just the phenomenon of Joan, as there is the phenomenon of a daisy or of the sky or of a bird. What pretentious creatures men are, if that's not enough for them.

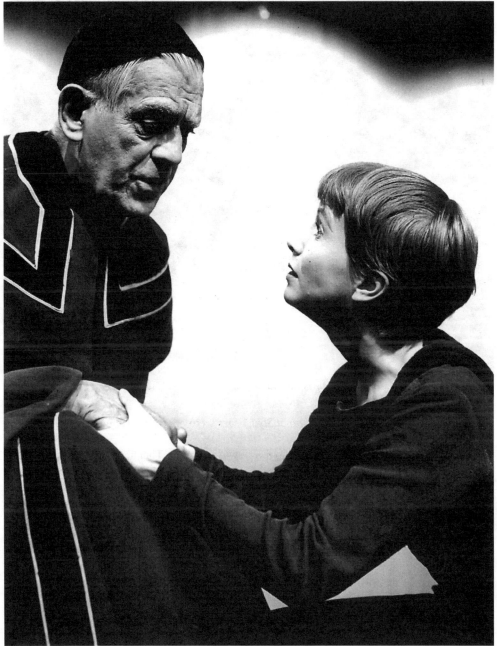

The Lark (1955). Julie Harris' Joan of Arc pleads with Boris' Bishop Cauchon at the Longacre Theatre, New York City.

> Children, even when they are growing older, are al-
> lowed to make a bunch of daisies or play at imitating bird-
> song, even if they know nothing about botany or ornithol-
> ogy. That is just about what I have done.

Perhaps Boris the philosophical anarchist agreed with Anouilh's undogmatic, impressionistic approach, but one fact is certain: *The Lark* was exactly the kind of serious drama that he wanted to sink his teeth into. Since the enormous success of *Arsenic and Old Lace*, Broadway had allowed him to prove his acting mettle outside the confines of the horror film genre; and

***The Lark*. Boris thoroughly in character as Cauchon.**

although *The Linden Tree* and *The Shop at Sly Corner* were box-office failures, he had received consistent critical praise.

On October 3, 1955, Boris reported to the New Amsterdam Theatre to rehearse with director Joseph Anthony and costar Julie Harris, who was considered one of the most gifted actresses in the nation. Then 29 years old, she had studied at the Yale Drama School and at the Actors Studio prior to making her Broadway debut in 1945. Portraying complex characters with great subtlety, she won acclaim as "Frankie Addams" in the play *The Member of the Wedding* in 1950, a role she repeated in Fred Zinneman's screen version two years later. A few months prior to concentrating on *The Lark*, she costarred with fellow method actor James Dean in *East of Eden* (1955).

Boris was absolutely thrilled to be sharing the stage with such a respected young performer. And to make the pairing even more interesting, his character (not the Inquisitor, as the papers had reported, but Bishop Cauchon) was based on Petain, the man who prosecuted and sentenced Joan of Arc to death. Boris later explained, "Both Cauchon and Joan suffer dreadfully, each in his own belief of what is best for France, and he with a tenderness for the girl and a deep desire to save her." Told from the Maid of Orleans' point of view as she recounts her life story for her judges at Rouen, the play—in the words of critic Peggy Doyle—transported the audience "with dramatic swiftness... to each progressive stage in Joan's brief, inspired existence."

Harris was familiar with Boris' Broadway work as early as 1942, when, as a teenager, she saw *Arsenic and Old Lace* at the Fulton. But after rehearsals for *The Lark* began, she developed an absolute adoration for him. Wanting to hone his portrayal of Cauchon to near-perfection, Boris constantly made notes in his script, reminders of how to deliver a particular line of dialogue, what emotions to indicate at certain moments, and how to position himself on stage. He penciled in the director's suggestions to other actors, as well as new lines when they were changed during rehearsals. Privately criticizing one dialogue change, he wrote, "The guts of the scene are gone."

194

On the very first page, he commanded himself, in dark blue ink, to be "not so solemn." He often made mincemeat of the script, crossing out half the dialogue and scrawling nearly indecipherable comments around what remained. Although his Cauchon was sympathetic toward Joan, the archbishop was forced to uphold his duty to the state—a character trait emphasized by Boris in his annotations. At one point, he noted that "Joan listens well... an island of grace," but early in the second act, he reminded himself to be "brutal," to deliver his speech "hard and cold at Julie." Not only did Boris view this role as an opportunity to prove what he was capable of, but also as an invaluable chance to further study the art of acting. At one point, he commented, "I've learned more since I got into *The Lark* than I ever did before."

One incident in the first act involved a debate between Cauchon and the Earl of Warwick over the state's knowledge about Joan. Interestingly, Boris' handwritten note referring to the medieval context of the play also pertains to modern notions of "national security" and the effects of mass media propaganda: "We pretend that our intelligence service is good and we say it so often that everybody believes it." Late in the second act, he penciled out the printed dialogue and wrote, "I knew the girl and I loved her."

One evening, while rehearsing at the New Amsterdam, the company was interrupted by the arrival of Maurice Chevalier, who, under the direction of Florenz Ziegfeld nearly 30 years earlier, had scored his first American success when the theater was still a nightclub. Chevalier took Boris and Julie on a tour of the building, pointing out the former locations of the orchestra, floor show and celebrity audience.

On Friday, October 28, the entire company began a two-week tryout of the play at Boston's Plymouth Theatre. Seven local newspapers reviewed the opening night, calling it "splendid," "spectacular and beautiful to see and to hear," "intense and incisive," and "magnificent." And the critics were equally impressed with Julie Harris, whose fervor for Boris they also shared. Cyrus Durgin of the *Daily Globe* referred to his performance as "noble and mellow," while Alta Maloney of the *Boston Traveler* called him "heart-rending... the audience's voice on the stage." But it was the *Sunday Post*'s Elliot Norton who praised his Cauchon as possessing "great power and impressive gravity." By October 31, *Hollywood Variety* already was reporting that "this play exhibits big film fare potential and negotiations... are under way with Allied Artists."

In many ways, Boris proved how much *The Lark* meant to him. Most conspicuously, he and Evie preserved every word written about it. While he had not collected reviews or mementos of his films, he had saved articles about his previous Broadway productions. This time, Evie bought a scrapbook and carefully pasted in all the newspaper clippings, carefully identifying the source of any information about the play and his performance.

On Sunday, November 13—the morning after closing its tryout in Boston and four days before its Broadway debut at the Longacre Theatre—*The Lark* made the front page of *The New York Times*. A large photograph of Boris and Julie, inset with smaller shots of Joseph Wiseman, Christopher Plummer and Theodore Bikel, impressively appeared directly below the newspaper's logo.

Although she had noticed it earlier, Julie began to worry about the back and leg problems Boris had after being on his feet for several hours. Not wanting to pry into the cause of his debility, which he never complained about nor mentioned, she politely insisted that he use the one dressing room located just off the stage and then claimed an upstairs chamber for herself.

On Friday, November 18, the New York critics who had attended opening night zealously echoed their Boston colleagues. While Walter Kerr of *The Herald Tribune* described Cauchon as "an agonized figure of great power and genuine warmth," Robert Coleman of *The Daily Mirror* wrote, "Boris Karloff, a fine and versatile actor, is moving as the kindly and compassionate Cauchon." When *Time* reviewed the first performance, the magazine claimed that, with the exception of Boris, "every member of the cast... was jittered off top form," needing to be "upbore" by Julie. And in the November 19 *Morning Telegraph*, Whitney Bolton claimed, "Here, too, looking like a portrait into which Rembrandt poured his gifts, is Boris Karloff as a Cauchon of richest dimension and heart." Had Boris, a true Renaissance man, become real Renaissance art?

Anxious to repay Julie for her dressing-room favor, Boris got his chance when her voice threatened to give out. She recalled, "He was always kind and thoughtful. When I had some strain on my throat, he suggested I get a little corncob pipe and stuff the bowl with cotton saturated with Vicks throat spray and just suck on it."

And Harris nearly put herself out of commission on one of the first nights:

> I fell during the first act. Well, really, I was supposed to
> faint but I misjudged the distance, and as I went down to
> my knees, my head—my mouth—grazed the side of the
> bench I sat on and I hit it with some force. I heard Boris
> behind me say—in a very low voice—"J-U-L-I-E!" And
> the next thing I knew, I felt something drip into my hands—
> my own blood, as I discovered a few moments later. I had
> split my lower lip open rather badly. I staggered through
> the next scene, spraying blood all over Joe Meilziner's
> blue carpet. I'll never forget how Boris said my name at
> that moment—full of such concern.

Boris' handling of Julie's predicament was indicative of the control and composure he had developed as a stage performer since his first Broadway run 15 years earlier. Not once did Harris observe any nervousness on his part and, in fact, she appreciated his occasional attempts to lighten the mood with humor:

> On Saturday nights—our eighth show of the week—places
> would be called, and he and I would walk on the set to our
> first position. And Boris would look at me and say, "You
> and I remind me of two old fighting cocks! Pretty soon
> we'll be going at each other."

On November 28, Julie as Joan appeared on the cover of *Time*, reflecting the coverage the play began to receive on a national level. *Variety*, *Newsweek*, the *Wall Street Journal*, the *New Yorker* and the *Christian Science Monitor* hailed it, as did West Coast publications such as *The Hollywood Reporter*. Two months later, Boris gave an interview to Associated Press reporter William Glover, admitting that Cauchon was the "high point of my career as an actor," a personal opinion reflected professionally by the *Montreal Star*'s Noel Mostert: "Boris Karloff gives a measured, moving performance that, for acting honors, steals the show."

In his interview with Glover, Boris, again demonstrating his common-sense philosophy, made a rare public observation about the acting profession:

> I have a theory that when an actor gets to the point where
> he may choose his own parts, nine out of 10 times he is in
> a very dangerous position. For myself, I know what I
> can't do, but I have no idea what I can do. That is rather
> putting the cart before the horse.

The day after Christmas 1955, producer Kermit Bloomgarden raised the price of *Lark* tickets from $4.60 to $5.75. The play had been critically acclaimed since opening night, but high production costs had created a deficit of $76,610 after only seven weeks in Boston and New York.

On Easter Sunday 1956, the American Theatre Wing held its annual Tony Awards ceremony at the Waldorf. Boris received a nomination for best actor, as did Julie for best actress, Jo Mielziner for best set direction and Alvin Colt for best costume design. Up against the heavyweight lineup of Paul Muni, Michael Redgrave, Edward G. Robinson and Ben Gazzara, Boris did not get enough votes to win. But he was not too disappointed that Muni, who had given a typical fire-and-grease paint performance in *Inherit the Wind*, was awarded the Tony, because Julie took one home, too.

During the run of *The Lark*, Boris appeared, as "a combination philosopher, doctor and bartender," in one television show, "Even the Weariest River," broadcast on NBC's *The Alcoa Hour* on April 15, 1956. Featuring a notable cast, including *Lark* colleague Christopher Plummer, Franchot Tone, Lee Grant and Jason Robards, Jr., it was one of the most unusual teleplays of the era. Alvin Sapinsley, who earlier had adapted versions of Cervantes' *Don Quixote* and Twain's *A Connecticut Yankee* in which Boris starred, wrote the script in iambic pentameter, concluding each scene with rhyming couplets.

Variety's "Gilb" found the drama "rich in poetic qualities and an ethereal mood": "By far the best lines were handed Karloff, and he handled them in dignified, scholarly fashion that accented the grim, fatalistic mood of the piece." Jack Gould of *The New York Times* considered it "one of the season's finest achievements," agreeing that "Mr. Karloff had the most inspired and rewarding lines. He spoke them with compassion and beauty." In fact, Boris and the drama made a clean sweep of the critics, including the *New York Herald Tribune*'s John Crosby:

> Not long ago, Sir Laurence Olivier, passing through town, observed that Americans mustn't feel too badly about the English doing Shakespeare better than we do because, after all, they'd had possession of Shakespeare for a long, long time. Then he added: "I'd hate to see an English Western."
>
> Well, if Sir Laurence had hung around long enough, he would have seen—not an English Western, exactly—but a sort of Shakespearean Western. It was a Western in blank verse, something I never thought I'd live to see. Actually the play... was almost Greek tragedy in its classic simplicity of line and predestined doom. It was one of those big gambles that only television seems prepared to make, something that could have been just awful and turned out to be almost perfect... it was all marvelously convincing and taut, the blank verse spilling out of the mouths of the barroom idlers as readily as if they spoke that way all their lives. There were genuinely fine performances by all the four principals... and a great job of direction by Robert Mulligan.

Alvin Sapinsley had realized he was taking a gamble with such an unorthodox hybrid of styles, so he was doubly grateful for the show's "resounding success" and the work of his "good friend":

> Boris was one of the... hardest working actors I was associated with during the days of live television, hard working in the sense that he rehearsed assiduously, studied his role and his lines unceasingly, made effort upon effort to sharpen, improve, and hone the part. During rehearsal breaks, while the others sat around the table drinking coffee, Boris would be off in a corner, working on his character...

> Boris was a wonderful person in addition to his quali-
> ties as an actor; gentle in his behavior, progressive in his
> outlook. He was also modest.

The Lark ran at the Longacre for 229 performances, closing on Saturday, June 2, 1956. Boris and Julie had developed a great rapport during the run of the play, but they had no contact off stage. Although she was an alumna of Yale and the Actors Studio, Harris never discussed acting technique or "the method" with the "just get out and do it" Boris, who had little faith in the value of drama schools. As Harris has explained, they both were accomplished performers, each from totally different training grounds: "You know, good actors, they don't really talk about technique. They appreciate each other, I think, and it doesn't matter *how* you get there, as long as you get there."

On the day of the final performance, Julie, ever the perfectionist, wrote the following note to Boris:

> Dearest Boris—I have never been so happy acting with
> someone as I have been with you—I love you and am
> grateful for the unspoken help and encouragement you
> have given me. I hope in my heart we will work together
> again and that the next time it will be a perfect experi-
> ence. I realize that this time there were disappointments
> but I know that you have made *The Lark* a beautiful and
> happy run for me.
> All my love. Julie

Harris believed Boris' uniqueness as an actor was an extension of his singular personality:

> *The Lark* was a very happy experience for me. Acting
> with Boris was a dream. He was so supportive and beau-
> tiful as Cauchon...
>   He would have been great in any play. He was just a
> great actor. He had an enormous warmth and humanity...
> and this fascinating darker quality. It was mysterious. You
> wanted to know where such a man came from. Well, of
> course, he had this great voice. It was a very compelling
> voice...
>   I *adored* Boris and Evie. He was a hero to me. A
> very loving, inspiring gentleman.

And Boris was no less enthusiastic about her, saying that he felt rewarded "just simply being in scenes with that girl, who is the most beautiful actress. A wonderful person to work with." In an interview with *Time*, he used a favorite artistic comparison to define her technique: "When Julie is at the height of her most emotional scene, she is always in complete control of herself, just as a fine pianist is always master of his music." Further commenting on her performance, he said, "That girl plays Joan with the hand of God."

The Lark simply was a triumph for all concerned. Boris not only interpreted a magnificent character and experienced one of the most satisfying working relationships of his career, he also encouraged and inspired a gifted young actress and earned the respect of Lillian Hellman, who, on June 11, wrote him a letter mentioning his "fine, honest work and... good friendship."

After closing at the Longacre, *The Lark* company went on a two-month hiatus before opening a touring version in Central City, Colorado, on August 4. Julie signed on for the tour, but Boris, Paul Roebling and Joseph Wiseman did not. In Central City on August 5, *The New York*

Daily News' John Chapman wrote, "Sam Jaffe now is the archbishop. His is a clear and intelligent portrayal, but it does not yet show the spiritual anguish which Boris Karloff bestowed on the role."

After closing in Central City on September 1, the company moved to San Francisco, where they opened four days later under the sponsorship of the American Theatre Society. Boris rejoined them for this three-week run, during which Sara Jane, now preparing to major in philosophy and political science at college, saw his acclaimed performance: "I can remember being picked up in a limousine several times during the time he was there." To keep himself mobile, he still walked as often as possible, and, on one particular morning, he ventured out into the streets of San Francisco, where he ran into future Hollywood writer Edmond Reynolds, then a university student who had seen *The Lark* after volunteering to usher during a performance:

> Yes, I met the formidable but charming Mr. Karloff... I am not an autograph hound but I do like to express appreciation when confronting a celebrity I admire. Mr. K. had sharp, penetrating eyes which belied his genteel countenance. He knew that I recognized him, so I felt I should acknowledge that I had recently seen his effective performance in *The Lark*. Since I am more of a theatre buff than a movie, I was brash enough to tell him that I wished he did more stage work, as I felt that his talent was barely touched in the movies. He, in turn, pointed out that in the U.S.A. there is not enough consistent stage work for the actor! I complimented him on his marvelous voice, its carrying power (he played Cauchon quietly and effectively) and the rich tonal qualities his voice possessed.
>
> Then he told me something I've never forgotten: "If you don't feel the vibrations in the diaphragm, and only in the head, you're not projecting correctly."

When *The Lark* closed in San Francisco at the end of September, the company once again said goodbye to Boris, heading to Los Angeles, where the play would run its course on December 15. Although a rewarding experience, it had been exhausting work for the 68-year-old actor. During the San Francisco performances, he had managed to sneak back to L.A. to play the vicar in H.F.M. Prescott's "Bury Me Later," broadcast on CBS's *Climax!* on September 6. Appearing opposite Boris was a 30-year-old actress who not only had earned an Academy Award nomination for her very first film performance, as Nancy the Maid in MGM's *Gaslight* (1944), but was an old acquaintance of his. Angela Lansbury remembered:

> I had the opportunity to work with Boris... It was a wonderful opportunity, of course, to re-awaken our kind of early friendship, when I was just a kid. I really was about 16 years old when I first met him...
>
> I had made my mark, my small mark, as it was, in *Gaslight* and [*The Picture of*] *Dorian Gray* and so on— and desperately trying to keep my professional boat afloat in the 1950s... He also, I think, at that time, was no longer playing Frankenstein, obviously—and parts... were not that many. So he was also doing television, and we landed in the same show together.
>
> It was a totally different world in those days—television was in its infancy, really. Except it was excellent in

its own way, because it was live, and I think there were some terrific productions done between *Climax!, Matinee Theatre, Playhouse 90*, all of those shows. Some of them were outstanding, and one got to play some *very* interesting characters, which you never would have done in movies. I mean, I'm sure he was cast many times in roles that he normally would never have had the opportunity to play in movies...

That was a wonderful experience... We felt we knew each other: He remembered me, and I remembered him from when we had first met. We were totally comfortable together. And being fellow Brits, shared a lot of the same kind of jokes and humor. And he was such a warm and friendly person.

And his Anglo-Indian background was always very interesting, I think. Most people don't realize that... That allowed for his color... He was always quite tanned.

Of Boris' achievements as an actor, Lansbury said:

I thought that he was far more of an actor than he ever got the opportunity to reveal. I think he was an extremely thoughtful and talented man, in many other areas. I don't know that he was a scholar, but he certainly... had an element of being a very rounded-out human being. And when you bring that kind of intelligence to your work, it helps enormously. And I think that's what he did.

I think... most great actors have to have that. They have to have, really, a rounded-out understanding of life, and so on. And he was no exception. As I say, I think he had depths that were probably never plumbed as an actor. But he could have been, probably, a great Shakespearean actor... He fell into the trap of being typecast in a role, but he was so good in that, that they wouldn't let him ever get away from it, obviously.

But... I think he would have been capable of all kinds of parts and roles. That's the tragedy of success: too much, too soon, you know. We all fall heir to that kind of problem at one time or another. I fell into it, you know, when I started playing people's mothers! I had a hell of a time getting away from that.

Quickly segueing from the sublime to the utterly ridiculous, Boris and Evie flew to Hawaii in November 1956 to shoot *Voodoo Island* for producer Howard W. Koch. Luckily, the beautiful locations and climate compensated for the film's plot, which cast Boris as a professional skeptic who, after investigating a voodoo-practicing tribe, admits that a supernatural realm might exist. As always, Boris and Evie enjoyed meeting the locals, posing for photographs with a Hawaiian family and taking long walks along the seashore. As she had done in Acapulco four years earlier, the beachcombing Evie collected driftwood, shells, stones and even sand to take back to New York.

Back on the mainland in late November, Boris made his first appearance on *The Red Skelton Show* at CBS. And for three straight weeks in December, he appeared on CBS's *The $64,000*

Voodoo Island **(1957). On location in Hawaii, Boris relaxes in the director's chair, November 1956.**

Question, correctly answering every query about one of his favorite literary genres: children's fairy tales. Reaching the highest plateau, he was asked if he wanted to try for the $64,000. Disappointing both the studio and home-viewing audiences, he refused, on advice from his lawyer that the income tax would reduce his winnings below the $32,000 he already had won.

Boris' stint on *The $64,000 Question* combined two of his favorite media, television and children's stories, both of which have been consistently attacked by would-be censors since the 1950s. After his appearance on the CBS show, he often refuted the claims that fairytale violence adversely affects children:

> I don't believe it for a moment. I think it's absolute non-
> sense. Children sort things out for themselves. They've
> got a perception which we know nothing about; and if we
> don't tamper with their minds, they take in the things that
> they want.
>
> It [television] is a tendency to be an alibi for the devo-
> lution of authority by parents. They want somebody else
> to be the policeman, not them—and I think that has a great
> deal to do with it.
>
> You should be able to say to your child, "Look, you
> look at television from five to six, or whatever it is, and
> *no more*." If you haven't got that amount of discipline in
> your home, it's too bad. It's your fault.

With Evie's technical assistance, Boris began recording a syndicated radio show, *Tales from the Reader's Digest*, during 1956. Broadcast on weekdays in three-minute installments, the series presented capsule summaries of articles featured in current or past editions of the popular magazine.

Boris and Sara Jane at the Chateau Marmont, Los Angeles, 1957.

But he began the New Year with more television work and, as 1957 wore on, matched every dramatic performance with a turn as a song and dance man on one of the musical variety shows. On January 9, he sang "You'd Be Surprised" on *The Lux Show Starring Rosemary Clooney*, but a month later, he re-teamed with "that girl," Julie Harris, for a 90-minute abridgment of *The Lark* that Lillian Hellman had prepared for director George Schaefer and *The Hallmark Hall of Fame* on NBC. Joining the cast was Boris' old friend Basil Rathbone as the Inquisitor, the role played by Joseph Wiseman in the Broadway production. Boris' fondness for television, particularly the medium's ability to give an actor "a much wider circulation," to "reach an enormous audience," was demonstrated by this critically acclaimed color broadcast, which reached 26 million viewers—125 times the number who saw it on Broadway.

In his *New York Herald Tribune* review of the TV version, John Crosby wrote:

> Miss Harris was surrounded by a very distinguished cast
> but, apart from Boris Karloff as a very sympathetic bishop
> torn between his humanity and his beliefs, I don't think

Arsenic and Old Lace (1957). Dr. Einstein (Raleigh C. Butterfield), Mortimer Brewster (Bill Trotman) and Jonathan Brewster (Boris) in Frank Brink's amateur production staged in Anchorage, Alaska.

any of them measured up to Miss Harris. As the Dauphin, Eli Wallach was much too full of little acting tricks and postures to be quite real. Basil Rathbone was a cold, implacable and altogether loathsome Inquisitor, but he didn't seem real either.

During the late winter of 1957, Boris received a letter from a Hollywood agent named Collins. Apparently, a community college in Anchorage, Alaska, was planning to stage *Arsenic and Old Lace*, hoping to raise enough money to build a theater. Asked if he was interested in starring in the production, he thought the request was an elaborate gag, but after several inquiries, realized that the college was making a serious gesture to hire him: "They were extraordinarily generous, and paid our expenses, our round-trip fare, from New York to Alaska and back, our expenses while we were up there, gave me a percentage—and off we went." Scheduling a one-day layover in Seattle, where Evie planned to visit her friends Elsa and Robert Coe, they booked a flight for Wednesday, March 13.

Boris enjoyed meeting the Coes, who were "grateful [to have] the privilege to know... truly a great man." Foul weather delayed their flight from Seattle, but they eventually left aboard Northwest Orient Airlines flight 583, with a scheduled landing at Anchorage International Airport at 1:15 p.m. on Saturday, March 16. Arriving safe and sound, Boris and Evie were greeted by city council members Frank Reed and I.M.C. Anderson, who acted for Mayor Anton Anderson and the Anchorage Community College Theatre Workshop. The first Hollywood or Broadway star ever to appear in an Alaskan production, Boris was deluged by the local press before he and Evie were driven away from the airport "like royalty."

Two hours later, Boris began rehearsing with English teacher-cum-director Frank Brink and members of "The Theatre Group," three of whom were acting for the first time. Hoping to build their own theater, the troupe currently used the stage at Anchorage's high school, which doubled as the community college during the evenings. The setting was familiar to Boris, as he had "sort of played high school auditoriums before": "We opened the door and stepped into the most magnificent, really modern theater that I have seen anywhere, practically. Seats two thousand people. An enormous, completely beautifully equipped stage... " Prior to Boris' arrival, the actors had rehearsed with his stand-in, Ernest Brown, and helped the technical crew construct the sets and collect props.

At 6:45 that evening, a chauffeur arrived at the Traveller's Inn to drive Boris and Evie to dinner at the home of General and Mrs. Frank A. Armstrong, Jr. Armstrong, whose World War II exploits are depicted in the 1949 film *Twelve O'Clock High* (via Gregory Peck's "General Frank Savage"), currently was in charge of all military operations in Alaska.

The following afternoon at 1:45, they were picked up by Mrs. Fannie Hoopes for a pleasant Sunday reception at the Loussac Public Library. Sponsored by the Theater Workshop, the Anchorage Little Theatre and the Anchorage Symphony, the fete was open to a public eager to meet the star whom the local papers had been touting for weeks. For two hours, Boris and Evie stood in a reception line to greet scores of locals as well as his amateur *Arsenic* colleagues. That evening, they retired to the home of Dr. and Mrs. George Hale for a cocktail buffet with 40 invited guests. Boris enjoyed discussing music with Mrs. Hale, who directed the 80-voice Anchorage Community Chorus, before the doctor whisked him to rehearsal at 7:30.

Boris and Evie were having a wonderful time, but Monday morning proved to be a unique thrill for them. At 9:45, local racing champion Dick Beaulieu, driving a team of nine dogs, took each of them on a half-hour adventure into the snow-covered countryside. Wrapping themselves in thick winter parkas, they held on tightly as Beaulieu maneuvered around drifts and over icy spots in the terrain. Hoping to see moose and polar bears, Evie was a bit disappointed when none reared their heads; but she loved the weather, and the fact that she was wearing a dress in the tundra did not bother her a bit.

That afternoon, Evie was even more excited when a new 1957 Packard was delivered to the hotel for their use until the following Sunday. Asking Boris to join her, she drove up and down Fourth and Fifth Avenues in Anchorage, "checking gift shops and purchasing postcards to send back home." Only three more evening rehearsals remained before *Arsenic* was to open on Thursday, March 21, for its three-night run. After the Monday night session, Boris, Evie, and some of the other cast and crew members congregated at Frank Brink's home for an impromptu party.

Imitating his Broadway schedule, Boris planned to sleep in each morning (or, as Evie referred to it, "keeping in shape for the active life") before appearing at luncheons, afternoon functions, radio and television interviews, and, finally, evening performances. Having one thing in common with Boris' previous wife, Evie liked to stay out late at social gatherings.

Tuesday, March 19, brought a luncheon of sourdough hotcakes at the home of Mr. and Mrs. Lloyd Hines, where six other couples joined them. Prior to the evening dress rehearsal, which was performed for military families unable to attend the upcoming performances, Boris was interviewed by local KTMI Radio at 6:30. When the cast and crew were assembled, Boris and Evie announced a decision they had made. Realizing that the company was truly in dire straits, Boris knew that accepting his salary would delay plans for the new theater:

> I thought, "How can I take that? I'm just a carpetbagger"... So... when we'd got to know each other a little bit, Evie and I sort of called the headsmen together and said, "Now look, this is what we'd like to do, because now we understand what this is for." And there was a terrific business. They wouldn't do it, and I said, "Well, then I don't go on"...

At 11:30 the next morning, Boris and Evie were driven by Mr. and Mrs. Robert Atwood to a nearby Army base at Ft. Richardson, where a luncheon was hosted by the commanding officer,

Evie and Boris try on parkas made by Alaskan National Guardsmen Pvt. George Allen (left) and Pvt. Herman Aishanna (right) at Fort Richardson, March 20, 1957.

Colonel Alexander N. Slocum, and his wife. Following lunch at the Officer's Club, they enjoyed another adventure into the ice, with Evie again supplementing her wool dress and pearls with a heavy parka and plastic tied around her shoes. At Camp Denali, they were given a tour of the post by Captain Lloyd Ahvakana of the 1st Scout Battalion, U.S. Army National Guard, who currently was engaged in an annual two-week training course. Under military escort, they then traveled on to a popular ski resort at Arctic Valley before returning to the hotel at 3:30. Prior to rehearsing, Boris was interviewed for 30 minutes by KTVA television.

That same day, an editorial, titled *"Arsenic* Provides Theatrical Highlight to Anchorage Story,"* appeared in the local *Daily News*. Throughout his acting career, Boris had blazed new trails, but now he was identified as a true pioneer and a factor in the development of a major city:

> When the curtain goes up on *Arsenic and Old Lace* to-
> morrow night [it] will mark the beginning of a new chap-
> ter of the theater in Anchorage and Alaska.

The vast scope of the play, the bringing to the territory of Boris Karloff and the sell-out of the huge high school auditorium all point toward the constant maturing process through which the city has been going for the last few years.

That evening, a final dress rehearsal was held, at which Boris continually conferred with Frank Brink on the most minute details of delivery and comic timing. *Anchorage Times* staff writer Dick Whittaker, who stayed for the entire post-10 p.m. session, reported the next morning:

> The problem worked on most last night was that of keeping action moving so swiftly as to stay ahead of the audience. The audience should have no trouble in being swept up into the spirit of the play if rehearsals are any indication. Even the cast, after almost two months of rehearsals, is still finding itself laughing at the amazing antics of some nine of the characters.

Having honored all scheduled public appearances, Boris was assured of event-free days from March 21-23, when he would be performing at 8:30 each evening. Thursday night's debut was sold out, but began late due to heavy traffic and parking problems created by patrons who did not foresee such a mob forming in their orderly town.

Minutes before the play began, Boris invited Brink to his dressing room. "Frank, would you have a small stool or ladder about 18 inches tall?" he asked.

Puzzled, Brink merely replied, "I'll get one" before walking to the janitor's closet, where he found a stool.

Thanking him, Boris placed it in the middle of the dressing room, immediately below a two-inch metal pipe that ran the length of the ceiling. Just as he stepped onto it, Boris solemnly announced, "I'm going to hang myself."

Brink was momentarily mortified before his star explained, "You needn't be alarmed. It's my arthritis. By hanging from that pipe, I can stop the irritation for a while!"

After Boris grabbed the pipe, Brink pulled out the stool and then replaced it when he had taken the pressure off his aching joints. Boris then let go, stepped down and headed for the stage.

Brink later recalled:

> I made a note in my diary reminding me of the many times Boris downplayed not only his personal physical problems, but problems created by the limited experience of some of the performers. The stool ritual went on each night of the show, and Boris insisted I tell no one. He did not wish the cast to be concerned about anything but the play itself.

Following the final curtain call, Brink ducked into Boris' dressing room to discuss the first performance. Elegantly attired, Evie, too, gave her opinion as the star relaxed in his comfortable tartan robe. Then Boris got dressed and joined the entire cast and 75 guests for an after-theater party at the Forest Park Country Club.

Not one to waste his free time relaxing, Boris agreed to more public appearances on Friday, March 22, when he and Evie became the honored guests of two local companies, the Federal Electric Corporation and Morrison-Knudsen, Inc. Picked up by Mrs. Frances Clark at 11:30

a.m., they were greeted at F.E.C. headquarters by the very enthusiastic "Li'l White Alice Gals," a group of female employees who "just couldn't wait" to meet Boris. The presidents of both companies were thrilled that he and Evie wanted to spend time talking with their workers. Patients and staff of the 5005th U.S.A.F. Hospital at Elmendorf Air Force Base also were thrilled that afternoon when the happy couple dropped by to cheer them up. Given a complete tour of the facilities, Boris chatted with surprised patients, including A-2c Charles R. Hendrickson, whose leg cast he autographed.

Following the sold out second-night performance, Boris and Evie attended another after-theater party, this time at the home of Anchorage Community College Director Dr. Leroy Good, who had invited the Theatre Workshop's executive board members. The final performance on Saturday night was capped off with numerous curtain calls, which Boris always took with the entire cast; however, this audience was so insistent that he literally was forced to do an additional solo bow—something that surprised Evie, who told Brink she was worried by his uncharacteristic response. In a brief speech, Boris told them how proud he was to appear with such a dedicated group "in a magnificent theater and a magnificent country." Brink later recounted:

> At that moment he poured out a rare and unusual response to an appreciative audience who saw in him something more than great skill and talent. He revealed a sense of humanity and generosity that evidently went beyond mere courtesy when he said, "This has been the most rewarding moment in my career."

The ensuing soiree, attended by the entire company, was hosted by Theatre Workshop president Don Gretzer. As a tribute to their star, most of the cast and crew members autographed Boris' personal copy of the play program. Kay Garvine, who portrayed Martha Brewster, wrote, "I shall surely never equal the thrill of all this!" But Frank Brink spoke for everyone involved in the production when he penned, "No words will ever be adequate enough to thank you." They also presented Boris and Evie with a carved mastodon tusk, a unique memento of their Alaskan adventure. Boris responded, "In the course of a long and simple life, I've never had a week like this. I love you all."

After the party, Boris took Brink aside. "I want to give you a gift, and I don't want it to be stupid or useless," he told him, "so I want you to tell what you would like."

Brink refused the gesture, telling Boris that it was unnecessary, that he "and Evie already had given us the greatest gift anyone could hope for—*themselves*."

Boris was adamant. "I shan't leave until you tell me," he insisted.

Mulling it over for a few seconds, Brink blurted out, "Your shoes! To have the shoes of the first great theater talent to walk on the Alaska stage would be the most wonderful gift I can think of. But, if you can't part with them, I will understand."

Unhesitatingly, Boris replied, "I can't think why you would want these old shoes, but if you want them, they're yours!"

Of the three performances, Boris later said:

> I've been in worse companies. There were some odd performances, but the play was so rich, they were so enthusiastic, and the audience was so keen—the place was sold out solid... And it turned into three of the most exciting... performances I've ever taken part in, because of the keenness of the company and the enthusiasm of the audience.

At 10 a.m. on Sunday, March 24, Boris and Evie boarded a Cessna 180 seaplane headed for Chinitna Bay on lower Cook Inlet, the location of the camp and operations of the Havenstrite

Drilling Co. Boris had purchased stock in his friend Russell E. Havenstrite's would-be oil company two decades earlier and now wanted to view the setup himself. Joined by Mr. and Mrs. A.B. Clark, Mr. and Mrs. Vincent J. Doran (of Morrison-Knudsen, Inc.) and pilots Ward Gay and Warren Wright, they were greeted at the site by John Havenstrite and camp supervisor Lee Brown. While aboard two Cessnas, the group circled Mt. Iliamna and Mt. Spurr, witnessing sporadic drilling activity and, much to Evie's delight, large herds of moose.

Prevented from exploratory drilling by restrictions imposed by the U.S. Department of the Interior, the Havenstrite operation had reopened in 1955. As a hopeful portent of things to come, Boris was presented with a quart of oil. Upon their return to Anchorage, he told a reporter, "I have been riding this horse since 1936, and I have always had complete confidence in it. The operations lay fallow for some time. But I am convinced that oil will come in. I was very impressed with the camp. It is comfortable and well organized."

Boris and Evie bade farewell to Alaska during the afternoon of Monday, March 25, but before the plane took off, told a reporter that they planned to return the following year. Boris, continuing to call the trip the "highlight of my life," was pleased to know that his percentage (about $1,500) would be added to the $6,000 profit the performances had netted, a good start toward raising the $40,000 that Brink estimated for his envisioned "intimate theater." Not only had Boris donated his percentage, but went an extra mile by offering to pay his agent's percentage out of his own pocket. Four days after they flew to Los Angeles, Don Gretzer wrote to Edd Russell, Boris' representative at Actors Equity:

> We would like you people to know of the great good which Mr. Karloff has done for the theatre movement here in Anchorage. The wonderful personalities of Mr. and Mrs. Karloff, their generosity, their understanding of people, and their wish to help us resulted not only in great admiration and respect for professional artists but heightened community respect for local players to a degree which we may have had to strive for over a period of a great many years.
>
> It is difficult to say exactly how we feel about Mr. Karloff and his gracious wife. Superlatives can never tell the story of their effect upon our community and upon the future of theatre here. Statistically, *Arsenic and Old Lace* drew the largest crowd ever to attend any performance of any kind of show in the history of the Territory. But statistics can never say as much about the Karloffs as the lump in our throats at their departure.

Back in Los Angeles, Boris honored several commitments. On April 25, 1957, he portrayed Montgomery Royle in "The Man Who Played God," a *Lux Video Theatre* adaptation of Jules Eckert Goodman's play *The Silent Voice*, which had been produced as a film starring his hero George Arliss in 1932. On the heels of this serious portrayal, he ventured back into Sinatra territory by singing "The September Song" on *The Kate Smith Special*, broadcast April 28 on ABC. Three weeks later, he again exercised his pipes, this time in humorous fashion, on "Mama Look a' Boo Boo" and the pop hit "Little Darlin'" for the May 17 broadcast of *The Dinah Shore Chevy Show*, one of the most critically acclaimed variety shows of the season. To play up Boris' macabre image, NBC altered the name of the sponsor to "Shiverolet" and released advance publicity claiming that he was shocked at the current "positively frightening" trend in popular music. While *The Hollywood Reporter* referred to him as "an inspiration" and "the surprise hit of the show," *Variety* called the entire broadcast "a thorough winner":

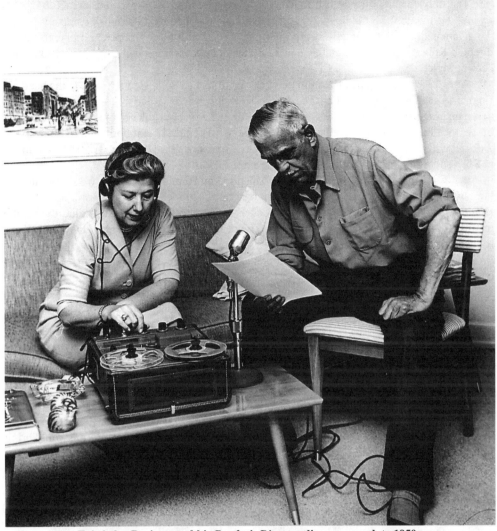

Evie helps Boris record his *Reader's Digest* radio program, late 1950s.

Betty Hutton, Boris Karloff and Art Carney came front and center for variegated chores, including tongue-in-cheeked rock 'n' roll, a hilarious calypso mockery and a load of finely wrought shenanigans. It was a crackerjack succession that made the hour pass swiftly—the acid test in 60-minute programs.

But it was television and radio columnist Bob Hull who made the most entertaining observation: "Boris turns out to be a real singer. He has aplomb and finesse in delivering the delightfully idiotic lines of the song, backgrounded by vampires Shore and Hutton in a Charles Addams-like cobwebby setting."

After dancing with Dinah, Boris exchanged the old soft shoe for an old bloody scalpel in his most rewarding film portrayal since the Val Lewton period. Although he had appeared in some prestigious films, particularly *The Secret Life of Walter Mitty*, since 1945, none of them had challenged or expanded his talents as a screen performer. While television and the stage offered him endless variety and artistic satisfaction, he simply had to return to the horror genre to play interesting roles on the big screen.

The only feature film he had made during the past four years was the dreadful *Voodoo Island*. Fortunately, his "comeback" horror vehicle, produced by the English company Anglo-Amalgamated, offered an intelligent script by Jan Read and John C. Cooper, and an enthusiastic director, Robert Day, whose technical and intellectual talents reminded Boris of Lewton's discerning style.

After 12 years in suspended animation, horror films had witnessed a rebirth at the hands of England's Hammer Films, when *The Curse of Frankenstein*, a garish color shocker loosely based on Mary Shelley's novel, was a huge box-office hit on both sides of the Atlantic. Directed by Terence Fisher, and starring Peter Cushing and Christopher Lee, it borrowed more from the 1931 Universal film than from Shelley's prose, but spawned *Dracula* (*Horror of Dracula* in the U.S.), a superior "sequel" featuring the same stars.

It was inevitable that a British company, inspired by Hammer's success, would call upon a famous native son who had specialized in horror roles. Immediately after Boris finished *The Dinah Shore Show* on Friday, May 17, he and Evie flew to New York. Intending to spend a restful holiday in France and England before work on "Stranglehold" began, they set sail the following day.

After reaching London, Boris' paramount concern was a reunion with Bernie Coleman and the Surrey Cricket Club. Coleman recalled:

> He and I developed a great friendship... Whenever these, what are called "test matches" between England and Australia, or England and India, or whoever—we would go to the test match at the Oval, and the test match at Lords. And we'd watch every bowler in a five day—bear that in mind—a *five-day* test match.

When visiting the test match held at Lords, Boris would arrive with a day's sustenance—a pint of his favorite bitter beer, and a bottle of tonic water for his pal—while Bernie would bring smoked salmon sandwiches and a veal and ham pie, "which [Boris] loved—it was a favorite of his."

During the lengthy matches, which sometimes failed to be fascinating, Coleman would lend an ear to Boris' true tales of Hollywood: "On occasion, I'd prompt him with a question about some of his colleagues in the film business, and away he'd go. And it was while we were watching the cricket—well, I'd listen to these marvelous stories."

Bernie's company, Coleman's Castle, now owned about a dozen pubs in south London. A World War II veteran who actually was born in a Bermondsey pub, he had worked his way up through sheer effort. As described by a London newspaper, he did indeed have several traits in common with his friend:

> He knows what he wants. He doesn't want to die the richest man in the cemetery, is bored to death by wealthy people who talk about money and, when things get on top of him, likes to slip away quietly to read.
>
> He's the perfect host, with a nod and a smile for everyone but if he knows someone is going to bore him he won't hang around until he falls asleep.
>
> His greatest love is cricket...

Bernie recently had purchased the Golden Lion, a pub he had transformed into "a vintage cider and wine lodge," located on the corner of Hawthorne Grove and Maple Road at Penge in southeast London: "I had one or two pubs at the time, and every time I took one, Boris would always come along to see the opening, and generally enjoy himself, and meet a few people."

For the opening of the new public house, however, Bernie asked Boris if he would do the honors. "Oh, I'd love to," he replied. "It's been one of my great ambitions."

Bernie said, "Well, let's negotiate a fee for this, because people get paid a lot of money to do this."

Boris paused only for a moment. "How about a pint of bitter beer?" he responded.

So, on the rainy evening of Tuesday, July 16, 1957, Boris, neglecting to wear a raincoat over his suit, stepped out of a car at the Golden Lion, where a crowd of wet fans waited to see him. Making his way through the throng, he ducked into the back door and thrilled Coleman's customers by appearing behind the bar.

Bernie recounted:

> When I had to pick him up to go to the opening, he was clutching a large brown paper bag with something in it, and, well, he wouldn't discuss what was in it. But when we got to the pub for the opening, there were a lot of people there, and he made a delightful little speech that his great ambition had been to open a pub.
>
> And then he said, "Now, I want you to stand in front of me." And then he suddenly... he said, "I now declare this pub open," and he hit me over the head with a specially made champagne bottle... Then he handed me one

Boris happily draws a glass of cider at Bernie Coleman's Golden Lion pub, located at Penge in southeast London, July 16, 1957.

and said, "Now you've got to hit me with this one, and we'll make it official."

The christening attended to, Boris ordered his pint of bitter before joining Evie to chat with both the invited guests and the young people who clamored for his autograph. After scrawling his moniker dozens of times, he told a reporter, "If they've got the patience to wait, I'm only too happy to sign for them."

Mucking in with the folks for most of the night, he drew glasses of cider for lucky patrons, enjoyed another pint of bitter and happily accepted a special gift from manager E. Peterson: a cigarette lighter decorated with the emblem of the Surrey Cricket Club. Several of the Surrey boys, including Alec Bedser and Jim Laker, took part in the festivities, joining Boris in autographing a wall in the "den" area of the lodge.

One of the local newspapers reported:

BORIS "LAUNCHES" NEW PUB
A 70-year-old former choir-boy, who decided years
ago that he would like to open a public house one day,
was given the chance of a lifetime at the Golden Lion,
Penge, on Tuesday. And he made a good job of it.
The former choir-boy is Boris Karloff, famed in
the film world as the monstrous "Frankenstein."

And the *Beckenham and Penge Advertiser* proclaimed: "No blood-curdling, horrific Boris Karloff was this. Just a nice, friendly chap it's a pleasure to meet anywhere."

His important work done for Coleman, Boris began shooting the tentatively titled "Strangle-hold" at the Walton studio in August. Drawing upon elements in Stevenson's *The Strange Case of Dr. Jekyll and Mr. Hyde*, he portrayed James Rankin, a social reformer in 1880 London, who decides to reopen a 20-year-old murder case. Theorizing that Edward Stiles, the "Haymarket Strangler," was executed because he could not afford a proper defense, Rankin sets out to discover the real killer, who, in the end, proves to be himself. Borrowing the message of *Bedlam* and inverting its casting, *The Grip of the Strangler* (*The Haunted Strangler* in the U.S.) presents a view of how past societies reacted to the mentally ill. Much to Boris' delight, Robert Day, following in Lewton's footsteps, chose to depict a strong, atmospheric portrait of Victorian attitudes toward poverty, mental illness and crime, while delivering several well-timed jolts to the audience. Without using heavy makeup or prosthetic appliances, Boris grotesquely twisted his face and contorted his limbs (à la John Barrymore in Paramount's 1920 *Dr. Jekyll and Mr. Hyde*) to create one of the most hellish, hideous creatures of his career, providing a stark contrast between the gentle, crusading Rankin and the homicidally maniacal "Dr. Tenant," a repressed identity that resurfaces each time he grasps the scalpel used in the original Haymarket murders.

While in London, Boris and Evie went to see an old friend, James Cagney, portray an even older friend, the late Lon Chaney, in Universal-International's semi-factual Cinemascope biopic *Man of a Thousand Faces* at the Odeon in Leicester Square. As guests of Douglas J. Granvill, U-I's British representative, they joined other stage and screen notables, including David McCallum and Jill Ireland, who had turned out to see Cagney's impersonation. The following day's publicity called Boris "himself a 'man of a thousand faces' whose macabre makeups have won him worldwide fame."

During the autumn of 1957, Boris and Evie flew back to California, where they rented an apartment at Hollywood's Chateau Marmont for the next seven months. Now in demand as much for his singing and comic acting as his ability to frighten and thrill, he again appeared live with Dinah Shore and on NBC with Rosemary Clooney, combining his horror and crooner personae for Clooney's Halloween show.

While at the Chateau, Boris was interviewed by a journalist who claimed to be preparing a press release about his upcoming television and film work in Los Angeles. Not knowing the true reason for the meeting, he went into great detail discussing his early years in England and Canada, his odd jobs and first film appearances in Southern California, *The Criminal Code*, *Franken-stein*, *Arsenic and Old Lace* and his other Broadway appearances. At his side throughout the interview, Evie interjected an occasional comment, but did not reveal that she knew why the journalist was really there. An entire year would pass before Boris discovered the truth.

Evie also demonstrated her control over Boris when learning that his daughter was planning to marry Richard Cotten, a 26-year-old Air Force pilot. Sara Jane revealed:

> The only time I can remember seeing my mother and fa-ther together [after their divorce] was when my father and Evie—they were in Los Angeles—flew up for a family conference, to try to dissuade me from getting married, and really, primarily because my husband-to-be was there also. Evie tried to dissuade me from having a wedding. She thought it would be better if they gave me $2,000, if we'd go off quietly and get married somewhere, and then we would have that money. But the real motivation for that was to keep my existence out of the newspapers.

Edgar Rowe persuaded Sara Jane to ask Boris to give her away at the wedding, scheduled for January 1958. But Boris declined, claiming that his presence at a large ceremony would cause a spectacle. "I rather snippily wrote back," Sara admitted, "that usually most eyes are on the bride, not on the bride's father":

> I was both disappointed and relieved that he wasn't, be-cause I really thought so much of my stepfather. It was certainly appropriate that my stepfather gave me away, and indeed my father would have created a spectacle amongst San Francisco society, because, to some, movie stars are movie stars. I think it was a very wise and prac-tical decision encouraged by Evie. And to what degree it was, I'm sure that she *absolutely* did not want him there, and *absolutely* did not want to be there herself, and *abso-lutely* did not want that sort of a tie between my father and myself. But, at the same time, no matter what her reasons were, it was the right thing—in the last analysis.

In November 1957 *Films and Filming* magazine published Boris' memoir "My Life as a Monster," in which he presents his views on filmmaking, including his belief that artists should create works that are governed by "taste and intelligence":

> I believe the British censor cut a scene from *Bride of Fran-kenstein* because of what he thought in his own mind were necrophile tendencies. I must say that I have never been in a scene that was objectionable to good taste. Some of my films have been stupid and silly, because they did not have good stories; but they have never been distasteful. I am opposed to censorship in any form. Censorship al-ways seems to me to be a mistrust of people's intelligence.

I believe that good taste takes care of license. It is also
worth remembering that one does not have to go and see a
film. Naturally, good taste plays a very important part in
the telling of a horror story on film. Some have taste,
others regrettably have not. As there are no rules laid down
to give an indication of good taste it is up to the film's
makers. You are walking a very narrow tightrope when
you make such a film. It is building the illusion of the
impossible and giving it the semblance of reality that is of
prime importance. The "horror" has to be done for the
sake of the story and not, as a few films have done, have a
story outline just for the sake of injecting as many shocks
as possible.

On December 16, 1957, Boris signed a three-picture deal with *Voodoo Island* duo Howard
W. Koch and Aubrey Schenck, although only one film, tentatively titled "Frankenstein 1975,"
had been written and slated for production. Less than a month later, on January 9, 1958, Boris
approved Allied Artists as the distributor, and Koch began directing the low-budget affair, re-
titled *Frankenstein 1970*, at Warner Bros., where he had rented still-standing sets from the Diana
Barrymore biopic *Too Much, Too Soon* starring Dorothy Malone and Errol Flynn.

Having vowed not to appear in another Frankenstein film, Boris relented because he now
was asked to portray, not the Monster, but its maker, in this case "Baron Victor von Frankenstein," grandson of the original scientist. Combining the old terror tale with modern elements
such as nuclear power and television—to raise money for a reactor, the baron allows an American company to film a show in his castle—*Frankenstein 1970* was a thoroughly forgettable
experience, merely providing Boris with another project (and $25,000) during his stay in Holly-
wood.

Two days after he had signed with Koch and Schenck, he entered into a contract with Hal
Roach Studios to host and appear in 25 episodes of "The Veil," a proposed television series. For
each half-hour installment, he was to be paid $2,000 plus an additional $1,000 as an advance
against syndicated re-runs, for a total of $75,000.

In early February, he and Evie enjoyed a pleasant, two-week holiday in France. Although
the trip did not involve a major film project, he could not resist an offer from Frank Sinatra, who
asked him to serve as "unofficial acting coach" during the location shooting of United Artists'
World War II drama *Kings Go Forth*, also starring Tony Curtis, Natalie Wood and the vibraphonic
jazz of the Red Norvo Quintet. Boris had become acquainted with Frank at Screen Actors Guild
meetings, but now he had the chance to contribute to one of "Old Blue Eyes'" best film performances, that of an infantry lieutenant who struggles with prejudice and racism before losing an
arm in combat. Frank evidently benefited from Boris' advice, as supported by the *Los Angeles
Examiner*'s Dorothy Manners: "The Thin Singer has never had a more difficult role and he has
never more completely mastered a characterization. Might as well admit it, he's a great actor."

Ironically, the screen's best bogeyman had told America's greatest popular vocalist, "You
must learn to act with your *voice* as well as your face." Forty years after the release of *Kings Go
Forth*, Frank's daughter Nancy wrote that Boris was "a profound influence on my father."

Back in the States, Boris, pleased with *The Grip of the Strangler*, signed to do a second film
for Robert Day, but prior to flying to London, appeared with Buster Keaton on *The Betty White
Show*, and narrated a color version of Washington Irving's "The Legend of Sleepy Hollow" on
Shirley Temple's Storybook. Portraying Irving himself, Boris was praised by *The New York
Times*' Jack Gould as the highlight of an uneven effort: "Karloff... was superb. His off-screen
narration enormously heightened the mood; indeed, his sensitive and understanding delivery at
times was more effective than the pictures on the screen."

The Doctor from Seven Dials (U.S. title: *Corridors of Blood*, 1958).   Boris as surgeon and medical researcher Thomas Bolton, with Francis Matthews (left) as his son, Jonathan.

Intending to spend the summer in England, Boris then began shooting *The Doctor from Seven Dials* at Elstree. Even more Lewtonesque than the previous Robert Day production, this stylish and atmospheric drama set in 1840 features him as Thomas Bolton, a physician who attempts to create a workable anesthetic to be used during surgical operations. Scorned by other members of the hospital committee, he returns to his clinic in Seven Dials, where he provides free medical treatment to the poor. Unfortunately, Bolton's charity work leads to his association with a local Burke and Hare, Black Ben (Francis de Wolff) and Resurrection Joe (Christopher Lee), who blackmail him into signing fabricated death certificates for people they have murdered in a seedy tavern. Combined with an addiction to the chemicals he has inhaled during his experiments, Bolton's relationship with the murderers results in his own death, but also in his son's successful demonstration of his anesthetic.

Boris noticed the thematic similarities between the two Robert Day films and the quartet of "mad scientist" films he had made at Columbia nearly 20 years earlier; but while shooting *The Doctor from Seven Dials*, he realized that the 36-year-old Day was truly the stylistic successor to Lewton. Rarely resorting to the blatant shock techniques of the Hammer horror films, Day created drama and terror by utilizing realistic performances and settings. Although Bolton is similar to Boris' earlier research scientists, he is developed to a much higher degree. Never exhibiting the "mad" behavior of the Columbia characters, Bolton does not actually commit any criminal acts, but is forced into a drug addiction and an alliance with murderers by the reactionary establishment that refuses to aid him in his humanitarian quest.

Portraying an iniquitous variation on Boris' John Gray in *The Body Snatcher*, Christopher Lee enjoyed his work on *Seven Dials*:

Boris was a very charming and delightful person... It was a wonderful experience for me, because it was the first time I ever really sat and talked to him and worked with him. We did indeed forge a great friendship. The sheer professionalism, the courage, the immense humor and the kindness of the man—everybody adored him.

During their behind the scenes discussions, Boris primarily talked about cricket and very little about his past work. Lee considered him "a brilliant, versatile actor" unaffected by typecasting. And although Boris must have known about *The Curse of Frankenstein*, Lee believed that professional courtesy prevented him from mentioning his colleague's interpretation of the "creature." Boris' self-deprecating admission to Lee that "All I'm fit for is to sweep up the lawns at night when the set is deserted and the players have all gone home" prompted the crew to give him a broom at the wrap party.

During production of *Seven Dials* (titled *Corridors of Blood* in the United States), Boris invited a 17-year-old fan named Stephen Sutherland to the set. An aspiring actor, Sutherland considered Boris his "theatrical godfather":

Whilst they were setting up the lights for the umpteenth time, I wandered over to another studio to watch the shooting there—and got into conversation with one of the studio electricians, a little man, nobody important or grand, but who by his very insignificance was the most important man of all. He was the man in the street, the man in the pub, the man who ultimately knows and makes a star— for he is the man who pays his money to go and see the movies and the people he likes.

He asked me what I was doing there, and on telling him that Boris had invited me down, he said... "Ah, Boris Karloff, now there's a *real* star—a real gentleman. He's the only one I know who has a kind word for everyone. Always stops to make a special point of talking to us blokes, and finding out our problems with lighting, etc. And always thanks us afterwards. Not only that, he knows us all by name and asks after our families. The missus loves that man, and so do we all. We wouldn't miss one of *his* films!"...

When I returned to the studio where Boris was filming, the scene had been going badly for Boris and he could not seem to get the hang of it, when the director... a man at least 40 years younger and less experienced than Boris, drew him aside and whispered something to him, whereafter the whole scene went all right...

Later Boris came to where I was sitting and said, "You might be interested to know what the director said to me. He said, 'Boris, don't *act* the scene, just *think* it.' And, do you know, he was right. It worked wonders!"

What could I possibly say to Boris as I sat there, a 17-year-old stage-door Johnny, when the great Boris Karloff tells you something like that! It was a humbling and unforgettable experience, and speaks worlds of his innate humility...

After another pleasant summer in England, the Karloffs returned to New York, but by the early autumn were back at the Chateau Marmont in Los Angeles. Boris looked forward to more live television work, particularly CBS's *Playhouse 90* on November 6. After enjoying and studying Joseph Conrad's works for much of his life, he now was given the opportunity to interpret one of the master's most important characters, Captain Kurtz, in the 1899 masterpiece *Heart of Darkness*. Costar Roddy McDowall remembered:

> I'll never forget him, because he was arthritic... and he would sit there for hours, and he would never, ever complain. He was in great pain. And I just loved him, because he was such a gentleman. He was just an impeccable man. I admired him immensely... because of his manner, because of his decency. Soft spoken, and he was very beautiful. He had a wonderful coloring, marvelous features... He had a marvelous head. He was a very, very fine looking man—and part of it, of course, was this gentleness. I liked him very much.
>
> He was underrated as an actor... because his fame was so enormous. And he took everything with such patience... There wasn't ever anything that I ever saw that Boris did that wasn't absolutely from the manor born. He was such an elegant man. And I will never forget that one image of him, just sitting hour after hour... in this cold studio, and in pain—he never, ever mentioned anything about it.

One of the aspects of Kurtz that Boris patiently tried to tolerate was a wig and beard that had been designed for him. Sitting in front of his dressing room mirror, he tried to find his features beneath all the hair, finally exclaiming that it made him look like Moses. Although the appliance had been created at great expense, director Ron Winston granted Boris' wish that it be relegated to the costumer's shelf.

Boris' performance in "Heart of Darkness" was not his only literary interpretation of the year, however. During 1958 he began a long-term relationship with Caedmon Records, the nation's foremost producer of spoken-word recordings, resulting in several albums of works by his favorite writers, including Kenneth Grahame, Rudyard Kipling, Lewis Carroll, Robert Browning and Hans Christian Andersen.

Exactly one week after giving his all as Captain Kurtz, Boris looked forward to an evening of relaxation and good company with Evie and their friends Ralph and Barbara Edwards. Ralph was still hosting *This Is Your Life*, and he offered a ringside seat to Boris if he cared to watch a broadcast of the show following dinner, with a promise of music and martinis afterwards.

Boris was not feeling "full marks," as he often said, but agreed to join them for a pleasant evening. On the afternoon of November 13, with only an hour or so before their scheduled rendezvous with Ralph and Barbara, and their mutual friends Milburn and Jane Stone, Boris began to feel even worse. Evie later recalled, "Boris was not well at all. He had a throat infection... but not sick enough to stay in bed... And he thought we were going to watch the show, and then we were all going out to supper afterwards."

A short time later, Boris and Evie, Mil and Jane Stone and Barbara Edwards were sitting comfortably in a corner, to the left of an NBC soundstage, ready to witness Ralph's embarrassing reminiscences of some star who had been suckered into the television studio.

"Let's turn the lights on, over there by the double door," Ralph's voice commanded as the show began. "And watch carefully to see what happens. Our honored guest, whom we're about to surprise tonight is known to all of you as one of the truly great and beloved stars of the theater, motion pictures, radio and television. Pan the camera, quickly please. He's not coming through those doors, because he's seated right there, innocently watching our producer's monitor."

And then Ralph put in a pregnant pause as his unsuspecting guest wondered who the victim would be.

"Tonight—This is your life—Boris Karloff," were the words that emanated from Edwards' mouth.

The audience applauded, but the guest, to say the least, was confounded.

Evie later said:

> So he was sitting at the back of the auditorium, and when Ralph said, "Boris Karloff, this is your life," Boris thought he was being introduced to the audience, and took a bow. And of course, the look of horror on his face when he found that he was the subject—and I think the look of hatred that he gave me before he stepped on the platform— was something.

Why the "look of hatred" toward his wife? It was Boris' incessant desire for privacy, as Evie explained:

> It was really very, very unfortunate, because... I knew [Ralph Edwards] before I knew my husband. And we saw a great deal of each other. And Boris said to me one day, "Now promise me you'll never let me go on *This Is Your Life*." And I said... "Yes." Well... Ralph said that he'd had some conversation at one time with Boris where he felt he would be quite happy to go on. So I agreed, I think wrongly. Boris always said I'd sold him down the river for a gas cooker... It was a very difficult time trying to keep it secret... at the Chateau Marmont... So I would have to go down in the lobby to take telephone calls...

When Boris finally realized that the show was really about *his* life, he put his hand to his mouth and walked forward a few steps.

"Okay, Boris," Edwards said cautiously. "All right, pal? Come here," he added, as if he were coaxing a family pet. "Boris, I think we really put the... "

Not yet certain of the circumstances, Boris let forth a forceful "Oh, my," again putting his trembling right hand to his mouth.

"This, believe me, is the greatest shocker, I think, of all time. He has been giving shocks all his life," Edwards continued, mentioning Jane and Mil Stone, trying to make Boris as comfortable as possible.

"And how many years have I been trusting you?" Boris asked facetiously, getting a huge laugh from the audience.

Introducing his nostalgic survey of Boris' life, Edwards described his friend, "the bogeyman," as "one of the kindest, most warm-hearted men among us, into whose arms little children run almost instinctively." Escorted to a sofa on the stage, Boris tried to mask his discomfort but literally could not sit still, wondering what skeletons would be dragged out of his closet. Worse yet, he was made even more uncomfortable by all the praise he received from Edwards and his guests. Typically, he used self-deprecation to ease the embarrassment. When a voice he had not heard since 1907 announced from backstage that "the young Bill Pratt was not a very distinguished scholar at Uppingham," and Edwards added, "I'll bet you haven't the slightest notion who that is," Boris laughingly replied, "So many people could have said that!"

This is Your Life (November 13, 1958). Boris is moved by the appearance of his good friend Frank Brink.

But before Edwards could fully identify the speaker, Boris recognized Geoffrey Taylor, whose entrance onto the stage left him speechless for a few moments. After reminiscing about cricket and his poor academic performance, he began to enjoy the show, but his illness was betrayed by a persistent cough.

Although he remembered his schoolmate, Boris was understandably confounded by the appearance of J. Warren Bacon from Minot, North Dakota, who jogged his memory with a photo of an old rooming house and talk of Magnussen's drug store. And stranger still was a gift of doorknobs from Jim Edwards, who had shared his dressing room at San Francisco's Majestic in 1919. When this actor-turned-salesman described his former colleague's attempts to "perfect the art of changing his appearance," Boris interjected, "Anything to cover myself up, in other words!"

As the director cut to a photograph from *Frankenstein*, another voice could be heard from backstage. Boris grinned and let forth a joyful laugh. "Hello, Jack!"

And when Jack Pierce came out to shake hands, Boris called him "the best makeup man in the business," admitting, "I owe him a lot." Like the others, Pierce brought a little memento for Boris, remarkably handing him two of the neck electrodes he had worn in one of the Frankenstein films.

The next guests, interestingly, were Howard Lindsay and Russel Crouse, who joined the show via a link from New York. Regardless of the disappointment he felt for their not allowing him to appear in the *Arsenic and Old Lace* film, Boris genuinely appreciated their kind words, again blushing over what he considered exaggerated praise.

"Jolly good to see you, Frank!" Boris beamed as he shook hands with his good friend from Anchorage, Frank Brink, who then proceeded with a reminiscence that *really* made him uncomfortable: "And from the very beginning, Boris became part of the group. Not a star, mind you, Ralph—but just one of us. And when he found out that we were trying to raise the funds... "

219

This is Your Life. **Ralph Edwards reunites Boris and Sara Jane as Frank Brink, Evie, J. Warren Bacon and Jim Laker look on.**

"Enough, enough, enough," Boris interrupted, motioning for him to stop.

"I'm going to tell it!" Brink stated forcefully. "Because it needs to be told." Informing Edwards and the audience of Boris' magnanimous donation for the Anchorage theater fund, Brink raised a great round of applause. Still grumbling under his breath and coughing lightly, Boris was ready to move on.

The well-timed appearance of champion bowler Jim Laker of the Surrey County Cricket Club brought out another childlike grin on Boris' face. Pleased to accept a ball signed by all "the Surrey boys," he then was joined by Evie, whom Edwards described as "the wonderful gal who's always at your side, who guides and counsels you in your career." As she sat down beside Boris, Edwards added, "Oh, what a time poor Evie's been going through!"

Cynthia Lindsay claimed that Boris actually "was furious. He was so angry that he didn't speak to her"—a comment that supports Evie's own interpretation of his "look of hatred." But Evie's manipulation of events did not end with tricking him into appearing on the show.

Edwards' usual policy was to allow the guest of honor's family members to join him on stage at the beginning of the show. But on this particular occasion, Sara Jane was not introduced until the very end, almost as an afterthought. Wrapping up the broadcast, Edwards mentioned Boris' upcoming birthday and asked him if anyone else's nativity fell on the same date.

"I believe so. Yes," Boris replied.

But Edwards was the one who actually mentioned "your daughter, Sara Jane": "Well, here she is, from Sausalito, California, where she's attending Munson Business School. From San Francisco, your daughter by a previous marriage, Sara Jane!"

As she joined her father on the sofa, Edwards inquired if they, whenever possible, celebrated their birthdays together.

"Yes," Sara Jane replied, "but not this year, because Dad and Evie will be on their way to New York." [1]

Edwards then emphasized that their meeting on the show was a birthday celebration and gave her a complimentary piece of jewelry as a brief flourish of "Happy Birthday" filled the soundtrack.

At the time, Sara Jane was confused by the way her part in the show was presented; but viewing it in retrospect, she saw the visible tension between daughter and stepmother as a product of Evie's possessiveness of Boris. During this period, she still visited them at the Chateau Marmont whenever they were in Hollywood, but she never had been invited to their apartment at the Dakota. Of her *This Is Your Life* experience, she recalled:

> My participation in it was minimal. I flew down from San Francisco and arrived the day of the show, and I think everybody else was there. I can remember, probably the most clearly, the cricket player, Jim Laker, and he is the person I visited with the most. I didn't get there much in advance of the show. And then I was given my one line, and we all waited backstage.
>
> I'm sure they had a tough job making up the program that night, and keeping a safe distance between those things my father didn't want discussed... Ralph really did a marvelous job pulling together some safe but special people in my father's life...
>
> After the show, in those days, it was shown later. It was done by live Kinescope. So, after the show was shot and shown live back East, there was a dinner party... We all went to that and then saw the show...

Boris rarely went to parties that were not work-related. Cynthia Lindsay claimed, "He wouldn't be around at a cocktail party, standing and chatting with people. People would come to him, but he never went up to anybody. He was very shy and very quiet. But with his friends, he was completely outgoing and very funny. But he had to know you."

During the party at the Hollywood Roosevelt Hotel, his shyness was magnified by the cough that had dogged him all evening. And although he was genuinely excited to see his long-lost friends, he began to feel increasingly worse. As the affair began to break up, Evie phoned a doctor and he was taken to the hospital. The malady she believed to be a throat infection was diagnosed as emphysema, brought on by decades of heavy smoking. Advised to abstain from cigarettes entirely, he asked for permission to smoke a pipe. Evie said, "He just gave up whatever he was told to and got on with it. But I wish he'd given it up many, many years earlier." The next day, Sara Jane visited him at the hospital, and then "was whisked away back to San Francisco."

---

[1] In fact, Sara Jane and Boris had not spent their birthday together since the 1946 divorce.

Chapter 10

Home

"I live in London. And in aeroplanes."

Nineteen fifty-nine was a year of major events for the Karloffs. After a 50-year absence from residing in his native land, Boris finally decided to forego the yearly summer trips and reclaim Britain as his full-time home. But before leaving the country that had provided him with so much work and success, he and Evie began the New Year by touring a few more of its sites, including some in California they had never visited.

On January 8, they delighted tourists at Marineland of the Pacific, particularly when animal lover Boris descended a platform to "shake hands" with Bubbles the Whale. And he earned the title of "Porpoise Jumpmaster" after participating in a feeding game, "successfully [making] the porpoises jump their entire length out of the water."

Boris also worked in one television show before flying to London, costarring with Edgar Buchanan and Jackie Coogan in "Indian Giver" on the April 27 broadcast of CBS's *General Electric Theatre*. It was the last small-screen performance he would give that year. Hal Roach Studios was to have completed all 25 episodes of "The Veil" by April 17, but instead, with only 10 in the can, declared bankruptcy. A far cry from the $75,000 he was supposed to have earned for the show, he only netted $12,500 for the episodes director Herbert L. Strock had completed. Having planned to appear in an additional 15 installments, he was not pleased when the series was left unsold and his additional "guaranteed" $62,500 vanished into thin air.

By May, all preparations had been made, and on the 21st of the month, he and Evie moved into a flat on the top floor of a Victorian House at 43 Cadogan Square, located in London's Knightsbridge district. Four days later, after settling in, he mentioned the "Veil" situation when writing to the Screen Actors Guild about another television program:

> I confess my heart quickened a bit when I found the enclosed among a lot of old letters in Putney, but then my damned conscience smote me and here it is.
>
> Last November some time, I think it was, MCA called me to find out if I had received the check for the rerun of the "Vestris." Of course for obvious reasons I hadn't, so after a long delay, a second check to cover it was issued and duly cashed some time in April. So most reluctantly I have to return this one. Maybe it will help Hal Roach, Jr., to pay off a bit of the sixty-odd thousand he owes me on "The Veil."

Since the early 1930s, when he had experienced problems with Universal and then helped to found the Guild, Boris had signed several contracts that subsequently were not honored by their producers. And, particularly after his marriage to Evie—an astute businesswoman and avid tax minimizer—he progressively grew less fond of those who reneged on mutual agreements.

Boris had lived in the United States for 45 years without ever applying for American citizenship. However, he had paid plenty of federal taxes and Social Security, under the number 562-18-9758. Of his decision to return to Albion's shores, he said:

I think everybody comes back to their roots eventually. You want to come home, and I was always homesick, but... for years, it just wasn't indicated. The early years, I had to struggle so hard just to keep going, and when things did begin to happen, I was sort of laying the foundation, as it were, and was frightfully occupied with work. And then... it was not until the '50s when I moved to New York, and I realized that you can be home in just a few hours, which we did, and thank heavens, here I am.

Enjoying a respite from the toils of film, television and radio, he wasted no time in getting to the Oval to watch cricket matches with Bernie Coleman. And at home he had an opportunity to rejuvenate his interest in horticulture. While carefully searching for a residence, he and Evie had "sort of made that a condition... to find a flat on the top floor with a roof garden that you could walk out on to."

Having proved so successful in his christening of the Golden Lion pub two years earlier, Boris accepted Coleman's offer to join Alec Bedser and fellow cricketers Tony Lock, Ken Barrington and Mickey Stewart at the grand opening of the Grove Public House in Balham. Featuring a photograph of the handsome quintet in its October 16 issue, *The News* identified the four athletes and then asked:

On May 21, 1959, Boris and Evie moved into a flat on the top floor of this Victorian House at Cadogan Square, located in London's Knightsbridge district. (1996 photograph by Sara Jane Karloff.)

[B]ut what about the distinguished bespectacled gentleman on the left?

Well, you might find it hard to believe, but he is none other than the film horror man himself, Boris Karloff, who really much prefers watching a game of cricket than sending chills up your spine.

Although he had not accepted any work all summer, Boris' first few months back in England—filled with cricket, gardening, reading, visits from friends and evenings at the theater with Evie—had literally flown by. But he did not abandon thoughts of working, and, on October 15, 1959, wrote a letter to SAG Executive Secretary John L. Dales, referring to Howard Koch and Aubrey Schenck's reluctance to fulfill the three-picture contract he had signed on December 16, 1957, prior to filming *Frankenstein 1970*:

As you may remember I have a contract with Koch and Schenck under the terms of which there are two pictures

Sara Jane, Boris and his second grandson, David Cotten, Chateau Marmont, Los Angeles, 1961.

remaining... and it is obvious to me and to MCA that they have no intention of making the remaining two films. The situation seems to have "stabilized itself" as follows: Every time I do a job they request and receive an extension. Obviously the time will come when the sooty fingers will snatch me away during an extension period and my rejoicing widow will be left high and dry so far as the contract is concerned.

Frustrated by Koch and Schenck's method of waiting for him to accept an offer from another company and then asking him to sign a contract extension for their nebulous "two more films," Boris asked Charles Belden of MCA to force the producers either to shoot them before July 1960 or pay him a cash settlement. At this point, neither option appealed to Boris: "I am inclined to gather that [Belden's] view is that Koch would only offer a very token sum at best and that only to protect his reputation." Although Boris was no longer an active member of the Guild board, he still lived by its principles, and considered untrustworthy independent producers little better than the greedy studio moguls of the 1930s.

With the onset of winter, Boris had the choice of attending rugby matches or flying back to warmer California for "a sort of television thing." Again using the Chateau Marmont as his base of operations, he costarred with Judith Anderson and Sam Jaffe in "To the Sound of Trumpets" on the February 9, 1960, episode of CBS's *Playhouse 90*. Depicting the World War I angst and obligatory love affair (with a nurse) of a British captain fed up at Flanders, the drama was praised by Cecil Smith of *The Los Angeles Times*: "In a series of brief yet marvelous vignettes, Dame Judith Anderson, Boris Karloff and Sam Jaffe etched three unforgettable portraits—proving again that where acting is concerned they wrote the book."

224

Boris went from the sound of trumpets to the clash of steel when he portrayed a thunderous Billy Bones in a *Du Pont Show of the Month* broadcast of "Treasure Island" on March 5. Written by Michael Dyne, this 90-minute abridgment of Robert Louis Stevenson's legendary novel was produced by David Susskind. Boris played the flamboyant role for all it was worth, drinking rum and singing to the patrons of the Admiral Benbow Inn, where the old pirate captain meets his untimely end. The show marked his fourth appearance in an adaptation of a Stevenson story.

Three days later, he acted as host of a one-hour pilot film, *Thriller*, for which Hubbell Robinson paid him $2,500 plus the offer of a series contract, should it be sold by December 3, 1960. Including above-the-title billing, $2,500 per show, an additional fee for any episode in which he also acted, a yearly salary increase of $250, and two first-class air fares from London to Los Angeles four times a year, the contract was particularly attractive. Boris also hosted NBC's musical variety show *Hollywood Sings* on April 3 before flying back to London for another season of growing flowers and eating meat pies at the Oval with Bernie Coleman. But he and Evie continued to record the syndicated *Reader's Digest* show, which Coleman remembered as one of Boris' steady sources of income: "He'd say, 'Another one of the pension checks has arrived this morning'."

Describing upcoming projects to Coleman, Boris would mention his next scheduled destination and departure date: "I'm just going off... to do this film they've offered me."

"What do you want to go all that way for?" Bernie would ask. "You don't need to."

"Well, when they offer you work, you can't refuse it," Boris would explain. "No actors *ever* refuse work."

Following suit, Boris was back at the Chateau Marmont in the early summer, ready to work on the *Thriller* series, which had been picked up by NBC. On July 18, while reading a *Screen Actor* article by John Dales on the founding of the Guild, he was pleased to see his name acknowledged in a list of founders but "saddened" by the exclusion of his old friend Ralph Morgan, who had passed away in 1956: "He, more than anyone else, was responsible for the founding... in 1933... I think he deserves to be remembered and numbered among the greats." Three days later, Dales replied, "How right you are," explaining that he had dashed off his comments in about 15 minutes.

Thriller debuted on September 13, 1960, with "The Twisted Image" starring Leslie Nielsen, Natalie Trundy and George Grizzard. Arthur Hiller directed the first two episodes, but after six had been broadcast, NBC, fearing that the show did not offer enough variety, threatened to cancel it. At that point, Lew Wasserman, the CEO of MCA, replaced producer Fletcher Markle with William Frye, convincing the network to give *Thriller* a second chance.

On a Sunday afternoon in December 1960 Frye invited Boris, Evie and the new production team to a cocktail party at his home in Coldwater Canyon. Frye's assistant Douglas Benton recalled, "I was amazed at how much energy Mr. Karloff had... and he was very happy that Bill had been put on the show and we already had begun to work out a new format. He was very enthusiastic about this... he took a great interest in all the stories." During the first week of production with the new crew, Evie invited Benton to lunch with them at Serrentino's, a seafood restaurant in Toluca Lake, an event he remembered as a tutorial from two fish experts:

> Mrs. Karloff... swore that California sandabs, which are little flounders... were the best fish she and Boris had ever tasted. He was equally enthusiastic, and we sat there on a Friday afternoon—Boris didn't have to work that afternoon—and polished off two orders of sandabs each. Mrs. Karloff said that was the first thing they did when they got in town. That, I guess, was [Boris'] favorite food.

I can tell you what his favorite drink was. He made the most potent martini, he was a prodigious drinker, although no matter how many of those lethal potations he tossed down, he never showed any reaction to it. Several occasions I've gotten flat-out roaring drunk sitting there watching him matching me drink for drink and never even getting a glow. He was amazing.

During the succeeding weeks, other Hollywood notables, including Mitchell Leisen, John Brahm, Hershel Daugherty, Ray Milland and Paul Henreid, directed episodes of *Thriller*. Allowed to film introductions for several stories during a single shoot at Revue Studios, Boris worked on the program for two seasons, appearing in a total of 69 episodes. Each prologue gave him a chance to play off his familiar horror image and display the narrative skill he had developed on numerous radio shows and recordings. He also acted in five episodes: "The Prediction" (November 22, 1960); "The Premature Burial," inspired by the Poe story (October 2, 1961); "The Last of the Sommervilles," directed by Ida Lupino (November 6, 1961); "Dialogues with Death," in which he played two roles (December 4, 1961); and "The Incredible Dr. Markesan" (February 26, 1962). Ironically, while filming "Dr. Markesan," one of the most truly spine-chilling productions of television's golden age, he was directed by Robert Florey, 30 years after the Frenchman lost *Frankenstein* to James Whale.

Douglas Benton remembered John Brahm's shooting of "The Prediction" on the Universal back lot as including a particularly uncomfortable situation for Boris:

> Brahm... was directing Mr. Karloff, and the scene was for him to be killed, and he fell in the gutter and this great wash of dirty water swept over him. As a matter of fact, it swept through him.
>
> He was lying on an incline with his head down and the water ran up his pants leg through his clothes and came out his collar. So Mr. Brahm, who was a man of 70, instructed Mr. Karloff where he wanted him to fall and then said, "Then we'll put in the double and run the water."
>
> And Boris looked at John, offended, and said, "Oh, *no*. I wouldn't allow anybody else to do that. That water was meant for *me*." And, by golly, he laid down and they made three takes, and every time he was drenched.
>
> I think that was the time I said, "Jesus, Boris, you're at a time in your life and on a plateau in this business that you don't have to do that sort of thing."
>
> "Have to?" he said. "I *want* to." And then he went into his speech about how marvelous it was to make a good living doing what you enjoyed so much.

And during the making of "The Last of the Sommervilles," Benton also witnessed the rapport between Boris and Ida Lupino: "She was a great favorite of Boris', as both used to tell slightly off-color English stories with a great deal of relish. He had a marvelous laugh. He really would laugh when he was amused, and she is one of the best storytellers I ever heard in my life."

While making *Thriller*, which spawned a popular comic book bearing his image, Boris was asked to play Gramps in a revival tour of *On Borrowed Time*, including performances at a theater in San Juan, Puerto Rico, during January 1961. Since the tour also involved dates in Monterey, California, he asked Hubbell Robinson to move forward the next *Thriller* shoot so he could complete the "fourth employment period" of the first season.

In Monterey on Saturday, March 11, he and Evie were the guests of honor at a midnight party held in the Country Club home of Mrs. Hugh Dormody. Intended to honor Boris' first stage performance at Monterey's Wharf Theater and Opera House that evening, the "gala" was one of the Peninsula's greatest social events of the season. Two days later, they joined Jean Arthur for dinner at her home on Carmel Point. Giving eight performances in *On Borrowed Time*, he then filmed scenes for several *Thriller* episodes at Revue Studios on March 28 before flying back to England.

While in Hollywood for a subsequent *Thriller* shoot later that year, Boris was the guest of honor at another cocktail party thrown by William Frye. Although he was not overly fond of such soirees, the fact that Frye's home was in Coldwater Canyon appealed to him, as did the chance to sit on the sidelines and chat with writer Robert Bloch, who had written *Psycho* before turning his suspenseful pen to eight episodes of *Thriller*. Engaged in a discussion about the nature of horror in the arts, Boris told Bloch:

> Think about it for a moment. There's nothing pleasant, nothing appealing, about the word "horror." It doesn't promise entertainment.
>
> You and I, each in our own way, have devoted a career to providing chills, shocks, shudders. But we've done so only to amuse—to fulfill the same function as the time-honored teller of ghost stories who offers a few cold shivers to his audience in front of a warm fireplace on a winter's evening. No harm in that, surely. But I'll be blasted if either of us ever deliberately set out to horrify anyone. All this violence and brutality today, shown against a "realistic" background—now that's downright horrible!

When Bloch asked him about his favorite characters, he replied, "The happiest role of my life was Jonathan Brewster... the man who looked like that fiend, Boris Karloff." Appropriately, his next performance was as Jonathan for a *Hallmark Hall of Fame* broadcast of "Arsenic and Old Lace" that reunited him with director George Schaefer on February 5, 1962. Afforded a 90-minute time slot by NBC, this color video version, less abridged than the 1955 *Best of Broadway* production, featured another excellent cast, including Dorothy Stickney, Mildred Natwick and Tom Bosley. In the top-billed role of Mortimer Brewster, Tony Randall appreciated the opportunity to work with Boris: "He was humorous, kind, very intelligent, friendly... He was a joy to work with and a good man." One week later, on February 12, Randall joined Boris on Mike Wallace's syndicated talk show *PM*. Turning this installment of the program into a real Karloff bonanza, Wallace also welcomed George Schaefer, Maurice Evans and Julie Harris. Prior to returning for the mandatory summer in England, he played Sir Simon Flaquer in a March 11 telecast of Robert Hitchens' "The Paradine Case" on NBC's *Theatre '62*.

Meanwhile, *Thriller* was in trouble. Pressured by Alfred Hitchcock, who saw the show as serious competition for his own anthology program, Lew Wasserman canceled it at the end of April 1962. Undaunted, Boris immediately moved on to host another series, *Out of This World*, a BBC production that lasted only a half season on British and Canadian television. Boris' first major brush with science fiction since *The Invisible Ray*, this one-hour program featured adaptations of stories by John Wyndham, Isaac Asimov and Philip K. Dick.

He also made more spoken-word recordings for Caedmon during 1962. Continuing his association with Kipling, he cut another disc of *Just So Stories*, including "The Cat that Walked By Herself," "The Butterfly that Stamped" and "How the First Letter Was Written," which garnered him a Grammy nomination. And under the direction of Howard Sackler, he played the title character in Shakespeare's *Cymbeline*. Costarring Claire Bloom, Pamela Brown and John

Fraser, this production for the Royal Shakespeare Society, released as a three-disc set, became Boris' first and only recorded interpretation of the Bard.

Although he had been appearing in many noticeable guest spots on television, Boris now was maintaining the lowest profile of his career. He had not acted in a feature film for four years, and yet his legend continued to grow, due in large part to the syndicated success of Screen Gems' *Shock Theatre* package. Nearly every major city in the United States with a respectable television station had its own Saturday night horror show hosted by a ghoul, mad doctor or sexy vampiress who quickly became a local celebrity. Just when the old Universal monster classics were first hitting the airwaves in 1957-58, introducing Boris to a whole new generation of viewers, he was finishing up his last major horror roles, in *The Haunted Strangler*, *Frankenstein 1970* and *Corridors of Blood*.

By the autumn of 1962 there were new fans of Boris Karloff and Bela Lugosi throughout the United States. And, though Bela, who had passed away tragically forlorn and largely forgotten in 1956, was unable to benefit from the success of *Shock Theatre*, Boris, however slowed by age and illness, was able and willing to produce a few more terrors. Nearly a quarter-century earlier, he had hung up his asphalt-spreader's boots, vowing never again to play the Frankenstein Monster. And he meant it.

Route 66: **"Lizard's Leg and Owlet's Wing" (1962). Evie and Boris, in his final appearance as the Frankenstein Monster.**

But his pronouncement of the Monster's "death" proved premature. His life in 1962 London bore little resemblance to that which he had led in Hollywood when *Son of Frankenstein* was released in early 1939. Now he was no longer just the "King of the Horror Films," but an older, well-respected English gentleman with a long string of stage, radio and television successes behind him. Now, when he wanted to work, he could fly to another continent, do what the role required, and then return to the coziness of his Cadogan Square flat to read Conrad, tend to his flowers and plan his next outing with Evie, Bernie Coleman and the Surrey boys, or American visitors like John and Francesca Beaufort. On one occasion, he accompanied Martin and Katie Manulis' daughters to Hampton Court Palace, where he led them and Evie through the maze. Later, the girls remembered it as "the most fun of anything we did in London!"

In 1948 Boris had said that he could not watch anyone "make sport of" his dear old Monster. But now he was willing to do it himself. Pushing 75, he certainly could not seriously portray Mary Shelley's creation again, but he could join some old colleagues in poking fun at his horror image.

On October 26, 1962, Karloff's Monster lived again, alongside Lon Chaney, Jr. (as the Wolf Man and the Mummy) and Peter Lorre, on "Lizard's Leg and Owlet's Wing," a special Halloween episode of *Route 66*, CBS's popular show starring Martin Milner and George Maharis. Using a publicity portrait from *Son of Frankenstein* as a guide, the makeup artist had attempted

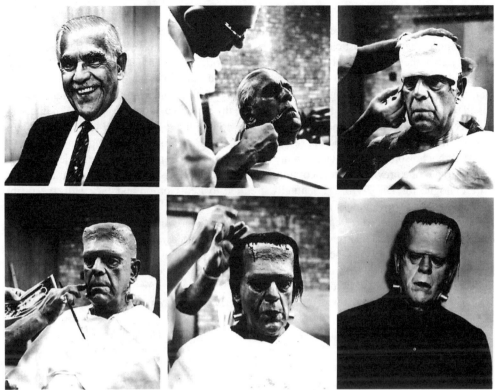

Route 66. **Having agreed to become the Monster one last time, Boris sacrifices his trademark mustache for makeup he considered unworthy of the character.**

to re-create Jack Pierce's original conception, while Boris, as patient as ever, received the only heavy makeup he had worn since that film wrapped nearly 24 years earlier. With a tinge of regret, he said, "It was a quick job, with no time to do the thing properly... the Monster was just a distant cousin to the original, which was a pity."

Atypically, Boris turned down a solid offer, from William Castle, who was shooting a farcical remake of *The Old Dark House* in London. "The new version... was simply not to my liking," he said. "I sent back the script—wanted no part in it." But he did accept another "monster burlesque," this time for American International Pictures, where he made his feature-film "comeback," in glorious Pathecolor and widescreen, again costarring with Peter Lorre. The latest in a series of low-budget films inspired by Edgar Allan Poe, *The Raven* was, in the words of director-producer Roger Corman, done "as a comedy, because I was tired of the Gothic stuff." Headlined by Vincent Price, who had starred in Corman's hugely popular *The Fall of the House of Usher* (1960), *Pit and the Pendulum* (1961) and *Tales of Terror* (1962), which also had brought Lorre and Basil Rathbone back to the horror fold, the new film gave the trio a golden opportunity to make fun of themselves.

Screenwriter Richard Matheson explained that *The Raven* "had to be a comedy because it's totally comic to take a poem and expect a horror film to come out of it." Cast as rival magicians during the Middle Ages, all three stars agreed with Matheson, particularly Lorre, who frequently ignored the script, surprising everyone on the set with new lines and physical improvisation—a tendency that delighted the equally rambunctious Price, but sometimes confused Boris. Corman commented, "Peter kept everyone on their toes, myself included. He would just begin to improvise unexpectedly. Vincent was always willing to play along with it but Boris, who was very methodical in terms of his craft, was a bit befuddled. Amused, but befuddled."

For Boris, one of the most amusing and unusual aspects of the script was his character's relationship with the presumably deceased wife (Hazel Court) of his mortal enemy (Price). In one scene, in which "Dr. Scarabus" makes amorous advances toward "Lenore," only to have his hand slapped away, Boris delivered his dialogue with obvious yet subtle relish.

Giving perhaps the most campy, wooden performance of his career, Jack Nicholson, who was only 26 at the time, remembered Boris as quiet, polite and spending most of his off-camera time reading *The London Times*. During a weekend that fell in the middle of the film's 15-day shooting schedule, Nicholson agreed to keep working when Corman's plans to play tennis were ruined by a rainstorm. Did the director want to use the extra two days to bring the film in ahead of schedule? Not Roger Corman, who surprised no one when he decided to begin shooting *another* film on the same sets before resuming with *The Raven* on Monday morning.

With Nicholson on board, Corman attempted to talk Price into joining the project, but the star had to honor a previous lecture commitment. However, Boris stayed, going so far as to help write dialogue for *The Terror*. Eventually credited to Leo Gordon and Jack Hill, the script became 80 minutes of plotless nonsense tied together by Boris' surprisingly effective performance as Baron Victor von Leppe, a Baltic nobleman who, while mourning the death of his wife, is visited unexpectedly by Andre Duvalier (Nicholson), a young Napoleonic officer.

Corman shot all of Boris' scenes over the weekend, and then assigned other portions of the loosely outlined story to Hill and Monte Hellman, who worked as assistant directors under associate producer Francis Ford Coppola. Having filmed entire features in one or two days, Corman now was satisfied to concentrate on completing *The Raven*. The director remembered:

> Boris was really not in good health during either *The Raven*
> or *The Terror*. He had an amazing spirit, an amazing heart.
> He was supposed to die in a terrible flood at the end of
> *The Terror*, so we came up with a tank of water, which we
> placed him in for the briefest amount of time, photograph-
> ing him with two cameras. After a little while, we then
> brought in a double to do all the really waterlogged scenes.

While waiting to meet with Corman in his office one day, Boris had a chance encounter with another artist who specialized in fantasy entertainment. Having contributed the stories for the 1953 thrillers *The Beast from 20,000 Fathoms* and *It Came from Outer Space*, Ray Bradbury was no stranger to fright films, and considered Boris a "rare competitor" and "a nice chap." Admitting that their meeting lasted "only about one minute," Bradbury recalled that each of them had enough time to compliment the other on his artistic work. Considering *Frankenstein* and *Bride of Frankenstein* as his favorite Karloff films—"Terrific, both of them"—the accom-plished writer also saw Boris "on stage... in the musical *Peter Pan*, playing Hook, and playing himself in *Arsenic and Old Lace*. Wonderful!"

Working harder than expected—and nearly having been drowned—Boris was relieved when his scenes for Corman were in the can. But American International planned an extensive public-ity campaign for *The Raven*, including personal appearances from all three stars, making his "comeback" auspicious indeed. Four days before the preview on January 30, 1963, Boris and Vincent Price teamed to promote the film in Los Angeles.

Recently, at the suggestion of his friend, Boris had signed with Hollywood agent Arthur Kennard, who had been representing Price for some time. For Kennard, picking up Boris at the airport was a memorable affair:

> In those days, the airplanes would land at LAX, but they
> didn't have that... thing that goes out and seals onto the
> airplane. You had to walk down the stairs in those days,
> and those were a long flight of stairs. And as soon as I
> saw what was going on, the first time he came over, I got
> ahold of a limousine... and they allowed me to... drive it

The Raven **tour (1963). Peter and Boris with two enthusiastic promoters, New York City.**

out to the airplane, so when he walked down the stairs,
with help, he got right into the limousine and we went off.
He never forgot that. And that established a precedent,
and so... he thought I was a hot-shot agent, and at that
point and time, my career was doing well—particularly
with the addition of Boris Karloff.

But he always remembered... "the young man" who
brought the limousine to the airplane. And from that point
on... every time... Boris would come to the United States,
I had a limo waiting at the bottom of those steps...

Now representing both Karloff and Price, Kennard, a native of Mamaroneck, New York,
who had worked as a musician and bandleader, became known as the "spook agent." He recalled his association with Boris as "truly one of the great, warm, loving relationships of my
whole career":

Boris had a way about him... unlike anybody I've ever
met in this business. Most actors have their own egos to
assuage and talk about. Boris was kind... He made me
feel important... He looked at you when he spoke to you.
He listened to you when you spoke. He was warm... He
was the most gentle man I've ever known in this business.

When *The Raven* opened in February 1963, Kennard accompanied Boris and Peter Lorre to
New York City on a tour sponsored by RKO Theatres, truly an adventure none of them would
ever forget:

It was the year that New York had the big blizzard, which
literally crippled the city. And it was RKO's intent to bring

231

The Raven tour. Boris' face graces the side of the bus that transported him, good friend Peter Lorre and agent Arthur Kennard through a New York City blizzard.

some live "spooks"... and we went to New York and were assigned this huge Greyhound bus and 23 off-duty policemen, New York's finest... They were to be our advance guard, so to speak, because at that period of time, the fans mobbed us. I mean, that was really Boris Karloff getting off that bus, right here in Brooklyn. And there was Peter Lorre behind him, with the big, hubcap eyes...

So we had a system worked out with the policemen... and the lead point man on this... flying wedge of policemen, was a fellow named "Chief," an American Indian... And Peter and Boris... just thought it was wonderful that we had an American Indian going through these crowds to protect us...

Well, the blizzard had started in the morning—became progressively worse. And I had a tentative date... who I had met in California, who was going to be in New York... a sort of tentative date at the Hampshire House— where RKO put the bunch of us up—at four o'clock. But here I am on this bus in the Bronx and all over New York, and the blizzard is picking up.

So I decided, "I've got to get out of this, so I can keep my date back at the hotel, and it's a good time to do it, because Boris and Peter will be out in the theaters, signing autographs, and I'll be back at the hotel having a drink with this lady."

And that's the way it went. I started... to cough at eleven o'clock. I said, "My throat's killing me. Gee, I don't feel well."

And I think Peter knew. He was instinctive. He knew I was faking it.

Boris brought himself up, sitting in the bus, and said, "Arthur, why don't you go back to the hotel?"

Peter picked it up and said, "That's a good idea. If you're catching cold, we're all going to have it... "

And I said, "No, no. I'm going to be macho and go on through the rest of the day's tour."

By one o'clock in the afternoon, there were snow drifts piling up, and it was questionable whether or not the bus would even continue... At any rate, it did, and by one-thirty, I said, "Oh... I can hardly talk."

And Peter said, "You should leave now and go back to the hotel and take care of yourself. Get in bed (great idea)... go back to the hotel."

So I did... and I felt in my stomach that Peter knew what was up. But how could he? I had it so well planned. Boris, he went along with it.

I got back to the Hampshire House. Met the young lady. Her feet were soaking wet. The drifts now were impossible... We got up to the suite. Peter and I shared a... two-bedroom suite, and Boris had a suite on one of the other floors. We were up on the 25th floor, I believe. And the young lady took her boots off, left them in the hallway, and we went into the living room...

They had lit a fire. I had planned this all out, to have the fire, have the champagne delivered—and the whole romantic sequence was to unfold. And you can imagine the surprise when about four o'clock—they weren't due back until about ten... the door burst open... Here was Peter... here was Boris right behind him, and here were the... 23 cops...

And they marched into Peter's half of the suite... And I was shocked. The girl turned white. She couldn't believe that here is Boris Karloff—Frankenstein—and Peter Lorre coming into this suite. It was pandemonium.

I hustled her out to... the freight elevator, so she wouldn't be embarrassed. I got back to the suite, went into the living room, and there was Peter, Boris, and 23 of New York's finest standing there, looking at me: "Uh, huh. You're *sick*."

Facing the man who supposedly was serving as their *chaperone* on the tour, Boris and Peter—actors, after all—staged a little drama:

By this time the blizzard was going full tilt, and the drifts were forming on the patio of the suite... And it was decided to have some drinks sent up for the policemen and some food, which Peter took care of. And they put a chair

233

in the middle of the room, and a chair at the other end of the room, and I was instructed to sit in it. The kangaroo court.

Boris became the judge. Chief became the prosecutor. Peter became my attorney... It was the funniest experience I've ever had in my life...

Peter would ask, "What was your intent, Arthur? Why did you lie to us on the bus?"

And I said, "Well, it wasn't a deliberate lie, Mr. Lorre. I had a previous engagement."

He said, "But what was your *intent*?"

And Boris would knock on the chair and say, "Out of order!"... And this went on and on, and it got funnier and funnier because Boris was being the judge.

Peter, with his insane way when he smoked cigarettes, would ask these vulgar questions.

Did I have any intent of molesting this young lady? Well, of course I did. Why do you think I made this whole thing up to leave the tour in the first place?

And Boris was continuing, saying, "He does not have to answer that. That's an uncalled for question," and so on.

And... the more we had to drink, of course, it got very interesting. The cops got a little tipsy. I got a little tipsy. Peter and Boris hardly drank anything, but the rest of us were getting intoxicated to the point where I've forgotten how the evening ended.

Everybody went to bed. I got up in the morning. Boris had gone to his suite... Peter was still asleep. And in the living room, hanging over chairs, on the lamps, on the mantelpiece, were guns, billy clubs, and coats, uniforms, hats, handcuffs... the same 23 policemen, all very hungover, as I was very hungover.

That was the kangaroo court when the agent tried to pull a shenanigan that never came off. Boris never forgot about it, nor did Peter, and we talked about it over the years. "Do you remember the blizzard of New York?" And everybody, when they said that... would kind of chuckle because they had me on the spot, guilty, nailed to the cross. I had no defense.

But blizzards, broads and booze did not stop Boris and Peter from promoting *The Raven*. On March 3, they appeared on WOR-TV's *Hy Gardner Show* to discuss their comic exploits both on and off the screen.

Completing the New York tour, Boris flew back to London for an extended rest. Other than recording material for the *Reader's Digest* radio show—which included topics as diverse as teenage rebellion, Swedish sailors, Herbert Hoover's philosophy of fishing and Halloween pranks on the farm—he remained professionally dormant for the remainder of the year. When the 76-year-old trouper did return to work, it was at American International, via LAX and Kennard's limousine, to shoot *The Comedy of Terrors* with Price and Lorre.

AIP's "moguls," James Nicholson and Sam Arkoff, were very pleased with the box-office performance of *The Raven*. And in true Hollywood fashion, they wanted more of the same,

The Comedy of Terrors (1964). The only teaming of all these horror greats—Basil Rathbone, Vincent Price, Peter Lorre and Boris in AIP's hilarious spoof.

perhaps an even funnier film, if possible. Hiring Richard Matheson to write another script, they assigned the project to Jacques Tourneur, who had directed five of the Lewton classics. And to boost the box-office power of the already formidable cast, they added Basil Rathbone, 1930s comic Joe E. Brown, high-decibel comedienne Joyce Jameson (who had played Lorre's attention-starved wife—and Price's lover—in *Tales of Terror*), topographically splendiferous "actress" Beverly Hills and the multi-talented Rhubarb the Cat.

Cinematographer Floyd Crosby, who had shot all the "Poe films," was retained, making *The Comedy of Terrors* Boris' third widescreen feature. And Richard Matheson did his best to fill Crosby's 2.35:1 aspect ratio with as many thrills and laughs as possible, creating an entertaining romp about New England funeral directors who, realizing that business is dropping off, decide to provide their own customers. While Price and Lorre comprised the twisted team of Trumbull and Gillie—Burke and Hare combined with Laurel and Hardy—Boris played Amos Hinchley, Trumbull's senile, nearly insane father-in-law.

Having visited the set of *The Raven*, Sara Jane, accompanied by her two young sons, came back to AIP to watch her father perform with his old friends. Her recollection that "he had a wonderful time making both of them—had a lot of fun" is openly apparent in *The Comedy of Terrors*. He even brought out the comic potential of his increasingly arthritic legs while shooting a scene in which Hinchley stumbles about the parlor, horribly bowing a violin as Trumbull drinks himself unconscious and Gillie dances with Trumbull's wife.

Outdoing all his compatriots, Rathbone mercilessly spoofed his Shakespearean career as John F. Black, landlord of the funeral parlor, who unwittingly becomes a customer when Trumbull cannot pay his rent. After being "killed" several times, Black refuses to stay dead, rising to his feet while reciting Macbeth's dialogue from Act V, Scenes 5-8, of Shakespeare's famous tragedy.

In his January 21, 1964, review of *The Comedy of Terrors*, Alton Cook wrote, "Boris Karloff is on hand to add his own touches to the act but he has limited opportunities as a doddering, deaf, old fool... The story is one of the thinnest to find its way to a movie screen." (Perhaps Cook had not seen Corman's *The Terror* before writing his review.) However, two days later, John G. Houser of the *Los Angeles Herald Examiner* wrote: "Boris Karloff, Peter Lorre, Vincent Price and Basil Rathbone... score in every reel. They ought to plan a series with them."

While shooting his scenes for *The Comedy of Terrors*, Boris narrated "A Danish Fairy Tale," a 60-minute documentary on the life of Hans Christian Andersen, for CBS's *Chronicle*. Reflecting his interest in children's literature, the program was broadcast on Christmas Day 1963. He also wrote an essay, "How Not to Be a Full-Time Bogeyman," for *Reader's Digest*, continuing his work for the popular magazine by promoting their "condensed books" series. Although allowed only one page for his remarks, Boris remarkably revealed a great deal about himself, including his modesty, his dry sense of humor, his belief in luck, his views on the nature of "horror" and his gratitude toward the genre, his acceptance of typecasting, his distaste for discussing his work and his striving for distinctiveness. Again demonstrating the influence of Conrad, he economically communicated a complex character with brevity and subtlety:

> As one who has made a career of playing fiends, demons, mad scientists and other assorted monsters, I admit to what may seem an unusual interest—the study of nursery tales. But the truth is that many of these children's favorites rank among the most chilling of horror stories.
>
> Do you recall, for example, the witch who fattened up boys and girls for the oven in *Hansel and Gretel*? Or the wicked queen who commanded the huntsman to kill Snow White and bring back her heart? And what about Bluebeard, and that collection of murdered wives he kept in a closet? These characters, I submit, are fully as terrifying as any of the weird and twisted characters I have portrayed.
>
> My predilection for the hair-raising, combined with the revival of many of my early films on television, has given me an unjustified reputation. The truth is, I am really a very gentle person. I do enjoy playing monsters, though, and I consider myself fortunate indeed to have frightened my way into the hearts of the public.
>
> But if I've submitted gladly to theatrical typing, I fight all the harder for variety and individuality in my private life. I'm a firm believer in limiting shoptalk to the shop. After hours, I like to get away from grease paint and box-office figures and talk about all the interesting happenings in other fields.

Though his emphysema and arthritis limited the amount of work he could accept, Boris agreed to act in several more films for AIP. His collaborations with Price, Lorre and Rathbone were the most enjoyable filmmaking situations he had experienced in many years, and the light-hearted tone of the material allowed him to demonstrate on the big screen the comic abilities he had honed in dozens of television performances. Of his deal with AIP, Sara Jane recalled, "He was at that point in his mid-70s, and he said to me, 'Well, I guess if they have that much confidence in my longevity, I'd better stick around and fill out the contract'."

Although he was far more bohemian than Boris, Peter Lorre was a fellow intellectual with common interests and a deep concern for his fellow performers. Boris had met the Hungarian actor for the first time at a dinner party in 1935, when the former Ladislav Loewenstein had come to the United States to appear in Karl Freund's *Mad Love* and Joseph von Sternberg's *Crime and Punishment*. Unlike Boris, Lorre tried to remain distinctly apolitical, and he applied for U.S. citizenship in April 1936 after returning from London, where he had appeared in Alfred Hitchcock's *Secret Agent*. On August 21 of that year, he was naturalized by the Department of Labor in Los Angeles.

In January 1937 Lorre, who was costarring in *Crack-Up* at Twentieth Century-Fox, visited Boris on the set of *Charlie Chan at the Opera*, where the two actors mugged for the still photographer. During this period, Lorre did get involved with the Screen Actors Guild, and became a member of the advisory board during the proposed strike of 1937. But it was the first round of HUAC witch hunts 10 years later that roused Lorre to political action. While Boris and Evie effortlessly escaped persecution, Lorre, who had a close relationship with the leftist Bertolt Brecht, joined the Committee for the First Amendment, which held meetings at the home of Ira Gershwin. In late 1947 two FBI agents visited him and produced a list, asking if he knew the people on it. "If you want to know who I know," Lorre replied, "you had better have more names."

Boris' first professional teaming with Lorre had occurred five years earlier in *The Boogie Man Will Get You*, a comic collaboration repeated for the 1955 *Best of Broadway* telecast of "Arsenic and Old Lace," and during the making of *Route 66*, *The Raven* and *The Comedy of Terrors*. Interestingly, they never were paired in a drama or straight horror film.

After *The Comedy of Terrors* was completed, AIP planned "Sweethearts and Horrors," a third Price-Lorre-Karloff spoof. But Price was preparing to shoot Roger Corman's latest Poe adaptation, *The Masque of the Red Death*, in England; and the Karloffs were off to Italy, where Mario Bava was making *Black Sabbath*, a three-part shocker. Boris was cast in "The Wurdalak," the third and longest episode, as a gentle Greek peasant who becomes a vampire feeding off the blood of his loved ones. Boris admired Bava's subtle approach to horror, particularly his shadowy visual style, spare use of dialogue and depiction of helplessly tragic characters. Not only did he portray the film's most dramatic character, a gentle man who cannot prevent the destruction of his family, but he also acted as a *Thriller*-style host, tying all three vignettes together with his eerie commentary. Released in the United States by AIP, the apocalyptic *Black Sabbath* proved a striking contrast to the horror spoofs Boris had made for the studio, providing him with his best big-screen character since *The Haunted Strangler* and *Corridors of Blood*.

With his costars occupied in other AIP projects, Lorre made a cameo appearance in *Muscle Beach Party*, the studio's first Frankie Avalon-Annette Funicello "beach" picture, and accepted a supporting role in Jerry Lewis' *The Patsy* at Paramount. His next performance was to be another AIP walk-on, in *Bikini Beach*, but unfortunately, fate intervened.

On the morning of March 23, 1964, Lorre was found dead on his bedroom floor. At noon that day, his physician discovered that he had suffered a cerebral hemorrhage. Three days later, while delivering the eulogy at Pierce Brothers Mortuary in Hollywood, Vincent Price reflected on the experiences he and Boris had shared with Lorre: "This was a man to be aware of at all times, for he was well aware of all who shared the stage with him and working with him never failed to fulfill the seventh and perhaps most sacred sense—the sense of fun."

The following month, Boris was back in Hollywood, to appear on the April 21 broadcast of *The Garry Moore Show* on CBS, and to fill in for his late friend in *Bikini Beach*. Spending a few hours on the set with producer Jim Nicholson, he walked through one sequence in which he observed a group of frantic teenagers. Turning to the camera, he remarked, "Monsters!" The fact that he was appearing in a film featuring Frankie and Annette, the Pyramids and Stevie Wonder was certainly a testament to his longevity.

And that longevity was a subject that Boris began to discuss publicly during this period, as he agreed to be interviewed on radio programs in both the United States and England. When asked about typecasting during a 1964 interview with the BBC, he explained exactly what his *job* as an actor was:

I think all actors are typed. I know it's fashionable to complain about being typecast, which I think is nonsense. We're all typed. If you're a young man, you play juveniles; and, I mean, as you get on, if you're lucky, you turn into a character man and you play that kind of part. And if you become known for a certain kind of role... that is not too restricted, I think you're a very lucky actor. If you're engaged... let's say in commerce, you'll spend a fortune trying to create a trademark that is known worldwide. Well, if you're typed in a certain line of country, it is handed to you on a platter, isn't it? I think you're lucky...

I haven't been hampered at all... I mean, it's a bit like the clown, I think, that is dying to play Hamlet. And if he has very bad luck, someday he'll have a chance to play Hamlet, and it'll be too bad. I think the cobbler should stick to his lathes, because I'm quite sure the public, the audience, the chap who pays his half-crown or whatever it is, in the final analysis is the best judge of what you can do and what he likes to see you do. And we are their servants, and we should bear that in mind.

Referring to his "terror" films, he acknowledged his debt to the *Shock Theatre* packages: "I think that practically every film that I was ever in has been revived at some time or other on TV. And I'm most grateful for it because it has served to keep me going and introduces me to a brand new audience." But, ever the consummate perfectionist, he still had no interest in viewing the films himself: "I never enjoy watching myself. You always long for the chance to do it over, you know."

In early 1965 Arthur Kennard was back at LAX to pick up Boris for his first acting job in nearly a year, a comedy guest spot on CBS's *The Entertainers* hosted by Carol Burnett. Broadcast on January 16, the program featured a skit in which he played himself—a mild-mannered gentleman—trying to check out a library book from Carol, who was absolutely terrified.

When she unleashed a bloodcurdling scream, he calmly requested, "I really wish you wouldn't do that. It frightens me." Then he explained, "You're making the mistake of mixing me up with the parts that I play in films. In real life, my great interest is in gardening. Why, only today, I planted a new flower bed."

Wide-eyed, Carol asked, "Who's under it?"

After two years of horror humor, Boris appeared to be spoofing his image in every performance, whether in films or on television. But his desire to work and dedication to his fans—combined with Evie's influence—prevented him from turning down serious offers. Arthur Kennard recalled:

Boris never complained about anything... If the director asked him to get up and run across the stage, he'd get up there and try. That's why he was so well respected, so well loved, so well thought about. He never had to ask for anything, wherever he worked. People were constantly going to him, "Can I get you this? Can I get you that?" and so on.

When a TV job came up, it was just as important as a movie, *any* movie... He seldom, if ever, asked me, "How much?"... I think it was a beautiful trust he had in me...

He was so aware and conscious of people who did nice things for him.

Sometimes in the terminals, they would get us an electric golf cart, have a guy drive us around the airport... and people walking in the hallways would stop and say, "Isn't that Boris Karloff?" And he'd always sit there with his cane... and he would always smile friendly... People would come up and ask him for autographs.

He would always say, "Arthur, loan me your pen."

Little... children, boys and girls, would come up, having heard about or seen the Frankenstein Monster, and there he is sitting in this golf cart, running around one of these airports.

I remember one little girl, in particular, stood there, and I thought she was going to wet her pants. "Oh, Mr. Karloff!" And her mother prompted her to get an autograph.

He said, "What is your name?" He wrote it down. This is the kind of man he was.

And he loved to work... he loved it. He was happiest when he was working or in his garden.

A lot of people today... they run from photographers, run from autograph-seekers. Boris never ran from anybody. He couldn't run anyway. But he was so gracious, so kind, so gentle, so giving. He was a remarkable man...

On January 24, 1965, a few days after Boris and Evie returned to Cadogan Square, Winston Churchill passed away, casting a pall over Britain. As the former prime minister lay in state in Westminster Hall, 300,000 people filed past his coffin, and more watched as the BBC broadcast his State Funeral, the first given a commoner in an entire century. As 6,000 Britons mourned their fallen countryman during the service at St. Paul's Cathedral, Boris sat silent in his chair, resting his work-weary legs and contemplating his own sense of Britishness. Soon after, when queried about his years in the United States, he explained:

I have a great regard for the American people, but watching that very moving funeral, I experienced that intangible something that tells a person if he "belongs." If I myself, never knew for certain why I never became an American citizen before that cold Saturday morning, I was left in no doubt later. Here I belong. Here is my ultimate home. And it goes a damn sight deeper than I can say.

In a later interview, he elaborated further about his Britishness:

Many things brought me back. An urge to return to my roots, homesickness, the countryside, the food, the way of life. The pace is easier. More comfortable. More human. Britain has contrived to make a society which is freer, gentler and fairer. Many parts of America are beautiful but there is nothing in the world to match the beauty of the English countryside... I didn't fancy renouncing my allegiance to Britain. It seemed nonsense. Had I escaped oppression or persecution in another part of the world, then a change of nationality would have been justified. Anyway, how can you become something else?

When interviewed by a London newspaper in 1965, Boris briefly stepped back into his Screen Actors Guild shoes to comment on the status of British performers. At the age of 77, he remained refreshingly undogmatic as he spoke of his common-sense "desire to right terrible wrongs, not to promote the labor movement, *per se*":

> The British actor is dreadfully treated. Far from being paid too much money, as popular opinion has it, he is not paid anything like enough—and I include film actors in that.
>
> Apart from money, conditions of employment are often bad—sometimes terrible. Our trade union, Equity, ought to act more strongly.
>
> Of course, the whole salary structure in this country is ridiculously low. How can you talk of a high standard of living when managements of all kinds are so mean to their employees?
>
> No other country would stand for it—look at the money paid in America.
>
> But the awful thing that has been accomplished by trade unions is this—you can't be given the sack. However rotten a man is at his job, he seems safe. The union protects him.
>
> One false move by the management and there's an unofficial strike. What nonsense. The words contradict each other. An unofficial strike is an illegal move and should be punished.

Boris returned to the truly "awful" and "rotten" in AIP's *Die, Monster, Die!*, a poor widescreen adaptation of H.P. Lovecraft's short story "The Colour Out of Space," shot in England by former Corman art director Daniel Haller. Released just before Halloween 1965, the film cast Boris as Nahum Whitley, an unfortunate man who is turned into a radioactive monster by a strange meteorite! But even stranger still, he followed the film with another trip to the States, to appear on the October 30 broadcast of the popular rock 'n' roll television show *Shindig*. Flanked by gyrating dancers, he dramatically recited the lyrics to the song "The Peppermint Twist." And as if to continue his establishment as a monster of rock, he then revisited AIP to shoot his scenes for *The Ghost in the Invisible Bikini*, in which he received special billing as Hiram Stokeley, a corpse visited by the spirit of his deceased lover (Susan Hart), an eye-popping blonde in a skimpy swimsuit.

Although he spent most of the shoot in a wheelchair, Boris was joined on the set by Basil Rathbone, silent star Francis X. Bushman, comedienne Patsy Kelly and a very young Nancy Sinatra, all of whom lent their diverse talents to this "beach horror film." Thirty years later, Sinatra recalled her "very good fortune to meet [Boris], a sweet, dear man." Perhaps the most inane moment of the *Ghost* filming occurred when the seminude Hart looked Boris in the eye and called him "Hiram, Baby!" Commenting on his client's participation, Arthur Kennard said, "I don't think he knew what a bikini was."

Having crowded themselves out of the flat in Cadogan Square, Boris and Evie purchased a new dwelling at Sheffield Terrace in Kensington and a lovely cottage called "Roundabout" in the village of Bramshott, near Liphook, Hampshire. Surrounded by a stone wall, the cottage provided them with great privacy, and Boris loved its two gardens, one of roses and flowering shrubs terraced with York stone, and the other a lawn extending toward the River Wey. Inside, he often relaxed with a book in the sitting room or lounge, each of which was heated by an open fireplace.

During the autumn of 1965 Boris invited editor Forrest J Ackerman and writer Peter J. Jarman of *Famous Monsters of Filmland* and *Monster World* magazines to visit Sheffield Terrace. Jarman, who acted as Ackerman's "British correspondent," had met Boris at Shepperton Studios during the filming of *Die, Monster, Die!*. Although Boris spent most of the afternoon answering their questions, particularly about the glory days at Universal, he and Evie made a rare appearance—as patrons—at a London movie theater that evening. This was a special occasion: Boris' first viewing of *Frankenstein* in nearly 34 years, and Evie's first *ever*.

"Roundabout," Boris and Evie's cottage in the village of Bramshott, Hampshire, as viewed from the road. (1993 photograph by Sara Jane Karloff)

Although his emphysema and arthritis were getting progressively worse, Boris spent the next year traveling back and forth between Europe and the U.S., acting in several productions for a variety of film and television companies. Before returning to London in the spring of 1966, he played "the Rat" in *The Daydreamer*, a Rankin-Bass children's film based on the work of Hans Christian Andersen; and during the autumn returned to Hollywood for episodes of *The Wild, Wild West* and *The Girl from U.N.C.L.E.*, in which he appeared in drag as the notorious "Mother Muffin."

He also made a small supporting appearance in a feature film starring *Man from U.N.C.L.E.* star Robert Vaughn, *The Venetian Affair*, a Cold War vehicle that shamelessly cashed in on the popularity of the Sean Connery James Bond films. Boris played Pierre Vaugiroud, a nuclear scientist with knowledge of a terrorist bombing, who is kidnapped by a nationalist party that is never identified. Is it the Soviet KGB, the American CIA or another destructive organization sporting a three-letter acronym?

But Boris' most memorable performance of 1966—and perhaps his most beloved since his first turn as the Monster—was broadcast on December 18. Always aware that his client hated to turn down work of any kind, Arthur Kennard had seen the *real* merit in a little piece of animation

Michael Cotton, Boris, Evie, Sara Jane and David Cotten, Chateau Marmont, c. 1966-67.

that Chuck Jones had concocted—a Yuletide cartoon based on Dr. Seuss' book *How the Grinch Stole Christmas*. Much like the narration work for Caedmon, this project required little more than Boris' arrival at the studio; beyond that, he could relax in a comfortable chair while reading a script—in this case, an absolutely brilliant teleplay by Theodor Geisel.

Geisel was impressed by Boris' dual performance: While providing a dramatic yet humorous narration, he also played the malevolent Grinch, a creature who progresses from a maligned miser to a generous "Grinchy Claus," ultimately learning the true meaning of Christmas and passing it on to his fellows.

Boris enjoyed recording anything for the children's market, but he was particularly fond of Geisel, who, as Dr. Seuss, had developed such a fascinating method of teaching basic human values to youngsters while entertaining them every step of the way. A huge hit upon its premiere broadcast, *How the Grinch Stole Christmas*, with its effortlessly unfolded morality tale, made an indelible impression on everyone who saw it. In the waning days of 1966 Chuck Jones realized that his images and Seuss' words benefited indescribably "through the skill of... Mr. Karloff." Arthur Kennard remembered that Jones "was in awe... when we recorded that, absolutely in awe—sketched pictures of Boris... It was a wonderful relationship."

As an accompaniment to the broadcast of the "Grinch," a children's recording of the soundtrack was released through Leo the Lion Records. An LP-length adaptation of Chuck Jones' script, the audio version thrust Boris' voice into venues all across America, into department stores in sections of the U.S. that may never have aired one of his films.

Narrating from a script by Forrest J Ackerman, Boris recorded another LP, *An Evening with Boris Karloff and His Friends*, during the autumn of 1966. Featuring audio excerpts from his three Frankenstein films and *The Mummy*, as well as Universal's *Dracula* and *The Wolf Man*, the album was a sonic equivalent of *Famous Monsters* magazine.

Barely settling down in England for a few days, Boris and Evie flew to Spain for the filming of a special episode of *I Spy* starring Robert Culp and Bill Cosby, a versatile performer and one of the first African Americans to receive a full television series contract (a fact that was not lost on Boris). Boris played another nuclear scientist, this time graced with shades of Don Quixote, who refuses to give his top-secret missile formula to "either side."

242

While still in Spain during February 1967, Boris, having learned that Claude Rains had passed away with a contracted role unfulfilled, agreed to play Franz Badelescu in *Blind Man's Bluff*, a film to be directed by Edward Mann. For the next two months, Boris stayed in Madrid, playing the Rains role, a blind sculptor who benefits from his wife's procurement, à la *Mystery of the Wax Museum*, of skeleton armatures from local graves.

Although he did not have the energy to attend many sporting events, Boris still supported local athletes; and during the spring of 1967, he became a vice president of the Bramshott and Liphook Cricket Club. Because he rarely was able to get to their matches, most of the players, who grew up watching him on television, knew him only by reputation.

In April 1967 Decca Records invited Boris and Evie to a Hollywood press party at the Magic Castle, a "spook house" on Franklin Avenue behind Grauman's Chinese Theatre. Accompanied by Arthur Kennard, they joined Forrest Ackerman, producer Alex Gordon, makeup artist Verne Langdon, writer Robert Bloch and others to celebrate the release of *An Evening with Boris Karloff and His Friends*, which had been selling-out in shops all over Los Angeles. As part of the festivities, Boris agreed to hold a "press conference," and while seated between Evie and Forry, gave an overview of his acting career. When asked about Evie's opinion of his work, he replied, "My wife is a woman of great taste. She has seen very, very *few* of my pictures!" filling the Magic Castle with laughter.

Back in Britain, "recharging between spells," as he liked to say, Boris regained enough breath and physical stamina to accept a role in Tigon Pictures' *The Sorcerers*, a film about telepathy directed by Michael Reeves, an enthusiastic but troubled young filmmaker who, amazingly in the 1960s, allowed his audience to exercise its imagination. Although the film is basically a drug-culture update of *The Devil Commands*, it gave Boris a well-developed character who, while demonstrating his method of mind control, is mercilessly manipulated by his wife (Catherine Lacey). *The Sorcerers*, which went into general release in June 1967, was entered in the Trieste Film Festival, where Catherine Lacey and Boris both won acting awards.

After working fairly steadily in both films and television over the past year, Boris eased up a bit, relaxing at Roundabout and visiting with theatrical friends like Mr. and Mrs. Walter Abel. The only professional offer he accepted during this time was another Arthur Rankin-Jules Bass film, *Mad Monster Party*, in which he provided the voice of "Baron Boris von Frankenstein," a role that reflected his eternal typecasting yet insured his continued appeal to filmgoing youngsters.

During the frantic preparation for the 1967 Grammy Awards, Arthur Kennard got a call. "Is Mr. Karloff going to be in Hollywood?" a female voice asked.

"No," Kennard replied. "Why?"

"He's been nominated for "How the Grinch Stole Christmas." And he's probably going to be getting a Grammy."

Politely ending the conversation, Kennard phoned Sheffield Terrace.: "Boris, I don't have anything other than an awards ceremony for you to come to."

"And what *is* that?" Boris inquired.

"It's the Grammy Awards," Kennard said.

A *long* pause ensued. "A Gra*nn*y?" Boris asked.

"No, Boris," Kennard replied. "Gra*mm*y—Gra*mm*y Awards."

Kennard could hear Boris quietly discussing the matter with Evie, who then got on the phone. "I don't understand at all," she said.

Kennard explained the significance of the award: "It's like an Oscar, only it's in the music business."

"Arthur wants you to come to some... *Granny* function," Evie said, turning away from the phone.

When Kennard contacted the Grammy committee, he again was informed that "The Grinch' probably would win the best children's album award. But Boris, having no interest in collecting a "prize," as he called it, would not fly to Los Angeles just to attend a ceremony. As the date of

Boris, as captured in a fan's snapshot, late 1960s.

the awards dinner drew near, Kennard called Boris back, attempting to change his mind. "It looks as though you're going to win this thing," he reiterated.

"What am I going to win?" Boris asked.

"The Grammy."

"You called a few weeks ago about that... Well, what is it?"

"It's a little statuette. It looks like a gramophone."

Boris asked Kennard to accept the "prize," and when "The Grinch" won, told him to keep it on his desk.

During Boris and Evie's next visit to Los Angeles, Kennard picked them up at LAX and then drove to the Sunset Boulevard Office. He recalled:

> [Boris] walked in and he looked around... and I said, "There it is... there's the Grammy." And he walked up to it, he looked at it, stood back. Evie walked up like they were examining a specimen... Evie said to Boris, "That's a Grammy."
>
> "Oh, a Granny." He was doing it on purpose... and he stood back and said, "It looks like a doorstop." And my secretary laughed. Evie laughed.
>
> And I said, "It's not a doorstop. It's an award."
>
> He said, "It's a marvelous prize. It looks like a doorstop. It looks marvelous on your desk with the other trophies that you have." And with that, he picked it up, opened my office door to the reception room, left it open, and put it on the floor as a doorstop. It stayed there for a long, long time..."

Chapter 11

A Very Good Year

It's a tough life. It's a rough life, and only a handful of
people are successful. They're the lucky ones, and it *is*
luck. You've learned the ABC of your craft, your business, your profession. Then, who's going to be lucky?
Who's going to be on the right corner at the right moment? And nine people out of 10 must resign themselves
to lives of depredation sometimes—more often. Certainly
frustration. And the handful who are lucky are very lucky
and should be very grateful. And the only thing that makes
it worthwhile, with the odds so heavily loaded against you,
is if it is the *only* thing you really love doing—the only
thing you really *want* to do. If you don't go into it with—
I think... Conrad called it—"the obscure inner urge," it's
no good. For God's sake, don't. But if you have it, then
for God's sake, *do*.

During the autumn of 1967 frugal Roger Corman discovered that Boris owed him two days'
work. When *The Terror* was filmed in 1963, he had not stayed on the project long enough to
fulfill his contract, Corman claimed. Unable to let a golden opportunity pass him by, the shrewd
filmmaker decided to churn out two days' worth of Karloff scenes for a new film. (After all, he
had shot complete pictures in less time.)

Acting as executive producer, Corman chose Peter Bogdanovich, a 27-year-old former actor and film critic who had assisted him on past projects, as director and producer of the new
film. Giving Bogdanovich a budget of only $125,000, Corman suggested that he shoot 20
minutes of new Karloff footage and integrate it with 20 minutes of *The Terror*. Then, if he
filmed another 40 minutes without Boris, he could edit it all together into a marketable 80-
minute feature.

Receiving a production schedule that only Corman could devise, Bogdanovich collaborated with his then-wife, Polly Platt, on the screenplay. They decided to invest the film with two
major subplots that eventually would merge in the final scene, combining the story of Byron
Orlok, an aging, somewhat disgruntled star of horror films, with the actions of Bobby Thompson, an "all-American boy" who becomes a vicious murderer. Using Boris' career and the story
of Charles Whitman, a 25-year-old man who committed mass murder in Austin, Texas, in 1966,
Bogdanovich and Platt created a vivid portrait of realistic modern horror. Bogdanovich recalled:

We started thinking about... how real horror is the kind of
random violence that the Whitman incident symbolized,
and that the kind of Victorian horror that Boris represented
really wasn't so horrible anymore—and, in fact, it was

cozy compared to the mindlessness of the Whitman incident.

The first draft of the *Targets* screenplay featured Orlok's death at midpoint, something that Bogdanovich's friend, writer-director Samuel Fuller, could not accept:

> Sammy said, "Why are you killing him off?"
>
> I said, "I've only got him for two days."
>
> He said, "Don't ever think about that... Why would you want to kill him off?"
>
> "I've only got him for two days!"
>
> "Don't kill him off!"
>
> I said, "How can I keep him going?"
>
> He said, "Don't worry about that, kid! Never worry about that! Write it the way you want it, and worry about how you're going to do it later."
>
> It was very good advice. He said, "You've got a better finish if he lives," and we worked out the ending where actually Karloff catches the killer. That was Sammy encouraging me to go that direction and have a totally different kind of ending. It was much better. Boris never saw the other version...

After Corman read the screenplay, he told Peter, "This is the best script that has ever been submitted to me... but there's no way you can shoot all of this with Karloff in two days. So you'll have to cut a lot of it out."

Bogdanovich protested, reminding Corman of the quality of the script. After arguing for some time, they reached a compromise, with Corman agreeing to book Boris for a longer shoot. The screenplay then was given to Arthur Kennard, who immediately saw it as a wonderful opportunity for Boris. Phoning him at Sheffield Terrace, Kennard described the film and the character based on his personality. Boris did not care for Corman's part in the project, but he jumped at the chance to work with the young and creative Bogdanovich. He agreed to do it without reading the script but, during a subsequent telephone conversation with Peter, asked, "Since this character is very much like me, do I have to say such terrible things about myself?"

"My feeling, Boris," Peter replied, "is that the more terrible things you say about yourself, the more the audience will say, 'No, it's not true. We don't agree.'"

"Well, I hope so," Boris said. "They might just agree."

As to why Boris was so quick to accept the part, Bogdanovich explained:

> I think he just recognized what it was, and he recognized that I was crossing the line between... who he was and what people believed he was.... I didn't ask him if this was really what he thought of himself. I doubt it is, because Boris was very self-effacing and humble... in every way... He was very unpretentious... He didn't put on any airs. And I think he recognized the potential of it and what he could bring to it.... I didn't realize how close to the bone it was...
>
> The picture took him seriously and what he'd done seriously. It was a serious picture, and he really responded to it, wonderfully... He liked working... but if he got some-

246

Targets (1968). An exhausted Boris rests as Peter Bogdanovich readies him for an upcoming scene.

> thing good, he responded, as he did with us, or as he did
> with *The Lost Patrol* or *Arsenic and Old Lace*.

The day after Kennard's limousine arrived at LAX, Boris and Evie joined Peter and Polly for dinner at their home. The meeting was the first time Bogdanovich had seen Boris in person. He later said:

> He was a proper English gentleman, really. Very polite.
> Very well read, intelligent. He looked most like... an ag-
> ing professor... of something esoteric: the study of coins,
> or an archeologist or something. He didn't seem like an
> actor. He didn't dress like an actor...

While seated at the dinner table, Boris told Peter, "You have written the truest line I've ever read in a script."

"That's quite a compliment," Peter gratefully replied. "What was that?"

"God, what an ugly town this has become," recited Boris.

While the interior scenes for *Targets* were filmed in a tiny studio across from a lumber yard on Santa Monica Boulevard, the extensive exterior work was done at a variety of locations in Los Angeles. On the first day of shooting in December 1967, Bogdanovich, who had scheduled night scenes that included Boris, did not require the crew to report until 11:30 a.m.

Targets. **At the age of 80, Boris still demonstrates his Stan Laurel–like comedic talent, as Byron Orlok is startled by his own reflection.**

At 11:30 sharp, Boris and the crew were waiting on the Sunset Strip, but Bogdanovich was nowhere to be found. After sleeping too late, he had driven out to the San Fernando Valley to scout another location and promptly got lost. When he finally did arrive, the limousine he had ordered was not there.

"Where is it?" he asked.

"Oh, well, they just didn't deliver it," a crew member replied. "Somebody's gone to get it, but it won't be here for an hour and a half."

Bogdanovich's schedule was already in jeopardy. He had only met Boris once, and his nerves were a bit shaky. "We can't wait," he explained. "With a 15-day schedule... we're going to wait? We can't wait a minute!"

Playing Sammy Michaels, a young filmmaker, in the picture, Bogdanovich changed his clothes and got made up for a shot in which the limousine did not appear. His nervousness increasing, he ran himself ragged all day, struggling to get all the shots of Boris in the limo completed before the sun went down. Then the crew packed up to move to the Reseda Drive-In, where they filmed all night.

By 1 a.m., the weather had turned colder, but Bogdanovich realized that the shoot would last several more hours. Approaching Boris, he "begged" him to stay longer:

> He had emphysema, so he was ill. I said, "This is our only chance. I can't get this stuff any other time. We can't afford to come back with you."
>
> "All right, we'll do it. It's only for you. It's not for Roger Corman." He didn't like Roger...

We finally wrapped it up at four in the morning, and I got in the car to drive to my house. I didn't feel tired at all. I started to laugh, and I said to myself, "I have never had more fun in my whole life than I had today!"

Bogdanovich and Platt's script provides a semi-factual look at Boris' career, habits and artistic philosophy. One scene set in Orlok's hotel room includes Byron and Sammy sitting down to watch *The Criminal Code*. Bogdanovich elaborated on his choice of this particular film:

> I wanted to use something where he was noticeably recognizable... so I was looking for a straight film, a non-horror film, and it was supposed to be something that he had made early in his career. And... when I told him about *The Criminal Code*, he said, "Oh, fine. That's the first really important part I ever had." We put that line in the picture... It seemed to me a good choice. It was Hawks, whom I love. And it was a very good scene for Boris, because he's threatening and kind of funny about it... that kind of quiet menace...
>
> He liked the clip, and he liked Hawks. He remembered Hawks fondly. He said, "He gave me my first really important part."
>
> And I had the line, "He sure knew how to direct."
>
> "He *certainly* did." He wanted to put that in. Boris threw that in, because he wanted to say something about Howard.

Although Bogdanovich patterned the character on his star's life and career, there are some major differences between Byron and Boris. At one point, Orlok admits:

> I know how people think of me these days—old-fashioned, outmoded. "Mr. Bogeyman," "King of Blood," they used to call me. The Marx Brothers make you laugh, Garbo makes you weep—Orlok makes you scream. Oh, it's not that the films have got bad; I've got bad. I couldn't even play a straight part decently anymore. I've been into the other thing too long.

Orlok's decision to retire contradicts the Karloff work ethic, and the character's appraisal of his own abilities is ironic, since Boris effectively plays "a straight part" throughout the film.

When not appearing in a shot, Boris, constantly aided by Evie, relaxed in a nearby chair or a wheelchair when he needed to move around. Arthur Kennard recalled:

> Peter looked after him, and the picture. Boris was pleased with it... He saw the dailies, and got along real well with Peter... Boris fell in love with Polly. And the both of them, they were two young, very, very smart, young picture makers who knew what they were doing. And Boris, because he was old at the time... was very happy to be there with them...

Of Evie's relationship with Boris, Bogdanovich recalled:

> They were very close. He was crazy about her, and she
> was crazy about him.... They were very warm, like a real
> old English couple.... Proper and cozy. She was mad about
> him. Took really good care of him, and he was very, very
> deferential and warm to her. They were very much in
> love... She loved him a lot... I think they were very happy.
> It was a very happy marriage.

Boris' greatest dramatic challenge involved his recitation of a two-minute macabre fable from John O'Hara's *Appointment in Samarra*. While writing the script during the holiday season, Bogdanovich had seen a re-run of *How the Grinch Stole Christmas* and, as a last-minute addition, decided, "How can we do a movie with Boris Karloff and not have him tell a story?"

Well after midnight one evening, Peter decided to shoot the scene. Although fatigued and in considerable pain from another very long day, Boris, refusing to display his discomfort, prepared to recite the tale.

"Do you want the words written on cue cards?" Peter asked.

"You mean *idiot* cards," corrected Boris, who was still a quick study at the age of 80. "I have the *lyrics*." (During the shoot, he referred to his dialogue as either "the lyrics" or "the jokes.")

Bogdanovich then explained how the scene would be filmed: "Boris, I'll start on you and then, as you're talking, I'll pan around the room and come back to you."

Boris was not pleased. "I want to do this without a script," he suggested.

Realizing that Boris was "quite right," Peter decided to begin the scene in long shot and then slowly dolly in on him as he spoke. Bogdanovich vividly remembered:

> It was a long speech. It was about a page. And it was a
> complicated shot because there was a room service table
> in the way. It had to be pulled out as the camera was going
> in, and I was in the shot, so it was tricky. We did the first
> take, and we had to stop after about 20 seconds, because
> something was screwed up.
>
> And then we started the second take. No cut. We
> went all the way through it. It was perfect, except for
> some technical things, which I ignored. And I had said to
> him, "Now, when you finish the speech... we'll be in a big
> head... so give me a beat afterward, where you think about
> your own death."
>
> "All right," he said. "Fine."
>
> So we did it, and we get into this big close-up... and
> he did this wonderful moment at the end, where he thought
> about it all.
>
> And I said, " Cut. Jesus! Brilliant. Print!"
>
> There was spontaneous applause from the crew... 25
> people. And I looked over at Evie, and she had teared up,
> and Boris had tears in his eyes. And I went over to Evie...
> and she said, "Wasn't that wonderful? Do you know how
> many years it's been since anybody gave Boris a hand on
> a set?... It never happens."
>
> So it was very memorable for him.

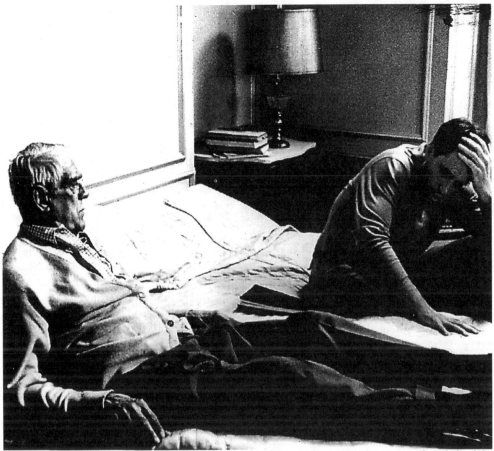

Targets. Byron Orlok and Sammy Michaels (Peter Bogdanovich), severely hungover after their night of drinking.

Running 10 days over schedule, *Targets* required an enormous effort from everyone involved. Originally contracted for two days, Boris stayed for five, and Evie literally became a member of the crew, helping to move props and sharing her husband's enthusiasm for the material.

Bogdanovich enjoyed the ease with which Boris "didn't need to be directed," and the scenes in which the two performed together proved to be a learning experience for the young film-maker. Having written the part of Sammy for another actor who became unavailable, Peter "reluctantly" took over, but ultimately was pleased because he "got to be in a movie with Boris Karloff!" One scene in particular—in which Byron and Sammy get drunk—briefly flustered the usually unflappable Boris:

> He was very good to act with—and it was difficult, because I hadn't acted in a movie... and directing and acting is not easy...
>
> So we had this scene in the bed, where we both pass out. And then I wake up in the morning and I see him, and I get scared and then I laugh... And we were shooting it... and I couldn't do the laugh. It was written by the writer, which was me... I look at him in the bed, and then I start laughing.
>
> And then he says, "What are you laughing at?"

251

And I say, "I just woke up and I was in bed with Byron Orlok"...

"Very funny. Very funny."

When we were shooting it, I couldn't do the laugh. It's very difficult to laugh on cue. So we did a couple of takes and I just kind of froze up. And he got irritated. He said, "If you're not going to laugh, then don't laugh!"

And I said, "I don't think I can."

He said, "Well, then *don't*, but let's get on with it!"

I said, "Well, maybe I don't need to laugh."

He said, "Well, then you don't. Don't laugh then! *Just don't laugh!*"

I said, "That's simple, isn't it?"

"Yes! Let's get on with it!"

But the scene was also a source of enjoyment for both men. As a coda to Byron and Sammy's hungover awakening, Boris wanted Orlok to frighten himself—a deft comic touch that pleased Peter: "There was a moment... where I get scared in the bed... and it was Boris who said, 'Well, I could see myself in the mirror and do a little take,' and so we did that. That got a big laugh."

By contrasting Boris' "horror" with the actual horror of 1960s America, Bogdanovich created a powerful cinematic exposé. Both Boris and Evie were thrilled, a very happy outcome to a project concocted by the fiscally minded Roger Corman. Of Boris' work, Bogdanovich said:

> He was so solid. He knew the words... on the first or second take. And he kept everybody on their toes, because of who he was and how good he was...
>
> When I think about Boris, the main thing I think of is a kind of warmth he projected... without being sentimental... It was a kind of dignity and warmth that he projected. And intelligence and taste that came across on a very high level...
>
> He was a real pro, a real professional... He never made fun of the material, tried to make himself better than the material. He was what you *hope for* in a star. If every star was like Boris Karloff was, life would be a lot easier.

However, finding a distributor for the picture was another matter. Bogdanovich revealed:

> We had a horrible time trying to sell it after it was all made. Couldn't sell it, because it was made for Roger, and Roger had a deal with AIP... and it was going to be released by them. And I said I wanted to see if I could get a major... and then we tried and failed a number of times...
>
> And then I was kind of desperate, so I had a couple friends of mine... I said, "Will you guys come down and see this movie, and if you like it, would you write about it in the trades? And if you don't like it, will you *not* write about it?"...
>
> And, at that point, Paramount came back into the story, because the reviews were very good... and they bought it, finally, and gave Roger his tiny profit.

And then it sat on the shelf for quite a while, because a lot of terrible things in history happened: Martin Luther King and Bobby Kennedy were killed in 1968. There was an outcry against guns and against violence in movies.... Now this movie, which is a very violent movie in many ways—didn't know what to do with it. And there was a faction at Paramount that said,

"Let's just never release it. Forget it." And another faction said,

"Let's release it with something about gun control"... and that's how it eventually got released, so it came across like some kind of documentary, at least in New York.

It got good reviews. They made eight prints... in 35mm...

Sara Jane considers *Targets* her favorite Karloff film:

I never saw it when it was playing in theaters, and Peter Bogdanovich nicely arranged for my children and myself to be able to view it at a special screening. And I know that my father liked and admired Peter Bogdanovich a lot, and enjoyed working with him, and admired the many facets of Peter's talent. I like the film a whole lot, too, because my father is essentially playing himself, and my father felt that the horror was happening on the streets, not up on the screen—that the way man was treating man was the real horror of today's world, and that really was what that film was all about.

On March 15, 1968, Boris' face appeared on the cover of *Life* to commemorate the sesquicentennial of the publication of Mary Shelley's *Frankenstein*. Of course he received many comments about his head hovering eerily over a flaming birthday cake, but perhaps the most satisfying remark came from the mother of a little girl who thought the magazine article celebrated the actor's own nativity:

My six-year-old daughter, Jenny, wants me to send this card to you for your birthday. She saw you in *Life* magazine and is afraid you will not get any birthday cards or presents because people are afraid of Frankenstein's monster, which you represent to her. In other words she feels sorry for the lonely monster.

There was a school holiday on your birthday and she believes that it was in honor of you. After all, you were on the cover of *Life* that week!

During the spring, Boris joined Christopher Lee and Barbara Steele for *The Curse of the Crimson Altar*, a Tony Tenser production shot on location at Grimsdyke House, the former home of composer William Gilbert, in Middlesex. Adapted from H.P. Lovecraft's "Dreams in the Witch House," the screenplay by Mervyn Haisman and Henry Lincoln was a poor one indeed, confusing everyone involved. Boris reported for eight days of work, including some night scenes filmed outdoors in a freezing rainstorm. Already hampered by considerable respiratory problems, he developed a serious case of bronchitis after insisting on taking part in the night shoot. Christopher Lee recalled:

> I saw him doing those takes... when he could barely breathe, and yet the precision, the sheer professionalism of it all never faltered, never flagged, not for one second... One part of me would literally shudder at the efforts that I saw him make and the pain that I knew it was causing to him, and the other part of me would stand there aghast in admiration and respect at the tremendous courage and vitality which he showed... He never complained; he always made light of his ills and his problems.

Both the cast and crew knew the film would be mediocre at best, but their positive attitudes, bolstered by the historical location, compensated. And lines of dialogue such as "It's a bit like one of those old houses in horror films. One expects Boris Karloff to pop up at any minute" added some self-reflective humor to the production. Director Vernon Sewell considered himself "very privileged" to have worked with Boris: "I admired him immensely and we got on so well together. His courage and enthusiasm were terrific."

While most 80-year-old performers would have taken a lengthy rest after such a life-threatening experience, Boris relaxed only long enough to recuperate from pneumonia before accepting an offer to appear in *four* films for Filmica Azteca, Columbia's subsidiary in Mexico City. Sara Jane believes that Evie convinced him to continue accepting such offers, but his acute emphysema, which necessitated frequent doses of oxygen, prevented him from making the trip. However, producer Luis Vergara, guaranteeing Boris $100,000 per film, made arrangements to shoot his scenes for all four at the Stage Studio in Los Angeles, and in May, the Karloffs flew to LAX, where Arthur Kennard again awaited.

Writer Bill Warren, who had been a mere face in the crowd of reporters at the Magic Castle party the previous year, was at Stage during the filming of many of Boris' scenes, and noticed one particular aspect of his acting method:

> He knew that he had to bring this part fully to life, for in a fantasy picture, obviously, believability is of enormous importance. Therefore, if a scene had several takes, Karloff would vary his delivery of his lines slightly on each take, changing pitch or accenting different words, but always keeping completely within the bounds of the personality he was portraying. This made the character more real both for himself and the other actors in the scene...
>
> I commented on this to him. "I've done it all my film career," he answered. "I've discovered that it keeps one from becoming too stale. This is a very great danger in working in films."
>
> I later have had occasion to discuss this with members of the movie business; they assured me that this practice was very rare, and most desirable. It was the mark of Boris Karloff, a true craftsman.

After Boris completed his final take and returned to the respite of his ever-present wheelchair, Vergara, speaking for the entire crew, thanked him for his cooperation, patience and fine acting. Visibly moved, Boris once again rose from the chair, long enough to express his gratitude for their hard work and satisfaction that he had completed scenes for four different films.

As everyone on the set applauded, his stand-in wheeled him to the dressing room. With Boris' work in the can, Vergara returned to Mexico City, where he and his native crew finished the films.

During the five-week sojourn at the Stage Studio, Boris and Evie were invited to dinner by Robert and Eleanor Bloch, who entertained them with a few select guests, including Fritz Lang and Forrest Ackerman, who recalled:

> Karloff... talked television, war, direction, politics, teen-age "monsters" and a whole spectrum of speculation. Karloff's mind was as alert and keen as Bertrand Russell when last seen on television; his dialogue sparkling as it welled up far more spontaneously than the wooden formulas he was often made to mouth by grade-B writers.

Boris had no choice but to spend the summer quietly at home with Evie, primarily among the flowers and fresh country air of Hampshire. But he still remembered that Hal Roach, Jr., owed him a substantial sum, and in June, SAG renewed its efforts to obtain what had been owed him for nearly a decade. Even though Roach Studios had been declared insolvent, Beverly Hills attorney William Berger stated the following:

> Karloff's claim for compensation must be determined by state law, and under California law he is entitled to full payment of his agreed compensation (*Payne vs. Pathé Studio*, 6 Cal. App. 2d. 136). I know of no provision in the bankruptcy law which limits, in any way, the amount of this claim. Consequently, Karloff is clearly entitled to have his claim allowed in the unpaid balance owing him under his employment contract, namely $62,500.

For the next three months, Boris accepted no work, until his old friend Red Skelton asked him to join Vincent Price on his annual "spook show" to be broadcast September 24. Arthur Kennard was delighted by this experience:

> Red regarded... Boris in such esteem, in such affection... He was catered to. Red loved Boris. Boris loved Red. Vincent loved them both... The three of them were like children, batting gags back and forth. Boris had a wit that wouldn't quit, sharp like a rapier, and he couldn't be more part of the gang... He sat and talked with the musicians, and they'd play him little tunes... It was a wonderful camaraderie that developed with Skelton and Boris and Vincent.

Boris and Vincent played a father and son team of mad doctors who, mistaking Red's Clem Kadiddlehopper for a robot, had him investigated by a general at the Pentagon (James Millhollin). They also donned black ties and tails to sing "The Two of Us" with Skelton and the David Rose Orchestra. Later, Price remembered Boris' dauntless professionalism:

> I knew of his suffering and even a little of his fear of stairs... Boris with braced legs was wheeled into the scene by a midget in Frankenstein makeup—in the audience dress rehearsal he came off and called me over to ask if I had

the same feeling he did that the humor of the scene was deadened by the audience sympathy for a man in a wheelchair. I had to admit I did—whereupon Boris with infinite courage played the rest of the rehearsal on his feet and the show as well. Later he and Evie and I discussed this. She was naturally worried, but Boris' concern was for the show.

Boris also performed on Jonathan Winters' Halloween program on October 30, fronting the Earl Browne Orchestra with an effective, touching rendition of "It Was a Very Good Year." And on November 29, he guest starred on NBC's *The Name of the Game*, as Dr. Orlov in "The White Birch," with Gene Barry, Susan Saint James and Roddy McDowall, who had not worked with Boris for a decade. Although he was anxious to be reunited with one of his favorite colleagues, McDowall, out of respect for Boris' physical condition, kept his off-camera contact to a minimum:

> He was in a wheelchair... the role allowed it, and it was very small. And we didn't speak very much... one doesn't wish to embarrass the man who's so reduced in a way, because we had worked together before. And he was quite reduced in ability, but again, never a word of complaint...

McDowall also commented on the essence of Boris' talent:

> The greatest thing that Boris radiated was a professionalism accompanied with discipline and elegance. He was a supreme professional. And very natural. I think probably that's one of the things that sort of worked so wonderfully as a monster—that he wasn't trying to be a monster, he was being a *human being*. And of course that's totally correct...
>
> He was a fine man. I never heard anybody say anything about him that wasn't a remark of praise or admiration or respect... He was a highly regarded working actor who sometimes was in very successful commercial ventures, and sometimes not. But he was highly, highly respected.

Having struggled to finish his scenes for *The Name of the Game*—an effort that greatly impressed the show's crew—Boris leaned on Evie a bit more than usual as he began another of the habitual transatlantic flights. During a stop at Kennedy Airport in New York, he caught another severe chill that seriously constricted his breathing. Upon landing in England, he and Evie were rushed to King Edward VII Hospital in Midhurst, Sussex, where he was diagnosed as having a weakened heart, as well as severe arthritis and emphysema.

He could hardly breathe. With only a portion of one lung remaining, he was in constant need of oxygen. Having acted as his private nurse for so many years, Evie devotedly stayed at his side, recording the *Reader's Digest* radio show as he struggled to speak.

For the next two months, Boris was cared for by 18 staff members who were surprised and impressed by his "calm geniality" and "cheerful and uncomplaining nature." Even spending the holidays in the hospital, bedridden and in constant pain, failed to dampen his spirits. One day nurse ranked him among "the best patients I've ever come across," while another described the pleasure all her colleagues experienced whenever they entered his room. A night nurse who called him "one of the nicest patients I've ever met" admitted, "It made an impression on my mind that a man so famous could be such a pleasant gentleman." Sensing that his end might be near, Boris made arrangements for a generous bequest to the hospital.

On January 23, 1969, while Evie was at the hospital, burglars broke into Sheffield Terrace and stole her silver, furs, jewelry (including the charm bracelet from *This Is Your Life*), wedding gifts from 1946 and Boris' gold medal from the Trieste Film Festival. Understandably distressed by this assault on their home, she was grateful that the criminals had overlooked Boris' Screen Actors Guild gold card, which he had received in 1951.

Arthur Kennard stayed in constant touch with Evie, speaking to Boris whenever he was allowed. Realizing that his client probably would not play another role, he fabricated tales about upcoming television and radio work, and capped off his exaggeration with a fictitious film offer from Federico Fellini:

> I told him how I had this picture in the works for him, and they wanted him to come to the United States, and the script and the whole thing. He was going to put on the harness again and go to work. He knew somehow I was lying... It made him feel good... I wanted him to go out on top.

Ever the protective spouse, Evie handled all the telephone calls and, as Boris' condition worsened, forbade close friends like Bernie Coleman from visiting his room on the seventh floor. Christopher Lee called several times, but Evie provided him with updates rather than putting Boris on the line. Lee recalled:

> She told me that he wasn't really at all well but was show- ing his usual tremendous guts. I said, "Well, look, I'd love to come down and see him. Do you think it would be all right?" And she said, "Oh yes. Twenty minutes... half an hour. He would love to see you."

But Lee did not make it in time. "One of my great sorrows," he said, "is the fact that I was not able to see him."

On February 1, Boris was very weak, and spent most of the day dozing. Occasionally he would awaken just enough to say a few words to Evie; and, suddenly at one point, with some surprise in his voice, whispered, "Walter Pidgeon," repeated the name a second time, and fell asleep once more. Considering that he had not seen or spoken of Pidgeon in many years, Evie was very perplexed by the incident.

One of the children's stories Boris always remembered was that of the groundhog stealthily climbing out of its hole, only to see its shadow and scamper back in. And as quietly as that legendary animal, he slipped into his final sleep on Sunday, February 2, 1969—Groundhog Day.

Literally worn out from six decades of performing, Boris did not possess the physical im- mortality of his Frankenstein Monster, Imhotep, John Elman and Dr. Henryk Savaard. In the movies, he had come back to life, both scientifically and supernaturally. Now the eyes that had fluttered open with resurrective light, to scare the souls out of millions, were closed. But the immediate outpouring of sympathy from his and Evie's friends and colleagues proved that Boris Karloff—not "Karloff the Uncanny," the actor and horror icon, but the bashful Anglo-Indian who became a star while leading a gentleman's life—lived on in the minds of those who knew him best.

On February 3, every major newspaper in Britain printed a notice of his death, and over the next two days, lengthy stories about his career flooded papers in the United States. Most Ameri- can articles included photos of the Frankenstein Monster: One (of Glenn Strange) in *The New*

York Times identified Boris as a "Master Horror-Film Actor." The *Tulsa Daily World*, however, hit closer to the mark by calling him a "Gentle Monster" and "Lover of Children," while *The Cleveland Press'* headline read, "Movie Monster Karloff Played Broadway Too."

Sara Jane had no idea that her father's illness had reached a fatal stage. At Boris' side, Evie did not call her after he passed away. However, at her home in Yucaipa, California, on February 3, she did receive a call—from someone next door.

"Turn on your TV," the neighbor suggested.

"Why?" she asked.

"You'll see."

Tuning her set in to NBC's *Today Show*, Sara Jane learned that her father was dead.

At 1:08 p.m., she sent a Western Union cable to Evie: "So grieved to have just learned of Dad's passing. Please call or wire arrangements for services. Love, Sara."

No word of funeral arrangements reached Sara Jane. And there was still no word from Evie.

Back in Sussex, Evie, who had spoken with several people in the U.S., including Arthur Kennard, Jane Stone and Mrs. A.J. Yardley, was being looked after by her sister, Barbara. During the afternoon, she began to receive dozens of telegrams from friends, including Mrs. Vincent Price, Christopher Lee, Peter Bogdanovich and Polly Platt, Mrs. Red Skelton, Lady C. Aubrey Smith, Tony Tenser, Katherine Cornell and Charlton Heston, representing the Screen Actors Guild.

After seeing the *Today Show* in Beverly Hills, George Schaefer wrote to Evie:

> For over 25 years, since I first met him in the Pacific, Boris represented to me the highest ideals, personally and professionally, and at the same time he was the warmest and wittiest of gentlemen. For what comfort it is, I assure you he lives on in the hearts and memories of all who loved him.

In Anchorage, Alaska, Frank Brink wrote of the "grand gentleman... one of the greatest men in American theatre." Telling Evie that he had "never known a person more dedicated nor more honestly related to his craft," Brink added, "We are presently producing *Hamlet* and our opening night production will be dedicated to Boris Karloff." In Los Angeles, Jane Wyatt wrote, "A great human being is gone."

As he was setting out on a tour, Vincent Price heard the shocking news. On February 4, at an out of the way Holiday Inn on U.S. Highway 10 in Bismarck, North Dakota, he penned a letter to Evie:

> The heartbreaking news met me here at the beginning of my lecture tour. I know you have heard from Mary but I just had to add my love.
>
> I think you would be cheered to know the tremendous concern and very real feeling of grief all people I have met have expressed to me. He certainly was a very beloved man.
>
> I feel a great personal sense of loss as Boris was always an idol of mine and from the beginning of my career one of the few actors I felt I could call a friend.
>
> How he adored you! In every word he spoke of you there was such love, such genuine devotion.
>
> I won't go on for I know you must be hearing from the world!

Indeed, the world was writing to Evelyn Karloff on February 4, 1969. At his home in Wimbledon, Bernie Coleman, who had stayed awake the previous night "thinking of the hundreds of hours... talking at cricket matches," wrote of the friendship and tutelage Boris had provided, but added that "he would not want us to indulge in too much sentiment, for it was not in his nature."

From North Hollywood, calling herself "The Bride-to-be in #1 *Frankenstein*," Mae Clarke wrote of "dearly remembered Boris," while "the depth of love that was expressed for him by his fellow actors" was noted by John L. Dales after a board meeting of the Screen Actors Guild. As a follow-up to her call of the previous day, Jane Stone wrote, recalling "all that we had done together, our meeting, our days at Selznick, and even our tea in Boris' dressing room on the lot when we had squashed fly biscuits." Also writing were actor Chester Morris, makeup artist Verne Langdon, producer Daniel Mayer Selznick, John Trevelyan of the British Board of Film Censors, Mary Helmore and both the widow and daughter of Boris' late friend, Nigel ("Willie") Bruce. But perhaps the most unexpected tribute came from Charlie Jackson, Boris' colleague during 1912-15, with the St. Clair Stock Company in Canada and when "the knife was at his throat" in Chicago.

Even more friends and coworkers paid their respects the following day. The man who animated "the Grinch," Chuck Jones, claimed that Boris' "thoughtful and understanding reading of the script" would allow "children for many generations [to] find joy and a deeper understanding of Christmas." His dear friend who embarrassed him on national television 11 years earlier, Ralph Edwards, wrote, "Boris was truly a man for all people and all ages and all time." Also writing were Joan Crawford, Maurice Evans, Mrs. Eli Wallach, James Nicholson and Samuel Arkoff of AIP, Robert Bloch, the Officers and Men of the United States Air Force Band in Washington, D.C., and many of Evie and Boris' friends in both London and Hampshire.

One of the London friends was Christopher Lee, who, for several years, had lived next door to them at Cadogan Square. He reiterated his boundless admiration for Boris, describing him as his favorite, "a superb actor" who was filled with "kindness, gentleness and humour." Like so many others who had heard the news, he offered to provide Evie with "anything at all you need."

On Thursday, February 6, Boris' remains were cremated at Guildford, southwest of London, where Evie, Barbara and her husband, and Evie's mother, Lina, attended the service. Afterwards, Boris' ashes were buried at the Garden of Remembrance.

Conspicuously absent from the funeral was Sara Jane, who still awaited word in Yucaipa. Having no idea if her cable of three days earlier had reached Evie, she decided to write; and regardless of her exclusion from the obsequies, she penned only compliments, thanking her stepmother for taking such good care of her father. A week later, she finally received a letter, more than 10 days after he had passed away. Evie claimed that she had wired the news. Sara Jane courteously replied that "evidently your cable was lost."

On February 20, Evie responded to Sara Jane's second letter, mentioning the lawyers who were handling the estate. Boris' will, executed by William Henry Pratt on June 3, 1964, named "Evelyn Pratt, a.k.a. Evelyn Karloff" as sole legatee and, as reported in *The New York Times*, "provided nothing for his daughter, Sara Jane Cotten."

However, the will did bequeath the Dakota apartment to Kit Helmore. But rather than give Kit their former quarters, Evie sold the property and gave her a check for $10,000. Even in death, Boris was still managed by Evie, who oversaw a process that excluded his own daughter, yet provided an inheritance for the daughter of his wife's ex-husband. Of her father's relationship with Kit, who called him "Uncle Boris," Sara Jane reveals:

> Evie encouraged the closeness with my father... She saw
> a great deal of my father, and Evie encouraged and engi-
> neered that—to replace having a daughter in his life, but
> something over which she had some control.
>
> And then she called Kit and said she thought it was
> best, instead of her having the apartment, if she sold it and
> gave her the money... despite my father's will.

According to the will, Sara Jane would have received the estate if Evie had predeceased Boris. Including American holdings valued at $250,000 and a $400,000 uncashed check he had received for the four Mexican films, Boris' bequest to Evie totaled about $2 million.

The letters to Evie continued to pour in, including condolences from Mr. and Mrs. Alfred Hitchcock, Mr. and Mrs. Cecil Kellaway, Alan Napier, Ann Baxter and Dr. Seuss, who admitted, "Working with him on 'How the Grinch Stole Christmas' was a privilege, an honor, and the experience will be an inspiration to me always." Sportsmen on both sides of the Atlantic also paid their respects. While Adrian Cole, Secretary of the Hollywood Cricket Club, noted Boris' "good innings," D.J. Lush, Honorary Secretary of the Bramshott and Liphook Cricket Club, wrote simply and eloquently, "We are all the poorer for his passing."

Two days later, Mrs. I. Goldsworthy of Caedmon Records in London wrote to Evie, informing her that the New York office wished to make a charitable donation in his memory. For more than a decade, this artistically satisfying company had allowed him to indulge in children's literature while giving the public a taste of his real personality, as well as earning him the first of two Grammy nominations. Now the company's offer to support "some specific charity in which Mr. Karloff was interested" was very comforting to Evie, as were donations by friends and fans to organizations like the March of Dimes and the Children's Blood Foundation of New York.

On February 26, Evie received a letter from the Secretary of King Edward VII Hospital, who expressed his gratitude for Boris' generous bequest, to be used only for "special purchases." And after the proper regulations were followed, Evie sent a second check, to be divided among the nursing staff who cared for Boris. Having appreciated the unusual experience, each staff member wrote back, thanking her for the unnecessary generosity. One of the night nurses refused to cash her check, deciding "to keep it in remembrance of Mr. Karloff."

The generosity of those who admired Boris also was in evidence as individuals made substantial donations to the Motion Picture Relief Fund in his memory. And friends in the entertainment industry continued to write, both to Evie and others who knew Boris, well into the spring of 1969. An agent at MCA who represented him only briefly, Paul Freeman, recalled their association as being one of "long time friends." On March 15, Rita Lynn wrote to John L. Dales, "Some years ago I had the privilege of working with Mr. Karloff—his warmth and his dedication to his work were an example to many of us in an industry so often cluttered with the bored or the instant glory seeker." Having torn up every letter she had written to Evie, Mrs. Alex Segal finally managed to mail one on March 24, noting that Boris' undaunted spirit had fooled her into believing that he was in good health. And Alec Guinness, a long-time friend of Evie's who also had a cottage in Hampshire, gave Boris an actor's tribute simply by writing, "I liked him so very much and so greatly admired him."

Chapter 12

The Man Who Lives Again

"He was a wonderful and gentle man, and just loved his life and being able to be an actor, which is all he had ever wanted to be... I am always happy to hear what people say about my husband—even those people who never met or worked with him know him as a sensitive, generous kind and modest man."
—Evelyn Karloff

"He was more than human, and if God weren't dead, and I wasn't an atheist to begin with, I'd say, 'God bless Boris Karloff.' I believe I'll say it anyway."
—Forrest J Ackerman

Boris' death had evoked responses from a literal "who's who" of the entertainment industry, professional colleagues who knew both the actor and, to some degree, the man. On February 9, 1969, *The New York Times* had published a brief but poignant tribute by Peter Bogdanovich, who explained how Boris "so completely transcended his vehicles." And on the next day, *Newsweek* had noted that, in *Frankenstein*, he "conveyed, in the slow, ponderous shuffle of his leaden feet and the sad, puzzled movements of his great head, all the tragedy of man's aspiration confounded and perverted by a deformed ideal."

But Evie also heard from many fans throughout Europe and the United States, "common" folks who knew nothing about the inner workings of show business and very little about the real Boris Karloff. Yet, by watching his sensitive and compassionate screen characterizations, they experienced a connection to the man behind the masks. They witnessed the humanizing element within even the most thoroughly evil Karloff characters. And less than a day after he passed away, these fans began to express their sentiments to Evie, who made the transition from Boris' care-giver and unofficial business manager to the guardian of his memory. A few years later, after magazines like Forrest Ackerman's *Famous Monsters of Filmland* had introduced yet another generation to the Universal horror films, she would be called the "unofficial curator of the cult of Boris Karloff."

On the day after Boris' death, two brothers in Philadelphia wrote:

If the mind is as strong as it's cracked up to be, then the combined memory of fans all over the globe will keep Boris Karloff alive for an eternity of sunrises and sunsets. The popularity Mr. Karloff enjoyed was well deserved. As an artist he was unparalleled; as a good man he was known and respected from the time his name first reached national prominence. Hardly a soul who ever saw Mr. Karloff felt anything less than love and respect for him.

We weren't privileged to know Mr. Karloff personally but his image rarely left our hearts. From the days of our childhood until the present time, the name, the face,

262

the voice and the warming personality that made up the man we all mourn for were a constant source of inspiration. We felt as if we knew him personally... For he was a man that any one of us would have wanted to call "Friend...." We truly hope that these words and the words of fans from all over the world will serve to remind you that your husband was a very great, great human being, and that we all loved him very deeply.

Eight months later, a fan in Forest Park, Georgia, typed:

I was utterly shocked on the morning of February 3, 1969, to hear of Mr. Karloff's passing. It seemed as if the world had split down the middle. Now my world (and the worlds of many fans) has been shattered. I do not exaggerate. I have loved Mr. Karloff since the first day I saw him on the screen.

And all this devotion was inspired by an actor who, according to most news sources, "played monsters."

In the March-April 1969 issue of *Screen Actor*, John L. Dales officially recognized Boris' contribution to SAG:

This was no honorary society—it was a dangerous bit of business. Boris was not the type to go along for the ride. He was a courageous and aggressive force. He felt injustice and reacted to it. He continued to serve his fellow actors as an active member of the Guild Board until the early 1950s. He served on every negotiating committee during that period—an outspoken, challenging advocate for the many who dared not speak for themselves, innovative, intelligent, and articulate.

On May 12, Dales wrote to inform Evie that Walter Pidgeon was planning to "make the motion that Boris' name be placed on a door of one of the [Motion Picture] Country Home's hospital rooms, at the next Trustees' meeting later this month." Imagine Evie's surprise when she returned from a trip to Bermuda to discover that the man whom her husband had mentioned shortly before his death had chosen to honor him in such a magnanimous way. On May 28, Pidgeon met with the Board of Trustees of the Motion Picture and Television Relief Fund, who immediately approved his suggestion. On June 11, Evie wrote a candid reply to Guild secretary Midge Farrell:

I wish I could say that I was finding this easier, but I have to confess that it is rather the reverse at the moment. I just seem to miss Boris more each day and life seems to have little point. But you can't have it both ways, and I have to try and make the past make up for the present, which I know has to get better. I have so much to be grateful for, and I am.

Before the estate was settled legally, Evie, per Boris' request, sent Dales a $5,000 check for the Relief Fund, an organization "devoted to serving those in the... industry who need... assistance."

Soon after, the memorial plaque was hung in the "Boris Karloff Room" at the Motion Picture Hospital. And on December 6, 1973, she sent Dales another $5,000 check, this time for a scholarship fund set up by the Guild, noting that Boris would have wished to support it.

Evie kept busy at Roundabout and traveling to various parts of the world, including France, Belgium, Switzerland, Germany and Italy. Every summer, she flew to California to visit old friends from the Hollywood days like Ralph and Barbara Edwards, Jane Stone and Jane Wyatt. But she also tended to business affairs, making certain that Boris' image was not being abused and that she received any royalties due the estate.

Boris' Screen Actors Guild pension amounted to $507 per month, and in July 1970 Evie had her accountant check into what, if any, percentage of this sum was taxable as earned income in Great Britain. Although she claimed that she could not bear to watch any of her husband's films or television shows, in early 1972 she caught wind of Universal's plan to syndicate his most famous series as "Boris Karloff Presents *Thriller*," immediately assuming that rerun royalties would be in the offing. Inquiring on her behalf, the Guild was informed (correctly) that Boris' original contract had included advance payments for all potential syndicated reruns.

As late as the spring of 1973, budget-minded executives at American International were still trying to wring some dollars out of their association with the King of the Horror Films. Aping Roger Corman's motivation for *Targets*, AIP planned to re-edit "certain scenes embodying the late Mr. Karloff's performance... in... *The Raven* and *The Comedy of Terrors*... in a new and different photoplay now tentatively entitled 'Revenge of Dr. Death'," paying Evie $200 for footage from each film. No such picture was ever produced.

After 14 years of marriage, Sara Jane and Richard Cotten were divorced in 1972. Soon after, she decided to strike out on her own and make a name for herself as a businesswoman. Although she had experienced a wonderful relationship with her stepfather, she and her mother were not as close, and Evie's distant attitude toward her was clearly illustrated when she divorced. Rather than offer support, Evie said, "Daddy would have been so disappointed"—an ironic comment, considering that Boris had been married five times. Displaying determination reminiscent of her father's, Sara Jane became a successful real estate broker and, in 1981, moved to Rancho Mirage, near Palm Springs.

Beginning in the early 1970s, Evie received many letters from young people who were being influenced by Boris, merely from seeing a few of his films on television. On February 22, 1973, a 15-year-old American girl visiting London with a school theater group wrote, "Only recently have I begun to watch his films... Through such contact with acting have I become interested in the same for myself."

On December 5, 1982, Evie noted that the BBC was running a season of Karloff films. Still receiving letters from fans on a regular basis, she always answered them cordially, but rarely offered information on Boris' life and, as far as his career was concerned, had scant knowledge of it. On May 6, 1988, she wrote, "I wish I had known him when he made all those films, as I never saw them." But she was very kind to admirers, thanking them for their devotion and even acting as a conduit between them. Answering one inquirer, she would write, "I hope you don't mind my giving your name to a[nother] great fan." And when prospective authors of books on Boris would drop a line, she always complimented them, adding, "When he was asked to write his life story, he always said no—'Local boy makes good. So what?'"

In 1987 educator and Uppingham alumnus Bryan Matthews' history of the school's most prominent students, *Eminent Uppinghamians*, was published. Among the 50 (post-1853) students profiled by the late Matthews are Sir Arthur Conan Doyle's brother-in-law, author E.W. Hornung and former Fircroft praeposter Charles E. Raven, who became a noted theologian, educator, scientist, pacifist, Master of Christ's College and Vice-Chancellor of Cambridge University. Looking back on his formative days at Uppingham, Raven called it a "perverse and philistine" school. But even with all his impressive accomplishments, he was outdone in at least one category by an Anglo-Indian underclassman named William Henry Pratt. As described by Matthews:

Mr. and Mrs. Joseph Cotten, Evie and Sara Jane at the Academy of Motion Picture Arts and Sciences 100th Birthday Tribute to Boris, Los Angeles, 1988.

> If the degree of a man's eminence is measured by the number of people in the world to whom his name is known, then Boris Karloff must be the most eminent OU [Old Uppinghamian] of all. Because of his fame as a film star,—most particularly as the monster created by Frankenstein—his name is familiar on the lips of people from every nation.

In 1988 Evie attended a 100th birthday tribute to Boris staged by the Academy of Motion Picture Arts and Sciences in Los Angeles. A host of clips from his greatest performances were interspersed with reminiscences by Vincent Price, Peter Bogdanovich, Robert Wise and George Schaefer. Sara Jane also attended but, as on *This Is Your Life* 30 years earlier, stood squarely in the shadow of her stepmother: "Evie never told me about the evening of the tribute. When I learned of it, I contacted the Guild. They were delighted to hear from me and said, 'We had never been given the information on how to contact you.'" Evie later wrote, "The tribute... was really fabulous. I thought it was almost better than an Oscar, which only takes a few minutes, and this took over two hours!"

Just before Christmas 1990 Evie was invited to London's 10 Downing Street by Prime Minister John Major, "a great admirer" of Boris. Shortly after their meeting, she wrote, "I think we are very fortunate to have him at the helm."

In 1991 *Frankenstein* turned 60, an event recognized by the press and by MCA-Universal, who marketed several Monster-oriented toys and products, as well as video releases of classic Karloff horror films. And a British television producer planned a documentary on Boris' life, but even Christopher Lee's participation in the filming of the pilot failed to generate the necessary financing. Another milestone of that year was the passing of Sara Jane's 91-year-old mother, who, following the loss of her beloved Edgar a few years earlier, had been living in Walnut Creek, California.

During the early 1990s, Evie, now in her late 80s, began to ease up on her constant globetrotting. In 1982 the British conflict in the Falkland Islands had troubled her considerably, and she expressed a similar fear of traveling during the Persian Gulf War in 1991. But more so than international conflicts, her failing health prevented her from enjoying the lifestyle she had grown accustomed to since Boris' death. In June 1992 she became seriously ill and, although she had visited a doctor during the past year, decided to return to the tenets of her Christian Science faith. Refusing to take medicine, she changed her own bandages and rarely left Roundabout. The following spring, concerned neighbors had to break into the cottage, only to discover her in a frightful state. On June 1, 1993, Evie passed away at the age of 89.

Although Sara Jane experienced a difficult relationship with Evie, she remembers her positive qualities as well as her overwhelming possessiveness, a trait that lasted a quarter-century beyond Boris' demise:

> Evie was attractive, always pin neat, conservatively dressed, proper, reserved. As to my feelings, she did not invite much in-depth conversation, but she was *absolutely* devoted to my father and to the memory of my father. She was very protective of him and his memory, and really didn't talk to me much about him, because I think: One, she had emotional difficulty in doing so. I think it was always very close to the surface for her, emotionally. And two, I don't think she *wanted* to discuss him with me—that would be an intertwining of the two worlds.
>
> But every year, when she came over, she and I would have lunch—once. And we just maintained that habit, and nothing more, nothing less. The last several years of her life, perhaps, we wrote four letters a year instead of one or two. But we both maintained the association, although one couldn't say it was any more arm's length than it ever had been—it simply remained arm's length.

Having witnessed—both personally and professionally—the collaborative nature of Boris and Evie's relationship, Frank Brink claimed:

> Evelyn Karloff was important, or better still, necessary to the middle and latter periods of Karloff's career. Her influence, I am convinced, had been constant as an essential part of the decisions that affected the roles Karloff accepted as well as the attitude he carried to those roles. I think this is true with any union of this nature, a union based upon genuine love and respect. They, I truly believe, were genuine partners in every sense of the word.

The estate left by Evie was valued at $2.5 million. While she bequeathed particular sums to friends, the remainder was placed in the Boris Karloff Charitable Trust, a fund overseen by two English attorneys.

The previous year, Sara Jane, after 16 years on her own, had married her "best friend," William J. Sparkman, a retired Air Force colonel and engineer for Martin-Marietta, whom she had known since 1962. She, Richard Cotten and their two children had met "Sparky," his wife and three children while stationed at Vandenberg Air Force Base outside Lompoc. Over the years, while living the itinerant military life, the two families saw each other whenever possible, and Sara Jane became very good friends with Sparky's wife, who unfortunately passed away in 1991. Of their 1992 marriage, Sara Jane revealed, "Nobody was more surprised than my husband and I when we got together. But it's delightful." It is indeed a remarkable relationship.

In October 1993 Sara Jane and Sparky flew to England, where they were allowed only limited access to the flat at Sheffield Terrace and Roundabout cottage, finding very few items that had belonged to Boris. For years, Evie had told fans that nothing remained of his personal belongings, but Sara Jane, aided by the executor of the estate, received a small number of objects that had been placed in the care of a neighbor at Bramshott. All told, she rescued his watch from *This Is Your Life*, a signature money clip, a French hat, two cricket balls and some books, papers and photographs.

When Sara Jane inquired about the future auctioning of the estate, she was told that a date had not been set. However, on Tuesday, October 26, 1993—11 days after she and Sparky returned to the States—the remainder of Evie and Boris' personal effects were sold off at a priory in Newbury, Berkshire. Among the items were many fine pieces of antique furniture and a collection of signed books and photographs that belonged to Boris. Roundabout also was sold by agents in Liphook. "They just didn't want me there," Sara Jane admitted. "I don't know why."

A couple who bought two of Evie's framed watercolors at the auction later discovered a canvas of Boris' Ardath Bey hidden beneath one of them. Evidently, Evie, choosing not to be haunted by her late husband's eerie image, had used the rare *Mummy* painting as a mount for a canvas that she preferred. According to the couple, "a series of weird mishaps" befell them after Ardath was unearthed.

As a result of California's Celebrities Rights Act of 1987, Sara Jane inherited family ownership of Boris' image, thus being able to license officially any future use of it. And more overwhelmingly, she inherited the mantle of "Curator of the Karloff Cult":

> As a way of dealing with not being close to my father, I felt that I really had no right to speak on the subject. That was one of the most difficult things after Evie died and people looked to me for answers... And I want people to understand that I *really do* understand that this has nothing to do with me. It has to do with my father.
>
> Of course, for a girl... who gets married—you change your name—and you can be as invisible as you like. And it isn't the first thing out of my mouth, nor has it ever been when I meet somebody. "Oh, my father's an actor. What does your father do?"
>
> People know it. People learn about it. And I can watch it go around a room. I have an absolute sixth sense when people are talking about it. And I had trouble—I don't anymore—when it was indeed the first thing out of people's mouths to me, because I think probably I was defensive, at least internally, that I didn't know more about him.

Sara Jane is very interested in the future of the Boris Karloff Charitable Trust. Since the fund is administered by two trustees from a firm that represented both Boris and Evie, she possesses no legal control, but nonetheless wants the donations to benefit organizations her father would have approved of.

Established in 1993, Karloff Enterprises is a partnership between Sara and her husband that resulted from their being invited to a *Famous Monsters of Filmland* convention in Arlington, Virginia, that June. Attending ostensibly to acknowledge Forrest Ackerman's role in the perpetuation of the horror-film genre, Sara Jane also was interested in another aspect of the event:

> I had heard that Bela Lugosi, Jr., and Ron Chaney [grandson of Lon, Jr.] were going to be there. We had never met, and we'd always been curious about what the other guy was like. And we found that we like each other tremendously, and we play together and we work together now. But they each had been actively involved in their ancestor's memorabilia, career, and fan following, and I had not, because that really had fallen to Evie... And she died, actually the weekend of the convention.
>
> So, given the information from Ron and Bela, and through the agent who represented my stepmother in licensing the use of my father's name and likeness, Roger Richmond, we became involved in the licensing process... The importance of my involvement is to oversee some standard of excellence, some standard of good taste in the way in which my father's name and likeness is used...
>
> So, by developing a high public profile during the last three years... we've made ourselves available to the fans, and it's been rewarding beyond belief. It's also been an education for me. I've learned much more about my father's career than I knew before. And I have the overwhelmingly marvelous experience of learning more about my father from people who knew and loved him. So, for me, it's been a total win-win situation.

Bela Lugosi, Jr., Sara Jane and Ron Chaney are happily menaced by monster impersonators at Universal Studios Florida in 1995.

Elisabeth Crowley, granddaughter of Julia Honoria Pratt Donkin; Rosamund James, daughter of Richard Septimus Pratt; and Sara Jane Karloff Sparkman, daughter of William Henry Pratt, a.k.a. Boris Karloff, England, June 1996. (Photographed by William Sparkman)

One major result of Sara Jane's collaboration with Lugosi and Chaney was the creation of "Classic Movie Monsters," a set of United States postage stamps honoring their ancestors' most recognizable film roles. Banding together, they petitioned the Post Office and, with the help of fans nationwide, gathered over 16,000 signatures. Sara Jane said, "The public support of it, the media attention to it, was unbelievable. They fell in love with the project. We had a lot of coverage on television, radio and in newspapers... and lots of letters written to the Post Office by individuals."

In October 1996 the Post Office announced that the stamps would be made available in time for Halloween 1997. Sara Jane enthusiastically admitted, "We would not have been successful without the overwhelming support of people across the country. We are very grateful to them all." While Chaney, Sr., Lugosi and Chaney, Jr. each appear on one stamp, Boris appears on two: one depicting the Monster and another featuring the Mummy. Sara Jane concluded:

> The tribute of having them each honored by his own stamp
> will be tremendous. It's a remarkable tribute. It's some-
> thing the three families have done together... something
> that we can share with the fans and it's something that we
> can leave for our children to be proud of.

If Boris were alive to see Sara Jane's efforts on behalf of his legacy, she feels he would tell her, "What's the big fuss?" But she observes, "No one would be more amazed or more gratified by the continuing adoration of his multi-generational fan base. He would just be astounded... He would be absolutely amazed at the reverence with which he is still held. He also would think it was a bunch of foolishness."

The East Indian strain in the Pratt lineage has carried on strongly. Both Sara Jane's son, Michael Cotten, and his daughter, Kacey, inherited the olive complexion, black hair and pierc-

Sara Jane, revisiting her childhood home at 2320 Bowmont Drive in Beverly Hills, recalls a fond memory for Fred Jordan, her husband William Sparkman and Harold Nollen, November 12, 1996. (Photographed by Scott Allen Nollen)

ing dark eyes. Aside from sharing what Boris called his "tan," Sara Jane also resembles her father in other ways: "A love of animals, certainly, and a love of sports and the outdoors. Probably a sense of privacy and propriety. I'm very self-disciplined, as was my father. I look like him, except for the pegs in his neck." As to her articulate speech, she credits the influence of her well-educated mother and stepfather as much as any genetic inheritance from Boris.

Although Boris' grandsons have no connections to the motion picture or theater industries, Sara Jane speaks of their admiration for his legacy: "They knew him. They loved him. They were proud of him, but they never showed any interest in following in his footsteps." Michael, who lives in California, has spent most of his adult life in the construction business. David Cotten, who bears almost no resemblance to his grandfather, works for an advertising firm in Colorado Springs, where he lives with his wife and two children, Kyle and Mackenzie.

Anyone who knows anything about Boris Karloff is aware that the man was the antithesis of monsters, killers and madmen. But the mistake most people make is believing that he was the antithesis of the *characters* he played—all of whom, in varying degrees, possess a depth, an inner soul, that other "horror actors" of his generation did not develop. And his successors who *did* demonstrate this quality were merely borrowing from the master. Boris Karloff was *not* the antithesis of the roles he played. He made those monsters, killers and madmen—no matter how iniquitous—*human*. He perfectly visualized the concept developed in 1885 by Robert Louis Stevenson in *The Strange Case of Dr. Jekyll and Mr. Hyde*: that each human being is *capable of being* a monster, a killer, a madman. By gaining an audience's empathy for his characters, he encouraged—and still encourages—them to look inside themselves, to discover what it is that makes us human.

As attested by scores of people who knew and worked with him, Boris Karloff was a true gentleman. People loved him, and filmgoers loved his characters because he was able to transmit his own unique personality into even the most one-dimensional villains. In light of the fact that each human being naturally possesses a morbid curiosity, the concept that villains are often more appealing and entertaining than heroes is a valid one. But people who admire Boris' characters do not do so just to satisfy a taste for the morbid; they do so because, without speaking a word, he stunningly captured the theme of Mary Shelley's *Frankenstein* and successfully varied it again and again for the next four decades. One does not have to see much of his work to know that the man and the actor are one and the same. The artist and his art are inseparable.

The fact that he accomplished this artistry in one of the most underrated and misunderstood film genres, thought of as "camp" by so many, makes his achievement even more staggering. There certainly have been better stage and film technicians, with more impressive professional backgrounds, more prestigious roles and more landmark performances; but only a truly remarkable actor leaves behind an artistic legacy that makes such a memorable and coherent statement. Directors and writers are better equipped for *auteurism*; but few performers have the talent, tools or opportunities to reach that esteemed level.

And Boris accomplished all this in the film medium, aside from his successes on stage, in radio and television shows and on spoken-word recordings. If he was confronted with this view of his achievement, he first would deny it, and then perhaps, begrudgingly, would attribute it to three things: luck, hard work and the "obscure inner urge" described by Joseph Conrad, who had an immeasurable influence on his life and art. He also would credit Lon Chaney, Sr., who had pioneered an earlier, more rudimentary version of the "sympathetic monster."

Chaney had told him to be "different," to "find something no one else can or will do," to express "individuality." But even if the Man of a Thousand Faces had not given him this advice, Boris may have realized it on his own, because he naturally possessed these qualities. Breaking away from family tradition and social prejudice in 1909, he expressed his individuality early, and kept doing so for the next 60 years. His acting style, social and political attitudes and philosophies of art, literature and film were all his own; and he expressed them through his performances, his literary essays, and his activism in the Screen Actors Guild. Thirty years after catching a lift with Chaney, he gave exactly the same advice to Christopher Lee, who made his own unique contribution to the terror genre by creating the screen's most powerful Count Dracula.

Women, in particular, noticed something special about Boris. They saw it in his eyes, which, demonstrated by his best performances, truly were the windows to his soul. The deep "inner aura," the "mysterious melancholy quality" that Valerie Hobson, Julie Harris, Angela Lansbury, Anna Lee, Cynthia Lindsay and his own daughter have described still exists in his art and, therefore, always will. To quote Bela Lugosi's Ygor in *Son of Frankenstein*, "Cannot be destroyed. Cannot die. Your father made him live for always."

Certainly Boris was a great actor, a great artist. But for what qualities would he wish to be remembered? According to Sara Jane: "That he was a man of integrity and compassion. That he was a consummate professional. This gentleness of spirit that he lived his life with and that he brought to his roles." She knows her father better than she thinks.

Boris' motion picture star on the Hollywood Walk of Fame. He also has a star honoring his two decades of television work. (1996 photograph by Scott Allen Nollen)

Appendix A

Stage Performances

Stock Companies (Canada and the United States)

The Jean Russell/Ray Brandon Players (1910-12)
Kamloops, British Columbia—Regina, Saskatchewan
The Devil (Written by Ferenc Molnar [Karloff as Hoffman]); *East Lynne*; *Charley's Aunt*.

The Harry St. Clair Players (1912-14, 1915-16)
Prince Albert, Saskatchewan—Minot, North Dakota
Paid in Full; *The Parish Priest*; *Charley's Aunt*; *Bought and Paid For*; *East Lynne*; *Way Down East*; *Baby Mine*; *What Happened to Jones?*; *Why Smith Left Home*.

Various Unidentified Stock Companies (1914-15)
Midwestern United States

Unidentified Stock Company (1916)
Virginia

The Billie Bennett Company (1916)
Chicago, Illinois—Minnesota, Iowa, Kansas, Colorado, Nevada
The Virginian (by Owen Wister and Kirk La Shelle [Karloff as Trampas]).

California

San Pedro Stock Company (1918)
Southern California

Maude Amber Players of Vallejo
San Joaquin Valley—San Francisco, California

Various Unidentified Stock Companies (1918-19)
California

Unidentified Vaudeville Act (1919)
San Jose, California

Robert Lawrence Players (1920)
San Francisco, California

Various Stock Companies (late 1920s)
San Francisco—Los Angeles, California
Hotel Imperial; *The Virginian*; *The Idiot* (Produced by Reginald Pole, 1926); *Window Panes* (Egan Theatre, 1928); *Kongo* (Capitol Theatre, 1929).

The Criminal Code (1930)
Credits: Written by Martin Flavin; Performances in San Francisco and Los Angeles.
Cast: Arthur Byron (Warden Brady), Boris Karloff (Ned Galloway).

The Tell-Tale Heart (1938)
Credits: Based on the Story by Edgar Allan Poe; touring production.
Cast: Boris Karloff (Narrator).

New York

Arsenic and Old Lace (January 10, 1941)
Credits: Written by Joseph L. Kesselring; Produced by Howard Lindsay and Russel Crouse; Directed by Bretaigne Windust; Settings and Costumes by Raymond Sovey; Theater: the Fulton (Broadway); Closed (Broadway) June 1942; Rehearsals: December 1940-January 1941; National Tour, June 1942-July 1943, including Performances in San Francisco, Sacramento, Portland, Denver, Salt Lake City, Minneapolis, and at West Point Military Academy; 1,444 Performances.
Cast: Boris Karloff (Jonathan Brewster), Josephine Hull (Abby Brewster), Wyrley Birch (the Reverend Dr. Harper), John Alexander (Teddy Brewster), John Quigg (Officer Brophy), Bruce Gordon (Officer Klein), Jean Adair (Martha Brewster), Helen Brooks (Elaine Harper), Allyn Joslyn (Mortimer Brewster), Henry Herbert (Mr. Gibbs), Edgar Stehli (Dr. Einstein), Anthony Ross (Officer O'Hara), Victor Sutherland (Lieutenant Rooney), William Parke (Mr. Witherspoon).

South Pacific

Arsenic and Old Lace (1945)
Credits: Written by Joseph L. Kesselring; Produced by the U.S. Army Special Service Office, by Arrangement with USO Camp Shows, Inc.; Directed by Sgt. George Schaefer; Officer in Charge: Major Maurice Evans; Stage Manager: Pvt. Robert Karnes; Assistant Stage Manager: Pfc. Bill Hammel; Set Design and Decoration: Sgt. Frederick Stover; Set Construction: Pfc. Frank Walkowiak; Electricians: Cpl. Lloyd Reed, Pvt. Melvin Glettner; Wardrobe: Pvt. E. Joseph Wilson; Program Design and Advertising: Sgt. Bill Beynon, Sgt. Ken Reid, Pfc. Ray Olivere; Publicity: Pfc. Bill Rowe.
Cast: Boris Karloff (Jonathan Brewster), Mary Adams (Abby Brewster), Mr. Arthur E. Wyman (Reverend Doctor Harper), Sgt. George Schaefer (Teddy Brewster), Cpl. Bill Leonard (Officer Klein), Cpl. Pat Iovinelli (Officer Brophy), Jean Bodge (Martha Brewster), Janet Slauson (Elaine Harper), Pvt. Robert Karnes (Mortimer Brewster), Pfc. Bill Hammel (Mr. Gibbs), Pvt. Werner Klemperer (Dr. Einstein), Pvt. Ross White (Officer O'Hara), Pvt. Harold Carol (Lieutenant Rooney), Pvt. Robert Dunavon (Mr. Witherspoon).

Hollywood and San Francisco

On Borrowed Time (November 1946)
Credits (Hollywood): Executive Producer: Richard Irving; Associate Producers: Keenan Wynn, Mort Werner, Tim Whelan; Press Representative: George Gale; Advisory Director: Gilda Dahlberg; Production Assistant: Belle Schwartz; Makeup by Jack P. Pierce; (Hollywood and San Franciso): Written by Paul Osborn; Based on the Novel by Lawrence Edward Watkin; Directed by Herbert Rudley: Set Design by Phil Raiguel; Lighting and Technical Director: Sol Cornberg; Stage Manager: Richard Reeves; Assistant Stage Manager: Maurice Kelly; Head Electrician: William Campbell; Carpenter: Lloyd Brierley; Production Assistant: Betty Buckner; Performances at the El Patio Theatre, Hollywood.
Cast: (Hollywood and San Francisco): Boris Karloff (Julian Northrup, Gramps), Tommy Ivo (Pud), Beulah Bondi (Nellie, Granny), Ralph Morgan (Mr. Brink), Margaret Hamilton (Aunt), Joseph Crehan, Richard Reeves (Mr. Grimes), Frank Cady (Sheriff), Ann Tobin, Edward Clark, Maurice Kelly, Dick Dillon, Herbert Rudley.

New York

The Linden Tree (March 2, 1948)
Credits: Written by J.B. Priestley; Produced by Maurice Evans, Directed by George Schaefer; Settings by Peter Wolf; Costumes by Frank Thompson; Theater: the Music Box (Broadway); Seven Performances; Closed March 1948.
Cast: Boris Karloff (Professor Robert Linden), Una O'Connor (Mrs. Colton), Noel Leslie (Alfred Lockhart), Barbara Everest (Mrs. Linden), Halliwell Hobbes, Jr. (Rex Linden), Viola Keats (Jean Linden), Cathleen Cordell (Marion Linden), Mary Kimber (Edith Westmore), Marilyn Erskine (Dinah Linden), Emmett Rogers (Bernard Fawcett).

Santa Fe, New Mexico

Unknown title (summer 1948)
Credits: Theater: El Teatro de Santa Fe.
Cast: Boris Karloff.

New York

The Shop at Sly Corner (January 18, 1949)
Credits: Written by Edward Percy; presented by Gant Gaither; Directed by Margaret Perry; Setting and Costumes by Willis Knighton; Theater: the Booth (Broadway); Five Performances; Closed January 1949; Rehearsals: November 1948-January 1949.
Cast: Boris Karloff (Decius Heiss), Una O'Connor (Mrs. Catt), Jay Robinson (Archie Fellowes), Mary MacLeod (Margaret Heiss), Jane Lloyd-Jones (Joan Deal), Ethel Griffies (Mathilde Heiss), Philip Saville (Robert Graham), Emmett Rogers (Corder Morris), Steve Hubbard (Alfred Hyslop), John Elliot (Reginald Mason).

Atlanta, Georgia

On Borrowed Time (January 1950)
Credits: Written by Paul Osborn; Based on the Novel by Lawrence Edward Watkin; Directed by Gerald Savory; Performances at the Penthouse Theatre.
Cast: Boris Karloff (Julian Northrup, Gramps), Richard Wilson (Pud), Rae Sterling Moore (Nellie, Granny), Robert McBride (Mr. Brink), Pamela Simpson (Aunt), Frank Lyon, James Reese, Carl Betz, Jean Barnes, Joe Starr, Joe Robinette, John Davis.

New York

Peter Pan (April 24, 1950)
Credits: Written by James M. Barrie; Presented by Peter Lawrence and R.L. Stevens; Directed by John Burrell; Associate Producer: Wendy Toye; Settings by Ralph Alswang; Costumes by Motley; Songs and Lyrics by Leonard Bernstein: "The Pirate Song" and "The Plank" sung by Karloff; "Who Am I?" "Build My House," and "Peter, Peter" sung by Marcia Henderson; Incidental Music by Alec Wilder; Orchestrations by Hershy Kay; Musical Coordination and Arrangements by Trude Rittman; Musical Conductor: Ben Steinberg; Theater: The Imperial (Broadway)—321 Performances; Closed late January 1951; National Tour, 1951, Including Performances in Boston (Shubert Theatre), Philadelphia (The Opera House), and Chicago (Opera House).
Cast: Jean Arthur (Peter Pan), Boris Karloff (Mr. Darling/Captain Hook), Peg Hillias (Mrs. Darling), Marcia Henderson (Wendy), Jack Dimond (John), Charles Taylor (Michael), Norman Shelly (Nana/the Crocodile), Gloria Patrice (Liza/Tiger Lily), Lee Barnett (Tootles), Richard Knox (Slightly), Philip Hepburn (Curly), Charles Brill, Edward Benjamin (the Twins), Buzzy Martin (Nibs), Joe E. Marks (Smee), David Kurlan (Starkey), Will Scholz (Jukes), Nehemiah Persoff (Cecco), Harry Allen (Mullins), John Dennis (Noodler), William Marshall (Cookson), Vincent Beck (Whibbles), Norman Shelly (the Crocodile), Gloria Patrice (Tiger Lily), Ronnie Aul, Kenneth Davis, Norman DeJoie, Loren Hightower, Jay Riley, William Sumner (Indians), Stephanie Augustine, Eleanor Winter (Mermaids), Ronnie Aul, Kenneth Davis, Jay Riley, William Sumner (Pirates).
Tour Cast included Joan McCracken (Peter Pan in Chicago), Jennifer Bunker (Wendy in Boston), Jackson Perkins (Mrs. Darling for all dates).

London

Night of 100 Stars (1955)
Credits: A Benefit for the Actors' Orphanage; Theater: London Palladium.
Cast: Richard Attenborough, Hermione Baddeley, Bernard Braden, the Crazy Gang, Marlene Dietrich, Diana Dors, Hermione Gingold, Alec Guinness, Gilbert Harding, Jack Hawkins, Boris Karloff, Evelyn Karloff, Danny Kaye, Pat Kirkwood, Beatrice Lillie, John Mills, Laurence Olivier, Eric Portman, Michael Redgrave.

New York

The Lark (November 17, 1955)
Credits: Written by Lillian Hellman; Based on the Play *L'Alouette* by Jean Anouilh; Presented by Kermit Bloomgarden; Directed by Joseph Anthony; Scenery and Lighting by Jo Mielziner; Costumes by Alvin Colt; Music by Leonard Bernstein; Theater: The Longacre (Broadway); 229 Performances; Closed June 1956; Rehearsals: October-November 1955; National Tour, August 4-December 15, 1956 (Karloff Appeared on the San Francisco dates).
Cast: Julie Harris (Joan of Arc), Boris Karloff (Bishop Cauchon), Christopher Plummer (Warwick), Ward Costello (Joan's Father), Lois Holmes (Joan's Mother), John Reese (Joan's Brother), Roger De Kovan (the Promoter), Joseph Wiseman (the Inquisitor), Michael Higgins (Brother Ladvenu), Theodore Bikel (Robert de Beaudricourt), Ann Hillary (Agnes Sorel), Joan Elan (the Young Queen), Paul Roebling (the Dauphin), Rita Vale (Queen Yolanda), Bruce Gordon (Monsieur de la Tremouielle), Richard Nichols (Archbishop of Rheims), Ralph Roberts (Executioner), Leonard Knight (English Soldier), Joe Bernard (Scribe).
Tour Cast included Sam Jaffe (Cauchon on all tour dates except San Francisco).

Anchorage, Alaska

Arsenic and Old Lace (March 21, 1957)
Credits: Written by Joseph L. Kesselring; Directed by Frank O. Brink; Assistant to Director: Lucille O'Brien; Technical Director: John Villesvik; Stage Manager: John Elliott; Stage Assistants: Ernest Brown, Sheryl Marquette; Crew Chief: Dave Davila; Lighting Engineer: Robert Cushman; Lighting Assistants: Dannie Caulfield, William O'Brien, Louise Rodgers; Sound Engineer: Ralph Daniels; Property Mistress: Monica Morton; Property Assistants: Gayle Hodgson, Don Clarkson; Costume Mistress: Mary Cushman; Costume Assistants: Lucille O'Brien, Jo Brink; Publicity Director: Pat Christensen; Publicity Assistants: Carmen La Rosa, Betty Brenner, Mary Ann Dehlin, Opal Everett, Bill Church, Daniel Hill, Don Gretzer, Clyde Rowen; Makeup: Dorothy Costello, Connie Hill, Claudia Davila; Set Design: William Trotman, John Villesvik; Set Construction Foreman: John Villesvik; Production Coordinator: William Trotman; Three Performances; Closed March 23, 1957.
Cast: Boris Karloff (Jonathan Brewster), Ellen Maxon (Abby Brewster), Cecil Abbott (Reverend Doctor Harper), Robert Yates (Teddy Brewster), Carmen La Rosa (Officer Brophy), Dennis Lynch (Officer Klein), Kay Garvine (Martha Brewster), Donna Peterson (Elaine Harper), Bill Trotman (Mortimer Brewster), Aubrey Mathis (Mr. Gibbs), Raleigh C. Butterfield (Dr. Einstein), Robert La Follette (Officer O'Hara), Maurice J. Costello (Lieutenant Rooney), Donald M. Gretzer (Mr. Witherspoon), Moose Moore, Dorothy Costello, Connie Hill, Ernest Brown (understudies), Paul Anderson (body).

Monterey, California

On Borrowed Time (March 17, 1961)
Credits: Written by Paul Osborn; Based on the Novel by Lawrence Edward Watkin; Theater: Wharf Theater and Opera House; Eight Performances; closed March 23, 1961.
Cast: Boris Karloff (Julian Northrup, Gramps).

San Juan, Puerto Rico

On Borrowed Time (January 1961)
Credits: Written by Paul Osborn; Based on the Novel by Lawrence Edward Watkin.
Cast: Boris Karloff (Julian "Gramps" Northrup).

Appendix B

Silent and Sound Films

Silents

His Majesty, the American (1919)
Credits: Directed by Joseph Henabery; Produced by Douglas Fairbanks; Written by Joseph Henabery and Elton Banks (Fairbanks); Based on a Story by Elton Banks (Fairbanks); Photographed by Victor Fleming and Glen MacWilliams; Released by United Artists; Running Time: 8 reels.
Cast: Douglas Fairbanks (William Brooks), Marjorie Daw (Felice, Countess of Montenac), Lillian Langdon (Marguerita), Frank Campeau (Grand Duke), Sam Southern, Jay Dwiggins, Albert MacQuarrie, Karla Schramm, Boris Karloff (extra).

The Lightning Raider (1919)
Credits: Directed by George B. Seitz; Screenplay by Charles Goddard and John B. Clymer; Based on stories by May Yohe; Released by Pathé Pictures; 15-chapter serial.
Cast: Pearl White, Warner Oland, Henry G. Sell, Boris Karloff.

The Masked Raider (1919)
Credits: Directed by Aubrey M. Kennedy; Released by Arrow Pictures; 15-chapter serial.
Cast: Harry Myers, Ruth Stonehouse, Paul Panzer, Boris Karloff.

The Prince and Betty (1919)
Credits: Directed by Robert Thornby; Produced by Jesse D. Hampton; Based on the Novel by P.G. Wodehouse; Released by Pathé Film Exchange; Running Time: 5 reels.
Cast: William Desmond (John Maude), Mary Thurman (Betty Keith), Anita Kay (Mrs. Wheldon), George Swann (Reggie Hayling), Walter Peng (President), Wilton Taylor (Benjamin Scobell), William Levaull (Crump), Frank Lanning (Shepherd), Boris Karloff (bit).

The Deadlier Sex (mid-March 1920)
Credits: Directed by Robert Thornby; Produced by Fred Myton; Based on a Story by Bayard Veiler; Released by Pathé Pictures; Running Time: 6 reels.
Cast: Blanche Sweet (Mary Willard), Winter Hall (Henry Willard), Roy Laidlaw (Huntley Green), Russell Simpson (Jim Willis), Boris Karloff (Jules Borney), Mahlon Hamilton (Harvey Judson).

The Courage of Marge O'Doone (early June 1920)
Credits: Directed by David Smith; Screenplay by Robert North Bradbury; Based on the Novel by James Oliver Curwood; Released by Vitagraph Pictures; Running Time: 7 reels.
Cast: Pauline Starke (Marge O'Doone), Niles Welch (David Raine), George Stanley (Michael O'Doone), Jack Curtis (Brokaw), William Dryer (Hauch), Boris Karloff (Tavish), Billie Benedict (Margret O'Doone), James O'Neill (Mukoki), Baree (the Outlaw Dog).

The Last of the Mohicans (1920)
Credits: Directed by Maurice Tourneur and Clarence Brown; Produced by Maurice Tourneur; Screenplay by Robert A. Dillon; Based on the Novel by James Fenimore Cooper; Photographed by Philip R. Dubois and Charles Van Enger; Released by Associated Producers; Running Time: 6 reels.
Cast: Wallace Beery (Magua), Barbara Bedford (Cora Munro), Albert Roscoe (Uncas), Lillian Hall (Alice Munro), Henry Woodward (Major Heyward), James Gordon (Colonel Munro), George Hackathorne (Captain Randolph), Nelson McDowell (David Gamut), Harry Lorraine (Hawkeye), Theodore Lorch (Chingachgook), Jack McDonald (Tamenund), Sydney Deane (General Webb), Boris Karloff (Huron Indian).

Without Benefit of Clergy (late June 1921)
Credits: Directed by James Young; Produced by Paul Brunton; Supervised by Randolph C. Lewis; Screen-

play by Randolph C. Lewis; Based on a Short Story by Rudyard Kipling; Released by Pathé Film Exchange; Running Time: 6 reels.

Cast: Virginia Brown Faire (Ameera), Thomas Holding (John Holden), Evelyn Selbie (Ameera's Mother), Otto Lederer (Afghan Money Lender), Boris Karloff (Ahmed Khan), Nigel De Brulier (Pir Khan), Herbert Prior (Hugh Sanders), Ruth Sinclair (Alice Sanders), E.G. Miller (Michael Revenish), Phillipe De Lacey (Tota, at five).

The Hope Diamond Mystery (1921)

Credits: Directed by Stuart Payton; Screenplay by Charles Goddard and John B. Clymer; Based on a Story by May Yohe; Released by Kosmik Films; 15-chapter serial.

Cast: Grace Darmond (Bibi/Mary Hilton), William Marion (Bagi/James Marcon), Harry Carter (Ghung/Sidney Atherton), George Cheseboro (Jean-Baptiste Tavanier/John Gregge), Boris Karloff (Priest of Kama-Sita/Dakar, Hindu Servant), Carmen Phillips (Miza/Wanda Atherton), May Yohe (Lady Francis Hope), Frank Seka (Saki), Harry Archer (Johnson), Captain Clayton (Lord Francis Hale), Ethel Shannon (Lady Francis Hale), William Buckley (Putnam Bradley Stone).

Cheated Hearts (December 1921)

Credits: Directed by Hobart Henley; Screenplay by Wallace Clifton; Based on the Novel *Barry Gordon* by William Farquar Payson; Photographed by Virgil Miller; Released by Universal Pictures; Running Time: 5 reels.

Cast: Herbert Rawlinson (Barry Gordon), Warner Baxter (Tom Gordon), Marjorie Daw (Muriel Beekman), Josef Swickard (Colonel Fairfax Gordon), Murdock MacQuarrie (Ibraham), Anna Lehr (Naomi), Boris Karloff (Nei Hamid), Al MacQuarrie (Hassam), Hector Samo (Achmet).

The Cave Girl (December 1921)

Credits: Directed by Joseph L. Franz; Screenplay by William A. Parker; Based on the Play by Guy Bolton and George Middleton; Photographed by Victor Milner; Titles by Katherine Hilliker; Produced by Inspiration Film Productions; Released by First National Pictures; Running Time: 5 reels.

Cast: Teddie Gerard (Margot Sperry), Charles Meredith (Divvy Bates), Wilton Taylor (J.T. Bates), Eleanor Hancock (Mrs. Georgia Case), Lillian Tucker (Elsie Case), Frank Coleman (Rufus Patterson), Boris Karloff (Baptiste), Jake Abrahams (Professor Orlando Sperry), John Beck (Rogers).

The Man from Downing Street (mid-April 1922)

Credits: Directed by Edward José; Produced by A.E. Smith; Screenplay by Bradley J. Smollen; Based on a Story by Clyde Westover, Lottie Horner, and Florine Williams; Photographed by Ernest Smith; Released by Vitagraph Pictures; Running Time: 5 reels.

Cast: Earle Williams (Captain Robert Kent), Betty Ross Clarke (Doris Burnham), Boris Karloff (Dell Monckton/Maharajah Jehan Dharwar), Charles Hill Mailes (Colonel Wentworth), Kathryn Adams (Norma Graves), Herbert Prior (Captain Graves), Henry Burrows (Major Bentley), Eugenia Gilbert (Sarissa), James Butler (Lieutenant Wyndham), George Stanley (Sir Edward Craig).

The Infidel (April 1922)

Credits: Directed by James Young; Produced by B.P. Schulberg; Screenplay by James A. Young; Based on a Story by Charles A. Logue; Photographed by Joseph Brotherton; a Preferred Pictures production; Released by First National Pictures; Running Time: 6 reels.

Cast: Katherine MacDonald (Lola Daintry), Robert Ellis (Cyrus Flint), Joseph Dowling (Reverend Mead), Boris Karloff (the Nabob), Melbourne McDowell (Bully Haynes), Oleta Otis (Mimi Pawliss), Charles Smiley (Mr. Scudder), Loyala O'Connor (Mrs. Scudder), Barbara Tennant (Hope Scudder), Charles Force (Chunky).

The Altar Stairs (early December 1922)

Credits: Directed by Lambert Hillyer; Screenplay by Doris Schroeder and George Hively; Based on a Story by G.B. Lancaster; Photographed by Dwight Warren; Released by Universal Pictures; Running Time: 5 reels.

Cast: Frank Mayo (Rod McLean), Dagmar Godowsky (Parete), Louise Lorraine (Joie Malet), Harry De Vere (Blundell), Hugh Thompson (John Strickland), Boris Karloff (Hugo), Nick De Ruiz (Tulli), Lawrence Hughes (Tony Heritage), J.J. Lanoe (Captain Jean Malet).

Omar the Tentmaker (January 21, 1923)

Credits: Directed by James Young; Produced by Richard Walton Tully; Screenplay by Richard Walton Tully; Based on the Play *Omar Khayyam the Tentmaker* by Richard Walton Tully; Photographed by George Benoit; Art Direction by Wilfred Buckland; Released by First National Pictures; Running Time: 8 reels.

Cast: Guy Bates Post (Omar, the Tentmaker), Virginia Browne Faire (Shireen), Nigel De Brulier (Nizam ul Mulk), Noah Beery (the Shah), Rose Dione (the Shah's Mother), Patsy Ruth Miller (Little Shireen), Douglas Gerard (Hassan), Will Jim Hutton (Little Mahruss), Boris Karloff (the Holy Imam Mowaffak), Maurice B. Flynn (the Christian Crusader), Edward M. Kimball (Omar's Father), Walter Long (the Executioner), Evelyn Selbie (Zarah), John Gribner (Mahruss), Gordon Mullen, George Rigas (Emissaries of the Shah).

A Woman Conquers (late February 1923)

Credits: Directed by Tom Forman; Produced by B.P. Schulberg; Based on a Story by Violet Clark; Photographed by Joseph Brotherton; Released by First National Pictures; Running Time: 6 reels.

Cast: Katherine MacDonald (Ninon Le Compte), Bryant Washburn (Frederick Van Cort), Mitchell Lewis (Lazar), June Elvidge (Flora O'Hare), Clarissa Selwynne (Jeanette Duval), Boris Karloff (Raoul Maris), Francis McDonald (Lawatha).

The Gentleman from America (February 1923)

Credits: Directed by Edward Sedgwick; Produced by Carl Laemmle; Screenplay by George Hull; Based on a Story by Raymond L. Schrock; Photographed by Virgil Miller; Released by Universal Pictures; Running Time: 5 reels.

Cast: Hoot Gibson (Dennis O'Shanc), Tom O'Brien (Johnny Day), Louise Lorraine (Carmen Navarro), Carmen Phillips (the Vamp), Frank Leigh (Don Ramon Gonzales), Jack Crane (Juan Gonzales), Bob McKenzie (San Felipe), Albert Prisco (Grand Duke), Rosa Rosanova (Old Inez), Boris Karloff.

The Prisoner (March 2, 1923)

Credits: Directed by Jack Conway; Screenplay by Edward T. Lowe, Jr.; Based on the Novel *Castle Craneycrow* by George Barr McCutcheon; Photographed by Benjamin Reynolds; Released by Universal Pictures; Running Time: 5 reels.

Cast: Herbert Rawlinson (Philip Quentin), Eileen Percy (Dorothy Garrison), George Cowl (Lord Bob), June Elvidge (Lady Francis), Lincoln Stedman (Dickey Savage), Gertrude Short (Lady Jane), Bertram Grassby (Prince Ugo Ravorelli), Mario Carillo (Count Sallonica), Hayford Hobbs (Duke Laselli), Lillian Langdon (Mrs. Garrison), Bert Sprotte (Courant), Boris Karloff (Prince Kapolski), Esther Ralston (Marie), J.P. Lockney (Father Bivot).

Riders of the Plains (1924)

Credits: Directed by Jacques Jaccard; Released by Arrow Pictures; 15-chapter serial.

Cast: Jack Perrin, Marilyn Mills, Ruth Royce, Boris Karloff.

The Hellion (July 15, 1924)

Credits: Directed by Bruce Mitchell; Produced by Anthony J. Xydias; Screenplay by Bruce Mitchell; Released by Sunset Pictures; Running Time: 5 reels.

Cast: J.B. Warner (Tex Gardy), Marian Sais (the Hellion), William Lester (the Father), Alline Goodwin (the Daughter), Boris Karloff (the Outlaw).

Dynamite Dan (October 3, 1924)

Credits: Directed by Bruce Mitchell; Produced by Anthony J. Xydias; Screenplay by Bruce Mitchell; Photographed by Bert Longenecker; Released by Sunset Pictures; distributed by Aywon Film Company; Running Time: 55 minutes.

Cast: Kenneth McDonald (Dan), Frank Rice (Boss), Boris Karloff (Tony Garcia), Eddie Harris (Sherlock Jones), Diana Alden (Helen), Harry Woods (Brute Lacy), Jack Richardson (Fight Manager), Emily Gerdes (Toodles), Jack Waltemeyer (Tim O'Rourke), Max Ascher.

Perils of the Wind (1925)

Credits: Directed by Francis Ford; Released by Universal Pictures; 15-chapter serial.

Cast: Joe Bonomo, Margaret Quimby, Jack Mower, Boris Karloff.

Forbidden Cargo (early May 1925)
Credits: Directed by Thomas Buckingham; Screenplay and Story by Frederick Kennedy Myton; Photographed by Silvano Balboni; an R.C. Pictures Corporation production; Released by F.B.O.; Running Time: 60 minutes.
Cast: Evelyn Brent (Captain Joe), Robert Ellis (Jerry Burke), Boris Karloff (Pietro Castellano).

The Prairie Wife (early May 1925)
Credits: Directed by Hugo Ballin; Based on a Story by Arthur Stringer; Photographed by James Diamond; Assistant Director: James Chapin; Edited by Katherine Hilliker and H.H. Caldwell; Released by Metro-Goldwyn-Mayer Eastern Productions; Running Time: 63 minutes.
Cast: Dorothy Devore (Chaddie Green), Herbert Rawlinson (Duncan MacKail), Gibson Gowland (Ollie), Leslie Stuart (Percy), Frances Prim (Olga), Boris Karloff (Diego), Erich von Ritzau (Doctor), Rupert Franklin (Rufus Green).

Parisian Nights (May 31, 1925)
Credits: Directed by Alfred Santell; Screenplay by Fred Myton and C. Doty Hobart; Based on a Story by Emil Frost; Photographed by Ernest Haller; Assistant Directors: Robert Florey and Roland Asher; an R.C. Pictures Corporation production; Released by F.B.O.; Running Time: 67 minutes.
Cast: Elaine Hammerstein (Adele), Gaston Glass (Jacques), Lou Tellegen (Jean), William J. Kelly (Fontaine), Boris Karloff (Pierre), Renee Adoree (Marie).

Never the Twain Shall Meet (July 26, 1925)
Credits: Directed by Maurice Tourneur; Produced by William Randolph Hearst; Screenplay by Eugene Mullin; Based on a Novel by Peter B. Kyne; Photographed by Ira H. Morgan and J.B. Shackelford; Art Direction by Joseph Urban; Edited by Donn Hayes; Titles by Peter B. Kyne; a Cosmopolitan Pictures production; Released by Metro-Goldwyn-Mayer; Running Time: 8 reels.
Cast: Anita Stewart (Tamea), Bert Lytell (Dan Prichard), Huntley Gordon (Mark Mellenger), Justine Johnstone (Maise Morrison), George Siegmann (James Muggridge), Lionel Belmore (Gaston Larrieau), William Norris (Squibbs), Emily Fitzroy (Mrs. Pippy), Princess Marie de Bourbon (Miss Smith), Florence Turner (Julia), James Wang (Sooey Wan), Ben Deeley (Doctor), Roy Coulson (Assistant Doctor), Thomas Ricketts (Andrew J. Carson), Ernest Butterworth (Captain Hackett), Boris Karloff (Villain).

Lady Robin Hood (August 14, 1925)
Credits: Directed by Ralph Ince; Screenplay by Fred Myton; Based on a Story by Clifford Howard and Burke Jenkins; Photographed by Silvano Balboni; Assistant Director: Pandro S. Berman; an R.C. Pictures Corporation production; Released by F.B.O.; Running Time: 65 minutes.
Cast: Evelyn Brent (Senorita Catalina/La Ortiga), Robert Ellis (Hugh Winthrop), Boris Karloff (Cabraza), William Humphrey (Governor), D'Arcy Corrigan (Padre), Robert Cauterio (Raimundo).

The Greater Glory (May 2, 1926)
Credits: Directed by Curt Rehfeld; Produced by June Mathis; Screenplay by June Mathis; Based on the Novel *Viennese Medley* by Edith O'Shaughnessy; Photographed by John Boyle and Arthur Martinelli; Art Direction by E.J. Shulter; Edited by George McGuire; Presented by Richard A. Rowland; Released by First National Pictures; Running Time: 106 minutes.
Cast: Conway Tearle (Count Maxim von Hartig), Anna Q. Nilsson (Fanny), May Allison (Corinne), Ian Keith (Pauli Birbach), Lucy Beaumont (Tante Ilde), Jean Hersholt (Gustav Schmidt), Nigel De Brulier (Dr. Herman von Berg), Bridgetta Clark (Mizzi, von Berg's Wife), John Sainpolis (Professor Leopold Eberhardt), Marcia Mannon (Kaethe, Eberhardt's Wife), Edward Earle (Otto Steiner), Virginia Southern (Liesel, Steiner's Wife), Isabelle Keith (Anna, Birbach's Wife), Kathleen Chambers (Irma von Berg), Hale Hamilton (Leon Krumm), Cora Macey (Marie), Carrie Daumery (Countess von Hertig), Thur Fairfax (Theodore von Hartig), Boris Karloff (the Scissors Grinder), George Billings (the Cross Bearer), Bess Flowers (Helga), Marcelle Corday (Maid), Manuel Acosta, Walter Shumley.

Her Honor, the Governor (July 1926)
Credits: alternate title: *The Second Mrs. Fenway*; Directed by Chet Withey; Produced by Joseph P. Kennedy; Screenplay by Doris Anderson; Based on a Story by Hyatt Daab and Weed Dickinson; Photographed by Andre Barlatier; an R.C. Pictures Corporation production; Released by F.B.O.; Running Time: 7 reels.

Cast: Pauline Frederick (Adele Fenway), Carroll Nye (Bob Fenway), Thomas Santschi (Richard Palmer), Greta Von Rue (Marian Lee), Stanton Heck (Jim Dornton), Boris Karloff (Snipe Collins), Jack Richardson (Slade), Kathleen Kirkham, Charles McHugh, William Worthington.

The Bells (July 30, 1926)
Credits: Directed by James Young; Produced by I.E. Chadwick; Screenplay by James Young; Based on the Play *Le Juif Polonais* by Emile Erckmann and Alexandre Chatrain; Photographed by William O'Connell; Released by Chadwick Pictures; Running Time: 7 reels.
Cast: Lionel Barrymore (Mathias), Gustav von Seyffertitz (Jerome Frantz), Edward Phillips (Christiane), Lola Todd (Annette), Boris Karloff (Mesmerist), Fred Warren (Baruch Koweiski), Otto Lederer, Lorimer Johnston.

The Golden Web (September 22, 1926)
Credits: Directed by Walter Lang; Produced by Renaud Hoffman; Presented by Sam Sax; Screenplay by James Bell Smith; Based on a Novel by E. Phillips Oppenheim; Photographed by Ray June; a Lumas Film Corporation production; Released by Gotham Pictures; Running Time: 62 minutes.
Cast: Lillian Rich (Ruth Rowan), Huntly Gordon (Roland Deane), Jay Hunt (John Rowan), Boris Karloff (Dave Sinclair), Lawford Davidson (George Sisk), Nora Hayden (Miss Philbury), Syd Crossley (Butler), Joe Moore (Office Boy).

The Eagle of the Sea (November 13, 1926)
Credits: Directed by Frank Lloyd; Produced by Adolph Zukor and Jesse L. Lasky; Associate Producer: B. P. Schulberg; Screenplay by Julian Josephson; Based on the Novel *Captain Sazarac* by Charles Tenney Jackson; Photographed by Norbert Brodine; Released by Paramount Pictures; Running Time: 73 minutes.
Cast: Ricardo Cortez (Captain Sazarac), Florence Vidor (Louise Lestron), Sam De Grasse (Colonel Lestron), Andre Beranger (John Jarvis), Mitchell Lewis (Crackley), Guy Oliver (Beluche), George Irving (General Andrew Jackson), Irvin Renard (Don Robledo), James Marcus (Dominique), Charles E. Anderson (Bohon), Boris Karloff (Pirate).

Flames (November 15, 1926)
Credits: Directed and Produced by Lewis H. Moomaw; Screenplay and Story by Alfred A. Cohn; Photographed by Herbert Brownell and King Gray; Edited by Frank Lawrence; Titles by Frank Lawrence; Released by Associated Exhibitors, Inc., Running Time: 6 reels.
Cast: Virginia Valli (Anne Travers), Eugene O'Brien (Herbert Landis), Jean Hersholt (Ole Bergson), Bryant Washburn (Hilary Fenton), George Nichols (James Travers), Boris Karloff (Blackie Blanchette), Cissy Fitzgerald (Mrs. Edgerton).

Old Ironsides (December 6, 1926)
Credits: alternate title: *Sons of the Sea*; Directed by James Cruze; Produced by Adolph Zukor and Jesse L. Lasky; Supervised by B.P. Schulberg; Screenplay by Dorothy Arzner, Walter Woods, and Harry Carr; Based on the Novel by Laurence Stallings; Assistant Director: Harold Schwartz; Photographed by Alfred Gilks and Charles Boyer; Special Effects by Roy Pomeroy; Titles by Rupert Hughes; Musical Score by Hugo Riesenfeld; Filmed partially in Magnascope; Released by Paramount Pictures; Running Time: 117 minutes.
Cast: Esther Ralston (Esther), Wallace Beery (the Boatswain), George Bancroft (the Gunner), Charles Farrell (the Boy), Johnny Walker (Lieutenant Stephen Decatur), George Godfrey (Cook), Guy Oliver (First Mate), Eddie Fetherston (Lieutenant Somers), Effie Ellsler (Esther's Mother), William Conklin (Esther's Father), Fred Kohler (Second Mate), Charles Hill Mailes (Commodore Preble), Nick De Ruiz (the Bashaw), Mitchell Lewis (Pirate Chief), Frank Jonasson, Frank Bonner, Duke Kahanamoku (Pirate Captains), Arthur Ludwig (Second Mate), Spec O'Donnell (Cabin Boy), Boris Karloff (Saracen Guard), Tetsu Komai (Pirate), Jack Herrick (Sailor), Edgar Washington Blue (Negro), William Bakewell, Dick Alexander.

Flaming Fury (December 1926)
Credits: Directed by James Hogan; Produced by Joseph P. Kennedy; Screenplay by Ewart Adamson; Based on the Story "The Scourge of Fate" by Ewart Adamson; Photographed by Joe Walker; an R.C. Pictures Corporation production; Released by F.B.O.; Running Time: 5 reels.
Cast: Ranger (Dog), Charles Delaney (Dan Duvall), Betty May (Jeanette Duval), Boris Karloff (Gaspard), Eddie Chandler (Bethune).

The Man in the Saddle (1926)
Credits: Directed by Lynn Reynolds and Clifford S. Smith; Screenplay by Charles A. Logue; Based on a Story by Charles A. Logue; Released by Universal Pictures; Running Time: 6 reels.
Cast: Hoot Gibson, Virginia Brown Faire, Fay Wray, Charles Hill Mailes, Clark Comstock, Boris Karloff (bit).

The Nickel Hopper (December 1926)
Credits: Directed by Hal Yates; Produced by Hal Roach; Supervised by F. Richard Jones; Titles by H.M. Walker; Released by Pathé Film Exchange; Running Time: 3 reels.
Cast: Mabel Normand, Michael Visaroff, Margaret Seddon, Theodore von Eltz, James Finlayson, Oliver Hardy, Boris Karloff (Masher).

Valencia (December 25, 1926)
Credits: alternate title: *The Love Song*; Directed and Produced by Dmitri Buchowetzki; Screenplay by Alice D.G. Miller; Based on a Story by Dmitri Buchowetzki and Alice D.G. Miller; Photographed by Percy Hilburn; Edited by Hugh Wynn; Art Direction by Cedric Gibbons; Costumes by André-Ani; Released by Metro-Goldwyn-Mayer Pictures; Running Time: 55 minutes.
Cast: Mae Murray (Valencia), Lloyd Hughes (Felippe), Roy D'Arcy (Don Fernando), Max Barwyn (Don Alvarado), Michael Vavitch (Captain), Michael Visaroff (Cafe' Owner), Boris Karloff (bit).

Tarzan and the Golden Lion (January 1927)
Credits: Directed by J.P. McGowan; Produced by Joseph P. Kennedy; Screenplay by William F. Wing; Based on the Novel by Edgar Rice Burroughs; Photographed by Joseph Walker; an R.C. Pictures Corporation production; Released by F.B.O.; Running Time: 6 reels.
Cast: James Pierce (Tarzan), Dorothy Dunbar (Jane), Edna Murphy (Ruth Porter), Frederic Peters (Esteban Miranda), Harold Goodwin (Burton Bradney), Liu Yu-Ching (High Priest Cadj), D'Arcy Corrigan (Weesimbo), Boris Karloff (Ozawa, Waziri Chief), Robert Bolder (John Peebles), Jad-Bal-Ja (Lion).

Let It Rain (March 5, 1927)
Credits: Directed by Edward Francis Cline; Produced by Douglas MacLean; Screenplay by Wade Boteler, George J. Crone, and Earle Snell; Story by Wade Boteler, George J. Crone, and Earle Snell; Photographed by Jack MacKenzie; Released by Paramount Pictures; Running Time: 67 minutes.
Cast: Douglas MacLean (Let-It-Rain Riley), Shirley Mason (the Girl), Wade Boteler (Kelly, the Gob), James Bradbury, Jr. (Butch), Lincoln Stedman (Bugs), Lee Shumway (Marine Captain), James Mason, Edwin Sturgis, Ernest Hilliarp, Boris Karloff (the Crooks), Frank Campeau (Marine Major).

The Meddlin' Stranger (April 1927)
Credits: Directed by Richard Thorpe; Produced by Lester F. Scott, Jr.; Screenplay and Story by Christopher B. Booth; Photographed by Ray Ries; Released by Pathé Film Exchange; Running Time: 5 reels.
Cast: Wally Wales (Wally Fraser), Nola Luxford (Mildred Crawford), James Marcus (Big Bill Dawson), Boris Karloff (Al Meggs), Charles K. French (Mr. Crawford), Mabel Van Buren (Mrs. Crawford).

The Princess from Hoboken (May 17, 1927)
Credits: Directed by Allan Dale; Produced by John M. Stahl; Screenplay by Sonya Levien; Photographed by Joseph Dubray and Robert Martin; Edited by James McKay; Art Direction by Edwin B. Willis; Released by Tiffany Pictures; Running Time: 6 reels.
Cast: Edmund Burns (Terrence O'Brien), Blanche Mehaffey (Sheila O'Toole), Ethel Clayton (Mrs. O'Brien), Lou Tellegen (Prince Anton Balakrieff), Julie ("Babe") London (Princess Sonia Alexandrovna Karpoff), Will R. Walling (Mr. O'Brien), Charles McHugh (Pa O'Toole), Aggie Herring (Ma O'Toole), Charles Crockett (Whiskers), Robert Homans (McCoy), Harry Bailey (Cohen), Sidney D'Albrook (Tony), Broderick O'Farrell (Immigration Officer), Boris Karloff (Pavel).

The Phantom Buster (July 1927)
Credits: Directed by William Bertram; Produced by Lester F. Scott, Jr.; Screenplay by Betty Burbridge; Based on a Story by Walter J. Coburn; Released by Pathé Film Exchange; Running Time: 5 reels.
Cast: Buddy Roosevelt (Jeff McCloud/Bill Turner), Alma Rayford (Babs), Charles Whitaker (Cassidy), Boris Karloff (Ramon), John Junior (Jim Breed), Walter Maly (Jack), Lawrence Underwood (Sheriff).

Soft Cushions (September 10, 1927)
Credits: Directed by Edward Francis Cline; Produced by Douglas MacLean; Screenplay by Wade Boteler and Frederic Chapin; Based on a Story by George Randolph Chester; Photographed by Jack MacKenzie; Art Direction by Ben Carre; Released by Paramount Pictures; Running Time: 7 reels.
Cast: Douglas MacLean (the Young Thief), Sue Carol (the Girl), Richard Carle (the Slave Dealer), Russell Powell (the Fat Thief), Frank Leigh (the Lean Thief), Wade Boteler (the Police Judge), Nigel De Brulier (the Notary), Albert Prisco (the Wazir), Boris Karloff (the Chief Conspirator), Albert Gran (the Sultan), Fred Kelsey (the Police), Harry Jones (the Citizen), Noble Johnson (the Captain of the Guard).

Two Arabian Knights (October 22, 1927)
Credits: Directed by Lewis Milestone; Produced by Howard Hughes; Supervised by John W. Considine, Jr.; Screenplay by James O'Donohue and Wallace Smith; Based on a Story by Donald McGibney; Adapted by Wallace Smith and Cyril Gardner; Assistant Director: Nate Watt; Photographed by Tony Gaudio and Joseph August; Titles by George Marion, Jr.; Art Direction by William Cameron Menzies; Technical Direction by Ned Mann; Released by Caddo-Howard Hughes Pictures; Running Time: 9 reels.
Cast: William Boyd (Private), Mary Astor (Anis Bid Adham), Louis Wolheim (Sergeant Peter McGaffney), Michael Vavitch (Emir of Jaffa), Ian Keith (Shevket), De Witt Jennings (American Consul), Michael Visaroff (Ship's Captain), Boris Karloff (Purser).

The Love Mart (December 24, 1927)
Credits: Directed by George Fitzmaurice; Produced by Richard A. Rowland; Screenplay by Benjamin Glazer; Based on the Novel *The Code of Victor Jallot* by Edward Childs Carpenter; Photographed by Lee Garmes; Edited by Stuart Heisler; Titles by Edwin Justus Mayer; Costumes by Max Ree; Released by First National Pictures; Running Time: 75 minutes.
Cast: Billie Dove (Antoinette Frobelle), Gilbert Roland (Victor Jallot), Noah Beery (Captain Remy), Raymond Turner (Poupet), Armand Kaliz (Jean Delicado), Emile Chautard (Louis Frobelle), Boris Karloff (Fleming), Mattie Peters (Caresse).

Vanishing Rider (1928)
Credits: Directed by Ray Taylor; Released by Universal Pictures; 10-chapter serial.
Cast: William Desmond, Ethlyne Clair, Bud Osborne, Nelson McDowell, Boris Karloff.

Sharp Shooters (January 21, 1928)
Credits: Directed by John G. Blystone; Screenplay by Marion Orth; Based on a Story by Randall H. Faye; Photographed by Charles Clarke; Titles by Malcolm Stuart Boylan; Released by Fox Pictures; Running Time: 6 reels.
Cast: George O'Brien (George), Lois Loran (Lorette), Noah Young (Tom), Tom Dugan (Jerry), William Demarest ("Hi Jack" Murdock), Gwen Lee (Flossy), Josef Swickard (Grandpere), Boris Karloff (Moroccan Bartender).

Vultures of the Sea (August 1928)
Credits: Directed by Richard Thorpe; Produced by Nat Levine; Released by Mascot Pictures; 10-chapter serial.
Chapter Titles: "The Hell Ship," "Cast Adrift," "Driven to Port," "Scum of the Seas," "Harbor of Danger," "The Stolen Ship," "At the Mercy of the Flames," "The Fight for Possession," "The Traitor," "The End of the Quest."
Cast: Johnnie Walker (the Boy), Shirley Mason (the Girl), Tom Santschi (the Mate), Boris Karloff, John Carpenter, George Magrill, Joe Bennett, Arthur Dewey, Frank Hagney, Joseph Mack, J.P. Lockney, Lafe McKee.

The Burning Wind (October 26, 1928)
Credits: Directed by Henry MacRae and Herbert Blanche; Screenplay by Raymond Schrock, George Plympton, and George Moran; Based on the Novel *A Daughter of the Dons* by William MacLeod Raine; Photographed by Harry Neumann and Ray Ramsey; Edited by Maurice Pivar and Thomas Malloy; Titles by Garner Bradford; Released by Universal Pictures; Running Time: 50 minutes.
Cast: Hoot Gibson (Richard Gordon, Jr.), Virginia Brown Faire (Maria Valdes), Cesare Gravin (Don Ramon Valdes), Robert Homans (Richard Gordon, Sr.), George Grandee (Manuel Valdes), Boris Karloff (Pug Doran), Pee Wee Holmes (Peewee).

The Little Wild Girl (October 1928)
Credits: Directed by Frank Mattison; Screenplay by Cecil Burtis Hill; Based on a Story by Putnam Hoover; Photographed by Charles Cronjager; Edited by Minnie Steppler; Titles by Gordon Kalem; Released by Hercules-Trinity Productions; Running Time: 6 reels.
Cast: Lila Lee (Marie Cleste), Cullen Landis (Jules Barbier), Frank Merril (Tavish McBride), Sheldon Lewis (Wanakee), Boris Karloff (Maurice Kent), Jimmy Aubrey (Posty McKnuffle), Bud Shaw (Oliver Hampton), Arthur Hotaling (Duncan Cleste)

The Fatal Warning (February 15, 1929)
Credits: Directed by Richard Thorpe; Produced by Nat Levine; Released by Mascot Pictures; 10-chapter serial.
Chapter Titles: "The Fatal Warning," "The Phantom Flyer," "The Crash of Doom," "The Pit of Death," "Menacing Fingers," "Into Thin Air," "The House of Horror," "Fatal Fumes," "By Whose Hand?" "Unmasked."
Cast: Helene Costello (Dorothy Rogers), Ralph Graves (Russell Thorne), Tom Lingham (John Harman), Phillips Smalley (Leonard Taylor), Lloyd Whitlock (Norman Brooks), George Periolat (William Rogers), Boris Karloff (Mullins), Syd Crossley (Dawson), Martha Mattox (Mrs. Charles Peterson), Symona Boniface (Marie Jordan).

The Devil's Chaplain (May 17, 1929)
Credits: Directed by Duke Worne; Produced by Trem Carr; Screenplay by Arthur Hoerl; Based on a Novel by George Bronson Howard; Photographed by Hap Depew; Edited by J.S. Harrington; Released by Rayart-Richmont Pictures; Running Time: 60 minutes.
Cast: Cornelius Keefe (Yorke Norray), Virginia Brown Faire (Princess Therese), Josef Swickard (the King), Boris Karloff (Boris), Wheeler Oakman (Nicholay), Leland Carr (Ivan), George McIntosh (the Prince).

The Phantom of the North (May 28, 1929)
Credits: Directed by Harry Webb; Screenplay by George Hull and Carl Krusada; Based on a Story by Flora E. Douglas; Photographed by Arthur Reeves and William Thornley; Edited by Fred Bain; Released by Biltmore Productions-All Star Pictures; Running Time: 48 minutes.
Cast: Edith Roberts (Doris Rayburn), Donald Keith (Bob Donald), Kathleen Kay (Colette), Boris Karloff (Jules Gregg), Joe Bonomo (Pierre Blanc), Josef Swickard (Colonel Rayburn), Muro (Himself), Arab (Himself).

Two Sisters (June 28, 1929)
Credits: Directed by Scott Pembroke; Produced by Trem Carr; Screenplay by Arthur Hoerl; Based on a Novel by Virginia Terhune Vandewater; Photographed by Hap Depew; Released by Rayart Pictures; Running Time: 6 reels.
Cast: Viola Dana (Jean/Jane), Rex Lease (Allan Rhodes), Claire DuBrey (Rose), Irving Bacon (Chumley), Boris Karloff (Cecil), Tom Lingham (Detective Jackson), Tom Curran (Judge Rhodes), Adalyn Asbury (Mrs. Rhodes).

Anne Against the World (July 2, 1929)
Credits: Directed by Duke Worne; Screenplay by Arthur Hoerl; Based on a Story by Victor Thorne; Photographed by Hap Depew; Edited by J.S. Harrington; Released by Rayart Pictures; Running Time: 6 reels.
Cast: Shirley Mason (Anne), Jack Mower (John Forbes), James Bradbury, Jr. (Eddie), Isabelle Keith (Teddy), Tom Curran (Emmett), Henry Roquemore (Folmer), Boris Karloff (bit), Billy Franey, Belle Stoddard.

Sound

Behind That Curtain (June 29, 1929)
Credits: Directed by Irving Cummings; Produced by William Fox; Screenplay by Sonya Levien and Clarke Silvernail; Based on the Story by Earl Derr Biggers; Photographed by Conrad Wells, Dave Ragin, and Vincent Farrar; Edited by Alfred DeGaetano; Sound Recording by George P. Costello; Assistant Director: George Woolstenhulme; Titles by Wilbur Morse, Jr.; Released by Fox Pictures; Running Time: 91 minutes.
Cast: Warner Baxter (John Beetham), Lois Moran (Eve Mannering), Gilbert Emery (Sir Frederic Bruce), Claude King (Sir George Mannering), Philip Strange (Eric Durand), Boris Karloff (Sudanese Servant), Jamiel Hassan (Habib Hanna), Peter Gawthorne (Scotland Yard Inspector), John Rogers (Alf Pornick),

Montague Shaw (Hilary Gatt), Finch Smiles (Gatt's Clerk), Mercedes DeValasco (Neinah), E.L. Park (Charlie Chan).

King of the Kongo (August 20, 1929)
Credits: Directed by Richard Thorpe; Produced by Nat Levine; Released by Mascot Pictures (silent and sound versions); 10-chapter serial.
Chapter Titles: "Into the Unknown," "Terrors of the Jungle," "The Temple of the Beasts," "Gorilla Warfare," "Danger in the Dark," "The Fight at the Lions' Pit," "The Fatal Moment," "Sentenced to Death," "Desperate Chances," "Jungle Justice."
Cast: Jacqueline Logan (Diana Martin), Walter Miller (Larry Trent), Richard Tucker (Secret Service Chief), Boris Karloff (Macklin/Martin), Larry Steers (Jack Drake), Harry Todd (Commodore), Richard Neil (Prisoner), Lafe McKee (Trader John), J.P. Leckray (Priest), William Burt (Mooney), Gordon Russell (Derelict), Robert Frazer (Native Chief), Ruth Davis (Poppy).

The Unholy Night (October 11, 1929)
Credits: Directed by Lionel Barrymore; Screenplay by Edwin Justus Mayer; Based on the Story "The Doomed Regiment" by Ben Hecht; Adapted by Dorothy Farnum; Photographed by Ira Morgan; Edited by Grant Whytock; Sound Recording by Douglas Shearer and Paul Neal; Titles by Joe Farnham; Art Direction by Cedric Gibbons; Gowns by Adrian; Released by Metro-Goldwyn-Mayer Pictures; Running Time: 92 minutes.
Cast: Ernest Torrence (Dr. Ballou), Roland Young (Lord Montague), Dorothy Sebastian (Lady Efrah), Natalie Moorhead (Lady Vi), Claude Fleming (Sir James Ramsay), John Miljan (Major Mallory), Richard Tucker (Colonel Davidson), John Loder (Captain Dorchester), Philip Strange (Lieutenant Williams), Polly Moran (Maid), Sojin (Mystic), Boris Karloff (Abdoul), Sidney Jarvis (Butler), Clarence Geldert (Inspector Lewis), John Roche (Lieutenant Savor), Lionel Belmore (Major Endicott), Gerald Barry (Captain Bradley), Richard Travers (Major McDougal), George Cooper (Orderly).

The Bad One (June 12, 1930)
Credits: Directed by George Fitzmaurice; Produced by Joseph M. Schenck; Screenplay by Carey Wilson; Story by John Farrow; Dialogue by Howard Emmett Rogers; Photographed by Karl Struss; Edited by Donn Hayes; Art Direction by William Cameron Menzies; assistant art director: Park French; Sound Recording by Frank Grenzbach; Assistant Director: Walter Mayo; Costumes by Alice O'Neill; Musical Score by Hugo Riesenfeld; Released by United Artists; Running Time: 70 minutes.
Cast: Dolores Del Rio (Lita), Edmund Lowe (Jerry Flanagan), Don Alvarado (the Spaniard), Blanche Frederici (Madame Durand), Adrienne D'Ambricourt (Madame Pompier), Ullrich Haupt (Pierre Ferrande), Mitchell Lewis (Borloff), Ralph Lewis (Blochet), Charles McNaughton (Petey), Yola D'Avril (Gida), John Sainpolis (Judge), Henry Kolker (Prosecutor), George Fawcett (Warden), Victor Potel (Sailor), Harry Stubbs (Sailor), Tom Dugan (Sailor), Boris Karloff (Guard).

The Sea Bat (August 8, 1930)
Credits: Directed by Wesley Ruggles; Screenplay by Bess Meredyth and John Howard Lawson; Based on a Story by Dorothy Yost; Photographed by Ira Morgan; Edited by Harry Reynolds and Jerry Thomas; Sound Recording by Douglas Shearer and Karl E. Zint; Titles by Philip J. Leddy; Art Direction by Cedric Gibbons; song, "Lo-Lo," by Reggie Montgomery and Al Ward; Released by Metro-Goldwyn-Mayer Pictures; Running Time: 74 minutes.
Cast: Raquel Torres (Nina), Charles Bickford (Reverend Sims), Nils Asther (Carl), George F. Marion (Antone), John Miljan (Juan), Boris Karloff (Corsican), Gibson Gowland (Limey), Edmund Breese (Maddocks), Mathilde Comont (Mimba), Mack Swain (Dutchy).

The Utah Kid (November 18, 1930)
Credits: Directed by Richard Thorpe; Screenplay and Story by Frank Howard Clark; Photographed by Arthur Reed; Edited by Billy Bolen; Sound Recording by Carson J. Jowett; Released by Tiffany Pictures; Running Time: 57 minutes.
Cast: Rex Lease (Cal Reynolds), Dorothy Sebastian (Jenny Lee), Tom Santschi (Butch), Mary Carr (Aunt Ada), Walter Miller (Sheriff Bentley), Lafe McKee (Parson Joe), Boris Karloff (Baxter), Bud Osborne (Deputy).

Mothers Cry (December 4, 1930)

Credits: Directed by Hobart Henley; Produced by Robert North; Screenplay by Lenore J. Coffee; Based on a Novel by Helen Grace Carlisle; Photographed by Gilbert Warrenton; Edited by Frank Hare; Released by First National Pictures; Running Time: 75 minutes.

Cast: Dorothy Peterson (Mary K. Williams), Helen Chandler (Beatty Williams), David Manners (Artie Williams), Sidney Blackmer (Gerald Hart), Edward Woods (Danny Williams), Evalyn Knapp (Jenny Williams), Jean Bary (Sadye), Pat O'Malley (Frank Williams), Claire McDowell (Mary's Mother), Charles Hill Mailes (Mary's Father), Reginald Pasch (Karl Muller), Boris Karloff (Murder Victim), Marvin Jones, Meredyth Burel.

King of the Wild (1931)

Credits: Directed by Richard Thorpe and B. Reeves Eason; Produced by Nat Levine; Screenplay and Story by Wyndham Gittens and Ford Beebe; Photographed by Benjamin Kline and Edward Kull; Musical Direction by Lee Zahler; Released by Mascot Pictures; 12-chapter serial.

Chapter Titles: "The Tiger of Destiny," "Man Eaters," "The Avenging Horde," "The Secret of the Volcano," "The Pit of Peril," "The Creeping Doom," "Sealed Lips," "The Jaws of the Jungle," "The Door of Dread," "The Leopard's Lair," "The Fire of the Gods," "Jungle Justice."

Cast: Walter Miller (Robert Grant), Nora Lane (Muriel Armitage), Dorothy Christy (Mrs. La Salle), Tom Santschi (Harris), Boris Karloff (Mustapha), Arthur McLaglen (Bimi), Carrol Nye (Armitage), Victor Potel (Peterson), Martha Lalade (Mrs. Colby), Mischa Auer (Dakka).

The Criminal Code (January 3, 1931)

Credits: Directed by Howard Hawks; Produced by Harry Cohn; Screenplay by Fred Niblo, Jr., and Seton I. Miller; Based on the Play by Martin Flavin; Photographed by James Wong Howe; Edited by Edward Curtis; Sound Recording by Glenn Rominger; Released by Columbia Pictures; Running Time: 96 minutes.

Cast: Walter Huston (Warden Brady), Phillips Holmes (Robert Graham), Constance Cummings (Mary Brady), Mary Doran (Gertrude Williams), DeWitt Jennings (Gleason), John Sheehan (McManus), Boris Karloff (Ned Galloway), Otto Hoffman (Fales), Clark Marshall (Runch), Arthur Hoyt (Nettleford), Ethel Wales (Katie), Nicholas Soussanin (Dr. Rinewulf), Paul Porcasi (Spelvin), James Guilfoyle (Doran), Lee Phelps (Doherty), Hugh Walker (Lew), Jack Vance (Reporter), John St. Polis, Andy Devine.

The Last Parade (February 27, 1931)

Credits: Directed by Erle C. Kenton; Screenplay and Dialogue by Dorothy Howell; Based on a Story by Casey Robinson; Photographed by Teddy Tetzlaff; Edited by Gene Havelick; Sound Recording by Russell Malmgren; Released by Columbia Pictures; Running Time: 82 minutes.

Cast: Jack Holt (Cookie Leonard), Tom Moore (Mike O'Dowd), Constance Cummings (Molly Pearson), Gaylord Pendleton (Larry Pearson), Robert Ellis (Marino), Earle D. Bunn (Lefty), Vivi (Herself), Jess De Vorska (Rosenberg), Ed Le Saint (Chief of Police), Edmund Breese (City Editor), Clarence Muse (Alabam'), Gino Corrado (Joe), Robert Graham (Danny Murphy), Boris Karloff (Prison Warder).

Dirigible (April 3, 1931)

Credits: Directed by Frank Capra; Screenplay by Jo Swerling and Dorothy Howell; Based on a Story by Lieutenant Commander Frank W. ("Spig") Wead; Dialogue by Jo Swerling; Photographed by Joe Wilbur and Elmer Dyer; Edited by Maurice Wright; Sound Recording by E.L. Bernds; Released by Columbia Pictures; Running Time: 100 minutes.

Cast: Jack Holt (Jack Bradon), Ralph Graves (Frisky Pierce), Fay Wray (Helen), Hobart Bosworth (Rondelle), Roscoe Carns (Sock McGuire), Harold Goodwin (Hansen), Clarence Muse (Clarence), Emmett Corrigan (Admiral Martin), Al Roscoe (Commander of the U.S.S. *Lexington*), Selmer Jackson (Lieutenant Rowland), Boris Karloff (bit).

Cracked Nuts (April 4, 1931)

Credits: Directed by Edward Francis Cline; Produced by Douglas MacLean; Screen play by Ralph Spence; Story by Douglas MacLean and Al Boasberg; Dialogue by Ralph Spence and Al Boasberg; Photographed by Nicholas Musuraca; Sound Recording by Hugh McDowell; Released by RKO-Radio Pictures; Running Time: 65 minutes.

Cast: Bert Wheeler (Wendell Graham), Robert Woolsey (Zander U. Parkhurst), Edna May Oliver (Aunt Van Varden), Dorothy Lee (Betty Harrington), Leni Stengel (Carlotta), Stanley Fields (General Bogardus), Boris Karloff (Revolutionary), Harvey Clark, Ben Turpin, Frank Thornton, Frank Lackteen, Wilfred Lucas.

Young Donovan's Kid (May 21, 1931)

Credits: Directed by Fred Niblo; Produced by Louis Sarecky; Screenplay by J. Walter Ruben; Based on the Novel *Big Brother* by Rex Beach; Photographed by Edward Cronjager; Sound Recording by John Tribby; Released by RKO-Radio Pictures; Running Time: 76 minutes.

Cast: Richard Dix (Jim Donovan), Jackie Cooper (Midge Murray), Marion Shilling (Kitty Costello), Frank Sheridan (Father Dan), Boris Karloff (Cokey Joe), Dick Rush (Burke), Fred Kelsey (Collins), Richard Alexander (Ben Murray), Harry Tenbrook (Spike Doyle), Wilfred Lucas (Duryea), Phil Sleeman (Mike Novarro), Charles Sullivan, Jack Perry, Frank Beal.

Smart Money (June 18, 1931)

Credits: Directed by Alfred E. Green; Screenplay and Dialogue by Kubec Glasmon, John Bright, Lucien Hubbard, and Joseph Jackson; Based on the Story "The Idol" by Lucien Hubbard and Joseph Jackson; Photographed by Robert Kurle; Edited by Jack Killifer; Musical Direction by Leo F. Forbstein; Makeup by Perc Westmore; Released by Warner Bros.-First National Pictures; Running Time: 90 minutes.

Cast: Edward G. Robinson (Nick ["The Barber"] Venizelos), James Cagney (Jack), Evalyn Knapp (Irene Graham), Ralf Harolde (Sleepy Sam), Noel Francis (Marie), Margaret Livingston (District Attorney's Girl), Maurice Black (the Greek Barber), Boris Karloff (Sport Williams), Morgan Wallace (District Attorney Black), Billy House (Salesman/Gambler), Paul Porcasi (Alexander Amenoppopolus), Polly Walters (Lola), Ben Taggart (Hickory Short), Gladys Lloyd, Wallace MacDonald (Cigar-Stand Clerks), Clark Burroughs (Back-to-Back Schultz), Edwin Argus (Two-Time Phil), John Larkin (Snake Eyes), Walter Percival (Dealer Barnes), Mae Madison (Small-Town Girl), Allan Lane (Suicide), Eulalie Jensen (Matron), Charles Lane (Desk Clerk), Edward Hearn (Reporter), Eddie Kane (Tom, Customer), Clinton Rosemond (George, Porter), Charles O'Malley (Machine-Gunner), Gus Leonard (Joe, Barber's Customer), John George (Dwarf on Train), Harry Semels (Gambler), Charlotte Merriam (Girl at Gaming Table), Larry McGrath, Spencer Bell.

The Public Defender (August 1, 1931)

Credits: Directed by J. Walter Ruben; Produced by Louis Sarecky; Screenplay by Bernard Schubert; Based on the Novel *The Splendid Crime* by George Goodchild; Photographed by Edward Cronjager; Edited by Archie Marshek; Released by RKO-Radio Pictures; Running Time: 70 minutes.

Cast: Richard Dix (Pike Winslow), Shirley Grey (Barbara Gerry), Edmund Breese (Wells), Paul Hurst (Doctor), Purnell Pratt (John Burns), Alan Roscoe (Inspector O'Neill), Boris Karloff (Professor), Ruth Weston (Rose), Nella Walker (Aunt Matilda), William Halligan (Auctioneer), Frank Sheridan (Charles Harmer), Carl Gerrard (Cyrus Pringle).

Pardon Us (August 15, 1931)

Credits: (French foreign-language version) Directed by James Parrott; Produced by Hal Roach; Screenplay and Dialogue by H.M. Walker; Photographed by Jack Stevens; Edited by Richard Currier; Sound Recording by Elmer R. Raguse; Musical Score by LeRoy Shield, Edward Kilenyi, Arthur J. Lamb, H.W. Petrie, Will Marion Cook, Irving Berlin, Cole and Johnson, Abe Olman, M. Ewing, Frederic Van Norman, L.E. De Francesco, J.S. Zemecnik, Freita Shaw, and Marvin Hatley; Filmed September-December 1930; Released by Metro-Goldwyn-Mayer Pictures; Running Time: 55 minutes.

Cast: Stan Laurel (Himself), Oliver Hardy (Himself), Boris Karloff ("the Tiger," a Wily Convict), James Finlayson (Schoolteacher), June Marlowe (Warden's Daughter), Charlie Hall (Dental Assistant/Delivery Man), Sam Lufkin, Silas D. Wilcox, George Miller (Prison Guards), Wilfred Lucas (the Warden), Frank Holliday (Officer in Classroom), Harry Bernard (Warren the Desk Sergeant), Stanley J. ("Tiny") Sandford (Officer LeRoy Shields), Robert ("Bobby") Burns (Prone Dental Patient), Frank Austin (Dental Patient in Waiting Room), Otto Fries (Dentist), Robert Kortman, Leo Willis (Pals of "the Tiger"), Jerry Mandy (Convict Who Can't Add), Bobby Dunn, Eddie Dunn, Baldwin Cooke, Charles Dorety, Dick Gilbert, Will Stanton, Jack Herrick, Jack Hill, Gene Morgan, Charles A. Bachman, John ("Blackie") Whiteford, Charley Rogers (Insurgent Convicts), Gordon Douglas (Typist at Desk), James Parrott, Hal Roach (Prisoners Marching in Formation Near Hardy), Eddie Baker (Plantation Overseer), the Etude Ethiopian Chorus (Cotton Pickers), Bloodhound (Belle), Guido Trento.

Five Star Final (September 10, 1931)

Credits: Directed by Mervyn LeRoy; Screenplay by Byron Morgan; Based on the Play *Late Night Final* by Louis Weitzenkorn; Adapted by Robert Lord; Photographed by Sol Polito; Edited by Frank Ware; Musical Direction by Leo Forbstein; Art Direction by Jack Okey; Filmed May 1931; Released by Warner

Bros.-First National Pictures; Running Time: 89 minutes.

Cast: Edward G. Robinson (Joseph Randall), Marian Marsh (Jenny Townsend), H.B. Warner (Michael Townsend), Anthony Bushell (Philip Weeks), George E. Stone (Ziggie Feinstein), Frances Starr (Nancy Vorhees Townsend), Ona Munson (Kitty Carmody), Boris Karloff ("Reverend" T. Vernon Isopod), Robert Elliot (Brannegan), Aline MacMahon (Miss Taylor), Purnell Pratt (French), David Torrence (Weeks), Oscar Apfel (Hinchecliffe), Gladys Lloyd (Miss Edwards), Evelyn Walsh Hall (Mrs. Weeks), Harold Waldridge (Arthur Goldberg), Polly Walters (Telephone Operator), James Donlin (Reporter), Frank Darien (Schwartz).

I Like Your Nerve (September 11, 1931)

Credits: Directed by William McGann; Screenplay by Houston Branch; Story by Roland Pertwee; Dialogue by Roland Pertwee and Houston Branch; Photographed by Ernest Haller; Edited by Peter Fritsch; Released by Warner Bros.-First National Pictures; Running Time: 70 minutes.

Cast: Douglas Fairbanks, Jr. (Larry O'Brien), Loretta Young (Diane), Edmond Breon (Clive Latimer), Henry Kolker (Pacheco), Claude Allister (Archie Lester), Ivan Simpson (Butler), Paul Porcasi (Patron), Andre Cheron (Franko), Boris Karloff (Luigi), Henry Bunston (Colonel).

Graft (September 21, 1931)

Credits: Directed by Christy Cabanne; Produced by Carl Laemmle, Jr.; Screenplay and Story by Barry Barringer; Photographed by Jerome Ash; Edited by Maurice Pivar; Released by Universal Pictures; Running Time: 72 minutes.

Cast: Regis Toomey (Dusty Hotchkiss), Sue Carol (Constance Hall), Dorothy Revier (Pearl Vaughan), Boris Karloff (Joe Terry), William Davidson (M.H. Thomas), Richard Tucker (Carter Harrison), Willard Robertson (Scudder), Harold Goodwin (Speed Hansen), George Irving (M.T. Hall), Carmelita Geraghty (Secretary).

The Mad Genius (October 23, 1931)

Credits: Directed by Michael Curtiz; Screenplay by J. Grubb Alexander and Harvey Thew; Based on the Play *The Idol* by Martin Brown; Photographed by Barney McGill; Edited by Ralph Dawson; set direction by Anton Grot; Choreography by Adolph Bolm; Released by Warner Bros.-First National Pictures; Running Time: 81 minutes.

Cast: John Barrymore (Ivan Tzarakov), Marian Marsh (Nana), Donald Cook (Fedor), Charles Butterworth (Karinsky), Luis Alberni (Serge Bankieff), Carmel Myers (Preskoya), Andre Luguet (Bartag), Frankie Darro (Fedor as a Boy), Boris Karloff (Fedor's Father), Mae Madison (Olga).

The Yellow Ticket (October 30, 1931)

Credits: Directed by Raoul Walsh; Screenplay by Jules Furthman and Guy Bolton; Based on the Play by Michael Morton; Photographed by James Wong Howe; Edited by Jack Murray; Sound Recording by Donald Flick; Released by Fox Pictures; Running Time: 78 minutes.

Cast: Elissa Landi (Marya Kalish), Lionel Barrymore (Baron Igor Andrey), Laurence Olivier (Julian Rolfe), Walter Byron (Count Nikolai), Sarah Padden (Mother Kalish), Arnold Korff (Grandfather Kalish), Mischa Auer (Melchoir), Rita LaRoy (Fania), Boris Karloff (Drunken Aide to Czarist Official), Edwin Maxwell.

The Guilty Generation (November 19, 1931)

Credits: Directed by Rowland V. Lee; Produced by Harry Cohn; Screenplay by Jack Cunningham; Based on the Play by Jo Milward and J. Kirby Hawkins; Photographed by Byron Haskin; Edited by Otis Garrett; Released by Columbia Pictures; Running Time: 82 minutes.

Cast: Leo Carrillo (Mike Palermo), Constance Cummings (Maria Palermo), Robert Young (Marco Ricca), Boris Karloff (Tony Ricca), Leslie Fenton (Joe), Jimmy Wilcox (Don), Elliott Roth (Benedicto), Phil Tead (Skid), Frederick Howard (Bradley), Eddie Roland (Willie), W.J. O'Brien (Victor), Ruth Warren (Publicity Woman).

Frankenstein (December 4, 1931)

Credits: Directed by James Whale; Produced by Carl Laemmle, Jr.; Presented by Carl Laemmle; Associate Producer: E.M. Asher; Screenplay by Garrett Fort, Francis Edwards Faragoh, John Russell, and Robert Florey; Based on the Novel by Mary Wollstonecraft Shelley and the Play by Peggy Webling; Adapted by John L. Balderston; Scenario Edited by Richard Schayer; Photographed by Arthur Edeson; Edited by Clarence Kolster; Editing Supervision by Maurice Pivar; Special Electrical Effects by Kenneth Strickfaden; Technical Assistant: Dr. Cecil Reynolds; Makeup by Jack P. Pierce; Art Direction by Charles D. Hall; Set

Design by Herman Rosse; Sound Recording by C. Roy Hunter; Musical Theme by David Broekman; Filmed August-October 1931; Released by Universal Pictures; Running Time: 71 minutes.

Cast: Colin Clive (Henry Frankenstein), Mae Clarke (Elizabeth), John Boles (Victor Moritz), Edward Van Sloan (Dr. Waldman), Boris Karloff (the Monster), Frederick Kerr (Baron Frankenstein), Dwight Frye (Fritz), Lionel Belmore (Burgomaster), Marilyn Harris (Little Maria), Michael Mark (Ludwig), Arletta Duncan, Pauline Moore (Bridesmaids), Francis Ford (Wounded Villager on Hill/Extra at Lecture).

Tonight or Never (December 26, 1931)

Credits: Directed by Mervyn LeRoy; Produced by Samuel Goldwyn; Screenplay by Ernest Vajda; Based on the Play by Lili Hatvany; Adapted by Frederick Hatton and Fanny Hatton; Photographed by Gregg Toland; Edited by Grant Whytock; Art Direction by Willy Pogany; Costumes by Chanel; Musical Direction by Alfred Newman; Released by United Artists; Running Time: 80 minutes.

Cast: Gloria Swanson (Nella Vago), Melvyn Douglas (the Unknown Gentleman), Ferdinand Gottshalk (Rudig), Robert Grieg (the Butler), Greta Mayer (the Maid), Warburton Gamble (Count Albert von Gronac), Alison Skipworth (the Marchesa), Boris Karloff (the Waiter).

Behind the Mask (February 25, 1932)

Credits: Directed by John Francis Dillon; Produced by Harry Cohn; Screenplay and Dialogue by Jo Swerling; Adapted from the Story "In the Secret Service" by Jo Swerling; Photographed by Ted Tetzlaff; Edited by Otis Garrett; Continuity by Dorothy Howell; Sound Recording by Glenn Rominger; Filmed November 1931; Released by Columbia Pictures; Running Time: 68 minutes.

Cast: Jack Holt (Hart), Constance Cummings (Julie), Boris Karloff (Jim Henderson, Dope Pusher), Claude King (Arnold), Bertha Mann (Edwards), Edward Van Sloan (Steiner), Willard Robinson (Hawkes).

Alias the Doctor (March 2, 1932)

Credits: Directed by Michael Curtiz; Screenplay by Houston Branch; Based on the Play by Imre Foeldes; Dialogue by Charles Kenyon; Photographed by Barney McGill; Edited by William Holmes; Art Direction by Anton Grot; Technical Adviser: Dr. Henry Morton; Filmed December 1931-January 1932; Released by Warner Bros.-First National Pictures; Running Time: 69 minutes.

Cast: Richard Barthelmess (Karl Muller), Marian Marsh (Lotti Brenner), Lucille La Verne (Mother Brenner), Norman Foster (Stephen Brenner), Adrienne Dore (Anna), Oscar Apfel (Keller), John St. Polis (Dr. Niergardt), Wallis Clark (Kleinschmidt), Claire Dodd (Mrs. Beverly), George Rosener (Von Bergman), Boris Karloff/Nigel De Brulier (Autopsy Surgeon), Reginald Barlow (Professor), Arnold Lucy (the Deacon), Harold Waldridge (Willie), Robert Farfan (Franz).

Note: In the original release print, Karloff appeared as the autopsy surgeon, but when the British censor objected to the "gruesome" nature of the character, his scenes were removed. Unable to recall him for re-shooting, Warner Bros. hired Nigel De Brulier as a replacement. Apparently, no copy of the original print exists.

Business and Pleasure (March 6, 1932)

Credits: Directed by David Butler; Produced by Al Rockett; Screenplay and Dialogue by Gene Towne and William Conselman; Based on the Novel *The Plutocrat* by Booth Tarkington and the Play by Arthur Goodrich; Photographed by Ernest Palmer; Released by Fox Pictures; Running Time: 76 minutes.

Cast: Will Rogers (Earl Tinker), Jetta Goudal (Madame Momora), Joel McCrea (Lawrence Ogle), Dorothy Peterson (Mrs. Tinker), Peggy Ross (Olivia Tinker), Cyril Ring (Arthur Jones), Jed Prouty (Ben Wackstle), Oscar Apfel (P.D. Weatheright), Vernon Dent (Charlie Turner), Boris Karloff (Sheik).

Scarface (March 26, 1932)

Credits: Directed by Howard Hawks; Produced by Howard Hughes; Screenplay by Seton I. Miller, John Lee Mahin, W.R. Burnett, and Fred Palsey; Based on the Novel by Armitage Trail; Adapted from the Screen Story by Ben Hecht; Photographed by Lee Garmes and L.W. O'Connell; Edited by Edward Curtiss; Editing Supervised by Douglas Biggs; Assistant Director: Richard Rosson; Sound Recording by William Snyder; Musical Production by Adolph Tandler and Gus Arnheim; Production Designed by Harry Oliver; Filmed May-November 1931; Released by United Artists; Running Time: 99 minutes.

Cast: Paul Muni (Antonio Camonte), Ann Dvorak (Cesca Camonte), Karen Morley (Poppy), Osgood Perkins (Johnny Lovo), Boris Karloff (Gaffney), George Raft (Guino Rinaldo), Vince Barnett (Angelo), C. Henry Gordon (Inspector Guarino), Inez Palange (Tony's Mother), Edwin Maxwell (Commissioner), Tully Marshall (Managing Editor), Harry J. Vegar (Big Louis Costillo), Bert Starkey (Epstein), Henry Armetta

(Pietro), Maurice Black (Sullivan), Purnell Pratt (Publisher), Charles Sullivan, Harry Tenbrook (Bootleggers), Hank Mann (Worker), Paul Fix (Gaffney Hood), Howard Hawks (Man on Bed).

The Cohens and Kellys in Hollywood (March 28, 1932)
Credits: Directed by John Francis Dillon; Produced by Carl Laemmle, Jr.; Screenplay and Story by Howard J. Green; Based on Characters Created by Aaron Hoffman; Dialogue by James Mulhouser; Photographed by Jerome Ash; Edited by Harry Webb; Released by Universal Pictures; Running Time: 75 minutes.
Cast: George Sidney (Mr. Cohen), Charlie Murray (Mr. Kelly), June Clyde (Kitty Kelly), Norman Foster (Melville Cohen), Emma Dunn (Mrs. Cohen), Esther Howard (Mrs. Kelly), Eileen Percy (Writer), Edwin Maxwell (Chauncey Chadwick), Dorothy Christy (Mrs. Chadwick), Luis Alberni (Solarsky), John Roche (Gregory Gordon), Robert Greig (Chester Field), Tom Mix, Lew Ayres, Sidney Fox, Boris Karloff, Genevieve Tobin, Harry Barris (Themselves).

The Miracle Man (April 1, 1932)
Credits: Directed by Norman Z. McLeod; Screenplay by Waldemar Young; Dialogue by Waldemar Young and Samuel Hoffenstein; Based on a Story by Frank L. Packard and Robert H. Davis and the Play by George M. Cohan; Photographed by David Abel; Art Direction by Hans Dreier; Released by Paramount Pictures; Running Time: 85 minutes.
Cast: Sylvia Sidney (Helen Smith), Chester Morris (John Madison), Robert Coogan (Bobbie Holmes), John Wray (the Frog), Ned A. Sparks (Harry Evans), Hobart Bosworth (the Patriarch), Lloyd Hughes (Thornton), Virginia Bruce (Margaret Thornton), Boris Karloff (Nikko), Irving Pichel (Henry Holmes), Frank Darien (Hiram Higgins), Florine McKinney (Betty), Lew Kelly (Parker), Jackie Searle.

Night World (May 5, 1932)
Credits: Directed by Hobart Henley; Produced by Carl Laemmle, Jr.; Screenplay by Richard Schayer; Based on a Story by P.J. Wolfson and Allen Rivkin; Photographed by Merritt Gerstad; Edited by Maurice Pivar; Musical Score by Alfred Newman; Musical Direction by Hal Grayson; Choreography by Busby Berkeley; Filmed March 1932; Released by Universal Pictures; Running Time: 60 minutes.
Cast: Lew Ayres (Michael Rand), Mae Clarke (Ruth Taylor), Boris Karloff (Happy MacDonald), Dorothy Revier (Mrs. Mac), Russell Hopton (Klauss, Show Producer), Bert Roach (Tommy), Dorothy Peterson (Edith Blair), Paisley Noon (Clarence), Hedda Hopper (Mrs. Rand), Clarence Muse (Tim Dolan, Doorman), George Raft (Ed Powell), Robert Emmett O'Connor (Policeman), Florence Lake (Miss Smith), Huntley Gordon (Jim), Gene Morgan (Joe), Greta Granstedt (Blonde), Louise Beavers (Maid), Sammy Blum (Salesman), Harry Woods (Gang Leader), Eddie Phillips (Vaudevillian), Tom Tamarez (Gigolo), Geneva Mitchell (Florabelle), Arletta Duncan (Cigarette Girl), Pat Somerset (Guest), Hal Grayson's Recording Orchestra (Themselves), Frankie Farr (Trick Walter), Alice Adair (Chorine), Amos Ingraham, Joe Wallace, Charles Giblyn, Dorothy Grainger, Frank Beale, John K. Wells.

Skyscraper Souls (August 4, 1932)
Credits: Directed by Edgar Selwyn; Adaptation by C. Gardner Sullivan; Dialogue by Elmer Harris; Based on the Novel *Skyscraper* by Faith Baldwin; Photographed by William Daniels; Edited by Tom Held; Released by Metro-Goldwyn-Mayer Pictures; Running Time: 90 minutes.
Cast: Warren William (David Dwight), Maureen O'Sullivan (Lynn Harding), Gregory Ratoff (Vinmont), Anita Page (Jenny), Verree Teasdale (Sarah Dennet), Norman Foster (Tom Shepherd), Jean Hersholt (Jake), George Barbier (Norton), Wallace Ford (Slim), Hedda Hopper (Ella Dwight), Helen Coburn (Myra), John Marston (Bill), Boris Karloff.

The Old Dark House (October 20, 1932)
Credits: Directed by James Whale; Produced by Carl Laemmle, Jr.; Presented by Carl Laemmle; Screenplay and adaptation by Benn W. Levy; additional Dialogue by R.C. Sherriff; Based on the Novel *Benighted* by J.B. Priestley; Photographed by Arthur Edeson; Edited by Clarence Kolster; Musical Score by Bernhard Kaun; Sound Recording by William Hedgcock; Art Direction by Charles D. Hall; Makeup by Jack P. Pierce; Special Effects by John P. Fulton; Assistant Director: Joseph A. McDonough; Filmed April 1932; Released by Universal Pictures; Running Time: 70 minutes.
Cast: Boris Karloff (Morgan), Melvyn Douglas (Roger Penderel), Charles Laughton (Sir William Porterhouse), Gloria Stuart (Margaret Waverton), Lillian Bond (Gladys DuCane), Ernest Thesiger (Horace Femm), Eva Moore (Rebecca Femm), Raymond Massey (Philip Waverton), Brember Wills (Saul Femm), John/Elspeth Dudgeon (Sir Roderick Femm).

The Mask of Fu Manchu (November 5, 1932)
Credits: Directed by Charles Brabin and Charles Vidor; Produced by Hunt Stromberg; Screenplay by Irene Kuhn, Edgar Allan Woolf, and John Willard; Based on the Novel by Sax Rohmer; Photographed by Tony Gaudio; Edited by Ben Lewis; Art Direction by Cedric Gibbons; Sound Recording by Douglas Shearer; Makeup by Cecil Holland; Costumes by Adrian; Special Effects by Kenneth Strickfaden; Filmed August 1932; Released by Metro-Goldwyn-Mayer Pictures; Running Time: 72 minutes.
Cast: Boris Karloff (Fu Manchu), Lewis Stone (Nayland Smith), Karen Morley (Sheila Barton), Charles Starrett (Terence Granville), Myrna Loy (Fah Lo See), Jean Hersholt (Professor von Berg), Lawrence Grant (Sir Lionel Barton), David Torrence (McLeod), E. Alyn Warren (Goy Lo Sung), Ferdinand Gottshalk (British Museum Official), C. Montague Shaw (British Museum Official), Willie Fung (Ship's Steward), Herbert Bunston, Gertrude Michael.

The Mummy (December 22, 1932)
Credits: Directed by Karl Freund; Produced by Carl Laemmle, Jr.; Presented by Carl Laemmle; Screenplay by John L. Balderston; Based on a Story by Nina Wilcox Putnam and Richard Schayer; Photographed by Charles Stumar; Edited by Milton Carruth; Art Direction by Willy Pogany; Makeup by Jack P. Pierce; Special Effects by John P. Fulton; Musical Score by James Dietrich, Heinz Roemheld, and Michael Brusselmans (Main Title Theme from Tchaikovsky's *Swan Lake*); Filmed October 1932; Released by Universal Pictures; Running Time: 72 minutes.
Cast: Boris Karloff (Imhotep/Ardath Bey), Zita Johann (Helen Grosvenor/ Princess Anck-es-en-amon), David Manners (Frank Whemple), Edward Van Sloan (Professor Muller), Arthur Byron (Sir Joseph Whemple), Bramwell Fletcher (Norton), Noble Johnson (Nubian), Leonard Mudie (Professor Pearson), Katherine Byron (Frau Muller), Eddie Kane (Doctor), Tony Marlow (Inspector), Arnold Grey (Knight), James Crane (Pharoah), Henry Victor (The Saxon Warrior).

The Ghoul (July 24, 1933)
Credits: Directed by T. Hayes Hunter; Produced by Michael Balcon; Screenplay by Leonard Hines, Rowland Pertwee, and John Hastings Turner; Adapted by Rupert Downing; Based on a Novel by Frank King; Photographed by Gunther Krampf; Edited by Ian Dalrymple; Art Direction by Alfred Junge; Musical Direction by Louis Levy; Sound Recording by R. Birch; Makeup by Heinrich Heitfeld; Filmed March-April 1933; Released by Gaumont-British Pictures; Running Time: 73 minutes.
Cast: Boris Karloff (Professor Morlant), Cedric Hardwicke (Broughton), Ernest Thesiger (Laing), Dorothy Hyson (Betty Harlow), Anthony Bushell (Ralph Morland), Kathleen Harrison (Kaney), Harold Huth (Aga Ben Dragore), D.A. Clarke-Smith (Mahmoud), Ralph Richardson (Nigel Hartley)

The Lost Patrol (February 16, 1934)
Credits: Directed by John Ford; Produced by Cliff Reid; Executive Producer: Merian C. Cooper; Screenplay by Dudley Nichols; Adapted by Garrett Fort; Based on the Novel *Patrol* by Philip MacDonald; Photographed by Harold Wenstrom; Edited by Paul Weatherwax; Art Direction by Van Nest Polglase and Sidney Ullman; Sound Recording by Clem Portman and P.J. Faulkner; Musical Score by Max Steiner; Musical Recording by Murray Spivack; Process Photography by Vernon L. Walker; Makeup by Carl Axcelle; Assistant Director: Argyle Nelson; Unit Managers: Wallace Fox, John B. Burch; Wardrobe by Sandeen; Technical Advisors: Major Frank Baker, Jamiel Hasson; Pilot: Garland Lincoln; Filmed on Location in Buttercup Valley, Arizona, August 31-September 22, 1933; Released by RKO-Radio Pictures; Running Time: 74 minutes.
Cast: Victor McLaglen (the Sergeant), Boris Karloff (Sanders), Wallace Ford (Morelli), Reginald Denny (George Brown), J.M. Kerrigan (Quincannon), Billy Bevan (Herbert Hale), Alan Hale (Cook), Brandon Hurst (Bell), Douglas Walton (Pearson), Sammy Stein (Abelson), Howard Wilson (Aviator), Neville Clark (Lieutenant Hawkins), Paul Hanson (Jock MacKay), Major Frank Baker (Arab), Francis Ford.

The House of Rothschild (April 6, 1934)
Credits: Directed by Alfred Werker; Produced by Darryl F. Zanuck; Screenplay by Nunnally Johnson; Based on the Play by George Humbert Westley; Photographed (partially in Technicolor) by Peverell Marley; Edited by Alan McNeil and Barbara McLean; Musical Score by Alfred Newman; Filmed December 1933-late January 1934; a Twentieth Century Production; Released by United Artists; Running Time: 94 minutes.

Cast: George Arliss (Meyer Rothschild/Nathan Rothschild), Boris Karloff (Baron Ledrantz), Loretta Young (Julie Rothschild), Robert Young (Captain Fitzroy), C. Aubrey Smith (Duke of Wellington), Arthur Byron (Baring), Helen Westley (Gudula Rothschild), Reginald Owen (Herries), Florence Arliss (Hanna Rothschild), Alan Mowbray (Metternich), Noel Madison (Carl Rothschild), Ivan Simpson (Amschel Rothschild), Holmes Herbert (Rowerth), Paul Harvey (Solomon Rothschild), Georges Renavent (Talleyrand), Murray Kinnell (James Rothschild), Oscar Apfel (Prussian Officer), Lumsden Hare (Prince Regent), Leo McCabe (Secretary), Gilbert Emery (Prime Minister), Charles Evans (Nesselrode), Ethel Griffies (Woman Guest), Lee Kohlmar (Doctor), Reginald Sheffield (Stock Trader), Gerald Pierce, Milton Kahn, George Offerman, Jr., Cullen Johnson, Bobbie La Mache (Rothschild Children), Wilfred Lucas (Page), Leonard Mudie (Tax Collector in Prussia).

The Black Cat (May 7, 1934)
Credits: Directed by Edgar G. Ulmer; Produced by Carl Laemmle, Jr.; production Supervised by E.M. Asher; Presented by Carl Laemmle; Screenplay by Peter Ruric; Screen Story by Edgar G. Ulmer and Peter Ruric; Suggested by the Story by Edgar Allan Poe; Photographed by John J. Mescall; Edited by Ray Curtiss; Art Direction by Charles D. Hall; Special Effects by John P. Fulton; Makeup by Jack P. Pierce; Musical Direction by Heinz Roemheld; Musical Themes by Pyotr Ilyich Tchaikovsky, Franz Liszt, Ludwig van Beethoven, and Robert Schumann; Assistant Directors: W.J. Reiter, Sam Weisenthal; Continuity by Tom Kilpatrick; Script Clerk: Moree Herring; Script Girl: Shirley Kassel; Camera Operator: King Gray; Filmed February 28-March 17, 1934; Released by Universal Pictures; Running Time: 65 minutes.
Cast: Boris Karloff (Hjalmar Poelzig), Bela Lugosi (Dr. Vitus Werdegast), David Manners (Peter Alison), Jacqueline Wells; later known as Julie Bishop (Joan Alison), Lucille Lund (Karen), Egon Brecher (Major-domo), Harry Cording (Thamal), Henry Armetta (Sergeant), Albert Conti (Lieutenant), Anna Duncan (Maid), Herman Bing (Car Steward), Andre Cheron (Train Conductor), Luis Alberni (Train Steward), George Davis (Bus Driver), Alphonse Martell (Porter), Tony Marlow (Patrolman), Paul Weigel (Stationmaster), Albert Polet (Waiter), Rodney Hildebrand (Brakeman).

Gift of Gab (September 24, 1934)
Credits: Directed by Karl Freund; Produced by Carl Laemmle, Jr.; Screenplay by Rian James; Adapted by Lou Breslow; Based on a Story by Jerry Wald and Philip G. Epstein; Photographed by George Robinson and Harold Wenstrom; Edited by Raymond Curtiss; Musical Direction by Edward Ward; Filmed July 2-24, 1934; Released by Universal Pictures; Running Time: 70 minutes.
Cast: Edmund Lowe (Philip Gabney), Gloria Stuart (Barbara Kelton), Ruth Etting (Ruth), Phil Baker (Doctor), Ethel Waters (Ethel), Alice White (Margot), Victor Moore (Colonel Trivers), Hugh O'Connell (Patsy), Helen Vinson (Nurse), Gene Austin (Crooner), Thomas Hanlon (Announcer), Henry Armetta (Janitor), Andy Devine (McDougal), Wini Shaw (Singer), Marion Byrne (Telephone Girl), Sterling Holloway (Sound-Effects Man), Edwin Maxwell (Norton), Leighton Noble (Orchestra Leader), Maurice Black (Auction-Room Owner), Tammany Young (Mug), James Flavin (Alumni President), Billy Barty (Baby), Richard Elliott (Father), Florence Enright (Mother), Warner Richmond (Cop), Sid Walker, Skins Miller, Jack Harling (the Three Stooges), Sidney Skolsky, Dennis O'Keefe, Dave O'Brien, Boris Karloff, Bela Lugosi, Alexander Woollcott, Paul Lukas, Chester Morris, Roger Pryor, the Downey Sisters, Douglass Montgomery, Candy and Coco, Douglas Fowley, Binnie Barnes, June Knight, the Beale Street Boys, Rian James, Graham McNamee, Gus Arnheim and His Orchestra (Themselves).

Bride of Frankenstein (May 10, 1935)
Credits: Directed by James Whale; Produced by Carl Laemmle, Jr.; Screenplay by William Hurlbut; Adapted by John L. Balderston and William Hurlbut; Based on the Novel *Frankenstein* by Mary Wollstonecraft Shelley; Photographed by John J. Mescall; Edited by Ted Kent; Special Effects by John P. Fulton; special Electrical Properties by Kenneth Strickfaden; Art Direction by Charles D. Hall; Sound Recording by Gilbert Kurland; Assistant Directors: Harry Menke and Joseph McDonough; Musical Score by Franz Waxman; Musical Direction by Mischa Bakaleinikoff; Makeup by Jack P. Pierce; Filmed January 2-March 10, 1935; Released by Universal Pictures; Running Time: 75 minutes.
Cast: Boris Karloff (the Monster), Colin Clive (Henry Frankenstein), Valerie Hobson (Elizabeth), Ernest Thesiger (Dr. Septimus Pretorius), Elsa Lanchester (Mary Shelley/the Bride), Gavin Gordon (Lord Byron), Douglas Walton (Percy Bysshe Shelley), Una O'Connor (Minnie), E.E. Clive (the Burgomaster), Lucien Prival (Albert, Chief Servidor), O.P. Heggie (the Hermit), Dwight Frye (Karl Glutz), Reginald Barlow (Hans), Mary Gordon (Hans' Wife), Anne Darling (Shepherdess), Ted Billings (Ludwig), Gunnis Davis

(Uncle Glutz), Tempe Pigott (Auntie Glutz), Neil Fitzgerald (Rudy), John Carradine (a Hunter), Walter Brennan (a Neighbor), Helen Parrish (Communion Girl), Rollo Lloyd (a Neighbor), Edwin Mordant (the Coroner), Lucio Villegas (Priest), Brenda Fowler (a Mother), Robert A'dair (a Hunter), Sarah Schwartz (Marta), Mary Stewart (a Neighbor), John Curtis (a Hunter), Arthur S. Byron (Little King), Joan Woodbury (Little Queen), Norman Ainsley (Little Bishop), Peter Shaw (Little Devil/Villager/Double for Thesiger), Kansas De Forrest (Little Ballerina), Josephine McKim (Little Mermaid), Billy Barty (Little Baby), Frank Terry (a Hunter), Frank Benson, Ed Piel, Sr., Anders Van Haden, John George, Grace Cunard, Maurice Black (Villagers), Monty Montague (Double for Thesiger), George De Normand (Double for Barlow).

The Black Room (July 15, 1935)
Credits: Directed by Roy William Neill; Produced by Robert North; Screenplay by Henry Myers and Arthur Strawn; Based on a Story by Arthur Strawn; Photographed by Al Siegler; Edited by Richard Cahoon; Art Direction by Stephen Goosson; Musical Direction by Louis Silvers; Costumes by Murray Mayer; Filmed May-June 1935; Released by Columbia Pictures; Running Time: 68 minutes.
Cast: Boris Karloff (Baron Gregor De Berghman/Anton De Berghman), Marian Marsh (Thea Hassel), Robert Allen (Lieutenant Albert Lussan), Thurston Hall (Colonel Hassel), Katherine De Mille (Mashka), John Buckler (Beran), Henry Kolker (Baron Frederick De Berghman), Colin Tapley (Lieutenant Hassel), Torbin Meyer (Peter), Egon Brecher (Karl), John Bleifer (Franz), Frederick Vogeding (Josef), Edward Van Sloan (Doctor), Lois Lindsay, Alan Mowbray, Herbert Evans.

The Raven (July 22, 1935)
Credits: Directed by Louis Friedlander (later known as Lew Landers); Produced by David Diamond; Presented by Carl Laemmle; Screenplay by David Boehm; suggested by the poem "The Raven" by Edgar Allan Poe; Photographed by Charles Stumar; Edited by Alfred Akst; Art Direction by Albert S. D'Agostino; Musical Direction by Gilbert Harland; Choreography by Theodore Kosloff; Dialogue Direction by Florence Enright; Makeup by Jack P. Pierce; Filmed March 20-April 5, 1935; Premiered July 4, 1935; Released by Universal Pictures; Running Time: 62 minutes.
Cast: Boris Karloff (Edmond Bateman), Bela Lugosi (Dr. Richard Vollin), Irene Ware (Jean Thatcher), Lester Matthews (Dr. Jerry Halden), Samuel S. Hinds (Judge Thatcher), Inez Courtney (Mary Burns), Ian Wolfe (Pinky Geoffrey), Spencer Charters (Colonel Bertram Grant), Maidel Turner (Harriet Grant), Arthur Hoyt (Chapman), Walter Miller.

The Invisible Ray (January 20, 1936)
Credits: Directed by Lambert Hillyer; Produced by Edmund Grainger; Presented by Carl Laemmle; Screenplay by John Colton; Based on a Story by Howard Higgin and Douglas Hodges; Photographed by George Robinson; Edited by Bernard Burton; Special Effects by John P. Fulton; Art Direction by Albert S. D'Agostino; Musical Score by Franz Waxman; Makeup by Jack P. Pierce; Filmed September 17-October 25, 1935; Premiered January 10, 1936; Released by Universal Pictures; Running Time: 79 minutes.
Cast: Boris Karloff (Dr. Janos Rukh), Bela Lugosi (Dr. Felix Benet), Frances Drake (Diana Rukh), Frank Lawton (Ronald Drake), Walter Kingsford (Sir Francis Stevens), Beulah Bondi (Lady Arabella Stevens), Violet Kemble Cooper (Mother Rukh), Nydia Westman (Briggs), Georges Renavent (Chief of Surete), Frank Reicher (Professor Meikeljohn), Paul Wegel (Professor Noyer), Adele St. Maur (Madame Noyer), Lawrence Stewart (Number-One Boy), Etta McDaniel (Zulu), Daniel Haines (Headman), Inez Seabury (Celeste), Winter Hall (Minister), Hans Schumn (Clinic Attendant), Fred ("Snowflake") Toones (Frightened Native), Lloyd Whitlock, Edwards Davis, Alphonse Martell, Daisy Bufford, Clarence Gordon, Ernie Adams, Walter Miller.

The Walking Dead (February 29, 1936)
Credits: Directed by Michael Curtiz; Produced by Lou Edelman; Screenplay by Ewart Adamson, Peter Milne, Robert Andrews, and Lillie Hayward; Based on a Story by Ewart Adamson and Joseph Fields; Photographed by Hal Mohr; Edited by Thomas Pratt; Art Direction by Hugh Reticker; Dialogue Direction by Irving Rapper; Costumes by Cary Odell and Orry-Kelly; Makeup by Perc Westmore; Filmed December 1935-January 1936; Released by Warner Bros. Pictures; Running Time: 65 minutes.
Cast: Boris Karloff (John Elman), Ricardo Cortez (Nolan), Warren Hull (Jimmy), Robert Strange (Merritt), Joseph King (Judge Shaw), Edmund Gwenn (Dr. Evan Beaumont), Marguerite Churchill (Nancy), Barton MacLane (Loder), Henry O'Neill (Warner, the District Attorney), Paul Harvey (Blackstone), Joseph Sawyer (Trigger Smith), Eddie Acuff (Betcha), Ruth Robinson (Mrs. Shaw), Addison Richards (Prison War-

den), Kenneth Harlan (Stephen Martin), Miki Morita (Sako), Adrian Rosley (Florist), Milt Kibbee, Bill Elliot, Wade Boteler.

The Man Who Changed His Mind (September 11, 1936)
Credits: U.S. title: *The Man Who Lived Again*; Directed by Robert Stevenson; Produced by Michael Balcon; Screenplay by L. DuGarde Peach and Sidney Gilliat; Based on a Story by John L. Balderston; Photographed by Jack Cox; Edited by R.E. Dearing and Alfred Roomer; Art Direction by Alex Vetchinsky; Makeup by Roy Ashton; Dresses by Molyneux; Musical Direction by Louis Levy; Sound Recording by W. Salter; Released by Gaumont-British Pictures; Running Time: 66 minutes.
Cast: Boris Karloff (Dr. Laurience), Anna Lee (Dr. Claire Wyatt), John Loder (Dick Haslewood), Frank Cellier (Lord Haslewood), Donald Calthrop (Clayton), Cecil Parker (Dr. Gratton), Lyn Harding (Professor Holloway), Clive Morton, D.J. Williams, Brian Pawley.

Juggernaut (September 18, 1936)
Credits: Directed by Henry Edwards; Produced by Julius Hagen; Screenplay by Cyril Campion and H. Fowler Mear; Adaptation and Dialogue by Heinrich Fraenkel; Based on a Novel by Alice Campbell; Photographed by Sidney Blythe and William Luff; Edited by Michael Chorlton; Art Direction by James Carter; Musical Score by W.L. Trytel; Released by Grand National Pictures; Running Time: 64 minutes.
Cast: Boris Karloff (Dr. Sartorius), Joan Wyndham (Eve Rowe), Arthur Margetson (Roger Clifford), Mona Goya (Lady Yvonne Clifford), Anthony Ireland (Captain Arthur Halliday), Morton Selten (Sir Charles Clifford), Nina Boucicalt (Mary Clifford), Gibb McLaughlin (Jacques), J.H. Roberts (Chalmers), Victor Rietti (Doctor Bousquet).

Charlie Chan at the Opera (January 8, 1937)
Credits: Directed by H. Bruce Humberstone; Associate Producer: John Stone; Screenplay by W. Scott Darling and Charles Belden; Based on a Story by Bess Meredyth and on Characters Created by Earl Derr Biggers; Photographed by Lucien Andriot; Edited by Alex Troffoy; Opera Music (*Carnival*) by Oscar Levant; libretto by William Kernell; Musical Direction by Samuel Kaylin; Orchestrations by Charles Maxwell; Sound Recording by George Leverette and Harry H. Leonard; Art Direction by Duncan Cramer and Lewis Creber; Costumes by Herschel; Filmed October 1936; Released by Twentieth Century-Fox Pictures; Running Time: 66 minutes.
Cast: Warner Oland (Charlie Chan), Boris Karloff (Gravelle), Keye Luke (Lee Chan), Charlotte Henry (Mademoiselle Kitty), Thomas Beck (Phil Childers), Margaret Irving (Madame Lucretia Barelli), Frank Conroy (Mr. Whitely), Guy Usher (Inspector Regan), William Demarest (Sergeant Kelly), Maurice Cass (Mr. Arnold), Tom McGuire (Morris), Fred Kelsey (Dugan), Emmett Vogan (Smitty), Selmer Jackson (Newspaper Wire-Photo Technician), Benson Fong (Opera Extra), Joan Woodbury, Stanley Blystone.

Night Key (May 2, 1937)
Credits: Directed by Lloyd Corrigan; Produced by Robert Presnell; Screenplay by Tristram Tupper and John C. Moffitt; Based on a Story by William Pierce; Photographed by George Robinson; Edited by Otis Garrett; Art Direction by Jack Otterson; Special Effects by John P. Fulton; Musical Direction by Lou Forbes; Makeup by Jack P. Pierce; Filmed February 1937; Released by Universal Pictures; Running Time: 67 minutes.
Cast: Boris Karloff (Dave Mallory), Jean Rogers (Joan Mallory), Warren Hull (Travers), Hobart Cavanaugh (Petty Louie), Samuel S. Hinds (Steve Ranger), Alan Baxter (John Baron, "the Kid"), David Oliver (Mike), Edwin Maxwell (Kruger), Ward Bond (Fingers), Frank Hagney, Frank Reicher, Ethan Laidlaw, George Cleveland, Charles Wilson, Antonio Filauri, Ralph Dunn.

West of Shanghai (October 30, 1937)
Credits: Directed by John Farrow; Associate Producer: Bryan Foy; Screenplay by Crane Wilbur; Based on the Play *The Bad Man* by Porter Emerson Browne; Photographed by L. William O'Connell; Edited by Frank Dewar; Art Direction by Max Parker; Costumes by Howard Shoup; Makeup by Perc Westmore; Technical Advisor: Tommy Gubbins; Dialogue Director: Jo Graham; Assistant Director: Marshall Hageman; Filmed March-April, 1938; Released by Warner Bros.-First National Pictures; Running Time: 65 minutes.
Cast: Boris Karloff (General Wu Yen Fang), Beverly Roberts (Jane Creed), Ricardo Cortez (Gordon Creed), Gordon Oliver (James Hallett), Sheila Bromley (Lola Galt), Vladimir Sokoloff (General Chou Fu Shan), Gordon Hart (Dr. Abernathy), Richard Loo (Mr. Cheng), Douglas Wood (Myron Galt), Chester Gan (Captain Kung Nui), Luke Chan (Chan), Selmer Jackson (Hemingway), James B. Leong (Pao), Tetsu Komai

(General Mu), Eddie Lee (Wang Chung), Maurice Lui (Conductor), Mia Ichioaka (Hua Mei), Paul Fung (Station Master), Frank Tang (Chinese Merchant), Bruce Wong (Steward), Sam Tong (Messenger), Tom Ung (Military Aide), Dara Meya (Chinese Officer).

The Invisible Menace (January 22, 1938)
Credits: Directed by John Farrow; Associate Producer: Bryan Foy; Screenplay by Crane Wilbur; Based on the Play *Without Warning* by Ralph Spencer Zink; Dialogue Direction by Harry Seymour; Photographed by L. William O'Connell; Edited by Harold McLernon; Art Direction by Stanley Fleischer; Gowns by Harold Shoup; Assistant Director: Elmer Decker; Sound Recording by Leslie G. Hewett; Filmed October 1937; Released by Warner Bros. Pictures; Running Time: 56 minutes.
Cast: Boris Karloff (Jevries), Marie Wilson (Sally), Eddie Craven (Eddie Pratt), Eddie Acuff (Corporal Sanger), Regis Toomey (Lieutenant Matthews), Henry Kolker (Colonel Hackett), Cy Kendall (Colonel Rogers), Charles Trowbridge (Dr. Brooks), Frank Faylen (Private of the Guard), William Haade (Private Ferris), Harland Tucker (Reilly), Phyllis Barry (Aline Dolman), John Ridgely (Private Innes), Jack Mower (Sergeant Peterson), Anderson Lawlor (Private Abbott), John Harron (Private Murphy).

Mr. Wong, Detective (October 5, 1938)
Credits: Directed by William Nigh; Produced by Scott R. Dunlap; Associate Producer: William T. Lackey; Screenplay by Houston Branch; Based on the Stories by Hugh Wiley; Photographed by Harry Neumann; Edited by Russell Schoengarth; Musical Direction by Art Meyer; Makeup by Gordon Bau; Released by Monogram Pictures; Running Time: 69 minutes.
Cast: Boris Karloff (James Lee Wong), Grant Withers (Captain Sam Street), Maxine Jennings (Myra, Dayton's Secretary), Evelyn Brent (Olga), Lucien Prival (Mohl), John St. Polis (Karl Roemer), William Gould (Meisel), Hooper Atchley (Wilk), John Hamilton (Dayton), Frank Bruno (Lascari), Lee Tong Foo (Tchain), George Lloyd (Devlin), Wilbur Mack, Grace Wood, Lynton Brent.

Son of Frankenstein (January 13, 1939)
Credits: Directed and Produced by Rowland V. Lee; Screenplay by Willis Cooper; Suggested by the Novel *Frankenstein* by Mary Wollstonecraft Shelley; Photographed by George Robinson; Edited by Ted Kent; Special Effects by John P. Fulton; Sound Direction by Bernard B. Brown; Art Direction by Jack Otterson; Associate Art Director: Richard H. Riedel; Set Direction by Russell Gausman; Makeup by Jack P. Pierce; Musical Score by Frank Skinner; Musical Arrangements by Hans J. Salter; Musical Direction by Lionel Newman; Assistant Director: Fred Frank; Technician: William Hedgcock; Costumes by Vera West; Filmed November 9, 1938-January 5, 1939; Released by Universal Pictures; Running Time: 99 minutes.
Cast: Basil Rathbone (Baron Wolf von Frankenstein), Boris Karloff (the Monster), Bela Lugosi (Ygor), Lionel Atwill (Inspector Krogh), Josephine Hutchinson (Elsa von Frankenstein), Donnie Dunagan (Peter von Frankenstein), Emma Dunn (Amelia), Edgar Norton (Thomas Benson), Perry Ivins (Fritz), Lawrence Grant (Burgomaster), Lionel Belmore (Emil Lang), Michael Mark (Ewald Neumuller), Caroline Cook (Frau Neumuller), Gustav von Seyffertitz, Lorimer Johnson, Tom Ricketts (Councillors), Edward Cassidy (Dr. Berger), Ward Bond (Guard at Gate), Dwight Frye (Villager; footage deleted), Bud Wolfe (Double for Karloff in pit fall), Jack Harris, Betty Chay, Harry Cording, Eddie Parker.

The Mystery of Mr. Wong (March 8, 1939)
Credits: Directed by William Nigh; Produced by Scott R. Dunlap; Associate Producer: William T. Lackey; Screenplay by W. Scott Darling; Based on a Story by Hugh Wiley; Photographed by Harry Neumann; Edited by Russell Schoengarth; Makeup by Gordon Bau; Released by Monogram Pictures; Running Time: 68 minutes.
Cast: Boris Karloff (James Lee Wong), Grant Withers (Captain Sam Street), Dorothy Tree (Valerie Edwards), Craig Reynolds (Peter Harrison), Lotus Long (Drina, Maid), Morgan Wallace (Brendan Edwards, Curio Collector), Holmes Herbert (Professor Ed Janney), Ivan Lebedeff (Michael Stroganoff), Hooper Atchley (Carslake), Bruce Wong (Man), Lee Tong Foo (Willie), Chester Gan (Sing, a Servant).

Mr. Wong in Chinatown (August 1, 1939)
Credits: Directed by William Nigh; Produced by Scott R. Dunlap; Supervised by William T. Lackey; Screenplay by W. Scott Darling; Based on a Story by Hugh Wiley; Photographed by Harry Neumann; Edited by Russell Schoengarth; Makeup by Gordon Bau; Released by Monogram Pictures; Running Time: 70 minutes.
Cast: Boris Karloff (James Lee Wong), Grant Withers (Inspector Sam Street), Marjorie Reynolds (Bobbie

Logan), Peter George Lynn (Captain Jackson), William Royle (Captain Jamie of the Orient Maid), Huntly Gordon (Davidson, Bank Manager), James Flavin (Sergeant Jerry), Lotus Long (Princess Lin Wha), Richard Loo (Aged Chinese), Bessie Loo (Lilly Mae), Lee Tong Foo (Willie), Little Angelo Rositto (Dwarf) Guy Usher (Commissioner).

The Man They Could Not Hang (August 17, 1939)
Credits: Directed by Nick Grinde; Produced by Wallace MacDonald; Screenplay by Karl Brown; Based on a Story by Leslie T. White and George W. Sayre; Photographed by Benjamin Kline; Edited by William Lyon; Art Direction by Lionel Banks; Musical Direction by Morris W. Stoloff; Filmed July 1939; Released by Columbia Pictures; Running Time: 65 minutes.
Cast: Boris Karloff (Dr. Henryk Savaard), Lorna Gray (Janet Savaard), Robert Wilcox (Scoop Foley), Roger Pryor (District Attorney Drake), Don Beddoe (Lieutenant Shane), Ann Doran (Betty Crawford), Joseph De Stefani (Dr. Stoddard), Dick Burtis (Kearney), Byron Foulger (Lang), James Craig (Watkins), John Tyrrell (Sutton), Charles Trowbridge (Judge Bowman).

Tower of London (November 17, 1939)
Credits: Directed and Produced by Rowland V. Lee; Screenplay and Story by Robert N. Lee; Photographed by George Robinson; Edited by Edward Curtiss; Art Direction by Jack Otterson; Associate Art Director: Richard H. Riedel; Set Direction by Richard Gausman; Orchestrations by Frank Skinner; Musical Direction by Charles Previn; Sound Direction by Bernard B. Brown; Makeup by Jack P. Pierce; Costumes by Vera West; Technician: William Hedgcock; Released by Universal Pictures; Running Time: 92 minutes.
Cast: Basil Rathbone (Richard III), Boris Karloff (Mord, the Executioner), Barbara O'Neil (Queen Elizabeth), Ian Hunter (Edward IV), Vincent Price (Duke of Clarence), Nan Grey (Lady Alice Barton), John Sutton (John Wyatt), Leo G. Carroll (Lord Hastings), Miles Mander (Henry VI), Lionel Belmore (Beacon Chiruegon), Rose Hobart (Anne Neville), Ralph Forbes (Henry Tudor), Frances Robinson (Duchess Isobel), Ernest Cossart (Tom Klink), G.P. Huntley (Prince of Wales), John Rodion (Lord Devere), Ronald Sinclair (Prince Edward), Donnie Dunagan (Prince Richard, as a Child), John Herbert-Bond (Young Prince Richard), Walter Tetley (Chimney Sweep), Georgia Cane (Dowager Duchess), Ivan Simpson (Retainer), Nigel de Brulier (Archbishop, St. John's Chapel), Holmes Herbert, Charles Miller (Councilmen), Venecia Severn, Yvonne Severn (Princesses), Louise Brien, Jean Fenwick (Ladies in Waiting), Michael Mark (Servant to Henry VI), C. Montague Shaw (Majordomo), Don Stewart (Bunch), Reginald Barlow (Sheriff at Execution), Robert Greig (Father Olmstead), Ivo Henderson (Halberdier), Charles Peck (Page Boy), Harry Cording (Tyrrel, an Assassin), Jack C. Smith (Forrest, an Assassin), Colin Kenny, Arthur Stenning (Soldiers), Evelyn Selbie (Beggar Woman), Denis Tankard, David Thursby (Beggars), Claire Witney (Civilian Woman), Ernie Adams (Prisoner Begging for Water), Russ Powell (Sexton/Bell Ringer), Ann Todd (Queen Elizabeth's Daughter).

The Fatal Hour (January 15, 1940)
Credits: Directed by William Nigh; Produced by William T. Lackey; Screenplay by W. Scott Darling; Based on a Story by Hugh Wiley; Adapted by Joseph West; Photographed by Harry Neumann; Edited by Russell Schoengarth; Makeup by Gordon Bau; Released by Monogram Pictures; Running Time: 68 minutes.
Cast: Boris Karloff (James Lee Wong), Grant Withers (Captain Street), Marjorie Reynolds (Bobbie Logan), Charles Trowbridge (Forbes), John Hamilton (Belden, Sr.), Craig Reynolds (Belden, Jr.), Jack Kennedy (Mike), Lita Chevret (Tanya), Frank Puglia (Hardway), I. Stanford Jolley (Soapy), Jason Robards, Sr. (Griswold), Pauline Drake (Bessie).

British Intelligence (January 29, 1940)
Credits: Directed by Terry Morse; Associate Producer: Mark Hellinger; Screenplay by Lee Katz; Based on the Play *Three Faces East* by Anthony Paul Kelly; Additional Dialogue by John Langan; Photographed by Sid Hickox; Edited by Thomas Pratt; Art Direction by Hugh Reticker; Musical Score by Heinz Roemheld; Makeup by Perc Westmore; Gowns by Howard Shoup; Sound Recording by Stanley Jones; Dialogue Direction by John Langan; Assistant Director: Elmer Decker; Released by Warner Bros.-First National Pictures; Running Time: 62 minutes.
Cast: Boris Karloff (Valdar), Margaret Lindsay (Helene von Lorbeer), Maris Wrixon (Dorothy), Bruce Lester (Frank Bennett), Leonard Mudie (Colonel James Yeats), Holmes Herbert (Arthur Bennett), Lester Matthews (Henry Thompson), John Graham Spacy (Crichton), Austin Fairman (George Bennett), Winifred

Harris (Mrs. Bennett), Clarence Derwent (Milkman), Louise Brien (Miss Risdon), Frederick Vogeding (Kuglar), Carlos de Valdez (von Ritter), Frederick Giermann (Jurtz), Willy Kaufman (German Corporal), Frank Mayo (Brixton), Stuart Holmes (Luchow), Sidney Bracy (Crowder), Jack Mower (Morton), Leonard Wiley (Captain Stuart), Morton Lowry (Lieutenant Borden), Evan Thomas (Major Andrews), Lawrence Grant (Brigadier General), Denis d'Auburn (Captain Lanark), Craufurd Kent (Commander Phelps), Carl Harbaugh (German Soldier), Ferdinand Schumann-Heink, Joseph DeStefani (German Officers), Jack Richardson, Bob Stevenson (Cockney Soldiers), Glen Cavender (Under Officer Pfalz), Henry Von Zynda (German), Hans Schumm (German Senior Officer), Arno Frey (German Junior Officer), Gordon Hart (Doctor), John Sutton (Officer), Leland Hodgson (Lord Sudbury), David Thursby (Mysterious Man), Paul Panzer (Peasant).

Black Friday (April 12, 1940)
Credits: Directed by Arthur Lubin; Produced by Burt Kelly; Screenplay and Story by Curt Siodmak and Eric Taylor; Photographed by Elwood Bredell; Edited by Philip Cahn; Special Effects by John P. Fulton; Art Direction by Jack Otterson; Associate Art Director: Harold MacArthur; Set Decoration by Russell A. Gausman; Sound Direction by Bernard B. Brown; Musical Direction by Hans J. Salter; Costumes by Vera West; Makeup by Jack P. Pierce; Technician: Charles Carroll; Filmed December 28, 1939-January 18, 1940; Premiered March 21, 1940; Released by Universal Pictures; Running Time: 70 minutes.
Cast: Boris Karloff (Dr. Ernst Sovac), Bela Lugosi (Eric Marnay), Stanley Ridges (Professor George Kingsley/Red Cannon), Anne Nagel (Sunny Rogers), Anne Gwynne (Jean Sovac), Virginia Brissac (Margaret Kingsley), Edmund MacDonald (Frank Miller), Paul Fix (William Kane), Murray Alper (Bellhop), Jack Mulhall (Bartender), Joe King (Chief of Police), John Kelly (Taxi Driver), James Craig (Reporter), Jerry Marlowe (Clerk).

The Man with Nine Lives (April 18, 1940)
Credits: Directed by Nick Grinde; Produced by Wallace MacDonald; Screenplay by Karl Brown; Based on a Story by Harold Shumate; Photographed by Benjamin Kline; Edited by Al Clark; Art Direction by Lionel Banks; Technical Advisor: Dr. Ralph S. Willard; Musical Direction by Morris W. Stoloff; Released by Columbia Pictures; Running Time: 73 minutes.
Cast: Boris Karloff (Dr. Leon Kravaal), Roger Pryor (Dr. Tim Mason), Jo Ann Sayers (Judith Blair), Stanley Brown (Bob Adams), Hal Taliaferro (Sheriff Stanton), Byron Foulger (Dr. Bassett), Charles Trowbridge (Dr. Harvey), Ernie Adams (Pete Daggett), Lee Willard (Jasper Adams), Ivan Miller (Sheriff Haley), Bruce Bennett (State Trooper), John Dilson (John Hawthorne).

Devil's Island (July 11, 1940)
Credits: Directed by William Clemens; Associate Producer: Bryan Foy; Screenplay by Don Ryan and Kenneth Gamet; Photographed by George Barnes; Edited by Frank Magee; Art Direction by Max Parker; Technical Adviser: Louis Van Den Ecker; Sound Recording by Robert B. Lee; Dialogue direction by John Langan; Assistant Director: Arthur Leuker; Released by Warner Bros.-First National Pictures; Running Time: 62 minutes.
Cast: Boris Karloff (Dr. Charles Gaudet), Nedda Harrigan (Madame Lucien), James Stephenson (Colonel Armand Lucien), Adia Kuznetzoff (Pierre), Rolla Gourvitch (Colette), Will Stanton (Bobo), Edward Keane (Dr. Duval), Robert Warwick (Demontre, Minister of Colonies), Pedro de Cordoba (Marcel), Tom Wilson (Emil), John Harmon (Andre), Richard Bond (Georges), Earl Gunn (Leon), Sidney Bracey (Soupy), George Lloyd (Dogface), Charles Richman (Governor Beaufort), Stuart Holmes (Gustav le Brun), Leonard Mudie (Advocate General), Egon Brecher (Debriac), Frank Reicher (President of Assize Court), John Hamilton (Ship's Captain), Alan Bridge (Captain of Guards), Earl Dwire (Priest), Harry Cording, Galan Galt, Frank S. Hagney, Douglas Williams, Henry Otho, Stanley King, James Blaine, Dick Rich, Sol Gorss, Don Turner (Guards), Ben Hendricks (Sergeant of Guards), Earl Smith (Servant), Alonzo Price (Captain Ferreau), Walter Sodeling (Waggoner), Glen Cavender, Cliff Saum (Gendarmes), Davison Clark (Captain of Gendarmes), Nat Carr (Court Clerk), Paul Panzer (Jury Foreman), Neil Clisby (Jules), Jack Mower (Sergeant), Lawrence Grant (First Official), Theodor von Eltz (Second Official), Eddie Foster (Supply Clerk), Dick Botiller (Pilot), Francis Sayles (Boatman), Billy McClain (Servant), Jack Wise (Convict), John Hamilton (Captain of Convict Ship), Jack Richardson.

Doomed to Die (August 12, 1940)
Credits: Directed by William Nigh; Produced by Paul Malvern; Screenplay by Michael Jacoby and Ralph G. Bettinson; Based on Stories by Hugh Wiley; Photographed by Harry Neumann; Edited by Robert Golden;

Makeup by Gordon Bau; Released by Monogram Pictures; Running Time: 68 minutes.

Cast: Boris Karloff (James Lee Wong), Grant Withers (Captain Street), Marjorie Reynolds (Bobbie Logan), Melvin Lang (Wentworth), Guy Usher (Fleming), Catherine Craig (Cynthia Wentworth), William Sterling (Dick Fleming), Henry Brandon, Wilbur Mack.

Before I Hang (September 17, 1940)
Credits: Directed by Nick Grinde; Produced by Wallace MacDonald; Screenplay by Robert D. Andrews; Based on a Story by Karl Brown and Robert D. Andrews; Photographed by Benjamin Kline; Edited by Charles Nelson; Art Direction by Lionel Banks; Musical Direction by Morris W. Stoloff; Released by Columbia Pictures; Running Time: 63 minutes.

Cast: Boris Karloff (Dr. John Garth), Evelyn Keyes (Martha Garth), Bruce Bennett (Dr. Paul Ames), Edward Van Sloan (Dr. Ralph Howard), Ben Taggart (Warden Thompson), Pedro de Cordoba (Victor Sondini), Wright Cramer (George Wharton), Barton Yarborough (Stephen Barclay), Don Beddoe (Captain McGraw), Robert Fiske (District Attorney), Kenneth MacDonald (Anson), Frank Richards (Otto Kron), Charles Trowbridge (Judge).

The Ape (September 30, 1940)
Credits: Directed by William Nigh; Produced by Scott R. Dunlap; Associate Producer: William T. Lackey; Screenplay by Curt Siodmak and Richard Carroll; Based on the Play by Adam Hull Shirk; Photographed by Harry Neumann; Edited by Russell Schoengarth; Art Direction by E.R. Hickson; Musical Direction by Edward Kay; Assistant Director: Allen Wood; production manager: Karl Lind; Sound Recording by C.L. Bigelow; Released by Monogram Pictures; Running Time: 61 minutes.

Cast: Boris Karloff (Dr. Bernard Adrian), Maris Wrixon (Frances Clifford), Gertrude Hoffman (Mrs. Clifford), Henry Hall (Sheriff Jeff Holliday), Gene O'Donnell (Danny Foster), Dorothy Vaughan (Jane), Jack Kennedy (Tomlin), Jessie Arnold (Mrs. Brill).

You'll Find Out (November 22, 1940)
Credits: Directed and Produced by David Butler; Screenplay by James V. Kern, Monte Brice, Andrew Bennison, and R.T.M. Scott; Based on a Story by David Butler and James V. Kern; Photographed by Frank Redman; Edited by Irene Morra; Special Effects by Vernon L. Walker; Art Direction by Van Nest Polglase; Musical Direction by Roy Webb; Music and Lyrics by Jimmy McHugh and Johnny Mercer; Costumes by Edward Stevenson; Filmed August 8-October 11, 1940; Premiered November 14, 1940; Released by RKO-Radio Pictures; Running Time: 97 minutes.

Cast: Kay Kyser (Himself), Peter Lorre (Professor Fenninger), Boris Karloff (Judge Mainwaring), Bela Lugosi (Prince Saliano), Helen Parrish (Janis Bellacrest), Dennis O'Keefe (Chuck Deems), Alma Kruger (Aunt Margo), Joseph Eggenton (Jurgen), Leonard Mudie (the Real Fenninger), Ginny Simms, Harry Babbit, Sully Mason, Ish Kabibble (Themselves), Kay Kyser's Band.

The Devil Commands (February 3, 1941)
Credits: Directed by Edward Dmytryk; Produced by Wallace MacDonald; Screenplay by Robert D. Andrews and Milton Gunzberg; Based on the Novel *The Edge of Running Water* by William Sloane; Photographed by Allen G. Siegler; Edited by Al Clark; Art Direction by Lionel Banks; Musical Direction by Morris W. Stoloff; Special Effects by Phil Faulkner; Filmed December 1940; Released by Columbia Pictures; Running Time: 65 minutes.

Cast: Boris Karloff (Dr. Julian Blair), Richard Fiske (Dr. Richard Sayles), Amanda Duff (Anne Blair), Anne Revere (Mrs. Blanche Walters), Ralph Penney (Karl), Dorothy Adams (Mrs. Marcy), Walter Baldwin (Seth Marcy), Kenneth MacDonald (Sheriff Ed Willis), Shirley Warde (Helen Blair), Erwin Kalser (Professor Kent), Wheaton Chambers (Professor Saunders).

The Boogie Man Will Get You (October 22, 1942)
Credits: Directed by Lew Landers; Produced by Colbert Clark; Screenplay by Edwin Blum; Based on a Story by Hal Fimberg and Robert B. Hunt; Adapted by Paul Gangelin; Photographed by Henry Freulich; Edited by Richard Fantl; Art Direction by Lionel Banks; Associate Art Director: Robert Peterson; Set Decoration by George Montgomery; Musical Direction by Morris W. Stoloff; Sound Recording by C. Althouse; Released by Columbia Pictures; Running Time: 66 minutes.

Cast: Boris Karloff (Professor Nathaniel Billings), Peter Lorre (Dr. Lorentz), Maxie Rosenbloom (Maxie), Larry Parks (Bill Leyden), Jeff Donnell (Winnie Leyden), Maude Eburne (Amelia Jones), Don Beddoe (J.

Gilbert Brampton), George McKay (Ebenezer), Frank Puglia (Silvio Baciagalupi), Eddie Laughton (Johnson), Frank Sully (Officer Starrett), James Morton (Officer Quincy).

The Climax (October 20, 1944)
Credits: Directed and Produced by George Waggner; Executive Producer: Joseph Gershenson; Screenplay by Curt Siodmak and Lynn Starling; Based on the Play by Edward J. Locke; Adapted by Curt Siodmak; Photographed in Technicolor by Hal Mohr and W. Howard Greene; Technicolor Consultant: Natalie Kalmus; Edited by Russell Schoengarth; Special Effects by John P. Fulton; Art Direction by John B. Goodman and Alexander Golitzen; Set Decoration by Russell A. Gausman and Ira S. Webb; Musical Score by Edward Ward; Musical Direction by Don George; Libretto by George Waggner; Sound Recording by William Fox and Bernard B. Brown; Assistant Directors: Charles S. Gould, Harry O. Jones; Costumes by Vera West; Makeup by Jack P. Pierce; Dialogue Director: Gene Lewis; Special Effects by John P. Fulton; Released by Universal Pictures; Running Time: 86 minutes.
Cast: Susanna Foster (Angela), Boris Karloff (Dr. Fredrick Hohner), Turhan Bey (Franz Munzer), Gail Sondergaard (Luise), Thomas Gomez (Count Seebruck), June Vincent (Marcellina), George Dolenz (Amato Roselli), Ludwig Stossel (Carl Bauman), Jane Farrar (Jarmilla Vadek), Erno Verebes (Brunn), Lotte Stein (Mama Hinzl), Scotty Beckett (King), William Edmunds (Leon), Maxwell Hayes (Aide), Dorothy Lawrence (Mrs. Metzger), Polly Bailey (Cleaning Woman).

House of Frankenstein (December 15, 1944)
Credits: Directed by Erle C. Kenton; Produced by Paul Malvern; Executive Producer: Joseph Gershenson; Screenplay by Edward T. Lowe; Based on a Story by Curt Siodmak; Photographed by George Robinson; Camera Operator: Eddie Cohen; Special Effects by Carl Elmendorf; Edited by Philip Cahn; Special Photography by John P. Fulton; Art Direction by John B. Goodman and Martin Obzina; Set Decoration by Russell A. Gausman and Andrew J. Gilmore; Musical Score by Hans J. Salter, Paul Desau, Frank Skinner, and Charles Previn; Sound Direction by Bernard B. Brown; Technician: William Hedgcock; Gowns by Vera West; Assistant Director: William Tummel; Makeup by Jack P. Pierce; Assistant Director: William Tummel; Properties: Eddie Keys; Filmed April-May 1944 as "The Devil's Brood"; Released by Universal Pictures; Running Time: 70 minutes.
Cast: Boris Karloff (Dr. Gustav Niemann), Lon Chaney, Jr. (Lawrence Talbot), John Carradine (Count Dracula), Anne Gwynne (Rita Hussman), Peter Coe (Carl Hussman), Lionel Atwill (Inspector Arnz), George Zucco (Professor Bruno Lampini), Elena Verdugo (Ilonka), J. Carroll Naish (Daniel), Sig Rumann (Burgomaster Hussman), William Edmunds (Fejos), Charles Miller (Toberman), Philip Van Zandt (Muller), Julius Tannen (Hertz), Hans Herbert (Meier), Dick Dickinson (Born), George Lynn (Gerlach), Michael Mark (Strauss), Olaf Hytten (Hoffman), Frank Reicher (Ullman), Brandon Hurst (Dr. Geissler), Glenn Strange (the Monster), Belle Mitchell (Urla), Eddie Cobb (Driver), Charles Wagenheim (Prison Guard).

The Body Snatcher (March 1945)
Credits: Directed by Robert Wise; Produced by Val Lewton; Executive Producer: Jack J. Gross; Screenplay by Philip MacDonald and Carlos Keith (Val Lewton); Based on the Story by Robert Louis Stevenson; Photographed by Robert de Grasse; Camera Operator: Charles Burke; Edited by J.R. Whittredge; Art Direction by Albert S. D'Agostino and Walter E. Keller; Set Decoration by Darrell Silvera and John Sturtevant; Musical Score by Roy Webb; Musical Direction by Constantin Bakaleinikoff; Sound Direction by Baily Fesler and Terry Kellum; First Assistant Director: Harry Scott; Second Assistant Director: Nate Levinson; Script Clerk: Pat Betz; Assistant Cameraman: Tex Wheaton; Men's Wardrobe: Hans Bohnstedt; Ladies' Wardrobe: Mary Tate; Makeup by Frank LaRue; Costumes by Renee; Hairdresser: Fay Smith; Gaffer: Leo Green; Best Boy: Frank Healy; First Grip: Marvin Wilson; Second Grip: Harry Dagliesh; First Propman: Milt James; Second Propman: Dean Morgan; Boom: D. Lent; Laborers: Joe Farquhar, Fred Kenny; Painter: Joe Haecker; Dialogue Director: Mrs. Charlot; Filmed October 25-November 17, 1944; Released by RKO-Radio Pictures; Running Time: 78 minutes.
Cast: Boris Karloff (John Gray), Bela Lugosi (Joseph), Henry Daniell (Dr. MacFarlane), Edith Atwater (Meg Camden), Russell Wade (Donald Fettes), Rita Corday (Mrs. Marsh), Sharyn Moffet (Georgina Marsh), Donna Lee (Street Singer), Robert Clarke (Richardson), Carl Kent (Gilchrist), Jack Welch (Boy), Larry Wheat (Salesman on Street), Mary Gordon (Mrs. Mary McBride), Jim Moran (Horse Trader), Aina Constant (Maid), Bill Williams.

Isle of the Dead (September 1945)

Credits: Directed by Mark Robson; Produced by Val Lewton; Executive Producer: Jack J. Gross; Screenplay by Ardel Wray and Josef Mischel; suggested by the painting *Island of the Dead* by Arnold Bocklin; Photographed by Jack MacKenzie; Edited by Lyle Boyer; Art Direction by Albert S. D'Agostino and Walter Keller; set direction by Darrell Silvera and Al Greenwood; Musical Score by Leigh Harline; Musical Direction by Constantin Bakaleinikoff; Sound Recording by Jean L. Speak and James G. Stewart; Assistant Director: Harry Scott; Costumes by Edward Stevenson; Filmed July 14-22 and December 1-12, 1944; Released by RKO-Radio Pictures; Running Time: 72 minutes.

Cast: Boris Karloff (General Nikolas Pherides), Ellen Drew (Thea), Marc Cramer (Oliver Davis), Katherine Emery (Mrs. St. Aubyn), Helene Thimig (Kyra), Alan Napier (Mr. St. Aubyn), Jason Robards, Sr. (Albrecht), Skelton Knaggs (Henry Robbins), Sherry Hall (Colonel), Ernst Dorian (Dr. Drossos)

Bedlam (May 10, 1946)

Credits: Directed by Mark Robson; Produced by Val Lewton; Executive Producer: Jack J. Gross; Screenplay by Carlos Keith (Val Lewton) and Mark Robson; suggested by the painting "Bedlam" (plate no. 8 of *The Rake's Progress*) by William Hogarth; Photographed by Nicholas Musuraca; Special Photographic Effects by Vernon L. Walker; Art Direction by Albert S. D'Agostino and Walter E. Keller; Set Decoration by Darrell Silvera and John Sturtevant; Musical Score by Roy Webb; Musical Direction by Constantin Bakaleinikoff; Sound Recording by Jean L. Speak and Terry Kellum; Costumes by Edward Stevenson; Assistant Director: Dorian Cox; Filmed July 18-August 17, 1945; Previewed April 1946; Released by RKO-Radio Pictures; Running Time: 79 minutes.

Cast: Boris Karloff (Master Sims), Anna Lee (Nell Bowen), Billy House (Lord Mortimer), Richard Fraser (Hannay), Glenn Vernon (the Gilded Boy), Ian Wolfe (Sidney Long), Jason Robards, Sr. (Oliver Todd), Leland Hodgson (John Wilkes), Joan Newton (Dorothea the Dove), Elizabeth Russell (Mistress Sims), Victor Holbrook (Tom the Tiger), Robert Clarke (Dan the Dog), Larry Wheat (Podge), Bruce Edwards (the Warder), John Meredith (First Maniac), John Beck (Solomon), Ellen Corby (Queen of the Artichokes), John Ince (Judge), Skelton Knaggs (Varney), John Goldsworthy (Chief Commissioner), Polly Bailey (Scrubwoman), Foster Phinney (Lord Sandwich), Donna Lee, Nan Leslie (Cockney Girls), Tom Noonan (First Stonemason), George Holmes (Second Stonemason), Jimmy Jordan (Third Stonemason), Robert Manning (John the Footman), Frankie Dee (Pompey), Frank Pharr (Second Commissioner), Harry Harvey (John Gray), Victor Travers (Sims' Friend), James Logan (Bailiff), Betty Gillette.

The Secret Life of Walter Mitty (September 1, 1947)

Credits: Directed by Norman Z. McLeod; Produced by Samuel Goldwyn; Screenplay by Ken Englund and Everett Freeman; Based on a Story by James Thurber; Photographed in Technicolor by Lee Garmes; Edited by Monica Collingwood; Special Effects by John P. Fulton; Art Direction by George Jenkins and Perry Ferguson; Set Decoration by Casey Roberts; Musical Score by David Raskin; Musical Direction by Emil Newman; songs by Sylvia Fine; Sound Recording by Fredlau; Costumes by Irene Sharoff; Assistant Director: Rollie Asher; Previewed July 10, 1947; Released by RKO-Radio Pictures; Running Time: 110 minutes.

Cast: Danny Kaye (Walter Mitty), Virginia Mayo (Rosalind van Hoorn), Boris Karloff (Dr. Hugo Hollingshead), Fay Bainter (Mrs. Mitty), Ann Rutherford (Gertrude Griswold), Thurston Hall (Bruce Pierce), Konstantin Shayne (Peter van Hoorn), Florence Bates (Mrs. Griswold), Gordon Jones (Tubby Wadsworth), Reginald Denny (RAF Colonel), Henry Corden (Hendrick), Doris Lloyd (Mrs. Follinsbee), Fritz Feld (Anatole), Frank Reicher (Maasdam), Milton Parsons (Butler/Tyler), Mary Brewer, Betty Carlyle, Lorraine De Rome, Jackie Jordan, Martha Montgomery, Sue Casey, Pat Patrick, Irene Vernon, Karen X. Gaylord, Mary Ellen Gleason, Georgia Lane, Michael Mauree, Lynn Walker (the Goldwyn Girls), Bess Flowers (Illustrator), Donna Dax (Stenographer), George Magrill (Wolfman), Joel Friedkin (Grimsby), John Tyrrell, Raoul Freeman (Department Heads), Sam Ash (Art Editor), Dorothy Grainger, Harry L. Woods (the Wrong Mr. and Mrs. Follinsbee), Lumsden Hare (Dr. Pritchard-Mitford), Hank Worden (Western Character), Vernon Dent (Bartender), John Hamilton (Dr. Remington), Henry Kolker (Dr. Benbow), Frank Larue (Conductor), Brick Sullivan (Cop), Charles Trowbridge (Dr. Renshaw), Minerva Urecal (Woman with Hat), Maude Eburne (Fitter), George Chandler (Mate), Vincent Pelletier (Narrator of Dream Sequence), Harry Harvey, Mary Anne Baird, Jack Gargan, Harry Depp, Dick Earle, Broderick O'Farrell, Wilbur Mack, Ralph Dunn, Jack Cheatham, Mary Forbes, Pierre Watkin, Ernie Adams, George Lloyd, Syd Sailor, Billy Bletcher, Eddie Acuff, Wade Crosby, Dorothy Christy, Dick Rush, William Haade, Billy Newell, Paul Newlan, Chris Pin Martin, Sam McDaniel, Betty Blythe, Ethan Laidlaw, Moy Ming, Beal Wong.

Lured (September 1947)

Credits: Directed by Douglas Sirk; Produced by James Nasser; Executive Producer: Hunt Stromberg; Associate Producer: Henry S. Kessler; Screenplay by Leo Rosten; Based on a Story by Jacques Companeez, Ernest Neuville, and Simon Gentillon; Photographed by William Daniels; Edited by John M. Foley and James E. Newcom; Art Direction by Nicolai Remisoff; Associate Art Director: Victor Greene; Musical Score by Michael Michelet; Musical Direction by David Chudnow; Sound Recording by H. Connors; Makeup by Don Cash; Assistant Director: Clarence Eurist; Previewed July 11, 1947; Released by United Artists; Running Time: 102 minutes.

Cast: George Sanders (Robert Fleming), Lucille Ball (Sandra Carpenter), Charles Coburn (Inspector Temple), Boris Karloff (Charles van Druten), Alan Mowbray (Maxwell), Cedric Hardwicke (Julian Wilde), George Zucco (Officer Barrett), Joseph Calleia (Dr. Moryani), Tanis Chandler (Lucy Barnard), Alan Napier (Inspector Gordon), Robert Coote (Officer), Jimmie Aubrey (Nelson), Dorothy Vaughan (Mrs. Miller), Sam Harris (Old Man at Concert Asking for Whiskey).

Unconquered (September 24, 1947)

Credits: Directed and Produced by Cecil B. De Mille; Screenplay by Charles Bennett, Frederic M. Frank, and Jesse Lasky, Jr.; Based on the Novel *The Judas Tree* by Neil H. Swanson; Photographed in Technicolor by Ray Rennahan; Edited by Anne Bauchens; Special Effects by Gordon Jennings, Farciot Edouart, W. Wallace Kelley, Paul Lerpae, and Devereaux Jennings; Art Direction by Hans Drier and Walter Tyler; Set Decoration by Sam Comer and Stanley Jay Sawley; Musical Score by Victor Young; song, "Whippoor-wills-a-Singing," by Ray Evans and Jay Livingston; Choreography by Jack Crosby; Sound Recording by Hugo Grenzbach and John Cope; Makeup by Wally Westmore; Costumes by Gwen Wakeling and Madame Barbara Karinska; technical advisers: Iron Eyes Cody and Captain Fred F. Ellis, BMM (ret.); Second Unit Director: Arthur Rosson; Assistant Director: Edward Salven; Released by Paramount Pictures; Running Time: 146 minutes.

Cast: Gary Cooper (Captian Christopher Holden), Paulette Goddard (Abigail Martha ["Abby"] Hale), Howard da Silva (Martin Garth), Boris Karloff (Guyasuta, Chief of the Senecas), Cecil Kellaway (Jeremy Love), Ward Bond (John Fraser), Katherine De Mille (Hannah), Henry Wilcoxon (Captain Steele), C. Aubrey Smith (Lord Chief Justice), Victor Varconi (Captain Simson Ecuyer), Virginia Grey (Diana), Porter Hall (Leach), Mike Mazurki (Dave Bone), Richard Gaines (Colonel George Washington), Virginia Campbell (Mrs. Fraser), Gavin Muir (Lieutenant Fergus MacKenzie), Alan Napier (Sir William Johnson), Nan Sutherland (Mrs. Pruitt), Marc Lawrence (Sioto, Medicine Man), Jane Nigh (Evelyn), Robert Warwick (Pontiac, Chief of the Ottawas), Lloyd Bridges (Lieutenant Hutchins), Oliver Thorndike (Lieutenant Billie), Rus Conklin (Wamaultee), John Mylong (Colonel Henry Bouquet), Raymond Hatton (Venango Scout), Julie Faye (Widow Swivens), Paul E. Burns (Dan McCoy), Clarence Muse (Jason), Jeff York (Wide-Shouldered Youth), Dick Alexander (Slave), Syd Saylor (Spieler for Doctor Diablo), Si Jenks (Farmer), Bob Kortman (Frontiersman), Edgar Dearing, Hugh Prosser, Ray Teal (Soldiers-Gilded Beaver), Chief Thundercloud (Chief Killbuck), Noble Johnson (Big Ottawa Indian), John Merton (Corporal), Buddy Roosevelt (Guard), John Miljan (Prosecutor), Jay Silverheels (Indian), Lex Barker (Royal American Officer), Jack Pennick (Joe Lovat), Byron Foulger (Townsman), Denver Dixon (Citizen), Fred Kohler, Jr. (Sergeant), Tiny Jones (Bondwoman), Charles B. Middleton (Mulligan), Dorothy Adams (Mrs. Bront), Davison Clark (Mr. Carroll), Griff Barnett (Brother Andrews), Francis Ford, Gertrude Valerie, Christopher Clark, Bill Murphy, Greta Granstedt, Ottola Nesmith, Al Ferguson, Constance Purdy, Rose Higgins, Inez Palange, Mimi Aguglia, Claire Du Brey, Fernanda Eliscu, Belle Mitchell, Charmienne Harker, Isabel Chabing Cooper, Anna Lehr, Lane Chandler, Mike Killian, Erville Alderson, Jeff Corey, William Haade, Iron Eyes Cody, Olaf Hytten, Eric Alden, Frank Hagney, Sally Rawlinson, Chuck Hamilton, Ethel Wales.

Dick Tracy Meets Gruesome (November 12, 1947)

Credits: Directed by John Rawlins; Produced by Herman Schlom; Screenplay by Robertson White and Eric Taylor; Based on a Story by William H. Graffis and Robert E. Kent and the Comic Strip by Chester A. Gould; Photographed by Frank Redman; Edited by Elmo Williams; Special Effects by Russell A. Cully; Art Direction by Albert S. D'Agostino and Walter Keller; Set Decoration by Darrell Silvera and James Attwies; Musical Score by Paul Sawtell; Musical Direction by Constantin Bakaleinikoff; Sound Recording by Jean L. Speak and Terry Kellum; Released by RKO-Radio Pictures; Running Time: 65 minutes.

Cast: Boris Karloff (Gruesome), Ralph Byrd (Dick Tracy), Anne Gwynne (Tess Trueheart), Edward Ashley (L.E. Thall), June Clayworth (Dr. I. M. Learned), Lyle Latell (Pat Patton), Tony Barrett (Melody), Skelton Knaggs (X-Ray), Jim Nolan (Dan Sterne), Joseph Crehan (Chief Brandon), Milton Parsons (Dr. A. Tomic), Lex Barker, Lee Phelps, Sean McClory, Harry Harvey, Harry Strang, William Gould.

Tap Roots (August 25, 1948)

Credits: Directed by George Marshall; Produced by Walter Wanger; Screenplay by Alan Le May; Additional Dialogue by Lionel Wiggam; Based on the Novel by James Street; Photographed in Technicolor by Lionel Lindon and Winton C. Hoch; Edited by Milton Carruth; Production Designer: Alexander Golitzen; Art Direction by Frank A. Richards; Set Decoration by Russell A. Gausman and Ruby R. Levitt; Musical Score by Frank Skinner; Sound Recording by Leslie I. Carey and Glenn E. Anderson; Makeup by Bud Westmore; Costumes by Yvonne Wood; Previewed June 22, 1948; Released by Universal-International Pictures; Running Time: 109 minutes.

Cast: Van Heflin (Keith Alexander), Susan Hayward (Morna Dabney), Boris Karloff (Tishomingo), Julie London (Aven Dabney), Whitfield Connor (Clay MacIvor), Ward Bond (Hoab Dabney), Richard Long (Bruce Dabney), Arthur Shields (Reverend Kirkland), Griff Barnett (Dr. MacIntosh), Sondra Rogers (Shellie), Ruby Dandridge (Dabby), Russell Simpson (Sam Dabney), Jack Davis (Militia Captain), Gregg Barton (Captain), George Hamilton (Quint), Jonathan Hale (General Johnston), Arthur Space, Kay Medford (Callers), William Haade (Mob Leader), Harry Cording (Leader), Bill Neff, Keith Richards (Lieutenants), Dick Dickinson (Field Hand), Elmo Lincoln (Sergeant), George Lewis, Helen Mowery, William Challee, John James, Hank Worden.

Abbott and Costello Meet the Killer, Boris Karloff (August 1, 1949)

Credits: Directed by Charles T. Barton; Produced by Robert Arthur; Screenplay by Hugh Wedlock, Jr., Howard Snyder, and John Grant; Based on a Story by Hugh Wedlock, Jr., and Howard Snyder; Photographed by Charles Van Enger; Edited by Edward Curtiss; Special Effects by David S. Horsley; Art Direction by Bernard Herzbrun and Richard H. Riedel; Set Decoration by Russell A. Gausman and Oliver Emert; Musical Score by Milton Schwarzwald; Sound Recording by Leslie J. Carey and Robert Pritchard; Makeup by Bud Westmore; Costumes by Rosemary Odell; Assistant Director: Joe Kenny; Filmed February 1949; Released by Universal-International Pictures; Running Time: 84 minutes.

Cast: Bud Abbott (Casey Edwards), Lou Costello (Freddie Phillips), Boris Karloff (Swami Talpur), Lenore Aubert (Angela Gordon), Gar Moore (Jeff Wilson), Donna Martell (Betty Crandall), Alan Mowbray (Melton), James Flavin (Inspector Wellman), Roland Winters (T. Hamley Brooks), Nicholas Joy (Amos Strickland), Mikel Conrad (Sergeant Stone), Morgan Farley (Gregory Milford), Percy Helton (Abernathy), Victoria Horne (Mrs. Hargreave), Claire Du Brey (Mrs. Grimsby), Vincent Renno (Mike Relia), Harry Hayden (Lawrence Crandall), Murray Alper (Joe), Patricia Hall (Manicurist), Marjorie Bennett (Maid), Harry Brown (Medical Examiner), Beatrice Gray (Woman), Frankie Van (Bozzo), Billy Snyder (First Reporter), Eddie Coke (Second Reporter), Jack Chefe (Barber), Arthur Hecht (Photographer), Ed Randolph (Bootblack), Phil Shepard (Bellboy).

The Strange Door (December 9, 1951)

Credits: Directed by Joseph Pevney; Produced by Ted Richmond; Screenplay by Jerry Sackheim; Based on the Story "The Sire de Maletroit's Door" by Robert Louis Stevenson; Photographed by Irving Glassberg; Edited by Edward Curtiss; Special Effects by David S. Horsley; Art Direction by Bernard Herzbrun and Eric Orbom; Set Decoration by Russell A. Gausman and Julia Heron; Musical Direction by Joseph Gershenson; Sound Direction by Leslie J. Carey and Glenn E. Anderson; Makeup by Bud Westmore; Costumes by Rosemary Odell; Assistant Director: Jesse Hibbs; Previewed October 29, 1951; Released by Universal-International Pictures; Running Time: 81 minutes.

Cast: Charles Laughton (Sire Alan de Maletroit), Boris Karloff (Voltan), Sally Forrest (Blanche de Maletroit), Richard Stapley (Denis de Beaulieu), Michael Pate (Talon), Paul Cavanagh (Edmund de Maletroit), Alan Napier (Count Grassin), William Cottrell (Corbeau), Morgan Farley (Rinville), Charles Horvath (Turec), Edwin Harker (Moret).

The Emperor's Nightingale (May 13, 1951)

Credits: Directed by Milos Makovec (Live Action) and Jiri Trnka (Animation); Screenplay by Jiri Trnka and Jiri Brdecka; Based on a Story by Hans Christian Andersen; English Narrative by Phyllis McGinley; Photographed in Agfacolor by Ferdinand Pecenka; Musical Score by Vaclav Trajan; Filmed and Released in Czechoslovakia by Czech State Films in 1949; Released in the United States by Rembrandt Films; Running Time: 71 minutes.

Cast: Jaromir Sobotna (the Boy), Helena Patockova (the Girl), Boris Karloff (Narrator of English Version).

The Black Castle (December 25, 1952)
Credits: Directed by Nathan Juran; Produced by William Alland; Screenplay and Story by Jerry Sackheim; Photographed by Irving Glassberg; Edited by Russell Schoengarth; Special Effects by David S. Horsley; Art Direction by Bernard Herzbrun and Alfred Sweeney; Set Decoration by Russell A. Gausman and Oliver Emert; Musical Direction by Joseph Gershenson; Dance Direction by Hal Belfer; Sound Recording by Leslie J. Carey and Joe Papis; Makeup by Bud Westmore; Costumes by Bill Thomas; Assistant Director: William Holland; Filmed March-April 1952; Previewed October 16, 1952; Released by Universal-International Pictures; Running Time: 81 minutes.
Cast: Richard Greene (Beckett), Boris Karloff (Dr. Meissen), Stephen McNally (Count von Bruno), Paula Corday (Elga), Lon Chaney, Jr. (Gargon), John Hoyt (Stricken), Michael Pate (Von Melcher), Nancy Valentine (Therese von Wilk), Tudor Owen (Romley), Henry Corden (Fender), Otto Waldis (Krantz).

Abbott and Costello Meet Dr. Jekyll and Mr. Hyde (August 1953)
Credits: Directed by Charles Lamont; Produced by Howard Christie; Screenplay by Lee Loeb and John Grant; Based on the Screen Story by Sidney Fields and Grant Garrett and the Novella *The Strange Case of Dr. Jekyll and Mr. Hyde* by Robert Louis Stevenson; Photographed by George Robinson; Edited by Russell Schoengarth; Special Effects by David S. Horsley; Art Direction by Bernard Herzbrun and Eric Orbom; Set Decoration by Russell A. Gausman; Musical Direction by Joseph Gershenson; Dance Direction by Kenny Williams; Dialogue Direction by Milt Bronson; Sound Recording by Leslie J. Carey; Makeup by Bud Westmore; Costumes by Rosemary Odell; Previewed July 21, 1953; Released by Universal-International Pictures; Running Time: 77 minutes.
Cast: Bud Abbott (Slim), Lou Costello (Tubby), Boris Karloff (Dr. Henry Jekyll), Craig Stevens (Bruce Adams), Helen Westcott (Vicky Edwards), Reginald Denny (Inspector), John Dierkes (Batley), Patti McKaye, Lucille Lamarr (Can-Can Dancers), Henry Corden (Javanese Actor), Carmen de Lavallade (Javanese Actress), Marjorie Bennett (Militant Woman), Harry Cording (Rough Character), Arthur Gould-Porter (Bartender), Clyde Cook, John Rogers (Drunks in Pub), Herbert Deans (Victim), Judith Brian (Woman on Bike), Gil Perkins (Man on Bike), Hilda Plowright (Nursemaid), Keith Hitchcock (Jailer), Donald Kerr (Chimney Sweep), Clive Morgan, Tony Marshe, Michael Hadlow (Bobbies).

Il Monstro del Isola [U.S.: *Monster of the Island*] (1953)
Credits: Directed by Roberto Montero; Produced by Fortunato Misiano; Screenplay by Roberto Montero and Alberto Vecchietti; Based on a Story by Alberto Vecchietti; Photographed by Augusto Tiezzi; Edited by Iolanda Benvenuti; Musical Score by Carlo Innocenzi; Released by Romana Films (Italy); Running Time: 87 minutes.
Cast: Boris Karloff (Don Gaetano Bronte), Franca Marzi (Gloria), Renato Vicario (Lieutenant Andreani), Patrizia Remiddi (Mirella), Germana Paolieri (Signora Andreani), Giuseppe Chinnici, Iole Fierro, Carlo Duse, Guilio Battiferri, Domenico De Ninno, Clara Gamberini, Salvatore Scibetta.

The Hindu (1953)
Credits: Directed and Produced by Frank Ferrin; Screenplay and Story by Frank Ferrin; Photographed in Eastmancolor by Allen Svensvoid and Jack McCoskey; Edited by Jack Foley; Art Direction by Ralph Ferrin; Musical Score by Daksnamurti; Sound Recording by Eugene Grosman; Previewed May 15, 1953; Released by United Artists; Running Time: 89 minutes.
Cast: Boris Karloff (General Pollegar), Nino Marcel (Gunga Ram), Lou Krugman (Maharajah of Bakore), Reginald Denny (Regent), Victor Jory (Ashok), June Foray (Marku), Jay Novello (Damji), Lisa Howard (Indira), Peter Coe (Taru), Paul Marion (Kumar), Vito Scotti (Rama), Lou Merrill (Koobah), Larry Dobkin (Aide).

Colonel March Investigates (1953)
Credits: Directed by Cyril Endfield; Produced by Donald Ginsberg; Screenplay by Leo Davis; Based on the Stories by John Dickson Carr; Photographed by Jonah Jones; Edited by Stan Willis; Art Direction by George Paterson; Musical Score by John Lanchberry; Musical Direction by Eric Robinson; Released by Criterion Films (Great Britain); Running Time: 70 minutes.
Cast: Boris Karloff (Colonel March), Ewan Roberts (Inspector Ames), Richard Wattis (Cabot), Sheila Burrell (Joan Forsythe), Anthony Forwood (Jim Hartley), John Hewer (John Parrish), Joan Sims (Marjorie Dawson), Ronald Leigh Hunt (Ireton Bowlder), Roger Maxwell (Major Rodman), Patricia Owens (Betty Hartley), Dagmar Wynter (Francine Rapport), Sonya Hana (Paula), Bernard Rebel (the Count).

Note: This feature was constructed from three pilot episodes of the British television series *Colonel March of Scotland Yard*.

Voodoo Island (February 5, 1957)
Credits: Directed by Reginald LeBorg; Produced by Howard W. Koch; Executive Producer: Aubrey Schenck; Screenplay and Story by Richard Landau; Photographed by William Margulies; Edited by John F. Schreyer; Special Effects by Jack Rabin and Louis De Witt; Musical Score by Les Baxter; Makeup by Ted Coodley; Assistant Director: Paul Wurtzel; Filmed November 1956; Released by United Artists; Running Time: 77 minutes.
Cast: Boris Karloff (Dr. Phillip Knight), Beverly Tyler (Sara Adams, Knight's Secretary), Murvyn Vye (Barney Finch), Elisha Cook, Jr. (Martin Schuyler), Rhodes Reason (Matthew Gunn), Jean Engstrom (Claire Winter), Frederick Ledebur (the Ruler), Glenn Dixon (Mitchell), Owen Cunningham (Howard Carlton), Herbert Patterson (Dr. Wilding), Jerome Frank (Vickers).

The Grip of the Strangler [U.S.: *The Haunted Strangler*] (June 1958)
Credits: Directed by Robert Day; Produced by John Croydon; Executive Producer: Richard Gordon; Screenplay by Jan Read and John C. Cooper; Based on a Story by Jan Read; Photographed by Lionel Banes; Edited by Peter Mayhew; Special Effects by Les Bowie; Art Direction by John Elphick; Musical Score by Buxton Orr; Musical Direction by Frederick Lewis; Costumes Designed by Anna Duse; Camera Operator: Leo Rogers; Assistant Director: Douglas Hickox; Sound Recording by Peter Davies; Sound Dubbing by Terry Poulton; Makeup by Jim Hydes; Continuity by Hazel Swift; Filmed at Walton Studios, London, August 1957; Previewed May 23, 1958; a MLC/Producers Associates Production; Released by Metro-Goldwyn-Mayer Pictures; Running Time: 78 minutes.
Cast: Boris Karloff (James Rankin), Jean Kent (Cora Seth), Elizabeth Allan (Barbara Rankin), Anthony Dawson (Superintendent Burk), Vera Day (Pearl), Tim Turner (Kenneth McColl), Diane Aubrey (Lily), Dorothy Gordon (Hannah), Peggy Ann Clifford (Kate), Leslie Perrins (Prison Governor), Michael Atkinson (Styles), Desmond Roberts (Dr. Johnson), Jessie Cairns (Maid), Roy Russell (Medical Superintendent), Derek Birch (Superintendent), George Hirste (Lost Property Man), John G. Heller (Male Nurse), George Spence (Hangman), Joan Elvin (Can-Can Girl).

Frankenstein 1970 (July 6, 1958)
Credits: Directed by Howard W. Koch; Produced by Aubrey Schenck; Screenplay by Richard Landau and George Worthing Yates; Based on a Story by Aubrey Schenck and Charles A. Moses; Photographed in Cinemascope by Carl E. Guthrie; Edited by John A. Bushelman; Art Direction by Jack T. Collins; Set Decoration by Jerry Welch; Musical Score by Paul A. Dunlap; Sound Recording by Francis C. Stahl; Makeup by Gordon Bau; Assistant Director: George Vieira; Released by Allied Artists Pictures; Running Time: 83 minutes.
Cast: Boris Karloff (Baron Victor von Frankenstein), Tom Duggan (Mike Shaw), Jana Lund (Carolyn Hayes), Donald Barry (Douglas Row), Charlotte Austin (Judy Stevens), Irwin Berke (Inspector Raab), Rudolph Anders (Wilhelm Gottfried), John Dennis (Morgan Haley), Norbert Schiller (Shuter), Mike Lane (Hans).

The Raven (February 1963)
Credits: Directed and Produced by Roger Corman; Executive Producers: James H. Nicholson and Samuel Z. Arkoff; Screenplay by Richard Matheson; Suggested by the Poem by Edgar Allan Poe; Photographed in Pathecolor and Panavision by Floyd Crosby; Edited by Ronald Sinclair; Special Effects by Pat Dinga; Photographic Effects by Butler-Glouner, Inc.; Art Direction by Daniel Haller; Set Decoration by Harry Reif; Musical Score by Les Baxter; Makeup by Ted Coodley; Costumes by Marjorie Corso; Raven Trainer: Moe Disesso; Assistant Director: Peter Bolton; Previewed January 30, 1963; Released by American International Pictures; Running Time: 86 minutes.
Cast: Vincent Price (Dr. Erasmus Craven); Peter Lorre (Dr. Adolphus Bedlo), Boris Karloff (Dr. Scarabus), Hazel Court (Lenore Craven), Olive Sturgess (Estelle Craven), Jack Nicholson (Rexford Bedlo), Connie Wallace (Maidservant), William Baskin (Grimes), Aaron Saxon (Gort), Jim, Jr. (the Raven).

The Doctor from Seven Dials [U.S.: *Corridors of Blood*] (April 1963)
Credits: Directed by Robert Day; Produced by John Croydon and Charles Vetter; Executive Producer: Richard Gordon; Associate Producer: Peter Mayhew; Screenplay and Story by Jean Scott Rogers; Photographed by Geoffrey Faithfull; Camera Operator: Frank Drake; Edited by Peter Mayhew; Art Direction by

Anthony Masters; Production Manager: George Mills; Musical Score by Buxton Orr; Musical Direction by Frederick Lewis; Sound Recording by Cyril Swern and Maurice Askew; Dubbing Editor: Peter Musgrave; Camera Operator: Frank Drake; Assistant Director: Peter Bolton; Continuity: Susan Dyson; Makeup by Walter Schneiderman; Hairdresser: Eileen Warwick; Dress Designer: Emma Selby-Walker; Wardrobe Mistress: Doris Turner; Filmed at MGM, Borehamwood, in May 1958; a Producers Associates Production; Released by Metro-Goldwyn-Mayer Pictures; Running Time: 85 minutes.

Cast: Boris Karloff (Dr. Thomas Bolton), Betta St. John (Susan), Finlay Currie (Superintendant Matheson), Christopher Lee (Resurrection Joe), Francis Matthews (Dr. Jonathan Bolton), Adrienne Corri (Rachel), Francis de Wolff (Black Ben), Basil Dignam (Chairman), Frank Pettingell (Dr. Blount), Marian Spencer (Mrs. Matheson), Carl Bernard (Ned the Crow), Yvonne Warren (Rosa), Charles Lloyd Pack (Hardcastle), Robert Raglan (Wilkes), John Gabriel (Dispenser), Nigel Green (Inspector Donovan), Howard Lang (Chief Inspector), Julian D'Albie (Bald Man), Roddy Hughes (Man with Watch), Bernard Archard, Charmion Eyre, Anthea Holloway, Frank Sieman.

The Terror (September 1963)

Credits: Directed and Produced by Roger Corman; Executive Producer: Harvey Jacobson; Associate Producer: Francis Ford Coppola; Screenplay and Story by Leo Gordon and Jack Hill; Photographed in Pathecolor and Vistascope by John Nicholaus; Edited by Stuart O'Brien; Art Direction by Daniel Haller; Set Decoration by Harry Reif; Musical Score by Ronald Stein; Sound Recording by John Bury; Assistant Director: Monte Hellman; Costumes by Marjorie Corso; Titles by Paul Julian; Location Scenes Filmed at Big Sur, California; Released by American International Pictures; Running Time: 81 minutes.

Cast: Boris Karloff (Baron Victor von Leppe), Jack Nicholson (Lieutenant Andre Duvalier), Sandra Knight (Helene), Richard ("Dick") Miller (Stefan, the Baron's Servant), Dorothy Neumann (Old Woman), Jonathan Haze (Gustaf, a Servant).

The Comedy of Terrors (January 20, 1964)

Credits: Directed by Jacques Tourneur; Produced by Anthony Carras and Richard Matheson; Executive Producers: James H. Nicholson and Samuel Z. Arkoff; Production Manager: Joseph Wonder; Screenplay and Story by Richard Matheson; Photographed in Pathecolor and Panavision by Floyd Crosby; Edited by Anthony Carras; Special Effects by Pat Dinga; Production Design and Art Direction by Daniel Haller; Set Decoration by Harry Reif; Musical Score by Les Baxter; Music Coordinator: Al Simms; Sound Recording by Don Rush; Assistant Director: Robert Agnew; Makeup by Charlie Taylor; Costumes by Marjorie Corso; Filmed December 1963; Released by American International Pictures; Running Time: 88 minutes.

Cast: Vincent Price (Waldo Trumbull), Peter Lorre (Felix Gillie), Boris Karloff (Amos Hinchley), Basil Rathbone (John F. Black), Joe E. Brown (Cemetery Keeper), Joyce Jameson (Amaryllis Trumbull), Beverly Hills (Mrs. Phipps), Paul Barsolow (Riggs), Linda Rogers (Phipps' Maid), Luree Holmes (Black's Servant), Buddy Mason (Mr. Phipps), Rhubarb (Cleopatra), Alan DeWitt, Douglas Williams.

Black Sabbath (May 1964)

Credits: Directed by Mario Bava; Produced by Salvatore Billitteri; Presented in the United States by James H. Nicholson and Samuel Z. Arkoff; Screenplay by Marcello Fondato, Alberto Bevilacqua, and Mario Bava; Based on the Stories "The Drop of Water" by Anton Chekov, "The Telephone" by F.G. Snyder, and "The Wurdalak" by Alexei Tolstoy; Photographed in Eastmancolor by Ubaldo Terzano; Edited by Mario Serandrei; Art Direction by Georgio Giovannini; Set Decoration by Riccardo Dominici; Musical Score by Les Baxter (United States) and Roberto Nicolosi (Italy); Sound Recording by Titra Sound Corporation; Makeup by Otello Fava; Costumes by Trini Grani; Released by Emmepi/Galatea/Lyre Films (Italy) and American International Pictures (United States); Running Time: 99 minutes.

Cast: "The Drop of Water": Jacqueline Pierreux (Helen Corey), Milli Monti (Maid); "The Telephone": Michele Mercier (Rosy), Lidia Alfonsi (Mary); "The Wurdalak": Boris Karloff (Gorca), Susy Andersen (Sdenka), Mark Damon (Vladimir d'Urfe), Glauco Onorato (Giorgio), Rika Dialina (Giorgio's Wife), Massimo Righi (Pietro).

Bikini Beach (July 4, 1964)

Credits: Directed by William Asher; Produced by Anthony Carras; Executive Producers: James H. Nicholson and Samuel Z. Arkoff; Screenplay by William Asher, Leo Townsend, and Robert Dillon; Photographed in Pathecolor and Panavision by Floyd Crosby; Edited by Fred Feitshans; Special Effects by Roger and Joe Zonar; Art Direction by Daniel Haller; Set Decoration by Harry Reif; Musical Score by Les Baxter and Al Sims; Songs by Guy Hemric, Jerry Styner, Gary Usher, Roger Christian, Jack Merrill, and Red Gilson;

Choreography by Tom Mahoney; Released by American International Pictures; Running Time: 100 minutes.

Cast: Frankie Avalon (Frankie/Potato Bug), Annette Funicello (Dee Dee), Martha Hyer (Vivien Clements), John Ashley (Johnny), Don Rickles (Big Drag), Harvey Lembeck (Eric von Zipper), Keenan Wynn (Harvey Huntington Honeywagon), Jody McCrea (Deadhead), Candy Johnson (Candy), Danielle Aubrey (Lady Bug), Meredith McCrea (Animal), Delores Wells (Sniffles), Paul Smith (First Officer), James Westerfield (Second Officer), Donna Loren (Donna), Janos Prohaska (Clyde), Timothy Carey (South Dakota Slim), Val Warren (Teenage Werewolf), Little Stevie Wonder, the Pyramids, the Exciters Band, Boris Karloff (Art Dealer).

Die, Monster, Die (October 1965)
Credits: Directed by Daniel Haller; Produced by Pat Green; Executive Producers: James H. Nicholson and Samuel Z. Arkoff; Screenplay by Jerry Sohl; Based on the Story "The Colour Out of Space" by H.P. Lovecraft; Photographed in Pathecolor and Colorscope by Paul Beeson; Edited by Alfred Cox; Special Effects by Wally Veevers and Ernest Sullivan; Art Direction by Colin Southcott; Musical Score by Don Banks; Musical Direction by Philip Martell; Sound Recording by Kenny Rawkins and Robert Jones; Sound Editing by Alban Streeter and Alan Corder; Continuity by Tilly Day; Makeup by Jimmy Evans; Hairdresser: Bobbie Smith; Assistant Director: Dennis Hall; Camera Operator: R.C. Cooney; Wardrobe Mistress: Laurel Staffell; Titles by Bowie Films; Filmed at Shepperton Studios; Released by American International Pictures; Running Time: 80 minutes.

Cast: Boris Karloff (Nahum Witley), Nick Adams (Stephen Reinhart), Freda Jackson (Letitia Witley), Suzan Farmer (Susan Witley), Terence De Marney (Merwyn), Patrick Magee (Dr. Henderson), Paul Farrell (Jason), Harold Goodwin (Cab Driver), Gretchen Franklin (Miss Bailey), Sydney Bromley (Pierce), Billy Milton (Henry), Leslie Dwyer (Potter), Sheila Raynor (Miss Bailey).

The Ghost in the Invisible Bikini (April 6, 1966)
Credits: Directed by Don Weis; Produced by Anthony Carras; Executive Producers: James H. Nicholson and Samuel Z. Arkoff; Screenplay by Louis M. Heyward and Elwood Ullman; Based on a Story by Louis M. Heyward; Photographed in Pathecolor and Panavision by Stanley Cortez; Edited by Fred Feitshans and Eve Newman; Special Effects by Roger George; Art Direction by Daniel Haller; Set Decoration by Clarence Steensen; Musical Score by Les Baxter; Songs by Guy Hemric and Jerry Styner; Choreography by Jack Baker; Sound Recording by Ryder Sound Services; Makeup by Ted Coodley; Costumes by Richard Bruno; Released by American International Pictures; Running Time: 82 minutes.

Cast: Tommy Kirk (Chuck Phillips), Deborah Walley (Lili Morton), Aron Kincaid (Bobby), Quinn O'Hara (Sinistra), Jesse White (J. Sinister Hulk), Harvey Lembeck (Eric von Zipper), Nancy Sinatra (Vicki), Claudia Martin (Lulu), Francis X. Bushman (Malcolm), Benny Rubin (Chicken Feather), Bobbi Shaw (Princess Yolanda), George Barrows (Monstro), Basil Rathbone (Reginald Ripper), Patsy Kelly (Myrtle Forbush), Boris Karloff (Hiram Stokeley), Susan Hart (the Ghost), Luree Holmes (Shirl), Alberta Nelson (Alberta), Andy Romano (J.D.), Piccola Pupa (Piccola), Myrna Ross, Bob Harvey, John Macchia, Alan Fife (Rat Pack), Ed Garner, Mary Hughes, Patti Chandler, Frank Alesia, Salli Sachse, Sue Hamilton, Jerry Brutsche (Girls and Boys), the Bobby Fuller Four, Elena Andreas, Herb Andreas (the Statues).

The Daydreamer (June 1966)
Credits: Directed by Jules Bass; Produced and Screenplay by Arthur Rankin, Jr.; Executive Producer: Joseph E. Levine; Based on the Stories "The Little Mermaid," "The Emperor's New Clothes," "Thumbelina," and "The Garden of Paradise" by Hans Christian Andersen; Animagic Sequences by Don Duga; Animagic Photography in Eastmancolor by Tad Mochinga; Live-Action Sequences Written by Ezra Stone; Live-Action Sequences Photographed by Daniel Cavelli; Art Direction by Maurice Gordon; Music and Lyrics by Maury Laws and Jules Bass; a Videocraft International Production; Released by Embassy Pictures; Running Time: 101 minutes.

Cast: Paul O'Keefe (Hans Christian Andersen), Jack Gilford (Papa Andersen), Ray Bolger (the Pieman), Margaret Hamilton (Mrs. Klopplebobbler), Robert Harter (Big Claus). Voices: Cyril Ritchard (the Sandman), Hayley Mills (the Little Mermaid), Burl Ives (Father Neptune), Tallulah Bankhead (the Sea Witch), Terry-Thomas (First Tailor/Brigadier), Victor Borge (the Second Tailor/Zebro), Ed Wynn (the Emperor), Patty Duke (Thumbelina), Boris Karloff (the Rat), Sessue Hayakawa (the Mole), Robert Goulet (the Singer).

The Venetian Affair (January 1967)
Credits: Directed by Jerry Thorpe; Produced by Jerry Thorpe and E. Jack Neuman; Screenplay by E. Jack

Neuman; Based on the Novel by Helen MacInnes; Photographed in Metrocolor and Panavision by Milton Krasner and Enzo Serafin; Edited by Henry Berman; Special Effects by Carroll L. Shepphird; Art Direction by George W. Davis and Leroy Coleman; Set Decoration by Henry Grace and Hugh Hunt; Music and Lyrics by Lalo Schifrin and Hall Winn; Makeup by William Tuttle; Released by Metro-Goldwyn-Mayer Pictures; Running Time: 92 minutes.

Cast: Robert Vaughn (Bill Fenner), Elke Sommer (Sandra Fane), Felicia Farr (Claire Connor), Karl Boehm (Robert Wahl), Boris Karloff (Dr. Pierre Vaugiroud), Roger C. Carmel (Mike Ballard), Edward Asner (Frank Rosenfeld), Joe De Santis (Jan Aarvan), Fabrizio Mioni (Russo), Wesley Lau (Neill Carlson), Luciana Paluzzi (Giulia Almeranti), Bill Weiss (Goldsmith).

Mondo Balordo (1967)

Credits: Directed by Robert Bianchi Montero; narrative by Castaldo and Tori; American version by Ted Weiss; Photographed in Eastmancolor and Stereorama by Giuseppe la Torre; Edited by Enzio Alfonsi; American Version by Fred von Bernewitz; Musical Score by Lallo Gori and Nani Rossi; Narration by Boris Karloff; A Cine Production Film (Italy); An Ivanhoe Production (United States); Released by Crown International Pictures; Running Time: 87 minutes.

The Sorcerers (June 1967)

Credits: Directed by Michael Reeves; Produced by Tony Tenser and Patrick Curtis; Executive Producer: Arnold Louis Miller; Screenplay by Michael Reeves and Tom Baker; Based on a Story by John Burke; Photographed in Eastmancolor by Stanley Long; Edited by David Woodward and Ralph Sheldon; Art Direction by Tony Curtis; Musical Score by Paul Ferris; Released by Tigon-Curtwel-Global (Great Britain) and Allied Artists Pictures (United States); Running Time: 87 minutes,

Cast: Boris Karloff (Professor Monserrat), Catherine Lacey (Estelle Monserrat), Ian Ogilvy (Mike), Elizabeth Ercy (Nicole), Victor Henry (Alan), Susan George (Audrey), Dani Sheridan (Laura), Ivor Dean (Inspector Matalon), Peter Fraser (Detective), Meier Tzelniker (Snack-Bar Owner), Bill Barnsley (Constable), Martin Terry (Tobacconist), Gerald Campion (Customer), Alf Joint (Ron).

Mad Monster Party (September 1967)

Credits: Directed by Jules Bass; Produced by Arthur Rankin, Jr.; Executive Producer: Joseph E. Levine; Screenplay by Harvey Kurtzman, Len Lorobkin, and Forrest J Ackerman; Based on a Story by Arthur Rankin, Jr.; Photographed in Anamagic and Eastmancolor; Music and Lyrics by Maury Laws and Jules Bass; Puppet Design by Jack Davis; a Videocraft International Production; Released by Embassy Pictures; Running Time: 94 minutes.

Voices: Boris Karloff (Baron Boris von Frankenstein), Phyllis Diller (Frankenstein's Wife), Ethel Ennis, Gale Garnett, Allen Swift.

Targets (August 13, 1968)

Credits: Directed, Produced, and Screenplay by Peter Bogdanovich; Based on a Story by Polly Platt and Peter Bogdanovich; Photographed in Pathecolor by Laszlo Kovacs; Edited by Peter Bogdanovich; Art Direction by Polly Platt; Associate Producer: Daniel Selznick; Production Manager: Paul Lewis; Assistant to the Director: Frank Marshall; Sound Recording by Sam Kopetsky; Sound-Effects Editor: Verna Fields; Musical Score by Charles Greene and Brian Stone; Makeup by Scott Hamilton; Filmed December 1967; Previewed May 2, 1968; a Saticoy Production; Released by Paramount Pictures; Running Time: 90 minutes.

Cast: Boris Karloff (Byron Orlok), Tim O'Kelly (Bobby Thompson), Nancy Hseuh (Jenny), James Brown (Robert Thompson, Sr.), Sandy Baron (Kip Larkin), Arthur Peterson (Ed Loughlin), Mary Jackson (Charlotte Thompson), Tanya Morgan (Ilene Thompson), Monty Landis (Marshall Smith), Peter Bogdanovich (Sammy Michaels), Paul Condylis (Drive-In Manager), Mark Dennis, Stafford Morgan (Gun-Shop Salesmen), Daniel Ades (Chauffeur), Timothy Burns (Walter), Warren White (Grocery Boy), Geraldine Baron (Larkin's Girl), Gary Kent (Gas-Tank Worker), Ellie Wood Walker (Woman on Freeway), Frank Marshall (Ticket Boy), Byron Betz (Projectionist), Mike Farrell (Man in Phone Booth), Carol Samuels (Cashier), Jay Daniel (Snack-Bar Attendant), James Morris (Man with Pistol), Elaine Partnow, Paul Belcher, James Bowie, Anita Poree, Robert Cleaves, Kay Douglas, Raymond Roy, Diana Ashley, Kirk Scott, Susan Douglas.

Curse of the Crimson Altar [U.S.: The Crimson Cult] (May 1970)

Credits: Directed by Vernon Sewell; Produced by Louis M. Heyward; Executive Producer: Tony Tenser;

Screenplay and Story by Mervyn Haisman and Henry Lincoln; Additional Material: Gerry Levy; Based on the Story "Dreams in the Witch House" by H.P. Lovecraft; Photographed in Eastmancolor by Johnny Coquillon; Edited by Howard Lanning; Art Direction by Derek Bannington; Musical Score by Peter Knight; Makeup by Pauline Worden and Elizabeth Blattner; Costumes by Michael Southgate; Filmed on location at Grimsdyke House, Middlesex, England; Released November 24, 1968, by Tigon Pictures (Great Britain); Released by American International Pictures (United States); Running Time: 87 minutes.

Cast: Boris Karloff (Professor Marshe), Christopher Lee (J.D. Morley), Mark Eden (Robert Manning), Barbara Steele (Lavinia Morley), Michael Gough (Elder), Virginia Wetherell (Eve), Rupert Davies (Vicar), Rosemarie Reede (Esther), Derek Tansey (Judge), Michael Warren (Basil), Ron Pomber (Attendant), Denys Peek (Peter Manning), Nita Lorraine (Woman with Whip), Carol Anne (First Virgin), Jenny Shaw (Second Virgin), Vivienne Carlton (Sacrifice Victim), Roger Avon (Sergeant Tyson), Paul McNeill (Guest), Millicent Scott (Stripper), Vicky Edwards (Bell Dancer), Tasma Bereton (Girl Who Is Painted), Kevin Smith (Drunk), Lita Scott (Girl with Cockerell), Terry Raven (Driver), Nova St. Claire (Girl in Car Chase), Douglas Mitchell (Driver).

Isle of the Snake People (March 1971)

Credits: Directed by Juan Ibanez and Jack Hill; Produced by Luis Enrique Vergara and Juan Ibanez; Screenplay by Jack Hill; Photographed in Eastmancolor by Austin McKinney and Raul Dominguez; Musical Score by Alice Uretta; Filmed May 1968 (Karloff's scenes); Released by Azteca Pictures (Mexico) and Columbia Pictures (United States); Running Time: 90 minutes.

Cast: Boris Karloff (Dr. Carl van Moulder/Damballah), Julissa (Deirdre), Charles East (Lieutenant William), Rafael Bertrand (Captain Laresh), Judy Carmichael (Mary Ann Vanderberg), Tongolee (Bondemo), Quentin Miller (Gomez), Santanon, Quinton Bulnes.

The Incredible Invasion (April 1971)

Credits: Directed by Luis Enrique Vergara and Jack Hill; Produced by Luis Enrique Vergara and Juan Ibanez; Screenplay by Karl Schanzer and Luis Enrique Vergara; Photographed in Eastmancolor by Austin McKinney and Raul Dominguez; Special Effects by Jack Tannenbaum; Musical Score by Alice Uretta; Filmed May 1968 (Karloff's scenes); Released by Azteca Pictures (Mexico) and Columbia Pictures (United States); Running Time: 90 minutes.

Cast: Boris Karloff (Professor John Meyer), Enrique Guzman (Paul), Christa Linder (Laura), Maura Monti (Isabel), Yerye Beirute (Convict), Tere Valdez, Sangro Alemez, Sergio Kleiner, Mariela Flores, Greselda Mejia, Rosangela Balbo, Tito Navarro.

Blind Man's Bluff (aka *Cauldron of Blood*) (August 1971)

Credits: Directed and Story by Edward Mann (Santos Alcocer); Produced by Robert D. Weinbach; Screenplay by John Melson, Jose Luis Bayonas, and Edward Mann (Santos Alcocer); Photographed in Eastmancolor and Panoramica by Francisco Sempere; Edited by J. Antonio Rojo; Art Direction by Gil Parrondo; Musical Score by Jose Luis Navarro and Ray Ellis; Songs by Edward Mann (Santos Alcocer) and Bob Harris; Filmed February-May 1967; Released by Hispamer Films (Spain) and Cannon Films (United States); Running Time: 101 minutes.

Cast: Boris Karloff (Franz Badulescu), Viveca Lindfors (Tania Badulescu), Jean-Pierre Aumont (Claude Marchand), Jacqui Speed (Pilar), Rosenda Monteros (Valerie), Ruven Rojo (Lover), Dianik Zurakowska (Elga), Milo Quesada, Mercedes Rojo, Mary Lou Palermo, Manuel de Blas, Eduardo Coutelen.

The Fear Chamber (1971)

Credits: Directed by Juan Ibanez and Jack Hill; Produced by Luis Enrique Vergara and Jack Hill; Screenplay by Jack Hill; Photographed in Eastmancolor by Austin McKinney and Raul Dominguez; Musical Score by Alice Uretta; Filmed May 1968 (Karloff's scenes); Released by Azteca Pictures (Mexico) and Columbia Pictures (United States); Running Time: 87 minutes.

Cast: Boris Karloff (Scientist), Yerye Beirut, Julissa, Santanon, Carlos East.

House of Evil (1972)

Credits: Directed by Luis Enrique Vergara and Jack Hill; Produced by Luis Enrique Vergara and Juan Ibanez; Screenplay by Jack Hill; Photographed in Eastmancolor by Austin McKinney and Raul Dominguez; Musical Score by Alice Uretta; Filmed May 1968 (Karloff's scenes); Released by Azteca Pictures (Mexico) and Columbia Pictures (United States); Running Time: 83 minutes.

Cast: Boris Karloff, Julissa.

Short Non-Fiction Films

Screen Snapshots No. 11 (1934)
Credits: Released by Columbia Pictures; Running Time: 10 minutes.
Cast: Boris Karloff, Bela Lugosi, Genevieve Tobin, Pat O'Brien, James Cagney, Maureen O'Sullivan, Eddie Cantor.

Hollywood Hobbies (1935)
Credits: Written and Narrated by Grantland Rice; Running Time: 10 minutes.
Cast: Boris Karloff, Clark Gable, Buster Crabbe, Richard Arlen.

Information Please No. 8 (March 21, 1941)
Credits: Released by RKO-Pathé Pictures; Running Time: 10 minutes.
Host: Clifton Fadiman; **Panelists**: John Kieran, Franklin P. Adams, Boris Karloff.

Information Please No. 12 (July 11, 1941)
Credits: Released by RKO-Pathé Pictures; Running Time: 10 minutes.
Host: Clifton Fadiman; **Panelists**: John Kieran, Franklin P. Adams, Oscar Levant, Boris Karloff.

Today's Teens (January 1964)
Credits: Narration by Boris Karloff; Released by Twentieth Century-Fox/Movietone Pictures; Running Time: 11 minutes.

Short Cartoon

The Juggler of Our Lady (December 1957)
Credits: Directed by Al Kousel; Produced by Bill Weiss; Supervised by Gene Deitch; Screenplay and Story by R.O. Blechman; Animation (Technicolor and Cinemascope) by Gene Deitch and Al Kousel; Narration by Boris Karloff; Musical Score by Philip Scheib; Released by Twentieth Century-Fox/Terrytoons; Running Time: 6 minutes.

Compilation Film

Days of Thrills and Laughter (March 1961)
Credits: Produced and Written by Robert Youngson; Narrated by Jay Jackson; Sound Effects by Alfred Dahlem and Ralph F. Curtiss; Released by Twentieth Century-Fox Pictures; Running Time: 93 minutes.
Cast: Douglas Fairbanks, Charles Chaplin, Stan Laurel, Oliver Hardy, Harry Houdini, Pearl White, Harry Langdon, Ben Turpin, Charley Chase, Snub Pollard, Mack Sennett, Fatty Arbuckle, Mabel Normand, Ford Sterling, Boris Karloff, Warner Oland, Ruth Roland, Monty Banks, Al St. John, Cameo the Wonder Dog, the Keystone Kops, the Sennett Bathing Beauties.

Boris acted as "unofficial acting coach" on the following film:

Kings Go Forth (early June 1958)
Credits: Directed by Delmer Daves; Produced by Frank Ross and Richard Ross; Screenplay by Merle Miller; Based on the Novel by Joe David Brown; Photographed by Daniel L. Fapp; Edited by William B. Murphy; Musical Score and Direction by Elmer Bernstein; Art Direction by Fernando Carrere; Set Design by Darrell Silvera; Costumes by Leah Rhodes; Makeup by Bernard Ponedel; a Frank Ross-Eton producton; Released by United Artists Pictures; Running Time: 109 minutes.
Cast: Frank Sinatra (Lieutenant Sam Loggins), Tony Curtis (Sergeant Britt Harris), Natalie Wood (Monique Blair), Leora Dana (Mrs. Blair), Karl Swenson (Colonel), Ann Codee (Mme. Brieux), Edward Ryder (Corporal Lindsay), Jackie Berthe (Jean Francoise), Marie Isnard (Old Woman with Wine), Jazz Combo: Pete Candoli (Trumpet), Red Norvo (Vibraphone), Mel Lewis (Drums), Richie Kamuca (Tenor Sax), Red Wootten (Bass), Jimmy Weible (Guitar).

Radio Programs

Unknown Title (January 3, 1932)
Format: Variety; **Network**: CBS.

Hollywood on Parade [aka: *Hollywood on the Air*] (October 7, 1933)
Format: Talk; **Host**: Jimmy Fidler; **Guests**: Boris Karloff, Victor McLaglen, Reginald Denny; **Network**: NBC; **Content**: the three stars promoted and performed a scene from *The Lost Patrol*.

Hollywood on Parade [aka: *Hollywood on the Air*] (January 27, 1934)
Format: Talk; **Host**: Jimmy Fidler; **Guests**: Boris Karloff, Maxine Doyle; **Network**: NBC; **Content**: Karloff promoted *The Lost Patrol*.

The Fleischmann's Yeast Hour (October 11, 1934)
Format: Variety; **Announcer**: Graham McNamee; **Performers**: Rudy Vallee, Boris Karloff, The Shaw Group, Lou Holtz, Crauford Kent, Margaret Braden, Katherine Hall; **Network**: NBC; **Sponsor**: Fleischmann's Yeast; **Broadcast Time**: Thursday, 8 p.m.; **Content**: Karloff portrayed the title character in "Death Takes a Holiday"; **Running Time**: 60 minutes.

Hollywood on the Air (May 1935)
Format: Talk; **Content**: Karloff promoted *Bride of Frankenstein*.

Shell Chateau (August 31, 1935)
Format: Variety; **Host**: Al Jolson; **Guests**: Boris Karloff, Maxine Lewis, Joyce Weathers, George Jessel, Jack Stanton, Peggy Gardner, Martha Creighton, Crauford Kent; **Network**: NBC; **Sponsor**: Shell; **Broadcast Time**: Saturday, 9:30 p.m.; **Content**: Karloff played the Rajah in a skit based on the play *The Green Goddess*; **Running Time**: 60 minutes.

Unknown Title (December 30, 1935)
Format: Fact-Based Drama; **Performers**: Boris Karloff, Murray Kinnell, Russell Gleason; **Content**: Karloff and his friends dramatized his "life history."

The Fleischmann's Yeast Hour (February 6, 1936)
Format: Variety; **Announcer**: Graham McNamee; **Performers**: Boris Karloff, Rudy Vallee; **Network**: NBC; **Sponsor**: Fleischmann's Yeast; **Broadcast Time**: Thursday, 8 p.m.; **Content**: Karloff appeared in a skit titled "The Bells"; **Running Time**: 60 minutes.

The Royal Gelatin Hour (September 3, 1936)
Format: Variety; **Announcer**: Graham McNamee; **Performers**: Rudy Vallee, Boris Karloff; **Network**: NBC; **Sponsor**: Royal Gelatin; **Broadcast Time**: Thursday, 8 p.m.; **Running Time**: 60 minutes.

Camel Caravan (December 8, 1936)
Format: Variety; **Performers Included**: Boris Karloff; **Music**: Benny Goodman and His Orchestra; **Network**: CBS; **Sponsor**: Camel; **Broadcast Time**: Tuesday; **Content**: Karloff reprised the title role in "Death Takes a Holiday"; **Running Time**: 60 minutes.

The Royal Gelatin Hour (November 11, 1937)
Format: Variety; **Announcer**: Graham McNamee; **Performers**: Rudy Vallee, Boris Karloff; **Network**: NBC; **Sponsor**: Royal Gelatin; **Broadcast Time**: Thursday, 8 p.m.; **Content**: Karloff appeared in a skit titled "Resurrection"; **Running Time**: 60 minutes.

The Chase and Sanborn Hour (January 30, 1938)
Format: Variety; **Announcer**: Wendell Niles; **Performers**: Edgar Bergen and Charlie McCarthy, Boris Karloff; Don Ameche, Nelson Eddy, Dorothy Lamour; **Music**: Robert Armbruster and His Orchestra; **Network**: NBC; **Sponsor**: Chase and Sanborn; **Broadcast Time**: Sunday, 8 p.m.; **Content**: Karloff read "The Evil Eye," an adaptation of Edgar Allan Poe's "The Tell-Tale Heart"; **Running Time**: 60 minutes.

Baker's Broadcast [aka: *Seein' Stars in Hollywood*] (March 13, 1938)
Format: Variety; **Host**: Feg Murray; **Performers**: Ozzie Nelson, Harriet Hilliard (Nelson), Boris Karloff, Bela Lugosi; **Network**: NBC Blue; **Broadcast Time**: Sunday; **Content**: Karloff read "The Supplication of the Black Aberdeen" by Rudyard Kipling and sang a duet, "We're Horrible, Horrible Men," with Lugosi.

Lights Out (March 23, 1938)
Format: Horror-Suspense Anthology; **Title**: "Darrell Hall's Thoughts"; **Performers Included**: Boris Karloff (as Darrell Hall); **Network**: NBC; **Broadcast Time**: Wednesday; **Running Time**: 30 minutes.

Lights Out (March 30, 1938)
Format: Horror-Suspense Anthology; **Title**: "Valse Triste"; **Performers Included**: Boris Karloff; **Network**: NBC; **Broadcast Time**: Wednesday; **Running Time**: 30 minutes.

Lights Out (April 6, 1938)
Format: Horror-Suspense Anthology; **Title**: "Cat Wife" by Arch Oboler; **Performers Included**: Boris Karloff; **Network**: NBC; **Broadcast Time**: Wednesday; **Running Time**: 30 minutes.

Unknown Title (April 11, 1938)
Format: promotional; **Content**: Karloff joined John Ringling Norton to promote the current New York performances of the Ringling Bros. and Barnum & Bailey Circus.

Lights Out (April 13, 1938)
Format: Horror-Suspense Anthology; **Title**: "Three Matches"; **Performers Included**: Boris Karloff; **Network**: NBC; **Broadcast Time**: Wednesday; **Running Time**: 30 minutes.

Lights Out (April 20, 1938)
Format: Horror-Suspense Anthology; **Title**: "Night on the Mountain"; **Performers Included**: Boris Karloff; **Network**: NBC; **Broadcast Time**: Wednesday; **Running Time**: 30 minutes.

Royal Gelatin Hour (May 5, 1938)
Format: Variety; **Announcer**: Graham McNamee; **Performers**: Rudy Vallee, Boris Karloff, Ed East and Ralph Dumke, Irving Caesar, Tommy Riggs and Betty Lou, Colgate Glee Club, Harold Vermilyea; **Network**: NBC; **Sponsor**: Royal Gelatin; **Broadcast Time**: Thursday, 8 p.m.; **Content**: Karloff appeared as a mysterious harbinger of death in a skit titled "Danse Macabre"; **Running Time**: 60 minutes.

The Eddie Cantor Show (January 16, 1939)
Format: Variety; **Announcer**: Bert Parks; **Host**: Eddie Cantor; **Performers**: Boris Karloff, Bert ("The Mad Russian") Gordon; **Music**: Edgar ("Cookie") Fairchild's Orchestra; **Network**: CBS; **Broadcast Time**: Monday, 7:30 p.m.; **Running Time**: 30 minutes.

Royal Gelatin Hour (April 6, 1939)
Format: Variety; **Announcer**: Graham McNamee; **Performers**: Rudy Vallee, Boris Karloff; **Network**: NBC; **Sponsor**: Royal Gelatin; **Broadcast Time**: Thursday, 8 p.m.; **Content**: Karloff appeared in a skit titled "Resurrection"; **Running Time**: 60 minutes.

Kay Kyser's Kollege of Musical Knowledge (September 25, 1940)
Format: Musical-Comedy Quiz; **Host**: Kay Kyser; **Announcer**: Ken Niles; **Guests**: Boris Karloff, Bela Lugosi, Peter Lorre; **Music**: the Kay Kyser Orchestra, including Ginny Simms, Harry Babbitt, Sully Mason, Ish Kabibble; **Network**: NBC; **Sponsor**: Lucky Strike; **Broadcast Time**: Wednesday, 10 p.m.; **Content**: the four stars promoted *You'll Find Out*; **Running Time**: 60 minutes.

Everyman's Theater (October 18, 1940)
Format: Dramatic Anthology; **Title**: "Cat Wife" by Arch Oboler; **Performers Included**: Boris Karloff; **Network**: NBC; **Sponsor**: Oxydol; **Broadcast Time**: Friday, 9:30 p.m.; **Running Time**: 30 minutes.

Information Please (January 24, 1941)
Format: Quiz; **Host**: Clifton Fadiman; **panelists**: John Kieran, Franklin P. Adams, Boris Karloff, Lewis E. Lawes (Warden of Sing Sing); **Network**: NBC Blue; **Sponsor**: Lucky Strike; **Broadcast Time**: Friday, 8:30 p.m.; **Running Time**: 30 minutes.

Inner Sanctum Mysteries (March 16, 1941)
Format: Horror-Suspense Anthology; **Title**: "The Man of Steel"; **Director**: Himan Brown; **Host**: Raymond Edward Johnson; **Announcer**: Ed Herlihy; **Performers Included**: Boris Karloff; **Network**: ABC; **Sponsor**: Carter's Little Liver Pills; **Broadcast Time**: Sunday, 8:30 p.m; **Running Time**: 30 minutes.

Hollywood News Girl (March 22, 1941)
Format: Talk; **Host**: Lydia Pinkham; **Network**: NBC; **Broadcast Time**: Saturday, 1:15 p.m.; **Content**: Karloff discussed *Arsenic and Old Lace* and his horror films; **Running Time**: 15 minutes.

Inner Sanctum Mysteries (March 23, 1941)
Format: Horror-Suspense Anthology; **Title**: "The Man Who Hated Death"; **Director**: Himan Brown; **Host**: Raymond Edward Johnson; **Announcer**: Ed Herlihy; **Performers Included**: Boris Karloff; **Network**: ABC; **Sponsor**: Carter's Little Liver Pills; **Broadcast Time**: Sunday, 8:30 p.m; **Running Time**: 30 minutes.

Inner Sanctum Mysteries (April 6, 1941)
Format: Horror-Suspense Anthology; **Title**: "Death in the Zoo"; **Director**: Himan Brown; **Host**: Raymond Edward Johnson; **Announcer**: Ed Herlihy; **Performers Included**: Boris Karloff; **Network**: ABC; **Sponsor**: Carter's Little Liver Pills; **Broadcast Time**: Sunday, 8:30 p.m; **Running Time**: 30 minutes.

The Voice of Broadway (April 19, 1941)
Format: Talk; **Host**: Dorothy Kilgallen; **Content**: Karloff discussed *Arsenic and Old Lace*; **Network**: CBS; **Broadcast Time**: Saturday, 11:30 a.m.; **Running Time**: 15 minutes.

Inner Sanctum Mysteries (April 20, 1941)
Format: Horror-Suspense Anthology; **Title**: "Fog"; **Director**: Himan Brown; **Host:** Raymond Edward Johnson; **Announcer**: Ed Herlihy; **Performers Included**: Boris Karloff; **Network**: ABC; **Sponsor**: Carter's Little Liver Pills; **Broadcast Time**: Sunday, 8:30 p.m; **Running Time**: 30 minutes.

Inner Sanctum Mysteries (May 11, 1941)
Format: Horror-Suspense Anthology; **Title**: "Imperfect Crime"; **Director**: Himan Brown; **Host:** Raymond Edward Johnson; **Announcer**: Ed Herlihy; **Performers Included**: Boris Karloff; **Network**: ABC; **Sponsor**: Carter's Little Liver Pills; **Broadcast Time**: Sunday, 8:30 p.m; **Running Time**: 30 minutes.

Inner Sanctum Mysteries (June 1, 1941)
Format: Horror-Suspense Anthology; **Title**: "The Fall of the House of Usher" by Edgar Allan Poe; **Director**: Himan Brown; **Host:** Raymond Edward Johnson; **Announcer**: Ed Herlihy; **Performers Included**: Boris Karloff; **Network**: ABC; **Sponsor**: Carter's Little Liver Pills; **Broadcast Time**: Sunday, 8:30 p.m; **Running Time**: 30 minutes.

Bundles for Britain (June 14, 1941)
Format: Propaganda; **Guests**: Boris Karloff, Constance Collier; **Network**: Mutual; **Broadcast Time**: Sunday, 3 p.m.

Inner Sanctum Mysteries (June 22, 1941)
Format: Horror-Suspense Anthology; **Title**: "Green-Eyed Bat"; **Director**: Himan Brown; **Host:** Raymond Edward Johnson; **Announcer**: Ed Herlihy; **Performers Included**: Boris Karloff; **Network**: ABC; **Sponsor**: Carter's Little Liver Pills; **Broadcast Time**: Sunday, 8:30 p.m; **Running Time**: 30 minutes.

Inner Sanctum Mysteries (June 29, 1941)
Format: Horror-Suspense Anthology; **Title**: "The Man Who Painted Death"; **Director**: Himan Brown; **Host:** Raymond Edward Johnson; **Announcer**: Ed Herlihy; **Performers Included**: Boris Karloff; **Network**: ABC; **Sponsor**: Carter's Little Liver Pills; **Broadcast Time**: Sunday, 8:30 p.m; **Running Time**: 30 minutes.

United Press Is On the Air (July 11, 1941)
Format: Talk; **Hosts**: Joan Younger and Russ Hughes; **Guests**: Boris Karloff, Dorothy McGuire; **Network**: Syndicated; **Content**: Karloff discussed his career, promoted *Arsenic and Old Lace*, and growled like the Frankenstein Monster; **Running Time**: 15 minutes.

Inner Sanctum Mysteries (July 13, 1941)
Format: Horror-Suspense Anthology; **Title**: "Death Is a Murderer"; **Director**: Himan Brown; **Host:** Raymond Edward Johnson; **Announcer**: Ed Herlihy; **Performers Included**: Boris Karloff; **Network**: ABC; **Sponsor**: Carter's Little Liver Pills; **Broadcast Time**: Sunday, 8:30 p.m; **Running Time**: 30 minutes.

Inner Sanctum Mysteries (August 3, 1941)
Format: Horror-Suspense Anthology; **Title**: "The Tell-Tale Heart" by Edgar Allan Poe; **writer**: Robert Newman; **Director**: Himan Brown; **Host:** Raymond Edward Johnson; **Announcer**: Ed Herlihy; **Performers**: Boris Karloff (as Simon), Everett Sloane, Santos Ortega; **Network**: ABC; **Sponsor**: Carter's Little Liver Pills; **Broadcast Time**: Sunday, 8:30 p.m; **Running Time**: 30 minutes.

Inner Sanctum Mysteries (October 26, 1941)
Format: Horror-Suspense Anthology; **Title**: "Terror on Bailey Street"; **Director**: Himan Brown; **Host:** Raymond Edward Johnson; **Announcer**: Ed Herlihy; **Performers Included**: Boris Karloff; **Network**: ABC; **Sponsor**: Carter's Little Liver Pills; **Broadcast Time**: Sunday, 8:30 p.m; **Running Time**: 30 minutes.

Time to Smile (December 17, 1941)
Format: Variety; **Performers**: Eddie Cantor, Dinah Shore, Boris Karloff; **Network**: NBC; **Broadcast Time**: Wednesday, 9 p.m.; **Running Time**: 30 minutes.

Keep 'em Rolling (February 8, 1942)
Format: Variety; **Performers**: Morton Gould, Clifton Fadiman, Boris Karloff; **Network**: Mutual; **Broadcast Time**: Sunday, 10:30 p.m.; **Content**: Karloff appeared in a play titled "In the Fog" in this program that supported the war effort; **Running Time**: 30 minutes.

Information Please (February 20, 1942)
Format: Quiz; **Host**: Clifton Fadiman; **Announcer**: Milton Cross; **panelists**: John Kieran, Franklin P. Adams, Boris Karloff, John Carradine; **Network**: NBC; **Sponsor**: Lucky Strike; **Broadcast Time**: Friday; **Running Time**: 30 minutes.

Inner Sanctum Mysteries (April 5, 1942)
Format: Horror-Suspense Anthology; **Title**: "The Fall of the House of Usher" by Edgar Allan Poe; **Director**: Himan Brown; **Host:** Raymond Edward Johnson; **Announcer**: Ed Herlihy; **Performers Included**: Boris Karloff; **Network**: ABC; **Sponsor**: Carter's Little Liver Pills; **Broadcast Time**: Sunday, 8:30 p.m; **Running Time**: 30 minutes.

Inner Sanctum Mysteries (April 19, 1942)
Format: Horror-Suspense Anthology; **Title**: "Blackstone"; **Director**: Himan Brown; **Host:** Raymond Edward Johnson; **Announcer**: Ed Herlihy; **Performers Included**: Boris Karloff; **Network**: ABC; **Sponsor**: Carter's Little Liver Pills; **Broadcast Time**: Sunday, 8:30 p.m.; **Running Time**: 30 minutes.

Inner Sanctum Mysteries (May 3, 1942)
Format: Horror-Suspense Anthology; **Title**: "Study for Murder" by Sigmund Miller; **Director**: Himan Brown; **Host**: Raymond Edward Johnson; **Performers**: Boris Karloff (as Dr. Herbert Lodge), Everett Sloane; **Network**: ABC; **Broadcast Time**: Sunday, 8:30 p.m; **Running Time**: 30 minutes.

Inner Sanctum Mysteries (May 24, 1942)
Format: Horror-Suspense Anthology; **Title**: "The Cone"; **Director**: Himan Brown; **Host:** Raymond Edward Johnson**; Announcer**: Ed Herlihy; **Performers Included**: Boris Karloff; **Network**: ABC; **Sponsor**: Carter's Little Liver Pills; **Broadcast Time**: Sunday, 8:30 p.m; **Running Time**: 30 minutes.

Inner Sanctum Mysteries (May 31, 1942)
Format: Horror-Suspense Anthology; **Title**: "Death Wears My Face"; **Director**: Himan Brown; **Host:** Raymond Edward Johnson**; Announcer**: Ed Herlihy; **Performers Included**: Boris Karloff; **Network**: ABC; **Sponsor**: Carter's Little Liver Pills; **Broadcast Time**: Sunday, 8:30 p.m; **Running Time**: 30 minutes.

Inner Sanctum Mysteries (April 7, 1942)
Format: Horror-Suspense Anthology; **Title**: "Strange Bequest"; **Director**: Himan Brown; **Host:** Raymond Edward Johnson**; Announcer**: Ed Herlihy; **Performers Included**: Boris Karloff; **Network**: ABC; **Sponsor**: Carter's Little Liver Pills; **Broadcast Time**: Sunday, 8:30 p.m; **Running Time**: 30 minutes.

Inner Sanctum Mysteries (April 21, 1941)
Format: Horror-Suspense Anthology; **Title**: "The Grey Wolf"; **Director**: Himan Brown; **Host:** Raymond Edward Johnson**; Announcer**: Ed Herlihy; **Performers Included**: Boris Karloff; **Network**: ABC; **Sponsor**: Carter's Little Liver Pills; **Broadcast Time**: Sunday, 8:30 p.m; **Running Time**: 30 minutes.

The Theatre Guild on the Air (1943)
Format: Dramatic Anthology; **Title**: "Arsenic and Old Lace" by Joseph Kesselring; **Performers Included**: Boris Karloff (as Jonathan Brewster); **Network**: CBS; **Broadcast Time**: Tuesday; **Running Time**: 60 minutes.

Information Please (May 17, 1943)
Format: Quiz; **Host**: Clifton Fadiman; **Announcer**: Milton Cross; **Panelists**: John Kieran, Franklin P. Adams, Boris Karloff; **Network**: NBC; **Sponsor**: Heinz; **Broadcast Time**: Monday, 10:30 p.m.; **Running Time**: 30 minutes.

Blue Ribbon Town (July 24, 1943)
Format: Variety; **Host**: Groucho Marx; **Performers**: Virginia O'Brien, Fay McKenzie, Boris Karloff; **Music**: Ray Noble and His Orchestra; **Network**: CBS; **Sponsor**: Pabst Blue Ribbon; **Broadcast Time**: Saturday, 10:15 p.m.; **Running Time**: 30 minutes.

The Charlie McCarthy Show (January 30, 1944)
Format: Variety; **Hosts**: Edgar Bergen and Charlie McCarthy; **Regulars Included**: Mortimer Snerd; **Guest**: Boris Karloff; **Music**: Ray Noble and His Orchestra; **Network**: NBC; **Broadcast Time**: Sunday, 8 p.m.; **Content**: Karloff agreed to have his head "read" in a skit dealing with phrenology; **Running Time**: 30 minutes.

Creeps By Night (February 15-June 20, 1944) [series]
Format: Horror Anthology; **Titles Included**: "Those Who Walk in Darkness" (**Director**: Dave Drummond; **Music**: Albert Sach), "The Voice of Death" (February 15, 1944), "The Man With the Devil's Hands" (February 22, 1944), "Dark Destiny" (March 14, 1944), "A String of Pearls" (March 28, 1944), "The Final Reckoning" (May 2, 1944), "The Hunt" (May 9, 1944); **Production Supervisor**: Robert Maxwell; **Performers Included**: Boris Karloff; **Network**: ABC; **Broadcast Time**: Tuesday, 10:30 p.m; **Running Time**: 30 minutes.

Blue Ribbon Town (June 3, 1944)
Format: Variety; **Host**: Groucho Marx; **Performers**: Virginia O'Brien; Fay McKenzie, Boris Karloff; **Music**: Robert Armbruster and His Orchestra; **Network**: CBS; **Sponsor**: Pabst Blue Ribbon; **Broadcast Time**: Saturday, 10:15 p.m.; **Running Time**: 30 minutes.

Duffy's Tavern (January 12, 1945)
Format: situation comedy; **Announcer**: Graham McNamee; **Performers**: Ed Gardner, Boris Karloff, Charles Cantor, Shirley Booth, Eddie Green; **Network**: NBC; **Sponsor**: Ipana; **Broadcast Time**: Friday,

8:30 p.m; **Content**: for a war bond rally, tavern manager Archie writes a play that pairs his "Dr. Frank" with Karloff's "Dr. Stein"; **Running Time**: 30 minutes.

Suspense (January 25, 1945)
Format: Horror-Suspense Anthology; **Title**: "Drury's Bones" by Harold Swanton; **Producer and Director**: William Spier; **Performers**: Boris Karloff (as Terrance Drury), William Johnstone, Debbie Ellis, Joseph Kearns; **Network**: CBS; **Sponsor**: Roma Wines; **Broadcast Time**: Thursday, 8 p.m; **Running Time**: 30 minutes.

The Fred Allen Show (October 14, 1945)
Format: Variety; **Host**: Fred Allen; **Guest**: Boris Karloff; **Sponsor**: Standard Brands, **Network**: NBC.

Inner Sanctum Mysteries (October 23, 1945)
Format: Horror-Suspense Anthology; **Title**: "Corridor of Doom"; **Director**: Himan Brown; **Host**: Paul McGrath; **Performers**: Boris Karloff (as John Clay), Richard Widmark; **Network**: CBS; **Sponsor**: Lipton Tea and Soup; **Broadcast Time**: Tuesday, 9 p.m; **Running Time**: 30 minutes.

Hildegarde's Radio Room (October 23, 1945)
Format: Talk; **Host**: Hildegard; **Guest**: Boris Karloff; **Sponsor**: Brown and Williamson Tobacco; **Network**: NBC; **Sponsor**: Raleigh; **Broadcast Time**: Tuesday, 10:30; **Running Time**: 30 minutes.

The Charlie McCarthy Program (October 28, 1945)
Format: Variety; **Hosts**: Edgar Bergen and Charlie McCarthy; **Announcer**: Ben Grauer; **Regulars**: Mortimer Snerd, Anita Gordon, Pat Patrick; **Guest**: Boris Karloff; **Music**: Ray Noble and His Orchestra; **Network**: NBC; **Sponsor**: Chase and Sanborn; **Broadcast Time**: Sunday, 8 p.m.; **Content**: Karloff took Bergen, McCarthy, and the gang to visit his "haunted house"; **Running Time**: 30 minutes.

Report to the Nation (November 3, 1945)
Format: Dramatic Anthology; **Title**: "Back for Christmas" by John Collier; **Adaptation**: Charles Monroe; **Announcer**: Ted Pearson; **Performers**: John Daly, Boris Karloff (as Professor Herbert Carpenter), Alan Young, Maxine Sullivan, Sgt. Ben Haroki; **Network**: CBS; **Broadcast Time**: Saturday, 1:45 p.m.; **Running Time**: 30 minutes.

Inner Sanctum Mysteries (November 6, 1945)
Format: Horror-Suspense Anthology; **Title**: "The Wailing Wall" by Milton Lewis (based on Edgar Allan Poe's "The Tell-Tale Heart" and "The Black Cat"); **Director**: Himan Brown; **Host**: Paul McGrath; **Performers**: Boris Karloff (as Gabriel Hornell), Jackson Beck; **Network**: CBS; **Sponsor**: Lipton Tea (represented by Mary, "the Lipton Tea Girl") and Lipton Soup; **Broadcast Time**: Tuesday, 9 p.m; **Running Time**: 30 minutes.

Theatre Guild on the Air (November 11, 1945)
Format: Dramatic Anthology; **Titles**: "The Emperor Jones" and "Where the Cross is Made"; **Performers Included**: Boris Karloff; **Network**: ABC; **Sponsor**: United States Steel Corporation.

The Fred Allen Show (November 18, 1945)
Format: Variety; **Host**: Fred Allen; **Regulars**: Portland Hoffa, Kenny Delmar, Minerva Pious, Parker Fennelly, Alan Reed; **Guest**: Boris Karloff; **Music**: the DeMarco Sisters, Al Goodman and His Orchestra; **Network**: NBC; **Sponsor**: Tenderleaf Tea; **Broadcast Time**: Sunday, 8:30 p.m.; **Content**: due to the postwar housing shortage, Karloff offered to rent his home to Allen; of course, it turned out to be haunted; **Running Time**: 30 minutes.

Textron Theater (December 8, 1945)
Format: Dramatic Anthology; **Title**: "Angel Street" by Patrick Hamilton; **Adaptation**: Robert Cenadella; **Announcer**: Frank Gallop; **Performers**: Helen Hayes, Boris Karloff (as Mr. Manningham), Cedric Hardwicke; **Music**: Vladimir Zalinsky (composer and conductor); **Network**: CBS; **Broadcast Time**: Saturday, 7 p.m.; **Running Time**: 30 minutes.

Exploring the Unknown (December 23, 1945)
Format: Anthology; **Title**: "The Baffled Genie"; **Narrator**: Charles Irving; **Announcer**: Andre Baruch; **Performers Included**: Boris Karloff; **Network**: Mutual; **Broadcast Time**: Sunday, 9 p.m.; **Running Time**: 30 minutes.

Information Please (December 24, 1945)
Format: Quiz; **Host**: Clifton Fadiman; **Panelists**: John Kieran, Franklin P. Adams, John Mason Brown, Boris Karloff; **Network**: NBC; **Sponsor**: Mobil; **Broadcast Time**: Monday; **Running Time**: 30 minutes.

Request Performance (February 3, 1946)
Format: Variety; **Performers**: Boris Karloff, Frank Morgan, Roy Rogers; **Network**: CBS; **Broadcast Time**: Sunday, 9 p.m.; **Running Time**: 30 minutes.

That's Life (November 8, 1946)
Format: Talk; **Host**: Jay C. Flippen; **Guest**: Boris Karloff; **Network**: CBS; **Broadcast Time**: Friday, 5:30 p.m.; **Content**: Karloff promoted *On Borrowed Time* and read a self-penned limerick; **Running Time**: 30 minutes.

The Lady Esther Screen Guild Theatre (November 25, 1946)
Format: Dramatic Anthology; **Title**: "Arsenic and Old Lace" by Joseph Kesselring; **Announcer**: Truman Bradley; **Performers**: Boris Karloff (as Jonathan Brewster), Eddie Albert, Verna Felton, Jane Morgan, Joseph Kearns, Herb Vigran; **Network**: CBS; **Broadcast Time**: Monday, 8:30 p.m.; **Running Time**: 30 minutes.

Show Stoppers (1946)
Format: Talk; **Host**: Knox Manning; **Guest**: Boris Karloff; **Production Company**: Textile Broadcasts; **Network**: Syndicated; **Sponsor**: Koret of California; **Content**: Karloff read "The Beggarman" by Ivan Turgenev and discussed his early career in Canada, *The Criminal Code*, *Arsenic and Old Lace*, and *Frankenstein*; **Running Time**: 15 minutes.

The Jack Benny Show (January 19, 1947)
Format: Comedy Variety; **Host**: Jack Benny; **Regulars**: Mary Livingstone, Phil Harris, Dennis Day, Eddie ("Rochester") Anderson, Don Wilson, Mel Blanc, Frank Nelson, L.A. ("Speed") Riggs, F.E. Boone; **Guest**: Boris Karloff; **Network**: NBC; **Sponsor**: Lucky Strike; **Broadcast Time**: Sunday, 7 p.m.; **Content**: in a skit titled "I Stand Condemned," Karloff played a mysterious stranger who gave Benny money; **Running Time**: 30 minutes.

Lights Out (July 16-August 6, 1947) [series]
Format: Horror-Suspense Anthology; **Titles Included**: "Death Robbery" (July 16, 1947), "The Undead" (July 23, 1947), "The Ring" (July 30, 1947); **Producer and Director**: Bill Laurents; **writers**: Willis Cooper and Paul Pierce; **Host and performer**: Boris Karloff; **Announcer**: Ken Niles; **Network**: ABC; **Sponsor**: Eversharp; **Broadcast Time**: Wednesday, 10:30 p.m.; **Running Time**: 30 minutes.

Philco Radio Time (aka *The Bing Crosby Show*) (October 29, 1947)
Format: Musical Variety; **Host**: Bing Crosby; **Announcer**: Ken Carpenter; **Guest**: Boris Karloff; **Music**: Victor Moore, John Scott Trotter and His Orchestra, Jud Conlin's Rhythmaires, Gail Robbins; **Network**: ABC; **Sponsor**: Philco; **Broadcast Time**: Wednesday, 10 p.m.; **Content**: Karloff traded quips and sang "The Halloween Song" with Crosby and Moore; **Running Time**: 30 minutes.

The Jimmy Durante Show (December 10, 1947)
Format: Musical-Comedy Variety; **Host**: Jimmy Durante; **Announcer**: Howard Petrie; **Regulars**: Arthur Treacher, Alan Reed; **Guest**: Boris Karloff; **Music**: Peggy Lee, Candy Candido, Roy Bargy and His Orchestra; **Network**: NBC; **Sponsor**: Rexall; **Broadcast Time**: Wednesday, 10:30 p.m.; **Content**: Durante described his visit to Karloff's "haunted house"; **Running Time**: 30 minutes.

Suspense (December 19, 1947)
Format: Horror-Suspense Anthology; **Title**: "Wet Saturday" by John Collier; **Adaptation**: Harold Medford;

Producer and Director: William Spier; **Performers**: Boris Karloff (as Fred Princey), Hans Conreid, Cathy Lewis, Wally Maher; **Music**: Lucien Moraweck (composer), Lud Gluskin (conductor); **Network**: CBS; **Broadcast Time**: Friday, 9:30 p.m.; **Running Time**: 30 minutes.

The Kraft Music Hall (December 25, 1947)
Format: Musical Variety; **Announcer**: Ken Carpenter; **Guest**: Boris Karloff; **Music**: Al Jolson, Oscar Levant, Lou Bring and His Orchestra; **Network**: NBC; **Broadcast Time**: Thursday, 9 p.m.; **Content**: Karloff played Santa Claus, visiting Jolson on Christmas Eve; **Running Time**: 30 minutes.

Unconquered (1947)
Format: Promotional; **Performers Included**: Boris Karloff; **Content**: re-enactment of a 15-minute scene from *Unconquered* (1947).

Guest Star (September 12, 1948)
Format: Federal Government Promotional; **Host**: Win Eliot; **Announcer**: Roger Foster; **Guest**: Boris Karloff; **Music**: Harry Sosnick and His Orchestra; **Network**: Syndicated; **Sponsor**: the United States Treasury Department; **Content**: Karloff appeared as escaped convict Spider Parsons in a skit titled "The Babysitter" and promoted the sale of Treasury Bonds; **Running Time**: 15 minutes.

The NBC University Theater of the Air (October 17, 1948)
Format: Dramatic Anthology; **Title**: "The History of Mr. Polly" by H.G. Wells; **Adaptation**: Clarice Ross; **Performers**: Boris Karloff (as Alfred Polly), Ramsay Hill, Constance Cavendish, Naomi Stevens, Terry Kilburn, Arthur Q. Bryan, Ben Wright, Gray Stafford, Donald Morrison, Monty Margetts, Ina Ronsley, Marlene Ames; **Commentator**: Harvey C. Webster; **Music**: Henry Russell (conductor); **Network**: NBC; **Broadcast Time**: Saturday, 2:30 p.m; **Running Time**: 60 minutes.

The Sealtest Variety Theater (aka *The Dorothy Lamour Show*) (October 28, 1948)
Format: Musical Variety; **Host**: Dorothy Lamour; **Guest**: Boris Karloff; **Network**: NBC; **Broadcast Time**: Thursday, 9:30 p.m.

Great Scenes from Great Plays (October 29, 1948)
Format: Dramatic Anthology; **Title**: "On Borrowed Time" by Paul Osborn; **Host**: Walter Hampden; **Performers**: Boris Karloff (as Gramps), Parker Fennelly; **Network**: Mutual; **Broadcast Time**: Friday, 8 p.m.; **Running Time**: 30 minutes.

Truth or Consequences (October 30, 1948)
Format: game; **Host**: Ralph Edwards; **Announcer**: Harlow Wilcox; **Guest**: Boris Karloff; **Network**: NBC; **Sponsor**: Duz; **Broadcast Time**: Saturday, 8:30 p.m.; **Content**: Karloff, disguised as a swami, surprised a local guest on the Halloween show; **Running Time**: 30 minutes.

Theater USA (February 3, 1949)
Format: Dramatic Anthology; **Producer**: ANTA (American National Theater and Academy); **Network**: ABC; **Broadcast Time**: Thursday.

Inner Sanctum Mysteries (February 14, 1949)
Format: Horror-Suspense Anthology; **Title**: "Birdsong for a Murderer"; **Director**: Himan Brown; **Host**: Paul McGrath; **Performers Included**: Boris Karloff (as Carl Warner); **Network**: CBS; **Broadcast Time**: Monday, 8 p.m.; **Running Time**: 30 minutes.

Spike Jones Spotlight Review (April 9, 1949)
Format: Musical-Comedy Variety; **Producer**: Joe Bigelow; **Host**: Spike Jones; **Announcer**: Michael Roy; **Guest**: Boris Karloff; **Network**: CBS; **Sponsor**: Coca-Cola; **Broadcast Time**: Saturday, 7:30 p.m.; **Running Time**: 30 minutes.

Theatre Guild on the Air (May 29, 1949)
Format: Dramatic Anthology; **Title**: "The Perfect Alibi"; **Performers**: Boris Karloff, Joan Lorring; **Network**: ABC; **Broadcast Venue**: Belasco Theatre, New York.

The Sealtest Variety Theater (aka *The Dorothy Lamour Show*) (June 23, 1949)
Format: Musical Variety; **Host**: Dorothy Lamour; **Guest**: Boris Karloff; **Network**: NBC; **Broadcast Time**: Thursday, 9:30 p.m.

Starring Boris Karloff (September 21-December 14, 1949)
Format: Suspense Anthology; **Titles**: "Five Golden Guineas" (September 21),"The Mask" (September 28), "Mungahara" (October 5), "Mad Illusion" (October 12), "Perchance to Dream," (October 19), "The Devil Takes a Bride" (October 26), "The Moving Finger" (November 2), "The Twisted Path" (November 9), "False Face" (November 16), "Cranky Bill" (November 23), "Three O'Clock" (November 30), "The Shop at Sly Corner" (December 7), "The Night Reveals" (December 14); **Host and Performer**: Boris Karloff; **Announcer**: George Gunn; **Organist**: George Henninger; **Network**: ABC; **Broadcast Time**: Wednesday, 9 p.m.; **Running Time**: 30 minutes.
Note: This radio series ran concurrently with the television version, which aired on Thursday evenings.

The Bill Stern Colgate Sports Newsreel (January 13, 1950)
Format: Sports; **Host**: Bill Stern; **Guest**: Boris Karloff; **Announcer**: Arthur Gary; **Network**: NBC; **Broadcast Time**: Friday, 10:30 p.m.; **Content**: Karloff briefly made sinister comments about Friday the 13th; **Running Time**: 15 minutes.

The Bill Stern Colgate Sports Newsreel (July 21, 1950)
Format: Sports; **Host**: Boris Karloff; **Announcer**: Arthur Gary; **Network**: NBC; **Broadcast Time**: Friday, 10:30 p.m.; **Content**: Karloff filled in for the vacationing Stern, relating sports stories with a murder theme; **Running Time**: 15 minutes.

Boris Karloff's Treasure Chest (September 17-December 17, 1950) [series]
Format: Children's Literature; **Titles Included**: "Casey at the Bat" (October 1, 1950), "Johnny Appleseed" (November 26, 1950), "Boris Karloff's Christmas Treasure Chest" (December 24, 1950); **Producer:** Richard Pack; **Director**: John Grogan; **Continuity**: Mort Levin; **Host**: Boris Karloff; **Organist**: Kay Reed; **Station**: WNEW, New York; **Broadcast Time**: Sunday, 7 p.m.

The Theater Guild on the Air (December 24, 1950)
Format: Dramatic Anthology; **Title**: "David Copperfield" by Charles Dickens; **Adaptation**: Robert Anderson; **Director**: Homer Thickett; **Executive Producer**: Imana Marshall; **Production Supervisors**: Lawrence Langer, Theresa Helborn; **Editor**: S. Mark Smith; **Host**: Roger Pryor; **Announcer**: Norman Brokenshire; **Performers**: Richard Burton, Boris Karloff (as Uriah Heep), Flora Robson, Hugh Williams, Cyril Ritchard, Isobel Elsom, Brenda Forbes, David Cole, Penelope Mundy, Patricia Marmont, John Merivale, Carl Harborg; **Music**: Harold Levy (composer and conductor); **Net work**: NBC; **Sponsor**: United States Steel Corporation; **Broadcast Time**: Sunday; **Running Time**: 60 minutes.

Stars on Parade (May 4, 1951)
Format: Dramatic Anthology; **Title**: "The Big Man" by Arnold G. Leo; **Announcer**: Joseph Ripley; **Performers Included**: Boris Karloff (as Al Carto); **Music**: Johnny Guarnieri (composer and conductor); **Sponsor**: Armed Forces Radio Service (AFRS); **Running Time**: 15 minutes.

Duffy's Tavern (October 1951)
Format: situation comedy; **Regulars**: Ed Gardner, Charles Cantor, Rudolph Weiss; **Guest**: Boris Karloff; **Network**: NBC; **Broadcast Time**: Friday, 9 p.m.; **Content**: when Duffy decides to sell the tavern, Archie hires his "old pal," Karloff, to scare off the potential buyer; **Running Time**: 30 minutes.

Phillip Morris Playhouse on Broadway (February 10, 1952)
Format: Dramatic Anthology; **Title**: "Journey into Nowhere"; **Performers**: Boris Karloff, Charles Martin; **Network**: CBS; **Broadcast Time**: Sunday, 10 p.m..

The Theatre Guild on the Air (February 24, 1952)
Format: Dramatic Anthology; **Title**: "Oliver Twist" by Charles Dickens; **Performers**: Boris Karloff, Basil Rathbone, Leveen McGrath, Melville Cooper; **Network**: NBC; **Sponsor**: United States Steel Corporation; **Broadcast Time**: Sunday; **Running Time**: 60 minutes.

The Theatre Guild on the Air (April 27, 1952)
Format: Dramatic Anthology; **Title**: "The Sea Wolf" by Jack London; **Host**: Roger Pryor; **Announcer**: Norman Brokenshire; **Performers**: Boris Karloff, Burgess Meredith; **Network**: NBC; **Sponsor**: United States Steel Corporation; **Broadcast Time**: Sunday; **Running Time**: 60 minutes.

Phillip Morris Playhouse on Broadway (June 1, 1952)
Format: Dramatic Anthology; **Title**: "Outward Bound"; **Performers**: Boris Karloff, Charles Martin; **Network**: CBS; **Broadcast Time**: Sunday, 10 p.m.

Inner Sanctum Mysteries (June 22, 1952)
Format: Horror-Suspense Anthology; **Title**: "Birdsong for a Murderer"; **Director**: Himan Brown; **Host**: Paul McGrath; **Performers Included**: Boris Karloff (as Carl Warner); **Network**: CBS; **Sponsor**: Pearson Pharmaceutical Company; **Broadcast Time**: Sunday, 8 p.m.; **Running Time**: 30 minutes.

Best Plays (July 6, 1952)
Format: Dramatic Anthology; **Title**: "Arsenic and Old Lace" by Joseph Kesselring; **Director**: Edward King; **Supervisor**: William Welch; **Adaptation**: Ernest Kinoy; **Host**: John Chapman; **Announcer**: Fred Collins; **Performers**: Boris Karloff (as Jonathan Brewster), Donald Cook, Evelyn Varden, Jean Adair, Edgar Stehli, Wendell Holmes, Joan Tompkins, Arthur Maitland, Ed Latimer, Ted Osborne; **Network**: NBC; **Broadcast Time**: Sunday, 6:30 p.m.; **Running Time**: 60 minutes.

Inner Sanctum Mysteries (July 13, 1952)
Format: Horror-Suspense Anthology; **Title**: "Death for Sale"; **Director**: Himan Brown; **Host**: Paul McGrath; **Performers**: Boris Karloff (as Mark Devis), Everett Sloane; **Network**: CBS; **Sponsor**: Pearson Pharmaceutical Company; **Broadcast Time**: Sunday, 8 p.m.; **Running Time**: 30 minutes.

MGM Musical Comedy Theater of the Air (November 26, 1952)
Format: Musical-Comedy Anthology; **Title**: "Yolanda and the Thief"; **Adaptation**: Melbourne Kelly (Based on the Screenplay by Irving Brecher and the Story by Jacques Thery and Ludwig Bememelmans; **Producer**: Raymond Cash; **Director**: Mark Lowe; **Announcer**: Ed Stokes; **Performers**: Boris Karloff (as Angelo, the Guardian Angel), John Conte, Lisa Kirk, John Griggs, Wendell Holmes, Eileen Heckart; **Songs Included**: "A Pocketful of Dreams," "Blue Moon," "You Stepped Out of a Dream," "Got a Date with an Angel"; **Musical Director**: Joel Harrisson; **Network**: Mutual; **Sponsor**: R.J. Reynolds; **Broadcast Time**: Wednesday; **Running Time**: 60 minutes.

Phillip Morris Playhouse on Broadway (December 10, 1952)
Format: Dramatic Anthology; **Title**: "Man Against Town"; **Performers**: Boris Karloff, Charles Martin; **Network**: CBS; **Broadcast Time**: Sunday, 10 p.m..

U.S. Steel Hour (April 5, 1953)
Format: Dramatic Anthology; **Title**: "Great Expectations" by Charles Dickens; **Performers**: Boris Karloff (as Magwich), Melville Cooper, Margaret Phillips, Tom Helmore, Estelle Winwood, Rex Thompson, Carl Harper, Sarah Burton; Anthony Kemble Cooper, Norman Barrs, Judson Reese, Veronica Cole; **Network**: NBC; **Broadcast Time**: Sunday; **Running Time**: 60 minutes.

Phillip Morris Playhouse on Broadway (April 15, 1953)
Format: Dramatic Anthology; **Title**: "Dead Past"; **Performers**: Boris Karloff, Charles Martin; **Network**: CBS, **Broadcast Time**: Sunday, 10 p.m.

Heritage (April 23, 1953)
Format: Historical Anthology; **Title**: "Plagues"; **Producer and Director**: Sherman H. Dryer; **Host**: Charles Irving; **Performers Included**: Boris Karloff; **Music**: Ralph Norman; **Network**; ABC; **Broadcast Time**: Thursday, 8:30 p.m.

Phillip Morris Playhouse on Broadway (June 17, 1953)
Format: Dramatic Anthology; **Title**: "The Shop at Sly Corner" by Edward Percy; **Performers**: Boris Karloff (as Decius Heiss), Charles Martin; **Network**: CBS; **Broadcast Time**: Sunday, 10 p.m.

The Play of His Choice (December 1953)
Format: Dramatic Anthology; **Title**: "The Hanging Judge" by Bruce Hamilton; **Writer**: Raymond Massey; **Producer**: Cleland Finn; **Performer**: Boris Karloff (as Sir Francis Brittain); **Network**: Aired in Great Britain.

Easy as ABC (April 27, 1958)
Format: Anthology; **Title**: "O Is for Old Wives Tales"; **Performers**: Boris Karloff, Peter Lorre, Alfred Hitchcock; **Network**: CBS; **Sponsor**: UNESCO (United Nations Educational Scientific Cultural Organization); **Broadcast Time**: 11:30 p.m.; **Running Time**: 25 minutes.

Tales from the Reader's Digest (1956-69)
Format: News-Talk; **Host**: Boris Karloff; **Network**: Syndicated; **Broadcast Time**: Weekdays, in 3-minute installments.
Note: This program also was aired as *Boris Karloff* on the Armed Forces Radio Service (AFRS).

Appendix D

Television Programs

The Chevrolet Tele-Theatre (February 7, 1949)
Format: Dramatic Anthology; **Title**: "Expert Opinion"; **Performers**: Boris Karloff, Dennis King, Vicki Cummings; **Network**: NBC; **Running Time**: 30 minutes.

Ford Theatre (April 11, 1949)
Format: Dramatic Anthology; **Performers Included**: Boris Karloff; **Network**: CBS; **Running Time**: 30 minutes.

Suspense! (April 26, 1949)
Format: Horror-Suspense Anthology; **Title**: "A Night at an Inn"; **Performers Included**: Boris Karloff; **Network**: CBS.

The Chevrolet Tele-Theatre (May 9, 1949)
Format: Dramatic Anthology; **Title**: "Passenger to Bali"; **Performers Included**: Boris Karloff; **Network**: NBC; **Running Time**: 30 minutes.

Suspense! (May 17, 1949)
Format: Horror-Suspense Anthology; **Title**: "The Monkey's Paw" by W.W. Jacobs; **Performers Included**: Boris Karloff; **Network**: CBS.

Suspense! (June 7, 1949)
Format: Horror-Suspense Anthology; **Title**: "The Yellow Scarf"; **Performers Included**: Boris Karloff; **Network**: CBS.

Celebrity Time (September 4, 1949)
Format: Quiz/Panel; **Host**: Conrad Nagel; **Panelists**: John Daly, Ilka Chase; Boris Karloff; **Network**: ABC; **Running Time**: 30 minutes.

Starring Boris Karloff (aka *Mystery Playhouse Starring Boris Karloff*)
(September 22-December 15, 1949) [series]
Format: Suspense Anthology; **Titles**: "Five Golden Guineas" (September 22), "The Mask" (September 29), "Mungahara" (October 6), "Mad Illusion" (October 13), "Perchance to Dream" (October 20), "The Devil Takes a Bride" (October 27), "The Moving Finger" (November 3), "The Twisted Path" (November 10), "False Face" (November 17), "Cranky Bill" (November 24), "Three O'Clock" (December 1), "The Shop at Sly Corner" (December 8), "The Night Reveals" (December 15); **Director**: Alex Segal; **Performers Included**: Boris Karloff, Mildred Natwick; **Announcer**: George Gunn; **Organist**: George Henninger; **Network**: ABC; **Running Time**: 30 minutes.

Inside U.S.A. with Chevrolet (1949-50)
Format: Musical Variety; **Guest**: Boris Karloff; **Network**: CBS.

Masterpiece Playhouse (September 3, 1950)
Format: Dramatic Anthology; **Title**: "Uncle Vanya" by Anton Chekov; **Performers**: Walter Abel, Eva Gabor, Boris Karloff; **Network**: NBC; **Running Time**: 60 minutes.

Lights Out (September 18, 1950)
Format: Suspense Anthology; **Title**: "The Leopard Lady"; **Narrator**: Frank Gallup; **Organist**: Arlo Hulls; **Network**: NBC; Running Time: 30 minutes.

Paul Whiteman's Goodyear Revue (October 29, 1950)
Format: Musical Variety; **Performers**: Earl Wrightson, Boris Karloff; **Network**: ABC; **Running Time**: 30 minutes.

The Don McNeil TV Club (April 11, 1951)
Format: Musical Variety; **Regulars**: Johnny Desmond, Fran Allison, Sam Powling, Patsy Lee; **Music**: The Eddie Ballantine Orchestra; **Network**: ABC; **Running Time**: 60 minutes.

The Texaco Star Theatre (aka *The Milton Berle Show*) (October 9, 1951)
Format: Comedy Variety; **Host**: Milton Berle; **Performers**: Fatso Marco, Boris Karloff; **Music**: The Alan Roth Orchestra; **Commercial Announcer**: Sid Stone; **Network**: NBC; **Running Time**: 60 minutes.

The Fred Waring Show (October 21, 1951)
Format: Musical Variety; **Music**: Fred Waring and His Pennsylvanians; **Network**: CBS; **Running Time**: 60 minutes.

Robert Montgomery Presents (November 19, 1951)
Format: Dramatic Anthology; **Title**: "The Kimballs" by Mitchell Wilson; **Performers**: Vanessa Brown, Richard Waring, Boris Karloff; **Network**: NBC; **Running Time**: 60 minutes.

Celebrity Time (November 25, 1951)
Format: Quiz/Panel; **Host**: Conrad Nagel; **Panelists**: John Daly, Ilka Chase, Kitty Carlisle, Boris Karloff; **Network**: CBS; **Running Time**: 30 minutes.

Studio One (December 3, 1951)
Format: Dramatic Anthology; **Title**: "Mutiny on the Nicolette" by Josepf Liss; **Commercial Announcer**: Betty Furness; **Sponsor**: Westinghouse; **Network**: CBS; **Running Time**: 60 minutes.

Suspense! (December 25, 1951)
Format: Dramatic Anthology; **Title**: "The Lonely Place"; **Performers**: Judith Evelyn, Robin Morgan, Boris Karloff; **Music**: the Westminster Choir; **Network**: CBS; **Running Time**: 30 minutes.

Lux Video Theatre (December 31, 1951)
Format: Dramatic Anthology; **Title**: "The Jest of Hahalaba" by Lord Dunsany; **Network**: CBS; **Running Time**: 30 minutes.

Columbia Workshop (January 13, 1952)
Format: Dramatic Anthology; **Title**: "Don Quixote" by Cervantes; **Writer**: Alvin Sapinsley; **Network**: CBS; **Running Time**: 60 minutes.

Stork Club (January 30, 1952)
Format: Talk; **Host**: Sherman Billingsley; **Network**: CBS; **Running Time**: 15 minutes.

Tales of Tomorrow (February 22, 1952)
Format: Science-Fiction Anthology; **Title**: "Memento"; **Performers Included**: Boris Karloff, Barbara Joyce; **Network**: ABC; **Running Time**: 30 minutes.

The Texaco Star Theatre (aka *The Milton Berle Show*) (April 29, 1952)
Format: Comedy Variety; **Host**: Milton Berle; **Performers**: Fatso Marco, Boris Karloff, Don Cornell, Jimmy Nelson; **Music**: The Alan Roth Orchestra; **Commercial Announcer**: Sid Stone; **Network**: NBC; **Running Time**: 60 minutes.

Studio One (May 19, 1952)
Format: Dramatic Anthology; **Title**: "A Connecticut Yankee in King Arthur's Court" by Mark Twain; **Performers Included**: Boris Karloff, Thomas Mitchell; **Network**: CBS.

Celebrity Time (May 25, 1952)
Format: Quiz/Panel; **Host**: Conrad Nagel; **Panelists:** John Daly, Ilka Chase, Vivian Blaine, Orson Bean, Boris Karloff; **Network**: NBC; **Running Time**: 30 minutes.
Curtain Call (June 27, 1952)
Format: Dramatic Anthology; **Title**: "Soul of the Great Bell" by Lafcadio Hearn; **Performers**: Raimonda Orselli, Boris Karloff; **Network**: NBC; **Running Time**: 30 minutes.

Schlitz Playhouse of Stars (July 4, 1952)
Format: Dramatic Anthology; **Host**: Irene Dunne; **Title**: "Death House"; **Performers**: Tony Gerri, Boris Karloff; **Network**: NBC; **Running Time**: 30 minutes.

I've Got a Secret (ca. September 9, 1952)
Format: Quiz; **Guests Included**: Boris Karloff; **Network**: CBS; **Running Time**: 30 minutes.

Lux Video Theatre (December 8, 1952)
Format: Dramatic Anthology; **Title**: "Fear"; **Performers**: Boris Karloff (as Sir George), Gene Lockhart, Bramwell Fletcher; **Network**: NBC.

The Texaco Star Theatre (aka *The Milton Berle Show*) (December 16, 1952)
Format: Comedy Variety; **Host**: Milton Berle; **Performers**: Fatso Marco, Don Ameche, Miriam Hopkins, Boris Karloff; **Music**: The Alan Roth Orchestra; **Commercial Announcer**: Sid Stone; **Network**: NBC; **Running Time**: 60 minutes.

Who's There? (1952)
Format: Quiz; **Host**: Arlene Francis; **Guests Included**: Boris Karloff; **Network**: CBS; **Running Time**: 30 minutes.

All Star Revue (ca. January 17, 1953)
Format: Musical-Comedy Variety; **Performers**: Martha Raye, Boris Karloff, Peter Lorre.

Hollywood Opening Night (March 2, 1953)
Format: Dramatic Anthology; **Host**: Jimmie Fidler; **Title**: "The Invited Seven"; **Network**: NBC; **Running Time**: 30 minutes.

Suspense! (March 17, 1953)
Format: Dramatic Anthology; **Title**: "The Black Prophet" (Karloff as Grigori Rasputin); **Network**: CBS; **Running Time**: 30 minutes.

Robert Montgomery Presents (March 30, 1953)
Format: Dramatic Anthology; **Title**: "Burden of Proof"; **Network**: NBC; **Running Time**: 60 minutes.

Tales of Tomorrow (April 3, 1953)
Format: Science Fiction; **Title**: "Past Tense"; **Performers**: Boris Karloff, Robert F. Simon, Katherine Meskill; **Network**: ABC.

Plymouth Playhouse (May 25, 1953)
Format: Various; **Host**: Cedric Hardwicke; **Title**: "The Chase" by John Collier; **Performers**: Philip Truex, Boris Karloff; **Network**: ABC; **Running Time**: 30 minutes.

Suspense (June 23, 1953)
Format: Dramatic Anthology; **Title**: "The Signal Man" by Charles Dickens; **Performers Included**: Boris Karloff, Alan Webb; **Network**: CBS; **Running Time**: 30 minutes.

I've Got a Secret (1953)
Format: Quiz/Panel; **Guests Included**: Boris Karloff; **Network**: CBS; **Running Time**: 30 minutes.

The Rheingold Theatre (1953)
Format: Dramatic Anthology; **Title**: "House of Death"; **Performers Included**: Boris Karloff (as Charles

Brandon); **Network**: NBC; **Running Time**: 30 minutes.

I've Got a Secret (October 13, 1954)
Format: Quiz/Panel; **Host**: Garry Moore; **Panelists**: Bill Cullen, Kitty Carlisle, Boris Karloff; **Network**: CBS; **Running Time**: 30 minutes.
Truth or Consequences (November 7, 1954)
Format: Game; **Host**: Jack Bailey; **Guest**: Boris Karloff; **Network**: NBC.

Climax! (December 16, 1954)
Format: Dramatic Anthology; **Host**: William Lundigan; **Title**: "The White Carnation"; **Performers**: Boris Karloff (as Dr. Philip Nestri), Teresa Wright, Claudette Colbert; **Network**: CBS; **Running Time**: 60 minutes.

Down You Go (December 17, 1954)
Format: Quiz/Panel; **Host**: Dr. Bergen Evans; **Panelists**: Professor Robert Breen, Toni Gilman, Carmelita Pope, Fran Allison, Phil Rizzuto, Boris Karloff; **Network**: Dumont; **Running Time**: 30 minutes.

Colonel March of Scotland Yard (December 1954-Spring 1955) [series]
Format: Drama/Mystery; **Titles**: 26 episodes, including "Death in the Dressing Room," "Death in Inner Space," "Error at Daybreak," "The Silver Curtain," "The Case of the Misguided Missle," "Hot Money," "Murder is Permanent," "The Case of the Kidnapped Poodle," "The Abominable Snowman," "The Stolen Crime," "The Invisible Knife," "The New Invisible Man," "The Talking Head," "The Case of the Lively Ghost," "The Headless Hat," "The Sorcerer," "Strange Events at Roman Falls," "The Devil Sells His Soul," and "All Cats Are Grey at Night" (with Christopher Lee); **Producer**: ITV (Great Britain); **Network**: Syndicated; **Running Time**: 30 minutes.

The Best of Broadway (January 5, 1955)
Format: Anthology; **Title**: "Arsenic and Old Lace" by Joseph L. Kesselring; **Performers**: Helen Hayes, Billie Burke, Peter Lorre, Boris Karloff (as Jonathan Brewster), Orson Bean, Edward Everett Horton; **Network**: CBS; **Running Time**: 60 minutes.

Down You Go (January 1955)
Format: Quiz/Panel; **Host**: Dr. Bergen Evans; **Panelists**: Professor Robert Breen, Toni Gilman, Carmelita Pope, Fran Allison, Phil Rizzuto, Boris Karloff; **Network**: Dumont; **Running Time**: 30 minutes.

The Donald O'Connor Texaco Show (February 19, 1955)
Format: Situation Comedy; **Performers**: Donald O'Connor, Sid Miller, Joyce Smight, Boris Karloff; **Music**: "The Human Thing to Do" and "'Arry and 'Erbert" sung by Karloff; **Network**: NBC; **Running Time**: 30 minutes.

The Elgin TV Hour (February 22, 1955)
Format: Dramatic Anthology; **Title**: "The Sting of Death" (based on "A Taste of Honey" by H.F. Heard) (Karloff as Mr. Mycroft); **Network**: ABC; **Running Time**: 60 minutes.

Max Liebman Presents (March 12, 1955)
Format: Musical Variety; **Title**: "A Connecticut Yankee in King Arthur's Court" (Based on the 1927 Musical by Richard Rodgers and Lorenz Hart, From the Novel by Mark Twain); **Writer**: Alvin Sapinsley; **Performers**: Eddie Albert, Janet Blair, Boris Karloff (as King Arthur); **Music**: "Knight's Refrain" and "You Always Love the Same Girl" sung by Karloff; **Network**: NBC; **Running Time**: 90 minutes.

Who Said That? (April 30, 1955)
Format: Quiz/Panel; **Host**: John K.M. McCaffrey; **Panelists**: Boris Karloff, Jimmy Cannon, Harriet Van Horne; **Network**: Dumont; **Running Time**: 30 minutes.

General Electric Theatre (May 1, 1955)
Format: Dramatic Anthology; **Host**: Ronald Reagan; **Title**: "Mr. Blue Ocean"; **Performers**: Susan Strasberg, Eli Wallach, Anthony Perkins, Bramwell Fletcher, Boris Karloff; **Network**: CBS; **Running Time**: 30 minutes.

I've Got a Secret (August 24, 1955)
Format: Quiz/Panel; **Host**: Garry Moore; **Panelists**: Bill Cullen, Kitty Carlisle, Boris Karloff; **Network**: CBS; **Running Time**: 30 minutes.

The U.S. Steel Hour (August 31, 1955)
Format: Dramatic Anthology; **Title**: "Counterfeit"; **Performers Included**: Boris Karloff (as George Redford); **Network**: CBS; **Running Time**: 60 minutes.

The Alcoa Hour (April 15, 1956)
Format: Dramatic Anthology; **Title**: "Even the Weariest River" by Alvin Sapinsley; **Performers**: Franchot Tone, Christopher Plummer, Boris Karloff (as Don Dixon); **Network**: NBC; **Running Time**: 60 minutes.

The Amazing Dunninger (July 18, 1956)
Format: "Mind-Reading"; **Network**: ABC; **Running Time**: 30 minutes.

Frankie Lane Time (August 8, 1956)
Format: Musical Variety; **Performers**: Boris Karloff, the Edith Barstow Dancers; **Music**: the Mellow Marks, the Russ Case Orchestra; **Network**: CBS; **Running Time**: 60 minutes.

The Ernie Kovacs Show (August 13, 1956)
Format: Comedy Variety; **Performers**: Bill Wendell, Peter Hanley, Henry Lascoe, Al Kelly, Barbara Loden, Boris Karloff; **Network**: NBC; **Running Time**: 60 minutes.

Climax! (September 6, 1956)
Format: Dramatic Anthology; **Host**: William Lundigan; **Title**: "Bury Me Later" by H.F.M. Prescott; **Performers**: Angela Lansbury, Torin Thatcher, Boris Karloff (as the Vicar); **Network**: CBS; **Running Time**: 60 minutes.

Playhouse 90 (October 25, 1956)
Format: Dramatic Anthology; **Title**: "Rendezvous in Black" by Cornell Woolrich; **Director**: John Frankenheimer; **Performers**: Franchot Tone, Laraine Day, Boris Karloff (as Ward Allen), Tom Drake, Viveca Lindfors; **Network**: CBS; **Running Time**: 90 minutes.

The Red Skelton Show (November 27, 1956)
Format: Comedy Variety; **Network**: CBS; **Running Time**: 30 minutes.

The $64,000 Question (December 11, 18, 25, 1956)
Format: Quiz; **Category**: Children's Fairy Tales (Karloff won $32,000); **Network**: CBS; **Running Time**: 30 minutes.

The Lux Show Starring Rosemary Clooney (January 9, 1957)
Format: Musical Variety; **Music**: "You'd Be Surprised" sung by Karloff, Paul Kelly and the Modernaires, Frank deVol and His Orchestra; **Network**: NBC; **Running Time**: 30 minutes.

The Hallmark Hall of Fame (February 10, 1957)
Format: Dramatic Anthology; **Title**: "The Lark" by Lillian Hellman, Based on *L'Alouette* by Jean Anouilh; **Adaptation**: James Costigan; **Performers**: Julie Harris (as Joan of Arc); Boris Karloff (as Bishop Cauchon); Basil Rathbone (as the Inquisitor), Eli Wallach, Denholm Elliot, Jack Warden; **Network**: NBC; **Running Time**: 90 minutes.

Lux Video Theatre (April 25, 1957)
Format: Dramatic Anthology; **Title**: "The Man Who Played God" (Based on the Play *The Silent Voice* by Jules Eckert Goodman and the 1932 film version starring George Arliss); **Performers Included**: Boris Karloff (as Montgomery Royle); **Network**: NBC; **Running Time**: 30 minutes.

Kate Smith Special (April 28, 1957)
Format: Musical Variety; **Music**: "September Song" sung by Karloff; **Network**: ABC; **Running Time**: 60 minutes.

The Dinah Shore Chevy Show (May 17, 1957)
Format: Musical Variety; **Performers**: Boris Karloff, the Tony Charmoli Dancers; **Music**: "Mama Look a' Boo Boo" sung by Karloff, the Skylarks, the Harry Zimmerman Orchestra; **Network**: NBC; **Running Time**: 60 minutes.

The Dinah Shore Chevy Show (October 27, 1957)
Format: Musical Variety; **Performers**: Boris Karloff, the Tony Charmoli Dancers; **Music**: Karloff, the Steiner Brothers, the Skylarks, the Harry Zimmerman Orchestra; **Network**: NBC; **Running Time**: 60 minutes.

The Lux Show Starring Rosemary Clooney (October 31, 1957)
Format: Musical Variety; **Music**: Boris Karloff, Paul Kelly and the Modernaires, Frank DeVol and His Orchestra; **Network**: NBC; **Running Time**: 30 minutes.

Suspicion (December 9, 1957)
Format: Suspense Anthology; **Host**: Dennis O'Keefe; **Title**: "The Deadly Game" by Friedrich Durrenmatt; **Performers**: Gary Merrill, Joseph Wiseman, Boris Karloff (as Judge Winthrop Gelsey); **Network**: NBC; **Running Time**: 60 minutes.

The Betty White Show (February 12, 1958)
Format: Comedy Variety; **Guests**: Buster Keaton, Boris Karloff; **Regular Performers**: Johnny Jacobs, Del Moore, Reta Shaw, Frank Nelson; **Music**: Frank DeVol and His Orchestra; **Network**: ABC; **Running Time**: 30 minutes.

Telephone Time (February 25, 1958)
Format: Dramatic Anthology; **Host**: Dr. Frank Baxter; **Title**: "Vestris" (Karloff as Dr. Pierre); **Network**: ABC; **Running Time**: 30 minutes.

Shirley Temple's Storybook (March 5, 1958)
Format: Children's Anthology; **Title**: "The Legend of Sleepy Hollow" by Washington Irving; **Narrator**: Boris Karloff; **Performers**: Shirley Temple, John Ericson, Jules Munshin, Russell Collins; **Network**: NBC; **Running Time**: 60 minutes.

Studio One (March 31, 1958)
Format: Dramatic Anthology; **Title**: "Shadow of a Genius" by Jerome Rise; **Performers**: Eva Le Galliene, Skip Homeier, Boris Karloff (as Professor Theodore Koenig), **Network**: CBS; **Running Time**: 60 minutes.

The Jack Paar Show (aka *The Tonight Show*) (April 22, 1958)
Format: Talk; **Regular Guests**: Hugh Downs, Dodi Goodman; **Music**: Jose Melis and His Orchestra; **Network**: NBC; **Running Time**: 105 minutes.

Playhouse 90 (November 6, 1958)
Format: Dramatic Anthology; **Title**: "Heart of Darkness" by Joseph Conrad; **Performers**: Roddy McDowall, Eartha Kitt, Oscar Homolka, Boris Karloff (as Captain Kurtz); **Network**: CBS; **Running Time**: 90 minutes.

This Is Your Life (November 13, 1958)
Format: Testimonial; **Host**: Ralph Edwards; **Guests**: Boris Karloff, Evelyn Karloff, Sara Jane Karloff, Jack Pierce, Frank Brink, Jim Laker, Geoffrey Taylor, Jim Edwards, J. Warren Bacon, Howard Lindsay, Russell Crouse; **Network**: NBC; **Running Time**: 30 minutes.

The Veil (1958) [unsold series]
Format: Suspense Anthology; **Titles**: "The Crystal Ball," "The Doctor," "Genesis," "What Happened to Peggy?" others; **Director**: Herbert L. Strock; **Producer**: Frank P. Bibas; **Executive Producer**: Hal Roach, Jr.; **Writer**: Fred Schiller; **Music**: Leon Klatzkin; **Host**: Boris Karloff; **Performers**: Boris Karloff, Booth Coleman, Roxanne Berard, Leonard Penn, Albert Carrier, Tony Travis, Argentine Brunett, Elvira Curci,

Paul Bryar, Gretchen Thomas, Robert Griffin, Ray Montgomery, Gene Collins, Vici Raaf, Connie Van, Bruno Della Santina, Dominick Delgarde, Ernest Sarrachino, Laurrie Perreau, Inez Palange, Dominica Hauser, Harry Bartell, Robert Hardy, Jennifer Paine, Patrick Macnee, Betty Fairfax, Terence De Marney, Donald Lawton, Kendrick Huxham; **Production Company**: Hal Roach Studios; **Network**: Series unsold; **Running Time**: 30 minutes.

Note: Twelve episodes (each featuring Karloff in a different role) were shot by Hal Roach, Jr., who declared bankruptcy before he was able to sell them to any of the major networks. Later, the series was edited into three four-episode features, *The Veil*, *Jack the Ripper*, and *Destination: Nightmare*, which have been broadcast on cable television and sold as pre-recorded videotapes.

The Gale Storm Show (January 31, 1959)
Format: Situation Comedy; **Title**: "It's Murder, My Dear"; **Performers**: Gale Storm, Zasu Pitts, Roy Roberts, Jimmy Fairfax, Boris Karloff; **Network**: CBS; **Running Time**: 30 minutes.

General Electric Theatre (May 17, 1959)
Format: Dramatic Anthology; **Host**: Ronald Reagan; **Title**: "Indian Giver"; **Performers**: Edgar Buchanan, Carmen Mathews, Jackie Coogan, Boris Karloff (as Henry Church); **Network**: CBS; **Running Time**: 30 minutes.

Playhouse 90 (February 9, 1960)
Format: Dramatic Anthology; **Title**: "To the Sound of Trumpets"; **Performers**: Judith Anderson, Stephen Boyd, Dolores Hart, Sam Jaffe, Boris Karloff (as Guibert); **Network**: CBS; **Running Time**: 90 minutes.

The Du Pont Show of the Month (March 5, 1960)
Format: Dramatic Anthology; **Title**: "Treasure Island" by Robert Louis Stevenson; **Adaptation**: Michael Dyne; **Director**: Daniel Petrie; **Producer**: David Susskind; **Performers**: Hugh Griffith, Max Adrian, Michael Gough, Boris Karloff (as Billy Bones), Barry Morse, Richard O'Sullivan, Douglas Campbell, George Rose, John Colicos, George Mathews, Tim O'Connor, Tom Clancy, Betty Sinclair, Woodroy Parfrey; **Production Company**: Talent Associates; **Network**: CBS; **Running Time**: 90 minutes.

Hollywood Sings (April 3, 1960)
Format: Musical Variety; **Host**: Boris Karloff; **Guests**: Tammy Grimes, Eddie Albert; **Network**: NBC.

Upgreen and At 'Em, or a Maiden Nearly Over (Spring 1960)
Format: Charity Performance of a 19th-century Melodrama about Cricket; **Performers**: the Company of Lord's Taverners; **Guest**: Boris Karloff (as the Faithful Butler); **Network**: British television.

Thriller (1960-62) [series]
Format: Suspense Anthology; **Executive Producer**: Hubbell Robinson; **Producers**: Fletcher Markle, William Frye, Maxwell Shane; **Directors**: Arthur Hiller, Mitchell Leisen, Maxwell Shane, Ray Nazarro, Douglas Heyes, John Brahm, Gerald Mayer, Maurice Geraghty, Herman Hoffman, Fletcher Markle, Herschel Daugherty, Richard Carlson, Jules Bricken, Lazlo Benedak, Ted Post, Ray Milland, Ida Lupino, Paul Henreid, John Newland, Boris Sobelman, Jess Carneol, William Claxton, Robert Florey, John English; **Story Consultant**: James P. Cavanagh; **Writers Included**: Maxwell Shane, Douglas Heyes, Donald S. Sanford, Philip MacDonald, Barre Lyndon, Robert Bloch, Cornell Woolrich, Richard Matheson, Hugh Walpole; **Director of Photography**: John L. Warren; **Makeup**: Jack Barron; **Music**: Pete Rugolo, Jerry Goldsmith, Morton Stevens; **Host**: Boris Karloff (69 episodes); **Guest Stars and Players Included**: Leslie Neilsen, Everett Sloane, Rip Torn, Alan Napier, Cloris Leachman, Ellen Corby, Elisha Cook, Jr., Conrad Nagel, Mary Tyler Moore, Beverly Garland, Warren Oates, Frank Albertson, Werner Klemperer, Jack Weston, Henry Daniell, William Shatner, Nehemiah Persoff, Torin Thatcher, Robert Vaughn, John Abbott, John Ireland, John Williams, Macdonald Carey, Glenn Strange, Hazel Court, Natalie Schafer, Tom Helmore, Ronald Howard, Tom Poston, Elizabeth Montgomery, John Carradine, Jane Greer, Otto Kruger, Leo G. Carroll, Ursula Andress, Ramon Novarro, David Janssen, Denver Pyle, Richard Carlson; **Titles**: "The Twisted Image," "Child's Play," "Worse Than Murder," "Mark of a Hand," "Rose's Last Summer," "The Guilty Men," "The Purple Room," "The Watcher," "Girl with a Secret," "The Prediction" (Karloff as Clayton Mace), "The Fatal Impulse," "The Big Blackout," "Knock Three-One-Two," "Man in the Middle," "The Cheaters," "The Hungry Glass," "The Poisoner," "Man in a Cage," "Choose a Victim," "Hay-Fork and Bill-Hook," "The Merriweather File," "Fingers of Fear," "Well of Doom," "The Ordeal of Dr. Cordell," "Trio for

Terror," "Papa Benjamin," "A Late Date," "Yours Truly, Jack the Ripper," "The Devil's Ticket," "Parasite Mansion," "A Good Imagination," "Mr. George," "Terror in Teakwood," "The Prisoner in the Mirror," "Dark Legacy," "Pigeons from Hell," "The Grim Reaper," "What Beckoning Ghost?" "Guillotine," "The Premature Burial" (Karloff as Dr. Thorne), "The Weird Tailor," "God Grante That She Lye Stille," "Masquerade," "The Last of the Sommervilles" (Karloff as Dr. Farnham), "Letter to a Lover," "A Third for Pinochle," "The Closed Cabinet," "Dialogues with Death": (1) "Friend of the Dead" (Karloff as Pop Jenkins); (2) "Welcome Home" (Karloff as Colonel Jackson), "The Return of Andrew Bentley," "The Remarkable Mrs. Hawk," "Portrait Without a Face," "An Attractive Family," "Waxworks," "La Strega," "The Storm," "A Wig for Mrs. Devore," "The Hollow Watcher," "Cousin Tundifer," "The Incredible Dr. Markesan" (Karloff as Dr. Konrad Markesan), "Flowers of Evil," "Till Death Do Us Part," "The Bride Who Died Twice," "Kill My Love," "Man of Mystery," "The Innocent Bystanders," "The Lethal Ladies," "The Specialists"; **Network**: NBC; **Running Time**: 60 minutes.

Out of This World (1962) [Series]
Format: Science Fiction; **Creator**: Irene Shubik; **Producer**: Sydney Newman; **Host**: Boris Karloff; **Titles**: 13 Episodes, including "Dumb Martian" by John Wyndham (pilot), "The Yellow Pill" by Rog Phillips (adapted by Leon Griffiths), "Little Lost Robot" by Isaac Asimov (adapted by Leo Lehmann), "The Cold Equations" by Tom Godwin (adapted by Clive Exton), "Botany Bay" by Terry Nation, and "Imposter" by Philip K. Dick (adapted by Terry Nation); **Production Company**: BBC-TV (Great Britain); **Network**: ABC; **Running Time**: 60 minutes.

The Hallmark Hall of Fame (February 5, 1962)
Format: Dramatic Anthology; **Title**: "Arsenic and Old Lace" by Joseph L. Kesselring; **Performers**: Tony Randall (as Mortimer Brewster), Dorothy Stickney, Mildred Natwick, Boris Karloff (as Jonathan Brewster), George Voskovec, Tom Bosley; **Network**: NBC; **Running Time**: 90 minutes.

PM (February 12, 1962)
Format: Talk; **Host**: Mike Wallace; **Guests**: George Schaefer, Tony Randall, Ed Wynn, Maurice Evans, Julie Harris, Kim Hunter, Boris Karloff; **Network**: syndicated.

Theatre '62 (March 11, 1962)
Format: Dramatic Anthology; **Title**: "The Paradine Case" by Robert Hitchens (adapted by Robert Goldman); **Performers**: Richard Basehart, Viveca Lindfors, Robert Webber, Boris Karloff (as Sir Simon Flaquer); **Network**: NBC; **Running Time**: 60 minutes.

The Dickie Henderson Show (June 1962)
Format: Variety; **Host**: Dickie Henderson; **Guest**: Boris Karloff; **Network**: British independent TV.

Route 66 (October 26, 1962)
Format: Drama; **Title**: "Lizard's Leg and Owlet's Wing"; **Performers**: Martin Milner, George Maharis, Lon Chaney, Jr. (as the Wolf Man and the Mummy), Peter Lorre, Boris Karloff (as the Frankenstein Monster); **Network**: CBS; **Running Time**: 60 minutes.

The Hy Gardner Show (March 3, 1963)
Format: Talk; **Guests**: Peter Lorre, Boris Karloff; **Network**: WOR.

Chronicle (December 25, 1963)
Format: Documentary; **Title**: "A Danish Fairy Tale" (the Life of Hans Christian Andersen); **Narrator**: Boris Karloff; **Network**: CBS; **Running Time**: 60 minutes.

The Garry Moore Show (April 21, 1964)
Format: Variety; **Guests**: Alan King, Dorothy Loudon, Boris Karloff, the Carol Henry Dancers; **Music**: the George Becker Singers, the Irwin Kostal Orchestra; **Network**: CBS; **Running Time**: 60 minutes.

The Tonight Show Starring Johnny Carson (June 1964)
Format: Talk; **Host**: Johnny Carson; **Guests Included**: Boris Karloff; **Network**: NBC.

The Entertainers (January 16, 1965)
Format: Variety; **Host**: Carol Burnett; **Guests**: Caterina Valente, Art Buchwald, Boris Karloff, the Peter Gennaro Dancers; **Music**: the Lee Hale Singers, the Harry Zimmerman Orchestra; **Network**: CBS; **Running Time**: 60 minutes.

Shindig (October 30, 1965)
Format: Rock 'n' Roll Music; **Guests**: Jimmy O'Neill, Ted Cassidy, Boris Karloff; **Music**: "The Peppermint Twist" recited by Karloff; **Network**: ABC; **Running Time**: 60 minutes.

The Wild Wild West (September 23, 1966)
Format: Western Adventure; **Title**: "Night of the Golden Cobra"; **Performers**: Robert Conrad, Ross Martin, Boris Karloff (as Singh); **Network**: CBS; **Running Time**: 60 minutes.

The Girl from U.N.C.L.E. (September 27, 1966)
Format: Spy Spoof; **Title**: "The Mother Muffin Affair"; **Performers**: Stefanie Powers, Noel Harrison, Leo G. Carroll, Randy Kirby, Boris Karloff (as Mother Muffin); **Network**: NBC; **Running Time**: 60 minutes.

How the Grinch Stole Christmas (December 18, 1966)
Format: Animated; **Director**: Chuck Jones; **Writer**: Theodor Geisel (Dr. Seuss); **Narrator**: Boris Karloff; **Network**: CBS; **Running Time**: 30 minutes.

I Spy (February 22, 1967)
Format: Adventure/Espionage; **Title**: "Mainly on the Plains"; **Director**: David Friedkin; **Producers and Writers**: Morton Fine and David Friedkin; **Executive Producer**: Sheldon Leonard; **Performers**: Robert Culp, Bill Cosby, Boris Karloff (as Don Ernesto Silvando), Carl Schell, Axel Darner, Mona Hamlin, Eduardo San Jose, Scott Miller, Felipe R. Armengol, Angel Jordan, Antonio Canal; **Network**: NBC; **Running Time**: 60 minutes.

The Red Skelton Show (September 24, 1968)
Format: Variety; **Guests**: Boris Karloff, Vincent Price, Spanky Wilson, James Millhollin, Jan Arvin, Melanie Alexander, the Tom Hansen Dancers; **Music**: "The Two of Us" sung by Karloff and Price, the Alan Copeland Singers, the David Rose Orchestra; **Network**: CBS; **Running Time**: 30 minutes.

The Jonathan Winters Show (October 30, 1968)
Format: Comedy Variety; Guests: Agnes Moorehead, Boris Karloff; **Regular Performers**: Abby Dalton, Dick Curtis, Pamela Rodgers, Jerry Pannow, Cliffe Arquette, Alice Ghostley, Paul Lynde, Georgene Barnes; **Music**: "It Was a Very Good Year" sung by Karloff, the Establishment, the Earl Browne Orchestra; **Network**: CBS; **Running Time**: 60 minutes.

The Name of the Game (November 29, 1968)
Format: adventure; **Title**: "The White Birch"; **Performers**: Gene Barry, Susan Saint James, Peter Deuel, Roddy McDowell, Ben Gazzara, Susan Oliver, Richard Jaeckel, Lilia Skala, Jean-Pierre Aumont, Beth Leslie, Boris Karloff (as Orlov); **Network**: NBC; **Running Time**: 90 minutes.

Appendix E

Recordings

Caedmon Spoken-Word Recordings

William Shakespeare: Cymbeline (Caedmon SRS 236)
Director: Howard O. Sackler; **Cast**: Boris Karloff (Cymbeline, King of Britain), Claire Bloom (Imogen), Pamela Brown (Queen), John Fraser (Posthumus Leonatus), Alan Dobie (Iachimo), Paul Daneman (Cloten), Walter Hudd (Balarius), John Dane (Guiderius), Robin Palmer (Arviragus), Wallas Eaton (Philario/Tribune/a Roman Captain/First Brother), James Cairncross (Caius Lucius), Stephen Moore (Pisanio), Harold Lang (a French Gentleman/First Jailer), Eric House (Cornelius/First British Captain/First Senator/Sicillus), Eric Jones (a Soothsayer/Second Gentleman/Second Brother), Douglas Muir (Second Jailer/First Gentleman/Second Lord), Richard Dare (Second Senator/Messenger/First Lord), Derek Godfrey (Jupiter), Judith South (Lady/Mother to Posthumus); **Music**: Owen Wayne (Countertenor), Desmond Dupre (Lute), Colin Chambers (Flute), Leslie Pearson (Organ), Bill Webster (Double Bass), Eric Allen (Percussion).

Rudyard Kipling: Just So Stories and Other Tales (Caedmon TC 1038)
Includes: "How the Whale Got His Throat," "How the Camel Got His Hump," "How the Rhinoceros Got His Skin," "The Jungle Book: Mowgli's Brothers" (abridged).

Kenneth Grahame: The Reluctant Dragon (Caedmon TC 1074)

Lewis Carroll: The Hunting of the Snark / Robert Browning: The Pied Piper (Caedmon TC 1075)

Rudyard Kipling: The Elephant's Child and Other Stories (Caedmon TC 1088)
Includes: "The Elephant's Child," "The Sing-Song of Old Man Kangaroo," "The Beginning of the Armadillos," "How the Leopard Got His Spots."

Mother Goose (Caedmon TC 1091)
Performers: Cyril Ritchard, Celeste Holm, Boris Karloff; **Includes:** 69 fairy tales; **Music**: Hershy Kay.

Rudyard Kipling: How Fear Came (Caedmon TC 1100)

Hans Christian Andersen: The Ugly Duckling and Other Tales (Caedmon TC 1109 [1959])
Includes: "The Ugly Duckling," "The Shepherdess and the Chimney-Sweep," "The Princess and the Pea," "The Collar," "Clod-Poll," "The Fir Tree."

Hans Christian Andersen: The Little Match Girl and Other Tales (Caedmon TC 1117)
Translator: Reginald Spink; **Includes**: "The Swineherd," "The Top and the Ball," "The Red Shoes," "Thumbelina," "The Little Match Girl."

Charles Dickens: The Pickwick Papers (Caedmon TC 1121)
Performers: Boris Karloff, Lewis Casson; **Includes**: "Mr. Pickwick's Christmas" and "The Story of the Goblins Who Stole a Sexton."

The Three Little Pigs and Other Fairy Tales (Caedmon TC 1129)
Includes: "Jack and the Beanstalk," "The Three Sillies," "Hereafterthis," "The Old Woman and Her Pig," "Henny Penny," "The Three Little Pigs," "King of the Cats," "The Three Bears."

Rudyard Kipling: The Cat That Walked by Himself and Other Just So Stories (Caedmon TC 1139)
Includes: "The Cat That Walked by Himself," "The Butterfly That Stamped," "How the First Letter Was Written."
Note: Karloff received a "Best Children's Album" Grammy Award nomination for this recording.

Rudyard Kipling: Toomai of the Elephants (Caedmon TC 1176)

Let's Listen Stories (Caedmon TC 1182)
Performers: Julie Harris, Boris Karloff, Gwen Verdon; **Includes**: "Petunia Beware" by Roger Duvoisin, "The Red Carpet" by Rex Parkin, Six Fables by Aesop, "Six Foolish Fishermen" by Benjamin Elkin, "The Pony Engine" by Doris Garn, "Maxie" by Virginia Kahl.

Rudyard Kipling: Gunga Din and Other Poems (Caedmon TC 1193)
Performers: Boris Karloff, Edward Woodward, Murray Melvin, Ronald Fraser, Nigel Davenport; **Includes**: "The Law of the Jungle," "Recessional," "Song of the Galley-Slaves," "To Thomas Atkins," "The Way Through the Woods," "The White Man's Burden," "A Song of the English," "The Song of the Dead, II," "The Ballad of East and West," "Gunga Din," "The Ladies," "Fuzzy-Wuzzy," "Mandalay," "Tommy," "Danny Deever."

Aesop: Aesop Fables (Caedmon TC 1221)
Includes: "The Ant and the Grasshopper," "The Fox and the Lion," "The Oak and the Reed," "The Wolf and the Crane," "The Vain Jackdaw," "The Mountain in Labor," "The Old Hound," "The Cock and the Jewel," "The Man and the Satyr," "The Flies and the Honey-Pot," "Mercury and the Woodman," "The Tortoise and the Eagle," "The Shepherd Boy and the Wolf," "The Ass and the Grasshopper," "The Fox and the Goat," "The Hare and the Tortoise," "The Frog and the Ox," "The Fox and the Grapes," "The Dog and the Shadow," "The Cow and the Pitcher," "The Country Mouse and the Town Mouse," "The Travellers and the Bear," "The Gnat and the Bull," "The Lion and His Three Counsellors," "The Eagle and the Arrow," "The Wind and the Sun," "The Mice in Council," "The Lion in Love," "The Hare and the Hound," "The One-Eyed Doe," "Hercules and the Wagoner," "The Lioness," "The Angler and the Little Fish," "The Farmer and Her Sons," "The Country Maid and Her Milk Can," "The Thief and His Mother," "The Goose with the Golden Eggs," "The Old Man and Death," "The Boy Bathing," "Venus and the Cat," "The Boys and the Frogs," "The Miller, His Son, and Their Ass."

Classics of English Poetry for Elementary Curriculum (Caedmon TC 1301)
Performers: Jeremy Brett, Katharine Cornell, Ronald Fraser, George Grizzard, Boris Karloff, James Mason, Frederick O'Neal, Ralph Richardson, Cyril Ritchard; **Includes**: "The Rime of the Ancient Mariner" by Samuel Taylor Coleridge; "The Lay of the Last Minstrel" ("Breathes There a Man") and "Lochinvar" by Sir Walter Scott; "How They Brought the Good News from Ghent to Aix," "Incident of the French Camp," and "My Last Duchess" by Robert Browning; "The Owl and the Pussycat" by Edward Lear; "How Do I Love Thee?" by Elizabeth Barrett Browning; "The Charge of the Light Brigade" by Alfred, Lord Tennyson; "Gunga Din" and "The Law of the Jungle" by Rudyard Kipling; "The Highwayman" by Alfred Noyes.

The Pony Engine and Other Stories for Children (Caedmon TC 1355)
Performers: Boris Karloff, Julie Harris, David Wayne; **Includes**: "The Pony Engine" by Doris Garn, "The Old Woman and Her Pig" and "The Country Mouse and the Town Mouse" by Aesop, "The Story of Minikin and Manikin" by Louis Untermeyer, "Silly Billy" and "Six Foolish Fishermen" by Benjamin Elkin, "The Little Boy with the Long Name" by Bryna Ivens Untermeyer, and "The Three Billy-Goats Gruff" by the Brothers Grimm.

Rudyard Kipling: How the Alphabet Was Made and Other Just So Stories (Caedmon TC 1361)
Performers: Boris Karloff, Anthony Quayle; **Includes**: "How the Alphabet Was Made," "How the First Letter Was Written," and "The Crab That Played with the Sea."

Other Spoken-Word Recordings

Washington Irving: The Legend of Sleepy Hollow and Rip Van Winkle (Pickwick CR-32/reissue SPC-5156)
Arranger and Producer: Ralph Stein; **Writers**: Sid and Helen Frank.

Michael Avallone: Tales of the Frightened, Volume One (Mercury 60815 [1963])
Michael Avallone: Tales of the Frightened, Volume Two (Mercury 60816 [1963])

Producer: Lyle Kenyon Engel; **Includes**: "The Man in the Raincoat," "The Deadly Dress," "The Hand of Fate," "Don't Lose Your Head," "Call at Midnight," "Just Inside the Cemetery," "The Fortune Teller," "The Vampire Sleeps," "Mirror of Death," "Never Kick a Black Cat," "The Ladder," "Nightmare!" "Voice from the Grave," "Theda is Death," "The Barking Dog," "Defilers of the Tombs," "Terror in the Window," "Tom, Dick, and Horror," "Portrait in Hell," "The Graveyard Nine," "Say Goodnight to Mr. Sporko," "Beware the Bird," "The Phantom Soldier," "Some Things Shouldn't Be Seen," "You Can Take It with You," "Children of the Devil."

Dr. Seuss: How the Grinch Stole Christmas (MGM S-901/Leo the Lion S-901 [1967])
Note: Karloff received a "Best Children's Album" Grammy Award for this recording.

Best-Loved Fairy Tales (Childcraft CLP 1206)

Prokofiev: Peter and the Wolf (Vanguard VRS-1208/VSP-2010/reissue SRV-174)

Theatrical Soundtracks

Joseph Kesselring: Arsenic and Old Lace (Command Performance LP5)

J.M. Barrie: Peter Pan (Columbia OL 4312/J-1526 [EP][1950]/reissue AOL-4312)
Presenters: Peter Lawrence and R.L. Stevens; **Director**: John Burrell; **Associate Director**: Wendy Toye; **Recording Director**: Robert Lewis Shayon; **Songs**: Leonard Bernstein ("The Pirate Song" and "The Plank" sung by Karloff; "Who Am I?" "Build My House," and "Peter, Peter," sung by Marcia Henderson); **Incidental Music**: Alec Wilder; **Musical Conductor**: Ben Steinberg; **Record Adaptation**: Henry Walsh; **Narrator**: Torin Thatcher; **Cast**: Jean Arthur (Peter Pan), Boris Karloff (Mr. Darling/Captain Hook), Peg Hillins (Mrs. Darling), Marcia Henderson (Wendy), Jack Dimond (John), Charles Taylor (Michael), Norman Shelly (Nana), Lee Barnett (Tootles), Richard Knox, Philip Hepburn (Curly), Charles Brill, Edward Benjamin (the Twins), Buzzy Martin (Nibs), Joe E. Marks (Smee), David Kurlan (Starkey), Will Scholz (Jukes), Nehemiah Persoff (Cecco), Harry Allen (Mullins), John Dennis (Noodler), William Marshall (Cookson), Vincent Beck (Whibbles).

Film Soundtracks

Mad Monster Party (RCA [1966])

The Daydreamer (Columbia OL-6540/05-2940 [1966])

Special Release

An Evening with Boris Karloff and His Friends (Decca DL 74833 [1967])
Producers and Writers: Verne Langdon, Milt Larsen, and Forrest J Ackerman; **Narrator**: Boris Karloff; **Original Music**: William Loose; **Includes**: Soundtrack excerpts from *Dracula* (1931), *Frankenstein* (1931), *The Mummy* (1932), *The Bride of Frankenstein* (1935), *Son of Frankenstein* (1939), *The Wolf Man* (1941), *House of Frankenstein* (1944).

Appendix F

Published Writings

Karloff, Boris. "Cricket in California..." *The Screen Player*, 15 May 1934.

Karloff, Boris. *Film Weekly*, 18 April 1936.

Karloff, Boris. "Houses I Have Haunted," *Liberty*, 4 October 1941.

Karloff, Boris. "Foreword." In *Drawn and Quartered*. Drawn by Charles Addams. New York: Random House, 1942.

Karloff, Boris, ed. *Tales of Terror*. New York: World Publishing Company, 1943.

Karloff, Boris, ed. *And the Darkness Falls*. New York: World Publishing Company, 1946.

Karloff, Boris. "My Life as a Monster," *Films and Filming*, November 1957.

Karloff, Boris. "Oaks from Acorns," *Screen Actor*, October-November 1960.

Karloff, Boris, with Arlene and Howard Eisenberg. "Memoirs of a Monster," *Saturday Evening Post*, 3 November 1962.

Karloff, Boris. "How Not to Be a Full-Time Bogeyman," *Reader's Digest*, January 1964.

Karloff, Boris, ed. *The Boris Karloff Horror Anthology*. New York: Avon Books, 1965.

Bibliography

Primary Sources

Interviews and Oral Histories

Beckham, Bob. Reminiscence. Montecito, California, March 1996.

Benton, Douglas. Reminiscence for Gordon Shriver, 4 March 1986.

Bogdanovich, Peter. Interview by Van Ness Films. Beverly Hills, California, 4 January 1995.

Bradbury, Ray. Telephone conversation with Scott Allen Nollen, 17 April 1996.

Brandon, Henry. Interview by Scott Allen Nollen. St. Paul, Minnesota, July 1988.

Brandon, Henry. Telephone interview by Scott Allen Nollen, 4 March 1989.

Coleman, Bernard. Reminiscence. London, England, 21 May 1996.

Edwards, Ralph. Discussion with Sue Clark Chadwick, October 1996.

Farrell, Midge Van Buren. Conversation with Scott Allen Nollen. Hollywood, California,
    11 November 1996.

Harris, Julie. Telephone interview by Scott Allen Nollen, 11 May 1996.

James, Rosamund, and Elisabeth Crowley. Conversation with Sara Jane Karloff and William Sparkman.
    England, June 1996.

Jordan, Fred. Conversation with Buddy Barnett, Sara Jane Karloff, Harold N. Nollen, Scott
    Allen Nollen, and William J. Sparkman. Beverly Hills, California, 12 November 1996.

Karloff, Boris. Interview. Chateau Marmont, Hollywood, California, 1957.

Karloff, Boris. Interview. BBC, London, 1962.

Karloff, Boris. Interview by Colin Edwards. Carmel, California, circa 1963.

Karloff, Boris. Interview by the BBC. London, circa 1964.

Karloff, Evelyn. Interview by Michael Pointon. London, England, 1991.

Karloff, Evelyn. Telephone conversation with Scott Allen Nollen, August 1991.

Karloff, Sara Jane. Interview by Van Ness Films. Rancho Mirage, California, 7 and 12
    December 1994.

Karloff, Sara Jane. Interview by Scott Allen Nollen and Barton H. Aikens. Rancho Mirage,
    California, 6 May 1995.

Karloff, Sara Jane. Interviews by Scott Allen Nollen. Tahoma, California, 27 July-1 August
    1996.

Karloff, Sara Jane. Discussions with Scott Allen Nollen and Harold N. Nollen. Rancho Mirage and Los
    Angeles, California, 9-16 November 1996.

Kennard, Arthur. Interview by Van Ness Films, 31 January 1995.

Lansbury, Angela. Telephone interview by Scott Allen Nollen, 17 July 1996.

Lee, Anna. Telephone interview by Scott Allen Nollen, 12 August 1989.

Lee, Christopher. Interview, 1969.

Lee, Christopher. Conversation with Sara Jane Karloff and William Sparkman, June 1996.

Lindsay, Cynthia. Interview by Van Ness Films, 23 January 1995.

McDowall, Roddy. Interview by Van Ness Films, 4 January 1995.

Mayo, Virginia. Reminiscence, *The Secret Life of Walter Mitty* laserdisc. Pioneer Special Edition, 1994.

Price, Vincent. Interview by Scott Allen Nollen. Omaha, Nebraska, March 1980.

Stuart, Gloria. Reminiscence, *The Old Dark House* laserdisc. Image Entertainment, Inc., 1996.

Walsh, Eugene. Reminiscence, 30 June 1971.

Wise, Robert. Reminiscence, *The Body Snatcher*, side 11 of "The Val Lewton Collection" six laserdisc
    set. Image Entertainment, Inc., 1995.

Wise, Robert. Interview by Van Ness Films. Los Angeles, California, 4 January 1995.

Letters, Postcards, and Telegrams

Abel, Mrs. Walter. Letter to Evelyn Karloff, 3 February 1969.

Albert, Eddie. Letter to Scott Allen Nollen, 7 May 1996.

Almirall, Lloyd. Telegram to Boris Karloff, 11 November 1941.

Baxter, Ann. Letter to Evelyn Karloff, 21 February 1969.

Beaufort, Francesca. Letter to Evelyn Karloff, 4 February 1969.

Beckham, Mae, and Rob Beckham and Bob Beckham. Telegram to Dorothy Karloff, 23 November 1938.

Beckham, Mae. Letter to Louise Stine, Autumn 1941.

Berger, William. Letter to Lynne Anderson Warren, 20 June 1968.

Bloch, Robert. Letter to Evelyn Karloff, 4 February 1969.

Bloomfield, S. Letter to Evelyn Karloff, 17 April 1969.

Bogdanovich, Peter. Telegram to Evelyn Karloff, 3 February 1969.

Bogdanovich, Peter. Letter to Evelyn Karloff, 9 February 1969.

Bossert, Derek. Letter to Evelyn Karloff, 22 October 1969.

Boulton, J.A. Letter to Evelyn Karloff, 26 February 1969.

Boulton, J.A. Letter to Evelyn Karloff, 26 March 1969.

Bradbury, Ray. Letter to Scott Allen Nollen, 10 May 1996.

Bradshaw, A A. Letter to John L. Dales, 24 July 1970.

Brandon, Henry. Letter to Scott Allen Nollen, April 1989.

Brink, Frank. Letter to Evelyn Karloff, 3 February 1969.

Brink, Frank. Letter to Evelyn Karloff, 27 July 1990.

Brink, Frank. Letter to Gordon Shriver, 27 July 1990.

Bruce, "Bunny." Letter to Evelyn Karloff, 4 February 1969.

Bryson, Helen. Letter to Evelyn Karloff, 22 July 1971.

Cantor, Eddie, Kenneth Thomson, and the Board of Directors of the Screen Actors Guild. Telegram to Boris Karloff, 26 December 1940.

Chadwick, Sue Clark. Letter to Scott Allen Nollen, 14 October 1996.

Children's Blood Foundation, Inc. Card to Evelyn Karloff, 17 February 1969.

Clarke, Mae. Letter to Evelyn Karloff, 4 February 1969.

Cleaves, Patricia. Letter to Evelyn Karloff, 9 April 1969.

Coe, Elsa. Letter to Evelyn Karloff, 5 February 1969.

Cole, Adrian. Letter to Evelyn Karloff, 9 February 1969.

Coleman, Bernard. Letter to Evelyn Karloff, 4 February 1969.

Coleman, Bernard. Letter to Scott Allen Nollen, 21 May 1996.

Coleman, Bernard. Letter to Scott Allen Nollen, 11 July 1996.

Cornell, Katherine. Telegram to Evelyn Karloff, 3 February 1969.

Crapp, Helen. Letter to Evelyn Karloff, 10 April 1969.

Crawford, Joan. Letter to Evelyn Karloff, 5 February 1969.

Crowley, Elisabeth. Letter to Scott Allen Nollen, 28 February 1997.

Edgley, Roy. Letter to Evelyn Karloff, 7 February 1969.

Dales, John L. Letter to Boris Karloff, 21 July 1960.

Dales, John L. Letter to Evelyn Karloff, 4 February 1969.

Dales, John L. Letter to Evelyn Karloff, 12 May 1969.

Dales, John L. Letter to William Kirk, 30 June 1969.

Dales, John L. Letter to Evelyn Karloff, 6 June 1972.

Dunlap, R. Scott. Telegram to Boris Karloff. 25 November 1938.

Edwards, Ralph. Letter to Evelyn Karloff, 4 February 1969.

Evans, Maurice. Letter to Evelyn Karloff, 6 February 1969.

Farrell, Midge Van Buren. Letter to Evelyn Karloff, 28 May 1969.

Foster, Alan. Letter to Evelyn Karloff, 5 February 1969.

Freeman, Paul. Letter to Evelyn Karloff, 6 March 1969.

Gabriel, Lt. Colonel Arnald D. Letter to Evelyn Karloff, 5 February 1969.

Geisel, Theodor ("Dr. Seuss"). Letter to Evelyn Karloff, 7 February 1969.

Gerard, Jennifer. Letter to Evelyn Karloff, 10 February 1969.

Gerard, Lillian. Letter to Evelyn Karloff, 20 February 1969.

Gerard, Philip R. Letter to Evelyn Karloff, 20 February 1969.

Ghaibi, Poura. Letter to Evelyn Karloff, 12 April 1969.

Gielgud, Sir John. Letter to Scott Allen Nollen, 23 April 1996.

Gilbey, Jenny Bruce. Letter to Evelyn Karloff, 4 February 1969.

Gleason, Lucile and James. Telegram to Dorothy Karloff, 23 November 1938.

Goldsworthy, Mrs. I. Letter to Evelyn Karloff, 13 February 1969.

Goodwin, Ella. Letter to Louise Stine. 30 December 1935.

Gretzer, Don. Letter to Edd X. Russell. 29 March 1957.

Guinness, Alec. Letter to Evelyn Karloff, 12 April 1969.

Harris, Julie. Letter to Boris Karloff, 2 June 1956.

Harris, Julie. Letter to Scott Allen Nollen, 5 May 1996.

Hellman, Lillian. Letter to Boris Karloff, 11 June 1956.

Helmore, Mary. Letter to Evelyn Karloff, 4 February 1969.

Heston, Charlton. Telegram to Evelyn Karloff, 4 February 1969.

Hitchcock, Alma. Letter to Evelyn Karloff, 10 February 1969.

Hope, Francis. Letter to Evelyn Karloff, 20 February 1969.

Hope, Jennifer L. Letter to Evelyn Karloff, 12 April 1969.

Houlston, H.F. Letter to Evelyn Karloff, 10 April 1969.

Hughes, Gareth R. Letter to John L. Dales, 7 July 1972.

Hughes, Gareth R. Letter to Chester L. Migden, 25 April 1973.

Jackson, Charlie. Letter to Evelyn Karloff, 4 February 1969.

Jarman, Peter J. Letter to Evelyn Karloff, 4 February 1969.

"Joan." Letter to Evelyn Karloff, 3 February 1969.

Jones, Chuck. Letter to Evelyn Karloff, 5 February 1969.

Jordan, Fred. Letter to Scott Allen Nollen, 7 December 1996.

Karloff, Boris. Letter to Kenneth Thomson, 22 September 1935.

Karloff, Boris. Letter to Kenneth Thomson, 22 October 1935.

Karloff, Boris. Telegram to the Screen Actors Guild, 3 March 1936.

Karloff, Boris. Letter to Kenneth Thomson, 15 May 1936.

Karloff, Boris. Letter to Louise Stine, 26 May 1936.

Karloff, Boris. Telegram to Sara Jane Karloff, 19 August 1939.

Karloff, Boris. Letter to Louise Stine, 22 February 1941.

Karloff, Boris. Letter to Pat Somerset and Jack Dales, 23 February 1941.

Karloff, Boris. Letter to Louise Stine, 3 February 1942.

Karloff, Boris. Letter to Louise Stine, 20 March 1942.

Karloff, Boris. Letter to Louise Stine, 16 April 1942.

Karloff, Boris. Letter to the Screen Actors Guild, 20 November 1951.

Karloff, Boris. Letter to K-B Productions, Inc., 9 January 1958.

Karloff, Boris. Letter to Ken Orsatti, 25 May 1959.

Karloff, Boris. Letter to John L. Dales, 15 October 1959.

Karloff, Boris. Letter to John L. Dales, 18 July 1960.

Karloff, Dorothy. Letter to Louise Stine, 9 March 1933.

Karloff, Dorothy. Letter to Louise Stine, 14 March 1933.

Karloff, Dorothy. Letter to Louise Stine, 23 March 1933.

Karloff, Dorothy. Letter to Louise Stine, 30 March 1933.

Karloff, Dorothy, and Boris Karloff. Letter to Louise Stine, April 1933.

Karloff, Dorothy. Letter to Louise Stine, 4 May 1933.

Karloff, Dorothy. Letter to Louise Stine, February 1936.

Karloff, Dorothy. Letter to Louise Stine, 9 February 1936.

Karloff, Dorothy. Letter to Louise Stine, 21 February 1936.

Karloff, Dorothy. Letter to Louise Stine, 2 March 1936.

Karloff, Dorothy. Letter to Nancy Smith, 17 March 1936.

Karloff, Dorothy, and Boris Karloff. Letter to Louise Stine, 25 April 1936.

Karloff, Dorothy. Letter to Louise Stine, 9 May 1936.

Karloff, Dorothy, and Boris Karloff. Letter to Louise Stine, 4 June 1936.

Karloff, Dorothy. Letter to Louise Stine. 7 July 1936.

Karloff, Dorothy. Postcard to Louise Stine, 17 July 1936.

Karloff, Dorothy. Letter to Louise Stine, 18 July 1936.

Karloff, Dorothy, and Boris Karloff. Letter to Louise Stine, 22 July 1936.

Karloff, Dorothy, and Boris Karloff. Postcard to Louise Stine, 25 July 1936.

Karloff, Dorothy, and Boris Karloff. Letter to Louise Stine, 26 July 1936.

Karloff, Dorothy. Letter to Louise Stine, 30 July 1936.

Karloff, Dorothy. Letter to Louise Stine, 10 August 1936.

Karloff, Dorothy. Letter to Louise Stine, 13 January 1941.

Karloff, Dorothy. Letter to Louise Stine, 23 April 1941.

Karloff, Dorothy. Letter to Louise Stine, April 1941.

Karloff, Dorothy. Letter to Louise Stine, 27 November 1941.

Karloff, Dorothy. Letter to Louise Stine, 4 December 1941.

Karloff, Dorothy. Letter to Louise Stine, 29 December 1941.

Karloff, Dorothy. Letter to Louise Stine, December 1941.

Karloff, Dorothy. Letter to Louise Stine, 11 January 1942.

Karloff, Dorothy. Letter to Louise Stine, 29 January 1942.

Karloff, Dorothy. Letter to Louise Stine, 16 February 1942.

Karloff, Dorothy. Letter to Louise Stine, 21 February 1942.

Karloff, Dorothy. Letter to Louise Stine, 24 February 1942.

Karloff, Dorothy. Letter to Louise Stine, 9 March 1942.

Karloff, Dorothy. Letter to Louise Stine, 16 March 1942.

Karloff, Dorothy. Letter to Louise Stine, 13 April 1942.

Karloff, Dorothy. Letter to Louise Stine, 15 April 1942.

Karloff, Dorothy. Letter to Louise Stine, 11 May 1942.

Karloff, Dorothy. Letter to Louise Stine, 19 May 1942.

Karloff, Dorothy. Letter to Louise Stine, 25 May 1942.

Karloff, Dorothy. Letter to Louise Stine, 12 October 1942.

Karloff, Dorothy. Letter to Louise Stine, 24 October 1942.

Karloff, Dorothy. Letter to Louise Stine, 8 April 1943.

Karloff, Dorothy, and Sara Jane Karloff (as dictated to her nanny, Mary Jane). Letter to Louise Stine, 24 June 1943.

Karloff, Dorothy. Letter to Louise Stine, 30 June 1944.

Karloff, Dorothy. Letter to Louise Stine, 5 July 1944.

Karloff, Evelyn. Letter to John L. Dales, 8 May 1969.

Karloff, Evelyn. Letter to Midge Van Buren Farrell, 11 June 1969.

Karloff, Evelyn. Letter to John L. Dales, 6 December 1973.

Karloff, Evelyn. Letter to Scott Allen Nollen, 28 August 1981.

Karloff, Evelyn. Letter to Scott Allen Nollen, 13 October 1981.

Karloff, Evelyn. Letter to Scott Allen Nollen, 8 April 1982.

Karloff, Evelyn. Letter to Scott Allen Nollen, 4 October 1982.

Karloff, Evelyn. Letter to Scott Allen Nollen, 5 December 1982.

Karloff, Evelyn. Letter to Gordon Shriver, 19 May 1983.

Karloff, Evelyn. Letter to Scott Allen Nollen, 19 May 1983.

Karloff, Evelyn. Letter to Scott Allen Nollen, 16 November 1983.

Karloff, Evelyn. Letter to Gordon Shriver, 1 August 1987.

Karloff, Evelyn. Letter to Scott Allen Nollen, 6 May 1988.

Karloff, Evelyn. Letter to Gordon Shriver, 3 August 1988.

Karloff, Evelyn. Letter to Scott Allen Nollen, 3 August 1988.

Karloff, Evelyn. Letter to Scott Allen Nollen, 20 June 1989.

Karloff, Evelyn. Letter to Gordon Shriver, 10 May 1990.

Karloff, Evelyn. Letter to Scott Allen Nollen, 18 May 1990.

Karloff, Evelyn. Letter to Gordon Shriver, 24 July 1990.

Karloff, Evelyn. Letter to Gordon Shriver, 15 August 1990.

Karloff, Evelyn. Letter to Gordon Shriver, 10 February 1991.

Karloff, Evelyn. Letter to Scott Allen Nollen, 18 February 1991.

Karloff, Evelyn. Letter to Scott Allen Nollen, 24 February 1991.

Karloff, Evelyn. Letter to Gordon Shriver, 15 July 1991.

Karloff, Evelyn. Letter to Scott Allen Nollen, 15 July 1991.

Karloff, Sara Jane (via Dorothy Karloff). Telegram to Boris Karloff, 19 August 1939.

Karloff, Sara Jane (as dictated to Dorothy Karloff). Letter to "Santa Claus," 8 December 1942.

Karloff, Sara Jane (as dictated to her nanny, Mary Jane). Letter to Louise Stine, 17 June 1944.

Karloff, Sara Jane. Telegram to Evelyn Karloff, 3 February 1969.

Karloff, Sara Jane. Letter to Evelyn Karloff, 6 February 1969.

Keats, Viola. Letter to Evelyn Karloff, 5 February 1969.

Kellaway, Mrs. Cecil. Letter to Evelyn Karloff, 22 February 1969.

Kennard, Arthur. Letter to Evelyn Karloff, 3 February 1969.

Kirk, William T. Letter to Evelyn Karloff, 2 July 1969.

Langdon, Verne. Letter to Evelyn Karloff, 4 February 1969.

Lovell, J.S. Letter to Evelyn Karloff, 11 April 1969.

Lee, Christopher. Letter to Evelyn Karloff, 5 February 1969.

Lee, Christopher. Letter to Evelyn Karloff, 7 February 1972.

Lush, D.J. Letter to Evelyn Karloff, 11 February 1969.

Lynn, Rita. Letter to John L. Dales, 15 March 1969.

McMichael, Marion. Letter to Evelyn Karloff, 11 February 1969.

Manners, David. Letter to Scott Allen Nollen, 6 July 1983.

Matthews, B. Letter to Boris Karloff, 9 June 1962.

Maydwell, K. Mary. Letter to Scott Allen Nollen, 3 June 1983.

Morris, Chester. Letter to Evelyn Karloff, 4 February 1969.

Mowbray, Alan. Telegram to Boris Karloff, 24 November 1938.

Munsell, Warren P. Letter to Evelyn Karloff, 18 February 1969.

Manulis, Katie. Letter to Evelyn Karloff, 24 February 1969.

Manulis, Martin. Letter to Evelyn Karloff, 20 February 1969.

"Marion and Lou." Telegram to Dorothy Karloff, 23 November 1938.

Meyer, Torbin. Letter to John L. Dales, 15 March 1969.

Napier, Alan. Letter to Evelyn Karloff, 6 February 1969.

Newport, Denyse. Letter to Evelyn Karloff, 6 February 1969.

Newport, Denyse. Letter to Evelyn Karloff, 6 April 1969.

Nicholson, James H. Letter to Evelyn Karloff, 5 February 1969.

Olivier, Sir Laurence. Letter to Scott Allen Nollen, 12 November 1981.

Oppenheim, Nancy. Letter to Evelyn Karloff, 22 February 1973.

Panikbutr, A. Letter to Evelyn Karloff, 16 April 1969.

Platt, Polly. Letter to Evelyn Karloff, 3 February 1969.

Porter, Joseph E., III. Letter to Evelyn Karloff, 21 May 1973.

Pratt, Mrs. James M. Invitation to the wedding of Louise M. Pratt and William F. Stine, 28 December 1892.

Price, Mary. Telegram to Evelyn Karloff, 3 February 1969.

Price, Vincent. Letter to Evelyn Karloff, 4 February 1969.

Price, Vincent. Letter to Cynthia Lindsay, early 1970s.

Randall, Tony. Letter to Scott Allen Nollen, 9 May 1996.

Reagan, Ronald. Letter to Cynthia Lindsay, 25 April 1974.

Reynolds, Edmond. Letter to Scott Allen Nollen, 30 January 1996.

Riley, Jay J. Letter to Evelyn Karloff, 12 February 1969.

Robinson, George. Telegram to Dorothy Karloff, 23 November 1938.

Sapinsley, Alvin. Letter to Gordon Shriver, 13 April 1983.

Savory, Gerald. Letter to Evelyn Karloff, 5 February 1969.

Schaefer, George. Letter to Evelyn Karloff, 3 February 1969.

Screen Actors Guild. Letter to Murray Kinnell, 5 November 1935.

Screen Actors Guild. Letter to Boris Karloff, 30 November 1935.

Segal, Ruth. Letter to Evelyn Karloff, 24 March 1969.

Selznick, Daniel Mayer. Letter to Evelyn Karloff, 4 February 1969.

Sewell, Vernon. Letter to Evelyn Karloff, 6 February 1969.

Sinatra, Nancy. Letter to Scott Allen Nollen, 16 December 1997.

Skelton, Georgia. Telegram to Evelyn Karloff, 3 February 1969.

Skinner, Cornelia Otis. Letter to Evelyn Karloff, 6 February 1969.

Smith, C. Aubrey, and Mrs. C. Aubrey Smith. Telegram to Dorothy Karloff, 23 November 1938.

Smith, Lady C. Aubrey. Telegram to Evelyn Karloff, 3 February 1969.

Stephenson, Dorothy, and Henry Stephenson. Telegram to Dorothy Karloff, 23 November 1938.

Stone, Jane. Letter to Evelyn Karloff, 4 February 1969.

Sutherland, Stephen. Letter to Evelyn Karloff. 16 February 1969.

Tavella, Marx F. Letter to Evelyn Karloff, 7 February 1969.

Taylor, Ann. Letter to Evelyn Karloff, 10 April 1969.

Tenser, Tony. Telegram to Evelyn Karloff, 3 February 1969.

Thomas, Ed. Telegram to Dorothy Karloff, 23 November 1938.
Thomson, Kenneth. Letter to Boris Karloff, 25 July 1933.
Thomson, Kenneth. Letter to Boris Karloff, 29 July 1933.
Thomson, Kenneth. Letter to Boris Karloff, 19 January 1935.
Thomson, Kenneth. Letter to Boris Karloff, 4 March 1936.
Trevelyan, John. Letter to Evelyn Karloff, 4 February 1969.
Vertlieb, Stephen and Erwin. Letter to Evelyn Karloff, 3 February 1969.
Vinton, Arthur. Letter to Boris Karloff, 3 August 1933.
Walch, Eugene. Letter to Evelyn Karloff, 30 June 1971.
Wallach, Mrs. Eli. Letter to Evelyn Karloff, 5 February 1969.
Williams, Lisa. Letter to Boris Karloff, 1968.
Wolfe, Ian. Letter to Scott Allen Nollen, 4 November 1983.
Wolfe, Ian. Letter to Scott Allen Nollen, 20 January 1989.
Wyatt, Jane. Letter to Evelyn Karloff, 3 February 1969.
Yardley, Mrs. A.J. Letter to Evelyn Karloff, 3 February 1969.
Yaros, Valerie. Letter to Scott Allen Nollen, 29 October 1998.
Young, Collier. Letter to Evelyn Karloff, 6 February 1969.
Zimmerman, Barbara. Letter to John L. Dales, 14 March 1969.

Karloff Family Records

"Boris Karloff (William Henry Pratt)." Geneology of Pratts and Millards (1815-1888).
Karloff, Boris, and Evelyn Karloff. "Karloff Social Schedule," March 16-24, 1957.
Karloff, Dorothy. Baby Book (for Sara Jane Karloff), 1938-42.
Karloff, Sara Jane. School Report Cards, 1944-49.
Stine, Mrs. Louise M. Rent Statement, 1 May 1947.

Official Documents

Breen, Joseph I. *Bride of Frankenstein*. 10, 16, 21 May, 7, 13 June, 17 July, 17 December 1935, 28
        January, 3 March, 28 April 1936.
Karloff, Boris. The Masquers, Application for Membership, Hollywood, California, 7 March 1926.
Karloff, Boris. Marriage Record, Clark County, Nevada, 22 April 1946.
Loewenstein, Ladislav (Peter Lorre). Petition for Naturalization, U.S. Department of Labor, Immigration
        and Naturalization Service, 21 August 1936.
Pratt, William Henry, and Evelyn Helmore. Marriage Certificate, State of Nevada, County of Clark, 11
        April 1946.
Screen Actors Guild, Inc. Application for Class A Membership. Boris Karloff, 19 July 1933.
Universal Pictures Corporation. Production Estimate and Picture Costs: *The Black Cat*. 2 March, 14 July
        1934.
Universal Pictures Corporation. Production Estimate and Picture Costs: *The Return/Bride of
        Frankenstein*. 10 January 1935, 26 March 1936.

Contracts and Contract Amendments

Karloff, Boris, with Hubbell Robinson Productions, Inc. 8 March 1960.
Karloff, Boris, with Hubbell Robinson Productions, Inc. 14 March 1960.
Karloff, Boris, with Hubbell Robinson Productions, Inc. 27 March 1961.

Scripts

The Lark. Karloff's personal, annotated copy, 1955.

Memoranda

Screen Actors Guild, "Inter-Office Communication," 6 February 1969.

School Records and Printed Materials

"Enfield Grammar School." Enfield, Middlesex, 1995.

The Epilogue. San Francisco: The Students of Sarah Dix Hamlin School, 1955.

Matthews, Bryan. *Eminent Uppinghamians*. Benenden, Kent: Neville and Harding Ltd., 1987.

Uppingham: "Prospectus," "Current Information," "Admission Information and Documents." Uppingham, Rutland, 1995.

Uppingham School Magazine. Vol. XLII, No. 332, July 1904. Uppingham, Rutland: John Hawthorn.

Uppingham School Magazine. Vol. XLIII, February-December 1905. Uppingham, Rutland: John Hawthorn.

Uppingham School Magazine. Vol. XLIV, February-December 1906. Uppingham, Rutland: John Hawthorn.

Uppingham School scrapbooks, 1903-06.

Playbills and Play Programs

Arsenic and Old Lace. U.S. Army: USO Camp Shows, Inc., 1945.

Arsenic and Old Lace. Anchorage: Anchorage Community College Theatre Workshop, 1957.

The Lark. New York: Playbill, Incorporated, 1955.

The Lark. New York: Program Publishing Company, 1955.

On Borrowed Time. Los Angeles: John F. Huber, 1946.

Peter Pan. New York: Program Publishing Company, 1950.

Peter Pan. Boston: The Jerome Press, 1951.

Peter Pan. Philadelphia: The Playgoer, 1951.

Peter Pan. Chicago: Chicago Stagebill, Inc., 1951.

Books, Articles and Essays by Karloff

Karloff, Boris, ed. *And the Darkness Falls*. New York: World Publishing Company,1946.

Karloff, Boris. "Cricket in California..." *The Screen Player*, 15 May 1934.

Karloff, Boris. *Film Weekly*, 18 April 1936.

Karloff, Boris. "Foreword," in *Drawn and Quartered* by Charles Addams. First draft manuscript, 16 May 1942.

Karloff, Boris. "How Not to Be a Full-Time Bogeyman," *Reader's Digest*, January 1964.

Karloff, Boris. "My Life as a Monster," *Films and Filming*, November 1957.

Karloff, Boris. "Oaks from Acorns," *Screen Actor*, October-November 1960.

Karloff, Boris, ed. *Tales of Terror*. New York: World Publishing Company, 1943.

Karloff, Boris, with Arlene and Howard Eisenberg. "Memoirs of a Monster," *Saturday Evening Post*, 3 November 1962.

Published Interviews

Karloff, Boris. "My Life of Terror," *Shriek*, October 1965.

McCluskey, Paul. *Movies: Conversations with Peter Bogdanovich*. New York: Harcourt Brace Jovanovich, 1974.

Parry, Mike, and Harry Nadler. "Castle of Frankenstein Interviews Boris Karloff," *Castle of Frankenstein*, no. 9.

Autobiographies

Arliss, George. *My Ten Years in the Studios*. Boston: Little, Brown, and Company, 1940.

Cagney, James. *Cagney by Cagney*. Garden City, New York: Doubleday and Company, Inc., 1976.

Lanchester, Elsa. *Elsa Lanchester Herself*. New York: St. Martin's Press, 1983.

Lee, Christopher. *Tall Dark and Gruesome: An Autobiography*. London: W.H. Allen, 1977.

Armstrong, Louise. "A Biographical Account of Rolf Armstrong." Unpublished manuscript, 1977.
Lindsay, Cynthia. *Dear Boris: The Life of William Henry Pratt, a.k.a. Boris Karloff*. New York: Alfred A. Knopf, 1975.

Commercial Publications

Isbell's Restaurant Menu. Chicago, 1951.
Marineland of the Pacific. "Porpoise Jumpmaster" membership card, 8 January 1959.

Newspapers, Trade Papers, and News Magazines

The Actor. May 1940.
"Actor Boris Karloff to Arrive Here Tomorrow," *Anchorage Times*, 15 March 1957.
"Actors Help Stage Hands," *Anchorage Times*, March 1957.
"Actors Speak Minds on Industry, Guild Action, and Future Plans," *Screen Actor*, September 1940.
Ames, Walter. "Karloff to Sing for Dinah," *Los Angeles Times*, 17 May 1957.
Anderson, John. "*Arsenic and Old Lace* Opens at Fulton" (New York), 11 January 1941.
"Arsenic and Old Lace with Karloff, Opens Tomorrow," *Anchorage Daily News*, 20 March 1957.
"Arsenic Provides Theatrical Highlight to Anchorage Story," *Anchorage Daily News*, 20 March 1957.
Atkinson, Brooks. "Theatre: St. Joan with Radiance," *New York Times*, 18 November 1955.
Atkinson, Brooks. "New Joan of Arc," New York *Sunday Times*, 27 November 1955.
Beaufort, John. "Julie Harris Starring in Role of Joan of Arc," *Christian Science Monitor*, 26 November 1955.
Belser, Lee. "Boris Karloff Does 'Little Darling': Calypso by 'The Monster'," 17 May 1957.
"Best Performance of August," *The Screen Guild's Magazine*, September 1935.
Bolton, Whitney. "All Hands Contribute Superbly to Stunning, Beautiful *Lark*," *Morning Telegraph*, 19 November 1955.
"Boris Karloff Arrives; Begins First Rehearsals" (Anchorage). 18 March 1957.
"Boris Karloff, Gentle Monster, Lover of Children, Dies." *Tulsa Daily World*. 4 February 1969.
"Boris Karloff Is Party Honoree," *Monterey Peninsula Herald*, 17 March 1961.
"Broadway Softens Up Boris Karloff...He's a Bishop," *New York Journal American*, 25 February 1956.
"The Call Board," *The Screen Player*, 15 May 1934.
"The Call Board," *The Screen Guild's Magazine*, May 1935.
"Chan." "New Telepix Shows: Colonel March of Scotland Yard," *Variety*, 9 December 1953.
Chapman, John. "Julie Harris and *The Lark* Co. Repeat Rave Show in the West," New York *Daily News*, 6 August 1956
Chapman, John. "Julie Harris Simply Magnificent in a Beautiful Drama, *The Lark*," New York *Daily News*, 18 November 1955.
Christian Science Monitor, 25 October 1955; 19 May 1956.
Clark, Norman. "Boris Karloff and Grand Cast in Maryland Play" (Baltimore), December 1940.
Coleman, Robert. "*Arsenic and Old Lace* at Fulton Theatre is a 'Killer'" (New York), 11 January 1941.
Crosby, John. "Television and Radio," *New York Herald Tribune*, April 1956.
Crosby, John. "Television and Radio," *New York Herald Tribune*, February 1957.
"Culinary Artist," *Los Angeles Examiner*, 16 February 1936.
"Daku." "The Chevy Show," *The Hollywood Reporter*, 20 May 1957.
Doyle, Peggy. "The Lark Scores a Huge Success," *Boston Evening American*, 29 October 1955.
Durgin, Cyrus. "At the Theatre," *Boston Daily Globe*, 29 October 1955.
Farrell, Nancy. "Of Boris Karloff," *New York Times*, 9 March 1969.
"A Fiery Particle," *Time*, 28 November 1955.
"Film Actors Linked Across Atlantic—Boris Karloff as Negotiator," *Daily Herald* (London), 15 May 1936.
"Film 'Monster' in London," *Morning Advertiser* (London), 20 February 1936.
"Film Monster Picks Farm Over Night Life," *New York Evening Journal*, 5 February 1936.
"First Night at The Theatre," *New York Times*, 25 April 1950.
"The Gentle Monster," *Newsweek*. 10 February 1969.

"Gilb." "Alcoa Hour," *Variety*, April 1956.

Goodwin, George. "Karloff and Atlanta Lad Score in 'Borrowed Time'" (Atlanta), October 1949.

Gould, Jack. "TV: 'Sleepy Hollow'," *New York Times*, 6 March 1958.

Gould, Jack. "TV: Western Tone Poem," *New York Times*, 16 April 1956.

Green, James. "London's Pride: The Gentle Monster Comes Home" (London), 1968.

"Groups Invite Public to Karloff Reception," *Anchorage Times*, March 1957.

"Guy." "Legit Tryout," *Hollywood Variety*, 31 October 1955.

Hall, Hal. "The Biggest Box-Office Attraction at the Fair," *The Screen Guild's Magazine*, July 1935.

Harris, Sydney J. "*The Lark* Soars Grandly into Artistic Stratosphere," *Chicago Daily News*, 26 March 1956.

Hawkins, William. "Julie Harris Captures Inner Beauty of Joan," *New York World-Telegram*, 18 November 1955.

"Hobe." "Shows on Broadway," *Variety*, 23 November 1955.

Hoffman, Leonard. "New York Play," *Hollywood Reporter*, 18 November 1955.

Howard, Steve. "Profile: Bernie Coleman" (London), 1969.

Hughes, Elinor. "Theater," *Boston Herald*, 29 October 1955.

Hull, Bob. "TV Talk: Karloff, Hutton, Carney on Dinah Shore Show," 17 May 1957.

"A Joan with Gumption," *Newsweek*, 28 November 1955.

Jones, Paul. "'Borrowed Time' Said Greatest of Season" (Atlanta), October 1949.

"Julie Harris: 'Best Actress'?" *Newsweek*, 28 November 1955.

Kanour, Gilbert. "Odd Plot Marks *Arsenic and Old Lace*, Comedy at the Maryland" (Baltimore), December 1940.

"Karloff Impressed by Alaskan Hospitality," *Anchorage Times*, 26 March 1957.

"Karloff Offers Proceeds to Help Build College Theater," *Anchorage Times*, 20 March 1957.

"Karloff Set for Lark," *New York Daily News*, 22 March 1955.

"Karloff Sings and Monsters Walk the Plank," *New York Times*. 1950.

"Karloff the 'Friendly Bogey'," *Star* (London), 19 February 1936.

"Karloff the Kind," *The Sunday Times* (London), 21 November 1982.

"Karloff to Inspect Havenstrite Oil Site," *Anchorage Times*, March 1957.

"Karloff's Visit Stirs Anchorage's Social World," *Anchorage Times*, 19 March 1957.

Kerr, Walter F. "*The Lark*," *New York Herald Tribune*, 18 November 1955.

Kerr, Walter F. "Theater: A Brisk New Joan," *New York Herald Tribune*, 27 November 1955.

Kronenberger, Louis. "So You Don't Think Corpses Are Funny," *PM Reviews* (New York), January 1941.

"Life Goes to a Party," *Life*, March 1942.

McClain, John. "Newest Joan, Julie Harris, Set to Conquer Broadway," *New York Journal-American*, 14 November 1955.

McClain, John. "Julie Depicts a Vital Joan," New York *Journal-American*, 18 November 1955.

McCord, Bert. "Boris Karloff Will Costar with Julie Harris in *Lark*," *New York Herald Tribune*, 22 March 1955.

McCord, Bert. "Julie Harris Will Open in *The Lark* Tonight," *New York Herald Tribune*, 17 November 1955.

Maloney, Alta. "Julie Harris as Joan, *The Lark*, Plymouth," *Boston Traveler*, 29 October 1955.

Melvin, Edwin F. "Drama of Joan of Arc from Anouilh," *Christian Science Monitor*, 29 October 1955.

"Mrs. Karloff Likes Crab, Travel," *Anchorage Times*. March 1957.

"Monster in Penge," *Beckenham and Penge Advertiser*. 18 July 1957.

Mostert, Noel. "Latest 'Joan' is Thrilling Theatre," *Montreal Star*, 26 November 1955.

Mostert, Noel. "'Mr. Frankenstein' Recalls Early Canadian Acting Days," 14 December 1955.

"Movie Monster Karloff Played Broadway Too." *The Cleveland Press*. 3 February 1969.

"Mrs. Beery is Looking for Rain—and Boris Karloff Gets a New Job—in England," *Daily Mirror* (London), 20 February 1936.

"A New Joan," *Wall Street Journal*, 21 November 1955.

New York Daily Mirror, 18 November 1955.

New York Daily News, 25 April 1950.

New York Herald Tribune, 12 January 1941, 3 March 1948, 20 January 1949, 25 April

1950, 18 November 1955.

New York Journal American, 25 April 1950.

New York Post, 11 January 1941, 18 November 1955.

New York Star, 20 January 1949.

New York Sun, 11 January 1941.

New York Times, 1931-69.

New York World-Telegram, 11 January 1941, 18 November 1955, January 1964.

The New Yorker, 3 December 1955.

"News of the Theater," *New York Herald Tribune*, 1 November 1950.

Norton, Elliot. "Remarkable Drama About Joan of Arc," *Boston Sunday Post*, 6 November 1955.

Norton, Elliot. "The Theatre," *Boston Post*, 29 October 1955.

"Officers of the Screen Actors' Guild, 1935-36," *Screen Actor*, August 1935.

Peper, William. "Karloff Has Role in Anouilh Play," *New York World-Telegram*, 22 March 1955.

"Sampling Sunlight as a Change from Limelight," *Daily Sketch* (London), 21 February 1936.

Screen Actor, June 1946, October 1946, March 1995.

The Screen Guild's Magazine, June 1935.

"Sell-Out Crowd Seen for *Arsenic* Tonight," *Anchorage Times*, 22 March 1957.

Smith, Cecil. "Karloff — Arsenic, Very Old Lace," *Los Angeles Times*, 5 February 1962.

Smith, Cecil. "Shirley Temple in Drama Role," *Los Angeles Times*, 5 March 1958.

Smith, Cecil. "'Sound of Trumpets' on the Right Scale," *Los Angeles Times*, 10 February 1960.

"South West Whispers: Tooting, Hollywood and Cricket" (London), 25 March 1959.

Sullivan, Frank. "Sullivan, the Angel" (New York), 1941.

"Tense Scene in Karloff Hit," *Anchorage Daily News*, 22 March 1957.

"Theater Cast Promises Top-Flight Production," *Anchorage Times*, 21 March 1957.

"Theatre Workshop Nets $6,000 from Play," *Anchorage Daily News*, 25 March 1957.

"This Karloff's No Monster," *The Advertiser*. 20 July 1957.

"Thriller Diller," *Newsweek*, 3 October 1949.

"Tickets Sell Well for Play," *Anchorage Times*. March 1957.

Time, 25 February 1957.

"22,300 Children Attend Book Fair," *New York Times*, 16 November 1950.

Variety, 1920-69.

Watts, Richard Jr. "Two on the Aisle," 18 November 1955.

Whittaker, Dick. "Karloff, Cast in Rehearsals for Arsenic and Old Lace," *Anchorage Times*, 18 March 1957.

"Who's That on Left?" *The News* (London). 16 October 1959.

Photograph Tags and Indentifications

ARCSC-591-1/AR-57. Ft. Richardson, Alaska: U.S. Army, 20 March 1957.

ARCSC-591-2/AR-57. Ft. Richardson, Alaska: U.S. Army, 20 March 1957.

ARCSC-591-2/AR-57. Ft. Richardson, Alaska: U.S. Army, 20 March 1957.

ARCSC-591-4/AR-57. Ft. Richardson, Alaska: U.S. Army, 21 March 1957.

"*The Big Cage.*" Universal, 1933.

Karloff, Boris. Identification of Marineland photo, 8 January 1959.

Karloff, Evelyn. Identification of Beverly Hills photo, 1947.

"Li'l White Alice Gals." Anchorage: Federal Electric Corporation, 22 March 1957.

"*Man of a Thousand Faces.*" Universal-International, 1957.

"The Pirate Ship," Macy's 24th Annual Thanksgiving Day Parade. New York: 1950.

Screen Actors Guild. No. 44, 13 September 1946.

Secondary Sources

Biographies

Ackerman, Forrest J, ed. *Boris Karloff: The Frankenscience Monster.* New York:
    Ace Publishing Corporation, 1969.

Blake, Michael F. *Lon Chaney: The Man Behind the Thousand Faces.* Vestal, New York: The Vestal Press,
    Ltd., 1993.

Bristowe, W. S. *Louis and the King of Siam*. London: Chatto and Windus, 1976.

Gifford, Denis. *Karloff: The Man, the Monster, the Movies*. New York: Curtis Books, 1973.

Gilbert, Martin. *Churchill: A Life*. New York: Henry Holt and Company, Inc., 1991.

Sinclair, Andrew. *John Ford: A Biography*. New York: Lorrimer Publishing, Inc., 1984.

Sinatra, Nancy. *Frank Sinatra: An American Legend*. Santa Monica: General Publishing Group, Inc., 1995.

Thorogood, Michael. "Arthur Donkin, Rector of Semer" (unpublished notes).

Underwood, Peter. *Karloff: The Life of Boris Karloff*. New York: Drake Publishers, Inc., 1972.

Books About Karloff's Films

Bojarsky, Richard, and Kenneth Beale. *The Films of Boris Karloff*. Secaucus, New Jersey: Citadel Press, 1974.

Buehrer, Beverly Bare. *Boris Karloff: A Bio-Bibliography*. Westport, Connecticut: Greenwood Press, 1993.

Jensen, Paul M. *Boris Karloff and His Films*. New York: A.S. Barnes and Company, Inc., 1974.

Mank, Gregory William. *Karloff and Lugosi: The Story of a Haunting Collaboration*. Jefferson, North Carolina: McFarland and Company, 1990.

Nollen, Scott Allen. *Boris Karloff: A Critical Account of His Screen, Stage, Radio, Television and Recording Work*. Jefferson, North Carolina: McFarland and Company, Inc., 1991.

Riley, Philip J., ed. *The Bride of Frankenstein*. Absecon, New Jersey: MagicImage Filmbooks, 1989.

Riley, Philip J., ed. *Frankenstein*. Absecon, New Jersey: MagicImage Filmbooks, 1989.

Riley, Philip J., ed. *House of Frankenstein*. Absecon, New Jersey: MagicImage Filmbooks, 1989.

Riley, Philip J., ed. *The Mummy*. Absecon, New Jersey: MagicImage Filmbooks, 1989.

Riley, Philip J., ed. *Son of Frankenstein*. Absecon, New Jersey: MagicImage Filmbooks, 1989.

Svehla, Gary J., and Susan Svehla, eds. *Boris Karloff*. Baltimore: Midnight Marquee Press, Inc., 1996.

Books About the American and British Cinema

Bogdanovich, Peter. *John Ford*. Berkeley: University of California Press, 1978.

Brunas, Michael, John Brunas and Tom Weaver. *Universal Horrors: The Studio's ClassicFilms, 1931-1946*. Jefferson, North Carolina: McFarland and Company, Inc., 1990.

Curtis, James. *James Whale*. Metuchen, N.J.: Scarecrow Press, 1982.

Mank, Gregory William. *It's Alive: The Classic Cinema Saga of Frankenstein*. New York: A S. Barnes and Company, 1981.

Naha, Ed. *Brilliance on a Budget: The Films of Roger Corman*. New York: Arco Publishing, 1982.

Nash, Jay Robert, and Stanley Ralph Ross, eds. *The Motion Picture Guide*. Vols. I-X. Chicago: Cinebooks, 1986.

Pohle, Robert W., Jr., and Douglas C. Hart, with the participation of Christopher Lee. *The Films of Christopher Lee*. Metuchen, N.J.: Scarecrow Press, 1983.

Robertson, James C. *The Casablanca Man: The Cinema of Michael Curtiz*. London: Routledge, 1993.

Schatz, Thomas. *The Genius of the System: Hollywood Filmmaking in the Studio Era*. New York: Pantheon Books, 1988.

Youngkin, Stephen D., James Bigwood, and Raymond Cabana, Jr. *The Films of Peter Lorre*. Secaucus, New Jersey: The Citadel Press, 1982.

Books About British History

Somerset Fry, Plantagenet. *The Kings and Queens of England and Scotland*. New York: Grove Press, 1990.

Wilson, Derek. *The Tower: The Tumultuous History of the Tower of London from 1078*. New York: Charles Scribner's Sons, 1979.

Magazines

American Cinematographer, Vol. 66, No. 1, January 1985.

Films in Review, August-September 1984.

Monster World, No. 5, October 1965.

Index

Page Numbers in **Bold** Indicate Photographs

"The Vestris" (TV show) - 222, 325
Vidor, Charles - 55, 57, 290
The Virginian (play) - 28, 272
Voodoo Island (film) - 200, **201**, 210, 214, 303

Wade, Russell - **153**, 155, 298
Waggner, George - 148, 298
Wallach, Eli - 191, 203, 323, 324
Wallis, Hal B. - 96
The Walking Dead (1936 film) - 95-97, **97**, 101,
    127, 167, 292-93
Walsh, Eugene - 60, 70, 108
Walsh, Raoul - 39, 287
Warner, H.B. - 38, 57, 287
Warner Bros. Pictures - 38-39, 49-50, 74, 95-98,
    109-11, 114-15, 128, 147, 214
Wasserman, Lew - 225, 227
Waterloo Bridge (1931 film) - 41
Way Down East (play) - 27, 272
Wegener, Paul - 67
Weinstein, Hanna - 185, 188-89
Wells, H.G. - 49, 62, 100, 176, 316
Wells, Jacqueline [aka: Julie Bishop] - 76-77, 80,
    291
Werewolf of London (film) - 88, 94
Werker, Alfred - 75, 100, 290
West of Shanghai (film) - 109-11, 293-94
West Point Military Academy - **143**
Westmore, Bud - 187, 301-02
Whale, James - 11, 41, 43-45, 47, 51-54, 62, 68-70,
    82, 84-87, 89, 116, 119, 226, 287, 289, 291
Wheeler, Bert - 38, 285
White, Betty - 214, 325
Whitman, Charles - 245-46
Widmark, Richard - 164, 314
The Wild, Wild West (TV series) 241, 328
Wiley, Hugh - 115, 294-96
Williams, Jeffrey - 80
Wills, Brember - 59, 289
Window Panes (play) - 35, 272
Windust, Bretaigne - 131-3, 135, 273
Winters, Jonathan - 256, 328
Wise, Robert - 152-56, 162, 265, 298
Wiseman, Joseph - 195, 198, 202, 275
The Wolf Man (film) 242, 331
Wolfe, Ian - 13, 89, 164, 292, 299
Wood, Natalie - 214, 308
Woolcott, Alexander - 100
Woolsey, Robert - 38, 285
Work, Cliff - 115-16
World Publishing Company - 147, 166-67, 332
World War I - 28, 157, 224
World War II - 139-42, 145, 147, **150**, 157-62,
    158, **159**, **160**, **161**, 164, 192, 204, 210, 214
Wyatt, Jane - 259, 264
Wyman, Jane - 168, **169**
Wynn, Ed - 140-41, 327

The Yellow Ticket (film) - 39, 287
You'll Find Out (film) - 129, 297, 310
Young, James - 15, 32, 277-80
Young, Roland - 35, 284
Young Donovan's Kid (film) - 38, 286

Zanuck, Darryl F. - 74, 290
Ziegfeld, Florenz - 195
Zucco, George - 172, 298

If you enjoyed this volume be sure to check out other titles from Midnight Marquee Press, Inc. For a catalog please send a SASE to Midnight Marquee Press, 9721 Britinay Lane, Baltimore, MD 21234 or call 410-665-1198.

MIDNIGHT MARQUEE ACTORS SERIES

BORIS KARLOFF

Edited by Gary J. and Susan Svehla

Midnight Marquee Actors Series

BORIS KARLOFF

$20.00 (plus $4.00 shipping), 356 pages

Various writers examine the film work of the legendary Boris Karloff. Included are analyses of films such as: **Frankenstein, Behind the Mask, Scarface, The Mask of Fu Manchu, The Mummy, The Old Dark House, The Black Cat, The Lost Patrol, The Black Room, Bride of Frankenstein, The Man Who Changed His Mind, The Walking Dead, Charlie Chan at the Opera, West of Shanghai, Invisible Menace, Devil's Island, British Intelligence, The Man They Could Not Hang, The Man With Nine Lives, Before I Hang, Black Friday, The Climax, House of Frankenstein, Arsenic and Old Lace (play), The Devil Commands, Frankenstein 1970, Grip of the Strangler, Corridors of Blood, The Comedy of Terrors, Die, Monster, Die!, Mad Monster Party?** and **Targets**. A must have for fans of the "Gentleman of Horror."